THE 20TH CENTURY LEGAL PHILOSOPHY SERIES

III

LATIN-AMERICAN LEGAL PHILOSOPHY

LONDON : GEOFFREY CUMBERLEGE
OXFORD UNIVERSITY PRESS

20TH CENTURY LEGAL PHILOSOPHY SERIES: VOL. III

LATIN-AMERICAN LEGAL PHILOSOPHY

BY

LUIS RECASÉNS SICHES
CARLOS COSSIO
JUAN LLAMBÍAS de AZEVEDO
EDUARDO GARCÍA MÁYNEZ

TRANSLATED BY

Gordon Ireland, Milton R. Konvitz,
Miguel A. de Capriles, and Jorge Roberto Hayzus

WITH AN INTRODUCTION BY JOSEF L. KUNZ

CAMBRIDGE · MASSACHUSETTS
HARVARD UNIVERSITY PRESS
1948

This book is published at this price in the interest of international cultural coöperation, and it is made possible through the coöperation of the Department of State of the United States of America acting through Science Service, Washington, D.C.

PRINTED AND BOUND BY
THE COLONIAL PRESS INC.
CLINTON, MASSACHUSETTS, U.S.A.

GENERAL INTRODUCTION TO THE SERIES

BY THE EDITORIAL COMMITTEE

THIS book is one of the 20TH CENTURY LEGAL PHILOSOPHY SERIES, published under the auspices of the Association of American Law Schools. At its annual meeting in December, 1939, the Association authorized the creation of a special committee "for the purpose of preparing and securing the publication of translations on the same general lines as the Modern Legal Philosophy Series, sponsored by this association at the annual meeting thirty years ago . . . the materials to represent as nearly as possible the progress of Continental Legal thought in all aspects of Philosophy and Jurisprudence in the last fifty years."

Whereas the earlier Series was a very daring venture, coming, as it did, at the beginning of the century when only a few legal scholars were much interested in legal philosophy, the present Series could be undertaken with considerable assurance. In 1909 only a few of the leading law schools in this country included Jurisprudence in their curricula, and it was usually restricted to the Analytical School. By 1939 Jurisprudence was being taught in many law schools, and the courses had been broadened to include not only Analytical Jurisprudence, but also the Philosophy and the Sociology of Law. The progress in logical theory, in ethics, and in social science between 1909 and 1939 was without doubt an important factor in the expansion of Jurisprudence. In 1939 there was not only the successful precedent of the earlier Series, now completely out of print, but also the known rise of a very substantial body of interested readers, including students and practicing lawyers as well as professional scholars. This thoroughly admirable change, especially in the English-speaking countries, has been widely recognized as productive of a great enrichment of Anglo-American law. The Modern Legal Philosophy Series has been justly credited with a major part of that influence by making readily available the Continental jurisprudence of the last century.

The primary task of the legal philosopher is to reveal and to maintain the dominant long-run influence of ideas over events, of the general over the particular. In discharging this task he may help his generation to understand the basic trends of the law from one generation to the next, and the common cultural ties of seemingly disparate national legal systems. He may, again, create from these common ideal goods of the world's culture general theories, beliefs, and insights that will be accepted and used as guides by coming generations. The works of great legal philosophers serve not only the needs of the practitioner and other utilitarian ends; they also contribute abundantly to our theoretical knowledge. Indeed, in a deeper sense, we have come to understand the superficiality of setting utility against theory. The day is past when jurisprudence can defensibly be regarded as a curious hobby or as "merely cultural" in the sense that the fine arts contribute to the rounded education of a gentleman at the Bar. The issues are now correctly formulated in terms of whether one wishes to be a highly competent lawyer or a technician. Since the question, thus put, is obviously rhetorical, it is but another mode of asserting the considered judgment of those best qualified to pass on such matters, that the science and philosophy of law deal with the chief ideas that are common to the rules and methods of all positive law, and that a full understanding of any legal order therefore eludes those whose confining specialties keep them from these important disciplines.

The recent revival of interest in American history also reminds us emphatically that the great Fathers of the Republic, many of them lawyers, were men of universal intellectual outlook. They were as thoroughly grounded in French thought as in English. Grotius and Pufendorf were almost as widely read as the treatises on common law. Indeed, Jefferson and Wilson, to select two of the many great lawyers who come to mind, were able philosophers and social scientists. They apparently regarded it as essential to the best conduct of their professional careers to study philosophy and, especially, jurisprudence, Jefferson remarking that they are "as necessary as law to form an accomplished lawyer." The current movements in politics and economics have raised innumerable problems which, just as in the formative era of the Republic, require for their solution the sort of knowledge and skills that transcend specialization and technical proficiency. They call for a competence that is grounded in a wide perspective, one that represents an integration of the practitioner's technical skills with a knowledge of the various disciplines that bear directly on the wise solution of the present-day problems; and these are by no means confined to public affairs—they equally concern the daily practice of the private practitioner. With many such legal problems, with methods relevant to sound solutions, with the basic ideas and values involved, the eminent legal philosophers whose principal works appear in this Series have been particularly concerned. If it seems to some that the literature of jurisprudence is rather remote from the immediate practical problems that occupy the attention of most lawyers, it is necessary to reassert our primary dependence for the solution of all such problems upon theory—a truth that has been demonstrated many times in the physical sciences but which holds, also, in the realm of social problems. The publication of such a Series as this rests on the premise that it is possible to discover better answers than are now given many problems, that a closer approximation to truth and a greater measure of justice are attainable by lawyers, and that in part, at least, this can be brought about through their greater sensitivity to the relevant ideals of justice and through a broader vision of the jurisprudential fundamentals.

In the General Introduction to the first Series, it was noted that "The value of the study of comparative law has only in recent years come to be recognized by us. Our juristic methods are still primitive, in that we seek to know only by our own experience, and pay no heed to the experience of others." As the nations are drawn closer together by forces not wholly in human control, it is inevitable that they should come to understand each other more fully. The legal institutions of any country are no less significant than its language, political ideals, and social organization. The two great legal systems of the world, the civilian and the common law, have for some years been moving toward what may become, in various fields of law, a common ground. The civilian system has come more and more to recognize actually, if not avowedly, the importance of case-law, whereas the common law system has been exhibiting an increasing reliance on legislation and even on codes. In a number of fields, e.g., commercial law, wills, and criminal law, there is such an agreement of substantive principles as to make uniformity a very practical objective. While economic interests will undoubtedly provide the chief stimulus to that end, in the long-range view the possibility of focusing the energies of leading scholars and lawyers, the whole world over, on the same problems is the most inviting ideal of all. The problems of terminology, legal methods, the role of precedent, statutory interpretation, underlying rationale, the use of different types of authority, the efficacy of various controls and their operation in diverse factual conditions, the basic issues concerning the values that are implemented—these and innumerable other fundamental problems of legal science and philosophy may and should receive collaboration on a scale never before attainable. The road to the attainment of these objectives is not an easy one, but if any such avenue exists it is surely that indicated by the best literature in jurisprudence.

These fundamentals are also invaluable aids to better understanding of one's own law. On the side of insight into legal methods and substantive doctrines alone, the gain is immeasurably great. The common lawyer, at least until very recent times, was wont to accept a rigorous adherence to the rule of precedent as axiomatic in any modern system. He was apt to regard the common law through Blackstonian eyes; and he can hardly be said to have been even initiated into the criticism of statutes from other perspectives than those required by an unquestioning acceptance of the primacy of case-law. The gains should be no less great as regards organization of the substantive law. A century and a quarter ago John Austin remarked that the common law was a "mess." Although much progress in systematization has been made since that time, we still have a great deal to learn from our civilian friends — particularly from those who have attained wide recognition for their jurisprudential analyses of the common problems of modern legal systems. In addition, there is that vast illumination to be had from the discovery that other advanced legal systems, representing cultures of high achievement, sometimes apply to the solution of many problems different rules of law and even different basic doctrines than does our own. What better avenue to sound criticism of our legal system, what easier road to its early enrichment than by way of intimate knowledge of the innumerable ideas, some identical with our own but otherwise enunciated, some slightly divergent, others directly opposite, that are supplied so generously in the works of legal philosophers!

With the above objectives in view, the Editorial Committee, appointed early in 1940, immediately took up its task. For almost an entire year it engaged in active correspondence with practically all the legal philosophers in the United States, with many European, including English, legal philosophers; and, later on, when the Committee decided to include in the Series a volume devoted to Latin-American jurisprudence, there was much correspondence with legal philosophers of the various countries of Latin America. In addition, like activities centered on the engagement of translators qualified to translate correctly great works of jurisprudence into readable English. Anyone who has undertaken such translation will realize the difficulties involved, and the very high competence that is required. The Committee was able to set very rigorous standards in this regard because of the presence in the United States of an exceptionally able group of European legal scholars, some of whom had for many years been well versed in the English language.

In making its selection of works for inclusion in this Series, the Editorial Committee has been guided in part by the originality and intrinsic merit of the works chosen and in part by their being representative of leading schools of thought. The first Series, the Modern Legal Philosophy Series, had made available some of the work of nineteenth-century European legal philosophers—including Jhering, Stammler, del Vecchio, Korkunov, Kohler, and Gény. That Series and other publications had brought Duguit to the English-reading public. In 1936 the Harvard University Press published a translation of Ehrlich's *Fundamental Principles of the Sociology of Law.* The present century has also seen the rise of a number of brilliant legal philosophers who have attained very wide recognition. Among those whose inclusion in this Series was clearly called for were Max Weber, Kelsen, Petrazycki, Radbruch, the French Institutionalists, chiefly Hauriou and Renard, the Interests-Jurisprudence School centering around Heck, and some others. The opinion of the Committee as to these men was abundantly confirmed by the numerous communications received from legal philosophers of many countries, and the chief problem was to decide which of their works should be translated. But distinction in jurisprudence is not confined to a few writers, and any choice solely on the basis of scholarly merit would be enormously difficult, if not impossible. The Committee, like its predecessors, sought "to present to Anglo-American readers, the views of the best modern representative writers in jurisprudence . . . but the selection has not centered on the notion of giving equal recognition to all countries. Primarily, the design has been to represent the various schools of thought." (General Introduction to the Modern Legal Philosophy Series.) Some schools of thought have been much more productive than others; especially has this been true of those of Legal Positivism and Sociology of Law, which number many very able representatives. Without further presentation of the numerous phases of this problem, it may be stated that the Committee, whose members represent various legal philosophies, has endeavored to make the best selection possible under the conditions of its appointment, the objectives set before it, and the rigorous restriction resulting from the size of the Series.

The success of such a project as this required considerable assistance of many kinds, and the Committee is pleased to acknowledge the abundant aid extended to it. Our greatest debt is to the late John H. Wigmore, whose broad experience as Chairman of the Editorial Committee of the Modern Legal Philosophy Series was placed at our disposal, and who advised us frequently on many problems that arose in the initial stages of the work. As Honorary Chairman of this Committee until his death on April 20, 1943, he participated in many of its conferences and took an active and highly important part in launching the project and assuring its success. It was Mr. Wigmore who, in the early uncertain days of the enterprise, interested his former student, a Trustee of Northwestern University, Mr. Bertram J. Cahn, and Mrs. Cahn to contribute a substantial sum to defray the expenses of translation. The publication of the Series involved the expenditure of a considerable sum of money, and would have been impossible had not the Committee received a very substantial subsidy from Harvard Law School. No less a debt does the Committee acknowledge to the authors who contributed their work and, in some instances, their close personal collaboration. The translators have earned the Committee's admiration for their splendid achievements in the face of serious obstacles and with very little financial assistance to ease their task. We of the Committee wish, also, to give our very hearty thanks to the many legal philosophers, American, Continental, English, and Latin-American, who made many valuable suggestions and encouraged us greatly by their interest in the project. They are far too numerous to be named, as are those many persons in various positions, some of them rather humble ones, who lightened our tasks by their kindly aid. Finally the Committee acknowledges the special help given by Harvard Law School, the University of San Francisco Law School, Columbia University Law School, and Indiana University Law School. Each of the first two schools provided at its own cost a member of its faculty to serve as a translator, as well as stenographic assistance, and the other schools provided considerable stenographic, clerical, and other help. To each of the above persons and institutions the Committee gives its grateful thanks for assistance, without which the publication of this Series would not have been possible.

CONTENTS

II. CARLOS COSSIO

III. JUAN LLAMBÍAS de AZEVEDO

IV. EDUARDO GARCÍA MÁYNEZ

V. EDUARDO GARCÍA MÁYNEZ

INTRODUCTION

By Josef L. Kunz*

Although Latin-American jurists have long been interested in the theoretical and philosophical problems of law, it is pertinent to ask whether there is a Latin-American philosophy of law. And since philosophy of law is a part of philosophy, the question amounts to asking: Is there a Latin-American philosophy?

To this question the Argentinian scholar, Risiero Frondizi answers: There is no Latin-American philosophy in the sense of original and typically Latin-American thought. What is usually known as Latin-American philosophy is a restatement of European philosophical ideas. "In all the Latin-American nations," states the Argentinian philosopher of law, Enrique Martínez Paz, "the juridical philosophical thinking has in its evolution, although somewhat tardily, followed the rhythm of Continental European thinking."

In the colonial period of Latin America, the scholastic philosophy prevailed. After the beginning of Independence, French influence was paramount in all Latin America; this meant, in philosophy of law, the predominance of the French eighteenth-century natural law. Conforming to the rhythm of Continental European thought, this was followed in the latter part of the nineteenth century by positivism, as a reaction against the long reign of natural law. Latin-American thinkers tried to destroy the dominating theological and metaphysical doctrines and, to achieve this end, they made use of the arguments of Herbert Spencer and, particularly, of Auguste Comte. Especially in the period from 1870 to 1925, Latin-American philosophy of law was dominated by positivistic agnosticism, contempt for metaphysics, hostility to natural law, repudiation of metaphysical speculation as unscientific, and the prestige of the natural sciences. The product was a somewhat vague "sociological-biological jurisprudence," in which the works of the influential Argentinian philosopher of law, Carlos Octavio Bunge, constitute a high mark.

II

About 1925, however, a reaction against this long reign of Comte's positivism set in. The influence of new philosophical tendencies made itself felt. Comte's influence, it is true, survived in some Latin-American

* Professor of Law, University of Toledo.

writings, especially in Brazil, where Francisco Pontes de Miranda is the most prominent representative of a sociological jurisprudence. It is, in addition, only natural that there always has been and that there is now in Latin America — an almost wholly Catholic continent — a scholastic philosophy of law based on St. Thomas Aquinas. Thus recent Continental European trends, again coming from France — the Institutionalist School (Hauriou, Renard, Delos) and the philosophy of Jacques Maritain — have given new impetus to a Latin-American Neo-Thomistic philosophy of law.

But neither the survival of Comte's influence nor Thomism is representative of the contemporary Latin-American philosophy of law. The present situation is characterized by the fact that Latin-American general philosophy and jurisprudence have again in the recent past followed the rhythm of Continental European thought, especially a twofold development in German and Austrian philosophy and jurisprudence.

The first change began about 1870 in Germany as a powerful philosophical reaction against the long dominance of positivism. The rediscovery of Kant and the return to Kant started a new period of philosophical idealism. In the quarter of a century prior to World War I, the Neo-Kantian School of Marburg (Cohen, Natorp, Cassirer) was the dominating philosophical movement. It reached Latin America after the beginning of this century. From that time on the influence of Comte was replaced by that of Kant, and French influence, by German and Austrian philosophy. The new trend in Latin America was encouraged in Spain, where Ortega y Gasset introduced German philosophy. His *Review of the Occident* terminated, as a Mexican scholar stated, French philosophical influence in Latin America. The movement toward Kant and Neo-Kantianism in Latin-American general philosophy is associated with the names of Alejandro Korn and Francisco Romero in Argentina, Antonio Caso and José Vasconcelos in Mexico, and Deustúa in Peru.

The same movement against positivism and toward Neo-Kantianism took place in Latin-American jurisprudence. As early as 1913, the Peruvian, Francisco García Calderón, could write that "after thirty years of influence positivism is losing its prestige." So, too, Martínez Paz stated that "juridical positivism is retreating before the penetration of the influence of Neo-Kantian criticism." Marburg Neo-Kantianism had found vigorous application in the field of jurisprudence both in Germany and in Italy, and the two outstanding representatives in these countries, Stammler and Del Vecchio, exercised strong influence in Latin-American jurisprudence. Many monographs were written on Stammler, and the outstanding Argentinian philosopher of law, Enrique Martínez Paz, is essentially a follower of Stammler. Certain ideas of Del Vecchio, for example, his thesis that legal norms refer to "human conduct in its inter-subjective relationship," have become fundamental in present-day Latin-American jurisprudence.

But the greatest influence on Latin-American theory of law is presently being exercised by Hans Kelsen. His writings are constantly being translated in Latin America and numerous monographs on his work have been published there. Even concerning Brazil, where Comte's influence has not only been strongest, but has also lasted longest, Karl Loewenstein in his book *Brazil under Vargas* could state in 1942: "In the legal realm the Austrian scholar (Kelsen) has taken the throne from which for the last two generations Auguste Comte ruled social thought."

Typical of Kelsen's influence is the *General Theory of Law* by the Cuban, Antonio S. de Bustamante y Montoro. It is, in general, no more than a very clear restatement of Kelsen's principal doctrines. The only original passages are to be found in the preface, where the author accepts Kelsen's doctrines but voices a longing to transcend Kelsen's relativism. Can we of this generation, the Cuban asks, accept Kelsen's dictum that law can have any content whatever? Can we be satisfied to regard law as a mere form, a mere social technique? Exactly by his demonstration of positive law in its nakedness, Kelsen provokes in us a "new thirst for justice," the Cuban author says, maintaining that the restoration of natural law is inevitable in the philosophy, as distinguished from the theory, of law.

What is thus stated incidentally in the preface of Bustamante's book constitutes the principal theme of the leading Latin-American philosophers of law of the present day. In varying forms and degrees they exhibit a tendency to accept Kelsen's theory of law but, in addition, to go beyond Kelsen in the realm of philosophy of law. The formula for this task has been supplied by Carlos Cossio: "To go beyond Kelsen without abandoning him."

III

The vanishing influence of Stammler in Latin America and the situation with regard to Kelsen are the result of the second movement in German philosophy, which was again followed in Latin-American philosophy and jurisprudence.

This movement constitutes a reaction against the Neo-Kantianism of the Marburg School. It started in Germany at the beginning of this century with the publication of Husserl's *Logical Investigations,* but gained particular momentum in the decade after World War I. The new philosophy arose from the great crisis of Christian Western culture and it seeks to meet the needs of men in this historical situation. A tendency toward the concrete, toward substantive richness, toward eternal values and natural law — in short, toward metaphysics — began to dominate philosophical speculation which, under the impact of the crisis, could no longer be satisfied with the merely scientific, the logical, and the formal.

Hence the attack on Marburg. It was charged that this Neo-Kantianism, by applying the transcendental method in the field of ethics and law, had misunderstood Kant, had "logicised" ethics, had identified philosophy with theory of knowledge and methodology, had neglected the investigation of reality (ontology) and of values (axiology); and had ended in mere formalism. Ethics against logic, history against reason, direct intuition against reflective thinking, realism against idealism, objectivism against relativism, and the independence of the cultural from the natural sciences: these were the inspiring ideas of this philosophical reaction against the Marburg Neo-Kantianism.

The new ideas presented themselves in Germany as "phenomenology," as philosophy of culture, as theory of values and as philosophy of life. Since the latter philosophies were developed phenomenologically, it can be said that the "phenomenological movement," taken in a broad sense, dominates this major development in recent Continental philosophy. It is the phenomenological movement which inspires much of contemporary Latin-American jurisprudence. It may, therefore, be helpful to describe briefly certain salient features of these phenomenological philosophies since the writings presented in this volume are closely related to them.

Phenomenology, in the strict sense of the word, is the creation of Edmund Husserl. He wanted to make philosophy a "rigorous science," the findings of which would be binding on all thinkers. He claimed to have brought about a revolution in philosophy, to have made possible a science of philosophy by delimiting the field of investigation and creating an adequate method. If philosophy is to be a rigorous science, it must have an absolutely firm starting point; nothing must be naïvely assumed. Husserl, therefore, applies Descartes' technique: Even if I doubt everything, including the existence of the world, my own consciousness, the thinking Ego, is something apodictically given to me that cannot be doubted. Husserl distinguished between sciences of fact and sciences of essence which he, adapting the Greek word *eidos* (essence), called "eidetic sciences." These essences constitute the "phenomena" of phenomenology; the term, which in Greek means "that which appears," was used by Kant as the appearance of things, as contra-distinguished from the "thing-in-itself" which, according to Kant, exists, it is true, but is not accessible to our cognition. These essences of Husserl are not, in

Kant's sense, subjective forms or transcendental categories of understanding; they are, instead, ideal objects, independent from and prior to human consciousness. The word "phenomena" is, therefore, used in phenomenology in a completely different sense from that of empiricism, and, in a sense contrary to its Greek meaning, since it means precisely that which does not appear to the natural attitude. Thus phenomenology claims to have discovered a new and immense *a priori* world, a realm, not only of a formal, but of a material *a priori*.

These essences are observable not by the inductive or deductive method, but by the phenomenological method, by intuition. The discovery of the new realm requires an appropriate method of gaining access thereto. To the things themselves! The things are not created by our thinking, they are given to us. We learn of them not mediately and indirectly, but immediately and directly by a neutral description of the essences as they present themselves to us. Here is the turning-point from Neo-Kantian transcendental idealism to ontological realism. Contrary to Bergson's and Scheler's "emotional intuition," Husserl's intuition is a special faculty of understanding, an "intellectual," an "eidetic" intuition. Since the things are immediately given to us and merely described, we can speak of them with absolute certainty, once and for all. As intuitionism has at all times claimed, so the truths discovered by Husserl's intuition are alleged to be self-evident, hence impossible of contradiction. In this way, it is claimed, an absolutely firm starting point is reached for philosophy — based on "eidetic intuition."

Phenomenology plays an important role in contemporary Latin-American philosophy of law, and more so in consequence of the fact that the dominating theories of values and of philosophy of life have been developed phenomenologically.

In the recent phenomenological development of the theory of values the most prominent name in Europe is Scheler. But Scheler later went ways, quite independent of Husserl, and the result is very different from Husserl's phenomenology. Whereas Husserl was primarily interested in mathematics and logic, Scheler's dominating interests were ethics, social philosophy, and philosophy of religion. Contrary to Husserl's "rigorous science," phenomenology in Scheler's hands became metaphysics and Husserl's intellectual intuition became an emotional intuition. Scheler combined his theory of objective values with scholastic philosophy, which has won for him a large following among Neo-Thomists in Europe and Latin America. Scheler, whose ideas stem from Brentano and Meinong, opposed the "formalism" of Kant's ethics of duty. He tried to show that Kant erred in identifying *a priori* with formal, and *a pos-*

teriori with material. There is also a material *a priori,* he insisted. The task — to establish an ethics of objective values — was later performed by Hartmann.

Values are essences in Husserl's sense, ideal objects; they are not created, but are only discovered by men; they are separate from and not dependent on things or human consciousness. They have both form and content; they are objective, not merely subjective. There exists between the values necessary, essential *a priori* relations. There is a necessary polarity of values — good – bad, and so on. There is a strictly objective hierarchy of values, ranging from the religious (the highest) to the least values of utility. Every duty must be founded on a value. Man is the being whose task it is to realize the values. Concerning the realization of values there are various axioms, e.g., the realization of a positive value is a positive value. But, contrary to other essences such as numbers or logical forms, values do not impose themselves on man. Man ought to realize them, but he may not do so. This is the locus of human liberty: thus Scheler's and Hartmann's theory of values is a philosophy of personalism.

The climax of this new philosophical movement is reached in the "philosophy of life" or "existentialism." This philosophy goes back to many sources and it has had many forms, including Bergson's "vitalism." But the philosophies of life which today largely dominate in Europe and in Latin America are those of Ortega y Gasset and Heidegger.

Heidegger united ideas of Nietzsche, Kierkegaard, Dilthey, and Husserl into a philosophy of life, an atheist "existentialism," which also dominates the present French existentialist movement. Heidegger, the "disciple and continuator" of Husserl, has accepted the phenomenological method, but in a very different manner. He seeks to apply the phenomenological method to a new subject — human existence. He does not start, as did Husserl, with the transcendental Ego, but with the "man-in-the-world." He is not interested in essence, but in existence. Or, rather, he holds that man's existence is his essence, that man is necessarily "here and at a specified time," that he is thrown into a world he has not made and lives under factual, historical conditions. Existing, not thinking, is the basic concept. Descartes had said: I think, therefore, I am. No, says Ortega y Gasset: You are, therefore, you think; you think because you are. Thinking is only done for life's sake. Life is the basic reality and, at the same time, the basis of all other realities. Human existence is for Heidegger the key to Being in general. His "analysis of existence," his "hermeneutics of Da-sein" purports to provide a fundamental ontology.

Man has not only a nature, but also a history, an idea which stems from Dilthey. All human existence, states Heidegger, is "being-in-the-world"; or as Ortega y Gasset expresses it: "co-presence of the world with me and of me with the world." The phenomenological analysis of this "Da-sein" begins with the ordinary everyday existence of banality. The fundamental feeling is anxiety, dread (Kierkegaard); the essential trait of banal, everyday life is "care," "concern." But man can also become an "authentic Ego," a real Self, through his resoluteness in the face of death. From all this "analysis of existence," "temporality" emerges as the very meaning of human existence. Temporality or "existential time" is distinguished from the "vulgar notion" of time, that time which is measured by clocks, which consists of instants, with no present and an unchangeable past. "Temporality" is existence in stretches, not in instants; it is defined by the past, present, and future. In the present, man realizes a future while the future determines the past. Man is, accordingly, a "temporal being."

The philosophy of life, especially the ideas of Ortega y Gasset, is basic in the philosophy of law of Recaséns Siches. Heidegger's existentialism and, particularly, his concept of "temporality," is one of the cornerstones of Cossio's "egological theory of law."

IV

Luis Recaséns Siches was born in Guatemala of Spanish parents and was taken to Spain in early childhood. In Spain, he became a professor of law in different universities and from 1932 until the Spanish Civil War he was professor of law at the Central University in Madrid. He is now professor of philosophy of law in the Law School of the National University of Mexico. At the University of Madrid, from which he received doctorates in law and in philosophy, he studied under Ortega y Gasset. He did postgraduate work at the University of Rome with Giorgio Del Vecchio, with Rudolf Stammler in Germany, and with Hans Kelsen at the University of Vienna.

A Spaniard of universal outlook, a profound student both of philosophy and of philosophy of law, a man of great talent and deep knowledge, an indefatigable worker whose enthusiasm for research and creative work could not be halted by bitter personal experience and difficulties, he has displayed an enormous productivity in the field of legal philosophy. His greatest work, *Vida Humana, Sociedad y Derecho* (*Human Life, Society and Law*), published in 1939 in Mexico City, is presented in this volume. This work is the only complete, modern, and original treatise on the whole field of philosophy of law in the Spanish language. It is a work of unusual and outstanding quality, synthesizing and, at the same time, developing the author's research and ideas, expressed in previous monographs. It shows its author, notwithstanding the influence of Kelsen, Kant, Scheler, Hartmann, Heidegger, and Ortega y Gasset, to be an original and independent thinker who exercises great influence over the whole Spanish-speaking world.

The Treatise consists of three parts: the place of law in the universe, the theory of law, and the philosophy of law. He begins by determining the place of law in the universe. Agreeing with Kelsen, he says that law is neither a corporeal nor a psychological thing, and that it cannot be explained in terms of causality. Even in this first part, the importance of the theory of values and the influence of the "philosophy of life" and of Spanish individualism are clear. Law belongs neither to nature nor to the realm of pure values. Law is a form of human life which has become objectivated. All philosophy must start from the central fact of human life; law is a part of human culture, a system of functions of human life. We must distinguish between the "collective life" of the individual and his "authentic life," where only is to be found the full, the real, the unique individuality. Law is a form of collective life. This indicates the major difference between law and ethics.

Law *is*, but its existence is not that of a thing of nature. Law is a specific significance, a complex of norms, a complex of norms of a special type, to be distinguished from other norms. Starting from the nondifferentiated norms of primitive times, Recaséns Siches distinguishes legal from ethical norms. Legal norms are characterized by their objectivity, heteronomy, bilateral structure, social, and inexorable imposition. Law is a standardized minimum social order. Ethics, on the other hand, fully regulate each person's individual, authentic destiny; hence ethical norms are necessarily autonomous. Then follows one of the most valuable and original chapters of the book on the distinctions between legal and conventional norms. Legal norms must finally be distinguished from "arbitrary" rules which are likewise inexorably imposed. "Arbitrary," the author warns, is not identical with "unjust." It means that the rule is made in violation of the positive law.

In the second part of the work — the theory of law — the author is a critical follower of Kelsen. Especially the chapters on the conception of the "person in law" and on the legal order are thoroughly Kelsenian. Recaséns Siches admits Kelsen's theory of the identity of law and State in so far as to the jurist the State is expressed in the legal order; but, as a whole, he rejects this theory. Kelsen, he says, recognizes that law is a historical work of man and that in order to be positive law, it must be effective, but he is not willing to accept the consequences of this insight. In order to uphold the purity of the normative system, Kelsen's basic norm would have to be a pure idea in the realm of values, having validity independent of any fact. But that is not the case; indeed, since law is not a pure value, that cannot be the case. Kelsen's basic norm, admittedly not a legal norm, but merely a hypothesis, derives from the reality of social power. That is why the jurist is not free in the choice of the basic norm; his choice is conditioned by certain social facts. The radical separation of the normative world from the world of fact fails with regard to the basic norm and fails in so far as the validity of the law, so rigidly separated by Kelsen from its efficacy in fact, is admittedly dependent on a minimum of efficacy. Similar criticisms have been voiced by García Máynez in his later writings. Kelsen has tried to meet this critique by modifying his theory in his recent work, *General Theory of Law and State,* published as the first volume of this Series.

For Recaséns Siches, in accord with Kelsen, justice is not part of the concept of law. Law is a form — its "juridical quality" does not consist in its contents, but in the inexorable imposition of norms which can have the most diverse contents. That, says the author, does not mean a philosophical relativism or an indifference to the ends of law. It means that the place for these investigations is not in the theory, but in the philosophy of law.

The philosophy of values and the philosophy of life furnish the necessary instruments for the development of a scientific philosophy of law. Hartmann's and Scheler's philosophy of values, valuable as it is, has separated the realms of phenomena and of values. They must be reunited, argues the author, and this can be done through Heidegger's and Ortega y Gasset's philosophy of life which, however, has neglected the theory of values. Human life is the radical reality which sustains all the other ones; the real man of flesh and blood is the intermediary between the real world of phenomena and the ideal world of values. The author's purpose is to found the philosophy of values in the philosophy of life.

The third part of his work gives his philosophy of law, i.e., a philosophy of juridical values. It is the problem of the justification of positive law, the problem of the criteria by which to evaluate a positive law, not of course, in a court of law, but *in foro conscientiae.* This problem cannot be evaded, but it transcends the theory of law. Justice is no part of the *concept* of law: positive law may be just or unjust, without ceasing to be law. But every positive law, whatever its contents, is necessarily *related to values* regardless of what these values may be and whether they are realized or not. Man can live only by making decisions and every decision is ultimately based on a value-judgment.

The problem of justice is discussed historically and critically and the conflict between history and reason since pre-Socratic times is emphasized. The author discusses the hierarchy of juridical values and their position within the world of values. Law, he maintains, can realize only the community's values, which stand on a lower level than the values of individuality; thus religion and ethics are higher values than law.

Recaséns Siches believes in an objective idea of justice. With intense and deep-rooted conviction he discusses the juridical value of human dignity. Man, as Kant has said, is an end in himself, not a means. State and culture are not only made by man; they also exist only for man. Hence the author eloquently opposes moral or political compulsion, State idolatry and any form of totalitarian government, whether fascist or bolshevist.

As noted, the juridical values are not of the highest rank. The conception of man as a "person in law" represents his participation in an inferior rank of values, in which all individuals are equal, generalized, schematized, typified. But the security of the legal order is the indispensable precondition for the real, the authentic, the unique individual participating in a realm of single and unequal values, superior in rank to law and State. This Spanish individualism is the author's inheritance; it is that individualism which is so characteristic of Spanish art, literature, and philosophy from the earliest times to Miguel de Unamuno's profound book, *The Tragic Sense of Life.*

V

While there are many interesting figures in the philosophy of law in Argentina, the outstanding and most original thinker is Carlos Cossio. Professor of philosophy of law at the University of La Plata and President of the Argentine Institute of Juridical and Social Philosophy, he exercises through his teaching, writing, adherents, and disciples a strong influence throughout Latin America. A "Cossio School," so to speak, is in the making, and various monographs on his work have already been published.

Stimulated by the Argentine revolution of 1930, Cossio's theoretical work began with the investigation of the concept of revolution and the relevant function of Kelsen's hypothetical basic norm. His ideas were developed in a great number of monographs on detailed problems. In 1944, in his book, *La Teoría Egológica del Derecho y el Concepto Jurídico de Libertad* (*The Egological Theory of Law*), he published a systematic discussion of his legal philosophy. A translation of the Introduction of this book, dealing with the phenomenology of the judicial decision, is included in this volume.

Cossio's theory is an attempt to go beyond Kelsen without abandoning him. It is an attempt to create an original philosophy of law, to shape an "Argentinian philosophy of law," so to speak, as a part of the ideal of "Argentinidad." In Cossio's thinking we see many of the same ingredients as in the thought of the other Latin-American authors represented in this book; yet the results at which he arrives are quite different. Cossio starts with Kelsen and his logical normativism. He pays great homage to Kelsen and he seems to this writer to be very much like Kelsen — a logician and theoretician rather than a philosopher of law in the metaphysical sense. He is the most positivistic, the least metaphysical of the four; hence his opposition to natural law, his lack of enthusiasm for Scheler and his admiration of the logician Husserl, his distinction between "pure axiology," the investigation of which he leaves to metaphysics, and the positive values of the positive law. He also shares with Kelsen a strongly polemical attitude in expounding his theory. More than the others he wants jurisprudence to serve the lawyer who, as practitioner, judge or scholar, deals with a positive legal order. Positive, dogmatic legal science is, accordingly, the correct starting-point of philosophy of law. More and more his investigations stressed the importance of the judicial decision, a rather rare thing in Roman Law countries.

Cossio's Introduction, presented herein, gives a summary of his whole theory, preliminary to its application to the special problem of the judicial decision. Like Llambías de Azevedo and Recaséns Siches, he starts with the problem of the essence of law and its place among the objects of the world. Law is a cultural object and, therefore, unlike ideal and real objects, it is not neutral toward values. The adequate method of knowledge of cultural objects is the empirical-dialectical method, the method of comprehension, of intuition, as Dilthey taught. Among the cultural objects he distinguishes the "objects of the world," the product of the activity of man, from the "egological" objects, i.e., human action in which human conduct, as such, is articulated. Contrary to Recaséns Siches, law is for Cossio not "objectivated human life," like a statue, but "living human life." Law is an egological object — hence the name of his theory. Law, on the basis of phenomenology, is human action in its inter-subjective relationship — a formula coined by Del Vecchio. This is the cornerstone of Cossio's theory. The science of law is, therefore, an empirical science, a science of reality. But this reality is an experience not of nature, but of liberty.

All science is cognition by concepts. The relevant method is not intuitive, but analytical. The object of the science of law is human conduct, the object of juridical logic is legal concepts. No science is possible without logic, but the logic must be adequate to it. Since the object of law is human conduct, an experience of liberty, not of necessity, of values, not of neutrality to values, the Aristotelian logic of "isness" is fruitless. Only a logic adequate to the egological object of the science of law, only a logic of "oughtness" can be serviceable. To have discovered and developed the "juridical logic," which is neither a logic of subsumption nor of formalization, but of individualization, is, according to Cossio, the outstanding achievement of Kelsen.

While highly praising Kelsen's work Cossio reduces it to formal juridical logic; in this field, Cossio feels, Kelsen has said definitive things. The Pure Theory of Law is indispensable for the science of law as its adequate logical tool; but it is not science of law. Not norms, but human conduct is the object of the latter. The norms are merely intellectual representations of the real object of legal science — concepts with which we think about human conduct. Unlike García Máynez and Recaséns Siches, Cossio does not distinguish between the theory and the philosophy of law, he distinguishes juridical logic from dogmatic science of law, and both from the theory of juridical values (axiology).

The science of law is the science of juridical experience. And since human conduct cannot be neutral to values, legal science must concern itself with juridical valuation. Contrary to the other authors, law is to Cossio not a mediation between human conduct and the values; the values are immanent in the law. Law has not only logical — formal and material — contingent elements but also a third element — juridical valuation — an element which is both material and necessary. Cossio fully accepts Kelsen's idea of liberating the science of law from both sociology and natural law theory. He insists that the scientist must have a neutral attitude toward the object of his investigation, and he believes that most jurists approach the positive law with subjective, preconceived ideologies. Values cannot be eliminated from the law; but if jurisprudence is to be a science, it must not deform its object by appraising it by reference to purely subjective, metaphysical ideals. The *positive* values (from order to justice) are *data given* to the jurist in the positive law. It is within the realm of an objective theory of values to inquire whether the actual ideals of positive law correspond to the "true ideals," an investigation of eminently metaphysical character. Cossio's theory of law is, therefore, quite different from that of the other three scholars. While fully acknowledging the value problem of law, he does not explain it metaphysically through ideal values above the law, but by the immanence of juridical values in positive law.

It is along these lines that Cossio gives us his phenomenology of the judicial decision. The judge is not outside the law, but within. Under any system he is necessarily a creator of law. Nowhere is he an automaton. He cannot be, for he deals with human conduct; his method must be the method of comprehension, his logic the logic of "oughtness." The judicial decision, as the structure of the concrete validity of the law, is an individual norm. Like every norm, it is a conceptual representation of a bit of juridical experience. It consists, therefore, of three elements: the logical structure (the Statute, the Constitution), the contingent contents (the "circumstances of the case"), and the juridical valuation of the judge. The critique of the positive law with reference to values is in the realm of metaphysics. But the judge deals with the positive values. He values not only the circumstances of the case, but also the Statute. As the juridical valuation is immanent in the law, the judge has necessarily an immense power, a fact which rationalist theories tried to conceal by treating the judge as a syllogistic automaton. On the other hand, the judge is not entirely free in creating normative imputations; even if he excludes the applicability of a Statute, his juridical valuation must necessarily accommodate itself to at least one of the legal structures of the legal order.

American lawyers will probably agree with much that Cossio has to say about the judicial decision. But he certainly would not want to have his theory classified as "Sociological Jurisprudence," or "Legal Realism." His theory is opposed to both the rationalist and empiricist types of legal science.

Is Cossio's interpretation of the Pure Theory of Law correct? Is Cossio's basic position that law is human conduct tenable? His theory is still in the process of development and no definitive critique is possible at this time. We must wait for the publication of his announced "Theory of Human Conduct." As it stands, his theory is an attempt to combine Kelsen's Pure Theory of law with Husserl's phenomenology, Heidegger's existentialism, and certain fundamental ideas of Dilthey, such as the concept of "structure" and the method of "comprehension" with regard to the cultural sciences. He vigorously denies that he conceives of "human conduct" in a sociological sense, and has recently said that "human conduct" necessarily means "regulated human conduct." In any case, this writer who appreciates the originality of Cossio's ideas and his vigorous manner of defending them, believes that law is not human conduct, but the regulation of human conduct. For the jurist, at least, law is a system of norms.

VI

Juan Llambías de Azevedo, professor at the University of Montevideo, Uruguay, has written some short, but valuable and original essays. He is not interested in the theory, but in the philosophy of law, not in the form, but in the essence of law. He, too, belongs to the phenomenological school which he combines with the aforementioned theory of values. In his essay entitled *Eidetica y Aporetica del Derecho* (The Eidetics and Aporetics of the Law), included in this volume, he takes as his starting-point the concept of philosophy, as theoretical speculation, a system of judgments which are alleged to be true.

The first task of philosophy is a rigorous description of relevant phenomena, that is, not empirical phenomena, but their essence. With Husserl, Llambías assumes the existence of these essences, apprehended by the phenomenological method of intuition. The science which deals with these essences is the "Eidetica." Applied to philosophy of law, the "Eidetica" seeks the essence of law which Llambías, after employing the method of intuition, describes in the following terms: "The positive legal order is a bilateral and retributive system of dispositions, made by man for the regulation of the social conduct of a group of men, and as a means of realizing the community-values." Law refers to human conduct; and as human conduct is impossible without values, law is, in the last analysis, an instrument at the service of values. Law is a phenomenon of mediation between values and human conduct.

Where is the place of positive law in the general sphere of objects? His criterion for making a division of the objects of the universe is the moment of time ("temporalidad"). Some objects begin and end, they have a development in a nonreversible direction, they stand in time — the objects of reality. On the other hand, there are nontemporal, immutable objects, which are what and how they are permanently — the ideal objects, e.g., essences, numbers, geometrical figures. Law is a temporal object: it has a life, it is "becoming."

The sphere of real objects can be divided according to the criterion of space ("especialidad"): temporal objects in space (the corporeal objects) and temporal objects without space (perceptions, cognitions, valuations). Law is noncorporeal. Although connected with space, it consists of thoughts, having no space.

And, finally, there are psychological objects (perceiving, thinking, valuing) and spiritual objects (thoughts, faiths, judgments, all the contents of art, science, ethics). The latter are objective and transmissible. The spiritual contents, as distinguished from the psychological acts in which they are given, manifest themselves in objectively outlined forms. Law is a spiritual object.

Having intuitively captured the essence of law in the "Eidetica," the author arrives at the second part of his discussion: the questions raised by the phenomenon, law. First of all, it is necessary to state the problems correctly. The "Aporetica" is the pure science of the problems of law and law is a mediation between human conduct and the community-values. Following Scheler, values are "objective essences," having an internal, axiological order, a hierarchic structure. Positive law must not be depreciated, but neither must it be over-valued, as was done in nineteenth-century juridical positivism. The end of law is not the realization of all the values, but only of the community-values. The highest values are the religious values; then follow the logical, ethical, and aesthetic values. Law is inferior to the foregoing values named, but it is superior to the values of biological life and to economic and technical values.

Only after the "Eidetica" has captured the essence of law and the "Aporetica" has stated the problems posed by the phenomenon, law, can the philosophy of law begin: as the answer which man gives to the questions (problems) asked by the phenomenon, law. Since the author limits himself to the two preliminary investigations, the subtitle of his study is Prolegomena to a Philosophy of Law.

Llambías is, among the authors represented, the closest adherent of Husserl's phenomenology. But he takes from Husserl only the conceptions of essences, of eidetic intuition and of regional ontologies. Moreover, he does not make a truly phenomenological investigation in Husserl's sense, namely an investigation of the intentional acts in which law is given; instead, he investigates law itself. The author is also a close follower of Scheler and Hartmann. The very structure of the essay — eidetica and aporetica as prolegomena to philosophy — follows Hartmann. The ideas of Husserl, Scheler, and Hartmann are, in the author's own words, accepted as the primary presupposition of his essay.

VII

Eduardo García Máynez, a Mexican of cosmopolitan outlook, an accomplished linguist, a man of wide learning and systematic knowledge in philosophy, is one of Mexico's eminent scholars, influential throughout Latin America. As editor of outstanding reviews and director of the center of philosophical study at the National University of Mexico, formerly Secretary-General of this University, he has made many contributions to philosophy and philosophy of law. His legal thinking is based largely on Kelsen's Pure Theory of Law and it is also influenced by the ideas of the eminent international lawyer, Alfred von Verdross, under whom he did postgraduate work at the University of Vienna. Philosophically he draws upon the phenomenological school (Husserl and Fritz Schreier), upon his teacher, the great Mexican philosopher, Antonio Caso, and upon the theory of values of Max Scheler and Nikolai Hartmann, under whom he studied in Europe.

The first essay, *El problema filosofico-juridico de validez del derecho,* presented here in English translation, was published in 1935 in Mexico City. It deals with the problem of the validity of law. García Máynez is interested in the theory of law, but the theoretical solutions alone do not satisfy him. The problem of the validity of law is for him a twofold problem: theoretical and philosophical.

In the theoretical treatment of the problem, he, too, is a critical follower of Kelsen: he accepts many parts of his theories, but attacks them at various points. Thus he emphasizes the normative character of the legal system and accepts Kelsen's doctrine of the "pyramid of law," anchored in the basic norm. And he recognizes that a theory of law can start from the hypothetical basic norm. But this solution does not suffice. As the basic norm does not and, by hypothesis, cannot depend on any superior legal norm, Kelsen, he feels, simply avoids the problem of the ultimate validity of the law, a fact which is not altered by Kelsen's doctrine of the primacy of international law. Not the theory, but only the philosophy of law can solve this problem by discovering the meta-juridical principle on which the validity of a positive legal order rests. Such philosophical justification, the author holds, is possible by reliance on the theory of values of Scheler and Hartmann.

The philosophical, as distinguished from the theoretical, problem of the validity of law is the problem of the justification of the positive law. Philosophically the problem can be solved only by considering a legal norm to be valid only in so far as it constitutes the expression of a moral "ought." And this problem has been solved by Hartmann's "material," not formalistic, ethics. The existence of objective values *a priori*, the author admits, cannot be proved satisfactorily by theoretical reason, but constitutes a metaphysical thesis; yet, the author insists, the conviction that there are objective values is not a simple faith, but an inherent necessity of the human spirit. Law, to be valid philosophically, must realize objective values, juridical values, of which justice is the highest. Justice is an absolute value, identical at all times and places, although the contingent conceptions which individuals and nations form of justice vary greatly. This is exactly the reasoning of Verdross and, like Verdross, García Máynez, is inevitably led by it toward natural law.

Since this early monograph, García Máynez has developed his ideas in many later books and writings. His monograph on *Liberty as Right and as Power* (*Libertad, como derecho y como poder*), included in this volume, is representative of his later work. The author distinguishes between liberty as a fact and legal liberty as a right, derived from and based upon a legal norm. Strongly opposing the thesis of Rocco, a leading jurist of Fascist Italy, that liberty admits only of a negative definition, the author maintains the possibility and necessity of a positive definition of liberty.

The author begins his discussion with a legal trichotomy of all human actions or omissions into those ordered, prohibited, or permitted by law. "Permitted" in the strict sence is only the doing or not doing of what the law neither orders nor forbids. His first definition of legal liberty is given as "the authority of everyone, subject to the legal order, to exercise or not to exercise his rights." The author emphasizes that "liberty" is not merely one among various rights, but is, instead, a category concerning the exercise of any right, whether absolute or relative, whether private or public. The right is only a normative possibility. "Liberty" is directly connected with its exercise or nonexercise.

Testing this definition, the author finds that there are certain rights, like the right to vote, which under some legal orders — e.g., in Mexico — is not only a right but also a duty, so that he who has the right to vote is not allowed any choice as to whether or not to exercise it. He thus arrives at a final definition: legal liberty is the authority, granted by the positive law to every person to exercise or not to exercise any right, in so far as the content of the right in question is not reduced to the performance of the person's duty.

In this monograph, too, the juridical analysis is followed by a philosophical discussion, which is again based on Hartmann's theory of values. A legal duty can be explained ultimately only as a function of the idea of value. The ultimate justification must be found in certain objective values which exist independently of any subjective perception and have, in Hartmann's phrase, a "being in themselves." Thus García Máynez' interest is primarily ethical rather than logical. So long as he holds that the legal validity of a positive legal norm must be justified philosophically, that is metajuridically, no objection can be raised. But when he later seems to imply that a positive law which is unjust is no law at all, he is in danger of espousing the one-sided, old-fashioned "natural law."

VIII

Since the jurisprudence of the above four authors accepts, in varying degrees, the philosophies of Husserl, Scheler, Hartmann, Dilthey, Heidegger, and Ortega y Gasset, it is pertinent to consider the status of these philosophies, which, while gaining wide adherence, have also been strongly attacked, not only by logical positivists, but also by Neo-Kantians and others. While far from subscribing entirely to these philosophies, this writer thinks they have made many great and lasting contributions. Moreover, these philosophies are the expression of our time, a time of immense crisis for the whole of Western Christian Civilization. "The story of modern axiology," states Wilbur M. Urban, "is in a sense the story of a culture — the European culture — fighting for its very life." This crisis — now a commonplace — was recognized eighty years ago; indeed, it may be said that Nietzsche's "transvaluation of values" is the theme of our epoch. The nineteenth-century faith in science and "progress" has been shattered. Technology has transformed the world. The bourgeoisie feels itself threatened and insecure in its ideals. Wars of a magnitude, never before imagined, have been fought. The atomic bomb hangs as a constant threat over humanity. Millions live in abject poverty, misery, and starvation, and under tyrannical governments. Art, music, painting, and poetry are in an uncertain period of transition. The appearance of the masses — the "vertical invasion of the barbarians," in the words of Ortega y Gasset — has posed problems not yet solved. Life, as William Barret says, is taking on a more and more drab, monotonous aspect; less and less is it possible to lead a distinctive personal existence.

In such periods of extraordinary crisis, metaphysical anxieties, such as the "dread" of Kierkegaard, become obsessive. There is a desire for salvation; e.g., Scheler, going back to Platonic-Christian ideas, emphasizes a "knowledge of salvation." Hence the revival of Thomism. Hence, on the other hand, the atheistic existentialism of Heidegger and Sartre, for whom the ultimate is that man exists. The longing for eternal, objective values, the return to natural law, the cry for the "authentic life" characterize the current temper of philosophical thought. All these philosophies are, in the words of Dilthey, the outcome of a specific historical situation and, in this sense, they are thoroughly "modern."

It is as modern men of the Christian Western culture in this historical period of crisis that Latin-American philosophers of law accept these philosophies. They try, in the field of jurisprudence, to find a way out of the crisis, to find better solutions, more adequate to man's present historical situation, as far as law is concerned. In this spirit they reexamine fundamental problems in order to arrive at satisfactory solutions which embrace the law in its totality. This also indicates the particular place of Kelsen's theory of law in their writing: a starting-point, a doctrine much of which is accepted, but also a target to attack. They think that the Pure Theory of Law is a product of intrinsic greatness which will remain definitively incorporated in the thinking of jurists and, at the same time, that Kelsen's theory is not sufficient, that the sociological substratum and the evaluation of the law must be included and, accordingly, that philosophical relativism must be overcome.

Ramón Alsina, professor of jurisprudence in the University of Buenos Aires, a few years ago surveyed the development of the legal philosophy of the last centuries: natural law, concerned only with the eternal and immutable values, stressing the element of reason; nineteenth-century positivism as a reaction, insisting only on sociological and historical factors; and the Neo-Kantian reaction against positivism, concentrating entirely on the formal, logical element of law. He suggests that we are now on the way toward a conception which will allow us to bring all the three aspects — logical, sociological and axiological — into one fundamental unity. The same problem was posed here by Jerome Hall, criticizing what he calls the "particularistic fallacies" of modern legal philosophies, and presenting an "Integrative Jurisprudence."

A knowledge of the most significant Latin-American writings in jurisprudence will obviously contribute to the understanding of our neighbors to the South. But apart from and transcending this inter-American aspect of good-neighborliness, these writings deserve to be known here because of their intrinsic merit. They constitute brilliant, original contributions to the solution of the most pressing legal problems of our times.

TOLEDO, OHIO

I

HUMAN LIFE, SOCIETY AND LAW. FUNDAMENTALS OF THE PHILOSOPHY OF THE LAW

BY LUIS RECASÉNS SICHES

Professor of the Philosophy of Law and of Sociology at the National University of Mexico, Vice President of the International Institute of the Philosophy of Law and of Juridical Sociology, Member of the Argentine Institute of Juridical and Social Philosophy

TRANSLATED BY

Gordon Ireland, Visiting Professor of Law, Catholic University of America, School of Law

PREFACE

This book is inspired with the purpose of making a systematic exposition — which may be comprehensible to any student, though not a specialist — of the philosophical problem of the Law. In part these pages present ideas from some earlier works of mine, now substantially rephrased. On the other hand, this new book which I now offer the reader contains new points of view which are the fruit of meditation during the last four years. I present at the same time, in a more mature and complete form, other subjects which have been only outlined in my previous publications. Above all, I have tried to accomplish a systematic articulation of the fundamental questions in the Philosophy of Law and of its integration into general Philosophy to the stage it has reached in our time. In fine, I have tried to state for juristics its primary truths of authentic philosophic rank; to understand essentially the Law as one of the tasks which man undertakes in his life. Therewith is an attempt to integrate the basic meaning of the Law in a complete Philosophy, in the direction of the Metaphysics of our time. Some years ago I formulated this theme as a program. Today, I have decided to offer some further advances in this attempt. It is clear that I do not consider my task finished, in any way. There yet remains much to be gone over. But I am confident that this systematic version of my work may constitute a point of departure for future speculations; and I hope, moreover, that this book may contribute somewhat to centering the philosophical reflection of our time on the Law, and that, in turn, it may serve as a manual of initiation.

MEXICO, D. F.
July, 1939

LUIS RECASENS SICHES

EXTRACT FROM THE PREFACE TO SECOND EDITION, MEXICO, NOVEMBER 1944

All the additions with which I have increased the present edition consist in part of the result of a deepening of my meditation upon the fundamental themes of this work, especially upon human life, society, and history; in part, of the benefit drawn from the experiences of these last years in the chair, to make comprehensibly more easily and deeply and with greater breadth many of the basic questions of the philosophy of society and juristics; in part, also, of the product of the urging of the events of our time; in part, as well, of the effect of important spiritual benefits received from the labors accomplished by illustrious colleagues; and, finally, of the consequence of putting my own thought in relation with other more or less near reflections.

HUMAN LIFE, SOCIETY AND LAW. FUNDAMENTALS OF THE PHILOSOPHY OF THE LAW

CHAPTER I

THE UNIVERSE, HUMAN LIFE, SOCIETY AND LAW

1. Preliminary Remarks upon the Multiform Complexity of the Universe

We are accustomed to call the Universe the totality of all things that are: external realities (such as a mountain), those which exist in my being (as a love), phantasies (as a centaur), ideas (as a triangle), ultra-realities (if there are any), any other properties of things there may be; and, above all, ourselves, who in some manner compose the Universe.

The spectacle of the Universe presents itself as a motley bulk of multiform and heterogenous things. In the Universe there are mountains, floods, trees, colors, geometrical forms, equalities, inequalities, toothaches, memories, chimeras, desires, numbers, moral ideas, automobiles, squares, judges, police, social usages, prices, immediate prospects, almost imperceptible (rather latent) backgrounds, friends, enemies, companions, etc. And, moreover, in the Universe I find myself, living, existing, with all the rest.

All the things mentioned, their respective kinds and many others besides which we have not mentioned, make up something which is in the Universe; they are elements or beings; in a word, they *are*. In any other way it would be impossible that we should be occupying ourselves with them, that we should talk of them, since it is not possible for us to refer to something which *is not* in any part, or in any form: to nothing. (When I try to think of nothing, it transforms itself into something, at least in my thought.) But if indeed all these things *are*, they are not in the same sense; if indeed all are *something*, those somethings differ radically among themselves. And the differences between those somethings do not consist of mere diversities of quality, nor of class, nor of species: it is a question of differences much more profound: it is a question of differences between multiple and irreducible meanings of the word being. It is manifest that the word being has a very different meaning when we apply it to a column than when we apply it to a color (for example, the white color of the column); and in turn it has a new and different meaning when we apply it to the equality which there may be between one column and another. The column is something which is in itself, which presents itself to me as being with its own existence. On the other hand, a color is something which *is* not independently of anything else, without support on another thing, that is, as the color of an object, as the color of the column; it is something which cannot *be* isolated and alone, but whose being rests upon or extends over the being of another thing. And if we now pass to the equality which we discover between two columns, we must recognize that that which we call equality is something which does not exist independently (like the column); nor is it something adhering necessarily to another thing (as occurs with the color); but it is something which exists between two things (two twin columns), when my mind compares them: in short, it is not a substantive thing, nor a quality, but it is a relation. We have, then, made manifest three radically different meanings of the word being; precisely the three fundamental meanings discovered by Aristotle. And Aristotle calls these several meanings or senses of the word being, categories; and so Aristotle explains in his Metaphysics that being is spoken of in various manners, that there are multiple meanings of the word being, in short, that there are various categories. But those three categories, to which we have just called attention, were discovered with respect to *real* being, of real things. However, in the world there are not only real things (mountains, rivers, trees, etc.), but many other things of a different kind, which are not real. Not all which is something, which is before me, is real; on the contrary, there are things which only *are in me,* as, for example, my dreams, my unfilled desires, my hallucinations. And, moreover, on the other hand, there are also some *ideals* which are not there among external things, neither are they only within me, for example, a pure triangle, a mathematical principle, the idea of full and perfect justice, which are objects which *are* something, but which are not there outside in space, nor in me as processes of my intelligence, but which have a spectral form of being, to wit, an *ideal being*.

And, moreover, we find also a multitude of other beings of a different kind from those heretofore mentioned, such as statues, paintings, melodies, tools, which have a reality external to us — of stone, wood, colors, sounds, various materials — but whose specific and peculiar being does not consist of those real ingredients, but in a meaning (aesthetic, utilitarian, etc.) which resides in them, in a human projection which is expressed in them. And, so, we distinguish a full, rich, aggregate of objects of which — though indeed they contain real elements — their being consists in a human feeling: it is the world of things which man makes in his life, by and large; the world of the human in an objectivated form, the realm of history, or, as it has also been called, the field of culture.

And, on the other hand, we take into account that we meet all those multiple classes of beings in the course of our existence, of our life, as ingredients of it. There are indeed many things which I find before me, upon which I happen, which I use or reject, which I like or abhor, which I construct or destroy or transform, which excite my liking or my repugnance; or things which occur within my personality; or principles which transcend me and by which I guide my understanding or my conduct. Hereby I discover myself not only as a subject — opposed to the idea of object — but, moreover, I contemplate something much more ample, namely *my life* as composed of two parts: I myself and the aggregate of things with which I occupy myself. In these complex terms the Universe appears to contemporary thought — to thought which is the protagonist of the present renaissance of philosophy. While in the second half of the nineteenth century there were favored monist trends (of many sorts) which arbitrarily and monomaniatically sought to reduce the Universe to one single formula, on the contrary, thinking of our time faces this problem with an attitude more honest and of greater theoretic responsibility; it emphasizes the pluralistic composition of the Universe. This is clear, without ceasing to aspire to a basic and universal primary criterion; to an underlying (primary) truth, fundamental to all else, since such is the goal inherent to all philosophy. But it tries to accomplish this in a rigorous and more profound manner, and consequently to avoid the precipitation and clumsiness of the monists, and not to fall into the arbitrary misconstructions which such unilateral formulas carry with them. As this book is dedicated not to a metaphysical exposition but to an examination of some fundamental themes concerning juristics, I cannot offer — even in a short summary — the story of the contemporaneous philosophic development. There will serve as a suggestive guide to this process the mere mention of the names of Brentano, Meinong, Dilthey, Husserl, Scheler, Nikolai Hartmann, Ortega y Gasset, Heidegger and Dewey,[1] through whose works runs the foremost line of contemporary philosophy.

[1] These notes do not pretend in any way to offer a bibliographic guide to the Philosophy of Law. They are only references to the allusions made in the text. For ample bibliographic information as to the Philosophy of Law, my book, The Themes of the Philosophy of Law, in historic perspective and vision of the future, may be consulted (1934).

Brentano, Vom sinnlichen und noetischen Bewusstsein (1928); Versuch über die Erkenntnis (1925); Entwicklung der Wertlehre (1908); Vom Dasein Gottes (1868): Vom Ursprung der sittlichen Erkenntnis.

2. Initial Setting of the Philosophic Problem in the Law

But the important purpose of this book is to obtain an essential knowledge of the Law: to find the primary and fundamental truth about juristics, that is to say, to understand it in itself and, at the same time, included in a total view of the world. To the degree in which we approach the fulfillment of this end, we shall obtain an authentically philosophic knowledge of the Law.

It is clear that all peoples have some idea with respect to the Law, as, indeed, they have with regard to all the things which they meet in their lives. In the world we find magistrates and police, sales, leases, deposits, salaries, statutes, lawyers, notaries, assignees, prisons, guardians, inheritances, etc. And for all it is obvious that those things — and an endless number of other similar ones — belong to the realm of juristics. This appears as obvious as that roses and peas belong to the field of botany.

Meinong, Psychologisch-ethische Untersuchungen zur Werttheorie (1894); Untersuchungen zur Gegenstandstheorie (1904); Über die Stellung der Gegenstandstheorie im System der Wissenschaften (1897).

Edmund Husserl, Logische Untersuchungen (1900); Ideen zu einer reinen Phänomenologie und Phänomenologischen Philosophie (1913); Meditations cartésiennes (1931).

Max Scheler, Der Formalismus in der Ethik und die materiale Wertethik (2d ed., 1922); Wesen und Formen der Sympathie (2d ed., 1923); Die Stellung des Menschen im Kosmos (1928); Philosophische Weltanschaung (1929).

Nikolai Hartmann, Grundzüge einer Metaphysik der Erkenntnis (1923); Ethik (1926); Das Problem des geistigen Seins (1933); Kathegorienlehre (1935).

José Ortega y Gasset, Descartes y el método trascendental (As. esp. para el progr. de las ciencias, vol. VI); Meditaciones del Quijote (1914); Verdad y perspectiva (t. 1 de El Espectador, 1916); Conciencia, objeto y las tres distancias de éste (*idem*); Biologia y pedagogia (El Espectador, IV, 1925); El tema de nuestro tiempo (1923); ¿Qué son los valores? Una introducción a la Estimativa (Rev. de Occidente, no. IV, 1924); Sobre la expresión, fenómeno cósmico (El Espectador, VII, 1929); Ni vitalismo ni racionalismo (Rev. de Occidente, no. XVI, 1924); Vitalidad, Alma, Espíritu (El Espectador, V, 1927); Kant, Reflexiones de Centenario (1925); Curso libre sobre ¿Qué es Filosofía? profesado en la primavera de 1929 (Véanse los resúmenes en El Sol de Madrid); Filosofía Pura (Rev. de Occidente, julio, 1929); La Filosofía de la Historia en Hegel y la Historiologia (Rev. de Occidente, no. 56, 1928); Goethe desde dentro (1933); Guillermo Dilthey y la idea de la vida (dos articulos en la Rev. de Occidente en 1934).

Martin Heidegger, Sein und Zeit (1927); Kant und das Problem der Metaphysik (1929); Was ist Metaphysik? (1930).

John Dewey, Human Nature and Conduct (1922); Individualism, Old and New (1930); Philosophy and Civilization (1931); How We Think (1933); Ethics (1932); Experience and Education (1938); The Unity of the Human Being (1937).

But so far it is a matter of merely approximate knowledge, superficial, unsure, haphazard; in short, of what is called popular knowledge, that is, at random, ignorant of reasons, without firm grasp, fluctuating and dangerous. We shall observe it — in the instance which interests us, that is, with reference to juristics — if we ask the man in the street why he includes in the Law all those things which we have mentioned (and many others, such as property, bill of exchange, governors, prisons and fines). Where is the legal quality in each of those things? Governors, judges, and policemen are men of flesh and blood like all other men, and do not differ from them by virtue of any peculiar reality; nevertheless there is embodied in them some juridical dimension. What is the juridical element in them? Codes and Regulations contain rules of conduct; but so also do the rules which regulate football or a game of cards, and, also, a cooking recipe or a manual on how to behave in a social gathering, and, as well, the precepts for a religious confession. Why, of the examples just put, do we say that some treat of judicial questions, and, on the other hand, we do not so consider all the other rules we have just mentioned? A prison and a fort are buildings, as is also a mansion or a stadium; why do the former have a juridical significance which the latter lack? With respect to all the multiple and heterogenous things mentioned, where in them does the juridical reside? What is it which permits me to group within one classification, that is, as Law, things so disparate? To what region of the Universe does the juridical belong, which makes itself evident to me in such diverse manifestations? Where dwells the Law? What class of thing is that we call Law and which presents such various faces? Whence arises all that we characterize as juridical? Why do we find juristics in all peoples and in all epochs? Why and to what end do men concern themselves with juridical problems in all latitudes and in all times?

And it is not to be thought that all these questions are a mystery only for laymen in Jurisprudence. Although the experts in the sciences of the Law know, it is clear, as to them immeasurably more than the layman, it sometimes happens that even jurists, so far as they are mere jurists — that is to say, as mere technicians of the Law — do not find themselves able to answer satisfactorily the questions which I have put. For the jurist — as jurist and nothing more, including the legal scholar — moves easily and skillfully in the trackless wastes of juridical provisions; he knows, understands, and applies all their elements; but he does not envision the problem of what is the situation and meaning which the Law has in the complexity of the Universe. Of the Law, the expert jurist knows perchance all its parts; but if he is only an expert jurist and nothing more than that, and does not emerge from the limited sector of his specialty — although that embraces all parts of the Law — he cannot have a perfect idea of the Law as a totality, of the Law by itself, nor of what the place is which it occupies with respect to the other types of things which there are in the world. Such problems can be stated and solved only so far as we put ourselves in another plane of knowledge, in a plane distinct from merely scientific knowledge, namely, in philosophic knowledge. Therefore, a Philosophy of the Law is alone able to tell the full and fundamental truth as to juristics, or at least to pose the problem.

3. Motivations of the Philosophy of the Law[2]

Formulated positive Law purposes to serve the exigencies of justice. In fact, as we shall show later, all positive Law is a proposal, an effort to translate into norms the exigencies of justice — and of other values connected with it — with respect to the determined social situation at one place and at one time. That effort may be successful, more or less successful, or a failure. But except in the last case, that is, except when that proposal of justice has failed, there will be a parallel, a concordance between the animating intention of the positive Law and the animating intention of the jurist; for the order as well as the judge desires to find the just solution. Now, although ordinarily the jurist may and ought to do much to accommodate the result of his work to the exigencies of justice — and in fact the work of the jurists has many times acted as a very important factor in juridical progress — he does not have full liberty in his work, for always he is inescapably restricted by the limits clearly and taxatively established by the positive norms.

Notice that in this aspect we find one of the limitations of the strict function of the jurist, so far as he is a jurist and nothing more than a jurist. And I say so far as he is jurist and nothing more, because it is clear that whoever may be a jurist can and even ought to be something more than a jurist, that is, he may and ought to set before himself the critique of the norms in force and to meditate upon the directives for their progressive reëlaboration. Now, when he does such a thing, he does not act strictly as a jurist, but as an explorer of future legislation. Moreover, as jurist, it is not proper for him to replace the norm in force by his personal criterion, however much superior that may be. But this does not prevent that, apart from his strict service of the positive Law in force, the jurist, beyond his office, should meditate upon the faults of the rules in force and should indicate the reforms which it is desirable and opportune to introduce into the precepts in force. Or, put in other words, independently of the juridical profession, in the strict sense, he has an-

[2] The two paragraphs of this section are from the Second Spanish edition of the book (Mexico, 1945). TRANSLATOR.

other distinct function to fill: the function of orientation of the future norms to dictate by new laws or regulations. Now, although this work is different from that strictly of the jurist, no one is in a better condition than he to bring it to success; for the jurist it is who possesses the fullest and deepest knowledge of the defects of the positive Law and the manner of remedying them. In truth, the jurist in his daily contact with the application of the Law in force acquires better experience than anyone else on the faults of the positive legislation; and he can orientate with greater and more certain capacity than any other person the reforms which it is desirable to introduce into it. But when he discharges that critical duty as to what there is and orientates as to what there ought to be, he does not function strictly as a jurist, although the knowledge acquired in his juridical office is of great usefulness to him for it. This knowledge is in fact very opportune for him; but his critical and orientating labor is based on other points of view, namely, on points of view strictly philosophical. Here is the root or motivation of one of the themes of the Philosophy of Law, the estimative or valuing theme.

4. The Question as to What Is the Region of the Universe to Which the Law Belongs

If the task which we set before the reader is that of trying to master the fundamental truth about the Law, what constitutes the first principle of all juristics, and what may be at the same time the truth which illumines and aptly grounds all the other questions to whatever themes they refer, it seems obvious that the first question to ask ourselves is: Where is the Law? Let us proceed to the search for and capture of juristics in its essence. Every effort for knowledge — and superlatively that for philosophical knowledge — resembles somewhat a police investigation. For that reason, we must first find our bearings with regard to where to find what we seek. Then we have to begin by inquiring in what part or zone of the Universe resides that which is called the Law. And if we succeed in answering satisfactorily this question, we shall have accomplished nothing less than determining the nature of that something which bears the name of Law.

5. The Law Does Not Belong to Physical Nature

All of a sudden, we conjecture that probably there are zones of the Universe in which dwell nothing which has to do with juristics. We have a presentiment that in no sector of nature, neither physical nor chemical nor organic, shall we find the Law. And certainly this conjecture is true, as we shall see presently.

The world of inorganic physical nature is composed of series of phenomena, linked by fatal bonds of causality, blind or indifferent to every point of view as to value or non-value, ignorant of all valuation, lacking all meaning; for the phenomena of physical nature are explained completely according to our success in placing them correctly in a chain of causality. There is nothing in nature which presents itself to us as a juridic element. And it does not argue to the contrary to say, for example, that the territory of the State — which is a juridic thing — constitutes a portion of the physical nature of our planet; because what there is juridical in the territory is not a physical reality, but a special significance, foreign entirely to its matter or body and which for that reason is absolutely inexplicable from the point of view of physical science. Nor, as ill assumed examples suggest, does the existence of tangible realities, such as prisons and flags, among the things in which the Law manifests itself, tend to the contrary. In the first place a prison and a flag, although composed of corporeal ingredients, are not natural things like mountains, or rivers, but are things constructed by man, the products of human activities, and as such wholly unintelligible to Physics or to any natural science. Moreover, it is plain that the juridical dimension in which we discover those things does not rest on any of their material components, neither in the stone or wood, nor in the textile fibers of the cloth, but on the *expression of a meaning,* of a purpose, completely foreign to the world of physical relations.

No more in the sector of corporeal organic realities do we find anything which evokes the Law for us, or presents any trace of juristics. But it suffices to say that, even in case they should have to be understood in the light of some principle of purpose, such idea of purpose would be of a kind entirely unlike what we understand by the word when we apply it to typically human activities (that is, to the intentional occupation of man). When very shortly, a few pages further on, we look at the realm of human realities, we shall understand that between the human and the biological intervenes a profound difference, an insurmountable heterogeneity.

Another consideration makes it evident that the Law is totally foreign to the world of nature. In nature, the elements present themselves to us always linked by causal bonds, by compulsory ties. Such bonds or ties receive the name of natural laws (physical, chemical, biological, etc.), which express how, in a compulsory manner, phenomena *actually* behave. On the contrary, the Law offers itself to us as an aggregate of *norms.* Although at this preliminary stage we may not yet attempt even a superficial definition of juristics, it is not too risky to say that the Law contains an aggregate of norms, since this much is discovered at the first common contact with it. Then a norm means an expression of an ought-to-be, that is, enunciation of something which we deem ought to be, although perhaps, in fact, it may remain unfulfilled. While natural laws (of Physics, Chemistry, etc.) denote something which takes place inevitably and necessarily; and are valid as such laws by virtue of their coincidence with reality; on the other hand, norms postulate conduct which — for some reason — is considered valuable, although in fact contrary behavior may take place. Precisely because such conduct cannot be relied on for necessary fulfillment, it is put forth as a *duty*. The world of nature is that of *material necessity;* the world of norms is a world of *necessity of ought-to-be*. What natural laws prescribe *has to be;* what norms prescribe is not assured by a natural necessity; precisely for that reason it is expressed as an ought-to-be directed toward conduct.

It appears then clearly that the Law does not dwell in corporeal nature; and consequently it is also plain that whoever remains confined within the ambit of the natural sciences and operates exclusively by their methods will never comprehend even from afar what the Law may be.

6. Nor Is Law Psychic Nature

For several centuries, indeed, there has been a tendency to call spiritual or psychological everything which appears not corporeal. And so there was a tendency to a sort of bipartite classification of the world: the material and the psychological. But it had to be recognized that this dual vision was very rough; since there are numberless things which plainly are not corporeal, which are not material, and which nevertheless do not belong to the domain of the psychic; nor can they for that reason be explained or understood by Psychology. Formerly some said: if the Law is not material, if Jurisprudence is neither Physics nor Biology, it will be somewhat psychological. Today, on the other hand, we have come to consider that the essence of juristics does not belong to the realm of psychic beings, even when it makes itself apparent to us by means of them. We call psychic a special complex of real phenomena which, although they are certainly not given in space, take place in time. The psychic is made up of an aggregate of resources, instruments, mechanisms (images, memory, impulses, emotions, etc.) which, however distinct and heterogenous they may be from the physiological, however irreducible they may be to those, nevertheless have that dimension of the mechanical, they are a temporal series of phenomena. Psychology — as a science — studies those intellectual, emotional, and volitional processes; and even though the points of view and the methods of understanding them are entirely distinct from those employed by the physical and biological sciences (since Psychology based on the concepts of natural causality and measurement has failed and has remained banished), nevertheless, it has in common with the natural sciences that it tries to explain some real phenomena, in its dimension of actual realities and in its peculiar connections. In contemplation then, of such psychological processes — intellection, feeling, volition — in the study of its structure and of its dynamism, the Law does not appear as such at all. It is true that the Law may present itself as an object or a term of reference for such phenomena. I may think of the Law with my understanding; I may feel the encouraging emotion of the Law triumphant or the sad emotion of a wrong committed; and my will may be on the way to the realization of the Law. But I do not find the essence of the Law, what the Law holds as such, by prying into those psychological processes, since those same psychological processes are present when I think, feel, or wish with regard to art, religion, love, or cooking. There has been talk, indeed, of an intuition as to what is just, of a juridical sentiment, and, also, one may talk of a juridical ratiocination and of a juridical will. But in all this juristics will be the content or the spoken of in a thought, an emotion, or a volition; but not those mental, emotional, or volitional processes, as psychic phenomena. What a juridical thought or a juridical feeling has of juristics is not what it has as thought or feeling but as a point of reference for that mental process. The juridical in an intuition or a feeling is not a real ingredient of those phenomena, but a *relational* quality, that is, something which creates them in relation to the object to which they refer, which in this case is something juridical. Resorting to similes — of course rough and with great inexactness like all metaphorical comparisons — it could be said that it is important not to confound the mirror with the image which it reflects, and to remember that it can reflect also many other different ones; and, also, we should not confound the chisel and the hammer with one of the marbles made with such tools, and we have to consider that using the same tools we can construct many other things.

It remains, then, clear that the Law is neither of a corporeal nature nor a psychic process.

7. The Ideal Being

But the world is not composed only of corporeal and psychic beings. There are other regions, other zones of being, besides those to which I have alluded at the beginning of these pages. And among these other kinds of objects are those called *ideal beings;* for example, mathematical principles, logical truths, etc. The ideal being has also been called unreal: it is something which *is,* but it *is* in a different manner from that in which the real being *is.* While the real is that which is encompassed in space and time — matter — or only in time — psychic things — the ideal occupies no space nor is it in any chronological series, but my mind meets with it as with an objective being.

We must carefully avoid the error of confounding the ideal being with the psychic world, as was done for a long time. Traditionally the world of the ideal has been confounded with the world of the spiritual. The spectral dimension which corresponds to ideas, its quintessential character, the valuing resonances which accompany many of them, all contributed to the tendency to define the ideal as spiritual, because in the spirit is made evident to us the world of ideas. But to think so is to confound lamentably the mental act with the content or object which by means of it is made evident to us. The psychic act by which I think of a number, a logical principle, or any other idea is a real fact of my mind, which extends over a definite time. On the other hand, the idea thought of has a consistency of its own, independent of the act of thinking of it. The manner of an idea's being, its entity or consistency, is not only ***not in space,*** but also ***not in time.*** Although the idea is present in my consciousness for some time, its being is distinct from that of my act of thinking about it, and infinitely exceeds the boundaries of that act. An example will make very clear what I am expounding. Let us, the reader and I, now think of the number 3. We shall have two thinking acts of the number 3: the psychic act of the reader and mine. But, on the other hand, the number 3 is one single and unique object: it is the same and identical as thought of by the reader and as thought of by me. Moreover, I think of the number 3 now, but I also thought of it yesterday, and may again think of it tomorrow. We shall have in the same person, three acts successive in time, of thinking of the number 3; but the number thought of, yesterday, today, and tomorrow, is exactly the same. Each act of thinking of it is a new real event which occurs in my mind or in that of the reader. But the idea, the 3 thought of by the reader or by me before, now or hereafter, is the same thing. Thus it is clear that the idea has a being distinct from the psychic realities in which it is thought of. These realities are multiple, they are produced in various persons and in successive moments of time. On the contrary, the being of the idea is one; it is something which is outside of space and outside of time, and independent of me although it reveals itself to me in a real act of my mind. My thinking the idea is indeed in time — and moreover in me — I am in a certain space; but the idea thought of is not in space and not in time. For the knowledge of the idea it is necessary that an intelligence should think of it, since it is obvious that we cannot know ideas which we have not thought of. But we may distinguish between the idea thought of and the act of thinking of it, and, consequently, take care that the being of the idea is not confounded with the ephemeral process of thinking of it.

There is, then, a world of ideas, which does not occupy space, which does not extend in time, which therefore does not have the dimensions of reality, but which has another manner of being. It would constitute a grave error to compare being with reality and reduce the former to the latter. There are real but there are also unreal or ideal beings, which offer to every judgment of the subject a resistance analogous to that of real objects. We find ourselves before them, as we find ourselves before a tree. Unlike the tree they do not have reality, but they do have an objective being which imposes determined requirements on our mind. That objective being of ideal objects is called validity. I find the principle 2 plus 2 equals 4 thanks to an effort of my mind, but this principle is not a piece of my mentality, but an ideality with its own consistency, with validity.[3]

8. Values

What I have just explained with respect to a mathematical principle we could also say with relation to moral ideas, or other criteria of valuation, that is, with relation to values. Values constitute ideal objects with a peculiar validity. We may discover them in things — in those things which we deem valuable — but they do not constitute a piece of their reality, but only a quality which they present to us, in so far as such things coincide with the ideal essences of value.

A slight consideration of those principles which we call values makes it manifest that they have characteristics different from other ideal objects. There are ideal structures like mathematics which, besides their ideal consistency, necessarily constitute also, in a certain dimension, peculiar structures of real being: for example, 2 plus 2 equals 4 is an ideal mathematical relation, but it is at the same time a structure in reality, something necessarily fulfilled, for it is not possible that two apples plus two apples should not add to four apples. The assembly of apples is incapable of any act of disobedience to this mathematical relation. While, on the contrary, values — ethical, juridical, aesthetic, ideas, the moduli of vitality, utilitarian points of view — constitute ideal qualities, with regard to which things or conduct may be intractable. The ideal validity of values is not necessarily accompanied by its embodiment in reality; it may happen — and many times it does happen —

[3] Cf. José Ortega y Gasset, ¿Qué son los valores?; Joaquín Xirau, El sentido de la verdad (1927) 173 and 174; José Gaos, La crítica del psicologismo en Husserl (1931); Husserl, Log. Unters. t. 1, pp. 129ff.; t. 2, pp. 98ff.; Ideen zu einer Phaenomenologie, t. 1, pp. 4ff.; Hartmann, Grundzüge einer Met. der Erk, 457ff., 478ff.; Ethik 137ff.; José Romano Muñoz, El secreto del bien y del mal (Mexico, 1938).

that reality shows itself disdainful of the voice of values. People ought to be truthful; but, nevertheless, we frequently meet with lying and treacherous persons. Some values are realized in some measure but not in another; some are absolutely realized in things; others only in a fragmentary manner; and others are not realized, that is, they are, consequently, denied.

Values are ideal objects which have a validity analogous to that which corresponds to other ideas; but, different from them, they possess also something special which we might name a calling to be realized, a pretension to rule in the world and to be embodied in it through the action of man. It is plain that the essence of values is independent of their realization; that is, a value has weight not because it may have been realized, but in spite of its not having been realized. Because something may be, is, here, does not signify that it embodies a value; it may represent precisely the negation of a value; that is, a nonvalue or an antivalue. And, vice versa, the validity of a value does not carry ready the effective necessity of its realization. Therefore we say that the categories of being and of value are independent. But if indeed it is plain that the essence and the validity of values are independent of their eventual fulfillment in facts, it is also plain that this independence does not indicate indifference in the face of their nonrealization. On the contrary, in the meaning of the values lies their pretension to be fulfilled. When the values which relate to a certain reality are not fulfilled or embodied in it, it results that such reality, without ceasing to be the reality which it is, seems not justified, as something which indeed *is*, but which *ought not to be*. And also, unrealized values have a dimension which consists in a sort of tendency or ideal trend to assert themselves in reality. Their meaning consists in wanting to be fulfilled, in fixing rules for behavior. Naturally when I speak of a "tendency," of "wanting," of a "calling," I use these words as metaphorical expressions, to denote the special meaning of values, and not in the strict acceptation of those words (as an effective power or as a real impulse). It is a question only of making clear the specific ideal dimension which belongs to values, like a tendency or reference of reality, as a pretension to rule over it.

Apart from other characteristics, the ideas of value have the peculiarity of appearing always in pairs, a positive value with a negative value (nonvalue or antivalue). That is, one single reference of value is bipolar: good-bad, truth-falsity, justice-injustice, aptitude-ineptitude, beauty-ugliness, largeness-smallness, etc. And so far as in the reality appears the negation of the value which belongs to it, that is, the nonvalue or antivalue — an immoral act, an unjust decision, a homely picture, a useless tool, etc. — it seems as if the positive value were clamoring for its realization; it seems as if the reality, or its anti-valuable or non-valuable side, were suffering a want or mutilation of its destiny.[4]

When we speak of the realization of values we do not mean to indicate that they are transformed into things, or into real qualities of things; to realize a value is not to transform it into a thing, nor into a real ingredient of a thing. The realized value of a thing constitutes a *relative* quality of that thing, that is, the quality which it has by virtue of comparing the thing with the idea of value. The morality of an act is not a psychological or biological component of the act, but is a quality which the act has of coinciding with the outline of an ethical idea. The beauty of a picture is not a material part of it, but its coincidence with an aesthetic value, etc. The valuable qualities of things are ideal qualities, which they have so far as they are compared with or referred to ideas of value.

Values present the show of keeping among themselves relations of rank or hierarchy. There are kinds of values which are more valuable than other classes, for example, ethical values are worth more than utilitarian ones. And, moreover, within each group of values it happens that some are more valuable than others; for example, purity is worth more than decency, sublimity is worth more than grace. If we compare this spectacle of the hierarchical relations of values with the picture of nature, a strange thing results; because nature does not know even remotely any idea of rank — so far as it is nature and nothing more than nature, that is, as a mere causal series of phenomena. In nature, so long as we do not introduce points of view of valuation, which are entirely alien to it, there are neither hierarchies nor scales; a phenomenon is or is not, but it cannot be more or less, in different degrees of being (reality). On the other hand, each value, in spite of continuing a value in itself, is less a value than some and more a value than others. This is a characteristic which differentiates the world of values from the world of nature; since, in the latter, the pure field of natural phenomena — and so long as we do not introduce into it any points of view alien to it — there are no degrees of reality; a phenomenon is or it is not; and between its being and its nonbeing there are no intermediate degrees: it is what it is and it is not what it is not. On the other hand, as I have shown, the being of values consists in their value, and in that there are degrees: some values are worth more than others. It is desirable to fix our attention on this, for it will serve us very soon to understand a peculiarity of human life and of the works produced in it, which consists of something analogous to what happens with values, namely, that human life and its works have a being susceptible of hierarchical gradations. And those

[4] NIKOLAI HARTMANN, ETHIK (1926) 144ff.

hierarchical gradations have two sources or dimensions, namely, the rank of different values and the degree of greater or less realization of each one of the values. This will put us surely on the track of the relations of the structure of the human to the structure of valuation. Some pages further on I shall develop this theme. And possibly in its light I may obtain some indications to resolve a question which has been forgotten by contemporaneous thought, and which it is urgent to consider.

I deem it desirable to add some considerations with respect to values, since, whatever may be the destiny which my theory may have in the near future, there are in it discoveries which show themselves firmly established.

Values are not elements *given* in a reality, they are not real ingredients of it. And, consequently, they are not known in the experience of things, they are not drawn from perception. A thing appears to have a positive value, as a *good,* by virtue of a primary intuition of value which it embodies in itself. That we value something as skillful, useful, beautiful, true, good, just, presupposes an ideal intuition of skill, utility, beauty, moral good, justice. In short, to deem such objects valuable consists in supposing that they coincide with ideas of value. Things in which there is an idea of positive value, we call *good;* those in which there resides a negative value are called *bad.* But it happens that things could not appear to man as good — or as bad — if there were not a judgment (independent of the perception of the reality of the things) which shows him that they possess a value — or a nonvalue. He judges only by virtue of an idea of value primarily intuitive. This distinction between reality and value — and consequently the difference between the perception of the real object and the intuition of its valuable quality — becomes clear if we observe the real object and are blind to its value; and that, vice versa, it occurs on some occasions that we have an intuition of the value of a thing, whose real texture we scarcely know; or that we simply think of the pure idea of value, without considering any concrete reality in which it is found fully embodied; for example, we think of perfect justice, which probably has never been realized.

This has sufficed to emphasize the independence between the category of reality and the category of value. The dimension of values shines in our consciousness in greater relief when they are not realized in life, because then we appreciate the enormous contrast between that which ought to be and that which is. Perchance we have never had the good fortune to see perfect justice completely realized; yet not on that account do we fail to recognize that justice is a value. On the other hand, we often meet injustices, whose reality here before us cannot be denied: but that very reality of unjust facts excites in us their rejection as unjustified in the light of value.

Also, we may suggest that every idea of ought-to-be, of normativity, is based on a judgment, that is, on an appreciation of values.

Again, there are essential connections between each one of the classes of values (ethical, utilitarian, etc.) and the respective media in which they are embodied. There are values, like the moral ones, which can be found only in persons really existing and not in things; juridical ones in a collectivity; others, such as those of utility, only in things and in processes; others, such as the vital ones (health, strength, dexterity), only in living beings, etc.

There are values which serve as foundations for others, that is, which function as a condition that other values may be realized. There cannot be the *founded* value unless there is the *founding* value. And the *founding* value, an unavoidable condition for the realization of the founded value, is of lower rank. So, for example, the *useful* is founded on the *pleasing* since without the pleasing the useful would not exist; and the pleasing, *founding value,* is lower in hierarchy than the useful, *founded value.* And, in the course of this work, the reader will have occasion to consider how in the world of the Law the values of justice and of security — among others — come in question; and we shall see that security is a founding value with respect to justice, which appears as a founded value; and security, as a founding value, is lower than justice, since it is an indispensable condition for the latter; or, put in other terms, there cannot be a postulation of justice without there being a postulation of security.

Finally, it will be desirable to mention — although very briefly — that the theory of values or Judgment has disclosed a series of pure, essential, rigorous principles and of laws or connections of the same sort with regard to them. By way of mere illustrative allusion, we shall mention some of these types of principles or connections. For example, the laws of the formal relation between reality and values: the existence of a positive value is a positive value; the nonexistence of a positive value is a negative value (antivalue), etc. So, also, the laws for the determination of the rank or hierarchy between values. And there could be instanced still many more examples; but it is not desirable to turn the course of these pages (dedicated to serve as an introduction to the essence of juristics) to a monographic study upon values.

9. Critical Appraisal of the Philosophy of Values. Indications of Its Superiority and for Its Insertion in the Metaphysics of Life

Perchance it is desirable that, even in a few pages of initiation to the Philosophy of the Law, I should formulate in a few words an appraisal of what the theory of values has signified in the immediate past, and its actual and future perspectives. The philosophy of values, especially that of the school of Scheler and of Hartmann, has represented one of the most resounding conquests of contemporary thought. But also it is necessary to recognize that, for something more than ten years now, it has entered into a strange situation. The theory of values, as it appeared in the work of Scheler, attained an enormous influence in the whole philosophic area of our epoch; and it was considered one of the most skillful and fertile discoveries of contemporary meditation. But then a rare event happened, in the final phase of philosophic thought, in the so-called existential Philosophy of Heidegger, in Metaphysics according to the principles of the vital reasoning of Ortega y Gasset, in short, in the thinking which we might label transcendental humanism — according to the happy designation of José Gaos.[5] That new thinking — protagonist of the present philosophic moment, and fertile creation which signifies the beginning of a new age in the history of Philosophy — seems to have left to one side, as almost forgotten, the theory of values. But the curious part is that there has been no critical confronting of it, with the intention of showing something superior to it. They have limited themselves simply to ignoring it — at least in appearance — we should say only to turn attention away from it. The themes which fifteen years ago were in the center of contemporaneous thought have been replaced by others in the thinking of Ortega y Gasset and of Heidegger; but without either of them having developed a sufficient explanation for it, in spite of the fact that some years before they were wont to live very near the source of the philosophy of values. It remains, consequently, as an urgent task for the thinking of the immediate future, to revise the philosophy of values and determine what may be its place in the doctrines of transcendental humanism. And as a contribution to this theme I should like to offer the following reflections, either in the form of pure outline or as a germinal suggestion.

Even when we appreciate everything there is in the philosophy of values of new conquest and the discovery of new zones, there stand out today some insufficiencies in it: matter which it leaves aside without explaining or even making a question of it.

So, for example, the basic separation between the realm of phenom-

[5] José Ortega y Gasset calls his philosophy Metafísica según los principios de la razón vital; the philosophy of Heidegger and of Jaspers has been called existential philosophy. José Gaos has proposed for the philosophy of these authors the accurate title of "transcendental humanism." It is founded on the fact that the primary reality of human life or existence plays a part analogous to that which was represented in transcendental idealism by the *consciousness* (*in absolute* terms).

enal reality and the realm of value may be, from a methodistic point of view, necessary and very useful; but it cannot constitute a final word, or, what is the same thing, it cannot be considered a first and deep basis for a general philosophy, that is, for a Metaphysics. Without disdaining the fruitful methodistic perspectives of the distinction between reality and value, we ought, on a deeper plane, to set ourselves the problem of joining again those two realms, to explain how one is designed for the other, and to find a more basic principle in which both are united. That is: on a plane of formal differentiation it is proper to distinguish between phenomenal reality and value; but, on the other hand, even from the point of view of formal characterization, being and value present themselves as independent and it is necessary to recognize that between them there is a relation which we might call reciprocal vocation; since there belongs to the very essence of values a pretension to be realized, to be fulfilled in definite facts; and, correspondingly, on the other hand, there are realities in which ought to be embodied certain values — and not others — to the point that if it does not so happen, those realities are unjustified for us, in spite of being real, that is, they are, but they ought not to be. It happens, then, that although the real and the valuable are distinct categories and formally independent — we remember that there are values not realized, and that there are realities not valuable — nevertheless here one seems to exist for the other reciprocally. That is, there are some values to be fulfilled in certain realities; and there are some realities in which certain values should be fulfilled. And all this supposes that between the two realms there is a connection, a linking, which was not satisfactorily studied in the philosophy of values. When the category of value was discovered distinct from the real being of nature, the philosophers experienced the enthusiasm which the explorer feels on setting foot for the first time on a land theretofore unknown, and they stressed strongly that the category "value" is as primary and basic as the category "real being," that it does not derive from the latter — from the simple consideration, already explained, that the fact that something is real indeed does not suppose that it is valuable, since there are in the world many nonvaluable realities; and from the inverse consideration that the fact that we recognize a quality as valuable does not imply that such quality is realized, nor that it has necessarily to be so, since the supreme values we have never yet seen fully embodied. The philosophy of values insisted strongly on that character which value has of constituting a category as primary as the category "real being" and so independent of it. Therefore, I believe that the philosophy of values has entered upon a crisis, because it will be necessary to note that in place of constituting what it offered a principle, that is, a new chapter of the treatise upon ideal objects, it will be transformed into something more important and basic, to wit, into a conditioning element of general Metaphysics. Because indeed we are in danger of believing that the category *value* is not just as primary as the category *being,* but that it is more primary than the latter, if I may be permitted such an expression. Surely, in the light of transcendental humanism (philosophy of existence or of life), we shall recognize that, since things present themselves to man with a serviceable function, and since things are ingredients of the life of man, elements in and for his life, and as human life is constituted of a series of acts of choice, which supposes judgments of value, it will happen that *judgment* conditions all the other forms of being, in short, conditions the entire Universe with all its zones and categories. In due season in later pages of this book I shall explain this idea, which then — after the reader has scraped acquaintance with the philosophy of life — will be evident in all its relief and significance. But it was necessary to suggest it here, in treating of the philosophy of values, although at this moment the reader can scarcely measure fully its scope.

And still I would wish to anticipate something more, to complete this sketch of the revision to which the philosophy of values must be submitted. This, in the works mentioned, has insisted strongly that values are not only pure essences independent of the experience of reality, but that moreover they constitute objective essences with absolute validity. And thereupon it seems that it is an established discovery that values are not a projection of my sentiments or of my desires, since I do not attribute greater value to that which gives me greater pleasure, nor even to that which I desire with most vehemence. That is, values do not constitute the result of a special configuration of my psychological mechanisms. But I beileve that this dimension of values — their independence of the psychic — which, at the beginning, constitutes a correct vision, has been transformed into a concept of abstract objectivity, which has led to many misunderstandings; and which, above all, has constituted the gravest obstacle to integrating the theory of values in a general philosophic conception. In the light of the Metaphysics of life, I consider that probably it will have to be established that, if indeed values are objective — that is, they are not projections of the psyche — this objectivity must nevertheless be understood as something immanent in human life; since human life is the basic reality which sustains all the others; and all the others appear in it. Very soon I shall explain and justify this assertion.

But the theme of this book is not values, but concretely the Law. We have met values in our excursion through the Universe in search of juristics. We have roamed in the zone of values to see if the Law dwells among them.

10. The Law Is Not Pure Value

Is the Law perchance purely and simply a value? Probably the reader will not feel inclined to answer this question in as sure and peremptory a manner as when, on asking if the Law belongs to the world of nature, he proffered quite clearly the negative response. The negative there seemed to fall of its own weight, like a ripe fruit, as a clear fact. Now, for the moment, we understand that the Law has something to do with the world of values, since it seems that one cannot speak of juristics without referring to some values. And this is true. But, on the other hand, we conjecture that the Law, in spite of its connection with the world of values, is not purely and simply a value, but that it is an aggregate of things which occur in the web of human life and in the area of history, and which has, consequently, a series of ingredients which cannot be domiciled in the realm of ideal objects, to which values belong.

Juristics — for example, the civil code, the penal code, parliament, judges, police, etc. — is constituted by an aggregate of activities and real works of men; works and activities inserted in their life, conditioned by it, in which lies the reference to various values (security, justice, common utility, etc.), that is, the intentional purpose of realizing them. Those values will be the criteria, the ideas, in which juristics tries to place itself; but positive Law is not constituted of pure essences of value, although it encourages the intention of being guided by them, and although it may contain a greater or less positive realization of them. The Law is not the pure idea of justice nor of the other qualities of value which it aspires to realize; it is an effort — a human labor — at interpretation and realization of those values, applied to various historic circumstances. And, for that reason, the Law contains elements of that historic reality.

Again, it is to be noted that the relation of positive Law to the values which it tries to mold is not always that of perfect correspondence: so, for example, it may be just, less just, or unjust. Many of the juridical rules and institutions elaborated by men may have definite results; but many others have been shown to be errors, inadequacies, and even failures for their purpose of justice. And the Law of a people at a given historical moment is composed of successes, of lesser successes, and also of failures in the intention to realize certain values. All Law, as we shall see, seeks to be something in which are embodied certain ideas of value, or, put in simpler terms, all Law is an attempt at just Law, a seeking of valuable Law. But it is not constituted simply of the pure values which it seeks to realize, but of a series of ingredients through which is offered a concrete interpretation of such values — an interpretation which, moreover, may turn out more or less correct or mistaken.

So, then, the Law is not composed purely of those values to which it refers, but it is the vehicle by which it tries to realize those values; it is something which may function as a medium or agent for the realization of such values, or for their failure; or, in other words, Law is something which may be just or unjust (taking these words now as the synthetic expression of the juridical values, positive and negative respectively).

The Law is something which men create in their lives and with which they live with the purpose of realizing certain values. Hereby we foresee that we shall have to embody juristics in human life.

11. Transition to the Philosophic Consideration of Human Life

A similar indication will make itself known to us if we ask the following question: Who ought to realize the values? Let us answer this question and thereby we shall have taken a step of extraordinary import. Who ought to realize the values? We shall have to answer immediately, man. For of all the beings we meet in the Universe, man is the only one who understands the so-called ideal of values, who is responsive to the ought-to-be which they carry with them, and capable of adjusting his conduct toward them. Nature — which is an aggregate of mechanisms controlled by the bonds of causality — is deaf to the call of values; it is inexorably subject to laws which are unaffected by the imperatives of values. On the contrary, man is the being who understands the call of values and can accommodate his behavior to them. Man is the channel by means of which the ideal dimension of values may be transformed into an effective power which operates in the world of reality. Man is the element thanks to which the ought-to-be may be converted into a real tendency acting upon facts. And, so, man presents himself to us as a sort of intermediate instance between the ideal world of values and the real world of phenomena; he hears the call of values; and through his conduct he can realize or fail to realize them. And, so, he acts as an example of transformation of reality, as a reëlaborator of it, from the valuing points of view.

So, then, it appears obvious that man is the agency of fulfillment or nonfulfillment of values. And therefore the question "where are values realized?" must be answered by saying that values are realized in human life. Now, with this reply we have made a great advance and we are in possession of a sure indication to discover in what zone of the Universe we find the Law; because we see that the Law is constituted by various labors and activities in which is an attempt to realize certain definite values. Now, we have just noted that the agent for realization of values is man, and that these are fulfilled — or violated — in human life.

12. Human Life

It is necessary that we now ask: what is that thing which is called human life? We have just found a being in the Universe, who already at first sight seems different from all the others which we have listed up to now. We have found human life. Now, the intellectual finding of that peculiar reality is going to furnish us other surprises — extraordinarily fertile ones. For we are going to see how that which we call human life is not only a being distinct from all the other beings in the Universe, but that it is the fundamental being. That is, we shall see that human life is the primary and basic reality, conditioning all the other beings. Human life is the primary and underlying reality and at the same time the base and compass of all the other beings and the key for the explanation of them. We shall see that everything that is, *is in human life,* and as a component of it.

What is that which we call human life? Before everything it is to be noted that in speaking of human life I do not refer in any way to biological life, but to the concept of life in the sense which we use when we speak of biography, that is, as that which we do and which happens to us.[6]

Human life in this sense is the most obvious. It constitutes our very existence, that of each one; everything which we do, desire, think, and which happens to us. But this so evident, so plain, reality has not been the object of special philosophic reflection until very recently, until the work of José Ortega y Gasset and of Martin Heidegger. Human life has been converted, in something more than ten years, into an object of central philosophic meditation. It is true that since consciousness sprouted Philosophy in the West, twenty-five centuries ago, human life appears in some fashion as an object of meditation; but not as a fundamental metaphysical theme. What transcendental humanism discovered is that life constitutes not only a reality distinct from all other realities, but that it is the *underlying, primary,* basic reality and that moreover it is the foundation and the explanation of all the others; since all the rest *is* in human life. And, in the light of this discovery, a whole new philosophy is begun, which signifies notable progress in the history of thought, and whose development offers itself to us as the theme of our epoch.

[6] I used not only the cited works of José Ortega y Gasset, but especially his lectures given at the University of Madrid, from 1924 to 1935.

We shall try to gain thoughtful contact with the reality of human life. And in this exposition I shall conform strictly and faithfully to the doctrine of José Ortega y Gasset, who has been the first to reflect upon this theme and definitely to elucidate it.

What is our life? It is clear that we refer to life in an immediate sense; and not, consequently, as biology. Biological definitions and points of view are theoretical constructions, and, therefore, mediate and not immediate or evident intuitions. And now we ask for the direct presence of that which we call life. To live is what we are and what we do; it is that which is nearest to us. Our life is everything which happens to us and which we do at each instant; and, finally, it is composed of a series of events, many of which — perhaps the greater part — seem lowly or trivial. It is true that, at times, life seems to take on a tension, to rise up, be concentrated, intensified. But those dramatic moments are as much life as the humble minutes.

"Life is all that we do; but that would not be life if we did not take note of what we do. Life is a reality of a most peculiar kind, which has the privilege of taking account of itself, of knowing itself. But this knowing is not an intellectual knowledge, but that character of immediate presence of life for each one. To feel, to note, to see oneself, is the first attribute of life." Life is then intimacy with ourselves, a knowing and a noting of oneself, an attending oneself and a taking possession of oneself. "To live is to find ourselves in a world of things, which serve us or which oppose us, which attract us or repel us, which love us or hate us; it is to find ourselves in a world of things engaging us. So, then, life consists of the *co-presence,* the *co-existence of the I with a world,* of *a world with me,* as inseparable, inescapable, correlative elements." For I am not, if I do not have a world to occupy me, if there are no things to think of, to feel, to desire, to reject, to preserve, to transform, or to destroy. But neither does it have meaning that I should speak of a world independent of me, because I am the witness of the world. For talk of the world to have meaning it is necessary that I should exist with it; and that I should exist, not only in the form of one of its parts or ingredients, but also as a guarantee of its existence. To talk of the world independent of me is an intellectual invention, fabrication, or hypothesis, but in no way a given reality. What is fundamentally given is the world witnessed by me.

We find life when we find ourselves with the world, the world with us in inseparable company. And who is the I? "The I is indeed not a thing; it is not my body, nor is it my soul, consciousness or character, since I have to live with these elements; the I has met these corporeal and psychic things and lives *with* them, *by means of them;* it is that which has to live *with* things, *among* things, of which there are some, the body and the psyche, which have greater nearness."

But life is not merely characterized as knowing oneself, as thinking of oneself; it has moreover to be added fundamentally that it consists of a *making* of oneself. Life is not a being already made, nor yet an object with a predetermined trajectory; life has not a reality already made like a stone, nor yet a predesignated route like the orbit of a star or the development of the vegetative cycle of a plant. It is quite to the contrary; it is something completely diverse: it is a *making of itself,* since life is not given to us all made; it is a *task;* we have to make it for ourselves each instant. And this not only in case of serious conflicts, but always every moment. "We live maintaining ourselves, carrying the weight of our own life which, each instant, finds itself obliged to resolve the problem of itself. A life which should live simply for itself, such as would be that of a ball which had consciousness, would not be life, for it would not have to make itself. And if indeed it is not given to us to choose the world in which we are going to make our life, and this is its dimension of fatality, we find ourselves always with a certain margin, with a horizon alive with possibilities, and this is its dimension of liberty" (since in the worst and most distressing case, there will remain at least two possibilities; to accept inexorable destiny or to quit life). Life is always making something, concrete, positive or negative — since to make nothing is in short also a vital making, a choosing of one of the possibilities. And the vital making consists in determining what I am going to be, what I am going to do in the next instant: life consists in having to decide each moment what we are going to be in the following one, in a making oneself by resolving each instant his future. "To live is to be completely occupied with something, preoccupied; to live is to have constantly stated the problem of oneself and to have to go on resolving it each moment. Our life is to decide our making, to decide upon ourselves, to decide what we are going to be; therefore, it consists in being that which we not yet are; in beginning to be for the future; in occupying ourselves with what we are to do, or what is the same thing, with *preoccupying* ourselves." To live is to realize a project of existence, is a business, a succession, and a simultaneity of *deeds.*

Now it is to be noted that the human *deed,* as such, does not consist in the activity of one's physiological processes, nor even in those of one's psychic mechanisms (of imagination, perception, thinking, emotion, will, etc.). Both those psychic mechanisms and the corporeal resources, are mere instruments by which man effectuates his *deeds.* The essence of doing, of all human deeds, is not in the spiritual and physiological instruments which intervene in the activity, but in the decision of the subject, in his determination, in a pure willing, prior to the volitional mechanism. That pure willing, that original and primary determination, sets to functioning the mechanisms, the activities which man commands (his imagination, his will, his arms, etc.). So it is — not to confound the *human deed* with its means or instruments — that we say: I *set about* reasoning, I *set about* imagining, I *set about* walking, etc. What basically proceeds from me is the *setting about* doing all those things, and not those things (reasoning, imagining, walking, etc.) which are mechanisms, activities, instruments. Life is based in my decision.

Each one of us consists of a being who has to decide, who has to decide what he is going to be (what he is going to do) in the coming instant. Sometimes it seems as if we did not decide what we were going to be, what we were going to do in the following moment; but what occurs in these cases is that we are maintaining, reiterating a resolution previously taken; but that prior decision could be modified or confirmed. By not modifying it and maintaining it, we confirm it.

Now, the structure of doing consists in wanting to do what one does, *for some reason* (for some motive, which is an urgency, an eagerness) and *to some end* (with a purpose which is the goal of the activity, that is, the work). So, then, human life, that is, what man does, is qualified by having a *why* (motive) and a *wherefore* (purpose), which constitutes a meaning, a possession of meaning. Let us note at this moment that we have just come upon something which we have not met in the world of nature: upon *meaning* or *significance.*

It is desirable to avoid a too simplified interpretation of the teleological or purposeful structure of human action, which was current in the thought of the past century. According to that thinking, which we ought to reject — as insufficient — purpose was understood as mental anticipation of reversed causality: they thought that the end was the desired effect, which was anticipated mentally; and the means was the cause, which was sought as adequate to produce the end (effect) desired. And I do not say that this is wholly inaccurate, but that it is insufficient, because in such explanation there does not appear the authentic human root of the teleological or purposeful process. For beneath and prior to that plan of intellectual anticipation of the causal process, there is a special human root, a peculiar *why* (which in this case does not signify cause) which consists in man feeling an urgency, a want, an emptiness, a need to have, which leads him to seek, to imagine something, with which he can fulfill that desire. This it is which constitutes the initial *why* of the deed, for example, man feels a fear of savage animals and this incites him to seek, to imagine something which may remedy this want: a hut. The *why* of what he is going to do consists of the want which he tries to meet. Already he has imagined that constructing a house will satisfy that urgency. Then the *imagined, proposed house* constitutes the *for what* of his act. And, this determined, he will seek the activities (strength of arm, for example, etc.) and the materials (stones, etc.) to construct his hut. Such activities, employed on those materials, constitute the *means* to arrive at the proposed end (the efficient causes whose effect will be the end desired). Now we note that the end-means plan (mentally inverted causality: effect-cause) enters upon the scene only after there has been produced the purely and typically human prior fact; the *motive* (why) and the *end* to that service (for what). Only after this, is the end set up as such, and does he seek the means to produce it effectively, to realize it. So it results that the *means-end* plan is supported by and inserted in a more basic supposition, which consists of the *motive-end* connection.

From all that has been said comes another of the essential characteristics of human life, namely, that any of its deeds needs to be justified, that is, that it constitutes a problem. To live is to occupy oneself with something "for" something. In the first place, I have to decide between various possibilities — few or many, at least two — which the circumstance in which I am put offers me. I am not obliged to do this concrete thing and nothing else, but I can do one thing or another. It is clear that those possibilities are limited in number; if they were unlimited they would not be concrete possibilities, but pure indetermination; and in a world of absolute indetermination it is not necessary to decide anything. In order that there should be a decision it is necessary to have, at the same time, limitation and breadth. The living world is made up of *circumstances,* something closed and, at the same time, open, that is, with a hollow interior in which to move. "Life goes on making its bed within an inexorable valley. Life is, at the same time, fatality and liberty, it is to be free within the space of a given fatality." To this I add the following reflection: to decide for one of the various possibilities which are offered, it is necessary to choose, and to choose it is necessary to prefer, there is necessary an act of preference in favor of this possibility, over all the others. But a preference is possible only by virtue of a valuation, that is, by virtue of valuing this possibility and estimating it higher than all the others. In short, to decide it is necessary to choose, to choose it is necessary to prefer and to prefer it is unavoidable that we should know how to judge or value.

For my part, I consider that the principles of the doctrine of life according to Ortega y Gasset — such and as I have been explaining them — necessarily lead us to affirm that our life is constituted, or, better, is formed, of an aggregate of valuations, of a succession of judgments.

And so, as I understand it, it will result that Judging is not a theory limited to certain ideal objects (as the philosophy of values pictured it), but has a much more basic structure, namely, it constitutes an essential structure of human life. Here we find, then, one of the perspectives which I announced, a few pages back, to reëlaborate the theory of values, inserting it in the very root of the philosophy of transcendental humanism.

Some years ago, in my lectures, I threw out the thought that the structure of life is estimative. That is, that if we should suppress the capacity of judging (to value, to prefer, to choose), human life would disappear; this would not be possible nor thinkable. The same phenomenon of attention, so much studied by the psychologists (although they have not observed its full scope), which conditions the possibility of knowledge, has an estimative structure. The man who could not choose (prefer, judge) could not think, could not do anything, he would be in pure suspension, in absolute abstention, in short, he would not live. More than once I have tried to exemplify this thought, applying the fable of Buridan's Ass who found himself starving between two mangers, without eating from either, because he could not decide for one or the other. I see the possibility of ascribing to this image a formidable and decisive metaphysical resonance. There is here, I would say, to my understanding, the reason why the theory of values would have to be inserted in the very root itself of Philosophy, to unite it to the theory of human life.

Likewise, we have to emphasize — what has been surely indicated by Ortega y Gasset — that every act of human life needs inexorably to be justified. And I will add not only the decision to do a deed, but also each one of the acts which compose it, for example, each one of the means employed to the proposed end. Each one of the acts, including the most lowly, requires to be justified before me, and therefore constitutes a problem. For example, when I am going to raise one foot to take a step, the question of knowing if the ground in front is going to sustain me or not presents itself; and only on the assumption that I believe that it is going to sustain me is the act which I am going to do justified to me. It is clear that most times we have resolved such problems by instinct or by habit, in a mechanical manner. But other times we have not; and then it is necessary that I should find a justification for what I am going to do. This justification may turn out to be correct, or incorrect, from an objective point of view; but, in any case, it will have to be sufficient for me: since if it is not, action would be impossible. Even when trying to decide something by pure chance (tossing a coin) there is in it a purpose of justification: not having found any motive sufficient to prefer one of two things, and because one recognizes that it is justifiable to do either, one resorts to this fortuitous process, to individualize one of the two acts between which one finds it necessary to decide. So we notice that another of the essential dimensions of life is the necessity which there is of justifying it to oneself at every moment. Whatever may be the decision which I take, it requires a justification before me. It is clear that many times we justify a determination and we take it, not alone in view of a single result the next moment, but with a long compass, for a prolonged time. So, for example, we decide to follow a career, etc. But in every case there always exists the possibility of revising that determination at any moment. And when we do not do it, we are corroborating it. Life cannot proceed, live, without resolving each instant — explicitly or implicitly — its particular problem, the question which it necessarily puts to itself, for which it is necessary that it should justify to itself its own attitudes and determinations.

Up to now, I have confined myself to explaining the reality of human life and describing its essential structure. But I have said nothing as to the dimension of "basicness" and fundamentality which this reality imparts to the new Philosophy. But such theme — which is one of the principal dimensions of this theory — does not belong directly to the matter which is concerned in this book. Therefore, I shall limit myself to a mere allusion to this point. Philosophy from its beginnings seeks basic and fundamental truth, that is, autonomous (which is sufficient to itself and does not support itself on any prior truth) and pantonomous (which serves as base and justification for all the others). Ancient and mediaeval Philosophy thought it found such truth in some element of the world outside of me; which was called *realism*. But at the dawn of the seventeenth century there was performed by Descartes the most formidable feat recorded in the history of culture — and which had been prepared for by the Renaissance: the inauguration of *idealism,* which gave rise to all modern culture and life (the new physics — with it, technique — rationalism — and with it, liberalism, democracy, etc.). Idealism consists in having taken into account that the external world, far from being a basic and incontrovertible datum, is something questionable and mediate; and that the only unquestionable, absolutely certain and primary thing, is my thinking; that the only indubitable thing is my own consciousness. Accordingly, thought, consciousness, constitute the primary truth, the basic reality, on which are supported all the other things, whose being will depend on what they receive from thought. But if idealism was right as against realism in emphasizing the dependence in which things find themselves with respect to me, it erred in not taking into account that I depend also on objects (since there cannot be an empty thought without an object, a thought of nothing). So, if indeed it is true that there cannot be an object without a subject, it is also true that there cannot be a subject without an object (which was not perceived by idealism).

The correlation[7] between the subject and the objects of his world, the interaction between them, does not prevent us from establishing the difference between truth and error; it is not in any way an invitation to skepticism, nor even to relativism, but rather the contrary. Because by discovering and emphasizing the factors which condition any thought of object, it becomes possible to appraise with precision the extent of any knowledge. In fact, when we discover the point of view of the relation of a subject to determined objects and the factors which influence that perspective, we can gage its extent and its significance. And that knowledge, although its extent and its significance may be partial, is true; true, that is, in its partiality and in its dependency. But all human knowledge is partial, and depends on the point of view and on the factors which operate in its determination. Absolute, ubiquitous knowledge, *sub specie aeternitatis,* can strictly be only Divine. Also it could be said that the world in itself, fully, without limitations of the point of view, that is, seen from all points of view at once, in true totality, can strictly be an attribute only of Divine Knowledge.

The new Philosophy has discovered that the primary and basic, and the fundamental, thing, is the *co-existence or inescapable co-presence* of subject and object, in a reciprocal relation of dependence, in inseparable correlation, which is called human life. And, so, transcendental idealism has been replaced by transcendental humanism (philosophy of life or of existence).

Now, human life is not only the primary and first base of Philosophy, but, moreover, it is also the fundamental reality, that is, the reality in which are given all the other realities, the reality in which all the others are based and explained. And, so, for example, the nature which physics encounters in its science is a familiar object of that science, a science which is something that man makes in his life; and the truths of biology will represent the results of one of the activities to which certain men, the biologists, have dedicated themselves; and so successively.

13. Free Will[8]

The philosophic analysis of human life has opened the road for me for a new focus and a new solution of the so much debated problem of

[7] This paragraph is from the Second Spanish edition of the book (Mexico, 1945). TRANSLATOR.

[8] This section is from the Second Spanish edition of the book (Mexico, 1945). TRANSLATOR.

free will. And it seems to me that in the light of the meditation which I have developed, and which I offer hereafter, this theme may be presented with a rigor not heretofore attained and put in route for its correct solution.

Man neither has nor does not have will, because the will is not something which one has or does not have or has in greater or lesser degree like muscular strength or memory. Will is not a psychological power. Man is will. The difference between employing the word *to be* or the word *to have* is not of small moment, but rather of great importance. When I say that man is will I do not say that he is in possession of a special resource, of a certain power, of a given energy, but I say something simply of his essential situation with respect to the circumstance which marks it and the process of his life: a situation which consists of finding himself always before a limited and concrete plurality of possibilities, that is, of roads to follow, and, consequently, in the necessity of deciding for himself, on his own account, under his own responsibility, to choose one of those ways. The will is not a thing, not an energy, not a power; rather is it simply the expression of a type of insertion of man in the world which surrounds him. This insertion does not constitute a strict, fixed enclosing, without movement, like that of the turtle within his shell; but an insertion with a certain margin of space, with a break in the circumference. Then this break, this ambit, offers the person, in each of the moments of his life, a repertory of various possibilities, small or great, but always in the plural number, among which man has to choose, deciding on his own account, because he is not predeterminedly forced to follow one only of such possibilities and to avoid the others. All life consists of having to elect at each instant among various roads which circumstance presents. These roads are concrete and in limited number; but they are always various. Hence the repertory of possibilities which is offered to each person is diverse; diverse as to the number and as to the quality of those roads. But to each person there are presented at each moment various possibilities and among them there is no predetermination to follow one and abandon the rest; but the election has to be pronounced by him, on his own account. To live is to find oneself always at a crossroads, having to choose between them. Therefore, man is will. He is it simply because he has to decide for himself among the various junctures which the situation presents to him. Our life is truly determined to have to move in each one of its moments within the situation which constitutes its concrete circumstance, that is, which constitutes a space within which various possibilities are opened. But within that space he is not necessarily and inexorably determined to have to follow a certain way. Even the life which we may imagine as the saddest and most grievous at any given moment, as offering nothing more than a tragic path, will not face one single possibility only, but two: that of accepting a dark destiny or of escaping from existence. Let it be said incidentally, however, that I subscribe to all the condemnations which have been uttered against suicide. If I bring now to the collocation the hypothesis of suicide, it has been to show that, even in the extreme case, there will be at least a duality of routes between which he will have to decide.

The concrete circumstance, which offers a multiplicity of paths at each one of the moments of the life of a human person is composed of a combination of very various elements. In that circumstance which determines which shall be the concrete paths of the life of a person, there figure not only the outline of exterior nature, the social structure and medium, but also the education and acquired capacities, and also the very body and the very soul. That, in truth, the very body and the very soul also form part of the circumstance or of the outline surrounding the person, and that they are not to be confounded with it, may be comprehended by virtue of the following considerations. Let us remember that life is, as José Ortega y Gasset has shown, a necessary and constant dealing of an I with the world, with its outline, that is, life is constituted of the inescapable copresence of the person with objects, with objects with which he has to get along whether he wishes it or not. Then, the body and the soul are not strictly the person himself in the strict sense, but the nearest, constant and inevitable envelopes of him. I am not either my body or my soul, but the person who has to live necessarily with the body and the soul which have fallen to his lot.

The combination of all those ingredients of the outline — psychic, biologic, geographic, and social — determines for each person the ambit of his life and the catalogue of possibilities which are presented to him. That ambit and those possibilities are different for each person, according to what may be the aptitudes of his body, the capacities of his psyche, the place where he is, the education which he has received, the social situation which he occupies, the economic means which he has at his disposal, the collective atmosphere which he breathes, and so forth. But each person, within the space of his own life, finds always the possibility of different conducts at each moment, whence is will, for he has to choose for himself among those conducts, not finding himself necessarily predetermined to undertake one single one of them.

There is, then, in our life, something determined, to wit: the concrete ambit within which we have to move, the series of possibilities in its extent, which is limited. But within that ambit and before the repertory of ways which it offers, man does not find himself determined, but rather has to resolve on his own account. Therefore, man is will; because he finds himself always at a crossing.

My affirmation that man is will differs radically as well from the classic indeterminist thesis as from the determinist one.

The traditional indeterminist supposes that man may do all; and that all men may in principle do the same. That thesis does not start from human concrete reality, but from an abstract figure of man, conceived as something universal. And, moreover, that abstract human figure considers itself, so to speak, as situated in a vacuum, in a vacuum of total indetermination, within which the person is permitted to do anything, which he resolves for himself, by virtue of a kind of power, that is, of free will, which is conceived as a creative potency. On the contrary, the thought which I am developing shows that man finds himself situated in a concrete, determined, limited circumstance, which he finds composed of multiple and diverse ingredients (psychic, biological, geographic, historic, social) and of various singular combinations of them in each one of the cases. Man cannot do it all, but only may do some of the things which are possible at each moment; and what those things are in each case the constellation of ingredients which form his circumstance determines. Nor can all men do the same things, because each one of them has his concrete circumstance, which outlines his ambit and determines the possible roads of his life.

Determinists maintain that man finds himself totally determined in his conduct, which, in each case, is the single effect of a complex aggregate of factors of multiple kinds, which are usually transformed in the final instance into motivations, of which the most vigorous triumphs at the end. Against that hypothesis — it is a matter only of a hypothesis and of a gratuitous hypothesis, for it has never been fully demonstrated — I maintain that, even if man is situated within a determined shell, on the other hand within that shell it is not determined that he has to follow necessarily one of the paths which figure in it, but that it is he who has to decide on his own account. For that *is* will. He does not have or fail to have will because will is not a power, is not a potency, is not a psychic recourse; it is simply the expression of our ontological situation with respect to the world which circumscribes our personality.

I have already indicated that the decision of the I, choosing any of the possible planes for its behavior, does not imply a suspension of nor an exception to the causal laws of nature, but the insertion into it of some new causes from the I and not contained, therefore, in the earlier part of the chain. The decision of the I, on being translated into behavior, does not come to break the normal fulfillment of the causal laws, but to bring at a certain moment an addition of causality, which is inserted under the form of a natural phenomenon, that is, under the form of a new cause, in the chain of what has previously occurred. This is possible by virtue of the fact that the human person, which has nature (body and soul) and which is in nature, is not nature, but something very distinct from it. The human subject is permeable with the so-called ideal of the world of values; he is capable of conceiving ideals of conduct, of proposing to himself purposes for his account and risk, and of undertaking means conducive to the realization of the chosen ends. Man is, in short, a citizen of two worlds, so to speak, of the world of nature and of the world of values and ends; and he stretches a bridge between the two. In taking decisions, he acts as a citizen of the world of values and ends; and he irrupts, as a new cause, into the world of nature.

Let us see how use may be made of these Kantian ideas, stripping them of the connection which they have in their author with transcendental idealism. The philosophical construction of Kantian transcendental idealism — according to which nature is nothing more than a phenomenon, an appearance, while behind or beneath it there is an intelligible world, which is real, but which does not appear, a world which irrupts as positive liberty in the phenomenological sphere — we may consider extinct. But it happens that Kant, as in all the great philosophers, many times is greater in the strictness of stating the problems than in the exactitude of the system. Now, the meaning of the doctrine referred to may be preserved as true by getting rid of transcendental idealism. Stripped of its connections with transcendental idealism, there remain firmly, of this Kantian theory, two important truths: the conception of the causal bond as a category and the emphasis upon the duplicity of ontological regions which meet in man. The Kantian duality of the sensible world and of the intelligible world, concurring in the human person, implies a discovery of great importance which does not have to be considered as integral with the transcendental idealist system. Beyond causal determination there is the decision according to the moral law, according to rational purposes, or, we should better say, in a terminology more adequate to contemporaneous thought, according to intentionalities of value. This was indeed seen by Kant and has been truly made use of by Nicolas Hartmann (*Ethik,* last part, 1926), but the latter did not come to take the decisive step in the conception of the will, because he followed inertly the tradition of stating this theme as integral with a form of will.

It happens that when one speaks of will in connection with this theme, he employs the word *will* in a double and equivocal sense. Sometimes he alludes to a psychic phenomenon, to an animated spring, which belongs to the field of internal experience; at other times he means the intimate and essential root of the I. From the confusion of these two notions has arisen an entanglement in the stating of the problem of the will. The will as a psychic fact forms part of my living circumstance, forms part of that which has been called the *me,* that is, my psychic and also biologic envelope. My tendencies, inclinations, desires, loves, hates, thoughts, temperamental strokes, are mine but are not I. The *me,* that is, the volume of my psychic phenomena, of my sensations, of my images, of my concepts, of my feelings, of my character, of my desires, of my appetites, of my force of will, of my propensities, is mine, but it is not I. The me is a part of the circumstances which surround me, of the outline which marks me; and that part has a very important role in the determination of the ambit of the possibilities which present themselves to my behavior, in the determination of their number and their quality. The one who is free is the I, by virtue of its special form of insertion with ample room in the outline which surrounds it. The I to decide, to resolve, between what it may do, pronounces a kind of "let it be done," a *fiat.* Precisely in that consists the decision, a kind of pure wish, *to resolve to.* That this decision may be fulfilled in effective deed, it is necessary among many other requisites (conditions of possibility), that the will which is going to act and to realize should have sufficient force to do so. Then, the will, a psychological mechanism, a kind of executor, is one thing, and the capacity of decision, of resolution, of command which the I emits on choosing between any of the possible behaviors, is quite another thing. The will is not a mode or quality of the psychological will, but the special situation of the I in the world, having to decide for itself among various paths. The will is a mode of the I, of the essential nucleus of the person, which, in the face of the multiple ways which circumstance presents, and many times striving against powerful solicitations of the outline, as well from the exterior as of its own soul, pronounces its judgment, decides, judges, upon the different suggestions which the exterior and its own soul send it. It is clear that to pronounce this judgment the I acts as a sort of motor, as a sort of discharge of energy, which acts upon the psychic mechanisms and these upon the corporal, entering so, in the form of action, into the kingdom of natural reality, that is, breaking into the causal series of the phenomena of nature. What it is important to emphasize is the necessity of not confounding the willing psychological mechanism with the special aptitude of the I, who, in the function of its situation as will, decides, judges, upon the different possibilities, choosing one of them. I shall have to confess with respect to this foreign motor that it is the I, so far as this decides upon its conduct, which is a matter of something very difficult to express, of something ineffable, but nevertheless of immediate maximum potency.

In fact, we feel the will — as in truth we are it — and this is something completely diaphanous, because we find ourselves before a number of possible behaviors to follow, of tasks to undertake, among which, although there emanate from them inducements to act in one direction, thanks to powerful motives, we have to decide on our own account. The decision is the moment of the I, the affirmation of what we may call a pure desire, the expression of a "resolve to." Now, this decision has the power to set in motion the willing psychic mechanisms of realization which we possess (whose vigor, agility, and skill are different in different people), that is, only of those which we actually have in their possibilities of concrete reality.

I insist on the difference between the decision of the I — who, being will, has to decide upon some of the possibilities which are presented to it — and the psychic mechanism of the will, which acts later as an instrument of execution, to put into practice that decision. The willing resources belong to the *me,* and this constitutes a part of my outline, the nearest and most inseparable part of my person. On the other hand, the decision is something strictly of the *I*.

This decision, this "let it be done," this fiat, which constitutes the expression of the I, being resolved as will within the vacancy which it occupies in the world, constitutes the basic beginning of human doing. It is not necessary that the decision should be put into practice immediately; but that a decision may be taken tonight which will not be actually perfected until tomorrow or even later and which may moreover serve for a great number of acts. In fact, if we examine our life, we shall see that decisions are relatively few. They usually form a small repertory, which serves as the permanent base for normal action.

We cannot explain how the decision, after the manner of a projection of the I, can operate to set in action the willing resources we have, which in turn will move to where they start the other mechanisms. But that we cannot explain it does not at all create any objection which invalidates what we have said; because, in any case, our exposition constitutes a rigorous and essential description of an obvious structure which I have succeeded in showing in an evident fashion. In short, it comes to make manifest, in another way, the singular character which the reality of our life has. Our life is the inescapable coexistence of the I with the world, of the subject with its circumstance; and, consequently, in our life, the dimensions or characteristics of the I are crossed with the dimensions or characteristics of the other realms of objects which constitute the world. In our life, the objects of nature, the natural phenomena concatenated by causal bonds, are crossed with the I. In our life ideal objects are also crossed with the I, so far as the I knows them as necessary validities, so far as the I is aware of the vocational call of the values. And responding — though not in a forced manner, but of its own account — to this call of the values, it interferes again in the sector of natural facts, it breaks into the series of them with its behavior, which comes to alter the succession of the phenomena of nature by the insertion of the new phenomena which its conduct produces; it being understood that these new phenomena which proceed from man arise already developed into natural phenomena.

14. Human Life Objectivated

I should like to complete the theory of Ortega y Gasset as to the individual human life with certain meditations, which I have developed for myself, upon human life objectivated.

The being of life, so far as one lives, operates a variegated instrumentality of psychic and corporeal realities: but it does not consist of those realities of which it makes use or by means of which it manifests itself, and in which it is realized, but in that the being of its acts consists in their *meaning,* in their intention, in their why or wherefore (with the valuating structure which this imports). So, the deeds of knowledge making a utensil, producing a work of art, founding a social institution, etc., are facts which are produced with and in certain psychic and corporeal realities — modifications in my body and in the world round about. But the peculiar and distinctive being of such facts does not consist either in their psychic ingredients nor in their material components, but in the human meaning of those acts, in their human purpose directed intentionally to determined values.

But many acts of human life after being realized leave behind them a trace, a trail. And this occurs not only with outstanding acts but also with lowly acts. *Don Quixote,* at the moment when Cervantes wrote it, was an episode of his individual life, a piece or segment of his own existence. But after that work was written — and even after the death of Cervantes — *Quixote* continues there, as something before us, as an aggregate of crystallized thoughts, which can be rethought by each one of us. It presents itself as a complex of objectivated, fossilized, materialized thoughts. It is something which has the structure of thought, but which is no more a live thought, which is living — he who thought it originally has disappeared — it is a thought which, if in its creation it was a living subjective process of someone, now appears as a thought converted into a thing, as an objective product at the disposition of all, for whoever will to rethink it, as a thing of communal use. But we may say the same with respect to a lowly example, for instance of a trivial letter. To write it was an event in the life of whoever did it; but afterwards it remains there, as a crystallization of that living thought, which it was before. This it is which I call *objectivated* or crystallized *human life*. But it will be desirable to consider other examples.

The so-called Franciscan virtues were originally facts in the life of the Saint of Assisi. But afterwards, the memory of that conduct has remained as a crystallized model, as a paradigm of conduct. Henry Ford invented new forms of behavior applicable to industrial production: they were facts in the life of Ford; but later one spoke of Fordism. The trace of those events in the life of the great North American industrialist remain as crystallized models of conduct; as possible rules for other behaviors.

Other human acts leave as their trail a modification of corporeal reality, for example, technical tools, sculptures, etc. A flint ax or an automobile are material realities; but their peculiar being does not consist of their corporeal components but in the dimension of being technical human works made for a utilitarian purpose; they are, then, also objectivated human life. The being of the Venus de Milo consists in its aesthetic meaning.

So, then, besides the authentic human life, which is that which is lived by the individual subject, we find another region of the universe, which also has a human structure, to wit, the works which man has realized, that is, the things whose peculiar being rests on their constituting objectivated human life: utensils, technical procedures, pictures, statues, musical works, scientific theories, moral rules, virtuous examples, signs, letters, altars, codes, magistracies, forms of usage, and so forth. Human deeds already realized, last as forms of life — conceived abstractly, separately from the concrete individual life which produced them — or as a modification or trace left in reality; and they come to acquire as it were a sort of objective consistency. It is clear that these crystallized forms do not constitute authentic life; for there is no other authentic life, in the correct and fullest sense, than individual life, that which a concrete man lives. Those objective forms are life which was, past, although, of course, susceptible of being revived by other individuals. (For we shall see, soon, the fundamental and interesting problems which that matter of revival raises, in copying forms of life which were; and how in their light we shall clear up the problem of what society is.)

Now, things, the forms of objectivated human life, human works, have a structure analogous to the deeds of life properly so called, that is, of individual life. Their being, what is peculiarly theirs, consists of their meaning, in having a purpose.

The realm of objectivated human life is that which some examined in the nineteenth century under the denomination of *objective spirit*

(Hegel) and others under the name of *culture* (for example, Windelband, Rickert). But, although some perceived the problem of these peculiar realities, nevertheless none succeeded in considering what is their nature. For in the objective spirit theory of Hegel there are, along with findings of genius, monstrous errors: as is the substantialization of the objective spirit, as a reality in itself and for itself, which would develop dialectically of itself. And in the philosophy of culture of the school of Windelband and of Rickert,[9] if indeed the attitude toward the question has been fertile, on the other hand the treatment which it received cannot be considered sufficiently correct.

The realm of the objectivated life is composed of all human works and the trace of human acts; in short, of everything to which is attached a human meaning. And these are of very diverse rank. For example, from the works of Einstein to a highway sign which says "Twenty miles to such a place"; from the primitive plow to the tractor of our day; from the civil code to the notice "smoking forbidden"; from the example of the hero or the saint to the trivial counsel of a friend; from the professions (social careers, with which I shall concern myself further along), to the rules of neatness at the table; from the most sublime religious rituals to the simplest prayers "made" by a devotee; from the organization of a modern industry to the form of production in the prehistoric epoch; from the structure of a bank to the contractual form of simple barter; from the philosophy and the science of our time to the vision of the world which primitive men had; from contemporaneous dietetics to the simplest cooking recipe; and so on.

A flint ax or an automobile are composed of physical reality; but their specific being, their peculiar being, that is, being an ax or being an automobile does not consist in the stone, nor in the metals and other components, respectively, nor in their geometric forms, but in constituting something which embodies a human meaning, that is, being utensils or implements to carry out a value of utility. A picture, a statue, consist of materials, of colors and of forms; but its "being a picture" or its "being a statue" does not consist in those shaped and colored materials, but in their peculiar meaning, in constituting works of art, human works with an aesthetic intention. A scientific treatise has birth in the living thought of its author — consequently it has been first a psychic phenomenon in the mind of the author, a psychic reality — and afterwards it has been fixed in writing on paper. But the special and peculiar being

[9] See principally RICKERT, NATURWISSENSCHAFT UND KULTURWISSENSCHAFT (1899). Also DIE GRENZEN DER NATURWISSENSCHAFTLICHEN BEGRIFFSBILDUNG (1896). Cf. LUIS RECASÉNS SICHES, ESTUDIOS DE FILOSOFÍA DEL DERECHO (Barcelona: Bosch, 1936) 75–77.

of the scientific treatise does not consist either in the psychic phenomena which served as the vehicle for its formation, nor — it is clear — in the paper and ink in which it afterwards remained written, but in the intended meaning of the thought — of significations, which aim at a value of truth, a purpose of knowledge.

And already the reader will have foreseen that where we find the Law is precisely in this realm of objectified human life. And, so, similarly to the examples which I have just put in the previous paragraph, we may adduce that of the Law. A code, for example, rests on real substrata (in the psychic acts of whoever drew it up, as to the process of its formation; in the consciousness of those who know it, who comply with it, and who apply it, after it is promulgated and in effect; and, as well, also as to the shape which a society receives from such a code); and, moreover, the Code is written in books, pronounced in articulate sounds, etc. But the Code as a Code, that is, as a juridical rule, does not consist in any of those real ingredients, but in the particular meaning which the thoughts crystallized in it have, in the meaning which the regulatory ideas of its precepts have, meanings which are based on aiming at the realization of certain values.

With respect to the knowledge of these objects, we have to note that it constitutes a type of science completely different from the type of the natural sciences. The sciences of nature explain their objects, natural phenomena, discovering their causes and recording the last effects to which they give rise; and nothing more. On the contrary, such method of causal explanation does not do for the sciences which concern themselves with human objects, that is, with the so-called disciplines of cultural or historic objects. These human objects, the objectivated life, escape a mere exclusive causal explanation; they are apprehended only in their peculiar being, in the degree in which they are *understood,* comprehended in their meaning. Consequently, the method employed by the human sciences (science of languages, science of law, science of economics, etc.) cannot be explanatory alone in the method of the natural sciences, but has to be *interpretative* of meanings. A natural phenomenon (for example, rain or lightning or the fall of bodies) is explained fully and exhaustively in the degree in which we determine its causes and record their effects. But, on the other hand, a ceramic, or a bow, are not understood for what they are, by the representation of the movements which produced them, but only so far as we understand their particular meaning — that is, so far we understand the human purposes which lie in the earthen pot or in a form of greeting. And the same occurs with all the facts and results of the activity of man.

Distinction should be made in objectified human work, especially in the so-called cultural products — religion, moral rules, science, art technique, economics, law, etc. — between the act (with a concrete meaning), which engenders them, and the objective, logical, autonomous meaning which they contain when they are already elaborated and crystallized. For example, we have said that the novel *Don Quixote* contains objectively a series of ideas, whose extent it is possible (or even probable) passed unnoticed by Cervantes, who did not even think of the full signification of some of his conceptions. Similarly, habitually jurists take into consideration the difference between the so-called authentic interpretation of the law — investigating what it was which the legislator really thought — and the so-called objective interpretation, which takes the law by itself, seeking its objective significations, the ideas which it contains, as well if they were explicitly thought of by the legislator as if they were not, and extracts their logical extent, although perhaps that was not wholly foreseen by the author of the law.

And this distinction between interpretation of the subjective meanings and the purely logical interpretation is not to be confounded with that other difference which is wont to be made between a vital act and its ideal content, that is, with the distinction between the vital reality which engenders the work and sustains it — on one side — and its meaning — on the other. Although this latter distinction may have fruitful methodical perspective for a series of needs,[10] I consider that it is not to be taken with the extent which some thinkers have done, since the same real act which produces the work is not a phenomenal reality, but vital reality which is already impregnated with meaning. And, on the other hand, the ideal content of the work of culture is not abstract ideality, but arisen in a process of human life, that is, it has a meaning in and for the human life in which it has grown.

15. The Law as a Form of Objectivated Human Life

We have seen that the Law is not corporeal nature, nor psychism; nor is it a pure idea of value. (Pure ideas of value will be those values which ought to orient the Law, but not real, positive, historic Law.) And, on the contrary, we have discovered clearly that the Law belongs to that particular reality which I call "objectivated human life."

The Law is an objectivated form of human life. It is constituted of an aggregate of ideas — better called significations — which constitute rules for human conduct. Those significations were formed by some human minds, and even originally lived by certain men — by those who have created a juridical standard. Then, those significations which were

[10] Cf. Freyer, Soziologie als Wirklichkeitswissenschaft (1930).

constructed, made, by certain men, once they have been produced, that is, once they have been objectivated in legislative precepts or in juridical customs, have acquired a distinct and autonomous consistency, similar to that of ideal objects. With pure ideal objects, like mathematics, logic, values, etc., they have in common the significations which the juridical norms integrate, the dimension in which they are nontemporal and non-spatial beings, spectral entities, ideas identic with themselves (that is, the same idea is capable of being thought of by multiple subjects and at different moments, without the idea in question being confounded with the multiple mental acts of thinking of it). Every crystallized, objectivated thought apart from the mental act in which it was created shares the dimension of the ideal being; it is non-spatial, it is nontemporal, it is identic with itself, that is, it constitutes an autonomous, separate, objectivated entity.

Then, the content of a legislative disposition, or of a regulation, although having in common with the ideal being that special consistency of ideality, of spectrality, of objectivity, differs from mathematical ideal objects and from pure values, in this way; a mathematical principle, a pure value, has a consistency and a validity all its own, entirely independent of and foreign to the accidental fact whether a human brain has thought of it or not; and so we note that many times it has been said that the radii to a circumference are equal before any geometrician may have thought of it. But, on the other hand, an article of the civil code was not, it did not exist until the legislator framed it. A mathematical idea has not been constructed, made, by the mathematician, who has only discovered something which already was, with entire independence of him. On the other hand, a regulation is born with the act of the legislator who enacts it, and thanks to him; though indeed after being made, after its birth, it collects a being of its own, independent of the acts which have created it; it acquires an ideal objective being of a crystallized thought, of an idea. The significations which make up the juridico-positive precepts do not have an absolute ideal entity, they do not have an eternal and necessary validity — in the degree in which they are not the pure, rigorous, and exclusive expression of certain values, and in the degree in which they contain other circumstantial ingredients. Those significations (in short, those concrete standards) have been elaborated, compounded, in some vital acts and by them, in human conduct, whether in the mind and will of the legislator, or in the producing community of juridical customs. Moreover, those juridical standards, so far as they are complied with, so far as they are effectively realized, constitute the configuration of a society, the form or structure of various human existences.

But those significations which make up the positive Law of a people in an epoch, apart from their historic origin (that is, from their creation at a certain moment), and also apart from their realization in certain effective human acts (that is, from their fulfillment and application in a concrete society), may be conceived abstractly as pure significations, as ideas, which have, as such, a being similar to that of ideal objects, an incorporeal and nonpsychic being, non-spatial and nontemporal, though, as we have seen, they lack an absolute and eternal validity. That is, those juridical significations — the positive standards — have a being analogous to the ideal being, so far as it consists in a spectral being, distinct from the psychic acts in which they are thought of or realized. All those historic cultural significations have in common with the pure ideas the possession of the dimension of the ideal; but, on the other hand, they cannot have the consistency of pure and necessary validity which characterizes mathematical or logical principles; since, while the latter were already what they are — that is they were already valid — before any mind pictured them to itself, were already what they are independently of any human act, on the other hand, the significations which make up positive Law (or the work of art, or the technical plan, or the scientific method, etc.), and in the form in which they compose it, have a historical origin, concrete in time and concrete as to the circumstances which conditioned their birth. But, once they have been born, have been created, those significations acquire an autonomous consistency, an objectivated being, susceptible of being thought of and realized by any person.

16. Structure of Objectivated Human Life

The structure of objectivated human life is analogous to the structure of human life proper, that is, of the individual; for finally and at last it is its product, its crystallization.

But, as crystallization, it lacks all dynamism — which is what characterizes the individual life — it is immovable; or, in short, if I may be permitted a paradoxical phrase, certainly expressive, we might say that it is dead life. It has the outline of human life; it possesses its same meaning, an equal teleological structure; but it does not live, that is, it does not move, nor change, it is not fluid, on the contrary it is immovable, permanent, solid; it does not make itself, but it was made and so it remains. It is not in the making, but is already made. It is not an act, but it is a thing. It is not an agent, but it is a pure trace, a pure track. And so, the objectivated, that is, fossilized, life is altogether incapable of being transformed, modified, recreated, living; because, in truth, it is not authentic life, but a rigid photograph of a life which was.

The observation which I have just expounded in the preceding paragraph is of superlative importance. It can destroy the phantasmagoria (to which German thought has so much tended) of substantializing the world of culture by considering it as something which lives in and for itself, which creates for itself, which evolves and becomes perfect by itself, as if it were a live and independent entity, which develops by itself. It will perhaps be objected that culture changes, is transformed, evolves; but to this I shall answer that culture does not realize such changes and developments by itself, but it produces them by the new action, the new interference of new individual lives, who reëlaborate and recreate what was previously elaborated by others. Science is not a subject which develops by itself, but the only ones who make it are living individuals. And the individuals of today revise the science which those of yesterday made, correct it, surpass it, augment it. Only by the intervention of new individual acts can this be produced. It is customary to say that artistic styles evolve, are changed, and initiated; but such manner of speaking is incorrect; styles are fossil outlines, incapable of transforming themselves; they change only thanks to the interference of new individual actions, thanks to new vital actions, which recreate, which create anew. Human work has no life of its own: it is the work of a life, but it does not possess life, but, on the contrary, it is dead, a pure thing; in a word, it is a fossil, a crystallized secretion. What happens is that in a work — of science, of art, of Law — there are in its thoughts some ideas which did not receive full and correct development, or there are premises not all of whose consequences were validated, or there are conjectures not developed, or contradictions not surmounted; and when it is thought of anew, rethought of in other acts of individual life, it happens that in these new live thoughts — of individuals — the ideas previously thought of by others — and which remain crystallized in the work — reach the development or the correction which in that prior work had remained frustrated; or consequences are drawn which were not extracted in the former work; or, in short, the prior work is replaced by another new one. The creation of cultural works belongs exclusively to authentic life, that is, to individual life. The individual will employ, as materials, elements contained in prior works, more, it always happens so by virtue of the process of vital reason and of historic reason (on these themes I shall say more later); but it is the individual — and only he — who transforms, reëlaborates, recreates, or replaces the former work.

And the same may be said as to social forms, and naturally as to the Law. Neither the social structure, nor economics, nor the Law, live in and by themselves, nor do they transform themselves autonomously, but only by the interference of new individual acts. The Law nor any of the social structures do not live by themselves, but they live only so far as men revive them, who cannot revive them only by repeating them rigorously, but by also correcting, transmuting, initiating them. But the change, the evolution, the superiority, which operates in the Law, or in economics, or in money, etc., is not a live process, immanent in the Law or in those other social forms, but is the fruit of new acts of human lives.

What I explain as the zone of objectivated human life constitutes a new version of the theme known in contemporaneous philosophy by the names of "sciences of the spirit," "realm of culture," or "realm of the historic." I consider that in the reëlaboration which I have offered of this theme are cleared up not a few of the points which, in those other theories, remained obscure and confused.

17. Culture as a System of Functions of Human Life

In that realm of objectivated works we see the expression of a series of functions of human life. We see what man has done and does in his life: religion, philosophy, morality, science, technique, economics, art, law, the state, etc. We conjecture that all those activities do not constitute mere chance episodes — which have been produced, but which also might not have been produced — but that, on the contrary, they represent constant and necessary functions of human life. This idea was skillfully outlined by Dilthey,[11] without being afterwards recognized in later thought.

The content of science, art, philosophy, law, technique, etc., has varied and varies historically: it is different in different peoples and times. But if as to its result, as to its structure, and as to its content, the Law has varied — the same as occurs with philosophy, with science, with art, with technique, etc. — on the other hand each one of these tasks (the Law, philosophy, science, art, technique, etc.) will have to keep an identity as functions of human life. The content of the Law today in one nation differs from that which the ordinances of other epochs and peoples

[11] See a summarized exposition of Dilthey in my book Estudios de Filosofía del Derecho (Barcelona: Bosch, 1936) 77ff. For Dilthey, cf. chiefly Einleitung in die Geisteswissenschaften (1910) 32ff.; Beitraege zum Studium der Individualitaet (1896) 296ff.; Das Natürliche System der Geisteswissenschaften. As to Dilthey see an enlightening study by the Argentine Professor Francisco Romero; also José Ortega y Gasset, the study cited in Note 1. Moreover, Georg Nisch, Die Idee der Lebensphilosophie in der Theorie der Geisteswissenschaften (1924); Lebensphilosophie und Phänomenologie (1930); Spranger, Gedächtnisrede (1912); Stein, Der Begriff des Geistes bei Dilthey; Hans Freyer, Theorie des objektiven Geistes (1923); and Soziologie als Wirklichkeitswissenschaft (1930).

had; but the *function* which the Law of here and now discharges in the human life of this historic situation is similar to that which the Law of yesterday and of other historic situations discharged. We shall see in the course of this work that such constant function is that of *security in the collective life*. So, we might say with respect to technique: the technique of the North American people is enormously different from that of a primitive collectivity or from that of the traditional Chinese; but both have in common the discharge of the same function, which perhaps we might define as the purpose of obtaining a certain power, a security and enjoyment with respect to the world of nature, and of creating in it for man a margin of comfort which permits him to devote himself to other tasks. And, in like manner, we might face the problem of art; perhaps all its multiple and heterogenous manifestations have in common a function expressive of service of an eagerness for sublimation. And also with respect to philosophy: however diverse may be the content of the thought of Thales, Plato, Aristotle, Descartes, Hegel, etc., they all respond to the same functional necessity, that of finding a basic and fundamental certitude, an autonomous and pantonomous truth. And, so, we might go on setting up similarly the problem of all the so-called branches of culture, which we should call the better — by virtue of what has been said — functions of human life. Necessarily in the structure of our life there have to be conditions which produce, with constant regularity, such creations, always as the situation permits. The structure of life — we might say, paraphrasing Dilthey[12] — brings into play the knowledge of things (science), domination over nature (technique), economic processes, art, religion, etc. And, as well, it organizes forms of coexistence and solidarity, rules of social behavior, law, the state, etc.

And each one of those functions would not represent something apart from and independent of the others; on the contrary, far from being isolated and unconnected, they would constitute a systematic articulation in the unity of life. There is in life a connection, an organic unity of everything which we think of, do, feel, desire. Each one of those functions (science, art, law, etc.) is not isolated elements, but abstractions, which our thought has made upon the effective reality of life, in which all are reciprocally interlocked.

And probably one should distinguish between functions of the individual life and functions of the social life. But this distinction is premature, for I have not yet explained the difference between individual life and social life, which I shall undertake in the following pages.

[12] Cf. Dilthey, Einleitung in die Geisteswissenschaften (new edition, p. 46); Beiträge zum Studium der Individualität; Der Aufbau der geschichtlichen Welt.

18. The Categories of Human Life. Reference to the Normative and to the Collective

The world of human life, as also that of its objectivation, has its system of categories. Discovery of this system is one of the tasks upon which the thought of our day is working; and this book is not the appropriate place to anticipate an exposition of this matter. But it is of interest and suffices here for me to refer to two of them: the *normative* and the *collective,* which are those which most directly affect the Law.

19. The Normative

In the significations which man thinks of, we may establish a formal classification in two groups; enunciative signification or propositions and normative signification or propositions.

Enunciative propositions are those which state in what a being consists, what a reality is, the existence of a fact, the effective manner in which that fact has happened, the regular way certain phenomena come about, etc. They are propositions with respect to being, they denote a being, they give an account of the existence of something, or of how that something is, or of the connection between various somethings. Such are, for example, the propositions relating to nature, as well of a particular type (for example, description of a mountain range), as of a general type (connection between various phenomena; the fall of bodies, their expansion, their vibration); also the propositions of psychological science, which declare the manner of being and producing animated phenomena; mathematical theorems (which express ideal connections); historical statements (Columbus discovered America in 1492) which declare facts which have been; the astronomical announcement of an eclipse, etc. All these propositions state something which is, something which was, or something which will be. These propositions, in their aggregate, constitute the plan of the world *really given;* they are valuable by reason of their coincidence with the actuality of the facts; and, consequently, they have validity only so far as they agree with the facts. Discrepancy between one of those propositions and the facts to which it refers involves the falsity of the proposition.

Normative propositions, on the other hand, do not state the reality of certain facts, nor the manner in which actually they happened, but they specify an *ought-to-be;* that is, they prescribe certain conduct as due. Such are, for example, moral precepts, the rules of decorum, the laws of the State. They refer to human conduct; but not as an explanation of its real facts, not as an enunciation of the effective connections in the real processes of human work, but *determining as due, as ought-to-be,* a certain behavior. Norms do not state what has happened, happens, or will happen, but what *ought to* be fulfilled, although perhaps in reality it may not have been fulfilled, nor is it going to be, since it is possible that one may violate the norm. It does not have to happen necessarily and inevitably in the world of facts that exactly the condition that a norm should be such that it may have meaning as a norm lies in what it ordains as ought-to-be. The norm prescribes what ought to be, which as well may be, as not be, in reality, since it depends upon human discretion. Precisely because in the real world there may not be fulfilled what the norm ordains, on that account the norm has meaning as such a norm. If what the norm says will always and necessarily, inevitably, be realized, then the norm would lose its character of "ought-to-be," it would cease to constitute such a norm, and would be transformed into a law (in the expression of a constant causal concatenation of phenomena). A norm which says "that ought to happen which actually happens" or "you ought to behave in the same manner in which you are actually behaving" would not be a norm, it would lack normative meaning. It would be as if we said that the flame *ought* to expand the column of mercury heated by it, which has no meaning, because the column of mercury is not capable of an act of disobedience to this law, and simply and necessarily it will expand when it is heated. So, then, the material possibility that it may be violated, that the conduct of the subject affected by it may contravene it, is an essential presupposition for the norm; since, in any other way, it would not be a norm but a mere statement of facts. When one says that the norm has been violated, injured, or broken, one does not mean by this to say that to the norm as such anything has happened, that it has suffered any diminution of its validity, but that the conduct of the subject represents a departure from it, a nonrealization of its demands; but that is so, precisely because the norm goes on being a norm despite its having been unfulfilled. The normativity of a rule is precisely affirmed in contrast with its inobservance in fact. The type of necessity of the normative demand is not causal, is not a real compulsion, but is a type of ideal demand. Norms are, then, propositions which are valuable, in spite of their noncoincidence with reality, because they do not try to express how it actually is, but how it ought to be; that is, they try to prescribe a conduct.

From this formal point of view, in which we have just contemplated the enunciative and the normative, it follows that these two categories (the being and the ought-to-be) are equally primary, that is, independent of each other. If we classify our thoughts from that purely formal point of view (as to their form), it follows that we meet some thoughts which give the expression of a being; and other thoughts which express an ought-to-be. The reality of anything tells us nothing about its adjustment or nonadjustment to a norm. A normative precept tells us nothing about what is or will be in fact the conduct to which it is directed.

What has been said does not judge adversely, nor contradict the attempt made by Husserl, to convert normative propositions into enunciators of qualities of value. According to that attempt, a normative proposition may be converted into one enunciative of the value or of the mandate which founds it. So, for example, the proposition "you ought to be truthful" would be transformed into the proposition "truth is morally good"; the norm "the bailee ought in such and such conditions to return the thing deposited to the depositor" would be converted into this: the civil code says that if the bailee does not return the thing, he will be subject to a proceeding enforceable by compulsory execution; etc. In spite of that possibility of conversion, there remains valid the special characterization of the normative, as I have explained it.

20. Formal Normativity and Material Normativity

Now, it should be noted that among the propositions of a normative type we may establish the following distinctions or classification: (A) Propositions of normative form, whose content has its origin in a human work, that is, which has been made by man; for example, the precepts of traffic regulations; and (B) Normative propositions whose content is the pure expression of an ideal value; for example, the pure and absolute principles of morals, the first principles of the value of justice; and in such principles it happens that not only is their form normative, but also their content is normative (valuable), in and for itself. It happens that to the essence of some values there belongs a dimension of "ought-to-be" and even of "ought-to-do" in the sense of ideal or pure duty. This ideal or pure ought-to-be — by virtue of the same kind of value, and within the conditions required by the same content and meaning of value — constitutes an absolute ought-to-be, which is founded on itself, whose validity does not derive from anything extrinsic to itself. And, so, it happens that in the principles which constitute a pure and perfect expression of ideal values, not only is the form in which they are presented normative, but so also is their matter, that is, their content.

It is to be noted that the normativity of the propositions of the objectivated human life, for instance, the example which we offered before of traffic regulations, is formal; but, on the other hand, its content springs from a human work, is the product of the thoughts and the will which some certain men of flesh and blood have had, and is not a pure essence of value, although, of course, it tries to found or to orient itself on certain values. Although this regulation orients itself toward some values and tries to found itself on them, the proximate or immediate basis of its ought-to-be, of its normativity, takes its root in a will, that is, in a mandate (of the competent authority). The positive Law rules as a norm not for its greater or less intrinsic correctness (for its greater or less attained justice), but for its operation, that is, for having emanated from the competent tribunal. And, moreover, again, the content of a positive precept (for example, the regulations to which I have referred), although it intentionally aims at certain values (for example, security, common good, liberty, etc.), shelters a series of historic, circumstantial elements, concrete, singular ends, conditioned to particular situations, and may embody only imperfectly the values to which it aspires.

21. The Collective. — Social Human Life

Society is not an entity in and for itself, with an existence apart from that of the individual men who form it; that is, society is not a subsisting reality, but the only substantive realities which compose it are men. So, for example, there does not exist apart from and independent of the Mexicans a reality *Mexico*. To suppose the contrary, to believe in the substantiality of social entities, as something in and for themselves, would be a caprice of romantic thinking (which talked of a mysterious and recondite national soul — as a spiritual reality — which acted as a protagonist of history and which gave birth to culture, art, language, law, etc.); or was also one of the most lamentable errors into which the doctrine of Hegel fell, and also its derivatives; or, as well, a manifestation of the crude biology of the nineteenth century, which, in an unpremeditated desire to resolve all problems with a unique and simple formula, sought to explain society as a biological organism — like the animals — of gigantic proportions. Contemporaneous thought has made sweeping criticism of all those doctrines, as well as of the phantasmagoria of the romanticists, as of the confusions in Hegel's theory, and the *naturalistic* thought of the organic theory. And it has been established, finally, with obvious clarity that the social has no reality apart from individuals, but that it constitutes something which happens to men and which they make. In short, I should say, the social is a form of human life.

Now, from the proof that the only substantive realities in the social are men, it does not follow by any means (as many have pretended with inexact vision) that society is only a fabric of individual lives. It is true that only men, that is, individuals, since we do not know other substantive human beings than individuals, compose and live society. But, as we shall see hereafter, when individuals act as members of a collectivity, what they live is not their own authentic individual life, but some special forms of objectivated life, that is, some forms of collective life. Or, anticipating in other words: the one who lives the collective life is the individual but those forms of collective life may be distinguished perfectly from the forms of true, authentic individual life.

But before developing the idea which I have just sketched in the preceding paragraph it is desirable that I explain what is the supposition of all interhuman relations. Among the many diverse things which I encounter in the world, I find other men. But I do not find them as I find a stone or a tree, but I find them as peculiar beings, which keep with me a distinct relation from that in which I am with the water spring or with the sun, or with ideas. I am affected by them in some way, and I know (or conjecture) that the same thing happens to them towards me. I have an intuition that they understand me and that I understand them. Although from a certain point of view we might say that I live with nature, nevertheless the relation of co-existence which I have with the things of nature is different from the way in which I am with other men: I am not only *in* society and *before* it, but also *with* it. I am with other men, I co-exist, I co-live. For it is a fatal error to conceive of society (the fact of interhuman relations and the fact of collectivity) under the figure of *association,* of *joining together,* as if it were founded primarily on the act of uniting or joining. For in order that people should unite to do something in common, or to join together, it is necessary that they should previously be in society, in relation; it is necessary that they should mutually understand one another and that they should feel that they have something in common.

Now, the individual may live two forms of life, as well in himself, as in relation to others. In some aspects or moments he lives *individual forms of life,* which he creates himself, which are private and exclusive to him, in his own manner, as something very characteristic and intransferable; but, in other aspects and moments, he lives by common recipes, according to formulas *already made* and generalized; in short, according to *collective forms of life.*

So, then, in the life of man, which certainly is always lived by individuals of flesh and blood, it is necessary to distinguish between the *purely individual deed or work* and the *deed or work according to common models* (which, of course, is also done by the individual, but not as an individual).

The *individual deed or work* is — as José Ortega y Gasset has truly characterized it — that which I live as an individual, so far as I am a certain being and different from all the others, so far as irreducible, as exclusive, peculiar and unchangeable, on my own account, under my fullest responsibility. It is the life in which I live my thoughts originally by strict adherence to them, my genuine desires, in which I take my decisions, wholly for my account, not only as to the act of deciding, but also as to the content of the decision, responding to my authentic convictions.

Now, the individual lives not only as an individual, in the manner and to the extent which I have just described in the preceding paragraph, but he may copy his deeds, taking his models from the models of objectivated human life, which are here, as crystallizations, which can be repeated, revived, by new persons. In this case, we find acts which are composed of two types of ingredients, to wit: an individual ingredient (the decision) and some objective ingredients, which consist in the content of what is done, which take something which is here already depicted, already formed, already made before by another person. In this case, the desire to do is what emanates from me as an individual; but what I do, the content of my action, does not proceed from me, but I take it from another; it is a form of human life already objectivated.

But, with this we have not yet come to characterizing the *collective form of life* (lived, of course, by individuals). For, in the class of conduct which I have just described — as conduct in which its content does not derive from the individual subject who lives it, but which he takes from yonder, from an objectivation of preëxisting human life — there may be two cases entirely distinct. In the first place, there may be the case of an individual taking the content of his work from the conduct which another individual lived, as his own original invention. Such is the case in which I copy or imitate the behavior which was original and characteristic with another person, because I consider that that conduct is valuable, is worthy of being taken as a model. This happens when I take as an example the conduct of a saint (guide myself by the virtues of St. Francis of Assisi) or of a hero (the general wishes to imitate what Napoleon did), or of a teacher (the writer wishes to imitate the style of another, because it seems to him that it is very good), or of a friend (whom I consider loyal, energetic and judicious), or of a stranger (whom I admire for his gentleness), or I let myself be guided by the opinion of another person whom I deem intelligent. In all these cases — and the numberless ones like them — it happens that an *individual,* by his own individual decision copies or reproduces the conduct of *another individual* (conduct which that other invented or fashioned as an individual). And, therefore, the first individual makes of his own invention the resolution to copy, to imitate, to reproduce; but what he copies is the individual conduct of another individual. The objectivated form of life which he reproduces is the crystallization of an individual life of another person. It is very desirable to note that, in these cases in which the conduct (which may be as well thought, as action) of another individual person is reproduced, although the content of that behavior is taken from without, nevertheless it is made intimate; full adherence is lent to it, and in that way it comes to be also the own conviction of the person who copies it. Although he has not invented that behavior he makes it intimately his, identifies himself with it because it seems to him valuable; it is precisely for that that he copies it. Naturally, I refer to the cases in which other conduct is taken as a model, consciously, by sincere adherence, by authentic devotion, and not only as the result of a mechanism of reactive imitation.

But, in the second place, we may record another type of work distinct from that I have examined in the preceding paragraph. There is also the case in which the individual copies an alien conduct but not the individual alien conduct of another individual (fixed and unchangeable so far as he is individual), but the general conduct of a group of persons, an impersonal conduct, for example, that which a *people* does, that which the *rest* do, what *colleagues, copartisans, co-religionaires, comrades,* do, in short, what the members of a group do, not as individuals, but as members of a collective circle. It is conduct which man does, not as an individual — untransferable, and unchangeable — but as one in a circle of men (class, profession, group, State, etc.) in his abstract quality as such, and therefore, as a generic being, interchangeable, replaceable, fungible. In this case — as José Ortega y Gasset has rightly emphasized — what is taken into account is not the conduct of other persons as individuals, but something generic, impersonal, abstract, functional. To be and to act as a member of a social class, a professional collectivity, or a belief or a party, as a citizen, as a functionary, is not to be nor to act as an individual, it is not to be nor to act as the authentic and original subject of a life, but it is to be and to exercise an abstract function, a part or *role;* it is to be not an authentic individual person, but a personage. In this case I execute a collection of acts which do not proceed from me as an individual, nor yet from another person as an individual, but which are defined impersonally, as something generic and unowned; it is to submit myself to something not individual but common. We have as the simplest example of this what happens with customs, which are something prototypically social. When we comply with a custom we do something which the rest do and because the rest do it. John wears a necktie because he has seen that the rest wear them; but, who are the rest? Perhaps Peter, Louis, Joseph, etc.? But, note well, the rest are not an assembly of individuals as individuals, they are not the meeting of Peter (as to what Peter has of Peter) and Louis (as to what Louis has of Louis), and so on; because it happens that Peter wears a necktie also because the rest wear one, and with those others also is included John (who is the one we have taken as the starting point); and so on. No one in complying with a custom starts out to take into account another person, as an individual, but a vague and generic totality — which naturally permits exceptions — the rest — within which concept I also am, as each one of all the others also takes into account the rest (among whom I am numbered). We find a deed which serves as a model for my deed (my life), and it follows that there is no one concretely and separately responsible for that deed, because each one complies also because all the rest do. It follows that the rest are almost all who belong to a certain circle; but not I in the concrete, nor John in the concrete, nor Peter separately. The rest, the people, are all, but no one in particular or in the concrete; they are all and none at the same time. And, therefore, it happens that when we seek for the person responsible for the social, we find that there is no such person concretely and definitely responsible, but the vague, generic, and diffused reference to "the rest." The social is a form of life which is not of any one in particular, but is something generic, communal, topical.

And when the individual — following along the example upon which I am commenting — complies with a social custom, the subject of this deed is not I the individual, but the fungible "I"; something like a store coat, like a mask, in short, what Wiese has skillfully noted, calling it "the social I in the individual." [13] In social conduct, that is, in the forms of collective life, the individual as an individual intervenes no more than as to the decision to behave according to those forms; since it is clear that he may resolve to respect the custom or to contravene it. The individual person places himself subject to the custom, to what the rest do. But that according to which he acts, the model of conduct which he follows, does not proceed from the individual in question, nor does it proceed from another individual whom the first copies, but from the collectivity, that is, from some persons in their condition as members of a group. The individual who complies with a custom does not do it without carrying out a scheme of conduct which he receives as something impersonal.

And so we might multiply examples. When I think something because it has occurred to me in complete solitude, or also when I have made the thought of another person sincerely mine, by intimate and basic conviction, to the point that it now belongs to my own profound brain, I think as an individual (fully and completely in the first case, and secondarily in the second). But, on the other hand, if I think something,

[13] Cf. LEOPOLD WIESE, SYSTEM DER ALLGEMEINEN SOZIOLOGIE (1933) 137ff.

because I have received it as a dominant opinion, in this case I am taking from something *not individual,* to wit, from something collective, from *public opinion* (that is, not private of one or another, but topical, communal). So, then, as a comment in the happy phrase of Bouglé, society manifests itself in phenomena of which the individual is the theater, but not the sufficient reason.[14]

When I act in deciding on my own life, on my private existence, I act as an individual. But when I act as a member or as a director of a group, my conduct is determined by a series of considerations foreign to my individuality, to wit, by taking into account the kind of group, its interest, its collective purpose, etc. It is common to hear phrases like "I willingly for my part would do such or such a thing, but as belonging to this social class, or as a member of this collectivity, or as a director of it, I cannot, since in my capacity as such I must take into account what the group signifies, the function which I represent in it."

So, then, although the individual also acts socially, so far as he submits himself to a plan of foreign, impersonal conduct and is the one who in fact executes it, the person to whom this behavior refers is not his deep I, but a sort of skin adhering to it, a kind of investiture, in short, what has been called by Wiese a *social I.* But it should be well understood that the bearer of this social I is the same individual person; that is, in speaking of a social I, we do not refer to a supposed collective I (an absurd hypothesis) distinct from the individual I's, but only and exclusively to a sort of mask borne by the individual I, to a part acted by him. This social I receives its shape, principally, from the collective forms. It is true that it keeps a union with the personal or individual I. But in social human life, what comes in question is not the totality of the man, his profound depth, but only his social component.

Moreover, note that we cannot speak of a single social I in each individual; on the contrary, upon a single individual I there are superposed and coexisting a multiple series of social I's, corresponding to the divers collective situations in which he participates, for example, as citizen, workman, sportsman, member of a singing society, affiliate of a party, etc. Each one of those social I's which the individual carries with him is a kind of personality, not for him, not for itself, but for the rest. It is shaped according to certain social exigencies, the product of the environment, crystallized in types. It is clear that the individual I is the only one which is an authentic subject; it is clear that it is the only one which suffers and enjoys, which desires and fears.[15]

[14] See Celestin Bouglé, Qu'est-ce que la Sociologie? (Paris, 1907).

[15] Miguel de Unamuno gave a true characterization of the individual person in his magisterial work, El sentimiento trágico de la vida.

The collective is a crystallization, an impersonalized objectivation.

It is true that in the subjection of a person to collective models of conduct he may be given a dose of sincere and profound adherence to them. But this is not in any way essential to the form of collective life. This may be in some cases desirable; but it does not belong to the essence of the behavior according to collective forms, on the contrary, it is something entirely accidental. I comply fully with a usage, behaving in accordance with it, although in the depth of my soul I feel a great contempt for it and find it ridiculous. Now, this which is possible — and admissible — in forms of collective conduct, is on the other hand not so in the case which we were examining before of the *individual* behavior of another person, that is, when, for example, one takes as model a saint, a teacher, a hero. Because then they are taken as an example, precisely because their behavior is deemed valuable, because one feels intimately an adherence, identification with it. But this is so because the relation with the teacher, with the model person, is not a social relation, but is an interindividual relation, as José Ortega y Gasset has skillfully shown. So also is something not social but interindividual, the relation with a friend, the relation with a beloved.

In fact, in a friendship, in a love, in an exemplary devotion, those who are inter-related are two individuals as individuals, as to what each has of individuality. One likes the friend, loves the sweetheart, follows the teacher, precisely for the individual and special qualities which are discovered in them. And, consequently, the beloved is irreplaceable; and the same occurs with the friend and with the teacher. These relations are established between individual I's, deep, and irreducible to other. This is exactly the opposite to what happens in the social relation: for that is established between interchangeable, exchangeable, fungible, persons; for example, the colleague, the copartisan, the comrade, the citizen, the car conductor, the associate, the vendor, the soldier, etc., expressions which designate social I's, pure parts or generic functions, which in their capacity as such may have substitutable agents.

Note with special firmness this characterization, which I have just expounded, with regard to the collective in general, because later we shall see how the same, with much more accentuated features — truly important — occurs in juristics. In the Law, which in fine is a form of collective life — the greatest in intensity and amplitude — occurs still more exaggeratedly that same which we have been commenting upon with respect to the social *in genere,* to wit: the subject of the social forms of life is not the authentic man, the individual man, but a mere functional dimension, a part or *role,* a mask, in short, a social I. The same, but with characters in bolder relief, occurs in the juridical life; in the established Law we never meet individual men, of flesh and blood, in their particular profundity, but we meet only the citizen, the foreigner, the functionary, the private person, the vendor, the purchaser, the principal, the agent, the shipowner, the overseer, the tax payer, the tax collector, the elector, the candidate, the judge, the policeman, the delinquent, etc., in short, abstract categories, types, functional crystallizations. But, on the other hand, there remains outside the Law, further from or nearer to it, my unique, untransferable, profound existence, my singular perspective to the horizon of the world, my life distinct from all other lives, that unique and most private instance which we each one of us are.

On the other hand, I said that when we ask who the collective person is, who commands or imposes the social models, who are "the people," "the rest," we find that there is no authentic collective person, but only an abstraction, an impersonal generalization. Then, we shall see later, with due attention, when we ask who the person is who commands the juridical norms, who imposes them, we shall again not find a real person, but a person constructed by the same norm, to wit, the State. This, different from the dominant subject in the social not juridical (the people), does not lack precise outlines, nor is it vague or hazy, on the contrary it is perfectly defined and rigorously bounded; but it is not a real person, but a conceptual, ideal, person, created by the juridical norm, personified by it.

The social,[16] constituted of objectivated forms of human life, with the characters which I have described, although it may be something which has no life of its own, but is inert, exercises a pressure upon men, in the measure in which it is lived anew by a circle of persons, that is, in the degree in which these forms are relived, fulfilled, or realized regularly by the totality or by the majority of a group of people. That pressure will be defined or better described, for the moment, as a kind of force which acts upon persons to accommodate their behavior to the collective form. It is a matter of a specifically collective pressure, that is, which flows from the fact that other people are behaving according to those forms.

Now, the characteristic of the collective behaviors which I now emphasize is not that action which every objectivated activity of human lives exercises over whomever contemplates it, but that other action which beyond that one is peculiar as to social forms when they are endowed with effectiveness, that is, with effective reality, to wit, when they

[16] This paragraph and the two following are from the Second Spanish edition of the book (Mexico, 1945). TRANSLATOR.

are in fact complied with by a multitude of persons. That characteristic action of the social over human behavior constitutes a sort of pressure, that is, sometimes something like an impulsion, or better, like a drawing force which the person experiences to conduct himself in the ruling social form; at other times, something like a conforming action which molds some aspects of his being according to the communal model; on occasions, something like the penetration in his life of the generic thoughts of the others. The existence of this pressure is shown in the fact that when one wishes to behave in a manner different from the current social one, he has to make an effort not to let himself be carried away by what the others do; it is necessary to oppose an internal energy to resist the influence of the communal thoughts or conduct. One can swim against the current, upstream, but it is necessary therefore to put in action a force sufficient to overcome the force of the current. Also, one may act in a manner distinct from and even contrary to that which usage determines; but, to do it, it is necessary to develop a strength capable of counteracting the pressure which usage exercises. One may dress in a manner contrary to the fashion, in a way contrary to the way the others dress; but, to do it, it is necessary to have the courage or the presence of mind to resist the critics, censors, or jokesters which such proceeding will arouse. One may think entirely contrary to what is general opinion, but therefore one must possess the necessary firmness not to yield before the influence of the common convictions. One may resist the employment of current fads of speech which do not please him, but he will have to develop a special attention and watchfulness, to avoid, by contagion, falling unwittingly into the same language. All these observations and numberless other analogous ones constitute the proof that current social conduct acts upon the person pressing him to accommodating himself to it.

This pressure may be of very different degrees and assume different forms, but in greater or less degree and in one form or another it exists always in all manifestations of the social. As to the degree of force of this pressure, it may range from very slight, for example, that which some unimportant usages exert, to so great that it becomes irresistible, such as that which juridical norms impose, which tolerate no rebellion but try to annihilate it, which I shall show later when I explain the peculiar form of dominion of juristics, which is inexorable imposition. Note how, in that character of peculiar pressure of social customs, we see that the Law represents the maximatization of the collective, that is, the social carried to its extreme.

Now, it is not at all to be thought that the social has, from these described characters, a purely secondary importance. By no means. The social forms an essential and necessary part of human life, as an inevitable component of it.

Man needs to rely, to solve many problems, on what he receives ready made from the rest and from the past. Man, as Rousseau noted very profoundly, is progressive. What essentially characterizes man, said Rousseau — whose well-informed doctrine has passed unnoticed — is his capacity of communication, that is, his power to learn from the rest. Man is defined not only by intelligence: we might even imagine a very intelligent man, capable of discovering for himself the most important truths and the surest maxims of morals and justice, we even might suppose the greatest lights in him — says Rousseau in his *Discourse on the Origins of Inequality* — if all that wisdom could not be communicated it would perish with that individual; and the rest — his contemporaries and his successors — would have to begin anew from the beginning, and so on, so that no improvement nor progress could be attained. What essentially characterizes man is his *perfectibility,* founded on communicability. Man begins to live not in a vacuum, but resting on what other men have done. To live, which is to choose between the limited possibilities which circumstance offers us, we proceed from an interpretation of it, we need a knowledge on which to depend with respect to the world and the rest; and that interpretation, for the moment, we receive from the rest. Upon the historical level of what men have already thought and done, my life commences; and upon this historical level, new individual ideas will bring innovations, rectifications, additions, so that a new generation will begin its life upon a level different from that from which ours took off. As to this, says Ortega y Gasset, man is always an *heir;* the man of today is necessarily different from the man of yesterday, because when the former began to live he found a heap of dogmas, of models, which were not there when the existence of the long ago man began; but, at the same time, the man of today, as he lives in new circumstances, in a different world (of knowledges, beliefs, experiences) from that of yesterday, will modify on his own account that legacy received. The tiger of today is as identically a tiger as the tigers of two thousand years ago: each tiger begins its being tigerish. But, on the contrary, man (who is characterized essentially by having tradition) never begins his being human, his humanity, but he receives it already shaped by the people of the immediate past; on that account man is always different from what he was; he does not have a fixed being; he of today is different from him of yesterday, because he knows or perceives that yesterday, and besides in each epoch he has to make for himself a new being. So it follows that man has not a *given, made* being, but he has to make it for himself; for him it commences starting from what the rest have done, on which level he will bring his own contribution (large or small). And it is the successive accumulation of theoretical and practical inventions which makes progress possible. Rousseau says that very much time must have elapsed before there could have arisen the institutions which today are habitual with us. It is clear that to be progressive, man needs, on the one hand, to free himself from what was yesterday and to remain at liberty to be in a different way; but, on the other hand, he needs also to be able to accumulate from yesterday, to make use of the past, to start from it; because otherwise, as Rousseau says, each human being would have to commence anew and no perfectibility would be possible. He can liberate himself from the past, correct it, supersede it, increase its heap, because he is an *individual,* with his own life, who can act on his own account. Even more, society begins on the level of the past. Society is necessary and essential to man: it is like a mechanism between the individual and his life, like an instrument or machine which makes progress possible. Now, let us take into account, as José Ortega y Gasset has noted, that the forms of social life are always representations of the past, of remote centuries, or recent days, but, in short, past; they are forms of life which *were before;* and so, archaic.

In accommodating ourselves in many of our tasks to what the rest do, there is implicit a confident credit which we extend to our predecessors and to our contemporaries. We believe that if the rest do so, this offers a certain guaranty of rightness: it may not be the best, but it is probable that neither is it the worst. It is not possible to imagine a man who copied nothing from the rest nor from the past: he would have to begin to decide on his own account all, absolutely all the problems of his life (what food to take, where to find it, how to dress, how to communicate with others since language is social, how to shelter himself, to form an interpretation of things, etc.); in short, he would have to invent *ex novo* all the business of his existence. Society gives us solved a series of problems, which permits us not to occupy ourselves with them and so facilitates the possibility of devoting ourselves to our own individuality, providing idleness in which we may for some moments live our own private life and in it invent some original forms (lowly or eminent); that is, it furnishes us occasions and time to live for our own account and risk. This would not be possible if we had to resolve each for himself all the problems of existence.

So, then, social life is as essential for man as his own individual life. Granting a confident credit to what the rest have done, the individual has resolved a series of peremptory problems; and, in this guise, can obtain sufficient ease to devote himself to his own private destiny; and, at the same time, he can bring, with his inventions and new experiences, progress in the legacy received from society.

Now, notice that the social — the crystallized forms of collective life — constitutes something inert, mechanical, and sterile; and it fructifies only in the degree in which there is produced on these forms the interference of a renovating individual action. As José Ortega y Gasset has very well commented, society is never original nor creative: it does not even feel necessities originally, because the one who feels them is the individual; he creates a work to satisfy them; and then, society adopts it; and, therefore, what first was the invention of an individual turns afterward into a social function.

So, then, it is erroneous to suppose, as some have done, that collective forms and social products are capable of themselves and by nothing more than themselves of engendering new forms, new institutions and creations. If indeed the collective life is something different from the individual life, nevertheless it is lived only by individuals; and, consequently, attains no real and actual existence except in the degree in which men live or, better, relive it. Then, if a social form to be real and actual needs indispensably the assistance of individuals, who fulfill and realize it, how can we imagine that a social form should be capable of itself and by nothing more than itself of originating new social forms, without passing through the crucible of new individual actions? It is in every way impossible. Everything which today is social, is collective, was once an individual invention, the creation of an individual or of several, which afterwards became communized, socialized, collectivized. The social is a crystallization, fossilization, mechanization, and, finally, it is sterile, and only renews itself, recreates itself, thanks to new individual contributions, which afterwards got socialized. And it evolves and changes thanks to a process of interaction between the social datum and the new fruitful contribution of the individual.

From all that has been said it follows very clearly that the social will play its part and will be beneficial in the degree in which it aids man to resolve a series of problems; but leaving to him at the same time a space, within which the individual may be himself, can move with freedom, to make his own individual life. And on that account, when one tries integrally to collectivize man, to make him static, to functionalize him, or, what is the same thing, to disindividualize him, then one exhausts the essence of what is human, one dehumanizes man, destroys him. And moreover therewith one cuts off irretrievably the future and all possibility of progress for society itself, which perishes desiccate, since it can progress only thanks to individual contributions.

22. Localization of Juristics

All that has previously been said has brought us to a precise and exact localization of juristics in the Universe. We have seen clearly, that the Law is not corporeal, nor biological, nor psychic nature, nor a pure idea of value (although it takes note of values). The Law belongs to the realm of *objectivated* human life; it is a human and, consequently, historic, product, which constitutes a *normative* form of a *collective* or social character. It is clear that with this we have not arrived, by far, at a determination of the *peculiar being* of the Law, of the specific essence of juristics. We have only succeeded in placing the Law in the zone of the Universe to which it belongs. But to this same zone belong also other forms of normative and collective human life, such as, for example, the social norms of decorum, of courtesy, etc. And, consequently, it will be necessary to pursue our search until we mark out the essentially juristic, as such, differentiating it from all the other norms and from all the other collective forms.

For the moment, it is possible to establish from the preceding study:

1. That the Law belongs to the zone of the Universe which I have characterized as objectivated human life; and that, as such, it is constituted of a complex of significations of a purposeful structure, with a meaning and intentionally directed toward certain values.

2. That those significations have a normative form.

3. That it constitutes a norm of historical content: the human interpretation, at any given moment of the exigencies of certain values, conditioned by given circumstances.

4. That it is something of a social or collective kind: a form of life not individual, but collective, abstract, common, functional.

But, on the one hand, we fail to learn the difference between the Law and other norms (of human conduct), as, for example, morals, decorum, etc.; and to differentiate it also from other social products. And, on the other hand, we fail as well to inquire what is the essential meaning of juristics, as such.

To define a thing is indeed precisely to learn to distinguish that thing from all other things, and especially from those which are nearest to it, or which present some feature of analogy with it. And, therefore, we shall undertake the search for the distinction between morals and juristics; between juristics and the rules of social behavior (decorum, decency, courtesy, etiquette, etc.); and between juristics and arbitrary commands (a task which has been attacked by almost all the contemporaneous works on the Philosophy of the Law).

But in having worked out this task of differentiating the Law from the other norms which are similar to it in appearance, we still have not succeeded in capturing mentally the whole essence of juristics. For to know a thing in its essence, from the bottom, it is not sufficient that we should know how to differentiate it from all the rest, but it is necessary, further, that we should make contact with the profound intimacy of that thing. Hence, we shall have to seek also the essential meaning of juristics, after having set apart the Law from all the other types of norms.

CHAPTER II

PRIMITIVE USAGE AS AN UNDIFFERENTIATED NORM. USAGE AS A MANIFESTATION OF DIFFERENT TYPES OF NORMS

Language and history record various types of norms directed to human conduct: moral, legal, rules of social behavior (decency, decorum, courtesy, etiquette, etc.), mandates of pure force. We shall see how in each one of those types of rule there lies a different meaning; how each one of those types of normation has essentially a peculiar and exclusive intent; how each one of those types of regulation of conduct aims at corresponding values. To inquire into the essential difference between Law and morals, between Law and rules of social behavior, and between Law and mandates of pure force, will consist in explaining the peculiar proper meaning of each one of those types of norm.

But the special essence of each one of those norms (morals, rules of social behavior, law, mandates of pure force) is not to be confused with the manifestations through which such norms reveal themselves to us. Because, as we are going to see hereafter, it happens that norms entirely distinct, with essentially diverse meanings, manifest themselves in a similar manner. So, through usage, from usages, moral norms can manifest themselves, as well as norms of social behavior, as also juridical norms. And the juridical norms, besides making themselves evident in usages (customary Law), may be manifested — and still manifest themselves in greater volume — by legislative provisions and regulations and by court decisions. And the norms of morals may be manifested much more purely and nobly through the strictly individual conscience.

We see also that there are usages of a non-normative character, that is, which constitute models of conduct without pretense of creating a duty in the rest. The usage of greeting (a rule of social behavior), the usage of paying an installment of rural rent on a certain festival day (a precept of customary Law), are usages through which are reflected respective forms of life with normative pretension — of behavior in the first case and of Law in the second. While, on the contrary, an artistic usage (for example, the prevalence of a style), the custom of eating certain dishes, public opinion, etc., are usages without normative pretension.

It remains, then, clear that usage, collective and impersonal repetition of a behavior, is a form of objectivated human life, by means of which very diverse meanings may be manifested: non-normative and normative meanings; and among the latter, as well moral norms, as juridical norms, as norms of social behavior. Indeed, many times, there is reserved for the norms last mentioned (those of behavior) the name of social usages. Moreover, the fact of usage constitutes the dimension of effectivity of a norm. I speak of effectivity and not of validity; and although this is not the moment to expound the difference between effectivity and validity, I will anticipate by saying that by effectivity I understand the fact that an objectivated and collective form of human life is actually practiced, is habitually relived by the people of the group.

Custom, usage, is the whole form of regulation of human life in primitive situations. It represents the most vigorous source of social power in primitive groups; and absorbs almost the totality of human life. It may be noted that primitive man scarcely takes account of individual life; he lives rigidly impressed in a collectivity, without having discovered himself, almost as a mere instrument of the collectivity. Progress is indicated always by a decollectivization of man, that is, by a discovery and liberation of individuality. Man entirely socialized, collectivated, carries on an existence similar to that of animals; since it is not he who acts and lives, but the collectivity through him.

In primitive custom there are involved religious precepts, moral imperatives, rules of behavior (decorum, decency, courtesy, etc.), juridical precepts, technical models, medical recipes, etc. Man in a situation of primitiveness (when I speak of the primitive I do not refer so much to a chronological stage, as to a special situation, of which there are also contemporaneous examples) rules his life almost exclusively by usages, which possess at the same time a religious, moral, decorous, juridical, political, and technical significance. But it is clear that those various aspects are not clearly distinguished: that primitive custom of multiple and diverse dimensions presents itself as something prior to their differentiation, as an undistinguished norm, which is all of these at once (religion, morals, decorum, law, technique, etc.) and none of them in particular and fully.

We have examples of this undistinguished normation in the dharma of the Hindus, the themis of the Greeks, the fas of the Romans, the Germanic sitte.

In proportion as man proceeds to gain consciousness of himself and of valuable events in his life, he outlines also the different types of regulation of conduct; the religious as such, the purely moral, social decorum, the Law, as different outgrowths of the primitive global norm. Now, it is not to be taken, in any way, that each one of those diverse types of regulation of behavior has an empirical, purely contingent, fortuitous origin. Although in the reality of history they come to arise in such manner, it is a question of different forms of normativity, each one of them with a pure and defined essence, which corresponds to a special necessary function of human life. Those diverse types of norm correspond essentially to different necessary and constant functions of human life. What occurs is that when life presents itself in primitive situations with rudimentary characters, then its corresponding norms appear also as rudimentary involved aspects of undifferentiated custom, which comes to fill imperfectly all those functions. But it is not fortuitous, as we shall see, but an essential something, which produces in human life morals, religion, law, decorum, technique, etc.

Now, it happens that among all those diverse types of norm, when the process of differentiation has operated, there is one of them which is wont to go on manifesting itself almost entirely through usage, namely, the norm of social behavior (decorum, decency, courtesy, urbanity, etiquette), on which account they are wont to be called on many occasions purely and simply "social usages." But it is important not to confound the essence of those norms, their peculiar meaning — which we shall study further along — with the fact that ordinarily they continue to manifest themselves in a customary manner. That customary form is not necessarily exclusive in such rules of social behavior, but it may also serve as a vehicle for other rules; for example, the juridical ones (customary Law). And, on the other hand, it happens — although not frequently — that some norms of social behavior find another medium of external expression, distinct from usage.

CHAPTER III

MY AUTHENTIC DESTINY AND THE COMMUNAL TOPIC OF SOCIETY. THE DIFFERENCE BETWEEN MORALS AND LAW

1. The Statement of the Problem

Romano Guardini, the great Christian thinker, once said: "The Sermon on the Mount is the most sublime moral document which humanity possesses; but let it be well understood, a moral document in the strictest sense; for if instead of seeing in it a source of inspiration, rigorously moral, we should try to take it as a direction for juridical or political organization, it would lose its grandeur and would appear to us as a testimonial of cowardice." Here he points clearly to the essential difference in meaning between the strictly moral and the purely juridical.

But, on the other hand, we frequently hear appeals to the ethical meaning of the Law, talk as if the Law were something moral, or at least that it ought to be so.

Here, then, is our problem: on the one hand it seems as if the Law were something essentially related to ethical ideas, something belonging to the field of Ethics; but, on the other hand, we feel that, although the Law resides in the area of the ethical, nevertheless it supposes a regulation animated by a meaning different from that which inspires morality — understood in the strictest meaning of the word. And, in confirmation of this, we find that the history of juridical thought offers us a series of attempts launched to establish the difference between the concept of Morals and the concept of the Law. And I think I may affirm that this theme, after innumerable episodes, has come today to a degree of satisfactory maturity.

Morals and Law are two regulations directed toward human conduct. Consequently, it seems obvious that both of them will have to be based on values pertinent to conduct, that is, on ethical values. Or, what is the same thing, that Ethics, as a consideration which embraces the fundamental problems of practical human behavior, would have to occupy itself not only with Morals but also with the Law. But what happens is that even though the values toward which the Law aims and on which it is based are ethical, such orientating values of juristics are different from purely and strictly moral values. And the diverse nature of moral values — in the rigorous and restricted acceptance of the word moral — and of those which refer to the Law, brings it about that the meaning of the moral and of the juridical norm necessarily have to be essentially distinct. To the study of this essential diversity I devote the pages of this chapter.

But first it is necessary to note that here I propound a problem exclusively of essential definition, and not the question of an ideal valuation. That is, we are going to inquire purely and simply about the universal concept of the Law and about the universal concept of Morals, and not about juridical ideals, about what *ought to be* Law; nor do we occupy ourselves with pure and authentic morals. What matters here is to inform ourselves of what is understood, in general terms, by moral regulation, and of what is understood, in general terms, by juridical regulation. And so the idea of juristics which we may obtain will be applicable to all the Laws which have ever been in the world, to all those which are now, and to all which may be in the future. And, in analogous fashion, the concept which we obtain of *morals* will be able to be referred to all morals which have been produced or which may be produced. It is a question, finally, of a work which consists only of defining the respective generic and essential meanings of the two functions of human life — the moral and the juridical — without proceeding to a critical valuation. Among the many laws which there have been and are in the world, we find just norms, others less just, and still others radically unjust and monstrous (such, for example as slavery or Nazi legislation). But there is no doubt that those unjust norms, such as those of the institution of slavery, belong to the juridical, and not to the religious nor to the artistic nor to the scientific nor to the sporting province. It is a matter of something which has been produced under a juridical form, though with an abominable result; it is something which was current Law at a given moment and place, although it may have been unjustified, although it ought not to have been Law. But it is something which we can understand only as something juridical — although unjust — and not as a work of art, nor as a product of science, nor as religion. It is something detestable, shameful, which appears unjust; but which adopted juridical form and meaning. In the same manner, we shall find in history convictions and moral doctrines which we regard as very grave errors, as frightful deviations from authentic moral values; but which — even though erroneous — belong to a moral intention (wasted), have the meaning of seeking to constitute morals (although the purpose is frustrated) and not art or law or science.

It is clear, moreover, that morals and juristics may and ought to be studied, not alone from the point of view of their definition, but from the point of view of their valuation; namely, to ask what are authentic, absolutely founded, morals; and to seek the criteria which ought to orient the Law, that it may find itself fully justified. Now, such study constitutes a point of view and a purpose different from that of a mere definition — it constitutes a study of the Estimative. But, on the other hand, what at the moment urges us to investigate here is the criterion which permits us to bound formally the field of juristics, marking it off from the field of morals. And in the last part of this book I shall put the other theme, the valuation, that is, the matter of a Juridical Estimative.

The historic juridical products — as well the Law which ruled or rules, as the doctrines about the Law which ought to be (natural Law, rational Law, ideal Law), the same as convictions and moral theories, constitute functions of human life, and involve, consequently, implications of values, first of juridical, second of moral, values. In order for us to include them, respectively, under the name of Law or of Morals, it is not necessary that they embody in a positive way the corresponding ideal values: it is enough that they intentionally postulate and offer the formal characteristics, some of the juridical sort, the others of the moral sort. Now, it is precisely for these characteristics that we are inquiring. We have to ask what is the universal concept common to every juridical phenomenon and thought; and, also, the universal idea common to every moral conception and fact; which is something very different from inquiring into the ideals corresponding to these two sectors of conduct.

Notice that the words "Law" and "Morals" are used in two distinct senses, which coincide, respectively, with the meaning of these two problems (that of definition and that of valuation). On one hand, "Morals" may signify the special field of a type of norms of conduct — the definition sense — for example: such a matter, such a norm belongs in people *X* to the field of morals. On the other hand, the word moral may signify an affirmative judgment of value — a positive estimation — for example: loyalty is moral (good). And an analogous thing occurs with the law: when we say that slavery is an institution of the Roman Law, we understand the word Law as a mere universal defining concept, which permits us to circumscribe, in historical realities or in our ideas, those things which have a juridical character. On the other hand, when we say "slavery is not of the Law," what is understood then by the word is not the concept of juristics pure and simple, but the idea of Justice, a juridical value; that is, what we wish to affirm is that slavery — in spite of having been Law in certain peoples and times — is unjust, unworthy, or, what is the same thing, *ought not* to have been Law.

2. The Point of View of Full Procedure of Human Life and the Point of View Relating to Society. Essential Meaning of Morals and the Special Meaning of Juristics

Recall what has been said with respect to the fact that every act of man constitutes a problem, and requires justification. Every decision calls for a justification, needs to be justified before me. Life cannot advance, cannot live, without trying to resolve its own problem, the questions which it sets for itself, for which it is inescapable that it should justify to itself its own attitudes and determinations. So, then, it seems that justification is a process to which all acts of life necessarily submit. Man cannot make any determination which he does not justify to himself. To act, it is necessary to find a justification of his acts to himself; which implies an estimation, an assembling of judgments of value. Now, this justification may be founded on a judgment of true value, or, on the contrary, on an estimation which rests only in a desire, or in a moment of passion, which try to contrive for themselves an appearance of justification, a deceitful justification. Such is the process which the sinner, the vicious man, follows when he tries to justify to himself the sins which he commits, when he tries to falsify his own life fleeing from his authentic destiny, when he tries to deceive himself.

Morals will consist, then, in the instance of justification of conduct according to the values which ought to inspire behavior, taking human life for itself, centering upon its authentic and most basic signification, mindful of its supreme destiny, contemplating it in its own reality — which is individual reality.

I said that every act of life needs to be justified to the man himself — which it may happen that he does correctly, according to the authentic values inspiring human destiny, or indeed falsely, with error; but in both cases, the justification (true or false) is produced with respect to the scope and the significance which a conduct has for the life of the person, in the light of which his destiny is judged.

But there are certain acts, or, better put, there is an aspect of behavior which, because it affects not only the person, but also directly and immediately other persons, living together with the rest, needs — besides a justification to the individual himself and for him — also another class of justification, to wit, an objective justification with regard to the rest, a justification which may satisfy not only my life, but also the other or others whom my conduct affects. That point of view, according to which my behavior, as to what directly and immediately affects the field of action of the behavior of other persons, requires a justification with regard to the others, constitutes the point of view of objective externality in which the juridical norm is placed.

The same ideas which I have just expounded as introduction to the difference in point of view between Morals and Law, may be examined in other of their respective sides, as to other of their respective aspects. But I ought to observe that it is not a matter of trying to found the essential difference between Morals and Law on a certain number of different characteristics, but of showing the diversity of the meaning which inspires Morals from the meaning which inspires the Law, from all the points of view from which they can be contemplated, and with all the consequences to which they give rise. The many characteristics which I shall proclaim as differentials between the Law and Morals — objectivity, bilateralness, heteronomy, social end, autarchy, inexorable imposition, etc. — are not definitely accumulated unlike dimensions, but various aspects of one same essence — of the essence of juristics — divers expressions of an identical meaning, corollaries or consequences which follow from the same principle.

It might be said that Morals considers human acts in relation to the person who performs them, determining among his possible acts which is the proper conduct: selects among the possibilities of behavior those which are proper or are licit and opposes those other behaviors which are possible, but undue, illicit, prohibited. The Law, on the other hand, places the acts of one person in reference to those of another (or others), establishing a bilateral or plurilateral objective coördination of the effects of one or the others, so that the due or licit possibility of an act of one person supposes the faculty in him of hindering all those acts of the others which turn out incompatible with the act which he ought to or may properly perform. And, vice versa, the prohibition of certain behavior by one person, follows from its being incompatible with due or permitted conduct of the others.[17]

It is fundamental for good understanding of the difference between the moral norm and the juridical norm that we should beware of the different meanings which, respectively, attach to both of them.

Morals values conduct for itself, fully, in an absolute, basic manner, in the integral and final signification which it has for the life of the person, without any reserve or limitation. On the other hand, the Law values the conduct from a relative point of view, as to the scope which it may have for the rest and for society.

The field of the sway of Morals is the conscience, that is, the intimacy of the person. On the other hand, the area over which the Law projects itself and seeks to act is that of social coexistence and cooperation.

As well Morals as the Law are intended to create an order; but the proper order of Morals is distinct from the proper order of the Law. The order of Morals is that which is to be produced within the conscience, within the intimacy, among the desires, the motives, the affections, etc., it is the interior order of our authentic life, that is, that which we each live for our own account, in an untransferable manner. On the other hand, the order which the Law tries to create is the social order, the order of objective relations between people, the order of hidden things made up of all the ties between various persons; in short, the order of collective structures, the order of the web in which are woven and mutually conditioned in an objective fashion the conducts of various persons.

[17] Cf. Del Vecchio, Filosofía del Derecho. con extensas Adiciones Originales de Luis Recaséns Siches (2d ed., Barcelona: Bosch, 1935). Roscoe Pound, Law and Morals (1926).

The moral norm values the actions of the individual with regard to their supreme and final end; on the other hand, the Law considers them exclusively in relation to the conditions for the ordering of the social life. Morals looks at the goodness or the badness of an act in absolute terms, in the full signification which it has for the life of the individual, as to the fulfillment of his supreme destiny, as to the realization of the supreme values which ought to guide his existence. On the other hand, the Law does not look at the good of an act for the subject who performs it, nor at the scope of the act for his own life, but at the relative value which it has for another or other persons, or for society, so far as it may constitute a positive or negative condition for the life of those other subjects. Moreover, Morals considers entirely the whole life of the individual, without omitting any of its factors and aspects, without excluding anything, and considering it in absolute terms, basically. On the other hand, the Law tries only to make possible a minimum harmonization of the conducts of people for collective living together and coöperation, and, therefore, that is the only aspect of behavior which it takes into account. The Law does not propose to bring men to the fulfillment of their supreme destiny, does not propose to make them fundamentally good, but only to harmonize the web of their external relations, with a view to coexistence and coöperation. And, consequently, the Law does not fully order conduct, but only those phases of it which refer in a direct way to living together and to solidarity.

Employing only for the present example an estimative expression, it might be said that Morals hopes to create a situation of peace; but its peace is interior peace. The juridical order also seeks to establish a situation of peace, but its peace is the external peace of collective connections, the exterior peace of society, the peace which flows from a certain, stable, and just regulation.

Morals, in short, asks us to be faithful to ourselves, that we should respond authentically to our mission in life. On the other hand, the Law asks of us only an external fidelity, an exterior adequacy for an established order.

I think it desirable to note, to avoid an inexact interpretation of all I have expounded, that with the established differences it is not a question, in any way, of dividing the field of human conduct into two sectors, of which one devotes itself to Morals and the other is assigned to the Law. It is not so; on the contrary, all human behavior is at the same time the object of consideration by Morals and by the Law, if indeed from a different point of view, and, moreover, attending to different aspects of it. So, for example: in some sectors of behavior, Morals imposes a positive conduct (for example, how sincerely we strive to find the truth), and, on the other hand, the Law guarantees all the possibilities as the sphere of liberty, as a privilege, as a zone exempt from the intervention of all the rest (liberty of conscience and of thought). So also, for example, in some situations, Morals prescribes a positive conduct (for example, in sexual matters), while the Law limits itself to prohibiting certain acts (violation, abuse of superiority, etc.), and guarantees as juridically permissible all the others, among which there may be some which are morally abominable. But it is true, as the ancients said, that not all which is juridically permissible is morally good (*non omnia quod licet honestum est*). It is seen here, then, how Morals, which assumes to realize an absolute value, determines what is good conduct; while the Law, which does not pretend to be anything more than a means for society, limits itself in some cases to establishing a zone within which a person may move without hindrance, because his behavior therein, good or bad, does not affect directly or immediately the others. And it happens also with respect to the same situation, although in some cases the moral imperative and the juridical precept may seem, nevertheless, to have different meaning and extent; so, for example, with respect to a pecuniary debt, Morals will require that it be paid with good intentions and without rancor or resentment to the creditor, so that the simple fact of payment, made with a hostile mind toward the creditor, does not leave the moral duty fulfilled; and, on the other hand, Morals is effectively fulfilled by having the good intention to pay, although it cannot be done materially for a cause not chargeable to the person. On the contrary, the Law claims solely and exclusively the material delivery of the sum owed. This diversity of point of view, this different meaning of juridical regulation, as compared with moral, does not imply in any way a contradiction between the two, nor opposition, within the same system (positive or doctrinal). It is simply a question of the moral norm and the juridical norm, although both are based on ethical values, having a different meaning. And this different meaning arises precisely because the ethical values which inspire the moral norm are different from those which inspire the juridic norm.

3. What Is the Motive of Morals and What Is the Motive of Juristics

We may also contemplate the difference between Morals and Law, by examining what is the subject which, respectively, embodies in one and the other the end result of the norm; or, in other words, what is the subject by reason of which the moral norm is set up, and what is the subject by reason of which the juridical precept is established. In Morals, the duty is imposed because of the person called on to fulfill it, because it is thought that such conduct constitutes an element for the fulfillment of the purpose of the person. On the other hand, the juridical precept is set up not in consideration of the person who ought to comply with it, but of that other person (possessing the claim), authorized to demand fulfillment of the conduct of another for his own benefit or that of society. That is, Morals looks directly and immediately towards the person obliged; it proposes purely and simply that he comply with the norm, because such compliance constitutes the realization of a value in and for the life of the person. On the other hand, the Law is not established in order that the person obliged should fulfill, by his compliance, a moral value, but only to assure to another person or to society a certain benefit. In Morals strictly there does not exist a person possessing any claim as to the conduct of the person obliged (since when to characterize the function of God in morality one speaks of the "rights of God," that constitutes a metaphorical expression to express a metaphysical idea of basic dependence, which is completely diverse from that of the juridical relation: since the bond between man and God would never be a "juridical" relation, but a relation of absolute dependence). In Morals there are *duties* pure and simple: in the Law, on the other hand, juridical duties have always the essential character of something *owed* to another person. A juridical duty is established for a person, because and so far as he wishes to authorize or yield to another the faculty of demanding certain acts or omissions from the first. The juridical duty of a person is the means to attribute certain possibilities or faculties to other persons. When a juridical duty is imposed on a person, we do not think of him, it is not done for a purpose of his, but to serve another person, who becomes authorized to demand the fulfillment of the obligation of the first.

4. Intimacy of Morals and Externalness of the Law

From another point of view, it follows that, because conduct is estimated morally according to the value which it has in an absolute manner in the life of its author, and, on the other hand, because it is valued juridically as to what may be its significance for the social community, it is to be deduced that the starting point of moral regulation is different from the starting point of juridical regulation. The starting point of moral regulation is the field of intentions, the ambit of conscience, the intimate root of action, its internal basis; and, on the contrary, the point of starting for the Law, and its center of gravity, is the external plane of conduct, the exterior dimension of acts. It is not a matter of dividing — which would be false — human actions into internal and external ones and attributing the first to Morals and the second to the

Law. It would be an error to seek to divide conduct into two classes, one internal and the other external; since all behavior possesses both dimensions, to wit, an intimate root and an external expression. Furthermore, the world of that behavior which seems purely intimate, like my thoughts, is accompanied by expressive corporeal resonances (however small these may be). And there is no exterior human behavior which does not have an intimate root (since when there is none, then it is not a question of human conduct, but of a biological or external fact which occurs in the body). We do not divide acts into internal and external — since all conduct possesses both dimensions — but we do distinguish between the internal root and the external aspect of the behavior.

Nor at this point do I try to formulate valuations, to establish an estimative control — that is, I do not try to determine now what may be the content of a juridical obligation, and of that other which ought not to be regulated preceptively by the Law (for example, the world of religious conscience and of thought). I am trying only to show that the meaning of every moral regulation is completed in the intimacy of the acts, while, on the contrary, the meaning of every juridical regulation looks preponderantly to the external face of the conduct and centers on that externality. And if indeed it is a possible fact — although it turns out monstrous and abominable — that a juridical system undertakes to regulate the sanctuary of the conscience (remember the Inquisition, and also German Naziism, and Bolshevism, etc.), nevertheless, even in such cases it follows that the Law starts from external signs of conduct — since it is altogether impossible to penetrate authentically into the intimacy of another — and prosecutes heresy not as an intimate process of conscience, as a moral evil, but on account of the social and political consequences which are attributed to it; in short, the behavior valued is external and the fundamental supposition adduced (detestable and unjust) is also of an exterior kind. And with respect to Morals, although this at times weighs also the external outcome of conduct — so far that it creates the duty not only of a good intention, but also the duty of positive effort for the success of a given behavior — nevertheless Morals gravitates always toward the internal root, since, in fact, including the cited case, it attends to what effort the person is willing to make and not to the external result. So, then, it may be affirmed correctly that the Law starts always from the external aspect of conduct; and that it centers about the same. Now, that dimension of exteriority of the Law does not mean to say that it necessarily has to refrain from every attempt to consider intentions, since juridical history furnishes us cases in which it has regulated such intentions (although sometimes this has been with an abominable affront to justice, as when it has denied the liberty of conscience); and we see, also, how the progress of penal Law has brought with it the distinction between wrong (intentional harm) and fault (damage by negligence), and the weighing of a long series of circumstances which modify criminal responsibility; and, also in private (civil and mercantile) Law certain effects have been connected to intention. But all that in no way contradicts the dimension of exteriority of the Law; because when the Law considers the intentional aspect of acts, it does it in the degree in which (truly or falsely) it considers that that intention has direct and immediate consequences for society, that is, so far as it believes that the state of conscience in which the conduct originated has an immediate result for the social life, and does not do it from the point of view of a pure moral valuation of good or evil. For example, the intentional assassin is much more terrible and much more harmful and much more dangerous for society than one who kills by rash imprudence (for example, without wishing to do it, when he was cleaning a pistol). But, moreover, when the Law wants to take into account the intentions, it has to judge them starting from the external signs of behavior, for nothing else is possible, since it is not given to any human being to transmigrate into the soul of another to see directly what is happening in it.

So then, summing up, we may say: (1) The Law attends always to the external aspect of conduct. (2) Ordinarily it limits itself to the external aspect. (3) When it takes intentions into account, it does so only so far as they could be externalized, and so far as it considers that such intentions have a direct and immediate importance for society; and, moreover, it judges them not as to the value which they have for the person whose they are but as to the effect which they may have for other persons or for society. (4) Even in the valuation of intentions, the Law has to start from external signs, since it is not possible to see directly the intimacy of the person.

The Law exists precisely by reason of the external dimension of life, by reason of its externalization in spatial magnitude. If only interior life existed, there would be no necessity either of Law or of the State, because there would be no possibility that there should be collisions. Thoughts may easily coexist. It is bodies which collide with each other in space. Therefore it is not with his thoughts, but with his acts, that a man may fall into conflict with the rest.

Since the realm of intentional intimacy is the proper field of Morals, it follows that as no one can look directly into the interior of another person and contemplate all the elements which are there, so no one can judge with full knowledge of the moral conduct of another person. Only the subject himself — and also God — has the possibility of passing a moral judgment on his behavior. But, on the other hand, juridical matters, as they consist in the external weaving of some acts with others, in what passes between one person and another, cannot be judged from the point of view of any of those bound in the relation, but from an objective, external, point of view; wherefore it is said that one cannot be judge in his own juridical cause.

5. Liberty of Compliance in Morals and Necessity of Realization in Juristics. Moral Autonomy and Juridical Heteronomy

Morals supposes and requires liberty in its fulfillment; since for conduct to be the object of a moral judgment, it is necessary that the person realize it for himself, that it correspond to a position of his own seeking. What I do — or better, what occurs in me — independently of my desire, is neither moral nor immoral; it is something foreign to all ethical judgment; if my arm is moved violently by another stronger, what it does has no moral meaning, it is not good nor evil, it is, in short, outside of the field of moral valuation. Morals does not remain fulfilled with what actually happens in the world to the external facts at which its content aims, but for it to be fulfilled it is altogether necessary that its norms should be realized by the person freely, free from all irresistible coercion, as acts wholly *his*. And, vice versa, Morals does not condemn events which seem, as to external appearance, to oppose its precepts, but only so far as the person is the genuine author of such acts. Man cannot fulfill his supreme destiny forced by the police; one cannot go to moral values led by the police, because one would not arrive; one has to go by his own efforts, freely, by his own volition, to them. On the other hand, the law may be imposed coercitively; the Law carries necessarily attached the proposition that its fulfillment may be imposed by force — including physical violence — because the intentional meaning of the Law consists in objectively producing the behavior which it establishes as necessary for social life, as necessary for the structure of collectivity and for its functioning. Some lines further on I shall insist on this dimension of juristics, but first, in order to measure fully its meaning, it is desirable to add some other reflections.

That a certain moral duty shall weigh as such, concretely and specifically, on a certain individual, it is necessary that he have consciousness of such obligation. Even when it is considered that the moral norms are founded on ideal values, objectives, with absolute validity, nevertheless it cannot be said that there is a concrete and specific duty for a certain individual in his case, while the person has not recognized, in his internal forum, the norm as obligatory. It is clear that when we speak of that recognition or adherence in intimacy, we do not refer to something which may be the product of a free voluntary act, so that it might be equally possible to give such recognition or to refuse it. It is a matter of an intimate conviction, which is not the product of the free will, but which is the result of an unbribable intimate conviction, which does not let itself be steered by the will. It is a feeling attached to the norm, to the values which inspire it — wanted or not — it is a feeling persuaded of the validity of the norm — although sometimes it would desire not to be so (to be able to give loose rein to a contrary passion). Then, although an objective validity is predicated of the moral values and norms, an obligation does not arise subjectively for an individual, but so far as he feels himself necessarily bound by it. Hence it may be affirmed that all morals are necessarily autonomous; that is, they do not create obligations if they have not become intimate in the person, if he does not see them as necessarily founded and justified. It is not a question here of the acceptation which the word autonomy has in the Kantian moral doctrine (according to Kant, only the morals of practical pure reason would be autonomous, since the rational person is at once legislator and subject), but it is a question of a different concept of autonomy. Here, in speaking of the autonomy of Morals, we refer to the following: whatever moral system or doctrine (upon which we are not now going to decide, since it is not our theme), whatever may be its foundation, its origin, and its content, for it to be considered to create duties in a person it is necessary that he should have recognized it, should have felt it as something obligatory, as something which he sees (willingly or not) as founded and justified. So also if its norms have been established by an intimate rational process, and are derived from an authoritarian source (religious revelation, tradition, paternal mandate, mandate of a teacher, etc.); because in these last cases, although the content of the moral norms has not been found by the person himself, nevertheless he accepts or recognizes them as such (because he believes that it is good and obligatory to comply with the mandates of revelation, tradition, father or teacher). And, therefore, even in such cases, those authoritarian Morals have to rest on a conviction of the person, on the conviction which he has of the goodness of such sources of authority. But, on the other hand, the juridical obligation is established by the Law in a purely and exclusively objective manner, that is, with total independence of what the person intimately thinks. And the person is obligated to the conduct which the norm imposes on him, whatever may be the opinion which it obtains in his intimacy. (This is to be understood, it is clear, on the plane of pure conceptual delimitation, and in no way as an estimative directive — since if we should take it in this valuing sense we should come to great absurdity.) In tracing the conceptual outlines of juristics, in delimitation from the strictly moral field, what I say is that the norm of Law is established with an objective exclusive force, that is, that it completely obliges as much if the person called to comply with it is in accord with it as if he is not; it rules, and it is imposed, with entire independence of what may be the intimate conviction of those subject to the norm; and, thus, it may be said, for example, that the articles in a Code which establish private property oblige exactly the same and without any limitation those who have a contrary opinion about this institution; and the regulations which establish the obligation not to appear naked in the streets oblige completely those who profess the nudist belief. This is so, as to the essential meaning of the juridical norm, as to the logical structure of the Law, whose validity and obligatoriness are imposed at any cost with entire independence of what may be the subjective state of mind of those called on to comply with it. But, on the other hand, from a point of view valuable for the establishment of norms, that is, of a political estimative adjusted to the legislative labor, we must declare that it is necessary that the Law which is going to be dictated correspond fundamentally to the manner of thinking and of feeling of the people whose conduct it is going to regulate; that is, it is necessary that it should have support in the general opinion of its subjects. And, more, from another point of view, from the point of view of the observation of reality, we could also say that a positive juridical system does not live practically, in fact, if it does not count upon a fundamental adherence of the collectivity; and so it is that it could be sustained that democracy before and apart from a special political system and a program, constitutes a law of forced gravitation in social life. Now, neither that political estimation, nor the sociological verification alter the dimension (upon which I am commenting) that the Law rules, obliges as such, when it is established without at all taking into account the subjective judgment of those called to comply with it, and without its obligatoriness ever being conditioned by whether or not the subject is in accord with the precept, since that is imposed unconditionally.

6. The Note of Inexorable Imposition as an Essential Characteristic of Juristics

This essential characteristic of juristics of being imposed unconditionally, as well if it has the will of the person as if that is adverse to it, has been traditionally called *coactivity* or *coercivity* and also *autarchy*. I prefer to call this dimension *inexorable imposition* or inexorability, because I believe that these words express much more exactly the characteristic in question. Whether this character is or is not essential to the

Law, and the nature of this dimension, has been discussed at length in juridical Theory for nearly a century. But in the light of the reflections which I shall explain, I understand that this point remains entirely cleared up, in the sense of affirming that the characteristic of *inexorable imposition* is essential to the Law; to the point that the thought of a Law which should not be inexorable (coercitive, autarchic) would constitute an absurdity, that is, an unrealizable thought, like a square circle or a knife without handle or blade.

Inexorable imposition is something which follows essentially from the very meaning of juristics. As the essential meaning of the Law consists in establishing reciprocal bounds and *necessary* connections between the conduct of various persons, to regulate in an *objective* and *external* manner social life, logically it cannot be conditioned on the chance of what may be the will of the persons whose behavior it is sought to subject to a collective structure. Precisely because the Law is an organization of the external relations between the members of society, in those points in which the conduct of some is an indispensable condition for the rest, this condition cannot depend on the fortuitous and unforeseeable will of those called to comply with it. Such thought would be absurd, simply contradictory. The Law desires that a person comply with what is reputed necessary and indispensable for another; then the realization of this cannot depend on the wish of the one who ought to comply with it, but it has to be imposed in an unconditioned, autarchic manner, that is, at all cost. As the Law seeks to subject necessarily one person to the interest or for the sake of another or others, it cannot leave the former at liberty to comply or not with the duties which it imposes. As the meaning of the Law — which, as I shall explain further on, is based on a purpose of security — consists in establishing necessarily and effectively a minimum of certainty and fixity in social relations, it excludes inevitably the mobility and insecurity which it would entail to confide its observance to the subjective free will. Therefore, the Law is Law because and so far as it can be imposed in an inexorable manner on all its subjects, at whatever price, with, without, or against their will (overcoming if necessary their violent resistance by force). And therefore, compliance with juridical obligations is enforceable in fact, by a coercive imposition which makes infraction impossible or which repairs it in the same imperative form if it has already occurred.

This dimension of "inexorable imposition" consists in the juridical norm — different from other norms, among them the moral one — not stopping before the will of the person, leaving to him to decide freely; but, on the contrary, it tries to annul the adverse will, tries to make impossible the realization of resistance to the norm. Other norms, for example the moral norm — we shall see how the same occurs with the rules of social behavior — direct themselves to the person to bind normatively his will, but without aspiring to annul it. That is, Morals expresses its imperative, but this imperative *ought* to be freely complied with by the person; moreover, as I have already explained, a forced realization of the proper conduct does not constitute compliance with the moral norm. This seeks to be complied with, but complied with by the free desire of the person and not in any other manner. Therefore, Morals — and also the rules of social behavior (as we shall see) — bind normatively the will, but do not try to restrain it, on the contrary leave it at liberty, in freedom, since that is the only situation in which the norm can be complied with. On the contrary, as the Law is grounded on the external result of behavior, it is directed toward controlling that, be it what it may — so much the better and more desirable if it is of free will and by sincere adherence, but, if not, it does it by force — at all costs, inexorably. So, then, the Law does not stop respectfully before the will of the person, but it encourages the purpose of enchaining it, if that is necessary, in order that the proper behavior may be produced. The inexorability consists in the norm not being projected upon the will, but it goes through it to apply itself to the external reality of the behavior. The essential meaning of the juridical norm consists in employing, if necessary, all means to avoid that there shall be produced behavior contrary to what it ordains and to impose that at any cost.

This character of inexorable imposition distinguishes the Law not only from Morals, but also from other classes of norms, such as the rules of social behavior (decorum, decency, courtesy, etc.), which, although they are different from those of morals, have in common with them the directing themselves to the will, but leaving it in freedom to decide without restraining it. Therefore, it will be necessary to return to treat of this dimension of inexorable imposition which essentially characterizes juristics, when we consider, in the next chapter, the difference between Law and the rules of social behavior.

In the thought of the eighteenth century this characteristic of the Law had been conjectured, calling attention to it to distinguish it from Morals (Tomasio). In the nineteenth century they went on elaborating this distinction on the same basis; and juristics was characterized essentially, as against morals, by the note of coaction (a somewhat rough and confused expression) or of coercitiveness (a more fortunate word to denote the dimension in question). But although the problem was truly defined and there was a correct direction for its solution, nevertheless the thought of the nineteenth century did not come to consider fully nor to mark with entire precision the meaning of the note. And, so, it followed that in spite of being on the right road for the characterization of the Law, in emphasizing in it the essential dimension of coercitive requirement, nevertheless, the defective formulation of this doctrine — true at base — gave occasion for the formulation of a series of anti-coercive objections. But all those objections, which were opposed to recognizing in the Law the essentially coercitive character, started from confusion and misunderstandings, and, consequently, none of them could maintain themselves. So it is that, in general, in the philosopho-juridical thought of the twentieth century, there is accentuated the emphasis in the Law, as an essential note of it, its autarchy, its coercitiveness (Stammler, Del Vecchio, Kelsen, etc.), to the point that all the objections which had been formulated against this thesis have vanished. Now, this theme remains still clearer and with more definitely precise outlines in the reëlaboration of it which I have just offered. The terms "coaction," "coactionability," "coercitivity," still may be somewhat equivocal. On the other hand, the expression of this doctrine as a character of "inexorable imposition" remains perfectly crystalline and evident.

7. Critical Examination of the Discussion upon Coercitivity

Nevertheless, although this is one of the themes of the Philosophy of Law which may be considered best mastered today, it is proper to inform the reader — even if very briefly — of some of the objections which, at another time, were made to the essentiality of this note, and to show how none of those objections can be considered operative, since all start from confusions which have today been entirely cleared away. Let us, then, pass rapidly in review those objections, which have today no significance other than as historic curiosities, although in their time they served to cause the purification of the coercitive doctrine.

It is said that the Law is complied with spontaneously in the greater number of cases, without inexorable coercion intervening for any purpose. That is true; but it does not indicate any objection to the thesis of inexorable imposition, since such thesis does not affirm in any way that the necessary manner of realization of the Law should be the employment of force, but only maintains that it is essential to the meaning of the juridical norm that, in case it should not be complied with voluntarily, compliance with it should be imposed by force.

It has been objected, also, that there are cases in which coaction turns out ineffective, as occurs, for example, when it has not been possible to avoid the commission of an antijuridical act, or also in certain relations in which it has not been possible to obtain by force the desired conduct (for example, rendering personal service, as painting a picture). To show the inconsistency of this objection with respect to the first example, I will repeat that the coercitive thesis of inexorable imposition does not refer to the fact, always contingent, that the police come in time or arrive too late to prevent the antijuridical behavior, but to the essential dimension that there belongs necessarily to juristics the principle of power and duty to employ force to overcome all resistance. A failure in the field of practical application says nothing against this essential dimension. And as to the second example, that of the case that it is not possible to compel the execution of a personal service, I have to declare that neither does this constitute an objection; since, on the one hand, it is clear that there can be no struggle against the material impossibility of imposing personal conduct (which alone is possible with the concurrence of the will of the person who ought to perform it); and on the other hand, when there is such a situation, the primitive content of the obligation is replaced by a subsequent conduct foreseen subsidiarily by the same norm (for example, payment of an indemnity in damages), a conduct which indeed is imposable by the use of force, namely, by an executory proceeding against the property. And in case of insolvency, the executory judgment will rest always against the future patrimony of the debtor.

It has been objected also that there are juridical relations whose fulfillment cannot be obtained by proceedings of coercitive imposition, nor can they either be replaced by a subsequent conduct, as occurs when we read, for example, that article of the Spanish Constitution of 1812, in which it is said that Spaniards ought to be honorable and kind; or when some civil code declares that children ought to love their parents. However, in these cases, the solution is clear: we must recognize that such norms, although inserted in legal texts, do not constitute juridical norms, since compliance with them is not enforceable. It is a matter of good proposals of a legislator, which does not result in making them authentic juridical precepts. It is a matter of another class of rules (morals, social behavior), which the legislator wished to convert into Law, but did not do so.

Another objection is based on an appeal to natural principles, to a Natural Law, an idea of justice; and, therefore, it is said that many times historic Law has ignored or openly violated such principles. But this argument starts from a lamentable confusion between what is really and actually the Law and the ideal principles which ought to direct the Law. When we find ourselves before the case of a juridical norm notoriously unjust, we say that this *ought not to be Law* (by which we recognize that it is, though improperly), and that on the other hand what ought to be Law is another ideal norm, correctly justified (by which it is recognized that this ideal norm is not Law, although it ought to be). Natural, rational, ideal Law, in short, the maxims of the juridical Estimative, are not real actual Law, but possible (and desirable) Law; then, within the realm of the possible, that is, of ideality, such norms possess also coercitive pretension; but what happens is that that coercitive pretension is a pure ideal and not a reality; no more nor less than a painted dog which has also fangs, but his fangs (like the rest of the animal) are not real, but painted. But so it is that a coercitiveness (which, naturally, is also only ideal) is attributed to the ideal scheme of Law and there are certain historic situations in which appealing to these norms results in violence, as occurs in revolutions. In fact, revolutions would remain inexplicable if we did not understand them as an appeal to something which it is thought ought to be future Law — and which, as such, offers a step for an inexorable imposition. On the other hand, to try to impose a moral or a scientific conviction or a religious belief by force, will always constitute, apart from being an abominable monstrosity, also a contradiction.

It is objected also that, independently of coaction by the State, men have in conscience a duty to comply with juridical norms. Indeed, that is true (although we cannot enter now upon this theme, which we shall do later); but I have to observe that discussion of the moral duty which people have to comply with juridical norms is a theme which belongs to moral philosophy, but not strictly to the Philosophy of the Law, nor to the essence of the juridical precept. Moral duties — among which may figure the duty in conscience of complying with juridical obligations — are something independent of the special bond which creates juridical precepts. Apart from whether or not there exists the moral duty to comply with a norm, there is a juridical duty, *specifically juridical,* simply because there is a juridical norm, that is, a norm of inexorable imposition; that is, because in case of not complying there will be a breaking loose from the proceeding of inexorable imposition.

It has been said that when a Law does not count actually on general adherence — of the most — of the society which it aspires to govern, it is inevitably condemned to failure or to catastrophic results. And this is true: I have already said that democracy, before being a political system or program, is a law of gravitation of political Society. But this refers to the aggregate of a juridical system, which cannot be maintained, cannot subsist, when it does not count on the free consent of the majority of the persons whose conduct it is going to regulate, in short, with the support of what is called public opinion; but this is not anything which belongs to the essence of the formal validity of a juridical norm. That is, a juridical regime, a state, does not maintain itself, does not subsist, if it does not count on general assent; but within that juridical regime, each one of its norms rules, is in force independently of the opinion and of the will of the individual person obliged to comply with it; and if it meets with resistance from him, then it is imposed on him at all costs, by means of force.

It has been said also, that it would be the best that men should act from the impulse of charity, of love, and not from juridical intimidation. And this also is true. But it is certain that not only are love and Law distinct points of view, but also that Law is given precisely for situations when love fails. Love and Law constitute two categories fundamentally and radically distinct, from which to view interhuman relations. Charity, love, has the superior rank. But as it cannot be guaranteed that there shall always be love or charity, exactly for that reason Law is established.

Another of the objections which it has been sought to raise against the essentiality of the coercitive dimension of juristics is that of noting that the sovereign power of the State cannot be subject to coaction; it is what constrains, but it cannot be constrained; and from this it is sought to argue that there is at least one exception to the coercitivity or the inexorability of the Law. This argument involves a lamentable confusion of ideas. For as Del Vecchio says, it is not sufficient to notice that in the whole juridical system there is one point to which coercion cannot reach; it would be necessary also to demonstrate further that upon that point might fall an authentic juridical duty, to prove that at that point might come to a halt as a passive subject an authentic power required of someone by imposition. Now, a juridical power or pretension of such type, that is, inexorable against the supreme organ of the State, against the State as sovereign, does not exist and essentially cannot exist in a positive juridical system. Against the State as sovereign may be raised requirements of a political character, it may be criticized in the light of certain values, but there cannot be exercised any "law." A law may be invoked against organs of the State in a question upon which the other organs of the State will decide, which, in such case, assume a rank superior to that of the defendant organ. But against the State as sovereign (for example, so far as it manifests itself through the Supreme Court of Justice, or when it expresses itself by the Legislative power — except appeals of unconstitutionality, which are heard before an organ which, for those purposes, functions as superior —) there is no exercise of any juridical power, and, consequently, it is absurd to speak of the possibility of coaction. But there is no coaction, because it is not a question in any way of a juridical power. There may naturally be a revolution: very well, in such case we step outside of the established system, because precisely it is what they wish to overthrow, to replace it by another. But when we speak of Law, we refer to the essence of real Law — which is not a pure idea, but a human work — to the Law formulated or recognized by the State, which supposes an inexorable command, that is, coercitive imposition. And when we speak of "laws" as against the State, they are laws established and recognized by it, which are given value, that is, which are imposed by organs of the same State charged by it with such mission — for example, in litigious-administrative jurisdiction. It is precisely a characteristic of constitutional systems among civilized peoples, in the liberal western democracies, to make possible by distribution of jurisdictions certain judicial actions by citizens against the State; but in such cases, the State, which on one hand is sovereign, appears on the other, here, as submitted by self-limitation to the dominion of a norm which emanates from itself as sovereign.

Also, they have argued against the thesis of coercitiveness taking as a basis the precarious reality of International Law. But to this it ought to be answered that International Law has the intention to constitute authentic Law, that is, to impose its norms; but in the degree that it does not have the possibility of doing so, it will follow that we shall be before a proposal of Law, which has not yet been able to succeed in establishing itself in reality. Just as States have suffered at times conditions of anarchy in their interior, so that having accepted norms, these do not succeed in being actually imposed, so it likewise happens that international society suffers today from a condition of anarchy, because peoples who make a profession of banditry are making difficult the application of the pertinent norms. But in the meaning of those norms, which are violated, appears the pretension of seeking to impose them at all costs; and so, although for some peoples war constitutes only the shameless operation of an aggressor, by others, on the other hand, it is interpreted as an instrument of juridical coaction, especially when it is a matter of defending the assailed International Law.

So then, by all that has been said, it may be roundly affirmed that Law is in its essence a norm of inexorable, irresistible dominion. A norm which should be based on a pure duty, without more, would not be a juridical norm. Law without the dimension of inexorable imposition is a contradiction, an absurdity, a thought mentally unrealizable. As to that, strictly speaking, the anticoercive thesis is at bottom anarchy, although its supporters do not take clear account of the fact. Tolstoi wished that humanity should be ruled solely and exclusively by Morals, by the Gospel; and as in the Gospel there is only Morals and it does not contain any strictly and peculiarly juridical point of view, he declared himself for the abolition of the Law, that is, for anarchy.

If the Law did not contain in itself, essentially, the possibility of forcing, of irresistibly compelling, in short, of inexorably imposing itself, then what foundation would that coercitive dimension have which actually develops in juridical life? If it were not a question of something essential to the Law it would be something foreign to its proper essence, it would be something which happened accidentally, by chance, and, therefore, something not founded in its very nature. And, then, it would become impossible to justify the actual use of coercion to impose fulfillment of the Law. If inexorable imposition were not an essential note of the Law, then the juridical power would constitute merely a mute material force. Therefore, to deny the essential implication between Law and inexorable imposition is equivalent to defending anarchy.

8. The Law as Maximum Social Form and Morals as Authentically Individual Destiny

By means of the differentiation between Morals and Law, it has appeared that the Law constitutes not a social norm, something inserted in the category of the collective life, but the maximum expression of the characters of the collectivity; constitutes the social reduced to exact and precise outlines, the maximum mechanization of the human. We might say that it constitutes the brutalization of the human, so far as it is that form in which human life seems most like nature, the mechanical, the inexorable.

And, on the other hand, by means of the differentiation between Morals and Law, it has also appeared that Morals constitutes that norm which takes into account the authentic individual life in all its fullness. Morals is what is referred to the absolute destiny of the individual as such. Morals considers the life of the individual in all its aspects, in its basic singleness, in its character of something private and untransferable. It considers the individual life with attention to all the elements which condition it singularly in each one of its situations, and regards it in absolute terms, from a basic point of view.

Now, this is the essential meaning of morals *sensu stricto;* but it may happen, and it happens in fact in the majority of cases, that the moral norms are received by way of social tradition. Except for a limited number of prominent individualities, of persons who have overcome their own individuality, who have arrived at the maximum consciousness of their destiny, the common run of people take the greater part of the moral norms from what they have learned from the rest. That is, there exist usages in whose content there is attempted to be manifested a norm of moral character (and not a juridical precept nor a rule of social behavior). That is, Morals many times is manifested, expresses itself, and is learned by means of customs. Moreover, this constitutes the etymological significance of the word *moral* (from the Latin *mos,* which means custom). But from this fact that morals manifests itself in social forms, which are usages or customs, there does not follow in any way a contradiction with respect to the individual character which belongs essentially to the moral norm. Because, even when the person may receive the moral norm from a social manifestation of objectivated life, nevertheless, the meaning of that norm expressed in a usage is that of constituting not something which refers to the collective topic, but something which refers to individual destiny — different from the meaning of the juridical norm (which also may be manifested in a custom), a meaning which consists in being referred to the communal topic of society. Although the moral norm may originate in society (usage, custom) it is given for the individual as an individual and not for society. In this case the interpretation given by society constitutes a moral value. The interpretation is given by society; but the value interpreted by society is a value whose meaning is referred to the individual life, to the full and authentic destiny of the individual.

But to the foregoing consideration I have to add another, to wit: the social manifestation (usage, custom) of a norm with moral meaning to create moral duties in an individual has to be internalized in him. That is, as we have seen, a moral value (although it may be objectively valid) determines the birth of a concrete duty in a particular individual, only in the degree in which he finds himself intimately and sincerely convinced of its goodness; that is, so far as the individual feels himself an adherent of and identified with such value. This involves a formidable essential difference from juridical norms (and also, as we shall see, from the norms of social behavior); for those norms, contrary to what occurs with the moral ones, oblige entirely independently of what may be the opinion of the person, as well if they count on his assent as if they do not. It follows, then, that although the moral norm may be received from a social source, it always refers to the fulfillment of individual destiny, to the supreme end for the person, and moreover only obliges him in the degree in which he feels himself an intimate adherent of the value expressed in the norm.

9. Extent of the Difference between Morals and the Law. The Law Oriented toward Peculiar Ethical Values, but with Special Juridical Meaning[18]

The theme of the differentiation between Morals and Law is a logical theme, that is, of delimitation of concepts and is not an axiological ques-

[18] This section is from the Second Spanish edition of the book (Mexico, 1945). TRANSLATOR.

tion, nor does it constitute an estimative study. It tries to clarify the meaning of all Morals and the meaning of all Law, showing the essential difference between them. It does not try to inquire what ought to be considered as Morals and what ought to be called Law. I have developed in the preceding pages this theme of the difference between Morals and Law from the logical point of view of the essence, leaving aside the estimative points of view referring to values or ideals. If now I am going to refer to an estimative theory — as to what Morals ought to command and what Law ought to order — it is not because I abandon in this part of the philosophic-juridical meditation the essential logical point of view, to enter upon a valuing study, but only take this doctrine which I shall cite as one of the possible examples — among others — in which there appears in full clarity not only the difference of meaning between moral and juridical norms but, moreover, how there may be a great discrepancy between what is ordered by Morals and that decreed by Law, within the same axiological system. The example which I am going to cite is the theory of Father Francisco Suarez, which is presented to one in the greatest relief, precisely because the religious character of the author and his ethical preoccupation better make real the meritorious truth of his clear differentiating intuition of the meaning of juristics against the meaning of morals. The eminent Spanish theologian does not properly put the problem of distinguishing formally between Morals and Law, but the question of what things can and ought to be the content of human law (understanding positive Law) as distinct from the matters which are ordered by the natural moral law. Suarez asks if positive Law ought to contain everything ordered by the natural moral law; to which he answers no, by no means, for positive juridical law differs from the moral law as to its end, as to its extent, as to its character, and as to its content. The Law is concerned not with the intrinsic purity of acts, as is Morals, but with that which the common good *directly and immediately* requires. Precisely from this diversity of end it happens that the content of juristics is less extensive than that of Morals and the meaning which animates the two regulations is also diverse. It is true, says Suarez, that positive Law ought not to order the realization of anything which Morals prohibits, nor prohibit anything which Morals requires to be fulfilled. But positive Law may not regulate behaviors which refer to the spiritual perfection of the individual; it ought not to ordain all the virtues, because those relating to the intimate are excluded from its end; neither ought the Law to prohibit many vices, however horrible and detestable they may be, if they do not have any immediate and direct repercussion upon the common good. The end of positive Law, Suarez affirms taxatively and unequivocably, is not the beatitude of the individual but only that which turns out necessary for the common good. So, for example, Suarez declares that positive Law cannot prohibit simple, non-scandalous fornication. But then, he asks, in a supposed argumentation directed to himself, "Then, if positive Law, in accordance with natural Law, ought not to prohibit simple non-scandalous fornication, does it result implicitly that it ought to permit it?" To which he answers, yes. "But does not this constitute a contradiction of the moral law?" No, by no means, replies Suarez, adducing two reasons. In the first place, as the end of Law is not to accomplish the beatitude, the salvation, of individuals, but only to ordain exterior peace and purity, that is, what is directly indispensable or very desirable for the common good, it ought to forbid only those vices which are immediately dangerous for the collectivity; but it cannot prohibit those other vices which do not prejudice the community in a proximate manner or those whose punishment might cause greater ills to it. And this is not saying, Suarez argues, that thereby the Law falls into an immorality, so far as the Law ought not to command the impure deed; because it ought at times, as in the example cited, to permit it, since to prohibit it is not within the aim of the Law. In the second place, moreover, for another reason: because, according to natural Law, there must be in the activity of man a certain sphere in which the imperative regulation of positive Law does not interfere in any way; that is, there must be a sphere free from the coercitive interventions of the Law, although moral duties fall within such sphere. And this sphere ought to be free from all intervention of the positive Law not only for the reason that it is not matter which affects the common good *directly and immediately* but, moreover, for another very important fundamental one: because natural Law requires the existence and guarantee of a sphere of liberty in the face of the political power. Precisely on that account natural Law does not admit either that positive Law should impose coercitively the realization of a series of morally virtuous conducts because although they may be good, it constitutes an aggravation to impose them without power to do so; and the political power, which ought to be ordaining solely for justice, peace, and external purity, cannot possess the faculty of imposing internal purity by means of positive laws. It may well be said that Suarez implies that the Law ought to be the condition for the possibility of morality, but it ought not to seek to convert itself into the positive and immediate agent for the fulfillment of morals, for that is impossible, since only such conduct can be moral as is realized by the free will of the person and never that imposed coercitively; and moreover because to impose the fulfillment of a purely moral duty, of internal purity, constitutes a monstrous affront to the ethical dignity of the individual, which requires an ambit of liberty for him to decide on his own account precisely in the sphere of moral duties. (Francisco Suarez, S.J., *De Legibus,* lib. III, caps. 2, 12, and 13. Upon Suarez, cf. Luis Recasens Siches, *La Filosofía del Derecho de Francisco Suárez, con un estudio previo sobre sus antecedentes en la Patrística y en la Escolástica,* Madrid, 1927; pp. 148ff.)

For analogous reasons, Suarez excludes in absolute terms positive Law from legislating upon internal behaviors, upon thought, upon inclinations. Conducts which are spent in intimacy in no way refer directly to exterior peace and purity nor to the common good (sole ends of Law). Moreover, these acts are outside the knowledge of the political power and, consequently, also are absolutely extraneous to its field. On the other hand, positive Law and the power of political society are coactive. Now, the intimacy of the conscience is uncoercible; so, then, this is another reason because of which positive Law ought not to legislate upon such matters.

In these thoughts of Suarez, it is seen clearly that since the meaning which animates the Law is so different from that which is characteristic of Morals, the precepts of those two types of norms are also many times different and even disagreeing, although never contradictory nor incompatible. I repeat that I have adduced this outstanding doctrine of Suarez — in this point worthy precursor of political liberalism as to what it has of capital and perennial truth — not to interfere with the logical study of the conceptual difference between Morals and the Law as estimative considerations; but only as an example in which, by means of this particular case, there appears with special light and precision the essential diversity which there is between the meaning of morals and the meaning of juristics; in which at the same time there is revealed how that diversity does not imply in any way contradiction or incompatibility between them; and in which it is made evident that to distinguish between Morals and Law does not conduce to the demoralization of the latter, that is, to deprive it of its foundation and orientation of ethical values, since those ethical values are not the same which give form to morality, in the strict sense, that is, intimate honesty.

CHAPTER IV

THE RULES OF SOCIAL BEHAVIOR, THEIR DIFFERENTIATION FROM MORAL NORMS AND FROM JURIDICAL NORMS

1. Description of the Rules of Social Behavior

On the horizon of human life we find a series of norms regulative of conduct, which are not Law, neither are they morals. There is an enormous and variegated repertory of norms which, in the aggregate, constitute a special category, which I shall call *rules of social behavior.* Some examples of such rules are: decency, decorum, good breeding, correct manners, courtesy, urbanity, social respect, gentility, norms of spoken style, of written style, requirements of dress, fellowship, gentlemanliness, gallantry, civility, social tact, politeness, etc. Think of the innumerable acts and prohibitions which such rules impose upon us. Commonly, these rules have been called "social conventions"; but I think that this designation is highly unfortunate, for it invokes the idea of agreement, of convention, which is wholly contrary to the essence of these norms, as we shall see further on. Also, they have been called social usages; and although it is true that they manifest themselves by means of usages and customs, this designation has the inconvenience that by usage may also be designated — as we saw — other normative types completely different (as, for example, moral principles and juridical precepts). On that account, I prefer to designate them with the generic title of "rules of social behavior," because that expression translates one of their essential characteristics, as I shall show; and, moreover, because within it falls the whole multiple and varied repertory of norms which I have mentioned and others of an analogous kind.

There is here, then, a different sort of norms, which present, above all, at first sight, as a dimension common to all of them, two negative characters: not being moral norms nor juridical norms, though many times they seem like the first and sometimes like the second. Exactly in this lies the difficulty of the problem which the purpose of characterization of such rules raises: in this seeming in some respect like the Law (for example, as to their social dimension and as to their exteriority); and in having from another point of view, a certain similarity to moral estimations (as happens, for example, with some principles of decorum). And, nevertheless, in the first mental contact with such rules we feel that they are not morals, neither are they Law. Although at times it seems that they resemble moral principles, nevertheless they do not fit within the concept of morals. And, in spite of their social character and of their gravitation toward the exteriority of conduct, nevertheless, they do not coincide with the essence of juristics. But it is not sufficient that thus spontaneously we should conclude that they are neither morals nor Law. It is necessary to investigate the essential difference between those rules of social behavior and moral norms; and also the difference of such rules from juridical precepts. Hereby we shall have taken another decisive step toward the essential characterization of the Law.

With respect to their form of appearance, remember what I said when I was considering briefly social usage. It usually happens that from the primitive undifferentiated custom (which constitutes the total regulation of conduct) are segregated types of specially delimited norms (Morals, Law, Religion, Technique, etc.) which determine the outline also of another class of norms with peculiar characteristics, to wit, the norms of social behavior.

To orient ourselves in this first reflecting contact with the rules of social behavior, it will be desirable to attempt a characterization of them, which, for the moment, I will make only as a provisional beginning.

Those rules of social behavior are usually manifested in customary form, as norms emanating from anonymous collective mandates (that is, from the people, from the rest, in short, from society), as due behavior in certain social relations, in a certain group or special circle and without counting on any coercitive apparatus at their disposal, which would force inevitably their compliance, although with the threat of a sanction of censure or repudiation on the part of the corresponding social circle.

As I have indicated, the habitual form of presenting the rules of social behavior is customary. Now, as we have seen, not all usages are expressive of those rules of social behavior, since there are also moral usages and also juridical customs. But, aside from that, there are social usages which are neither moral, nor juridical, nor even the manifestation of rules of social behavior. For there are collective usages of an intellectual character, as is, for example, language; as, of another order, is public opinion. And there are those, also, which refer to practical and external conduct, but which lack any normative pretension. Not every practical social custom has a normative pretension: there are some — and in much abundance — which announce a collective conviction, but which do not pretend to create a duty for anyone; so, for example, to lunch at a certain hour, to take this or that dish at a private meal, to take excursions on certain days, to walk on the street at one or another hour, to devote oneself to some or other games, etc. The English distinguish with precision, in idiomatic usage, between the not normative and the normative custom: the former (pure repetition of acts without any idea of duty) they call *habit;* and on the other hand those usages which, with reference to practical conduct, have the tendency to constitute norms, they call *custom.*

Observe that the volume of rules of social behavior and of the duties which they impose is formidably great and embraces innumerable aspects of our social life. Note also that the effective pressure of these norms is very intense; so that many times we feel them with greater intensity than the voice of moral conscience or the intimidation of the Law. On some occasions the Law, in spite of its coercitive pretension to impose itself inexorably, has weakened in practice, has shown itself ineffective to suppress certain behaviors which had a deep root in the usual rules of social behavior: so, for example, in the case of duelling in other times, which disappeared only when the usual rules which supported it lost social approval, and were replaced by other normative convictions, according to which the jousts of honor were considered ridiculous. That illustrates the effective potent vigor which many rules of social behavior have.

Notice, moreover, that the rules of social behavior do not have any universal version, not even generalized, but are rather a series of particular and various versions for each social circle. An act which is permissible in a boy may, on the other hand, be indecorous in an old man; and what is plausible in an old man may be unsuitable in a youth. The perfect clothing for a manual laborer would be unsuitable for a functionary. What is licit for a secular might be scandalous for a priest. Diversions permitted socially to a mountebank are closed to a magistrate. The medieval concept of honor for knights did not rule among peasants. In the Middle Ages there were some customs for merchants and others for the aristocracy. What is permitted to a native may turn out intolerable in a foreigner. Words which would not be criticized when a muleteer uses them would be held vulgarities in a domestic servant, etc. This assigning of the rules of social behavior to a fixed collective sphere is one of the most notorious of the characteristics of this type of norm. Decorum, decency, fitness, courtesy, are things very diverse as to their content according to the social circle of which they treat. Those rules apply always in a certain circle (more or less ample) of persons, in a special collective sphere which gets its delimitation by virtue of various points of view for each sphere: by age, by relationship, by the profession, by residence, by race, by religion, by politics, by the economic position, by class, by devotion to certain activities (singers, athletes, students, tourists). Now, it is by no means necessary that the collective circle which comes into question should constitute an association; moreover, at the moment at which there is an association, with its regulations, many of those norms cease to be pure rules of social behavior and are changed into juridical precepts. While morals considers the individual in his entirety, as such individual (irreplaceable) and the Law considers him as a version of the great generalization, that is, as a citizen, or in other situations which, in principle, are all possible (vendor, bailor, etc.), on the other hand, the rules of social behavior consider the social conduct of each one according to his actual assignment to certain social circles. And, therefore, it could be said that the rules of social behavior are situated between the great circle in which men are submitted to the Law and absolute individuality, which is the subject of morality.[19] A violation of the usages of social behavior may be innocent before the moral conscience (and even praiseworthy in certain cases). On the other hand, only those belonging to the circle in which its usage ruled react to a violation of the rules of social behavior; while a violation of the juridical order provokes the reaction of all the community in which it governs, represented by the State.

2. Essential Differentiation between Morals and Rules of Social Behavior

It is not sufficient to consider the difference which there is between juridical norms and the rules of social behavior; since if I limit myself to showing why these are not Law, I should then run the risk that they might be confused with Morals. And it is important to leave perfectly examined the different essential types of normation of conduct; and, hence, it is necessary that each one of them should remain perfectly marked off from the rest.

The rules of social behavior have in common with Morals the lack of any coercitive organization to overcome the resistance of the subject and to force compliance. However much vigor moral motives acquire in the intimacy of the person, they never constitute a fatal and irresistible force, they do not constitute an inexorable imposition of the proper conduct. Also, however strong may be the external expression which supports a rule of social behavior, and however much scope that social influence may acquire in the conscience of the person, if the individual wishes to neglect the rule, the social circle in which it governs lacks power to force compliance on him.

But this dimension common to Morals and to rules of social behavior — which I have just commented on — that is, that both lack an apparatus with force to compel inescapably their realization, does not imply

[19] Cf. Jorge Simmel, Sociología (ed. of the Rev. de Occidente), t. i.

in any way that these two types of norms (the moral and that of social behavior) have an identical essence; rather, on the contrary, we are going to see that they are essentially different. In fact, I shall show how the meaning of the norms of social behavior (decorum, decency, courtesy, etc.) is radically different from the meaning of the moral norms. Now, to that end, it will be necessary to complete the analysis with the object of discovering rigorously and precisely what the essential differences are between the two types of norm. The difference may be conjectured at first glance, but, on the other hand, it is not so easy to define it with exactitude. Twenty centuries ago Cicero said that the difference between modesty and decorum was easier to understand than to explain.[20] But it is important that we should have better success in this theme than Cicero. Therefore let us expound that difference with care.

If we attend to the meaning which the rules of social behavior (decorum, decency, courtesy, etc.) have we shall notice that they refer predominantly to the external aspect of conduct in relation to other persons. They are rules which affect the exterior manner of behaving, referred to other persons and in consideration of them. Note that we do not qualify the strictly moral virtues (for example, veracity, temperance, charity, fortitude) as decorous, as decent, but simply morally good in themselves, intrinsically, in an absolute manner. On the other hand, the decent, the decorous, is that which appears to another person externally adequate, suitable, fitting for a given situation, on its superficial levels. That is the meaning of the Latin *decet* (decency in our tongue); and also of *decus*, that is, decorum. The norms of decency, of decorum — and also those of courtesy, of good breeding, etc. — affect the superficial layer of man, the external levels of conduct, that is, those on which occur contact with other people, what we may call the social skin. The depth of life, the intimacy, the sphere of original intentions, in short, the authentic individuality is that affected by morals and is never reached by the rules of social behavior. And, therefore, it may happen that a perfectly moral person is in a *deficit* with respect to the rules of social behavior: as happened with St. Francis of Assisi who embodied an exemplar of moral conduct and who on the other hand was unadaptable to the rules of social behavior; in another view, something of this sort happens to the character of Charlot (created in fiction by Charles Chaplin in his films), who represents a pure spirit and nevertheless perpetual discord in social behavior. And, on the other hand, we all know persons very correct in compliance with the norms of social behavior who, nevertheless, have a rude soul within.

[20] Cf. Cicero, De officiis, 1, 27.

The character of externality which I have just emphasized in the rules of social behavior does not imply that the rules do not possess an intention of value. Certainly, the norms of social behavior aim at the realization of certain values, to wit, of those values which are accustomed to be called decorum, decency, politeness, good manners, etc. What happens is that those values, which naturally belong to the ethical family, that is, to the axiological region of ethics nevertheless are distinguished within it from the moral values *sensu stricto*, from those values which are called of pure morality. And, so, it would result that the ethical values should be classified in three great species: those purely moral, those of juristics, and those of decorum.

And in the same manner as we distinguish between pure moral values and the positive moral convictions of peoples (which may be more or less correct, that is, which may embody better or worse, or may not embody authentic moral values), and in the same manner as we distinguish between pure juristic values and historic positive Law (which may be more or less just and even unjust), so, in a similar manner, we may distinguish between the values of decorum and the positive rules of social behavior manifested in usages.

This dimension of externalness of the rules of social behavior (and also of their corresponding values) is made evident in the words of which language makes use to designate them. Of the man who complies with these rules, it is said that he is *well-behaved,* and the rules themselves are called good *modes,* good *form,* good *manners.* The word *decoro* signifies ornate, the same as the Latin *decorum;* also the corresponding German word, *Anstand,* denotes the same idea of externality, and similarly the French word *façon,* which is used as signifying good social manners. The same applies to the English equivalent *fashion,* which also signifies good tone, correct. But it is not only this generic qualification which expresses the idea of exteriority, it is revealed in a series of words which designate different phases of social behavior, in which is evoked an analogous representation of an exterior surface. So, the qualifiers: formal, formality, refined, politeness, suave, suavity, polish, *poli, politesse, fein, glatt,* etc. Another word in which that same idea of externalness appears distinctly is *etiquet,* which means something superficial which adheres to the face of a thing.

We may emphasize also that dimension of exteriority in the rules of social behavior and in their corresponding values, by noticing that they govern only those moments in which we are in present real company. When the door of my room shuts behind me, there are not felt to apply to my behavior judgments based on those rules or their values. Alone, in the isolation of my quarters, I cannot be decent or indecent, decorous or indecorous, discreet or indiscreet, courteous or discourteous. It does not happen so, on the other hand, with the moral duties, which continue always weighing upon me and whose voice gains power when I am alone, for then is the most propitious hour to reflect upon my destiny; because the moral values affect the innermost depths of my life.

The difference between Morals and the rules of social behavior is made patent to us from another point of view, in the following characteristic. However the rules of social behavior rule in delimited collective circles, and in their positive form manifest themselves in customs, they govern only so far as they belong in fact and at present to the social circles to which they belong and in the degree in which their use is current, that is, as their use effectively rules. So, for example, referring to national or local customs, I may say that on going on a journey I leave them at home and they do not oblige me; I remain free from them; and, on the other hand, I ought to submit myself to the rules of the country which I visit. On the contrary, the moral norms weigh on the individual as such individual, at every moment; and moreover their validity is entirely independent of whether other persons comply with them or not (even when it is a matter of a moral norm which has been received by tradition).

When, in the preceding chapter, I was describing the moral norm and contrasting it to the meaning of the juridical norm, I emphasized that for the moral norm to create concrete obligations upon a particular person, it was necessary that the person should have recognized it as valid in his conscience, that he should feel himself intimately adherent to it, bound by it; in short, I explained that, whatever might be the origin of a moral norm, to create obligations it was necessary for it to have been made autonomous, that is, to belong sincerely to the intimacy of the person. On the other hand, the rules of social behavior ask of me only an external conduct and not an intimate adherence; and, therefore, assume to oblige me, whatever may be my opinion, favorable or adverse to them. They imply a regulation which comes only from without, which for its effectiveness does not require a process of interiorization, of sincere adherence, or of loyal recognition. As they ask of the person only something due externally to the others, they do not demand intimate devotion; and they seek perfect obligation entirely independent of the opinion of their subjects. That being founded exclusively on an external instance, entirely alien to the feeling of the individual, is called *heteronomy*.

The characteristic difference between Morals and the rules of social behavior may be summed up by saying that Morals is a valuation of the conduct of the individual, as such individual, in his authentic, peculiar, and untransferable being, in his fully responsible life, in his basic intimacy and with reference to his ultimate destiny; and that, on the other hand, the rules of social behavior constitute a form of collective life. Precisely because they constitute a *collective* model of conduct the rules of social behavior have the characters which I have explained and which may be summed up as follows.

1. The rules of social behavior do not take into account the person as an individual in his full particular life, but consider him as a subject functionary of a collectivity, as a fungible member of a circle, that is, as the interchangeable, generic, member of a group. They do not refer to what the individual does as such individual, but to what there is in his communal, vagrant, topical life, of a generic bed or path, as belonging to a social sphere.

2. The norms of social behavior refer to the external dimension of the acts of a person in consideration with the other persons of a social circle (wide or narrow).

3. The positive rules of social behavior govern only so far as they have present social efficacy, so far as they constitute a usage complied with by most, or a conviction which lives in the members of the collective circle.

4. The rules of social behavior proceed from an external instance and their pretension to compulsion is not conditioned on the intimate sincere adherence of the person; that is, they are heteronomous.

3. Differentiation between the Norms of Social Behavior and Juridical Norms

As to the proposition of distinguishing essentially between Morals and rules of social behavior it seems that I have succeeded in setting forth the difference rigorously. But, it turns out that here we have arrived at a disturbing point with regard to the intent to differentiate between Law and rules of social behavior. For it happens that all the characters which I have emphasized in the rules of social behavior to contrast them with the essence of moral norms, are, in turn, peculiar notes of juristics. Indeed, I have shown how the rules of social behavior constitute a form of *collective* life, which is also essentially a peculiarity of the Law. And as a consequence of the differentiating study of the norms of social behavior and those of morals, I have discussed also the following notes: *exteriority, positivity* (that is, their existence is supported by *facticity,* that is, by the fact that they are observed as usage), and heteronomy. Now, it happens that the collective character, and the notes of exteriority, positivity and heteronomy are also essentially peculiarities of the Law. I have here, then, our problem in a dogmatic phase: the coincidence of the rules of social behavior with juristics in four essential characters common to both. But let the reader not be disheartened: he may go on believing that in spite of such coincidences there is a radical diversity between the rules of social behavior and the Law. The measure of one essential difference has been already foreshadowed or conjectured, although ordinarily I should not have come to explain with rigor and precision in what that difference consists. It is time now that the Theory of the Law should complete its analysis on a point as basic as this, since on its happy solution will depend the establishment in clear form of the essential concept of juristics.

Contemporaneous juridical production has elaborated various doctrines to solve this topic of the essential differentiation between juridical norms and the norms of social behavior.[21] But considering the character of this book, which is at the same time that of radical foundations and beginnings, I wish to save the reader — as I have done also on other topics — the burden of an erudite relation of the multiple theories which have been tried; and so I will go directly to the topic to raise it to the height which I reached by the development of the various preceding thoughts, in a special work which I have devoted to the subject.[22]

The distinction between rules of social behavior and Law cannot be referred to the actual origin of one or the other of the norms; for there is also customary Law, which, although it appears in the form of custom, is also authentic Law.[23]

Nor can the difference between rules of social behavior and juridical norms either be referred to an essential diversity of content between them;[24] since the content of the Law as well as that of rules of social behavior varies in the course of history and in different peoples. And, therefore, we see that what yesterday constituted matter for mere regulation by the rules of social behavior is today the object of restrictive juridical precepts; and, vice versa, we observe also that many aspects of conduct, which formerly were submitted to a juridical normation,

[21] This is a theme which could not be avoided in almost all the treatises on juridical Philosophy and on the general Theory of the Law; but the greater part of these treatises pass rapidly and summarily over the question, without reaching either a correct view of it, or much less a satisfactory solution. So, among many other examples, we may cite AUSTIN, THE PROVINCE OF JURISPRUDENCE, included in his lectures on Jurisprudence or the Philosophy of Law (1861) which contents itself with relegating the rules of social behavior to the sphere which he calls that of positive morality, as an imperfect form of it, which does not constitute properly a mandate, but the mere expression of feelings and opinions.

[22] Cf. LUIS RECASÉNS SICHES, LES USAGES SOCIAUX ET LEUR DIFFERENTIATION D'AVEC LES NORMES JURIDIQUES (Paris: Sirey, 1936).

[23] Cf. HATSCHEK, in an article in the JAHRBUCH DES ÖFFENTLICHEN RECHTES III, 1ff.; and SOMLO, JURISTISCHE GRUNDLEHRE (2d ed., 1927) 72ff. As to the criticism of this thought, see my work cited in the preceding Note.

[24] This is the thesis of JHERING, ZWECK IN RECHT, t. II, pp. 79ff.

have since remained relegated to simple disposition by the rules of social behavior. So, for example, etiquette and good breeding at the table, in the great majority of peoples and times, have been and are matters regulated by the usual rules of social behavior; but, on the other hand, it happened in a primitive Greek people that at royal banquets to turn the fish in the dish was considered a grave wrong and punished with a cruel penalty.[25] And, also, let us remember that clothing and headgear, which for the most part belong today solely to the rules of social behavior, have been at times juridically regulated — as formerly in the Venetian Re-

[25] I cannot pass over the cleverness of the ambassador who outwitted the wise men of Greece. When he, with some of his companions, came in autumn to the royal city, they were lodged some here, some there, but he himself was entrusted to the care of a bishop who incessantly fasted and prayed. This brought the ambassador to his wits' end. In spring, when the weather was somewhat milder, the bishop introduced him to the king, who wanted to know what he thought about the bishop. Sighing deeply, he said: "Your bishop is quite holy so far as it is possible without God." To this the king asked in astonishment: "How can anybody be holy without God?" To this the ambassador answered: "It is written, God is love; but this the bishop has not."

Afterwards the king invited him to dine with him and placed him amid the eminent people. These had introduced a law (*Gesetz*) that nobody at the table of the king, native or foreign, was allowed to turn an animal or a part thereof on the other side, but to eat only as it lay on the platter. On one of these platters was brought a fresh-water fish covered with a well-seasoned sauce. But as the guest, who did not know of the custom (*Sitte*), turned the fish on the other side, they all sprang up and said to the king, "Sire, you have been dishonored as your forefathers never were." And the king said to him, "I cannot prevent them from putting you to death, but demand of me something else that you want and I shall comply with your request." The ambassador thought for a while, then said, "I entreat you, emperor, in accordance with your promise to grant me a small wish." The emperor said to him, "Ask what you desire and it shall be granted to you, only I cannot, contrary to the law (*Gesetz*) of the Greeks, spare your life." Thereupon the ambassador said, "If I must die, I request only this, that whoever saw me turn the fish around on the other side shall lose his eyesight." Dismayed by such terms, the emperor swore by Christ that he himself had not seen him turn the fish, but believed those who told him about it. Then the queen began to justify herself as follows: "By the Mother of God, St. Mary, I have not noticed it." All the other distinguished people, one after the other, tried to extricate themselves from such danger. One swore by St. Peter, who carries the keys of heaven, another by the teacher of the heathen, others by the virtue of all the angels, and others by the host of all saints. In this way they sought to free themselves by means of terrible oaths.

Thus the wily Frank outwitted proud Hellas and returned as victor safe and sound to his fatherland.

BALBULUS NOTKER DER STAMMLER (c. 840–912 A.D.), DIE GESCHICHTEN VON KARL DEM GROSSEN, II 6. Translated into German by Karl Brügmann. (Leipzig, n.d., Inselverlag.) Referred to by RUDOLF STAMMLER, LEHRBUCH DER RECHTSPHILOSOPHIE, Sec. 38, p. 79 (Berlin, 1922; Berlin, 1928). The translation from the German is by the kindness of Professor Emeritus Paul V. C. Baur of Yale University. TRANSLATOR.

public, as Montesquieu tells; also in some precepts of the Mosaical legislation of the Hebrews, in Japanese law, in the Colonial Ordinances of 1542, and in the Turkish Law of our time, which has prohibited certain traditional garments, requiring their replacement by western articles. And it is not only a matter of variations chronologically and between different countries, but also, moreover, it happens that in one people at one moment, a matter may fall partly under the rules of social behavior and partly under juridical rules; so, for example, dress, which in most of its aspects is determined by the rule of social behavior, on the other hand constitutes an object of juridical regulation for the military and for other functionaries on whom a uniform is imposed. Analogously, a greeting has been and is on most occasions and in social circles a mere usage of courtesy; but, on the other hand, in the army a salute in prescribed form constitutes a juridic duty. Similarly we recall that priority to occupy the seats in public vehicles has been and is in general a matter of mere politeness and gallantry; but, after the war of 1914–1918, many cities established juridically by municipal ordinances the obligation to yield seats to the mutilated. The formulas for written style in our communications with others are, also, an object of mere rule of social behavior; but, on the other hand, in relations with the Public Administration they answer to juridical norms. All these examples — which we might multiply interminably — show us that it is not possible to establish an essential difference between strictly juridical material and matter strictly of social behavior. And we begin to conjecture that the essential difference between these two types of norms cannot in any way proceed from their content, nor from the different form in which they govern.

Neither can it be sustained, as some have claimed,[26] that the rules of social behavior constitute nothing more than invitations from a social circle to behave in a certain manner; since when one disregards a rule of decorum or of courtesy he is not considered to have declined an invitation, but to have violated a norm which obliged him. The rules of social behavior aspire to constitute authentic norms; they have a normative pretension and, so far, to determine duties. (We leave aside now the problem of the justification or not which belongs to each concrete norm of courtesy, etc., according to a critical valuation, and we consider in a formal sense what such rules essentially are.) A norm which should be no more than an invitation, which should condition its pretension to validity on the pure free will of the person, is an impossible concept, a

[26] This is the doctrine of STAMMLER, LEHRBUCH DER RECHTSPHILOSOPHIE (1923), paragraphs 37 to 42. See a full criticism of it in my book ESTUDIOS DE FILOSOFÍA DEL DERECHO (Barcelona: Bosch, 1936).

logical absurdity; for such conditioning is incompatible with the meaning of normative. The meaning of normative consists in seeking to bind the conduct of the person, to create a duty in him; consequently, a supposed norm which should not rule over the person, which should determine no duty in him, whose validity should remain entirely subordinate to what the person might accept in the functioning of his pure free will, would not be properly a norm. Consequently, it is not possible to obtain the difference between juridical norms and rules of social behavior by assigning to the latter the character of pure invitation; since, as I have shown, when in a social circle someone fails to behave as social usage requires, the other members do not consider that he refused an invitation, but that he violated a duty.

Some have indicated,[27] as a difference between the Law and rules of social behavior that while the former has organs by which to impose itself, the latter have none; that is, that the rules of social behavior lack any organized apparatus of coaction to act on persons imposing themselves and demanding responsibilities. At the bottom of this attempt at a distinction, perhaps there is very much in the background a correct idea, although confused and mistakenly conceived. But formulated simply in that manner, the distinction is very rough and is formally erroneous: it in no way offers an essential delimitation. In fact, for Law to be Law, it is not necessary for it to rely on judicial and executive organs which should be rigorously differentiated in the social division of the work, which is what happens in the modern constitutional States of the civilized peoples of the West. For in the primitive juridical orders those organs do not always exist, and in them it happens that it is the injured person himself who undertakes the coercitive reaction of the Law against the offender: so it is with private vengeance as a juridical institution in many primitive peoples; and so also, in imprisonment of the debtor by the creditor that he may work for the latter's benefit until the extinction of the debt. And, vice versa, we may note in several cases that certain rules of social behavior do count on means to impose on their transgressor certain sanctions of censure or of exclusion, which, for example, happens with tribunals of honor, which can only declare an incompatibility without juridical effects.

Now, it is necessary to attain to good understanding of the essential meaning of the juridical norm — as well if it has diverse organs for its application, as if it lacks them — in view of the entirely different meaning which rests in the rules of social behavior — even if in some cases

[27] Cf. JULIUS BINDER, PHILOSOPHIE DES RECHTES (1925) 811ff.; CONSTANTIN TSATSOS, DER BEGRIFF DES POSITIVEN RECHTES (1928) 101ff. The criticism of such doctrines is in my book ESTUDIOS DE FILOSOFÍA DEL DERECHO (1936).

they may have organs of an appearance similar to the juridical ones.[28]

The essential difference between the rules of social behavior and the juridical norms, as I understand it, consists in a fundamental difference between the forms of their dominion and, consequently, also in a difference between the types of their sanction. The rules of social behavior have the pretension of norms, that is, they claim normative validity, they constitute mandates for their subjects. Moreover, noncompliance with the rules of social behavior involves a sanction of social reprobation or of exclusion from a certain collective circle, a sanction which may turn out to be very serious for the person, and fear of which may exercise a vigorous influence — to the point, in some cases, of being stronger than the threat of juridical sanctions. (There are those who violate a juridical duty, to comply with a rule of social behavior, for fear of what "they will say" in the social circle to which they belong — of which we have had an example before in the case of the duel.) Now, that sanction for noncompliance with the rules of social behavior is expressive only of a censure, which may extend even to exclude the infractor from the corresponding social circle; but it is never the forced imposition of observance of the norm. The effects of that sanction of the rules of social behavior may result for the person as terribly as you please; but that sanction never consists of imposing on the person the proper conduct in a forced manner. The sanction of the rules of social behavior may be included previously in the norm — which is what Max Weber did not see — as happens in the so-called codes of honor; but that sanction does not consist in compelling inevitably compliance with what the rule commands. On the contrary, as I have explained in the preceding chapter, the essential characteristic of the Law is the possibility of imposing forcibly in an inexorable, irresistible manner, the performance of the proper conduct, or of a consequence provided in the norm itself (or of avoiding at all costs the prohibited behavior, or of imposing other conduct as an equivalent). The juridical sanction as *forced execution* of the prescribed conduct — which constitutes the primary and normal form of the inexorability of the Law — is an essential note of juristics; and, on the contrary, the absence of this form of sanction consisting in forcing compliance, is what essentially characterizes the rules of social behavior, as a difference in them from the juridical rules. And it is not to be said that in juridical life it is not always possible to impose forcibly com-

[28] Cf. HANS KELSEN, HAUPTPROBLEME DER STAATSRECHTSLEHRE (2d ed., 1923) 30ff.; MAX WEBER, WIRTSCHAFT UND GESELLSCHAFT (1925) 221 and 376; FRITZ SCHREIER, GRUNDBEGRIFFE, UND GRUNDFORMEN DES RECHTES (1924). See an exposition and criticism of the doctrines of these authors in my book ESTUDIOS DE FILOSOFÍA DEL DERECHO.

pliance with the proper conduct and that what happens is that there is imposed either other behavior or a punitive sanction; for to this it must be answered that indemnity and penalty are not the primary expressions of the inexorability of the Law, but substitute manifestations, in case the primary form (which is forced execution) is made impossible in fact. Although of course also in these secondary forms is made evident the same essential inexorability of the Law. Actually, the primary, exact, natural manifestation of the autarchic or inexorable meaning of the Law consists in that when the person does not comply spontaneously with the precept, execution of the right is imposed violently on him or he is well prevented, by force, from doing the forbidden. When by limitation of reality it is not possible to force a person to do personal acts, which are practicable only with the will, then the same juridical norm anticipates the imposition of a compensating behavior, which may be realized by irresistible external pressure; for example, execution against the property to satisfy a judgment for damages. And in the case in which some anti-juridical act has been committed with an irremediable effect (of offense or social alarm), then a penalty is imposed as an inexorable retribution — as paying, in another way for what he does not wish to do. [It is necessary to recall that the penalty has always, necessarily and essentially, a sense of retribution, which is entirely independent of the motive or foundation for the penalty (which may indeed be for social defense alone) and of the functions which further are attributed to the penalty (which may be the correction of the delinquent). The foundation of the penalty will be social defense; but society may defend itself in many ways — for example, also by educative proceedings, by economic prosperity, etc., and by norms of penal Law; now when the means of defense adopted is this last, to wit, penal Law, then there is employed something — the penalty — which has, whether or no, a retributive meaning. The retributive meaning, which is objective payment, compensation, is not to be confused with the expiatory meaning, which can be given only in morals. On the other hand, there is no difficulty, rather it is praiseworthy progress, in having the penalty be of such nature that it operates correctionally, as a reëducation for the delinquent; but such effect — very desirable — does not at all destroy the essentially retributive meaning of the juridical penalty. A penalty without a retributive meaning would be a round square, a flagrant contradiction. One may speak of penal substitutions, but it is an absurdity to suppose that if there is a penalty there is not a meaning of retribution.]

A rule of social behavior commands a certain conduct; inobservance of it may be sanctioned by censures, reproofs, and exclusions (which perhaps may come to be very serious); but that sanction never consists of the forced imposition of the proper conduct, nor does it have the meaning of inexorable retribution — of paying in another way for what he does not wish to do — but it constitutes a simple reproving or excluding reaction on the part of the collective circle in which the rule prevails, against the member who violates it. From the norm of social behavior is essentially excluded inexorable imposition; because at the moment in which it should be given such dimension, it would cease to be a pure rule of social behavior and would be transformed into a juridical precept. Or, put in another way, the norm of mere social usage commands or reigns; but its formal manner of governing is essentially different from the formal manner of governing which is characteristic of the Law; for the norm of social behavior pauses before the free will of the person, who is the one to decide on its compliance or violation, which always are free for him; while, on the contrary, the juridical norm, by virtue of its inexorability, does not pause before the free will of the subject, but tries to annul it in case it intends to depart from the precept; and tries to annul it by all means, at all costs, physically. The Law seeks essentially to annihilate the will adverse to it. On the contrary, the rules of social behavior, although sanctions are derived from them in case of noncompliance, do not annul the will of the person. In the face of social usages, I may place myself in an attitude of rebellion and maintain that rebellion, without those rules being able to annul my desire hostile to them; they invoke sanctions and more sanctions, under which, if I am disposed to endure them, I may continue to violate the usage as many times as I like; which, on the contrary, is impossible with respect to a juridical norm.

Let us look now, in the light of some examples, at what I have explained. Whoever while breaking the norms of social behavior fails to respond to the call of a companion, will be the object of censure by him and even by the whole social circle to which they both belong, and even may be excluded from it; on the other hand, whoever receives from a competent juridical authority an order to present himself before it, and does not do it, will be taken by force. If a person does not pay a gambling debt he will be disgraced in a certain social circle, but he cannot in any way be forced specifically to pay; while, on the contrary, whoever does not pay the debt arising from a juridical contract, will be definitely deprived of a portion of his property. Who does not comply with the usual norms of greeting will be censured — or even excluded from corresponding social relations — but not forced to bow; while, on the contrary, the soldier who breaks the military order to salute will be forced to salute and will suffer a retributive sanction. And so it would be possible to continue giving innumerable examples, in all of which appears the difference which I have explained.

It turns out then that here, on considering the difference between norms of social behavior and juridical norms, we have found anew the dimension of *inexorable imposition* as an essential characteristic of the Law, a dimension with which we have already had contact when I explained the distinction between Law and Morals. It seems, then, that a special form of dominion, which is peculiar to it, characterizes juristics, the inexorable dominion, the formal pretension to impose itself at all costs.

4. The Problem of Customary Law

Perhaps someone may believe at first sight that the existence of customary Law, that is, of juridical customs, raises some difficulty with regard to the difference between it and the rules of social behavior, from the fact that, similar to what is true of them, it manifests itself by means of the usual forms of collective behavior. But, in truth, there is no difficulty whatever, for customary Law is as much Law as is statutory: it has exactly the same essential meaning as the latter. The fact that a norm manifests itself by means of a usage, tells nothing at all as to its particular nature. By means of usage there may be revealed forms of human life of essentially different types (intellectual, technical, moral, juridical, social). The juridical norm constituted by custom has an identical meaning with that established in a statute; it has the same logical structure, the same formal pretension of validity, the same type of inexorable compulsion. On the other hand, there are rules of social behavior reduced to written form and codified (for example, the so-called laws of duelling, the epitomes of how to behave in society, etc.); and, nevertheless, such rules do not change their nature from the fact of having been formulated in writing and in the form of articles; and they continue to be pure norms of social behavior — and in no way Law — because they lack the inexorable imposition.

5. Dynamic Relation between the Law and the Rules of Social Behavior in History

Juridical material and the material of decorum, courtesy, etc., are subject to flux in two directions: what today is governed by Law was yesterday a matter only of decency or politeness; and what yesterday constituted a juridical precept passed afterwards into a mere rule of social behavior.

But it has to be noted, moreover, that in that movable boundary between the two classes they are not found situated on the same level of strength, but, on the contrary, the primacy belongs to the Law. Precisely the fact that the Law has the note of coercive imposition is what determines the bounds of its content, i.e., it is what decides the matters which are going to be the object of juridical regulation and those others which by exclusion will remain relegated to a mere rule of social behavior. The Law may restrict the sphere of the norms of social behavior, may forcibly annul these or those usages. So, it happens that the usages of social behavior may domicile themselves in those places alone which the Law leaves free to them. And there are times when the Law enters upon a struggle against certain usages of social behavior.

Finally, it is necessary to note also that, at times, the Law takes up, in certain cases, some norms of social behavior and converts them into juridical norms for certain persons who find themselves in a certain situation. Thus, for example, in certain cases the Law transforms into a juridical norm a rule of decorum, of modesty, of neatness, of decency, etc., and takes to its bosom what good customs require, what modesty determines, what decorum establishes, what correct neatness demands. Consequently, the Law prohibits that which offends good customs, and attacks on modesty, and indecorous behavior in a chamber of administration, of justice, or in a hall, or in Parliament. Now, the juridical norm does not define what it is which is meant by good customs, decorum, decency, modesty, neatness, but it leaves it to the provisions of the social usages which are in force as to these forms.

CHAPTER V

JURIDICAL MANDATES AND ARBITRARY MANDATES. (LAW AND ARBITRARINESS)

From all that has been said up to this point, it follows that the Law is essentially a form of objectivated human life, of a social character, with a normative pretension, referring to the exteriority of living together and of collective coöperation, and with a command of inexorable imposition. We need to establish another differentiation of the juristic from a diverse form of mandate (the arbitrary mandate), with which it might perhaps be confused; and, moreover, we must also clarify what the functional meaning of Law is in human life, that is, what the typical basic motivation is by virtue of which men make Law in their lives.

Let us see, first, what it is which we are wont to call an arbitrary mandate and in what it differs from the juristic mandate. It happens that at times we find ourselves in the presence of mandates which are provided with a force of irresistible imposition, but to which we deny a juridical character and call them *arbitrary*. Upon what is founded such qualification of arbitrariness? And, consequently, what is the note which differentiates a juridical order from an arbitrary order? This is the theme which I am now going to develop.

Let us notice, before all, that when we speak of arbitrariness as contrasted to the Law, we understand that it is something negativing the latter, something which radically opposes it. But it is to be noticed also that the qualification of arbitrary is not applied to all acts which are contrary to the Law, but only to those acts which proceed from whoever possesses the supreme effective social power and which are understood as antijuridical, that is, to antijuridical acts dictated by the public powers, with an unappealable character. The antijuridical acts of private persons and also those of subordinate organs of the public power and all those susceptible of appeal, are classified — according to the case — as civilly illegal, wrong, crime, administrative violation, but in no way as arbitrary in the strict sense of the word; and they are punishable and rectifiable by superior authorities. It seems that, in the strict sense, there are called arbitrary those antijuridical and unappealable mandates (with irresistible imposed force), dictated by organs of the public power; and that, on the other hand, strictly, the antijuridical acts of the public powers which are rectifiable and punishable by another authority superior to them, deserve simply the qualification of illegal (in the civil, administrative, penal, order, etc.).

We say to define arbitrariness that it constitutes an antijuridical mandate, dictated by an irresistible public power. Now, on what does the qualification of antijuricity depend? It is important not to confound this judgment of antijuricity with the censure of injustice, a crass error into which some authors have fallen. Arbitrary does not mean the same thing as unjust. The qualification of justice or injustice is predicated upon the contents of a precept; it constitutes an estimative judgment (in the light of several values) upon what the precept requires. On the contrary, the qualification of arbitrariness does not refer to the correctness or incorrectness, to the justice or injustice of a precept, but to the characteristic that a mandate is formally a denier of the juridical mandate. An arbitrary mandate is something which not only does not constitute Law, but which moreover represents its basic negation, the negation of the essence of juristics, purely and simply. Within the essential notion of the Law, within its universal, formal, concept, fall alike the just norms, those less just, and also the unjust ones, if there concur in them all the formal notes of juricity. Even when the Law ought to realize justice, even when it is essential for it that it should intentionally refer to values, even when it remains justified only in the light of such values, nevertheless, for a precept or a mandate to deserve the qualification of juristic, it is not necessary that it should have positively succeeded in the realization of that ideal: it is sufficient that, implying an intentional meaning of justice (that is, an aspiration to mold the pertinent values), it possesses the formal notes characteristic of juristics, an aggregate of notes — juricity — which is the only means or vehicle in which juridical values can be realized. So, there may be successful Law, that is, just Law, and unsuccessful Law, that is, unjust Law, but Law finally and at last (although failing in the light of values), in which there is distinguished from it what is not Law, that is, in what it differs from other non-juridical imperatives (among which are arbitrary mandates). Arbitrariness is not an estimative qualification within the world of juristics, but something which denotes a power alien and contrary to the Law: it is the negation of the formal essence of juristics.

But in what does that negation of the essence of juristics consist? On perceiving that it is a question not of a qualification as to content — of what is commanded — but of a formal characterization, one might be inclined to define juristics as the legitimate (as that proceeding from legitimate positive authority sanctioned by the Law), as against the arbitrary, which would be defined as the illegitimate, that is, as that originating in an illegitimate power, of a usurper who seizes power by a *coup d'état* or by a revolution. But this formal criterion of origin will not do. Because it is an undeniable fact that a triumphant revolution or *coup d'état* determines the end of the prior Law and the creation of a new juridical order — always and when there concur in the new regulation which arises the essential characters of a juridical form and it gains the assent of the community. That this is so constitutes an undeniable fact, although its explanation constitutes one of the most intricate problems of Juridical Philosophy.[29] Now, this being so, it is not possible to tie up juristics to the legal formality of its primitive origin, and to call arbitrary every norm which in its origin lacks such character of formal legitimacy. It should be noted that if one tries to establish that criterion, it must be concluded that there is actually not, in the whole world, any juridical order whatever, since the history of no nation is free from revolutions and *coups d'état* which have broken the continuity of the Law. The formal criterion for distinction between juridical mandates and

[29] See chap. IX of this book.

arbitrary mandates cannot be in the initial legitimacy or illegitimacy of their origin.[30]

In general, the Juridical Philosophy of our time has accepted as the essential distinction between the juridical mandate and the arbitrary mandate the doctrine elaborated by Stammler. Following this source — though giving it some shades of greater precision — it may be said that for juristics the note of *inviolable regularity* is essential, while on the contrary the arbitrary mandate presents itself as a *capricious irregularity*. This doctrine has hardened in the heat of a controversy over a case which arose in Prussian history in the time of Frederick II.[31] The facts

[30] Cf. STAMMLER, *op. cit.*, paras. 43–45. Cf. also LUIS RECASÉNS SICHES, DIRECCIONES CONTEMPORÁNEAS DEL PENSAMIENTO JURÍDICO (Manuales Labor, 1929) 59–60.

[31] Miller Arnold's upstream neighbor constructed a fish pond and filled it with water from the river so that there was not enough left to drive the mill properly. The decision in first instance by the court (*Regierung*) of the Neumark (part of the Province of Brandenburg) on Oct. 28, 1779 dismissed the claim of the miller, because "the mill-river was but a private water; the owner was entitled to deal with it according to his will, without regard to the damage inflicted upon someone else (Lex 24, Sec. 12 and Lex 26, Dig. de damno infecto 39,2; Mevius, Decisiones IV dec. 39; Horn in Polacks Mathesi forensi sect. IV ad Sec. 52; Stryck, Usus modernus pandectarum ad tit. serv. praed. rustic. Secs. 8, 9; Oraculum juris, tom. X paras. II chap. 8, 70—et doctores ibi allegati)." The division (*Senat*) of the Supreme Court of second instance (*Kammergericht*) ruled on Dec. 8, 1779 that the neighbor of the miller "was entitled to make use of the water of the river in order to water his pond; for insofar as it is running through his own estate, it belongs to him as his own property, and he who exercises his own right does not hurt anyone." At the request of Frederick the Great, the Criminal Division of the Supreme Court of the Province of Brandenburg (*Kriminalsenat des Kammergerichts*) gave a report on Dec. 26, 1779, upon the question of whether the Judges of the *Kammergericht* who had decided the case in second instance had behaved incorrectly or were liable to punishment; which the *Kriminalsenat* denied explicitly, and said further: "As any customary law (*Landrecht*) or any explicit law of the country was lacking, both Courts (*Collegia*) agreed upon the following legal sentence, in accordance with the generally accepted Natural Law and with some laws of the Roman law, which had to be applied according to the regulations, if laws of the country (*Landesgesetze*) did not exist. Each owner or landlord is entitled to build or construct anything on his own estate at his pleasure, therefore he is entitled to make use of the water of a river running through his estate at his pleasure. He does not need to take into consideration the convenience (*Convenienz*) of his neighbors, insofar as he is not limited by regulations of the local police or by treaties or conventions (*Conventionen*) with his neighbors . . ." "He (the neighbor) uses but his right, and according to Natural Law and the statutory laws the principle is valid: he who exercises his own rights does not do injustice to anyone." There was at the time no Prussian law of waters justifying the decisions, but they were rather based on Roman law and general principles. The authors cited in the lower opinion were authorities of the German Common Law (the Roman law valid in Germany) in the seventeenth and eighteenth centuries. Frederick caused the pond to be destroyed, the mill put in order, Arnold's loss to be reimbursed from the private property of the judges, and the

were as follows: a miller of Potsdam owned a piece of land on the lower part of a slope, which received a stream of water which previously crossed a neighboring piece of land. The proprietor of the latter, from motives solely of enmity and without any benefit to himself, turned the stream so that it no longer entered the miller's premises. The miller thereupon sued the neighbor, but abuse of the law not being known in the legal rules in force at that time in Prussia, the judge dismissed the action. The poor miller took an appeal to the Superior Court, but that court affirmed the decision. As this was a matter of life or death for the miller, he went to tell his troubles to the monarch, Frederick II, who on hearing the case and considering the judgment unjust, revoked it by personal mandate and further punished the judges who had rendered it by several months of arrest in a fortress. There is no doubt that the order given by Frederick II had a more just content than the judgment of the courts; and furthermore it is obvious that Frederick II was the legitimate monarch; and nevertheless the order which he issued was arbitrary. Why? Because although Frederick II, as an absolute monarch, had power to abrogate one law and decree another in its place, still what he could not juridically do was to violate an existing law — which he did not abrogate — and apply to a particular case his whim — however just it might be in that concrete case — and still less punish judges who had complied faithfully with the existing Law. Arbitrariness consists, then,

members of the Supreme Court Council (*Senat*) to be removed and imprisoned in the fortress for a year. It is said that this case caused Frederick to order at once the preparation of a new civil code (*Preussische Allgemeine Landrecht*) in which the law of waters was regulated differently. 2 ADOLF STÖLZEL, BRANDENBURG-PREUSSEN'S RECHTSVERWALTUNG UND RECHTSVERFASSUNG 272–281 (Berlin, 1888). 1 RUDOLF STAMMLER, DEUTSCHES RECHTSLEBEN IM ALTEN REICH 412–429 (Charlottenburg, 1928). RUDOLF STAMMLER, DIE LEHRE VON DEM RICHTIGEN RECHTE 212 (Halle (Saale), 1926). English translation of an earlier edition by ISAAC HUSIK, THEORY OF JUSTICE 243 (New York, 1925). I am indebted to Prof. Eberhard F. Bruck, of Harvard University, for the foregoing summary of the Prussian law of the case.

That by the civil law of Europe, both before and in the Code Napoleon (1804), as in the common law, the free flow of water in natural surface streams was secured from undue interruption and the riparian proprietors were protected from undue interference with the flow by obstructions, deflections, or additional burdens, above a reasonable use, see White, C. J., in Cubbins v. Mississippi River Commission (1916), 241 U. S. 351, 36 Supr. Ct. 671, 60 L. Ed. 1041. For the English law, see Miner v. Gilmour (1858), 12 Moore P. C. 131, 14 Eng. Reprint 861, 10 Eng. Rul. Cas. 195. The United States (comprising only the thirteen original eastern seaboard states until 1791), at first applied only the doctrine of riparian rights for ponds in natural streams; III Kent's Commentaries 439, 544. Wood v. Edes (1861), 2 Allen (84 Mass.) 578. Weare v. Chase (1899), 93 Me. 264, 44 Atl. 900. Fisher v. Feige (1902), 137 Cal. 39, 69 Pac. 618, 92 Am. St. Rep. 77, 59 L. R. A. 333. Pierson v. Speyer (1904), 178 N. Y. 270, 70 N. E. 799, 102 Am. St. Rep. 499, 70 A. L. R. 220 (1931). TRANSLATOR.

in the public power, as a mere act of force, going over the current norm or criterion in a particular concrete case, without regard to any rule of a general character, and without creating a new rule of a general character which should annul and replace the former one. The arbitrary mandate is one which is not founded on a general principle — applicable to all analogous cases — but responds to a simple *because,* because it pleases me; in short, to a caprice or whim which does not spring from any general criterion. On the other hand, the juridical mandate is founded on objective norms or criteria in a regular manner, which have validity for all similar cases which occur. It is precisely an essential characteristic of the juridical norm to control necessarily even the very power which enacted it — that is, while such power does not derogate that norm generally, in employment of its power of equal force with that which dictated such norm previously. The juridical power is bound by the current norms; and it operates juridically only so far as it accommodates itself to them and within the powers which they give it. It is then characteristic of the Law to constitute a regular, inviolable, stable order (until it may be derogated) which while it lasts binds equally subject and ruler. On the contrary, the arbitrary mandate consists of acts of force, which are not founded on any general prior criterion, but obey the fortuitous whim of him who exercises the power: it is characterized by putting itself above every norm, making a caprice prevail over it, that is, something not reducible to a fixed criterion.

We may notice that arbitrariness, in reference to these cases of public mandates, has the same meaning as when this word is habitually applied, in daily speech, to other situations: it is said that someone is arbitrary when he does not follow any rule in his work, neither proper, nor erroneous; when we do not know what to expect of him; a thought is called arbitrary when it not only is erroneous but it has no basis; and so, continually, there always lies in the concept of arbitrariness the indication of an absence of rule, the lack of a fixed criterion, capriciousness, whimsicality.

It is important not to confound an arbitrary mandate with a discretional decision, of which there are such abundant examples in the field of the Law. In arbitrariness there is pure caprice, which does not respond to any general rule or principle. On the contrary, the discretional power of many organs of the Law — judges, governors, etc. — is subject to norms as inviolable as the determined fixed rules. What happens is that sometimes the formulated juridical norms — law, regulation, custom, etc. — with regard to the complex variety of factors which intervene in various relations, instead of providing definitely and minutely the solution to be given to each type of case, confides to some authority the task of applying to each situation with its circumstances certain general principles, and in this way obtaining the proper solution. So, in the case of discretional powers, authority has not prescribed its decision by a detailed precept, but as to each solution submitted to its jurisdiction, it must determine the most just and adequate precept; but it must do so, in no way by particular caprice, but by attending to objective directions and criteria, which are the same which must be applied to all analogous cases that present themselves. To operate with discretion does not mean to operate arbitrarily, but to be ruled by general principles, and to apply them to the circumstances of each concrete case, and to deduce the consequences. So it is that in the most perfect juridical systems there has been introduced the *administrative action for excess of power,* that is, appeal against the public Administration for one of its acts which, even though it has not infringed any law or regulation and the Administration has acted in the exercise of its discretional powers, has done it in a way which contradicts the purpose for which such discretional powers were granted.

If indeed in a concrete case it is possible that the content of an arbitrary mandate seems just and proper — and even more just than what would be derived from the existing Law — nevertheless, it must be recognized that arbitrariness, as such, would be the worst evil which society could suffer. Because, even in the case in which the arbitrary mandate is guided by a good intention, it destroys the essential element of juridical life, stability, inviolability of norms, in short, security.

CHAPTER VI

SECURITY AS THE BASIC MOTIVATION OF JURISTICS

In the light of the theme examined in the preceding chapter, the basic motivation of juristics begins to dawn, that is, its primary vital root (why and wherefore men construct Law). It is true that in the Law must be embodied superior values such as that of justice; it is true that the Law ought to be the realization of such values in the social life; it is true that the Law will not be justified except so far as it serves those values; but it is also true that the Law does not arise primarily as a mere exercise of devotion to those values of a superior rank, but from the impulsion of an urgency for security.

If we ask ourselves why and wherefore did men establish Law, and if we try to discover the germinal meaning of the origin of Law, in order to consider its essence, we shall find that the basic motivation which determined the origin of Law is not derived from the high regions of the superior ethical values, but from a value of a lower rank, namely, from the *security* of social life.

Truly, if indeed justice, and the other highest juridical values, represent the axiological criterion which ought to inspire the Law, and if indeed this does not remain justified except so far as it meets the exigencies of such values, nevertheless, Law was not born into human life by reason of the desire to render tribute or homage to the idea of justice, but to fulfill an inescapable urgency for security and certainty in social life. The question of why and wherefore men make Law is not answered in the structure of the idea of justice, nor in the suite of outstanding values which accompany it as presupposed by it, but in a subordinate value — security — corresponding to a human need.

This function of security which is embodied in the law may be explained by way of comparison with the function of security which technique develops in another order of things. Primitive man stands terrified before the spectacle of nature; he witnesses an aggregate of facts in tumultuous succession, whose secret he does not know; and this compels him to live upset, dependent on his environment, constantly on the alert, possessed by panicky fear. And he feels a necessity to dominate nature, to know what to expect with regard to it, and on this impulse he elaborates a technique (properly as such or as magic) to create a margin of comfort or of relative security in the cosmos. But man experiences the affliction of insecurity not only as regards nature, but a similar problem is also presented to him as to other men; and he feels the urgency of knowing what to expect with regard to those others; to know how they will behave to him and what he ought to do with regard to them; and it is necessary to know not only what to expect as to what ought to happen, but also to know that it will necessarily happen; that is, a need of *certainty* as to social relations, but moreover *security* that the rule will be complied with, that it will be powerfully guaranteed. It is necessary to know what will happen to the cattle which he was grazing or the tree which he was cultivating when he is sleeping or absent; what will occur to his companion when he is not at her side; in short, he needs to know what the others may do with respect to him and what he may do with respect to the others; and not only this, but he also needs to have the security that this will be necessarily complied with, guaranteed, defended in an efficient manner. And the Law rises as a given instance of what man has to expect in his relations with the others — *certainty;* but not only theoretical certainty (to know what ought to be done), but also practical certainty, that is, *security:* to know that this necessarily is what has to happen, because it will be imposed by force, inexorably if necessary. The Law is not pure dicta, a mere maxim, but a true norm sure of fulfillment (of inexorable imposition), a norm guaranteed by the maximum social power, by the State whose command cannot be escaped. And it is at the call of such need for security, for unbreakable guaranty, that Law arises. This is its primary motivation, its deepest root in human life.

Now it is clear that men need to do many things as individuals — for which they require guarantees of liberty, comfort, room — and as members of society, for which they need solidarity — assistance. Among these multiple individual and social deeds which men propose to themselves, there are some which are considered by them as more urgent, more necessary, more indispensable; and conduct concerning these is that which they are most interested in establishing as *certain* and *secure* in an effective manner, that is, to make it a content of the Law. The Law is security; but security in what? In that which society of any epoch thinks it important to guarantee fundamentally, considering it necessary for its ends. Hence the content of the Law varies among peoples and in the process of history. But at any moment, whatever may be the content, the Law constitutes a function of security, of certain and efficient order.

The superior values which ought to inspire the Law are referred to those ends which ought to be accomplished by it; and it is clear, as I have already said, that a juridical order will not be justified, will not be just, except so far as it fulfills the values which ought to serve to guide it. But the juristics of the Law are not based on those values, but on the form of their realization by means of it. Or, to put it otherwise, juristics is not an end, but a special means put at the service of the realization of various ends. There are social ends, which in the beginning may be pursued by means foreign to juristics: education, apostleship, propaganda, individual initiative, social organization, etc. Now when a collectivity interests itself in *assuring* in a firmer manner the realization of certain ends, it gathers them into juridical norms, that is, it imposes compliance with them in an inexorable manner, by forcible execution. So, the function of the Law is always security, assurance; the same in a traditional regime as in a revolutionary regime; for, in one case as in the other, it tries to assure the realization of certain tasks, although these are radically different in the one case and the other.

What I have just explained does not imply in any way that I believe in the indifference of purposes. By no means. From the point of view of valuation, of the Juridical Estimation, there must be distinguished bad ends and good ends; and even so not all the good ends can be pursued juridically, since there are many values — for example, pure moral ones — whose realization it is not proper to pursue by Law, nor does it have a meaning which so intends. And so in the Juridical Estimation (that is, in the Theory of juridical valuation, of the ideals of the Law) will be determined the purposes which ought to guide the Law, the criteria for its perfecting and for its progressive reëlaboration; what the supreme values are which ought to be molded into the Law will be made clear; and what may justifiably enter into the content of the Law will be established, and what cannot rightly constitute an object of juridical norms (for example, religious and scientific thought, as to which the Law ought to do nothing except to guarantee their liberty, but in no way to regulate them by way of any limitation; or pure morality, which also in no way can be imposed by Law, etc.). And the Juridical Estimation ought also to determine in what cases and under what conditions certain ends may enter into juridical normation and to what limitations they should be subjected. But all of these problems will concern me in another part of this book. I have brought them together here only to avoid the error of having it thought that the affirmation that the Law is nothing more than a *means* or *form* of realization of very diverse ends may signify that there is indifference with respect to those ends, pure relativity of a skeptical type and disregarding any axiological criteria; but I have shown that it is by no means so, and when I develop the doctrine of the Juridical Estimation it will be seen how all this material is subject to a judgment as to value. Here, what matters at this stage of the argument is not an expression of certain ends, but only the special manner or form of the realization of social ends. Now it is clear that in the light of the Estimation the problem of which are the social ends which may and ought to be pursued juridically cannot be indifferent, since not all social ends can rightly enter into the world of the Law; and, on the other hand, there are some which ought necessarily to be the object of juridical regulation; while with respect to many others according to the circumstances it will or will not be desirable that they should be set forth juridically.

What matters here is, as I have said, to show that there is a series of ends whose accomplishment may be sought by various means, one of which, but not the only one, is juridical regulation. Hence *juristics* does not consist of this or that content, but in the form of imposable and inexorable normation which the most diverse social contents may adopt. So, for example, the social task of aid or assistance to the needy has many times been confided to the free initiative of individual generosity; at other times to pure (unofficial) social aid organizations; but when the collectivity (represented by its supreme organ, the State) has considered it altogether necessary to *assure* the full realization of this end, it has then converted social assistance into a juridical institution, and has subjected it to the norms of inexorable imposition (for the functionaries who are charged with it, and for those who must necessarily make a contribution to it). So also, the function of teaching has been confided in some epochs to private initiative, to free (that is, nonjuridical) social institutions; but when the State has judged that the collectivity needs to be assured in unescapable form of the accomplishment of this task and that it should be performed upon certain bases (for example, on the fundamental principle of liberty of thought, etc.), then it has organized the pedagogic function juridically. So also there have been epochs in which it has been thought that the welfare of the people was a matter which they ought to realize by virtue of individual and spontaneous action of free social beings, but in no way a task of the State; and that nothing more belonged to the State than to guarantee liberty and the just application of it; and hence, in some phrase of liberalism it was said that the government was not to be asked to make its citizens happy (which was their own concern), but only that liberty be just and respected; but on the other hand after the conviction (which indeed existed also in other times) began to be felt in society that to the State there belonged the mission of realizing to the fullest extent possible the common good of its members and that, consequently, it ought to intervene in the regulation of economics and in the realization of a series of welfare aims, because it was necessary to *assure* the accomplishment of such tasks, they then became *juristic,* that is, they came to be set forth in juridical norms. So, also, it may be noted that in former times it was considered necessary for society to *assure forcibly* the religious life (which is a great error and a monstrous aberration, since religion may be founded only on free adherence and sincere conviction) or also a scientific doctrine (which is as great an error as the former, and moreover a stupidity), and so such functions were converted into something juristic, they were subjected to a regulation of precepts and limits by norms of Law; and, on the other hand, when the liberation of conscience — without which there can be no authentic culture — became a human aim, the content of religious conscience and of theoretical thought was taken out of the domain of the State, that is, the domain of juridical regulation; and then what mattered was to assure the liberty of conscience and of thought, and to such end there was imposed inexorably on all, functionaries and private persons, full respect for the inviolability of the person.

I repeat that all these matters, which I have adduced as examples, do not constitute pure historic accidents, which we have to accept without any criticism, as if they were governed by mere relative and fortuitous circumstances. By no means: they are matters upon which there may and should be exercised a judgment of values, as to which there should be formed a critical estimation, which, probably, in some cases will turn out positive, in others negative. The only thing I wish to emphasize here is that juristics is not a concept of end, but the concept of a special *means,* which may be put at the service of very different ends. This has been seen with a true stroke of genius by Kelsen, in declaring that the Law is not a matter of ends, is not a subject which proposes aims for itself, but that its ends are simply human (for liberty, technical, salubrious, economic, pedagogic, etc.); it is men who propose them; and the Law is not an end but a special *means* which society constructs for the accomplishment of such or such ends. The Law does not consist of *what* society proposes but in *how* it proposes to attain some of the ends which it pursues, to wit, in an inexorable impositive fashion, which corresponds to the necessity of *assuring* with full certainty and efficacy the realization of those ends.

And the essence of juristics corresponds to the function of security. If we suppress from the knowledge of what to expect fundamentally in collective relations the knowledge of what may be expected *certainly* and with the *security* that it will actually be so (because to make it so there will be employed all necessary compulsion), there has disappeared the meaning of the Law.

It should be understood clearly that security is the fundamental value of juristics, without which there can be no Law; but it is not the sole nor the supreme value, since there must be in the Law a series of values of superior rank — justice, common utility, etc. Then, although the Law refers to those values, and moreover finds its justification in them (to the degree that it realizes them), it does not contain them within its concept. But, on the other hand, it truly contains in its formal very essence the idea of security. Without security, there is no Law, either good or bad or of any sort. It is true, moreover, that the Law ought to be just, to serve the common good, etc.; if it does not, it will be unjust, it will be unjustified, it will represent a failure. But, on the other hand, if it does not represent an order of security, then it is not Law of any sort. Injustice is opposed to justice; error in certain aims is opposed to common utility; but, on the other hand, the absence of security denies the very essence of juristics.

Security is the basic motive or the reason for being of the Law; but it is not its supreme end. This consists in the realization of values of a superior rank. Indeed security is also a value, but in relation to justice it is an inferior value. Now it is to be remembered that the fulfillment of inferior values conditions the possibility of the realization of superior ones.

So, then, we have found in security the functional meaning of the Law. And this functional meaning is an ingredient of the essence of juristics, of its universal concept.

It is not to be thought that by including in this determination of the essence of juristics its functional purpose we have diminished the universality of the concept. Contemporaneous Philosophy of Law has shown that into the universal concept of juristics there cannot enter any idea of purpose; for it is said that to include an idea of purpose, since whatever may be the ends, they are always specific, suited to a given community or moment, or fitted to a valuing system, it would result that we should not obtain an absolutely universal concept, but only the concept of certain historic orders or of a certain estimative system; and then this concept could not be applied to all the Laws which there have been, are, and will be in the world. But this argument does not affect in any way the doctrine I have explained. Truly, the inclusion of a reference to a concrete end would invalidate the universality of the concept, its assumed essentiality; but here I do not include any idea of a concrete end, but an idea of functional purpose, which is as a whole formal, fully universal. What varies in history and in the various philosophical and political systems is the assured ends, but on the other hand it is a constant character of all Law that its function consists of assuring those conditions or ends which society considers indispensable in realization. Security may be established with respect to the most disparate contents, as the history of Law shows us; but wherever there is Law we recognize it as constituting an assuring function that certain conduct, independent of any hostile will it may meet, will be imposed and realized, and that contrary behaviors will be effectively made impossible.

CHAPTER VII

LEGAL RIGHT IN THE SUBJECTIVE SENSE

1. Use of the Word Legal Right in a Subjective Sense

The word Law ("Derecho") is employed in popular usage as well as in juridical doctrine with two distinct meanings: to designate the juridical norm which is the meaning in which up to now we have employed the word; and also to express the faculty which a person has to determine normatively and forcibly the conduct of another, which is the meaning which it presents in the phrase "to have a legal right to —." Naturally it is a question always of the faculty to require of *another* certain conduct; since even if sometimes we say "I have a legal right to do such a thing," from which it appears that we refer the faculty to our own behavior, what is really expressed in such proposition is that "I have a legal right to demand from another or others that they should not prevent or disturb this certain activity of mine."

But this which is called *having a legal right to,* or, what is the same thing, the word *legal right in a subjective sense,* as an attribution of faculties to a person, presents three typical features. Let us examine them in the light of some examples taken from habitual expressions. When I say "I have a right to walk on the street," that is, I have the right of free locomotion, and so also when I say "I have the right to preserve my own property," I express the sphere of free activity which a person has by virtue of the juridical duty which lies upon others to behave in such manner that they do not injure the free field of my conduct. In those cases, my subjective right is the transfer to my life of the consequences of certain juridical duties which lie upon other persons; it constitutes what has been called the material reflection of the juridical duties of other persons. On the other hand, the expression "to have a right to collect a debt, to receive a salary, that there should be returned to me a thing which I have deposited," means that there is attributed to the person the faculty of requiring of another person certain conduct, being able to accomplish it to put in motion the whole apparatus of coercitive imposition of the Law. It is a matter, in this type of case, of the person being possessed of a *pretension* over certain conduct of another, which may be demanded imperatively, putting in motion the coercitive mechanism of the Law. But we may discover still a third meaning of the phrase "to have a legal right to — " when we speak of having a "right to contract marriage, to make a will, to sell my property," which in the foregoing examples means a power to create, modify, or extinguish certain juridical relations. There are, then, three different types of situations which are usually designated by the name of "subjective right": (a) one's own conduct, juridically authorized and protected, which is determined by the duty which others have not to do any act which may disturb that conduct or make it impossible; (b) power to demand certain conduct of another; (c) juridical power of creation, modification, or extinction of juridical relations.

In spite, however, of these three meanings of the expression "subjective right" we shall see how these three forms have a common denominator which justifies the use of that name for all three.

2. The Essence of the Subjective Right

Let us try then to ascertain the essential concept of the "subjective legal right."

First of all, we must note that there is to be avoided an error, which the traditional terminology tends to suggest. Whether we speak of "subjective legal right" or of "legal right in a subjective sense," it may seem at first sight that the opposing extreme and correlative of this will be Law in an objective sense (norm); but it is not so by any means. The subjective legal right is opposed, or, better, refers correlatively, to obligations or duties. The Law in an objective sense, that is, as a norm, in projecting itself on concrete situations, determines subjective legal rights and juridical duties, in correlation. The subjective legal right is opposed correlatively to or agrees with the juridical duty; and the two are derived from the norm as an inseparable pair.

The subjective legal right is not a real thing but an entity belonging to the world of juristics; consequently, of an ideal nature; that is, it constitutes an originating character of the norm. The subjective legal right is not a phenomenon of the will, because juristics is not of a psychic nature, as I have already explained; and, for fuller proof, it is evident also that it is not a phenomenon of the will, because we see that subjective legal rights are attributed to persons who actually lack an effective will (children, the insane, associations); because also subjective legal rights are given without any real support of the will, either of the owner or of any representative (when for example the Public Minister proceeds *ex officio* in defense of my rights, of which perhaps I did not think); and because subjective legal rights are sometimes given even against the will of the owner (for example, irrenounceable rights, such as the indemnity for work accidents).

Nor can the subjective legal right be defined as an interest juridically protected, because the essence of the subjective legal right does not consist in the reality of interest but in the special juridical protection. And, in short, to speak of the interest is no different from speaking of the will, since one only exercises that on a thing in which one has some interest; and, on the other hand, one exercises it on whatever subjectively inspires a preferential interest.

And if it is not correct to define subjective legal right either as a phenomenon of the will, nor as a reality of interest, it is clear that neither is it permissible to define it as both those things at once, since thereby one would combine the errors of both those mistaken characterizations.

To obtain with all strictness the essential notion of the subjective legal right, it is not necessary to recur to elements foreign to the concept of *juristics,* but it is sufficient to regard this in a special perspective. The juridical norm (of inexorable imposition) regulates or coördinates social activities from an objective point of view, so that it concedes to certain conduct of a person (the owner of the legal right) the normative capacity to determine in another person (the obligated one), or, in several, a certain positive or negative behavior. Or put otherwise: the situation or conduct of the owner of the subjective legal right constitutes according to the norm the determining supposition of a duty in one or more persons. So then, in general, to have a subjective legal right is to say that the norm binds to a situation or conduct of one person the duty of a certain type of behavior by another person. It results, then, that a subjective legal right — in its most general and fullest meaning — is the quality, which the norm attributes to certain situations of some persons, consisting of the possibility of determining juridically (by inexorable imposition) the duty of a special conduct in one or more other persons. As I have already noted, it is not a question of a real phenomenological quality but a projection of the juridical precept, of a normative qualification, which is derived from it with respect to a certain real situation. This qualification consists in attributing normatively to a certain situation of one person a correlative conduct in one or more other persons. Among the elements of this situation foreseen in the norm, as conditions of the subjective legal right, may be — and many times is — a declaration of the will of the person; in which case it will be necessary that such declaration be produced to make real the subjective legal right. But, on the other hand, at other times the norm attributes subjective legal rights without requiring any declaration of will as a necessary element of the situation which conditions or bases them.

The norm may condition on a declaration of will the actualization — but not the attribution — of a subjective legal right, as for example in the case of a civil debt, for which an executory demand can operate only as the result of a claim by the creditor. But, on the other hand, subjective legal rights correlative to the juridical duties whose fulfillment is imposed *ex officio,* that is, by the same juridical order without any complaint being necessary (as occurs with respect to obligations to respect the life of another, others' property, guaranteed by penal precepts), are not conditioned, either in their existence or in their realization, by any declaration on the part of the owner. Now it happens that in positive statutes these grounds are wont to be combined, at times, forming jointly and in parallel the figure of public action exercised by the representative of the law and private action exercised by the owner of the subjective legal right, threatened or injured.

Sometimes the situation or conduct of the owner of the subjective legal right is a determining element in the creation of juridical duties (in other persons), which cannot be realized or complied with immediately but only later; which is what happens in the cases of juridical power to create, modify, or extinguish juridical relations.

With all that has been said there has been explained the essential notion of subjective legal right which is common to all the manifestations of it, since, as I have shown, in all of them — in spite of their diversities — we find a common element, which is this: by virtue of the norm, the situation or conduct of a person (the owner of the subjective legal right) is the determining presupposition of the existence or the realization of juridical duties in other persons.

3. The Three Forms of Subjective Legal Right

Even though at the beginning of this chapter I mentioned the three typical features of subjective legal rights, now when we know their essence, it will be desirable to examine more closely these typical features, which moreover are susceptible of being combined to present mixed figures.

(1) *Subjective legal right as the mere material reflection of a juridical duty to others imposed by the norm independently of the will of the owner of the right.* This feature, of which the so-called rights to life, liberty, to enjoy private property, etc., may be used as examples, consists of the margin of free and reputable conduct which a person has by virtue of the duty which others have to abstain from all behavior which shall disturb or make impossible such sphere of action in the first person. Strictly, it ought not to be said that he has the right to do this or the other (to be quiet or to walk about, to choose this occupation or another, to think in this manner or that) but that he has the right to act freely, without being prevented or molested by others, within the limits the norm indicates. For the realization of these rights there is not necessary any special declaration of will on the part of the owner, because they are actively protected and guaranteed by the norm itself, through the action of the representative of the law, that is, the public ministry; since all attacks against such rights (penally sanctioned) are prosecuted, repressed, and penalized *ex officio,* without the necessity of a complaint by any party; and, in every case, even if the interested party does not wish to make any claim, and even if he wishes that the wrongs should not be penalized (for example, attacks upon physical integrity and against property are repressed and in proper case punished even if the victim forgives the aggressor). If the prosecution against the attack depends on the will of the victim, then the subjective legal right does not belong to this first aspect, but to the following one.

(2) *Subjective legal right as a pretension.* This consists in the situation that a person in a juridical relation occupies by virtue of the norm in having at his disposal the power to demand of another person compliance with a juridical duty, making use of the coercitive apparatus of

the Law. A person is owner of a subjective legal right as a pretension when the last step of the realization of a juridical duty by another person is at the former's disposition; that is, when it depends on his will to impose the juridical coaction of the State, or not to do it. The juridical norm with respect to certain situations determines a duty for some person, but it puts the necessary execution of this duty at the disposition of another person (whom such duty benefits), who is therefore the one who appears as owner of the subjective legal right (as a pretension). For example: the civil norm as to a loan contract provides that when anyone has received a sum on loan he must return it within the agreed time, and that if he does not do so, then *if the lender presents a demand* to the competent court, he may proceed executorily against the borrower; that is, his goods will be attached and sold to meet the payment. Here is given a "subjective legal right" (as a pretension) to the lender, because there is made to depend upon his will the coercitive imposition against the borrower. If the borrower does not return the amount due and the lender does not claim it by means of the coercitive apparatus of the Law (that is, judicially), the organ of the juridical order cannot proceed spontaneously against the delinquent debtor. Notice that it is not the attribution of the subjective legal right which conditions the pretension of the effective fact of the will of the owner, but the subjective legal right is considered as a pretension, because it leaves to the creditor the possibility that he may freely exercise (or not exercise), at his free will, the power of asking fulfillment of the duty through the means of coaction, that is, by way of forced execution. So, then, to have a subjective legal right (as a pretension) to the return of a loan is to say that one has the power, in case payment is not made, to start a proceeding of coercitive imposition against the debtor.

The juridical precepts which establish the duty of the State to maintain administrative activity will give rise to subjective legal rights in other persons only when there is placed at the disposition of such persons the power to require forced compliance. For example, if a juridical precept requires certain officials to take the necessary steps to build schools, without more it does not give any right to citizens to claim compliance with this duty coercitively. There is truly a juridical duty upon the officials, whose fulfillment may be demanded or required by their hierarchical superiors in the Administration, but there is no subjective legal right (as a pretension) on the part of the citizens. On the other hand, this subjective legal right will exist (as a pretension), if the norm makes the construction of the schools depend on an act of the citizens as, for example, on a petition of the inhabitants of the town benefited by the provision.

(3) *Subjective legal right as a power of juridical formation.* This consists in the power which the norm attributes to a person to determine the creation, modification, or extinction of certain juridical relations. In this meaning, it is said: the proprietor of a thing has the right to give, sell, encumber it; the creditor has the right to transfer his credit to any other person; persons of full age or legally emancipated have legally the right to make all lawful contracts; at a given age and on certain fixed conditions one has the right to contract marriage, to execute a will, etc. In all these cases, the expression "subjective legal right" is taken in the sense of juridical power; that is, that the activity of the owner is the decisive determinant for the creation of rights of the kinds I have just defined, or for the modification or extinction of those already in existence. In such cases, the acts of the owner are an element productive of the concrete juridical precepts; that is, of the individualized precepts which will govern the relation in question, which will determine the particular duties of the passive persons, to which duties will correspond certain subjective legal rights (of the other two types previously studied).

4. Priority between Objective Law and Subjective Legal Right

It is clear that the subjective legal right is always a consequence of what is established in the juridical norm (called Law in the objective sense). We might represent the attribution of a subjective legal right to a person as the conclusion of a syllogism, whose major premise is the norm and whose minor premise is proof that there is a situation in fact whose subject unites the conditions established by the norm. This is somewhat evident in juridical logic.

Now if, instead of studying the logical relation between the norm and the subjective legal right — a relation which consists, as we have demonstrated, in that the latter represents a consequence of the former — we consider the chronological order in which such ideas have firmly appeared in human consciousness, we shall have to make a different observation. This consists in that then we shall have to note that, ordinarily, man thinks first of juristics as his own subjective rights; and that only later, by mental operations of reflection, does he think about the norm. And there is nothing strange in the happening thus, for the order of logical connection of ideas does not usually coincide with the order of their appearance in consciousness; and so, frequently, the first principles in the logical structure are the last with which the human understanding deals. The logical *a priori* constitutes at least a psychological *a posteriori*. And so it has happened many times with the two meanings of the word law: although the apriority, the primacy, logically belongs to the idea of Law as a norm, nevertheless, consciousness has ordinarily thought first of law as a power, that is, in the subjective meaning. On many occasions the idea of the law in the sense of power, of subjective legal right, arises as a spiritual emotional reaction regretful of an unjust attack. And this especially in the whole political process of the formation of the Law, from the point of view of the Law it is desired to establish (from which it is called the problem *de jure condendo*). And from the fact that man feels himself rightfully the owner of certain powers, he deduces later the ideal norm on which they are founded. Also there may be noted some analogy with respect to positive or enacted Law with those persons who are not experts in juridical matters, who, in the face of an attack upon them, react with a sense of injury and suspect the existence of some subjective legal right in their favor, which they find afterwards confirmed on reference to the existing norm.

CHAPTER VIII

THE JURIDICAL DUTY

1. Distinction between the Juridical Duty and Moral and Other Similar Duties; and the Difference between the Juridical Duty and the Moral Duty of Complying with the Law

Norms determine the conduct which a person *ought* to put into practice, that is, they create duties. This is common to all norms; and, consequently, also to juridical ones. Now, to the particular essence of each one of the types of norms (moral, of social behavior, juridical) there corresponds a special kind of duty to which it gives rise. Here we are interested to discover what is the characteristic essence of the juridical duty as such; that is, as something determined by the norm of Law.

Consequently, we shall have to consider the juridical duty, strictly as juridical, as something based exclusively on the juridical norm. We have especially to emphasize this, because otherwise we run the risk of two serious mistakes which, for more than two millennia, have proved fatal for the Theory of the Law and given rise to grave errors and muddlement. On the one side, we have to separate the juridical duty so far as it is strictly juridical, from those other possible duties of similar content, which derive from moral norms or from norms of social behavior; for example, a debtor has the juridical duty to discharge his debt to the creditor (by virtue of the norm of Law); but moreover he also has, probably, the moral duty to pay; and it is possible that certain social usages also oblige him to it. However, it must be clear that although the moral duty to pay seems like the juridical duty, nevertheless these duties deal with separate things. The juridical duty exists only and exclusively because there is a norm of current positive Law, which so provides; and the only thing this norm requires is the objective and exterior fact of payment, without demanding any special internal state of mind towards the creditor. On the other hand, the moral norm will also require payment, but founded on other values; for example, in that one ought not to let himself be prompted by avarice and egotism, that he ought not to permit an unlawful passion to dominate his conscience, that he ought to profess love of his neighbor; and, on account of all this, it demands not only external payment but a sympathetic feeling with the creditor. And the usage of social behavior, which also prescribes the duty of payment, is founded on other grounds; to wit, on ideas of decorum, of mutual consideration. In this example, there are three similar duties superposed: the juridical, the moral, and the social; but we may separate each one of them and consider it as independent of the others. The juridical duty is based purely and exclusively on the existing norm; and so, for example, it happens that in the case of a pact null or nonexistent for lack of having been executed with the legal formalities (for example, a notarial instrument, which is prescribed for certain matters) we have to say that it does not give rise to any juridical duty to comply with it; and, on the other hand, morally, it is very probable that we might have to recognize that duties have arisen; and, possibly, also according to the current social norms of decorum. The player in games of chance does not have a juridical duty to pay, according to the majority of civil codes; probably neither does he have the moral duty to do so; but on the other hand, according to the norms of social behavior, he will have the duty of decorum to meet his debt within the space of twenty-four hours. Consequently, it is necessary to have clearly in mind that each type of norm determines a special corresponding type of duty, which it is necessary to distinguish with all neatness; so much the more because it often occurs that one simple situation is regulated by various norms (moral, social, juridical) and sometimes the several duties of each one of them are similar in appearance. And what matters here is to clarify the concept of juridical duty, isolated and independent of all the others which may occur with it.

On the other hand, it is also necessary to distinguish between the specifically juridical duty, created by the juridical norm, and the moral duty of complying with what the norms of the existing Law command. They are distinct duties although they appear superposed and as coincident. The juridical duty is founded solely and exclusively on the existence of a norm of positive Law which imposes it; it is an entity belonging strictly to the world of juristics. Apart from this, men have the moral obligation (and also the obligation of decorum) to comply with what the norms of positive Law ordain; but this is a moral duty, whose content is specified in Law, and is not the specific juridical duty created by the juridical norm. The moral duty to comply with what is ordained in the juridical norms has those norms as content, but is not founded on them, but is based on moral values. On the other hand, the juridical duty properly as such is a situation which rests on the juridical norm and proceeds from it; apart from which, moreover, for moral reasons, there is the moral duty to adjust one's conduct to that prescribed by Law. If every norm determines duties, and if we have recognized that juridical norms exist with a particular outline and a peculiar essence, distinct from moral norms and from rules of social behavior, it is evident that there will also be juridical duties perfectly distinguishable from the other types of duties.

The moral duty to accommodate one's conduct to existing juridical precepts raises the question of what is the fundamental ethics of this obligation to submit oneself to Law; and, indeed, this problem implies that of the justification of what Law is, that is, the rejection of anarchistic doctrines. But the theme which we are studying here is not this; it is not the justification of Law, the reason why its norms also compel morally; but the question now raised is that concerning the formal concept of juridical duty, within a systematization of pure juridical ideas.

2. The Essence of Juridical Duty

From what has been said, when we formulate the question of what may be the essence of juridical duty, we necessarily have to seek the solution within the same concept of juridical norms, leaving aside the circumstance that the contents of juridical duty may concur with and be like the contents of moral and social duties; and, on the other hand, leaving aside also the question of what may be the reason by which the Law also compels morally. It is not a question, in any way, of denying these two problems, now left aside, nor of denying them importance; I especially recognize the seriousness and the extent of these themes. What is done is only to distinguish and separate them from the problem we have now put, namely, that of the pure concept of juridical duty, as something which is founded on the norm of law and exists by virtue of it.

For the moment, and to affirm still more the autonomy of the juridical duty, it is to be remembered that it is an essential postulate of all Law that ignorance of the norm does not relieve from compliance with it; and, on the contrary, there cannot exist any single actual moral duty for any person if he does not know the norm and moreover is convinced of its rightness, because although the moral values have objectivity they do not create a present obligation on the conscience except so far as they are known and recognized as such.

Kelsen has skillfully noted [32] that a concrete juridical duty may be spoken of as something annexed to the juridical precept, as something springing from it, in so far as and because it is capable of subjectivation, that is, is capable of being applied to a certain individual. The objective precept existing for all is converted into a subjective legal duty for a given person, because and so far as it ordains the imposition of a sanction upon the person who behaves in the manner which is prescribed in the norm as a condition of such coactive acts; that is, which imposes a sanction on him who behaves in a manner contrary to that prescribed in the norm. Or, to put it otherwise: that anyone has a juridical duty to behave in a certain way means that he is situated with respect to the norm in such a way that, if he does not conduct himself in this manner, he may be the object of an act of impositive coaction of an inexorable character.

Where it is not possible, by reason of what comes from the norm, to impose an inexorable coaction on the person, it is evident that there is no juridical duty. There may be a moral duty or a social or religious duty to behave in a certain manner; but there is no juridical duty.

3. Reference to Other Problems

I repeat that here I treat solely of the concept of juridical duty in the strict sense, and not of anything else. Among other questions, apart from that which I have just examined here, might be raised the following, which properly belongs to moral philosophy, but which also interests the philosophy of Law: In what manner is one morally obliged to comply with positive Law? This question implies the following: the theme as to what are the values which ground the moral duty to comply with positive Law; and again the theme as to what is the type of adherence which Ethics claims of the Law (the kind and extent of such adherence, its limits and its lawful exceptions). As to this last perhaps one would reach the conclusion that the ethical duty of complying with positive Law has a structure different from that of other moral duties; since the moral duty of complying with the Law does not require any intimate adherence of the person to the contents of the norm, but the mere relation of submitting to the Law and of formal compliance with its provisions, so far

[32] Cf. Kelsen, Hauptprobleme der Staatsrechtslehre (2d ed., 1923) 311ff.; Reine Rechtslehre (1934), para. 23.

as they are merely juridical; and there is required only intimate adherence to the moral value which grounds this duty of submission to the Law.

CHAPTER IX

THE PERSON AND PERSONALITY

1. Preliminary

Properly the concept of person has its base in the juridical field. But it happens that later this word, used to designate the subject of juridical relations, has been used metaphorically in various other meanings in Ethics, in Metaphysics, and also in Sociology. Now it is necessary to make it clear that the concept of person employed in Philosophy to express the peculiar reality of man (and even other spiritual beings) differs very greatly from the meaning of person in the juridical sense. As to the concept of person in sociology, although it differs from the juridical, it is closely related to it; indeed we shall see that it comes to be represented as an embryonic or attenuated form with a meaning analogous to the juridical; or, better, the juridical personality (of individuals and groups) constitutes the maximum development and culmination of the social form of personality.

But before all it is necessary to call attention to the totally diverse meaning which the word person has as it is employed in Philosophy to designate the peculiar form of existence of man and as used in Law where it signifies not the authentic human reality but an abstract and generic category. We are going to treat first the concept of person as a human being; and afterwards I shall consider the meaning of what is called person in social life and the meaning which it has in Law.

2. The Authentic Individual

Here again we find ourselves in the necessity of contemplating human life, of which I have spoken at length in Chapter I of this book; because one of the two essential ingredients which in inseparable union constitute human life is the person. The world and I, I and the world, in copresence, in essential correlation, in constant intercourse, are the elements which constitute my life. Now let us try to penetrate a little deeper the theme of whom I am, that is, of who is the subject of human life.

At the height of the present philosophic thinking of transcendental humanism (Metaphysics of life, existential Philosophy) there has appeared a clear vision of the peculiar nature of the human person, by its position in that reality which is called life. To attain better comprehension of this thinking, it will be convenient to compare it with the philosophical tradition of other times: because, thanks to this contrast, there will appear in greater relief the extent of the great progress which has been made today in this theme.

In the ancient philosophy above all, and in the medieval, the concept of person was employed to designate the rational being as a conscious individual, with a view to applying it fundamentally to man, although it was used also with reference to God and the angels. Person was defined as "an indivisible substance of a rational nature"[33] or as "that which is one by itself"[34] or as "the individual of a rational nature."[35] And even in the first period of modern Philosophy there were those who defined the person as a reflecting and self-conscious rational being.[36] Now it is to be noted that these definitions try to explain the person — so far as it is the true human being — as a *thing,* which differs from other things by virtue of there concurring in it certain special characteristics (indivisibility, rationality, will, etc.); but finally a *thing,* one of many beings in the world, distinct from the rest by some peculiar dimensions: it would be a substance (so far like other substances) but indivisible, with rationality and with will. That is, a person is inserted on the plane of classic Ontology, as a being among other beings, which if indeed it has some separate qualities which distinguish it from other beings, has also some dimensions in common with them.

On the other hand, with Kant arose the idea that it is not possible to define a person if we do not place ourselves on the plane of Ethics; that is, that the person is not to be understood by examination of his being, but only when we perceive that it enfolds an ethical idea. And so he says that personality is "liberty in independence of the mechanism of all nature,"[37] that rational beings are called persons so far as they constitute an end in themselves, a self goal, that is, something which ought not to be employed as a mere means, something which consequently (by virtue of this ethical idea) includes will; and the person is a being entirely different from things, different by its rank and its dignity.[38] Now it is to be noted that the ideas of rank and dignity represent something

[33] BOECIO, DE DUAB. NATURIS ET UNA PERSONA CHRISTI, chap. 3. Cf. GELLIUS, NOCT. att., v. 7.

[34] According to San Isidro, cited by Alberto Magno, in Sum. Th. 1, 44, 1.

[35] St. Thomas Aquinas, Sum. Th. 1, 29, 3 ad 2. Cf. also FRANCISCO SUÁREZ, MET. DISP. 34S. 1.

[36] For example, LOCKE, ESSAY CONCERNING HUMAN UNDERSTANDING, II, chap. 27, para. 9.

[37] KANT, CRITIQUE OF PRACTICAL REASON.

[38] KANT, ANTHROPOLOGIE 1.

entirely new with respect to other things; they represent not only some special characteristics, but something which is on a plane alien to things, something which is not derived from a special mode of being, but which depends on an ethical consideration. That is, the person is defined with regard not only to the special dimension of a being (for example, rationality, indivisibility, etc.), but by discovering in it the projection of another world distinct from that of reality, to wit, the world of moral law; and emphasizing that a person is that being which has a particular end to accomplish and who must accomplish it by his own determination: that being which has its purpose in itself, and who, precisely on that account, possesses *dignity,* different from all other beings, from things which have their purpose outside themselves, which serve as mere means for alien ends, and which, so far, have a *price.* And this is so because the person is the subject of the autonomous moral law: and so far the person is the only thing which does not have a solely relative value or a price (which is the nature of all things) but which has a value in itself (dignity) and constitutes a self-goal. As a natural being, man is inserted in the mechanism of nature; but as a rational being he is situated above that mechanism, is superior to it, because he opposes the law of ought-to-be to all the laws of natural necessity.

But where this theme took a great step forward was in Fichte. His thought as to the person displays such genius that we may well consider it a substantial anticipation of the ideas of our time, and it still preserves full reality. According to Fichte, the essence of personality consists in a free being who proposes ends for himself: "I am not a being already made, but I am one who makes myself; I am a duty facing my task; I am individualized action." "My being is to seek myself, it is my liberty; alone in my moral determination, I am given to myself as determined." "We are in truth nothing else than the vital movement of a subject will, and now and again freed from subjection making objective that liberty which duty expresses." We are finite as essences which act, and nevertheless infinite at the same time; we are limited as individuals, expressing the subjection of the body and of nature; but at the same time we rise above those limits, soaring freely in election and then in the absolute act of concentration, in the determination which establishes ends and which again binds us to realities.[39]

In the Philosophy of our century, the definition of man as a person has rested predominantly on this ethical meaning; that is, emphasizing that the concept of person denotes that man is the subject of a moral world, or, put more exactly, of a world of values. So, in very different schools,

[39] FICHTE, DAS SYSTEM DER SITTENLEHRE; GRUNDLAGE DES NATURRECHTS; DIE BESTIMMUNG DES MENSCHEN; DAS WESEN DES GELEHRTEN; DIE STAATSLEHRE.

but in a special manner in the philosophy of values, according to Max Scheler and Nicolai Hartmann.

Scheler has clearly accentuated the basic and irreducible individuality of the person. He denies that being a person denotes being a subject of rational acts, since that represents but a word juggling which leads to forgetting that the person is a concrete and singular individuality. A person "is a real concrete unity of itself, with acts of various essence or nature." That is, a person is not a mere logical subject of rational acts, nor of acts of will; but a person is the reality in which are realized all those acts phenomenologically diverse. The person is not a pure empty point of departure for acts, is not a sort of mere connection or link for them, but is a concrete being, without which we could not find anything more than abstract essences of phenomena, but not the fully adequate essence of an act. Scheler emphasizes that the person is something concretely individual, in each one of whose acts is seen something his own, peculiar and characteristic. The correlative of a person is his world; to each individual person there corresponds his individual world. (Note that this idea of Scheler is similar to that developed by the Metaphysics of life, as I explained.) Everything is the concrete world, and the world of one person only. Objects considered apart have only an abstract objectivity; they are converted into fully concrete things, so far as they are parts of a world, of the world of a person. A person is the only thing which never is a part, but which is always the correlative of a world, of its world; of the world in which it lives for itself. The aggregate of the worlds of all the different individual persons would constitute *the world.* But the world which should comprise all the individual worlds in that abstract and general sense *is not given to us,* but we refer to it only by way of mention, as an abstract construction, but not as given.

As a commentary[40] on and derivation from that thought of Scheler, it occurs to me to present a series of considerations which make clear that correlation between the person and his world. Our world of the west in the second third of the twentieth century is very different from the world of the Greeks. In the world of the Greeks, for example, there were no electricity, no microbes, no vitamins. I do not say that in reality in that time there were not actually those things; but even if there had been, they would not have belonged to the world of the Greeks, because they did not know them. The world of the Greeks was limited; on the contrary the modern world, since Descartes, and since the new Physics and the new Mathematics presents itself as unlimited. Let us consider some examples all relating to the present epoch. The worlds of the

[40] This paragraph is from the Second Spanish edition of the book (Mexico, 1945). TRANSLATOR.

banker, of the lawyer, of the philosopher, of the football player, etc., are different. In the world of the banker, there figure in first place the prices and operations of the exchange, which if they exist in the world of other persons — which does not always happen — will occupy a much more remote and vague place. In the world of the scientist and in that of the philosopher there appear in first place the theoretical intellectual disciplines and perchance there do not figure even remotely the things which constitute the greatest concern for the merchant. For the lawyer, the world puts in the first position the juridical dispositions which he has to manipulate in the practice of his profession; while many of those norms form no part of the world of the football devotee or the musician. For the football fan, in his world he singles out with great importance the life of the players, of the teams, of the sides; and, on the other hand, all that has no existence in the world of one who has no inclination for that sport. All the examples which I have indicated refer to generic differences among the different worlds of the different epochs, of distinct professions, of various preferences; and to those differences there could be added many other analogous ones, founded on belonging to a certain social class, on the grade and type of education one has, etc. But within each group there are also individual differences, perhaps in many cases of minor weight, but always existing. Each person has his own world. It is true that the different worlds of the various persons have many common elements, but they never constitute identical frames, but each one of them will constitute a singular combination and perspective.

From another point of view Scheler emphasizes also the concrete individual dimension of the human person. A person constitutes an individual measure or instance of value, which ought not in any way to be interpreted as subjectiveness in the estimation, but in a very different sense, to wit: without impairment of the ideal dimension of values (of their objective entity in themselves, of their *apriority*) Scheler says, they are related in their "duty to be realized" to the individual concrete person; that is, the individual person, or better, each concrete individual person, precisely by his concrete reality and situation, is called to the fulfillment of certain values, whose grouping constitutes his "personal safety or salvation," his individual or singular ideal destiny. In the same ideal content of values is implied reference to a given situation. In this sense, it ought to be declared that each person constitutes a single ethical ideal; that to each person there corresponds an ideal projection of himself; the complex of values to whose realization he is particularly "called"; summarized by virtue of his concrete personal being. The value in itself does not cease to be *in itself* because the duty of realizing it is referred concretely to a person in a particular situation; because that value in itself has in its own essence a kind of vocational direction. It is a matter of evident knowledge of some good in itself, but at the same time good in it for me; in which there is no contradiction, since it is not that its worth depends on me, but that it is good in itself and only refers to me and perhaps not to others. It is good in itself, because its worth does not depend on me; but at the same time it is good in itself "for me," because in its content of good in itself there is an indication which I experience as directed to me; there is the existence of a sort of calling which rising from the valuable content signals to me, which cries or whispers as if to say "for you." And by virtue of this correlation between my person and the values of its calling, there is a place left indicated for me in the moral cosmos; and the duty of certain acts bears upon me, the fulfillment of a destiny which represents me as saying to myself "I am for you" and "you are for me." So, then, it happens that the criterion to define personality is not, as Kant supposed, the dimension of being the subject of a universal abstract ought-to-be, but constituting precisely an individual instance of values, the person itself being a concrete structure of value. It is clear that there are also general values, that is, values from which are derived duties for all men; and those general values represent a minimum of conduct without the realization of which no person can attain the fulfillment of his ideal destiny. But those general values do not include all the duties whose realization implies the fulfillment of the destiny of the individual person; they do not include all the values, by means of which is attained the full moral value of the person; they do not contain a response to the "exigency of each hour." [41]

Nikolai Hartmann, in a certain aspect continuer of the ethical thought of Scheler[42] with new original points of view, has offered a study upon personality which is very suggestive and which has certain attainments, though I think that it ought to be improved by integrating this theme into the philosophy of life. But, even considering that this theory of Hartmann requires some complementary points of view in the way indicated, I think that there is in it much of positive value. According to Hartmann, personality in man constitutes the point of insertion of the ought-to-be in the world of reality. (I understand that one ought to begin by emphasizing that life is made up of a "chore," a "task," from which, as I have explained, follows its estimative structure.) Values are essential ideals: from them spring the exigencies of "ought-to-be," that is, "normative pretensions." This "ought-to-be," those normative pre-

[41] Cf. MAX SCHELER, DER FORMALISMUS IN DER ETHIK (2d ed., 1921) 384ff., 397ff., 629ff.

[42] Cf. NIKOLAI HARTMANN, ETHIK (1926) 159ff.

tensions, proceed from the ideal sphere of value, but they transcend it, knocking so to speak at the doors of reality and succeeding in entering it, in greater or less degree. Now for the ought-to-be of the values, which springs from an ideal dimension, to be converted into a real acting factor, and to make itself felt in the world of reality, that is, to be inserted in the blind happening of phenomena, it has to have in reality some point at which it can penetrate the scale of values; it has to have an Archimedes' lever, from which and thanks to which ideal power may be capable of moving the world of reality, converting itself into a real acting factor. In short, there has to be a real being, capable of acting as an effective factor in reality, sharing in its conditions, but who may have the power of producing movements of its own and of being inspired to so doing by the ideal world. This instance, capable of transforming the ideal ought-to-be into a real factor acting on the events of the world, is man. Man is something real, he is part of nature, he participates thereby in the natural laws of reality; but, at the same time, he is different from all the other real beings, for he has a connection or contact with the realm of values, is in communication with them. Man as a moral subject is the administrator of normativity in the world of real being; but it is not fatally necessary that he should have to be a faithful administrator; he may be a traitor to the values, since it is in his hands to decide whether or not they are to be realized. Here is then the weakness of the bond of the insertion of values in reality; because the mediating agency through which the fulfillment has to operate is free to follow them or not. Now this weakness of the ideal principle is precisely what constitutes the grandeur of man, his qualitative greatness, his situation of power in the world. In this sense man is the constructor, reformer, and shaper of being; he acts as a kind of creator *in parvo*. What man forms and produces transcends the reality of nature which there may be in man; he is something which hears the voice of the other world, of the ideal world, for which he has a special organ of perception. But what man perceives of that ideal world does not imply for him an irresistible coaction, but is a good which is entrusted to him, from which springs an ideal exigency but not a necessity. The human person is the point of intersection or the crossing of two heterogenous dimensions and — so to speak — the scene of their collision. Hence it is that the being of man consists in a never resting, in a constant having to take decisions. (Here Hartmann suggests what afterwards the Metaphysics of life of Ortega y Gasset puts in clear relief.) The ideal ought-to-be, proceeding from the world of the ideal penetrates the person, flows through it and issues from it in the form of real action; and in traversing the person in this way lends it a special dignity, a dignity which is not only an accent of value, but which constitutes a *categorical novum*, something radically new, to wit, *personality*.

The person, according to Nikolai Hartmann, is constituted of two ethical dimensions, and both refer to the relation of the person to values. One of the dimensions consists of the following: values do not compel the person fatally; when they have been perceived by him, they implant in him a pretension, but they do not force him inexorably; above all, they leave him a freedom to decide for himself. This power to put himself or not at the service of the values, equalizes the person, in a certain way, with the great metaphysical powers of being, as well the ideal as the real; raises him to an autonomous factor, to a means joined with the other means represented by the other powers of creation. In this sense it is said that the person is *free*. The other dimension of the person, consists, according to Hartmann, in the accents of value which he receives in his acts; that is, the person — his intentions, his purposes, his acts — constitutes the only support or ground for strictly ethical values. The strictly moral values do not aim or direct themselves to objective results, to works in their real consistency — as occurs with other values, such as the aesthetic, the utilitarian — but they aspire to dwell in the acting subject himself. The person is the intersection of the ideal world of values with the world of reality, as a free means and moreover as possessor of the ethical.

This theory of Hartmann, which I have just summarized briefly, contains much of merit. But, as I have indicated, I understand that it cannot constitute a final word, because it would be necessary for it to be inserted in a philosophy of life, such and as I explained in Chapter I; and then it would be seen that reality, as well as values, are ingredients of my life, components of my existence, since all that *is*, is in life; that is, that being, in all its meanings, zones, and categories, has a vital significance. It must be noted that one should avoid carefully any subjective interpretation of the preceding assertion, for that would be gravely erroneous. Remember that life is the inescapable coexistence of the subject and the object, of me with the world and of the world with me, in essential correlation; and that this doctrine is not in any manner subjective, for if indeed it emphasizes the dependency of the world on me (in this it coincides with idealism), it emphasizes also the dependency in which I am on the world (in which it essentially corrects idealism) and it does not admit in any way whatever that the world is a creation, emanation, or projection of the I. Now, all that Nikolai Hartmann says, I understand ought to be carried to a more basic, more primary, plane, in the light of the metaphysics of life; and, then, we should understand the person not only as the intersection of the region of values with the zone of reality, but we should take account of what basic being is, which does not have to be a given or made being, but consists in having to be making itself at each moment; which carries with it that the structure of life itself should be estimative (to determine — select — prefer — value); and, moreover, we should understand that, although we have to recognize that values are objective ideals, their objectivity is held within human life, since everything it has is in life and not outside of it. This is the orientation which I offer to bring about an insertion of the philosophy of values in the metaphysics of transcendental humanism.[43]

The philosophy of transcendental humanism offers, to the theory of the person, perspectives of renovation and of greater novelty. It will be desirable to mention here some of the thoughts of José Ortega y Gasset. This great Spanish master says that Philosophy has always fallen into incredible error in calling "I" the most extravagant things, but never that which we call I in our daily existence. Before asking ourselves *what* I am, we have to ask with firmness and peremptoriness *whom* I am. The I which is each one is not his body, nor is it his soul; the I — as I have explained in Chapter I — has met these corporeal and psychic things and has to live with them, by means of them. The soul remains as far from the I as the landscape around the body. The I is not a thing; it is one who has to live with things, among things; and life is not something which is given to us ready made, which has a predetermined being, but it is something which has to be made, which has to make the I which each one of us is; and its structure is of the future, it is to decide at each moment what is going to be in the following moment, and, so, is liberty. But not an abstract liberty (as absolute and limitless indetermination), but liberty fitted into circumstance, among those concrete possibilities it has to choose. But each one has to live not any life whatever but a certain life. One cannot live an abstract life. Life signifies the necessity of realizing the project of existence which each one is. This project, of which the I consists, is not an idea or plan imagined by man and freely chosen. It is prior to all the ideas which his intelligence forms, to all the decisions of his will. Moreover, we ordinarily have of it only a vague knowledge; and nevertheless it is our authentic being, our destiny. Our will is free *to realize or not* that vital project which ultimately we are, but it cannot correct, change, avoid, or replace it. We are indelibly that sole planned personage whom we must realize. The world in due course, or our own character, make that realization more or less easy or difficult for us. Life is a continuous drama, because it is a mad struggle with things and even with our character to attain being in fact what we are

[43] I make it understood that priority in the formation of this thought belongs to me.

in project.[44] I am a certain individual pressure upon the world: the world is no less determined and individual resistance to that pressure. The soul, character, body are the sum of the apparatus *with* which I live, and are equivalent to an actor charged with representing that personage who is the authentic I. And here arises the most surprising fact of the vital drama: man possesses an ample margin of liberty with respect to his I or destiny. He may refuse to realize it, he may be unfaithful to himself. Then his life lacks authenticity. If by vocation is meant an integral and individual program of existence, it will be clearer to say that our I is our vocation — to which, after all, we may be faithful or not. We have to seek our circumstance, such and as it is, precisely with what it has of limitation, of peculiarity, the fixed place in the immense perspective of the world. Not to stand perpetually in ecstasy before the hierarchy of values, but to attain for our individual life a proper place among them. In short — says Ortega y Gasset — "the reabsorption of circumstance is the concrete destiny of man."

The theory of the person finds also fruitful suggestions in the work of Martin Heidegger. So, for example, when he emphasizes that being is the basic existence in man; that the existence of man is to be in the world, preoccupied with it. And there are two types of preoccupation (*Sorge*): (a) that of daily, banal, existence, which is the preoccupation of everyone and of no one in particular (here we should find, in my point of view, an important light on the determination of social life); the banal or daily existence, which is made up of that which we have in common with the rest and not peculiar to each one, that is, in short, an existence which avoids itself; (b) the preoccupation with the existence which he has found for himself, the very deep existence, the existence of liberty; the basic and undetermined anxiety which makes nothing clear to us; the sense of death as the place where man is fully himself and separated from other beings (in which I understand that we may find light to characterize the individual person, that is, the authentic person, who has fully succeeded for himself).

I have developed the foregoing exposition of some of the thoughts of Fichte, Scheler, Hartmann, Ortega y Gasset, and Heidegger not with the purpose of giving an erudite relation of various doctrines, but rather as a selection of a series of points of view of various authors who, in spite of their diversity, have a kind of similar style, a common denominator; for, although under different form, there appears in all of them a similar *leitmotiv*, and the whole exposition of such theories is, so to speak, determined by my own thinking, by the thread of which the selection has been

[44] Cf. José Ortega y Gasset, Meditaciones del Quijote (1914) 42–44; ¿Qué es Filosofía? (tenth lecture, 1929); Goethe desde dentro 11ff.

made, picking in each of the authors considered those themes which I consider the most successfully treated, and omitting or leaving aside other aspects which I believe either unessential or deficient.

What I have expounded is to be related to what I said in Chapter I upon the individual life and its estimative structure; upon the individual life as an untransferable, unique, uninterchangeable, most private task. And of what is said in this Chapter let us remember, especially, that personality is not the concept of a thing, but is a concept which is comprehensible only in the light of a moral idea, or better, of values and their realization; that each person is such precisely because he embodies an individual and unchangeable magnitude, which has its correspondence in a peculiar and individual collection of values, in a particular destiny; which represents a unique point of view on the world and on the task of life; in short, which involves a theoretical and practical, individual, exclusive perspective.

Consider the peculiarity offered by the concept of the individuality of the person. The concept I is a general concept (which seeks to include all the I's), but what it denotes in itself is precisely the exclusion of all generality. Each one of the I's is an I; thus, the concept is general; but to be an I means to be a basically individual person, that is distinct from all the rest, unique. Notice, now, that the word individual has two meanings: (a) as signifying the attribute of indivisibility (for example, applied to the atom); (b) as individual reality, totally determined and different from any other reality. Here, referring to the human person, we employ the word individual not only in the first of the meanings, but also and *above all* in the second, that is, as signifying something singular, peculiar, and exclusive.

3. The Concept of Person in Social and Juridical Life

In the preceding pages I have explained what *person* means as an expression concerning the human, that is, the concept of person as a human individual, offering the reader a vision of the main dimensions of a philosophy of man. But it happens, as I have observed at the beginning of this chapter, that the word person is also used profusely in the social sciences and especially in juristics, in which it has its principal seat. And, so, in social life, and especially in Law, we speak of persons, of individual persons, of social persons, and of juridical persons. And it is to be noted that the sociologists and the jurists have produced a huge and varied literature on the concept of person; which makes one strongly suspect that the sense in which one speaks of person in the Law and in social life does not coincide with the philosophic idea of person.

In a properly systematic order, I ought to treat first of the concept of person in the purely social life, foreign to Law; and then treat of the concept of person in the Law. But it happens that, in many cases, the juridical turns out to be a maximum of the social, a superlative expression of the social, in short, the social carried to its extreme limits and to the full extent of its outlines; and on that account it makes comprehension easier to begin the exposition with the study of the juridical forms, which represent the largest degree of the social; and afterwards to examine the non-juridical social forms, which are lesser, sometimes embryonic. And so it happens with the theme of personality: it will be easier to understand what constitutes personality in the merely social (not juridical) life, if we have first considered what is personality in the Law.

It is usual to say that to be a person in Law means to be the subject of rights and of juridical duties. And it is affirmed that there are two classes of persons in Law: physical persons or individuals; and collective persons (corporations, associations and foundations) which are usually called moral persons, juridical persons, or social persons. Individual persons in Law are today in civilized countries all men (slavery was the negation of this principle). Among the so-called moral or juridical persons (which ought more properly to be called "collective persons") are public corporations (for example, municipalities, member States of a Federation, the State, official banks, autonomous administrative agencies, etc.); associations (religious, scientific, artistic, sporting, etc.); civil and mercantile societies (collective, special partnerships, anonymous, limited); foundations (religious, beneficent, cultural, etc.), and also other masses of property, as, for example, the estate in bankruptcy.

Now in what is usually said in Law treatises upon personality are involved very various and heterogenous problems, the confusion of which has lamentably muddled juridical thinking for centuries. And it is time now to clear up this confusion and to perceive each one of the questions in full clarity and with mental rigor. In this matter have been mingled diverse questions, which it is necessary to keep separate with accuracy. These diverse questions may be specified in the four following inquiries, which we may refer as well to so-called physical persons as to the so-called moral (collective) persons.

1. What does person mean in juridical terms; what does it mean to have the quality of person in a juridical order; in short, *what* is it to be a person in Law; a concept which is applied equally to individuals and the collective entities considered as persons. (This is a theme of the *general theory of Law.*)

2. *Who* are the entities upon which falls this juridical qualification of person; that is, to ask ourselves, referring to the individual entities in

the Law, what are the men to whom the Law concedes personality; and to ask ourselves, referring to collective persons, what are the entities to which the Law grants personality. (Each positive order answers this.)

3. In what does the being of these entities (individual and collective) to which the Law concedes personality consist; as for example referring to individual persons, to inquire of what the essence of the human consists, its forms and its manifestations (which is what I have done in the preceding pages), the theme of philosophic anthropology; and as to what concerns collective persons, to make clear in what consists the being of an association, a corporation, a foundation. (This is a theme of Sociology.)

4. To put from an estimative point of view, for example, in legislative policy, the question of to whom the Law *ought* to concede personality. This, for example, is what is done when one criticizes the institution of slavery, declaring that juridical personality ought to belong to all men; or when one discusses whether the State ought to admit other collective persons than those it creates, or if on the contrary it ought to concede personality to all collective entities which arise spontaneously. (This is a theme of juridical estimation or of political philosophy.)

In the copious juridical literature upon the person this theme appears sunk in a sea of equivocations and confusions, because these four problems which I have just enumerated have been confounded and confused. The only possibility of creating a clarity of ideas in this theme is to bound with rigor and precision each one of these four questions.

This systematization of problems which I have offered may be applied equally to the consideration of individual persons as to that of collective juridical persons. It has the same value for the first as for the second. We must distinguish carefully the question as to the *juridical concept of person* from the other inquiries with respect to the *who are, how,* and *who ought to be* the realities which the Law constitutes persons.

4. The Juridical Concept of Personality

More than a century ago there was launched in the theory of the Law the thought that the personality of collective entities is a juridical fiction, created by the norm (Savigny). This doctrine of the founder of the historic school of Law refers only to social persons; but there is no doubt that in it lies the idea that juridical personality is something *constructed by the Law.* This shrewd conjecture receives and collects new forms of expression in a series of doctrines which were successively produced in the past century: that called "comparative" (Böhlau, Bruns, etc.); that of "rights without a subject" (Winscheid, Brinz, Gianturco, Bonelli); that of the "consignees of property" or of the "person as a technical instrument" (Jhering); that of "the privileged social relations" (Van der Heuvel); that of the "special regime" (Vareilles-Sommières); and so forth. It is important to note that in all of them, in one way or another, lies the idea that juridical personality applied to social entities is a construction of the Law. It is not that they deny that beyond the Law the collective entities have a reality; but they emphasize that that which functions as the subject of juridical relations is not that reality, but a construction created by the Law.

The doctrines of Ferrara and of Kelsen have given decided progress to this theme. Ferrara has seen clearly that the juridical personality (with independence of its real substratum, which it always has), as well in reference to the individual as to the collective entity, is not a reality, nor a fact, but is a juridical category, a product of the Law, which the Law may tie to any substratum, and which does not imply necessarily any special corporeality or spirituality in the one who receives it.[45]

But these same thoughts are found in a stage of greater maturity and better managed in the doctrine of Kelsen. Although it is thought that the pure theory of Law of this great master needs substantial rectifications, from the weakness of his fundamental suppositions;[46] and even when it is considered, as I believe, that it has been surpassed, it is necessary to recognize that it contains not a few very skillful points and fruitful achievements. Perhaps then of all Kelsen's doctrine, one of the themes best developed, which will survive the rest of his work, is that of personality. And, further, the thought of Kelsen on this point not only represents a decided success, as to this theme, but it probably will have a much greater effect than even its author suspected; for, though the theory arose with the purpose of being purely and exclusively juridical (as to this matter, as in all the others), I understand it to offer an important inspiration by which to elaborate some essential concepts of social Ontology (social circle, the social I of the individuals, social personality). To understand duly the doctrine of Kelsen upon personality, it is desirable to explain first one of the fundamental concepts which occur in it, to wit, that of the *normative imputation*. The logical structure called imputation is the characteristic method of connecting two facts in a norm. Facts, phenomena in the world of nature — and in general of reality — are related among themselves causally, they are bound

[45] Cf. FERRARA, TEORIA DELLE PERSONAE GIURIDICHE (in the DIR. CIV. DE FIORE; there is a Spanish translation published by Ed. Reus); and 1 TRATTATO DE DIRITTO CIVILE ITALIANO (1921), 697ff. KELSEN, HAUPTPROBLEME DER STAATSRECHTSLEHRE (2d ed., 1923); REINE RECHTSLEHRE (1934).

[46] See my ESTUDIO SOBRE LA TEORÍA PURA DEL DERECHO Y EL ESTADO, as an extensive prologue to the Second Spanish edition of the COMPENDIO DE TEORÍA GENERAL DEL ESTADO of Hans Kelsen (1934).

to each other by causality; some are the effects of others, and in their turn function as the causes of other new ones. Now in the norms we see how the divers elements contained or foreseen in them are related to each other; but that relation is not real, of causality, but normative. For example, in the juridical norm there appear certain determined suppositions with certain determined consequences: given such a fact (for example, a contract of sale, let us say) there ought to be produced such and such consequences (the buyer ought to pay the price and the seller to deliver the thing). Here we find ourselves before two facts, which are not related to each other by any process of real causation, but only by a normative connection by the juridical precept, which is called normative imputation. Another example: if the buyer does not pay the price and the seller demands it judicially (suppositions), the State will impose a compulsory executory proceeding against him (consequence); that is, to the fact of the default of the buyer joined to the claim of the seller is imputed normatively another fact, to wit, compulsory execution; and it is not a matter of any relation of effective causation, but of juridical connection. Another example: whoever kills another man intentionally (supposition), shall be condemned to the punishment of thirty years at hard labor (consequence); the thirty years at hard labor are not a true effect of the fact of the homicide, but a juridical consequence of it, which is imputed to it by virtue of the norm. In all these given examples we find present the normative imputation of one fact upon another fact, that is, of a juridical consequence upon a juridical supposition. But *there is another kind of normative imputation,* to wit, the imputation of a fact to a person. It happens in juridical life that, while many times — indeed most times — a fact is imputed to the person who actively has desired and has realized it, in many other cases, on the contrary, it does not happen so. For example: when a person makes a declaration of will under the influence of an overwhelming fear, that declaration in spite of being real and of being voluntary (for the compelled one, even compelled wills — as the Roman Law rightly says *coactus tamen voluit* —), in spite of representing a real effect of the conduct of the person, on the other hand juridically is not imputed to him, does not produce consequences; the fact of the fall of a flowerpot from a balcony because of a strong wind is not a fact of which the tenant of the house is the real author, and nevertheless juridically it is imputed to him, although he is not the physical cause of that event; the act which a public employee (judge, administrator, policeman, etc.) performs in the exercise of his official functions, although indeed he does it, is not imputed to him, but is imputed to another person, to wit, the State; when the president of an association acts as such his acts are not imputed to him but to the association. In all the cases mentioned, and in innumerable others which we might go on enumerating indefinitely, it happens that the imputation takes place, without there having to be any chain of real causality between the person and the fact, because the juridical norm so provides. The *normative personal imputation* is the form of juridical connection between the subject of the duty and the object of the same (positive as to fulfillment; or negative as the result of a violation or the omission of due care) such and as the precept establishes. When we compare a fact (which is matter for regulation by a norm) with the content of the juridical norm in question, there arises at once the question as to the person to whom we ought to attribute the observance or the violation, that is, the problem with regard to the subject of the duty. The norm only can give the answer which is what contains in itself the juridical bond between what it commands and who ought to obey it, between the object and the subject of the ought-to-be. As I have indicated, in the great number of cases, it happens that by the rule of the norm the fact is juridically imputed to its intentional and real actual author; but it also happens in many other cases that an act juridically sanctionable is not the voluntary effect of the behavior of a person (results of negligence); or it even happens that it is an external fact, neither desired nor foreseen by the person, and which, nevertheless, is imputed to him, because he ought to have foreseen and consequently to have avoided it (responsibility for the fall of a tile from one's house); or it also happens that the act of a person (for example, damage caused by a child, by a servant) is imputed to another person (for example, to the father, guardian or master); and this is what happens as to all the acts done by agents of another person, by representatives of associations, corporations, and foundations, by state officials, for these acts are not imputed to their physical authors but to other persons, to wit: (with regard to the examples given) to the principal, to the entity represented, and to the State. So, then, juridical imputation, from the inherent normative point of view, is not founded on the causal series, has nothing to do with it; it expresses simply the relation which the norm establishes between an object and a subject. The imputation starts from a fact external to the person (the object or fact in question) and connects it to an ideal point or center, at which that imputation stops. This ideal point, which functions as the terminus of an imputation, is what jurisprudence calls will. The will, juridically, is not the real psychological fact (which is called by the same word), but is a pure normative construction which represents a final point or terminus of imputation. Many times the juridical will coincides with the real psychological will; but other times it does not coincide with it, as in the given examples. This is the doctrine of

Kelsen as to normative imputation, which constitutes a cornerstone for comprehension of juridical personality.

So, then, being the subject of a juridical relation (of a juridical duty or of a subjective right) does not represent any real fact, is not the expression of any natural actuality, does not denote any situation of causality; it is purely and simply the result of a normative imputation established by the Law. That is, on raising the problem of the juridical person (as well individual as collective), we do not find ourselves on the plane of reality, but we are within the inherent sphere of juristics, which has its own context and its own logic. This problem does not consist in asking ourselves about any reality, but in asking ourselves about normative imputation. Kelsen believes that the current concept of person in a juridical sense is no more than a duplicate expression for juridical duty and subjective right, conceived in substantialized form. The person for the Law is not a reality, but an inherent concept of the same juridical order, common to all its possible manifestations; and, consequently, within the field of Law there does not arise any question as to what may be the reality which the substrata of the various persons may have beyond and independent of it; and, consequently, on establishing the general concept of juridical personality, there is no question of distinguishing between physical persons and collective persons, since that difference relates to extrajuridical or metajuridical realities. For the moment, to formulate the juridical concept of personality, there is only juridical personality, whose essence is the same if it is of an individual as if it is of a collective entity. Kelsen says that the individual collective person is not man as a biological or psychological reality (here Kelsen does not penetrate sufficiently deeply, for he ought to say that it is not man as the complete human person), but is a juridical construction of his conduct, so far as that constitutes the contents of juridical norms. Consequently, it is not the total man which may form the content of the juridical precept, but only some of his acts and omissions, that is, certain aspects of his conduct, to wit, those aspects which are in direct relation to the juridical order. Human conduct may be found positively or negatively related to the Law. The first, that is, the positive and direct relation of the human conduct of a person to the Law, may occur in two ways: (a) his behavior may be the content of a juridical duty; and (b) the behavior of a person may be a condition for the juridical duty of another person, or rather for a subjective right;[47] that is, that a certain

[47] Although this idea is due to an inspiration from Kelsen, nevertheless I have rectified his theory in the exposition in a double sense: first, distinguishing between positive and negative relations of conduct with the juridical norm; and, second, including in the concept of subjective law the three manifestations which I have

declaration should be voluntary constitutes the condition upon which the State will undertake some compelling act; or also as a juridical power, that is, that the act of a person may be the condition upon which a juridical precept arises (for example, suffrage, the beginning of any juridical action whatever, etc.). The negative relation of the conduct of a person with the Law consists in that conduct not constituting material for juridical duties nor for a subjective right nor juridical power, but it is entirely irrelevant, inoperative, indifferent to the Law. This conduct which is not related directly and positively to the Law, but maintains a negative relation with it, this conduct which is free from the Law, does not come into question for the determination of the concept of personality. For that, one must attend to the two cases given of positive relation. In both cases, Kelsen says, it is a question of juridical norms which are presented to us with regard to a person, that is, which appear subjectivized. Now it happens that an individual juridical person, or individual person in the juridical sense, will be the aggregate of all those norms which have for their object the conduct of a man, as well to juridical duty as to a subjective right. The individual juridical person is, then, a sector of the juridical order: that sector which regulates the rights and duties of a man, the aggregate of those norms which refer to the conduct of a man, a sector or aggregate which we conceive abstractly in a unified manner. The individual juridical person consists, then, of the ideal common terminus of reference or imputation for all the acts which form the contents of this part of the juridical order. The concept of the individual person is the unified and synthetic expression of the rights and duties of a man; it is the portion of the juridical order which establishes them, conceived as a partial system upon the basis of a common point or center of imputation of such duties and rights. We shall see at once how the concept of person applied to collective entities is analogous.

Now it happens that on many occasions the juridical order attributes certain conduct (duties and rights) of certain individual men, not to them (who are its real authors), but to an ideal person supposed behind them (corporation, association, etc.) which is the one who functions as the central and common terminus of imputation of all the acts (which may be done by various physical persons: president, secretary, manager, etc.). In this case, we have what is called a "collective juridical person." This is then, according to Kelsen, a complex of juridical norms, which regulate the reciprocal conduct of an aggregate of men directed toward a

explained in chap. VI of this book and consequently also what Kelsen calls mere reverse materials of the juridical duty of other persons, and which he excludes from the concept of subjective law.

common end. The collective juridical person is, then, also a part of the juridical order, limited according to a certain point of view, conceived as a unified system of rights and duties referred to a common center of imputation; a common center of imputation which consists of an ideal point, an ideal person, constructed by the Law. Now this ideal person is no more than the expression of the unity of this aggregate of norms, bounded and separated according to a certain point of view.

When this process of personification is applied not to a partial order or limited aggregate of juridical norms, but to the totality of them, conceived unifiedly, then we have what has been called the *person of the State,* which is no more than the totality of the positive order in force, converted into an ideal and common subject of imputation of all the mandates contained in the Law, acts which are realized by those men whom the juridical norms invest with the character of state or juridical organs.

Now, the collectivity is not a substantive reality, with its own conduct; there are no conducts other than those of individuals; only those conducts can be the content of the juridical norm; and so, the juridical personality of the collective entity is solely the expression of the unity of the order which governs its relations, that is, the reciprocal relations of the behaviors of the men who compose it; it is, in short, the expression of a common ideal terminus of the imputation of the conducts of the men who act not for themselves but in the name and for the account of the collectivity.

It follows then, clearly, that the individual juridical personality and the collective juridical personality are entirely homogeneous. It is understood that they are homogeneous *juridically,* for the enormous differences which appear between them refer to the special reality foreign to the Law which each one has.

It should be noted that, in every case, the one who has the duties and the rights is man. The juridical personality is not the support of those duties and rights, but their unified expression, under the form of personification of that part of the juridical order which establishes them and which is conceived as forming a relatively independent system. The juridical precept concerns only human conduct, that is, of individuals; only thanks to the attribution of such conduct to the unity of a partial order or partial system of juridical norms, arises the concept of person. And so, Kelsen sums up his doctrine by saying: when the basis for limiting this partial system or order is the human unit, we have the *individual juridical person;* when the criterion for the limiting is the reciprocal conduct of various individuals in view of a certain end, then we create the concept of the *collective juridical person.* And if we conceive unifiedly the whole of the current juridical system, referred to a common ideal point of imputation of such acts as belong to such systems, then we have created the concept of the *personality of the State.*

But I believe that upon the basis of the disclosure by Kelsen, one ought to go still further: that is, one should draw other consequences, some of which are not indicated nor even suspected in the work of the founder of the so-called Viennese school.[48] So, then, next I shall explain the derivations and consequences which I have found for myself from this theme, and some new critical clarifications which I deem necessary to introduce in it.

The juridical personality which is attributed to the individual person is as artificial as that conceded to the collective entity. In saying artificial, I mean to express the quality of being "constructed by the Law," springing from the Law, and not constituted outside it. Outside of the Law, there are deep and irreducible individuals, men of flesh and blood, authentically individual persons (each one with his own little heart), unique, unchangeable; and there are, besides, social relations and collective complexities. But none of these, none of those realities, functions as a person. What juridically functions as an individual person is not the totality of the human person, is not the fullness of the individual subject, but only some of its aspects and dimensions, and certainly aspects not strictly individual, but *generic,* dimensions not purely privative but *topical, functional,* which are that part of his eternal typical conduct which is foreseen in the juridical norm, which is described in it as suppositions with determined consequences. A great part of my human being, precisely what I have of individual depth, of uniqueness, of intransferability, of irreducibility to any abstract scheme, of concrete radicalness, remains outside of the Law, remains beyond its perceptive regulation, and only in the quality of guaranteed, as free from or foreign to taxative normativeness. So, then, it is to be noted that for the Law there does not come into question the totality of my human person, but only some of its acts. But, moreover, let us note also that there does not come into question for the Law the dimensions of my acts which are strictly individual and untransferable, but only those generic, common, typical, interchangeable, fungible dimensions. That part of my reality and of my behavior which the Law takes into consideration is not that which I have strictly as individual, is not my real authentic person, nor even aspects of my conduct as a genuine individual, as a true concrete human person, but generic schemes and types of conduct, described in

[48] I insist that this is one of the ideas which must turn out most fertile and decisive for the Theory of Law.

the norm and applicable in principle to all persons. In short, I am not I myself, the unique and deep person whom I carry within, who functions as a juridical personality, but it is as a kind of part or *role* planned beforehand, as a sort of mask or disguise which all may wear whom this form fits. And this idea is found present in the original meaning of the word person, in which state the Law borrowed it. The word person signified originally and in the proper sense a mask — the disguise which actors used — and the Law employed it metaphorically to denote the subject of juridical relations. Now, in such usage, person has come to indicate a part, a function previously determined, preëstablished, designed beforehand, that is, not the man, whom they represent in the theater, but the *role* performed by him.

To be an individual is to be I and no other; it is to constitute a unique, untransferable, unchangeable existence, irreducible to any other; it is the reality of my own life, a perspective on the horizon of the world distinct from all the other perspectives of other lives. The authentic, profound, intimate person constitutes that unique and untransferable instance of decision which each one of us is. On the other hand, the juridical personality attributed to the individual is supported and founded precisely on those dimensions of it which are not individual, but collective, common, generic, schematic. The dimension of the man who functions as a person in the Law is the dimension which he has in common with other juridical subjects, all those others which can fit in the figure foreseen by the juridical norm. Nor do the various singular concretions of juridical personality in each individual subject represent complexes or clusters of an aggregate of generic dimensions which occur in the subject, who for example is at the same time citizen, adult, husband, father, owner of real property, tenant, buyer, mortgagor, bailee, principal, public official, tax payer, etc. Man in the fullness and basicness of his own private individual life never comes in question for the Law. In the Law there functions as subject the citizen, the seller, the ward, the guardian, the son, the father, the lessee, the heir, the party in default, the delinquent, the tax payer, the soldier, the judge, etc. In principle, there may be any other human being found in the same juridical situations (as citizen, professor, buyer, lessee, etc.) in which my juridical personality shows itself; all the dimensions of my juridical personality, so to speak, functions or parts previously written, disguises molded beforehand, store suits (and not to measure), which, just as by me, may be occupied or discharged by anyone else in whom the provided conditions concur. On the other hand, my authentic personality, my basically individual life, my own and exclusive, unique and untransferable, is found always apart from juridical relations; it is found either nearer to or farther from the Law. This is comprehensible, since the Law is always something social or collective.

It has been seen how human behavior may be found with respect to the Law in three classes of relations (two of them positive and the other negative): (a) positively, as material or object of duties; (b) positively, as a conditioning element of the production of juridical precepts or of their fulfillment by others, that is, as subjective right (in its three manifestations); (c) negatively, as free from limiting regulation, and consequently, as permitted and guaranteed. So, then, juridical regulation is always partial with respect to the plenitude of human life (which is not true of the moral values, which embrace, circumscribe, and penetrate the plenitude of life). It results, therefore, that only one part of my behavior is preceptively and limitingly regulated by the Law, the other part remaining free, that is, permitted and guaranteed. But, moreover, another observation must be made: in the part of conduct which comes in question for the Law, it does not take into account the plenitude of that work, but solely and exclusively some dimensions of it, to wit, those foreseen in the norm, which are the external dimensions relating to the other subjects of law. So that of that conduct relevant for the Law, it picks only the generic dimensions (those typified in the norm) and leaves aside from its juridical content the individual shades and accents, which are exclusively individual and not fungible. However much one may try to singularize or make concrete the juridical precept, it will remain always a typical formula which necessarily escapes the authentic individuality of the singular and nonduplicatable I, with its peculiar accents and modalities, which are irreducible to any general concept.

So there is contemplated in the light of this theme something which I have already indicated in defining the essence of juristics: that the Law is always and necessarily a schematic regulation of conduct. These schemes may be more or less general, slightly or very detailed, but, finally, always and necessarily they are schemes, and consequently they always have a minimum of generality which excludes the essence of what is authentically individual. They are schemes of conduct which do not refer to the individual essence, but regulate communal aspects, topical forms, functional dimensions, in short, forms of collective life. On the contrary, moral values *sensu stricto* take into consideration the full individuality, as such; moral values take into account all the concrete, singular, and special elements which concur in one human person and which determine at any moment the untransferable situation in which he finds himself. Thus Morals constitutes the point of view which envelops the totality of the person and penetrates it to its deepest essence; it constitutes the instance individualized *par excellence* for behavior.

Man comes in question for the juridical norm, constitutes a juridical personality like a will unburdened of the totality of its real relations: a will, not understood as a psychological phenomenon, but as an objectified signification, as an exteriorized situation, loosed from its real connections and appraised in a sense prefigured by the norm. So, then, to have personality in Law signifies to be the subject of parts foreseen in juridical regulation. And the individual juridical person is constituted by the unity of imputation of a series of actual and possible functions foreseen in the norm. Now, in the case of the individual person, this center of imputation coincides with the real living unity of the man, who is its substratum or support, although it is understood that what functions as an individual juridical person is not that living full reality of the individual, but a united or unified scheme of objectified functions, a scheme which the norm projects upon the real human subject.

As to what concerns the juridical personality of the collective and foundational entities, there is little more to add after what I have set forth in the preceding pages. The personality of a social group consists of the unity of imputation of a multiple series of the conducts of certain men; conducts which the Law does not ascribe to the persons who make them, but to another ideal person constructed by the norm, as a terminal point of imputation for a determined repertory of juridical relations. Now while under the individual juridical personality — also constructed by the Law — there exists a real person, a subjectivity conscious of itself, an I, a human person in the basic sense, on the contrary under the juridical personality of collective entities, although there may be support for a social reality, that reality does not have the dimension of subjectivity, of an authentic *I*. It is clear that if this juridical entity has a juridical life, we ought to ask ourselves of whom is that life, that is, its subject. But the subject of that juridical life is a juridical subject, that is, created or constructed by the Law; it is merely a logical synthesis of a multiplicity of relations determined by the Law. By this I do not deny that under the collective juridical personality there is a special social reality, independent of the Law; but what functions in the Law as a collective personality is not the full social reality of the collective entity which serves as a substratum or support for its juridical personality. The juridical personality is so only the synthesis of the juridical functions imputed by the norm not to the men who exercise them, but to an ideal subject, constructed, pretended, consisting in that common ideal terminus of imputation.

In the same way as I explained that the juridical personality of the individual person does not exhaust nor even remotely translate the full and concrete human reality of each one, analogously I must note that the juridical personality of collective entities does not express all the social reality which serves them as substratum. The juridical personality of the collective entities does not translate nor reflect all the social reality which they have apart from or independently of the Law. A great part of that social reality remains outside of the juridical personality. Notice that the juridical personality of the collective or foundational entity is something constructed by the Law; it constitutes a normative figure of unified imputation, which the norm projects upon a complex of relations. But not only is there no equation between the social reality which the collective entities have and their juridical personality; there is, moreover, an independence between that reality and the category of juridical person. The juridical personality of collective entities is not the same as the social personality which they may have, and of which I shall speak more later. The social personality of a collective entity, independent of the Law, will be, as I shall explain presently, a kind of organization for the service of a common end, its members being conscious of that teleological unity. On the other hand, the juridical personality of a collective entity is a unification produced by the Law for the external activity of the group in juridical commerce with the rest, something thus like a mask put on over a face, but which does not reflect it exactly, according to the expression of Hauriou (notice how inevitably there arises again the figure of the mask).[49] The concept of juridical personality does not clarify at all for us the internal constitution of the group.

Notice, in the first place, that, given the existence of social configurations, groups, collective entities, with strict cohesion and clear outlines, they nevertheless do not have juridical personality; and this is so, simply, because the Law has not attributed it to them. In the second place, we observe that the relation between the juridical personality and the reality of the collective entity, by which the former is made clear, may be of very diverse kinds. There are collective entities which, apart from the juridical personality which the Law attributes to them, and even before it attributes it, have a social reality perfectly constituted, of a clear and vigorous structure — for example, a religious community, independently of whether or not the Law attributes to it juridical personality; for example also, certain beneficent or cultural institutions, which may or not have juridical personality, according to whether the Law grants it or not. In all these cases — and in many other similar ones — when the Law impresses juridical personality, it happens that it projects or attaches to it something which already constituted a collective entity

[49] Cf. Hauriou, De la personalité comme élement de la réalité sociale (R. g. d. D., 1898); Précis de Droit administratif et Droit public (1921); Droit constitutionnel; La Théorie de l'institution et de la fondation (1925).

with social reality. It is clear that the juridical regulation of the reality of a group as a personality has influence afterwards as an effective factor in the real configuration of the group and in its life. On the other hand, there are other cases in which the collective entity is constituted as such for the first time by operation of the Law and thanks to it, as occurs for example with an anonymous mercantile company. In this case, the collective entity has been created by the Law, not only as to its juridical personality, but also as to its social reality apart from the Law. Now, even in this case, in which the collective entity owes the birth or origin of its social reality to the Law, once it has arisen, its social reality is not exhausted in its juridical personality, nor is the latter an exact expression of the former.

5. Extrajuridical Social Personalities of Individuals and the Extrajuridical Social Personality of Groups

The themes which the heading names do not belong strictly to a reflection upon the Law; but they have their place in a treatise upon Sociology. But, apart from the interest which such themes offer, it is desirable to consider them here, although somewhat summarily, to complete the panorama of questions which the word personality raises; and, moreover, because in the light of this complementary study we shall cover in greater relief and more rigorous significance everything which I have said on the one side with regard to the authentic human person and on the other side as to the juridical personality.

The extrajuridical social personalities of individuals. Recall that in characterizing the social life, the social work of individuals, I explained that the subject of that social conduct (that is, of the compliance with a usage) is not the authentic individual and deepest I, but a social I, attached to the individual, as its mask, as far as it is a member of a collective circle, as a crust left by the social medium. What the authentic individual puts into his social work is the decision to accommodate his conduct to the collective models: but as those models are not his original work, but a communal form of behavior, it follows that in complying with them what he manifests is not individuality but a kind of collective mask which that carries, in short, a social I which carries the subject, a sort of costume, belonging to the social circle in question. The personality of a subject so far as he is a member of a collective circle is not the reality of his full individuality, but a common dimension, functional, schematic, fungible. In the collective, in the strictest sense, there does not come into question the individual as such individual, fully responsible for his own life, as a peculiar and exclusive subject, unique and insubstitutable, but what is socially relevant is a generic quality of member of a collective circle, or owner in it of determined functions. Put in other words: the subject which acts in collective life is not the deepest individual, but is the "neighbor, the colleague, the comrade, the gentleman, the aristocrat, the member of the middle class, the workman, the coreligionary, the copartisan, the sportsman, the professional," etc. That is, never the intimate individual whom he is, but the objectivized, generalized, schematized magnitude, of a function, which is complied with not for its own account but for the account of the collectivity. We see, then, that those social personalities which play the subject are like their juridical personalities (for example, they act as citizen, employee, seller, lessee, etc.), but at the same time as this, they are functionaries, objectified, artificial, molded from without. And so it happens that if we take a social relation isolated from every other ingredient, in a situation chemically pure, let us say, we observe that this relation is established between fungible, changeable subjects, and not between authentic individuals (that is, in what each one has of individuality); which is also what happens in our juridical relations; the seller of whom one buys is of course a man who has his own individuality, who has, as the saying goes, his soul in his wallet; but as such seller he comes in question for me only in that quality, in that mask of seller, and he is perfectly replaceable by any other person who fills the same part; and the same occurs with a colleague who is nothing more than colleague (that is, who is not besides a friend or enemy — for in that case I should have something more than a social relation, I should have also an interindividual relation). Now then, those social personalities which we all carry and wear (like ready-made clothes) differ from the juridical personality as follows: in the juridical personality there is a responsible instance, to wit, the juridical order, whose unity is expressed in the State; while in the social personalities there is no such definite and responsible instance, because the subject responsible for the collective life does not exist as a determined thing, but as an anonymous thing, to wit, the people, the rest, all and none in particular. From this it follows that while the social personality of the individual is always something vague and diffused, on the other hand, the juridical personality has rigorously defined outlines. We might say here that in the light of this comparison, it appears here — as in so many other aspects — that the juridical represents the extreme form of the social, the maximization of the social, its most intense and most rigidly crystallized expression. In juristics, the social attains its solidest and most definite outlines, and all its characters reach their culmination.

The extrajuridical social personality of collective entities. Neither does this theme, any more than the preceding, belong to the philosophy of Law, but is appropriate to Sociology. But for the same reasons presented with respect to the former, it is desirable to say something about it here. It is clear that I shall have to limit myself to some very summary considerations, since to treat fully of this theme, although it should be in the most concise manner, would require the development of one of the principal parts of Sociology, that which refers to collective products, complexes or entities. I am going to refer only to one kind of those entities, namely, to those so-called institutions or entities with a special purpose, among which may be included corporations, foundations, and many associations (scientific, artistic, etc.).

And as a mere allusion to this theme I think it most opportune to recite the theory of the institution (of Hauriou and of Renard), or, rather, my interpretation of it (with some of my own points of view and shadings). Also, I shall refer to some great thoughts of Wiese with regard to the same theme.[50]

Hauriou has elaborated his theory of the institution in view of the doctrine of the collective juridical person; but his doctrine, strictly and for the most part, is not juridical but sociological. Here I shall leave aside the juridical aspect of those collective entities which have juridical personality, to attend only to the problem of their social reality. Hauriou calls institutions those collective entities which consist of the idea of an undertaking which is realized and lasts in a collective medium, raising in it, to that end, an organization and some peculiar rules of conduct and producing common phenomena among the members who compose it. The institution is a practical idea which has been objectivated and positified, being embodied in a peculiar structure and social organization. And as it is an idea of work, that is to say, of an undertaking, the institution is something active, clearly it is active by means of the individuals who compose it. The end ought not to be confused with the idea of the work in common; for the end is something exterior to the undertaking, as to its directing idea (its inspiring thought), it is something interior with it: the end is something strictly determined, concrete and limited, while that idea of the undertaking or mission has a quality of persistence and of renewed enrichment. The institution as a social group is determined by the participation of its members in that idea of undertaking; by their sharing in that idea. Such sharing produces an equilibrium in internal forces; moreover it originates action according to certain objective pro-

[50] Cf. Hauriou, the works cited in the preceding Note; GEORGES RENARD, THÉORIE DE L'INSTITUTION (1930); L'INSTITUTION (1933); DELOS, LA THÉORIE DE L'INSTITUTION. LA SOLUTION RÉALISTE DU PROBLÈME DE LA PERSONALITÉ MORALE ET LE DROIT À FONDEMENT OBJECTIF (ARCHIVES DE PHILOSOPHIE DU DROIT, I. 72); WIESE, SYSTEM DER ALLGEMEINEN SOZIOLOGIE (1933).

cedures, which consist of adherence to certain facts; and finally it engenders an organized structure. So, then, this idea of undertaking, on taking root in a human medium, informs it, configures it, organizes it, endows it with a different outline and makes a power arise in it. And the institutional group may attain a social personality (Hauriou says moral) which is something entirely distinct from and independent of the juridical personality, which it may have or not have, solely by virtue of what the positive Law provides. It acquires this social personality when the idea of work or undertaking is interiorized in the consciousnesses of the individuals who are members of the group; and then they act freely and consciously as such members, that is, discharging a function which is not individual but of the collective entity. From this moment the collective entity shows itself as an aggregate of social activities, directed to a definite undertaking, in view of determined ends; activities which are fulfilled by the members, but with the consciousness that they are not dealing with something individual of their own, but rather with something which belongs to the common undertaking. When that occurs, we may say that the group constitutes a social personality. If indeed it is true that the institution can do nothing except by means of the men who compose it, nevertheless, its action is specifically different from any other; it is presented as attributable to a person distinct from the individual persons who have in fact acted. Notice, moreover, that we are not treating in any way of a gratuitously and phantasmagorically supposed collective consciousness as something real, in the strict and proper sense, since it is plain that such does not exist; such collective consciousness is only an arbitrary creation of romantic wordiness. We do not treat of such, or of anything like it. But the acts of the institution as a social personality, if indeed it is true that they have for authors the men who make up the group, also have in the collectivity their motive as a final end, and I would say, further, their center of imputation. Although it is true also that the responsibility will fall in the last instance upon the individual consciences of the members, it is as true that there will not weigh upon each anything more than by virtue of his function in the institutional entity, and that it will be measured taking as a criterion that same function. In a social person, the subjects who compose it are called upon to behave as conscious members of the institution; and, therefore, the existence of the group, constituted by the hierarchical aggregate of functions, consists of an organization which is reflected in the consciousness of its members. It is necessary that it should be clear that, according to what has been said so far, the institution is a purely sociological concept and in no manner whatever has anything in the least to do with Law. Not all the collective entities or institutions which have social personality have juridical personality. The juridical personality of the collective entities to which the Law concedes such personality constitutes a pure juridical expedient, a creation of the Law, to unify externally, from without, in juridical commerce, the aggregate of relations which make up the group; it is a species of simple unity constructed by the juridical norm, something thus like a mask which does not reflect nor translate what is under it, in the reality to which it is applied.

As I have explained it, I understand the theory of the institution — and I believe that this is the fertile meaning which resides in the works of Hauriou, Renard, and Delos, which will acquire full outlines in the degree in which they are inserted and understood in the form in which I have just interpreted them.

But, as a complement to this sociological theme, I would like to offer some reference to several points of analysis which Wiese has raised as to abstract collective entities (or corporations), as he calls them. Wiese insists strongly, by means of a minute and decisive analysis, that collective entities — which some Hegelian and romantic sociologists wished to materialize — are reduced solely and exclusively to a complicated texture of interhuman relations and processes. Those social formations or collective entities constitute condensations or accumulations of social processes, which are repeated in given or complex figures; are woven of human forces, united by multiple or durable combinations; they are gathered and connected human energies, whose existence depends upon what has been done by the men who effectively desired them. The supposed independent reality, which by some is wont to be attributed to social formations or collective entities, exists only in our images and not as a "thing" outside of ourselves. In the face of the concrete individual, the collective entities are no more than the influences of other men which exist contemporaneously, which existed before, or which will exist afterwards. The collective entities called associations and corporations are complicated combinations of social processes; and are characterized by the presence in them of the thought that the functions which the collectivity exercises constitute a good, which deserves to be preserved and cared for independently of the men who are living at any given moment. So, then, it may be said that an abstract collective entity exists when a group of men who are living at the same time operate and feel as a unit, possess relative permanence, and must subsist finally by means of some spiritual production.

The qualitative material of corporations — according to Wiese — is constituted of common human experiences, which are of two classes: technical experiences and strictly social experiences, that is, experiences of living together and of organization. These experiences come to constitute a kind of common conviction which enjoys general currency and acceptance. On the other hand, what originally might constitute an individual desire is sometimes objectivated, converted into ideal forms of conduct and crystallized as a type of collective entity.

The compelling force which many collective entities possess over the individual is explained — Wiese says — if we take into account: (1) That ordinarily men do not see the complex totality of the factors which intervene in the texture of all those interesting human acts of the association or corporation; nor even succeed in giving a clear account of the extent of their own actions; (2) That many times men act under the influence of abstract entities already preëxisting and contribute to their conservation and to their ultimate development. To a dull and superficial glance it would perhaps appear that it is the same entity which is acting with independent life and which even breeds new entities on its own account; but this is not what happens in reality; what happens is that those who act are solely and exclusively individual men, influenced by the images which they have formed of the collective entity — I would say further, influenced by the forms of objectivated social human life. Existing corporations last or are modified only to the degree to which men, members of them, wish to preserve or modify them. When a generation arrives which forgets or wishes to ignore them, they disappear and disintegrate like soap bubbles.

I wish to note, as the final word of this comment, that the social personality of collective entities — apart from whether or not they have juridical personality — constitutes something relatively diffuse and tenuous, which we may conceive in its aggregate, but without rigorous and exact outlines. This is contrary to what occurs with juridical personality, which is strictly limited and outlined by the norm of the Law, which creates an ideal center of imputation, which constructs an ideal subject drawn with great precision. But, nevertheless, the type of that collective personality — purely sociological — is analogous to that of the juridical personality, if indeed much more embryonic and less fixed, since it consists also of constituting a sort of common center of imputation of conducts realized by persons of flesh and blood, which are not attributed to such persons but to the entity. So, for example, when a man acts as director or member of an institution (without juridical personality), he realizes such conduct not as any individual, but as a function of the group, and it is attributed to it, and creates a responsibility for it. And this is so because the organization of the group consists precisely of this process of attribution or unified imputation of the various conducts which make it up, not of its respective persons, but of the group as a group. Now, then, this imputation takes place not by virtue of a norm of precise and unequivocal terms — as occurs with juridical personality — but by virtue of some forms of objectivated social life which so indicate, forms which ordinarily are less exact than those of the Law, and above all are norms which rule internally in the group, but which can have no force in the relations of it with the outside, that is, with other men and with other groups. Notwithstanding that it is a matter, as I have indicated, of a process analogous to that of the juridical personality, it is indeed less crystallized than of the latter. That is, the context of what we call the social personality of the collective entities consists also in a special measure of imputation. Now, in this theme there happens what we have already seen in others, to wit: that juristics represent the maximization of the collective characters, their culminating intensity, their rigid crystallization, their extreme expression.

CHAPTER X

THE ELEMENTS, SOURCES, AND SYSTEM OF POSITIVE LAW IN FORCE

1. Different Classes of Juridical Norms

Until now, when I have spoken in these pages of the positive juridical norm, I have studied it in its essence; but no reference has been made to the different types of norm, nor to their various sources, nor to the relations which they bear to one another. We shall now occupy ourselves with these themes.

There are juridical precepts of very diverse classes, according to their greater or less generality, or their lesser or greater concreteness, according to their range, and according to their source, apart from other classifications, with which I shall concern myself further on.

The juridical order current in a State, at any given moment, is composed of a series of precepts of diverse generality. There are those of maximum generality, for example, those contained in the laws, which in abstract terms bind to a determined type of situations a determined type of juridical consequences. There are those of greater concreteness, like many of the provisions of regulations and administrative directives, which make concrete, in more restricted terms, principles contained in the laws. There are other juridical precepts which have a purely concrete and singularized material and ambit, such as, for example, the pacts of a certain contract celebrated between Peter and John, which constitute the Law in force to regulate certain relations between those two persons.

And finally still there are those of a maximum concreteness, as happens with the provisions of a judicial judgment or of an administrative resolution, in which, within a certain time, a definite performance or consequence is commanded by name.

From another point of view, to wit, from the point of view of their apparent origin, we may also distinguish various types of juridical norms. There are those which appear in provisions emanating from the State (laws, public regulations, administrative orders, judgments of the courts). Others, on the other hand, reveal themselves by means of juridical customs, and consequently have as origin the juridical conviction of the community, expressed by the repetition of the same conduct with regard to certain relations. Others are the product of collective entities, of institutions, which beget spontaneously their own ordinances, as happens with some corporations, syndicates, etc. Finally, there is a series of juridical dispositions of a concrete character, whose contents emanate from the will of particular persons, for example, the clauses of a contract, those of a will, etc.

We shall leave until later other classifications of juridical norms (necessary and supplementary; formulated or not formulated, etc.).

It is necessary now to attain principles of orientation in the motley cluster of juridical norms, from the two points of view of difference which I have noted, that is, from the point of view of the diverse generality and range, and from the point of view of the various sources of their contents.

2. The Positive Law Is the Will of the State

Then, that multiform and disparate bulk of juridical precepts (laws, regulations, judgments, contracts, corporation statutes, customs, etc.) must constitute an organic or systematic whole, since otherwise the positive juridical order would not be possible. And it would not be possible, because we should meet a multitude of precepts of different origin, of distinct range, and even of disparate contents, without knowing how to articulate them. The principle of connection between all the juridical precepts of a positive order consists in their all being effective and ruling so far as and because they are the will of the State. The common reference of all juridical precepts to the will of the State is what permits the juridical order to be conceived as a unified and connected whole.

The affirmation that all juridical norms are the expression of the will of the State is not rendered untrue by adducing that there are juridical norms which have not been elaborated by the State, for example, the customary Law created spontaneously by a collectivity, the Law of corporations emanating from their own bosom, the rules of contracts dictated by the parties who celebrate them, etc. This objection is not admissible, because when we speak of the will of the State as the unified and sole source of the being in force of all and each of the juridical precepts, we do not mean that all the norms of Law have been made by the State — for it is notorious that this is not so — but that all which are valid as norms of the Law in force, whatever was their true origin, *are required and applied as such by the State.* And, on the other hand, we notice, moreover, that when we speak of the will of the State we do not refer to any real phenomenon of the psychological will of any men, but to a formal juridical construction, to wit, the personality of the State as a common center of imputation for all the mandates contained in the juridical order.

A juridical custom has not been elaborated by a qualified organ of the State, but has arisen by spontaneous social gestation in the bosom of a community. True; but that custom is Law in force only in case the State (the courts of justice) apply it, only if it is imposed inexorably by the organs of juridical coaction. If these do not take it into account, if they do not decide in accordance with what is determined by such custom, we may perhaps censure such disregard from an estimative or political point of view, but it is true that such custom does not constitute, in such case, current Law, although we may believe that it ought to constitute it. We may say the same with respect to the bylaws of a corporation: they have been made by it and not by the State, but they will constitute current Law only in the degree to which the State raises them and recognizes them as Law. And, similarly, we may say that the clauses of a contract it is true have been drawn up by the contracting parties, but they have effect as Law because the State permits private persons to establish, within certain limits, the juridical norms which will control certain reciprocal relations between them; and so it is that contracts made contrary to what is determined by the Law are considered juridically nonexistent.

3. Four Different Problems as to the Sources of the Law

Therefore, when we treat of the sources of the Law, we must differentiate carefully between two entirely different problems, to wit: (1) The problem of the common source of juridical force of all the norms, a problem which is solved by answering that this source is unitary and consists always and necessarily in the will of the State, understood as the common center of imputation of all the mandates contained in the juridical order; and (2) the theme with regard to how in fact there have been developed in history the concrete juridical contents, that is, what are the social processes by means of which the contents of the Law have arisen, which constitutes an investigation of genetic Sociology.

On the other side, it is necessary also to put the problem of the sources of the Law from two other points of view distinct from the two mentioned in the preceding paragraph, to wit: (a) to ask with relation to a given positive system — for example, the Mexican of today — what are the instances which it establishes for the production of juridical norms, that is, to whom and to what procedure is granted authority to establish juridical norms; and (b) the estimative consideration, that is, appraising, as to what procedures ought to be considered preferable for the formation of the Law, that is: the discussion as to whether statutory regulation is better than customary regulation; whether it is better to leave a broad margin of discretionary judgment in the courts, or if, on the contrary, it is more desirable to proceed with a rigidly preëstablished normation, etc.

So, then, we have outlined four distinct problems, which it is important to keep separate, since otherwise chaotic disorder would result in this matter. And exactly this is what has occurred in the greater part of juridical literature, produced with regard to this subject: that by having mixed up these four points of view, there has befallen a maximum of confusion.

4. The Formal Unitary Source of Positive Law

As to its fundamental of juridical validity, all Law (customary, jurisprudential, legislative, contractual, institutional, etc.) derives from the will of the State. What is called the will of the State, in juridical language, is no psychological reality, for the State, as we shall see, is not a real person who has consciousness or a will, in the proper meaning of those words. What is called the will of the State is simply a case of the *general law of normative imputation,* to wit: a series of acts done by certain individuals (administrative functionaries, legislators, courts of justice, contracting parties, etc.) are not attributed to such individual persons, but to an ideal subject supposed behind them, that is, to the State, which constitutes and signifies the total and unified personification of all the juridical norms. The State, or, what is the same thing, its will, consists of a central and common point of imputation, which constitutes the unity of the juridical order. The will of the State, or, what is the same thing, its personality, is an ideal term of imputation, created by the Law. Notice, by way of digression, that the State and Law are in juridical consideration two words which refer to one and the same object. I am not going to treat here, but I reserve for one of the later chapters, the much discussed problem of whether the reality of the State exceeds the juridical consideration of it, that is, if, in absolute terms, the State is the same as positive Law, or if, on the contrary, it is necessary to distinguish them and, consequently, to establish what are the relations which subsist between them. But, even being, as I am, adverse to the *Kelsenian* thesis of the full identification of State and Law, nevertheless I have to proclaim that for the jurist, that is, from a point of view purely and exclusively juridical, the State manifests itself solely in the Law and exhausts itself in the Law. For juridical consideration, State and Law appear as two forms or modes of the same thing, to wit, as the constituting order and the constituted order, respectively. For the jurist, the State exists only and so far and as it expresses itself in the Law; not as a social power (which it also is), not as a historic product (which it also is, indisputably), but as the subject and object of its norms, that is, of juridical norms. The State is the Law as normative activity; the Law is the State as a normated situation.

All positive Law (customary, jurisprudential, legislative, contractual, institutional, etc.) is such positive Law so far as we may refer it to the will of the State. That is then the sole formal source of positive juridical norms in force. And it is so because every positive norm, whatever may be its true origin, will constitute Law in force in the degree in which it must be applied, imposed by the State, that is, by its organs. Organs of the State are those which the Law establishes as such, because certain acts of them are not attributed to them but to the State. But the organs of the State cease to be such when what they enact is not what is provided in the juridical order as the will of the State. And all that they do, within the orbit of their formal and material competence, is effective as will of the State (although in fact it has been created by other sources: customary, institutional, contractual, etc.). That custom or that contractual or institutional norm is not positive Law, is not current Law, which is not susceptible of obtaining enforcement from the courts or the other organs of the State which may come in question, that is, a norm whose compliance is not going to be inexorably imposed by the State. If the custom (or the institutional norm) is applied by a state organ competent for the purpose, it is so far a manifestation of the will of the State; or, better, because it is considered that the State makes its will express in this norm, it is thus applied by the state organs. A custom may in fact exist, but if the state organs do not apply it, if they do not impose compliance with it, it will not constitute Law in force, it will not be Law in reality; it will remain something which would like to be Law, but which has not been able to attain being it; and, naturally, the way for critical judgment remains open, to consider the non-recognition of such custom proper or improper.

5. Sociological Allusion to the Generating Sources of Law

As I have indicated, it is necessary to undertake a study of the real genesis of the juridical norms. And, proceeding inductively in this historico-sociological observation as to the sources from which flow juridical rules, there may be established a picture of the more important typical sources of the contents of the Law and of those factors which — in greater or less proportion — we find always, or almost always, as producers of juridical determinations. This observation will show us that the Law has gone on developing concretely in history thanks to different social processes: judicial decisions not based either on a legal norm nor on precedents; customs; doctrine applied by the courts; laws, regulations; recognition of the autonomy of the private will to create juridical norms (for example, contractual ones); foreign Law incorporated in judicial practice; ideological movements which may penetrate the decisions of the State; social convictions which are received by the Law and made lawful; professional usages which attain the status of juridical obligation; etc.

Among the enumerated sources — and all the possible others — three stand out for their constancy and permanency and for their power of absorption with respect to the others. They are jurisprudence, custom, and Statute.

Custom has had great importance above all in primitive societies, and of course still persists, although in lesser degree — and even preserves enormous effect in peoples of a maximum civilization like the Anglo-Saxons. But with this exception, in general, in the course of historical progress, custom is in a great part being displaced by the Statute, that is to say, by the written Law, dictated by the competent public power, in which a general rule is formulated for the future.

Now, jurisprudence, that is, the decisions of the courts, has had the part of greatest protagonist in the formation of the Law; and, although in much less volume, it continues today of great importance. And it is understandable why it has been so and still goes on being so (although in much diminished proportions); because in fact the last and greatest expression of juristics is always the executory judgment. The state will of inexorable imposition always manifests itself in final instance in concrete decisions.

Not all customs are juridical; since by custom are manifested also moral norms, rules of social behavior, technical maxims, etc. Custom by means of which are manifested social rules with the character of inexorable mandate is juridical, that is, as of forced imposition. Juridical custom is that custom which rules in a collectivity and is considered by it as juridically obligatory. There are to be distinguished in it on one side that which properly constitutes the juridical norm, which is the current conviction in the collectivity of what certain behavior is juridically obligatory, which has been called *animus* and also *opinio juris* or *opinio necessitatis;* and, on the other side, the fact of the effective reiteration of that conduct in the bosom of a collectivity, by means of which is manifested that conviction, a fact which creates the positive existence of the norm.

In spite of the fact that codification has lessened enormously the importance of custom and has restricted in great measure its field of action, nevertheless it still subsists in the field of private law, since the greater part of the civil laws — as also the mercantile laws — grant it authority as a subsidiary source of Law, in case there does not exist any law applicable to the given case; and also in other cases their own normation is completed by a reference to a customary rule (for example, when the law says that the payment of a rural rent shall be made on the date which local custom requires). In constitutional Law, custom still has great importance: English constitutional Law is based on very few texts and in great part rests upon customs; the delegation of competence by the legislative power to the executive in France is founded upon a customary precedent; the procedure of the head of the State in consulting the principal political leaders in cases of ministerial crisis, in Spanish constitutional law — when Spain was a constitutional State — had also a customary base; etc. Custom also has great importance in the matter of public international Law; precisely because of the embryonic, rudimentary character which International Law still has, custom plays a great part. On the other hand, custom is excluded from the Penal Law of civilized peoples, because in that there is established the principle that there can be no crime without a law which previously made it such; and also that no penalty can be imposed unless it has been established previously by a law. And also for reasons of security, custom has been excluded from the field of procedural Law, because in it certainty and the rigor of forms play the greatest part.

It must be noted that the observations which I have just made as to the part and the importance of custom summarize the situation of the countries of the European Continent and the Spanish American ones; but on the other hand it happens otherwise in English Law — and also in the North American Law. England has not let itself be attracted by the codifying movement; and its Law has gone on following customary

Law, or rather judicial usages (case laws) reported in the numerous collections of decisions (Law Reports); and the legislative Law is enacted to supply the deficiencies which customary law may leave upon certain points.[51]

From the material point of view, that is, from the point of view of the genesis of the juridical contents, it is usual also to indicate as one of the sources of the Law scientific doctrine and juridical philosophy; because it is observed how, many times, there are incorporated in the juridical order in force the opinions of the jurisconsults and the philosophers. But the science and the philosophy of the Law do not function directly as sources of the Law except to the degree in which they penetrate the other sources formally recognized as such, that is, to the degree in which they influence the thought of the legislator, or react upon popular juridical convictions, or upon the ideas of the courts.

This is not the opportune place to consider the problem as to the advantages and disadvantages which each of the sources referred to has, and especially law and custom. Let us say only that custom has the inconveniences that ordinarily it constitutes an instance of very vague outlines, and that, consequently, it serves less the urgency of security and certainty, which is the vital root of the Law; and that, moreover, it is insufficient to regulate the complicated relations of an advanced society; but it has the advantage that being deeply rooted in reality, it takes account of decisive probabilities upon which it will regulate effectively and successfully the relations for which it arises. The law has the advantages that it serves fully for juridical security and certainty; that it can meet all the necessities which are being presented; that in it may be embodied better a progressive rhythm; but on the other hand it may run into the danger that it departs too much from the reality of the collective situations, that it wants to go too far in its eagerness for reform, and then fails (remains merely a dead letter) or produces catastrophic results by its enormous aloofness with respect to certain historic conditions. In any case, both law and custom represent manifestations of a predominant social will.

6. The System of the Juridical Order in Force

All the different precepts which make up the juridical order in force, at a given moment, have different origins, of various range: but nevertheless they keep among themselves a formal connection, that is to say, they have an organic articulation, in spite of the different sources of their origin and of their disparate characters. We cannot interpret all these

[51] Cf. W. M. Geldardt, Elements of English Law (2d ed., London, 1931); Roscoe Pound, Outlines of Lectures on Jurisprudence (1928).

components as constituting a mere inorganic and disorderly aggregate, a mere fortuitous juxtaposition, but they form a unified and connected whole, a systematic order, whose parts keep relations of coördination and dependence among themselves. Then, what is the principle which gathers in the form of a system all these juridical norms of disparate origin, range, and extent? It is a question of a common title of formal effect, of a common base of validity which is precisely what makes them all norms of the order in force. An aggregate of norms constitutes an order, that is, a relatively independent system, when the *raison d'être* or validity of all of them is derived from one single or the same norm, upon which all formally rest, which receives with reference to all the others the description of fundamental norm. We owe this theory for constructing the system of the juridical order in force to the masters of the Vienna Kelsen school, Merkl and Verdross.[52] The creation or determination of some juridical norms is regulated by other juridical norms. So, for example, the establishment of the ordinary laws is regulated by the constitution; by whom and in what manner are to be issued regulations is directed in certain laws; judgments and judicial steps are conditioned by legal and regulatory juridical norms, as well of a substantive nature (civil, penal, administrative, etc.) as of a procedural character (personal); local ordinances are founded on legal and regulatory precepts which determine the conditions and the competence of the municipal authorities; contracts are valid when they have been made by persons whom the law declares competent, within the range permitted by the law, and according to the forms required by it, etc. Therefore, the principle of internal connection of a juridical order or system is a relation of the foundation of the validity of certain norms to the validity of others: if it is asked what the reason is for the validity of a juridical norm, that is, the reason why it is an integral part of an order or system of Law (for example, current Mexican Law), we shall see that it rests upon another norm which regulates the production of the first. A valid

[52] Cf. KELSEN, DAS PROBLEM DER SOUVERANITÄT UND DIE THEORIE DES VÖLKERRECHTS (1920); ALLGEMEINE STAATSLEHRE (1925); COMPENDIO DE TEORÍA GENERAL DEL ESTADO (not published in German), translation of Luis Recaséns Siches and Justino de Azcárate (2d ed.), corrected, with a preliminary STUDY OF THE PURE THEORY OF LAW AND THE STATE, by LUIS RECASÉNS SICHES (1934); ADOLF MERKL, DIE RECHTSEINHEIT DES ÖSTERREICHISCHEN STAATES (1927); ALFRED VERDROSS, DIE EINHEIT DES RECHTLICHEN WELTBILDES AUF GRUND DER VÖLKERRECHTSVERFASSUNG (1923). Strictly, Merkl was the originator of this doctrine, which afterwards Kelsen took from him, and which Verdross applied to the problem of the relations of state Law with international Law. In the consideration of this theme with respect to International Law, Josef L. Kunz has attained important successes. (Cf. LA PRIMAUTÉ DU DROIT DES GENS, 1925.)

norm, that is, is such juridical norm in force, because and so far as it was established by the person and in the manner which a superior norm provides; so, for example, the individualized precept of a judicial judgment finds the reason of its validity in certain laws of the State (the substantive law which applies, the organic ones by which are established the judicial organs and the procedural ones which regulate their activities); and all of them in their turn in the constitution.

It happens then that each part of the juridical system, that is, each class of norms, rests on other parts superior to it; and moreover constitutes in its turn the base or support for other inferior sets. The totality of the juridical order (in force) constitutes then a system constructed in echelon or graduated form, in a hierarchical structure, in which each one of the steps or links depends on its superior and in turn sustains its inferiors. The Law regulates its own creation, its ulterior production, and its reform, in such way that the production of a norm appears conditioned on its validity by another norm; and then in its turn is the fundamental determination for the issuance of other precepts; and so successively until we arrive at executive mandates.

Now, the validity of all the norms of a juridical order comes to lean, finally, that is, to rest in final instance, on the *constitution* — understanding by constitution the norm which determines the supreme competence of the juridical system, that is, the supreme authority of the State. But, upon what is the constitution based, from whence does it derive its reason for being? It may happen that a current constitution is derived from other prior constitutional laws, which were modified by the means and according to the procedure established in themselves; so that the new constitution springs up supported entirely by what was provided in the former one. But finally one will arrive at a constitution which was not established in conformity with the precepts of any other older one, either because it was the first for the juridical community in question, or because it arose by means of a revolution or *coup d'etat,* that is, with a break in the continuity of the juridical history; in short, we arrive at the *first constitution in the juridico-positive sense.* Now, that this first constitution should have validity, that it should be positive Law, is something which cannot be founded on pure juridical arguments, in the strict sense, drawn from the system itself, because precisely the whole of the juridical system and everything derived from it is supported on the constitution — while we remain within the sphere of the juridical order of a State which we are considering as fully sovereign. The validity or base of this first constitution — born in the ordinary manner, for example, by reason of the establishment of a new State, or by means of a revolution or *coup d'etat* — cannot be justified by *juridico-positive reasons.* Its justification has to be founded on other considerations, on political and historical considerations, which, in fine, require a judgment of valuation. The jurist, so far as he is purely that, and from the exclusively juridical point of view, *takes for granted* the validity of the constitution. It is clear that the validity of this supposition may be discussed in an estimative field, and there may be adduced opportunely reasons for and against the justification of that supposition. But this does not belong to the strict juridical function; the jurist dwells in a determined system, and within it he proceeds to reason out the basis of each one of its parts; but he cannot rise outside of the system in which he dwells; and on this account cannot construct juridically the connection of the fundamental norm of the system, or, what is the same thing, the connection of the totality of the system. The formula of this *supposition* or *hypothesis,* which grounds the unity and the validity of a juridical system, would read approximately: *one ought to behave as the organ which established the first constitution commands;* or again: *that organ which orders the establishment of the first constitution shall be the positive base of the Law in force.* This supposition Kelsen calls the *hypothetical fundamental norm* or the *constitution in the logico-juridical sense,* to differentiate it from the first positive constitution, which was established founded on it, which he calls the *constitution in the juridico-positive sense.* In saying that the fundamental norm has only a hypothetical function, we refer to the strictly juridical point of view immanent in the system; but we do not mean to say that it lacks foundation: it has it certainly, but of a different sort, not juridical in the restricted sense of that word, but historical, sociological, in the last instance founded on estimative considerations. But from the purely and exclusively juridical angle of a system, it results that the primary juridical norm, the constitutional one, as the basis or cornerstone of the whole order, cannot have a foundation within it, but outside of it. In fact, each one of the parts of a juridical system is supported upon other parts of the same, in a similar way to that in which each of the stones or bricks of a building rests upon others; but the totality of a positive juridical order cannot be supported upon a positive precept, but upon something which is prior to that system, as the foundations of a house cannot rest upon any element of the construction, but upon a lower plane. At bottom, the base of a juridical system consists of a phenomenon of predominant social will, in the formulation of which there is implicit an estimative political judgment. But this point will be elaborated further on.

7. The Forms of Production of the Law: the Original and the Derivative Ways

From what has been said, it follows that we must distinguish between two manners of production of juridical norms: (a) *Original production,* which is that in which is created the fundamental norm of a system or order and which gives birth to it, without support in any previous positive juridical norm, for example: the establishment of a juridical community in a territory not belonging to any State; the foundation of a new State, as occurred with the German Empire in 1870, and, also, with the foundation of the Czechoslovakian Republic and the Republic of Poland in 1918; so also a revolution, a *coup d'etat* and the triumphant conquest. (b) *Derivative production,* which is that which takes place when norms are produced, according to the provisions of a juridical system already constituted, by the competences and under the procedures established in it; for example, the ordinary laws enacted by the legislative power which is sanctioned by the constitution; regulations decreed by the authorities competent for the purpose; judgments rendered by competent courts, as provided in the applicable laws; contracts made by private persons with capacity for it, according to the law and within the field permitted by it, etc.

8. The Original Production. The Constituting Power

When a juridical order arises for the first time, that is, without support upon any other previous positive order, it is clear that it represents an original production; that is, there arise norms which do not find their reason for validity in other norms, because they are going to inaugurate a system, and, consequently, they constitute prime norms. Such first norms cannot adduce a foundation of juridical *legitimacy* derived from any previous system, since there is none such. They may adduce another type of historic, political, ethical, explanation or justification, in short, a judgment of value; but not any juridical legitimacy.

The problem does not seem so grave when it is a matter of the creation of a new State. But, on the other hand, it presents itself as troublesome for the Philosophy of Law when the original production arises from a violent rupture of the previous juridical order (revolution, *coup d'état* or conquest). Revolution, a *coup d'état,* and triumphant conquest — which represent a violation of the previous juridical order — in many cases create new Law, originate a new juridical system. This cannot be explained by the pure jurist, by the jurist *sensu stricto,* because he moves within the contained field of a positive juridical system in force; and when the violent fact occurs which ruins that system, the jurist finds that thereby there has been destroyed the sphere in which he dwelt. He may move to the new sphere or system created by the triumphant movement; but he cannot adduce for it juridico-positive reasons, but only another type of reasons (historic, political, always in conjunction with estimative points of view). What these reasons may be constitutes a grave problem for the Philosophy of Law. And it may happen that when one speaks of estimative reasons one does not mean thereby necessarily a sincere political devotion to the new regime which has arisen, but, even feeling hostility to it, if it adopts the juridical character and obtains a normal majority sentiment — that is, not by continued violence, but by the adherence of the predominant social conscience — he lends obedience to the new system, because he considers it necessary that there should be Law; and once the previous one has been ruined, it is preferable to accept the new — if it has juridical form — than that there should not be any. And so, then, it is recognized that a new law has been born.

Now, the recognition or proof that a new law has been born — although it is given for the considerations that I have just mentioned — does not necessarily imply, in any way, either a favorable estimative judgment upon what the revolution or triumphant *coup d'état* has created, nor much less the need to lower the head before the accomplished facts. It may be recognized that a new law has been born, and judged nevertheless, that it is so abominable that one feels the duty to make every effort to overthrow it, even by resort to violence. That is, one may register the *legality of today;* and, notwithstanding, by virtue of certain estimative considerations, in the service of an idea of justice, judge that one ought to make every effort to strike down that legality of today and to substitute for it tomorrow a more just legality, whether renewing that of yesterday or establishing another new one on better bases.

Notice that here[53] I speak of revolution in a purely juridico-formal sense, as a break of continuity in the development of the Law, that is, as a lapse of the previous system and the original production of another new system. I speak from a juridico-formal point of view, because I consider that a system lapses so far as its fundamental norm loses the minimum of actuality, of true reality, which it needs for its existence; and because I consider that the new system is *new,* so far as it is based on another fundamental norm, which is first, in that it is not founded on any in the previous regime. So, then, one juridical system dies and another is born (always and when there are fulfilled the two requisites

[53] This paragraph and the three which follow it are from the Second Spanish edition of the book (Mexico, 1945). TRANSLATOR.

which I shall speak of further on), because the fundamental norm is replaced without the new one having any support in the old. The new system, which is formally new because it has a different base of validity from that which served as ground for the former one, may be very different from the preceding as to its content or, on the contrary, may keep many of the norms which composed the other. But, although this may be so, it is a matter of a new system, because the reason for the validity or formal existence of those norms, which already formed part of the former, is, in the new, distinct from that which they had in the preceding; they are valid in the new system because the power triumphant in the revolution or in the *coup d'état* has accepted them as worthy and not by virtue of the formal foundation which they had in the preceding regime. So, then, the revolution, the *coup d'état,* and the conquest are considered here as cases of original production of Law; are considered within it as cases of basic rupture of the previous juridical order, of break in continuity of juridical development. Consequently, I take here revolution only in this sense of formal rupture of the prior juridical order and replacement of it by another system with a new base, independently of what may be the magnitude of novelties which the new system offers as to the material content of many of its norms.

But it is clear that apart from this formal concept of revolution as a rupture or break of continuity in juridical history, the word revolution has other meanings; that is, there are other concepts of revolution from other points of view. So, for example, from the point of view of content, not every rupture of juridical continuity can be considered revolution in the profound sense, politically and socially. From the point of view of the political and social content, only that rupture with the past can be called revolution which takes place in a sudden manner, that is, with scant respect for the past situation and the installation of a new system, which shall be new not only as to its formal base but also as to the content of a great part of its norms.

On the other hand, also with the meaning of content, but with more ample extent or comprehension, there may be called revolution also any deep transformation of the historic life, in culture and in society, founded on the discovery of new values, a discovery which arouses a radical change in the attitude of men to existence, in the orientation of their tasks, in their preferences, in their social structures. In this sense one may, for example, speak of the revolutions brought about by Christianity, by the Renaissance, and by modern mentality. Carlos Cossio, in a very interesting and valuable book, has tried to find a pure concept of revolution applicable not only to those manifestations but to all cases includable under this word, a concept which shall constitute a category of historical knowledge. Cossio characterizes this pure concept of revolution as facts of the historic man, which break the logic of their antecedents and refer to and directly affect society.

Finally it is necessary to speak not of revolution but of what we might call a specific form of revolutionary activity, which is a phenomenon characteristic above all of the modern age. It consists of a rationalist attitude or state of mind of contempt for the real structures forged in the historic process of the past, of a desire to overthrow them and to replace them by putting in practice a conception of the intellect, in which one has full confidence. In this sense, the revolutionary attitude constitutes a state of mind of hypertrophic devotion to pure abstract reason, of a mathematical type, which tries to impose itself on life to mold it to its form; that is, it entertains the proposition of adapting social reality to an ideal scheme, to the square of concepts which pure reason has forged; which it carries, on the wings of a superlative enthusiasm, in a radical posture and at the same time with a kind of fervent love and exaltation for the revolutionary task; so that, for example, in a violent revolution nothing is seen so much as a severe surgical necessity, for which there is no more remedy than to call upon the dramatic moments of history, in which all the other paths have been closed, and above all there is seen in revolution the normal and magnificent proceeding of sweeping out past traditions and structures, basely engendered (that is, not according to schemes of the intellect) and putting into practice the plans made by reason. It would be very suggestive to develop the themes outlined upon the different concepts or meanings of revolution and to trace the relations which there may be among them. But this treatise upon the fundamental theory of Law is not the adequate place to develop those themes. This digression has already become too long, whose only object was to allude to those other concepts of revolution; and it is time to close this parenthesis, to return to the theme of the present section, which is that of the original production of Law and, within it, the cases of revolution, *coup d'état,* and conquest which all three constitute a rupture of the juridical order in force and the creation of a new order on a different fundamental base, that is, which represent a break of continuity in the history of Law.

One would ask, perhaps, why it must be admitted that from a violent rupture of the juridical order a new Law may in some cases be born; and why, on the other hand, the principle of legitimacy is not sustained, that is, the principle that the Law only can reform and reshape itself by the procedure established in the juridical order in force. But it is to be noted that if we should establish such a criterion, we would have to conclude that there is not actually in the whole world a single juridical order, since revolutions and *coups d'état* which have broken the juridical continuity are not lacking in the history of any nation. Note, moreover, that, even admitting hypothetically such criterion of legitimacy, the problem set by the original appearance of the Law remains integrally present, since the chain which unites the successive phases of the legitimate development of the Law has to have a beginning; that is, it will have a first link or step, which will not be supported on any prior ones, but which will represent a moment of original juridical creation, without previous juridico-positive support. And we have seen already that there are other cases of original production of the Law, apart from revolution, *coup d'état,* and triumphant conquest.

At the depth of the explanation and justification that such facts (of breach of continuity in juridical history) can — with regard to certain conditions — create new Law lies the feeling of certainty and security which is the vital root of the Law. Once the anterior juridical order has been overthrown and broken to pieces, society remains without Law; and then the necessity which this vacuum creates is filled by the new Law which the revolution creates, or the *coup d'état,* or the conquest. And so from an estimative point of view the new Law arisen from the violent event may be preferable — although it is not considered good — to the absence of all juridical order.

Now, I must repeat two warnings, which I have already outlined. *In the first place,* it is to be noted that the statement that a new Law has been born does not imply in any way an estimative approval of its contents. The new Law may turn out better than the former, more just, more adequate for the social circumstances and to the necessities of the collectivity, as for example occurred with the Law arising from the French Revolution, in relation to that of the old destroyed regime. Or, on the contrary, the new Law arisen from the violent event may represent something much worse than that destroyed, such as for example occurred with the order created by some revolutions in our time, on the old continent, which signified a pure regression and an agency of rebarbarization — apart from the fact that in such regimes there is a great amount of arbitrariness, which is not Law either just or unjust, but brute force at the service of caprice.

In the second place, it is to be noted that not everything done by the triumphant power in a revolution, *coup d'état,* or conquest, represents the creation or birth of new Law. To register an original production of Law, there are essentially necessary two requisites: (1) That the new product, which aspires to be valid as Law, possesses the essential characters or notes of the formal concept of juricity, that is, that it treats of mandates in juridical form and not of arbitrary mandates; (2) That the predominant social will is in accord with the new regime, by virtue of adherence to it and not by the mere crushing influence of brute force.

The first requisite refers, as I have indicated, to the difference between Law and arbitrariness. For the mandates issued by the new regime to constitute Law, it is necessary that they should not be arbitrary mandates. That is, it is necessary that they should not be mandates which correspond only to the fortuitous and unforeseeable caprice of whoever controls the supreme power, unconnected with any general rule, foreign to any fixed principle; but, on the contrary, it is necessary that, whatever be their content, they should constitute an expression of general rules which are imposed as valid for all, obliging even him who enacts them; that is, it is necessary that they should represent inviolable principles with general validity, with stable effect, until they are repealed or supplanted by others of equal nature. With this first requisite we do not formulate any estimative judgment upon the justice or injustice, nor upon the adequacy or inadequacy of the contents of the new norms; but we only trace the line between those which have juridical form — and which by virtue of it satisfy the urgency for certainty and security — and those which represent solely and exclusively the manifestation of the peculiar whims of the holder of the power, without regard to any fixed and stable criterion, in short, those which constitute pure arbitrariness — and which, in such measure, represent the destruction of all certainty and security.

The second requisite consists in that for the new system of norms to be able to be considered as Law in force, it is necessary that in its aggregate it obtains the recognition or adhesion of a majority of the community, whose life it proposes to regulate. It is true that there belongs to the essence of juricity the dimension of inexorable necessity or coercitive imposition; but this dimension refers to all and each of the norms within a system *in force*. Now, for a system, in its aggregate, to be considered as *in force*, it is necessary that it be supported upon the effective predominant social will; that is, that it should count upon a real basis of assent of the majority of the collectivity; that it should constitute an expression of the predominant manner of thinking and of feeling of the society. The root of the being in force of a juridical system cannot consist in a pure relation of brute force. On the contrary, it must consist of a resultant of the wills which form the social texture. The deepest root of the juridical command is never material force. The juridical command has at its disposal the greatest concentration of power and of force which there is in society, to cause inexorably, compulsorily if necessary, compliance with its precepts. But its installation as a juridical command is not founded on the holding of the instruments of material force, but on the support of public opinion. Precisely because a regime is installed with the acquiescence of public opinion, because it counts on the resultant of the wills which make up the collectivity, on that account it has at its disposition the apparatus which is called force.

This adherence[54] of public opinion may be given in very different degrees. But a minimum of adherence which represents the tranquil and normal acceptance of the greater part of the people is always indispensable for it to be able to be said that a new juridical regime has been born, because otherwise we should find ourselves in the presence only of a phenomenon of brutality. The new regime may arise supported from the first moment by a fervent enthusiasm of the immense majority or of almost the whole of the community, as, for example, happened with the Spanish Republic in April, 1931, exalted in ardent devotion by more than three quarters of the nation. In this case, there is no problem of any sort, because the new regime counts not only on the acquiescence of the people, but also on something more intense and vigorous: on the phenomenal activation of the result of an enfervored will. It may happen also that the new regime counts only on the enthusiastic support of a majority and on the passive compliance of the other groups. And it may happen that the new system has for its support only the passive conformity of the people, without any fervent devotion. This would be the minimum to which I have referred as indispensable for the new system to be considered as Law. That passive acceptance, though pacific and normal — we might say, conformist — constitutes a deference without identification with what the new regime represents, inspired by motives distinct from any enthusiasm or even from full satisfaction. These motives, for example, may be that, considering it difficult for the moment to overcome the regime newly installed and thinking that it would be worse to live without Law in a situation of anarchy, one chooses to join with it, in the hope of some more favorable juncture to modify or defeat it. Or even the people, without wishing to be identified with the new regime, consider it as the lesser evil among all the other immediate possibilities and agree to defer to it for that motive. In such cases, although there does not exist a feeling of full satisfaction nor any enthusiastic coincidence with what the regime represents, there is produced a normal and peaceful accession; a customary habituation. This is sufficient to comply with that second indispensable requisite that the order which has arisen with a juridical aspect — containing therefore the first requisite — may be considered as new Law. On the other hand, if the new

[54] This paragraph (though not there paragraphed, but running along with the preceding and following text) is from the Second Spanish edition of the book (Mexico, 1945). TRANSLATOR.

order, although it has a juridical aspect, is maintained solely by the brute force of arms and terror, against not only the manner of thinking and feeling of a majority of the people, but also of their taxative will, only because they have been reduced to impotence by atrocious violence, then the new regime cannot be considered as juridical, even though it issues norms which have juridical form.

Whoever counts solely and exclusively on the brutality of material force may direct an aggression against a people, and even maintain it for some time, but properly speaking will not exercise any juridical command over them. In this respect, José Ortega y Gasset says: "It is necessary to distinguish between a fact or process of aggression and a situation of command. The command is the normal exercise of authority. It is always founded upon public opinion — always, today as ten thousand years ago, among the English as among the Botocudos. The truth is that one does not command with Janizaries. So Talleyrand to Napoleon: 'With bayonets, Sire, one may do all, except one thing: sit on them.' And to command is not the gesture of snatching power, but the tranquil exercise of it. In short, to command is to be settled. Throne, seat, curule, the blue bench, ministerial chair, see . . . The State, finally, is the state of public opinion." [55] Who commands juridically disposes, as I have said, of all the force to impose his norms on rebels. But the global fact of his command, or, what is the same thing, the fundamental base of the juridical system, of the regime as a totality, cannot be force, but must be the adherence of the national community.

9. The Constituent Power

Not every replacement or reform of the constitution represents an original production of Law, nor, consequently, does it inaugurate a new juridical system, nor indeed finally does it determine a break of continuity with respect to the prior order. A constitution may be modified or replaced normally, legally, that is, following therefor the procedure for reform explicitly or tacitly provided in the previous constitution, that is, as to what is modified or replaced; and then the continuity of the juridical life is not broken in any way, since on the prior constitutional foundation is placed another new one linked with it, founded on it; so that the validity of the new constitution does not represent anything primary; is not anything radically original, is not something of a new base, but is derived from the validity of the preceding constitution, which serves as foundation for the new.

Now, the normal or legal reform of the constitution is limited by in-

[55] Cf. José Ortega y Gasset, La rebelión de las masas (1929).

surmountable barriers: it may comprise a number of points, but never that relative to the titular legitimacy of the supreme power. That a modification of the constitution may be considered as a legal reform, normal — and not as another completely different type of alteration — it is necessary that it respect the original title of the supreme power, that it continue being supported upon the same power primarily accepted as legitimate. A normal or legal reform of the constitution cannot go to the point of changing the essence of the constitution, it cannot modify the supreme power of the State; for example, it cannot transform a democratic regime into a regime of absolute monarchy by divine law, nor vice versa; since either of those two changes represents a break of continuity, represents the rising of a new regime, not supported in the former, but based precisely on the negation of what was essential in the former. This is so for the following consideration, which is entirely clear and evident: the organ or power authorized to reform the current constitution is such, precisely because that constitution confers competence upon it for that purpose; and, consequently, it can modify those points of the constitution for whose reform such competence is granted, but in no case can it modify — even if such competence has not been expressly limited — what refers essentially to the authority of the supreme power. At the moment at which the organ competent for the reform of the constitution pretends to modify this point — the authority or source of the supreme power — it would negate the foundation of its own legal competence; and, then, what it might do in that direction would constitute the original foundation of a new juridical system, without connection with the former, without any foundation upon the preceding; it would represent a total break with the preceding juridical order, even in case it was produced in a peaceful and bloodless manner. Notice that to cause a break of continuity in juridical history it is by no means indispensable that events of material violence should occur. Although this latter is the most frequent, nevertheless history records cases in which without any act of violence, an old regime falls and a new regime then appears — as the original production of a new Law.[56]

The original production of Law implies what is called *constituent power*. When a state community is formed for the first time (and also when in an old State the former regime has been defeated), there arises the constituent situation, which is characterized by there being no positive prior Law which is in force, and because it goes to found the new juridical system.

[56] As, for example, the proclamation of the Spanish Republic on April 14, 1931, a sweeping—and at the same time pacific—expression of the will of an immense majority of the Spanish people.

With respect to the constituent power there have to be put two questions: (1) In what does the constituent power consist? (2) To whom should the constituent power belong? The first of these themes consists of asking ourselves for the essential or pure essence of the constituent power. The second is properly a problem of the Juridical Estimative or of political philosophy.

Let us concern ourselves, before all, with the first of these questions: of the nature of the constituent power. The constituent power is by its nature unlimited, absolute, so far as it does not find itself submitted to any positive order, and so far as it does not derive its competence from any other power, but is founded on itself, in itself, as primary and original. The acting of the constituent power represents an original form of Law; and, consequently, is not regulated by any preëxisting positive juridical order. The constituent power is precisely the condition for having afterwards constituted Law; and, therefore, is not conditioned by any prior positive norm. The constituent act is the primordial and original act of sovereignty, superior and prior to the acts of ordinary sovereignty, whose future regulation it will itself have to establish. The constituent power cannot find itself submitted to any previous positive precept — if there was an order before, it falls — and consequently, the constituent power is superior and prior to every established norm, for in it there will be founded the validity of all the norms to be established. Hence, the constituent power is not bound by any positive bond: it represents an immediate will, prior and superior to every provided procedure. As it does not proceed from any prior positive norm, it cannot be regulated by previous juridical precepts. On this account, said Sièyes, the constituent power "can do anything." [57]

Now the preceding affirmations are not to be misinterpreted by giving them a meaning and an extent different from what they have. In speaking of the unlimited and absolute character of the constituent power, I was declaring only that it was not subjected to any prior juridical norm, simply because there is no prior juridical norm which is still in force — those which continue in force while the constituent power may act do not derive their efficacy from any former title, but from a tacit or express validation on the part of the constituent power. But this formal absence of limitation of the constituent power in no manner implies that we

[57] Cf. my book El poder constituyente. Su teoría aplicada al momento español (Madrid: Morata, 1931). Cf. also Sièyes, Arch. Parlam. 1st ser., t. viii, pp. 256ff.; Carré de Malberg, Contribution à la théorie générale de l'Etat (1922) 517; Vattel, Le Droit des gens ou principes de la loi naturelle (1758) 33; Zweig, Die Lehre vom pouvoir constituant 117ff.; Jellinek, Allgemeine Staatslehre, t. II; Carl Schmitt, Verfassungslehre (1928).

have to consider that the constituent power is not subjected to other non-positive norms or that it ought not to follow certain estimative orientations. That is, the constituent power is not subjected to any positive bond, but it is subject to ideal juridical values and to the exigencies of the common good in a certain historic circumstance. The constituent power does not find itself restricted by any human juridical authority, but it must obey the principles and the other juridical values and the social opinion which has originated it.

The constituent power is essentially unified and indivisible; that is to say, it is not a coördinate power with other divided powers (legislative, executive, judicial); above all, it is the foundation of all the other powers which are going to arise and of their respective competences. The elaboration of a *first* constitution (written or not written, of one type or another, express or tacit) supposes a constituent power; and, so, from the very concept of a constitution is deduced the difference between the constituent power and the constituted powers. All the competences or faculties of the constituted powers rest on the fundamental norm, basis of the first constitution, and as this is the work of the constituent power, it results finally that they are derived from it. The whole juridical system is based on the fundamental norm which instituted the constituent power ("what the constituent power orders will be Law"). The constituent power rises precisely when there is no prior juridical system — either because it is a matter of the foundation of a new sovereign political community, or because in a preëxisting one the ancient regime has fallen — and, consequently, there then exists no constituted power with a juridico-positive title; the only legitimate power is the constituent one; in it the fact of its reality is founded with the Law; since all the Law which is going to arise will be supported on the fact of the constituent power.

It will be argued, perhaps, that despite the changes of regime, there subsists in the new order a series of juridical norms accepted from the prior one — for example, the civil code, etc. — which has occurred in more than one revolution. But such objection is not justified against the thesis which I have explained, for the simple reason that it confounds the norms with their real origin and the title of their formal efficacy. If after a triumphant revolution there subsists the civil code which had been born and which ruled in the prior defeated regime, although it is a question of the same civil code, the foundation of its validity has changed substantially. It rules in the new regime, not by virtue of the title which it possessed in the past one, but thanks to the new regime's having expressly or tacitly approved it. So, for example, in Spain, after the proclamation of the Republic in 1931, the old civil code continued in force; but from that date it ruled not because it had been approved by the

Cortes of 1888 and the Crown had sanctioned it, but because the Constituent Power of the Republic had tacitly ratified it.

Up to now, I have examined the question of what the constituent power essentially is; that is, of what it consists. But there remains the other question which I have already mentioned, that of *to whom ought to belong* the right of the constituent power. But this is indeed not a problem of the general theory of Law, but a question of the Juridical Estimative and of political Philosophy. Consequently, this question ought to be postponed to the latter part of the book, in which the Juridical Estimative will be treated. But in order not to break the unity of the material relating to the constituent power, I shall deal here with this theme, although it represents a point of view formally distinct from those which make up the content of this investigation; since, now, it is not a question of seeking the essence of a juridical concept, but of asking ourselves for an appraising exigency.

The conceptions of an absolute monarchy founded on a supposed Divine Right held that the constituent power belonged to the king, who received it fully in his concrete person, by virtue of a taxative and determined Divine Will. This thesis more than a century ago entered into a sharp decline, even in the very bosom of monarchial traditionalism, which tried to find democratic foundations for its thesis, which occurred within the actual parties of German Lutheranism, since Bismarck himself adduced the will of the people as the basis for the Prussian crown and the imperial institution. In recent times, the totalitarian political movements have tried to maintain other theses, which do not withstand serious examination, for they represent the expression of frantic gyrations — the enthronement of myths: violent audacity, race, etc. — and such myths have even been proclaimed without full conviction, since at the same time that they were declared with noisy paroxysms, they tried to find a democratic support (real or fictitious) for such regimes. (Note that the totalitarian regimes are not characterized so much by their antidemocracy, since they are typically revolutions of the masses, as by the denial of human dignity and of liberty; and it is fundamentally in this denial of liberty in which reside their barbarity and monstrosity[58] consisting of a proposition of integral bestiality and at the same time in a satanic attitude, that is, of subversion of all the values.)

The zone of western culture maintains the democratic conception, according to which the constituent power belongs to the national community in the fullest manner, the holder of the constituent power must be the nation, as the unity capable of acting, as the aggregate of persons

[58] The rest of this sentence is added from the Second Spanish edition of the book (Mexico, 1945). TRANSLATOR.

who have a consciousness of their national integration and the will to affirm it. According to the classic democratic theory,[59] the constituent power belongs legitimately to the national sovereignty, one, full, and indivisible; and is inalienable, permanent, intransmissible and imprescriptible. It remains always potent, latent under every constitution derived from it. And, therefore, when the positive constitution falls and with it falls all positive juridical order, then the constituent power of the full national sovereignty assumes the character of sole legitimate authority.[60]

10. The Derivative Production of Law. Constitutional Legislation. Ordinary Legislation. Regulations. Juridical Business. The Judicial Judgment. The Administration Resolution. The Executive Act

It has already been made manifest that the positive juridical order itself regulates its own production, that is, the production of its norms. Whatever may be the real concrete origin of the different norms and even the chronological order of their production, all of them are bound together — as I have explained — in a unified hierarchical or scaled system; so that each has in another superior one the formal foundation of its validity; and, at the same time, it constitutes the base for the validity of other inferior ones. The grades or steps of the juridical system are organized in a series, which comes from the fundamental norm, passing through the more abstract and general superior norms — positive constitution, ordinary legislation, regulations — by way of other intermediate grades (orders, bylaws, juridical business) to the most concrete and individualized ones—judgments, resolutions, executive acts — .

Against this doctrine of Merkl and of Kelsen it has been argued that it might be valid to explain certain juridical orders — for example, that of the Austrian Republic, that of the Czechoslovak Republic, that of the Spanish Republic, 1931, etc. — which have been constructed according to this pattern of hierarchical system; but that, on the other hand, it would not be applicable to other juridical orders, such as the English. But a grave error rests in this objection. It supposes undoubtedly that the doctrine of the hierarchy of the norms or the scaled construction of

[59] I refer to the doctrines of St. Thomas, Marsilio de Padua, Occam, Vitoria, Suárez, Bañez, Soto, Altusio, Locke, Sidney, Milton, Rousseau, etc.

[60] Cf. Luis Recaséns Siches, Las teorías políticas de Vitoria con un estudio sobre desarrollo de la idea del contrato social (Anuario de la Asociación Francisco Vitoria, 1931, published also in separate pamphlet). El poder constituyente. Su teoría aplicada al momento español (Madrid: Morata, 1931).

the juridical order tries to affirm that in history, really and truly, juridical orders have been produced according to this pattern; and then it would result that this is not applicable to the English Law, nor to many other orders. But this is not the meaning of the doctrine; it does not pretend in any way to be a photographic copy of the reality of the elements which constitute a juridical order, whose actual origin may be heterogenously disparate and various in time; but this theory proposes something else. It proposes to interpret all these various elements, that is, all the multiple and diverse precepts — whatever may have been the true episode of their creation — as forming a *juridical system,* which can only be based on a hierarchical articulation of formal competence. It proposes to explain, not the real chances by which the diverse norms have arisen, but above all the fundamental formal validity of each one of them. For example, two persons make a contract not knowing the civil legislation and consequently not having a clear knowledge that they are dealing with a matter of accepted competence of the civil code; yet, nevertheless, the clauses of that contract are valid, as Law in force in certain relations between the parties, by virtue of the delegation which the code establishes in favor of private persons, within the ambit granted by it, to regulate their relations contractually. A judgment may enunciate expressly for the first time a norm, which was not theretofore formulated; but, nevertheless, it is considered that that norm, although it had not been formulated before, was already previously valid, and that it is precisely that which gives validity to the decision decreed by the judgment, which otherwise could not be considered other than as a precept inserted in the juridical order in force. A purely private corporation makes its own bylaws, without the intervention of any official authority; but those bylaws form part of the Law in force, only by reason of the fact that a superior norm permits that this should be one means of the production of Law. In some American States, in fact, the Executive may be the strongest power, which in reality operates with decisive preëminence; but its determinations are effective juridically, so far as we can interpret them as the exercise of competences which the constitution grants, or as delegations received from the Legislature. So then, the theory of the hierarchical structure of the norms or scaled construction of the juridical order is not a tale of realities, nor a historical narration, but is a methodical instrument by means of which the jurist may construct the system of the positive juridical order in force, with the materials which he receives.

This scaled system starts from the fundamental norm in the logico-juridical sense (whose meaning I have explained), for example, "that will be Law which the constituent power *X* establishes." From this fundamental norm or first constitution in the logico-juridical sense is derived the first constitution in the juridico-positive sense, that is, the aggregate of norms (established by the constituent power, supposed to be valid) which regulates the creation of the later other norms.

The positive constitution may establish a difference in rank or degree between its norms and the later ordinary laws, so far as it determines that its own modifications or amendments must be elaborated by a different procedure from that of ordinary legislation (whether because it confines their production to a special legislative organ, different from the ordinary legislative organ; or confers it on that one, but requires a special procedure or certain extraordinary requisites). When there is this difference between constitutional law and ordinary law, we may then formulate a formal concept of the constitution, which represents a supreme rank in the hierarchy of the positive norms, above ordinary laws. And under this constitutional form may be regulated diverse matters; ordinarily it happens that by this form of constitutional legislation is determined not only the elaboration of the laws, but also the exercise of the executive power, the administration of justice, the supreme law of trade; on the other hand, also, the so-called fundamental rights or those of individual liberty (conscience, thought, movement, security, inviolability of the home and of correspondence); the political rights (equality before the law, petition, suffrage, access to public office, etc.); the rights to positive acts by the State (those related to labor, social assistance, education, etc.). But some constitutions include moreover the regulation of other matters, with the purpose of endowing their regulation with a special and stronger protection. Naturally this has meaning only when the constitution cannot be changed by the procedure of ordinary legislation; because in case the constitution can be modified by an ordinary law, there is no practical use in including such matters within the constitutional norm.

Ordinary legislation represents, in the juridical system, the grade immediately below the constitution. In the material sense every written juridical provision, of a general character, is called law; and, consequently, within this concept fall all regulations, and, in short, all general juridical rules, deliberately and knowingly dictated by the organs with competence for that act. Also, in a stricter sense, in a formal sense, the general rules emanating from the legislative power and according to the procedures which the constitution prescribes for the legislative function are called law. Also, there usually receive the name of laws in the formal sense, though improperly, all the resolutions and resolves of the legislative power, although they do not establish norms of a general character, as for example the grant of citizenship to a person by resolution of the Legislature, or the grant by it of pensions to illustrious citizens, the naming of a Regent, the declaration of war, a vote of funds for a celebration, etc. So, then, law in the material sense is equivalent to a written juridical norm of a general character. And law in the formal sense is the norm emitted under the form established by the constitution for ordinary legislation whatever may be its content — general or particular.

Regulations are general provisions issued by organs of the so-called executive power (Head of the State with the advice of a Minister or a Secretary, Ministers or Secretaries by themselves, General Directors, authorities of the local administration).

On the other hand, we find norms of a particular character which regulate the reciprocal relations of various persons, and which represent a lower grade in the hierarchy of the juridical order; they are the *contractual* or *corporative norms* and those arising from juridical business (contracts, wills, etc.). It is usual to call corporative Law the contents of the bylaws of foundations, autonomous corporations, and associations. The rules contained in those bylaws do not proceed materially from organs of the State, since they have arisen in the very bosom of those entities. But those rules are juridical norms, inserted in the system of Law in force, because that grants to such entities (corporations, associations, foundations, etc.) competence within a certain sphere and with regard to fixed conditions to dictate juridical norms which shall determine reciprocal relations among their members and even of the group with other persons. They have the dimension of juridical norms in force, because those who have dictated them have received from the law competence delegated for the purpose. So it is that such bylaws — in whose elaboration no public organ has materially intervened — if they are applied by the courts, are so because it is understood that they are formally valid by the will of the State. And if, on the contrary, they are not applied by the courts, because they understand that such rules cannot be valid with the will of the State, then we shall have to recognize that such norms will not constitute juridical norms in force, and have merely the character of social rules, which seek to be Law, but which do not attain to being it.

We may say the same with respect to the concrete and individualized norms, which are created in juridical business, by a declaration of will, to which the Law attributes competence to produce precepts applicable to certain relations. The parties who intervene in a contract make for themselves its clauses, which will constitute the juridical rules which will have to regulate certain relations between them. But that declaration of mutual will, which constitutes the juridical business called a contract, is a norm of Law, because the Law authorizes private persons to establish concrete rules as to certain aspects of their behavior, within certain limits and with subjection to some special requisites.

The lower grades in the juridical system are constituted of norms of a more concrete and individualized type: judicial judgments and administrative resolutions. General norms regulate situations of fact abstractly determined, ascribing to those suppositions (that is to say to those situations of fact) some consequences also abstractly determined. But the general norm (law, regulation, bylaw, etc.) to be carried into practice and so to obtain its effective application, requires an individualization, as well with respect to its subject, as of the conduct which it imposes. It is this part which the individualized and concrete norms of the judicial judgment and of the administrative resolution fulfill. By the judicial judgment — or the administrative resolution — it is proved in a certain manner whether there is present concretely the situation of fact foreseen in the abstract by the law, as a condition for the juridical duty which that establishes; there is determined concretely also the specific content of that juridical duty, and finally it is imposed on a person particularly determined. Many times, between the law and the judgment there is interposed the norm created in some juridical business; and then, the judgment complies not only with the prescriptions of the law, but also with the more concrete norms established in the juridical business (for example, in the contract).

Finally, we arrive at the end of the juridical chain, to wit, at the act of actual execution, in which is imposed — by force if necessary — compliance with an individualized juridical precept; for example, the acts of the representatives of authority who carry out the execution of a judgment or of an administrative resolution, or who prevent the commission of a crime, etc. by means of force.

11. Relation between General and Individualized Norms

I have just shown how among general, less general, concrete, and fully individualized norms there are always relations of delegation. There now arises the question of what may be the types of that relation of delegation between the general and the individualized norms.

Now, it may be said that that relation of delegation between general and individualized norms can be of three types.

(a) Taxative. The general norm indicates taxatively the pattern to which those who have to elaborate the concrete and individualized norms have to attend. So, for example: the cases in which the law determines beforehand — in a general way — what must be the contents of judicial judgments or of administrative resolutions, without leaving to the tribunal any margin of discretionary action; also the contents of certain contracts, whose norms are taxatively determined by the law, without permitting the parties to elaborate them on their own account, for example, marriage so far as concerns the personal relations between the spouses; for one is free only to decide if it is to be celebrated or not (one is free to marry or not); but not free as to the content of the matrimonial relations (it cannot be agreed by mutual consent of the parties for a temporary marriage for a term, or exemption from the duties of fidelity and mutual aid, or without the obligation of living together, etc.).

(b) Supplementary. The law gives to the parties who intervene in an autonomous juridical relation the right to determine for themselves by their own will the norm which is to control the relation created by the business in question; and only in case the parties, in creating a certain juridical relation, do not make use of those faculties which are granted them, does the law then determine supplementarily the norms to which the development of the created relation must accommodate itself. So, then, in this case, the norm determined by the law comes into effect only on condition that the parties have not provided otherwise. For example, when some civil codes provide that, in the absence of any stipulation to the contrary, civil deposit (bailment) shall be considered gratuitous. And also there are some cases in which that type of regulation, although in form supplementary, is given with respect to the judge; that is, the law indicates to the judge a solution, not of a necessary character, but only for the case in which he feels that no other different solution is specially justified, for reasons which the law cannot foresee, but which may be concretely weighed by the judge. So, for example, it is provided — with respect to the effects of a judgment of divorce — that "if the judgment shall not have provided otherwise, the mother shall have the custody in every case of the children less than three years of age." This is the type of regulation which is advanced by the so-called movement of "free Law" or "free Jurisprudence" (Magnaud, Kantorovicz, etc.), which proposes the decrease of taxative Law and its replacement by regulations of a supplementary type.

(c) Delegation to the parties, to the judges, or to administrative functionaries. The law neither imposes a taxative fixed norm nor offers a supplementary rule to control some special relations, but delegates to the parties or — in some cases — to the authorities, to fix the norm which they deem most just and adequate; and grants the effect of a juridical norm to what the parties provide or to what the judge (or the administrative functionary) resolves. The delegation (express or tacit) may be *particular* for certain relations; or *general* for all cases not prescribed in the law or in custom (or in other norms previously formulated).

Let us look at some cases of particular or singular delegation. One of them is that of the so-called innominate contracts, by which the law grants to the parties full faculty to determine, within the general conditions of contracting, such pacts as they consider desirable, without offering supplementary regulation (which would not be possible, precisely because they treat of figures not delineated beforehand in the law). An example of special delegation to the judge is found when the law confides to him the determination of the term of obligations which have none indicated, or when the term shall have remained at the will of the debtor. Another example of particular or special delegation is that of all those cases in which the law or regulation confers on certain functionaries a sphere of discretionary faculties, to carry out the articulation and the execution of certain administrative activities.

The type of general delegation is the essential principle, of every juridical order, that the courts cannot in any case refuse a decision because there does not exist any previously formulated norm, but then they must decide according to the general principles of Law. There are some juridical orders which explicitly contain this principle, in the form of a precept inserted in the civil code; and which expressly order the judge when he finds himself confronted by a case not foreseen by the law, nor by custom, nevertheless to decide it according to the criterion which he considers obligatory: according to the general principles of law, say the Spanish, Mexican, Argentine, Peruvian codes; according to equity, says the Honduran code; according to natural Law, says the Austrian code; according to the rules which the judge would establish if he had to act as legislator and relying on the most authorized doctrine and jurisprudence, says the Swiss code. But there are various juridical orders which do not contain the manifest expression of any similar precept, which occurs for example with the French, Belgian, German, and other civil codes, which do not occupy themselves with the question of any lacunae, nor indicate the subsidiary sources for the cases in which there is no formulated rule applicable. Now, in such orders there governs exactly the same principle expressed in the others, that the judgment shall not in any case be denied if there is a lack in law and custom and that then the judge ought to give judgment with attention to the rule which he considers relevant. And this principle does not constitute a positive juridical precept which the legislator has enacted in certain orders and which on the other hand does not appear in others; but it is an essential principle of every juridical order, equally if it has been explicitly formulated as if it has not; it is an absolute necessity of every juridical order; it is a necessary postulate of all positive Law. This principle we call: the *hermetic fullness of the juridical order in force.* The Law is essentially a relation of social security autarchically imposed; and on this account, when a social conflict arises, the Law has to pronounce necessarily some solution, either of positive regulation, for example, attributing to someone a certain duty; or of negative guarantee, protecting a sphere of liberty (for example, no one may be forced to any religious belief); but in either case it is a matter of a solution which is inexorably imposed, and which circumscribes the uncertainty which the posed conflict implied. On this account, says Del Vecchio,[61] there is no social interference or controversy between men, however complicated it may seem, or however unforeseeable, which occurs to us, which does not require or have a solution in the field of Law in force. And the solution must be executory. Doubts may persist for a long time in the field of theory — the same philosophy of Law may discuss its questions for centuries — but the practical juridical life does not permit delay. To every juridical question a decision must be given — which theoretically may not be infallible, but — which practically has to be final. This the basic meaning of the Law requires, which consists in creating a practical situation of certainty and security in social life. The Law aspires to constitute necessarily a total regulation — it is understood, from its juridical point of view — from which there may be essentially predicted its hermetic fullness, that is, there may be affirmed that there ought to be a juridical solution given to every stated conflict. And it is not to be said against this thesis — as my dear master Diez Canseco argues — that it is possible that some will have resort to the courts seeking that they should resolve a controversy which may be entirely foreign to the Law, as for example would be the discussion of a philosophic question; because, even in that case, it ought to have a juridical solution — which of course would not be the solution of the philosophic problem, but the solution of the practical conflict presented with regard to it. Let us take the example which Dr. Diez Canseco proposes; as if the philosophic polemic presented to the courts should be in the following form: John demands of Peter before the court that he should be required to recognize the truth of a certain philosophic doctrine which he denies; and then what would happen would be that the judge would give judgment relieving the defendant of the claim of the plaintiff, because he would decide it was a principle of the juridical order in force that conscience and thought should be free and that no one should be disturbed for his opinions and, consequently, would order that the plaintiff should abstain from molesting the defendant. Thus the ineffectiveness of this objection remains evident.

But if indeed the system of the juridical order in force has to be con-

[61] Cf. Giorgio del Vecchio, Los principios generales del Derecho (Spanish translation by Juan Ossorio Morales, with a prologue by Felipe C. de Diego, Barcelona: Bosch, 1935); Filosofía del Derecho, with Extensive original additions by Luis Recaséns Siches (2d ed., Barcelona: Bosch, 1935); Carlos Cossio, La plenitud del orden jurídico (Buenos Aires: Losada, 1939).

sidered necessarily as complete, as full, as hermetic, without spaces, that is, without lacunae, on the other hand it is evident that in fact such do exist in the aggregate of material of the positive Law. But these actual vacancies must necessarily be filled by whoever exercises the jurisdictional function (judge or administrative functionary). The juridical order in force, which in its essence must be total — hermetically full — contains in principle a reply for every practical controversy; because if there is any space, it must necessarily be filled by the judge. It is clear that this is true of Law in force. On the other hand, historical orders, which ruled in the past but do not rule today, as they do not discharge any practical function, show many vacancies. Radbruch says with a fortunate expression: "There is offered us the spectacle that the apparel of the law while he wears it appears to the jurist as a royal mantle; but as soon as he has put it off, or wishes to put it off, or another wears it, it is then transformed into the ragged and stained cape of a beggar." [62]

And the same that we have said of vacancies may be applied to contradictions. The aggregate of materials (laws, customs, regulations, etc.) that make up a positive juridical order in force presents more than one case of norms contradictory among themselves; but the juridical order as such, as in force at a given moment, cannot harbor any contradiction. Then, as in fact its parts have some, the jurist must proceed by his methods of interpretation and of juridical construction to eliminate those contradictions; for the order in force must give an unequivocal response to every case brought before it.

It is to be noted[63] that under the word interpretation it is usual to include two different functions. On one hand, interpretation strictly speaking, that is, clarification of a legal precept. On the other hand, it is customary also to call interpretation something else: the activity of the judge consisting of surmounting contradictions and filling vacancies, a task which he always has to perform, in greater or less proportion, since laws and regulations are never so perfect or so complete that they do not require that judicial function of eliminating contradictions and filling vacancies. (Roscoe Pound, *An Introduction to the Philosophy of Law,* pp. 104ff. Upon the problem of the methods of interpretation, cf. Fritz Schreier, *Die Methode der Rechtsinterpretation,* 1927.) But how ought the vacancies to be filled? It will be desirable that we examine, if indeed very summarily, the problems which create the necessity that the judge should fill the vacancies in the formulated Law, determining the norm

[62] Cf. Gustav Radbruch, Grundzüge der Rechtsphilosophie (1914).

[63] This paragraph is from the Second Spanish edition of the book (Mexico, 1945). Translator.

applicable to the case put, which was not prescribed either in the law or in custom.

When neither the law nor custom resolve the case put, it is the jurist who ought to determine the norm. Now, the judge does not have the same margin of decision as the legislator; since the judge cannot apply purely and without restriction his own personal criterion, but he is bound by the cardinal principles which inspire the positive order. In the first place, the judge ought to try to extract from the general principles formulated in the positive order those consequences which should be applicable to the case which he has to decide and which were not especially provided. And if this should not be possible, that is, if he should not come to any result by such procedure, then he ought to try to obtain it by the *method of analogy,* which consists of transferring to a factual situation *a* a rule *b,* which is not directly applicable to it, but which refers to an analogous situation of fact. That is, analogy is founded not on identity of the juridical facts, but on identity of the motive of the norm; that is, he discovers that the two cases raise equal juridical reasoning, and then he applies to one of them (not foreseen) the law enacted for the other, since between the two he discovers that there ought to be the same point of view of regulation.

When it still has not been possible to determine the norm by the analogous means, then the judge ought to resort to other procedures. To what ones? Shall he decide according to the rules which he would establish if he had to act as legislator (as the Swiss civil code says)? I think that this formula of the Swiss code is not fully proper; because the judge does not possess the space which the legislator has. The judge is not free to be guided by his personal conviction, but he must fill the vacancy in the order according to the positive principles effectively inspired by it and regarding moreover the mass of social convictions actually in force which mark and condition the interpretation of the law. On the other hand, such limitations do not exist for the legislator, who is bound only by the constitutional precepts of the formal superior rank.

It is clear that in the last instance and in lack of any positive criterion in force, the judge must have recourse to an operation of ideal estimation, that is, to what he considers as ideal principles of the Law. And this is actually the situation which is found in truth and in all rigor in the presence of a vacancy. If it should not be the case of an authentic vacancy, but rather only of an apparent deficiency, then a norm could be obtained by the concrete application of general formulated principles, or by the proceeding by analogy, or by an inductive generalization, or by the application of the estimative criteria which in fact and actually inspire the order. But the extreme case which we have now put, that of the authentic vacancy, is otherwise: it is that for which a solution could be obtained neither in law nor in custom, but neither in generalization, nor in analogy, nor in the cardinal criteria of the order, nor in the social convictions which integrate it. And then, in the last subsidiary instance, the judge ought to be inspired by a judgment of value, by an ideal juridical estimative.

The belief in some principles of justice, the idea of some principles of natural Law or of rational Law — it would be better to say in some values which ought to inspire positive Law — has always been the inheritance of individual as well as collective convictions, through the historic development of humanity. This belief has suffered only some short eclipses in theory, with the irruptions of skepticism. But the human spirit has always overcome satisfactorily all these short skeptical crises, emerging from them more fortified. This idea also dominates in jurisprudence, which constantly refers to it, under various expressions ("good customs," "morals," "ethical exigencies," "nature of things," "equity," "good faith," "correct reasoning," "spirit of justice," etc.). I cannot develop here this reasoning, which refers to the theory of juridical values, but I concern myself with it in the latter part of this book, devoted to the *juridical estimative;* and then I shall rigorously justify this theme, that is, the theme of the ideal criteria for the procedure of the Law.

It will be sufficient to say that the legislator provides for unforeseen cases, signing a document in blank, to be filled in by the judge, who ought to be inspired by a principle of justice, in an ideal valuation, which is, in short, the same intentional proposition which animates the formulated legislation. And so, the judge recognizes in those principles a positive currency within the juridical order.

It is to be noted that the judge deems that those ideal principles, the basis of his judgment, constitute juridical norms, which were already in force before he proclaimed them, although they were not formulated in an explicit manner. He understands that already, before he dictates the decision, the norm upon which it is founded was in effect. Since if it were not so, the decision would have to contain a special pronouncement in which there should be declared the retroactive force of the norm formulated in it; but this is not what occurs.

The ideal norms to which the judge resorts in case of a rigorous vacancy cannot be in contradiction with other formulated norms of the positive system; because if it were so, it would not be permissible for the judge to be inspired with those ideal criteria, which would be equivalent to making the positive order appear in pieces; would be equivalent to destroying certainty and security, the essential root of all Law. But, on the other hand, there is recognized in such ideal principles a positive control over the gaps in the formulated norms, thanks to the judicial function, which, by delegation of the law, applies them to the cases not foreseen in it. So, then, there is no duality nor opposition in the systems, positive and ideal, but one single system, the positive. Because the ideal principles applied by the judge constitute authentic positive Law, and the essential note of this is inexorable imposition or coercive protection, which obtains its sanction in the judgment or resolution endowed with executoriness.

CHAPTER XI

THE STATE (STATE AND LAW)

1. Statement of the Problem of the Relation between State and Law

All through the previous chapters allusions to the State have occurred. It was so, when I was trying to explain the essential characteristic of inexorable imposition, which is distinctive of the Law; so also, when I was putting the problem of the difference between norms of Law and rules of social behavior; also on distinguishing between arbitrary mandates and juridical mandates. Also I made reference to the State when, in expounding the concept of collective juridical personality, I mentioned in what the personality of the State consisted as such. Finally, in the preceding chapter I have explained positive Law as the will of the State (in the formal sense, that is, as juridical imputation); and in constructing the system of the positive juridical order, the same as in speaking of the original production of Law, there has been constant mention of the State.

Now, this series of allusions to the State, when I was trying to expound the concept of Law and the system of the juridical order, has not been by chance, but has been inevitable. This at least makes us presume with sufficient motive that between the concept of the Law and the concept of the State there truly exists a very close connection, perhaps essential and necessary. This chapter, then, is to be devoted to examining with all strictness what may be the type of relation which exists between the positive Law in force and the State.

2. The Question, What Is the State?

But this problem is joint with the consideration as to what is the State. Therefore, it is necessary to put the question, what is understood by the State?

At first view, it seems as if the reality of the State were indeed plain. And, nevertheless, when we try to determine it in a rigorous fashion, it presents itself to us as confused and with fugitive outlines. We find the State forming part of our life and we find ourselves forming part of the State. Practically, we refer to it on innumerable occasions: we feel it weigh upon us, imposing on us multiple and onerous exigencies; we enroll, at times, in its service with enthusiasm; at others, we feel it as an obstacle to our desires; we know that without it life would be impossible for us, or at least very difficult; but also, on occasions, it demands of us the sacrifice of our very own life. To the extent to which we take part in politics, we work to procure that it shall be of a certain sort; on one side, we find ourselves ingredients of it; on the other side, we consider it a supra-individual magnitude; we have never perceived it in its authentic and total being, but we see it acting in various manifestations, as legislative activity, as administration, as army, as police, as social assistance, as courts of justice; it seems to us symbolized in a shield, in a flag, in a hymn. We address ourselves to it, asking that it do certain things; and also we confront, it, demanding that it do not act, that it abstain, that it leave us at liberty to fulfill our own individual actions, which we do not wish to see violated by its interference. And, nevertheless, in spite of the State being something so near to us, with which we are in constant touch, when we try to grasp its essence, to determine its being, to apprehend it in a clear and precise concept, it escapes us and wavers among all the representations of it which we have formed for ourselves.

Apart from the confused knowledge, merely approximate, which we have of the State by daily intercourse with it, human thought has put several interrogatories with regard to it.

On one side, there were thinkers who asked what were the most efficacious means to dominate the life of the State and to obtain a decisive influence in it; that is, problems of what might be called preparation for the political career and for success in it; examination of the technique which permits one to make use of the resources of the State and to manage them with effective success. Now, since to manage a thing it is necessary to have some knowledge of it, it follows that such studies contain much of interest with regard to some aspects of the reality of the State and its functioning.

In general, during all the history of thought, the problem with respect to the State which has been of chief consideration is the ideal which ought to inspire its organization. How ought men to plan, to organize, and to direct the State? What ought men to do with the State? What is the best type of State? What are the principles which ought to inspire it, and in the light of which it is justified?

But, apart from these two problems (the pragmatic and the ideal), contemporaneous thought — with precedents in other epochs — has put with regard to the State another problem, to wit, that of what may be its *reality.* The State is something which is here; well then, of what does this something consist? What is the State? Of what nature is its being? We say that it *is;* what meaning or acceptance has that word is? Of what ingredients is the State composed? What is it which truly occurs or happens in it? This theme is prior to all other questions as to the State; with respect to the pragmatic question of political technique and also with respect to the problem as to the political ideal.

This problem as to *what is* the State has been attempted to be answered on various planes as to depth and breadth. On one side there have been produced studies descriptive of the various state realities; also considerations of empiric sociology as to the texture and the dynamic processes of the State. On the other side, as in the State there is a juridical organization, which seems to discharge a predominant and essential part in it, other studies have attended preëminently to this juridical angle.

But none of these types of studies reaches the basic root of the problem as to the essence of the State; none of them answers satisfactorily the question, what is essentially the State?

What is the State? Is it perhaps a thing, a natural organism, similar to other biological organisms — as some school of the nineteenth century maintained? [64] Is it a national soul or popular spirit, as romanticism declared? Is it a form or manifestation of objective spirit, as Hegel taught? Or is it a complicated mixture of multiple and heterogenous ingredients (land, men, norms) as has been affirmed for a long time by the most widespread doctrine? Does it constitute perhaps a mere mental form, a synthesis of knowledge, which unifies from the point of view of finality a series of various and disparate elements, as Jellinek explains? Is it purely an ideal system of norms, with objective and coercitive being in force, limited as to the persons subject to such norms, as to space and as to time, as Kelsen affirms? Is it perhaps a complex of phenomena of culture, as a historic movement in constant reëlaboration, in incessant becoming, as other authors maintain, as for example Litt and Smend?

[64] Cf. BLUNTSCHLI, DERECHO PÚBLICO UNIVERSAL, Primera parte, *Teoría general del Estado* (transl. of G. Moreno y Ortega) 16ff.; SCHAEFFLE, BAU UND LEBEN DES SOZIALEN KÖRPERS (1875); ABRISS DER SOZIOLOGIE (1906); LILIENFELD, GEDANKEN ÜBER DIE SOZIALWISSENSCHAFT DER ZUKUNFT (1873–77); HAECKEL, GENERELLE MORPHOLOGIE DER ORGANISMEN (1856); NATÜRLICHE SCHÖPFUNGSGESCHICHTE (1886); MONISMUS UND NATURGESETZ (1906); KJELLÉN, DER STAAT ALS LEBENSFORM (4th ed., 1924); HERTWIG, DER STAAT ALS ORGANISMUS (1922); WORMS, ORGANISME ET SOCIÉTÉ (1896); PHILOSOPHIE DES SCIENCES SOCIALES (1903–1907); LA THÉORIE ORGANIQUE DES SOCIÉTÉS, DEFENSE DE L'ORGANICISME (1899).

Is it a supreme source which formulates decisions in view of legitimate and adequate fundamentals, through the coördination of different grades of separate wills to act in a manner which shall reach a determined end, as Harold Laski explains? Is perhaps the reality of the State an institutional reality personified juridically, that is, the juridical personality of the nation, as Hauriou says? Is it a dialectic unity of being and ought to be, of act and feeling, embodied in a social reality, as the thesis of Hermann Heller maintains? I have here, enunciated in rapid outline, a series of diverse doctrinal efforts, elaborated to answer this question with regard to what is the State. I have collected here these references not as erudite data — of which this book desires to be free — but that the reader may form more easily the idea of the question which we are asking. It is a strictly philosophic question; in short to determine in what consists the essence of the State.

Now the reader will have noticed that in this theme of determining what the State may be, the question with regard to the relation between State and Law plays a very principal part. It appears in all the various answers to which I have summarily alluded. But above all it is plain in the fact that many essential themes of the theory of Law carry with them an implication of themes as to the State. And, surely, the solution of the theme as to what is the State will carry implicitly the reply to the question as to what are the relations between State and Law; or, vice versa, this reply will contain the solution to the query as to the nature of the State.

It is desirable, before developing the study of this problem of the relation between State and Law, to call attention to the following. Almost always — if not always — when we think of the Law, we find implied in it the notion of the State, understood as an objective instance which imposes inexorably compliance with juridical precepts; understood as an organ of coercitivity; and understood as a personification of the positive juridical order. On the other hand, it seems that when we think of the State we imply also a reference to the Law: we represent it to ourselves as the organ of the Law. It is to be conjectured then, even at first sight, that there is a reciprocal implication between the concepts of Law and of the State. In such manner we state the problem. Now, to try to inquire rigorously if in truth it is so, or if on the contrary essential examination does not confirm this appearance. At the thread then of this theme, arise the following questions which are the specification of it. Do the State and Law constitute distinct entities, related in some essential manner? Is it a question, on the contrary, merely of two words which designate one single and identical thing, so that, in truth, the concept of the State and that of the positive juridical order will fully coincide? In case of its not being so, that is, if the State is not the same as the juridical order in force, what is the type of relation which exists between them? Is it a relation of essential implication, so that there cannot be a concept of the State without implying a concept of the Law, or, on the contrary, is there a purely and exclusively sociological concept of the State, absolutely foreign to every juridical point of view? Is there on the other hand a relation of essential implication between the concept of the Law and the concept of the State, that is, does the concept of Law imply a mention of or reference to the State? If State and Law do not exactly coincide, if they are not one and the same thing — although they are linked between themselves — what would be the type of relation between them?

3. Examination of the Typical Doctrinal Positions

Although I wish to keep this book free from erudite recitals — and from a critical examination of others' doctrines — which I have already presented in other of my works, nevertheless it will be indispensable to make some allusions to the divers typical positions which have been advanced in the doctrine upon this theme.

There have been a great number of theories which have tried to define the State as a pure reality, leaving aside every juridical point of view. Other doctrines have maintained that the State offers two faces or dimensions; one juridical and the other sociological, but without succeeding in determining with precision what may be the type of connection which exists between them. Another theory — that of Kelsen — has affirmed strict identity between State and Law (the juridical order in force), to the point of saying that it is a matter of two words designating the same object. Finally, present thought has returned to consider that in the State there are sociological realities but also dimensions essentially juridical; but it has tried to understand rigorously the relation between the social reality of the State and its normative order.

To undertake to examine critically the typical positions with respect to a problem offers the advantage of a kind of vaccine, which prevents us from relapsing into thoughts which have already shown their error, or which at least were already superseded; and in this way it is possible to attain greater probability of approaching the correct road in which we may find the solution of the problem put. Only with this end I will pass in review — if indeed very briefly and summarily — a series of doctrines upon the being of the State.

Theories which consider the State as a being of nature. Among the various forms of these doctrines, which declare that the State is a natural being, a piece of nature, and which, consequently, try to explain it as a science of the natural type, that is, similar to the other natural sciences, there must be distinguished especially those called *organistic theories* in the strict sense.

According to these organistic theories in the strict sense, the State constitutes a biological organism — similar to the animal organisms — enormously great with epithelial texture (the protective institutions of patrimony, health, internal order, exterior security); with bony texture, composed of the land, the streets, the buildings; with vascular texture, made up of the economic institutions; with muscular texture, composed of the technical labor organizations; with nervous texture, represented by the government, and by the telegraph and telephone lines, which transmit its orders. This organism would be subject to the biological laws of creation, birth, growth, development, illnesses and death; it would have sex (there are masculine States like John Bull, Uncle Sam; and feminine ones like la Belle France), and would subsist by means of the change and decline of its component elements. At the height of our time, it is not necessary, in truth, to spend many words in rejecting entirely these organistic theories. They are a manifestation of naturalistic sociology — today overthrown — which pretended to explain all the objects of the cosmos as pieces of nature. This sociology was blind to see and understand all the multiple and various things which there are in the *cosmos* which do not constitute nature — for example, ideas; so, also, human life strictly as such (that is, not as biology, but as biography); also the cultural and historical realities (that is, objectivated human life) — and also it does not take account of the fact that all those objects which are not natural cannot be known by the methods of the natural sciences, but need, besides the explanation of their causes, *comprehension of their meaning*. The State is a human reality which, as such, is irreducible to the natural reality of the biological; and which possesses a privative system of categories, which have no correspondence in the world of nature. On the other hand, the concept of organism which these theories employ is extremely vague and unprecise; and many times one does not know if they are trying to apply to the human-social a notion of organism taken from the biological sciences or if, on the contrary, the concept of organism which they employ represents a transposition of the idea of organization — taken from the social sciences — to the field of the biological. Moreover, the greater part of these organistic theories, in spite of pretending to use only methods of phenomenological observation, nevertheless are inspired by the desire to found a certain political criterion (and in that direction there have been efforts for all tastes).[65]

Other doctrines[66] have wished to see in the State a mere complex of *relations of force* so that those who possess more dominate the weaker. But although it is evident that in the State there are relations of power and the use of force, the reality of the State is not exhausted in those pure relations of physical violence. True — as will be seen — the State is a special power; but the power is a social relation, which cannot be compared in any way to pure physical domination.

Romantic and Hegelian theories. These are the theories which exhibit the State as a substantive spiritual reality.

Those with a basis preponderantly romantic (Savigny, Stahl, etc.) affirm the existence — although mysterious and secret — of a national soul, as a real psychic substance, but not conscious, which is the source of historic life, and from which emanate the manifestations of culture (law, usages, language, art, etc.), and which constitute the basic substratum of the State.

The doctrine of Hegel — and all those inspired by it — affirms that the State is the objective Spirit which is determined for itself as an ethical idea conscious of itself; and that each State constitutes a manifestation or phase of the objective Spirit, that is, a system of juridical, moral, artistic ideas, in which are given form the subjective spirits of the individuals who participate in it.

The thesis which seeks to explain the reality of the State as a national soul is inspired in the romanticist ideas, to wit: universal animism, antirationalistic tendency, exaltation of the historic realities of each people, and a passionate devotion to the mysterious. In short, this doctrine represents a poetic phantasmagoria, perhaps very beautiful, but without any serious scientific or philosophic argument in its favor: it is a purely mystic creed, which has inspired political traditionalism to the death — which makes it manifest that there lies in it a political purpose and not so much a serene knowledge of what the State may be.

As to the theory of the State as autodetermination of the objective spirit, its detailed critical examination would lead us to a very extensive series of considerations of the main points of the philosophy of Hegel,

[65] So, for example, the works of Hertwig are filled with a poisoned imperialist and traditionalist political passion. Others, like Kautsky, influenced by a pacificist desire, have maintained that in nature there is normally an equilibrium, and there does not exist war nor crime nor egoism.

[66] Principally the theory of LUIS DE HALLER, ZUR RESTAURATION DER STAATSWISSENSCHAFT. In another more moderate style, also LEÓN DUGUIT, MANUEL DE DROIT CONSTITUTIONNEL (1918) 14 and 15.

which it is not proper to make here within the limited bounds of this reference. I will only note that I have shown already that what Hegel explains as objective Spirit is not a substantive and independent reality, but reduces purely and simply to what I have explained as objectivated human life. This theoretic substantiation of the cultural and of the collective has since constituted the foundation — more or less proximate or remote, but definitely the foundation — of the political systems which deny human dignity and suppress liberty — fascism, bolshevism, national-socialism.

Reference to the purely sociological theories of the State. There have been produced many doctrines which have defined the State as a social reality, that is, the State is a reality but not a physical nor biological reality, nor a reality exclusively spiritual; but its reality is that which all collective entities have, although with special characteristics. And, so, there is a series of theories which define the State as a social organism;[67] others as an institution;[68] others as a corporation with peculiar characters, etc.

In principle, it does not seem wrong to affirm that the State is a social reality. Now, the problem which is put, at this moment, is based on knowing if the State can be comprehended solely and exclusively as a pure social reality, without essential reference to the normative order of the Law; or if, on the contrary, we cannot succeed in establishing the concept of this special collective reality which we call the State, if we do not apply the notion of an ideal normative order, that is of the juridical order.

The greater part of the sociological doctrines as to the State mingle in their definition the juridical point of view; such happens, for example, with the theory of social organism, which has been especially elaborated by the jurists (such as Gierke); so also happens with the theory of the institution of Hauriou, who defines the State as the juridical personification of the nation.

But there have been some doctrinal attempts which have proposed to give a purely and exclusively sociological concept of the State, without alluding at all to the concept of Law. They have tried to define the State as nothing more than a complex of social facts, leaving aside every juridical consideration. And, following this direction, it has been said that the State constitutes a phenomenon of command; a phenomenon of command which differs from all the non-state mandates by a series of peculiar characteristics: (1) Because it would constitute a supreme mandate, that is, a mandate which would not tolerate any other mandate

[67] So, for example, Spencer, Gierke, etc.

[68] Cf. HAURIOU, works cited in Note. 41.

above it; "a power which is not only stronger than the weak, but also stronger than the strong, and which is imposed on all," as Wiese explains.[69] (2) Because this mandate is objectified in an external regulation, in a regulation of the conduct of relation. (3) Because this mandate has the pretension of being legitimate. There are mandates which are not legitimate, nor even pretend to be so, for example that which the kidnaper exercises over his victim; while, on the contrary, there are other mandates, which have essentially the pretension of being legitimate — whether they are so or not is a problem for critical discussion in each case; but here we do not speak of what may be really legitimate, but of what possesses the characteristic of pretending to be so. (4) Because this mandate proposes to secure a lasting and ordered living together among men and groups. (5) Because in the State mandate there is always intentional reference to the principles of justice; this may or may not be realized, more or less realized; but there never completely fails to be some reference to it.

Now then, in this characterization of the State, which pretends to be exclusively sociological, that is, which pretends to define it with entire absence of every juridical and political consideration, as a mere complex of a series of collective facts, we find nevertheless a series of references to juristics, although camouflaged.

In the first place, on characterizing the State as a fact of mandate, it is said that this mandate is supreme, that it does not admit any superior instance situated above it, that it pretends to impose itself upon all, including the strongest; but this constitutes precisely the sociological version of the dimension of *inexorable imposition,* which constitutes the essential characteristic of Law.

In the second place, notice also that in speaking of the fact of the state mandate, it is characterized by being objectified in a regulation or ordinance; that is, it is not a matter of some sporadic and unconnected phenomena of command, but of a stable mandate, according to objective rules; by which we have an allusion to another of the essential notes of the Law. And also that it is a matter of organization of the conduct of external relation (since otherwise it would be a matter of a Church and not of a State); but this is clearly another dimension of juristics.

In the third place, it is said that this mandate is characterized also by pretending essentially to be legitimate; but this pretension is another of the ingredients of the essence of juristics.

In the fourth place, it is affirmed that the sociological fact of the state mandate has as meaning the purpose of securing an ordered and lasting

[69] Cf. Wiese, System der allgemeinen Soziologie (1933) 135, 139, 158, 284, 387, 397, 509–549.

living together among men. It is precisely this mention of security, of a true and sure order, of guaranty, which is precisely the root of all Law!

And finally, in the fifth place, the sociological study of the State tells us that in it there is always a reference to a spirit of justice; which is also one of the essential characteristics of the Law; for the Law is a proposition of realization of some fixed values presided over by justice.

So then, to know the social facts which constitute the reality of the State, although they are human facts and not facts of nature, it is necessary to interpret them in their meaning; and this meaning consists precisely in being facts in which it is sought to constitute Law. Suddenly the real facts in which the State manifests itself to us are the social facts in which is constituted a supreme mandate, with a pretension of legitimacy, to determine an external regulation, which guarantees an ordered and lasting living together, according to some principles of justice. Now, this is equivalent to saying that the reality of the State is composed of those facts in which is sought to be constructed the juridical order. That is, it is a matter of facts, of social human realities, whose meaning consists of its intentional reference to juristics. It remains, then, clear, that in these sociological definitions of the State is implied an essential reference to the concept of juristics. With this, we limit ourselves to stating simply that there is an essential implication between the concept of the State and the concept of Law; but still we have not fixed with precision the type of this connection between State and Law.

Reference to the theory of the facets or the double aspect of the State. Having taken account in general that the State is a social reality, but that the juridical aspect is essential to it, was what determined that a great number of doctrines[70] should say that in the State there are two sides: one real, phenomenal, which demands a sociological study; and the other ideal, normative, which has to be considered by Juridical Science. Jellinek says:

> The sociological consideration of the State has for object the study of it as a social phenomenon: those subjective and objective real facts in which the concrete life of the State consists . . . ; the doctrine of the origins, transformation and decadence of States; the investigation of the social suppositions of the State, of its social action . . . The second consideration has as object the juridical aspect of the State; but the Law has a double existence: it is on the one side actual juridical practice, and, as such, appears to us as a social power, which forms part of the concrete life of the culture of a people; and, on the other side, is an aggregate of norms, which must be transformed into acts. In this last sense, the Law does not belong to the world of being, but to

[70] This theory has been held by Gerber, Jellinek, Hauriou, Max Weber, Posada, etc.

the world of ought to be. In this sense, it constitutes an aggregate of concepts and of propositions, which do not serve to know given reality but to judge reality normatively. Juridical knowledge of an object is then, fundamentally, distinct from knowledge of the real facts which compose it. The juridical conception of the State has as object knowledge of the juridical norms which determine and serve as guide for its institutions and functions, as also of the relations between the real facts of the life of the State and those normative judgments upon which juridical thought rests. The juridical conception of the State proposes, therefore, to complete the social doctrine of it; but they cannot in any way be confused with each other.[71]

I believe that, in principle, the program for this doctrine of the two facets is well formulated. But I think that this doctrine does not go beyond being the formulation of a program which has as basis the having taken account of the State's being a social reality, in which is produced and applied the normative order of the Law, and that, consequently, the Law has to be studied from these two points of view. But, on the other hand, I consider that this doctrine of the two facets or the double aspect — in the majority of its versions — has not tried to investigate with sufficient depth and sagacity what may be the type of connection which exists between these two dimensions. They have limited themselves to juxtaposing a series of sociological studies and a series of juridical studies, without finding the essential point of articulation between them. And this insolidarity between the two studies, this having remained in the middle of the road, being content with having offered two heterogenous considerations as to the State, has been one of the principal motives which has brought about the criticism formulated by Kelsen, who has come to deny the double dimensionality of the State and to sustain the absolute identity between the concept of the State and the concept of Law (as a positive order in force) — a thesis which, as I shall explain further on, I deem inadmissible but which has been advanced by the loose ends left by the theory of the two facets in its first phase.

Theory of identity between State and Law. I am going to expound at relative length this theory of the identity between State and Law, because precisely by means of the criticism which afterwards is to be made of it will develop with greater relief the correct doctrine as to the reality of the State. And as such theory of the identity arises in a polemic position against the purely sociological thesis and against the affirmation that the State has two facets; and as the solution which I propose

[71] Cf. JELLINEK, TEORÍA GENERAL DEL ESTADO, Spanish translation by F. de los Rios (Madrid, 1914) 169–172, 224–228.

will be elaborated in its turn as critical of the theory of identity and as an attempt at replacement of that as well as of the preceding doctrines — sociological and that of the two facets — hence it is indispensable to grant special attention to this theory of Kelsen.

If indeed there are precedents for this theory of identity,[72] it is formulated in its extreme and rigorous manner in the work of the great theorist of Law, Hans Kelsen.[73]

Kelsen affirms that the State is purely and simply a normative system, to wit, the system of the juridical order in force; nothing more. He tries to found this assertion on the following considerations.

Kelsen criticizes the sociological doctrines of the State, arguing that they, when they try to explain the State as a social reality, have to seek a differentiating criterion which permits them to discriminate between the state social facts and those other social facts which do not belong to the area of the State; and he says that this limiting criterion of the state sphere with respect to the other non-state social facts is always the reference to the juridical order. It is always the perimeter of the Law which comes to trace the frontiers of the state sphere. But then it happens that what the State has from the State is what it has from the Law, since only by the light of the latter do we limit the state sphere. The State is reduced, then, to a system of norms, to wit, the system of positive Law. The so-called State facts have from the State their insertion in the juridical order, either as conditioning facts of the production of juridical norms, or as facts of human conduct regulated by the Law. And Kelsen maintains that it is not permissible to say that the State may be known in two distinct ways, to wit: juridically, with attention to the norms of the Law; and sociologically, mindful of the facts which are the content of juridical regulation, because one single object is not capable of being treated by two absolutely different and disparate methods, such as are the juridical method, which is a normative method — knowledge of norms — and the sociological method, which is a method for understanding realities, phenomena. The first is inscribed in the world of ought-to-be, where its object (the juridical norms) dwells; and the second belongs to the world of being, since the social facts are realities.

[72] There are precedents in HERMANN COHEN, ETHIK DES REINEN WILLENS (3d ed., 1921) 64; STAMMLER, DIE LEHRE VOM RICHTIGEN RECHT (1902) 232–233; RADBRUCH, GRUNDZÜGE DER RECHTSPHILOSOPHIE (1914).

[73] Cf. KELSEN, ALLGEMEINE STAATSLEHRE (1925); COMPENDIO DE TEORÍA GENERAL DEL ESTADO, translation by Recaséns Siches and J. de Azcárate (Barcelona: Bosch); DER SOZIOLOGISCHE UND DER JURISTISCHE STAATSBEGRIFF (1920). [See a review by Recaséns of KELSEN'S GENERAL THEORY OF LAW AND STATE (Cambridge, 1945), in 8 REVISTA DE LA ESCUELA NACIONAL DE JURISPRUDENCIA (Mexico, 1946) 180–184. Cf. also review in 59 HARV. L. REV. 1946) 1184. TRANSLATOR.]

Kelsen, starting from the Kantian thought that the knowing activity is a determinant and formative of the object of knowledge, argues that a special method of knowledge produces a determined object, and that, consequently, another method, entirely different, cannot produce the same object as the first. On this account — he says — it is not possible that the State should be knowable by two diverse methods; for the juridical method — devoted to the category of ought-to-be — produces the norms of Law, is correlative of them; and the sociological method — inserted in the category of being — cannot produce the same object as the former. If the correlative of the juridical method is the State as a system of juridical norms in force, the correlative of the sociological method cannot indeed be the State but will have to be something different.

The State is, in short, nothing more than the system of Law in force, which is called the State when we think of it personified, unified, that is, in the form of a person. Here Kelsen applies his doctrine of the collective juridical person, which I explained in Chapter VIII. Now, this doctrine of the juridical personality, which I consider one of the best achievements in the whole Kelsenian work, is used here — although I think unduly — to found the thesis of the identity of State and Law. Let the reader remember here the Kelsenian conception of the collective juridical person, as the synthesis or unified system of an aggregate of norms which regulate the reciprocal conduct of a series of men. When this synthesis embraces a partial order of norms (limited according to a certain point of view) we have the juridical personality of corporations, associations, etc. But when we embrace in one synthesis or system the totality of the juridical order, conceived as a unity, as a common center of imputation of all the actions determined as of the State, then we obtain the concept of the State as a person. There is to be understood, then, by the State, the metaphorical personification of the totality of the positive juridical order.

That the State is a coercitive normative order, that is, that it consists of the system of positive Law — says Kelsen — no one will deny; but many argue that besides it is a reality, an effective power, a social force. And, in support of this second affirmation, many authors adduce the well-known existence of state realities, in which is manifest this dimension of power; prisons, fortresses, army, police, etc. Now — Kelsen argues — all these facts and similar ones in which the State makes itself evident to experience, taken in themselves and without more, are material or psychical realities, pertaining to the realm of nature (material or spiritual) or to the field of technique, realities which are ruled by their peculiar laws (physical, chemical, psychological); and are nothing else while we contemplate them purely and exclusively as realities, without it appearing from this point of view even remotely that they are ingredients of the State. Such realities obtain a state significance only so far as we contemplate them through the Law, from the juridical point of view; that is, when we take account of the fact that men make use of those objects to determine their needs, needs which are ordained in the juridical norms. What makes the prison a prison is none of its component materials, none of its technical forms, but that it has to serve as a coercitive element for compliance with the juridical order, as provided in it. What makes the judge a judge, the policeman a policeman, is no real component of those human beings, but the special qualification with which they are invested by the juridical order, that is, that it institutes them as its organs.

One speaks of a power of the State, referring to a real substratum of it, foreign to the Law; but this — says Kelsen — is not correct. Whence comes the power of the State? In the last instance, what we call the power of the State is not a material force but a psychological force, to wit, the fact that certain men — legislators, functionaries, military men, police, citizens, etc. — behave in a certain manner, to wit, conduct themselves in compliance with juridical norms. Now, this psychological power, which constitutes the warp or texture of the reality of the State, consists of the motivating force which the psychic representations of the juridical norms exercise over such men. The juridical norms, taken by themselves, are not realities, but they are idealities, normative significations, normative ideas, and, consequently, unreal beings, spectral, like all ideas. But it happens that men represent those ideas, represent such norms in their consciousness; and such psychological representations — which are already some realities — originate certain spiritual forces, of adherence, of fear, etc., which are the motive for some special behaviors; of the behavior of the functionary who carries out the state acts foreseen in the juridical order and who moreover develops it finally within the ambit of the competence which the order grants to him; of the soldier who obeys the voice of command of the person instituted as his superior by the Law; of the citizen who acts and complies with the precepts of the juridical order, etc. All that aggregate of psychological forces originated by the representation of the juridical norms is what constitutes what is called power of the State. But all this is of the State precisely because it has juristics as its content.

Inasmuch as the concept of the State coincides with the concept of juristics — says Kelsen — the relation between State and Law is a relation of identity. It is a matter of two words to designate the same object. They are not distinct things but things united in a certain way; but they treat of the same and unified thing; then the supposed dualism between State and the Law is only a superfluous duplication of the same object. It happens that the image of personification, which is merely an auxiliary means of knowledge to understand this object with more facility which is only an auxiliary representation to express the unity in the multiplicity of juridical norms, is unduly hypostatical and converted arbitrarily into a supposed independent object. And so, this superfluous duplication creates the apparent problem of the relation between two things which, at bottom, are but one thing. Now, the apparent problems cannot be resolved satisfactorily, but can only be *dissolved,* that is, made to disappear, because in pureness they do not exist as problems.

Many have maintained that the State is the support, the creator, and the protector of the Law, and that, consequently, it is necessary to distinguish between them, though indeed they are intimately related. As to this, Kelsen argues as follows: for there to be a juridical norm it is necessary that there should also be an instance of coercitive imposition of it, for otherwise we should not have a norm of Law, but some other class of norm. Now, this connection between the conduct required by the norm and the coercitive imposition of it is what constitutes the essential logical structure of the Law. It is a matter of a logical relation, of an essential connection. But it happens that the dualists have transformed unduly this relation of logical condition into a supposed genetic relation. There is no Law without coercitive imposition; there is no State without a juridical norm; this expresses an indissoluble logical bond; but it does not express a genetic relation between distinct things. The logical structure of the juridical precept, which consists of the essential connection between due conduct and the sanctions against its noncompliance, cannot be disintegrated from the manner which is called Law first and State second.

All the problems of the general theory of the State are posed and resolved by Kelsen as juridical questions, affirming that this is their unique and peculiar meaning. The theory of the State — says Kelsen — does not concern itself either with sociological studies (which can never lead us to capture the essence of the State), nor with disquisitions of a political character, that is, of justice or injustice, convenience or inconvenience of such or such institutions (which belongs to Ethics and to Politics). All the themes of the general theory of the State are questions either as to the validity or the being in force of the juridical order. I will show some examples of how Kelsen develops his general theory of the State. Territory, which was considered by most authors as a real element of the State, is simply the special sphere of the being in force of the juridical order, that is, the space within which a positive juridical system has validity. People, who have also been held one of the realities of the State, are purely and simply the human sphere of the being in force of the juridical order. The power of the State is no more than the being in force of the Law. Sovereignty is reduced to a logical quality of the juridical order as a totality, to wit: this quality of sovereignty consists in being a supreme and total juridical order, whose positive validity is not derivable from any other superior normative order. To designate a juridical system as sovereign means precisely that it is intended to make it valid as a total order. The questions with respect to centralization and decentralization, as to the federations, and as to the autonomous corporations, are problems with regard to spatial articulation and material for the being in force of the juridical order. The object of the doctrine as to the powers or functions of the State is the series of the diverse ranged steps in the production of the Law. The organs of the State are situations in the production of the Law. The various forms of a State are different methods of production of the juridical order, which is called in a figurative sense the "will of the State."

4. Relation between State and Law. The Reality of the State

I gave some amplitude to the exposition of the Kelsenian doctrine for two reasons. On one hand, it has contributed by its criticism to clarifying not a few confusions in the prior thinking, and on the whole has contributed to the necessity of restating with greater acuteness and precision a series of themes. Although I consider that the Kelsenian thesis of the identification between State and Law contains grave errors and is, consequently, inadmissible, nevertheless, I recognize that the work of Kelsen has served greatly on its critical side, and, above all, has made evident the urgency of revising the statement of many themes and of carrying them to a deeper and more basic plane than they have heretofore had. On the other hand, the doctrine which I shall propound as correct has been elaborated exactly as a superstructure on the Kelsenian theory and also at the same time as superstructure on the prior thought.

It will be helpful to notice, at the commencement of this critique, that Kelsen has reduced all consideration of the State to a juridical consideration, alleging that the sociological problems which are usually included in the theory of the State (nation, people, race, determination of geographic factors, processes of formation of public opinion, forms of political integration, etc.) are *metajuridical* themes. And he also qualifies as metajuridical all the questions of political valuation. Some themes are considered metajuridical because they do not form strictly a part of the positive juridical order: so the sociological factors, to the extent that they have not obtained a coercitive normative expression, do not form part of the Law and consequently not of the State; and, so, too on the other hand, political disquisitions upon the ends and means of the State, whether they have been transformed into the juridical norm in force, in which case they belong indeed to the positive Law, or whether this has not yet occurred, and in this case they are not positive Law and do not fall within the order called State. Now, to this reduction of the State to mere juridical themes — which Kelsen proposes — there must be formulated the following objection. The Law is concrete, that is, the juridico-positive order is here, and it is so in a determined way and in no other, and it has this content and not that, and in it is embodied a certain estimative signification, some true political values, thanks to the joining of a series of elements and factors in certain processes of human reality, processes which have essentially peculiar political meanings. All these elements and factors, which condition and determine the birth of a juridical order and its special configuration, are not strictly Law, except to the extent to which they have succeeded in a normative transcription, that is, to the extent to which they have been translated into rules of Law in force; so, for example, a process of public opinion in a political matter is not Law, until this opinion has succeeded in being transcribed into juridical norms in force. While it is nothing more than a process of public opinion, not yet triumphant, not yet precipitated into juridical norms, it does not belong to the system of Law, nor, consequently, strictly to the State order. But possibly this which today is only a movement of public opinion will tomorrow be transformed into an official criterion, which will be carried into new juridical norms. This shows that those processes of public opinion — as also other series of social processes (of political integration, of an economic character, etc.), social processes which, being human ones, have peculiar meanings — condition and circumscribe the system of the juridical order in force. And, consequently, all those problems ought to be taken account of in a philosophy of Law and State, which will have to take into consideration all those elements which operate as suppositions and as markers of the Law. These themes may exceed a strictly pure juridical theory, because they do not yet constitute Law; and, consequently they might be called metajuridical themes; but they cannot be left aside by a philosophy of Law and State, because precisely those elements constitute the basis of the social reality in which Law operates and for which Law is produced. Such elements and factors, as they do not yet constitute Law (to the degree that they have not yet precipitated into juridical norms), may be called, if one wishes, metajuridical. But note that this particle *meta* denotes that they transcend the perimeter of positive Law in force; on the other hand, the qualifier *juridical,* to which such particle meta is prefixed, expresses that it is something connected with the Law, and, consequently, something which has a series of close relations with it. The base upon which an edifice is built and the ideas which engendered it do not belong in a strict sense to that edifice; but without such foundation and without such plans, the construction could not be raised nor sustained, nor, either, could it be understood and totally explained without considering such points of view. And, then, we take account of there being a special social reality, to wit, the state reality, which creates, formulates, gives life to and circumscribes the Law.

Having made the preliminary observation which precedes, and which may serve as the first critical point of view with regard to the Kelsenian doctrine, we are now going to examine it in more detail, and, at the same time, construct a concept of what the State is and what it contains.

In the doctrine of the identity of State and Law, there is much of error and that is inadmissible, as the reader will already have surmised. But not all that is in it is untrue. In general terms, the State does not coincide by a great deal with the normative system of the juridical order in force, as I shall explain very soon in the next pages. But, on the other hand, from the purely and exclusively juridical point of view, it is true that there is no more State than that which is expressed in the system of Law in force. That is, for the jurist, in the strict and rigorous meaning of the word, placed exclusively in the juridical point of view, the essence of the State is the system of Law in force, and, consequently, it coincides with it. For the jurist, the State exists solely *so far and as* it is expressed in the juridical order, and in no way as a social power, nor as a complex of historical forces, nor as a nation, nor as public opinion, nor as economic conditions, nor as a process of political integration, etc. For the jurist the State exists solely and exclusively as the subject and object of the juridical norms in force; that is, as a system of all those acts which in the juridical order are attributed to this unity, in short, attributed to the State. For strict juridical consideration, it is not necessary to distinguish between State and Law, nor to ask about the priority of one or the other, because they are both merely two different modes or aspects of the same entity; they are only different points of view as to the same thing. So, for example, legislation, considered as an activity, seems to us as State; and, on the other hand, seen as a result, that is, as law, as the product or content of that activity, it receives the name of Law. Understood as *ordering* order is the State; as *ordered* order is the Law. So, then, from the exclusively juridical point of view, the State is the Law as a norm creating activity; and the Law is the State as a regulated situation. It is possible that within the state command shall be produced sometimes phenomena of arbitrariness; but these cannot be taken as of the State by the jurist. When the jurist finds himself faced by an arbitrary mandate — purely such, that is, which has not anything which deserves any other qualification (for example, a crime, an illegality against which one may appeal to a higher instance) — he cannot take it as of the State, precisely because it is outside the system of Law in force. This phenomenon of arbitrariness represents for the jurist the intrusion of a fact of bare brute force, which cannot be ascribed to the State, simply because there is no juridical norm by virtue of which such act may be imputed to the State. For the jurist, the State is simply the unity of the organs of creation and application of the Law; and nothing else, which cannot apply within the juridical system. For the jurist there is no other State than that which appears foreseen and sketched in the order in force.

That the affirmation which precedes may be correctly understood and that possible mistaken interpretations may be avoided, it will be necessary to utter certain cautions.

In the first place, I will repeat that this equivalence between State and Law is produced only within the domestic ambit of the juridical sphere; that is, it does not mean to say that the existence of the State is exhausted in the order of Law in force; it does not mean to maintain that there is not a complex of state realities; but it denotes only purely and simply that for the Law there is no more State than that which is determined in its own norms.

In the second place, it is to be noted that this equation (of mere juridical extent) between State and system of positive Law, refers exclusively to the juridical order in force and does not pretend — as some have wrongly interpreted it — that there are no measures of an ideal character by which to judge the positive norms. The juridical equivalence between State and Law does not suppose in any manner that above the positiveness there are not valuing criteria and political ideals for the criticism of existing norms and for proceeding to their reëlaboration and reform in a more just sense.

On the other hand, it is necessary to call attention to the following: the equivalence between State and positive Law does not mean to say that the content of every juridical norm in force has been truly and actually elaborated by an official organ of the State; for it is evident that this did not happen, either with the rules of customary Law, nor with those established by the parties to a contract, nor with the bylaws framed by an association, etc. But those norms (customary, contractual, institutional, etc.), nevertheless, are valid as the will of the State, and only as such can be considered as juridical precepts in force. The equivalence implies only that for a norm to be considered as Law in force it is necessary that it should be included within the unitary system of the juridical order and referred to a common instance which gives validity to all the norms; that is, referred to the will of the State, in the formal sense, although in fact it has not been elaborated by any of the strictly State organs. Juridically, the State is only an ideal point of convergence, to which must be referred all the juridical determinations which belong to a system.

In the sense which I have just explained, it is said that for the jurist, strictly as such, that is, from the purely juridical point of view, the State exhausts itself in the system of positive Law in force.

But the preceding affirmation in no way implies that therefore the State remains totally identified with the normative system of the Law. It is a matter of a purely domestic assertion of the juridical consideration: but not of a full concept of the State. For the simple reason that the system of the juridical order in force, at a fixed place and time, is not a system of pure and absolute ideas with validity in and for itself — as might be, for example, the system of mathematical ideas — but is a historic human work; and, moreover, a work which, that it may go on existing as something real, has to be effectively vivified by a society; and, I may add to this, the juridical order in force is not something quiet and static, but is a thing subject to the processes of renovation and of change. The State as a normative system, as juridical order, is not a magic product which is brought here by the art of enchantment, which has arisen miraculously, but is a sort of precipitation or of normative expression of a series of happenings of social life; which is, in short, the resultant of an aggregate of real phenomena of collective integration with a special meaning, to wit, a political meaning, with the meaning of organizing a supreme mandate and with dimensions of legitimacy.

But, moreover, as the State is not a quiet thing, but something acting and always in reëlaboration and change, those movements are produced by the action of the historic social facts, as the effect of a certain collective reality. That is: the State, as a positive juridical order, is initially produced, sustains itself, lives and evolves, falls and is replaced — either normally or with interruption of continuity (revolution, etc.) — thanks to the real processes of integration of the effective factors which constitute the juridical society and thanks to the phenomena of the preponderant will in it.

Notice that, suddenly, the basic separation between the normative region and the world of real facts — proposed by Kelsen — fails necessarily at the base of the system. The base of the system is the so-called fundamental norm or constitution in the logico-juridical sense, which is not supported upon a juridical precept; Kelsen says that it is not strictly positive but hypothetical. Now, having reached this point, the pretended logical autonomy of the normative-juridical system breaks down before the social reality; and breaks down because, in order that we may suppose a system of Law in force, it is absolutely necessary that there should be a social reality which in fact supports this system and which actually corresponds to it, at least in a certain minimum degree. Because unless there is produced a phenomenon of preponderant social will in favor of a certain juridical system, it cannot be considered that this has really been born; that is, we cannot formulate the hypothetical fundamental norm which is going to be the base of the whole juridical system. If an order does not attain any efficacy in reality, if in its greater part it does not obtain effectiveness, if it is not generally and ordinarily complied with, then it cannot be supposed to be positively in force. It is true that Kelsen recognizes this when he says that to admit the dimension of being in force or positiveness of a given juridical system, it is necessary that the conduct of the men to whom it is directed should actually coincide, at least to a certain minimum degree, with the content of the norms of the system; that is, that the positiveness or being in force of the system requires a minimum of actuality. But Kelsen, despite such recognition, does not take account of the decisive extent of this observation; for he does not come to comprehend that this carries the definite proof that the juridical system is supported from without, as to its first base, as to its lowest fundamental, on a fact of collective power, upon a human reality; and that, consequently, the choice or supposition of the fundamental norm is not a moment which belongs to juridical logic or the pure theory of Law, but is something derived from some actual social facts. The positiveness or being in force is founded on an actuality. And so it happens that the theoretical Law does not have liberty to choose the fundamental norm or logico-juridical constitution which permits it to construct, that is, to systematize the positive juridical order or the one in force; but that its decision on this point is conditioned by the result of some social facts, to wit, by the facts of the predominant collective power; and so it has to suppose as fundamental norm that which it derives from those facts. Thus it results that the construction of the system of the juridical order is not a pure autonomous construction, but a post-construction of certain phenomena. And so it appears that the whole juridical system is conditioned by a sociological base.[74] To maintain the purity of the normative system, it would be necessary that its primary base (its fundamental norm), should be a pure idea belonging to the

[74] Against the point of view of the text: CARLOS COSSIO, EL CONCEPTO PURO DE REVOLUCIÓN (Barcelona: Bosch, 1934).

realm of values, with ideal validity in itself and for itself, independent of every fact; or, expressed in another way, it would be necessary that its being in force should not be derived from any real contingent phenomenon, but from the intrinsic rightness or justice of the norm. But it happens that the actual being in force of a juridical system is not an expression of its intrinsic justice, but is the effect of its *positiveness*, of its *actuality*. And this brings us to what Kelsen has not wished to see: to the fact that the first constitution or fundamental norm of a juridical system is a reality of social power.

The State as a normative system, that is, as a system of Law in force, is based, maintained, and conditioned by a complex of social phenomena. What constitutes and acts as the real sociological fundamental of the State is a phenomenon of collective power which constitutes the actual resultant of the wills of the men who compose it. This real phenomenon of power consists in the existence of an effective unity of supreme decision upon the regulation of the common life. It is not a matter of a collective will understood mystically, as an entity apart from and independent of the men who compose the State and of their separate wills; it is not a matter of supposing phantasmagorically a real soul of society, in the arbitrary way in which romanticism does; it is not a matter of a collective spirit apart and distinct from the individuals; but it is a matter only of an actual unified resultant of the conjunction of forces which make up the political community. Among all the private wills — many times diverse and even contradictory — there arises a process, from which flows a certain unified direction, which appears as a decisive resultant, as the final product individualized and formed by all the social mechanisms which make up the woof and the dynamics of the political collectivity. So, then, the fundamental norm of the State as Law, as a system of juridical order in force, is the normative expression of the fact of the resultant of the will which is embodied in the predominant power. The whole juridico-positive edifice at its base rests upon that social reality which constitutes the supreme instance of collective decision.

What I have just explained is not to be interpreted in the sense of a consecration of physical force as the ultimate foundation of the Law. Ethically the Law will need to be founded always on reasons of value; it will have to justify itself estimatively in ideal rights. When it lacks these, we find ourselves in the presence of an order which could or may have positiveness, but which will always lack justification, and finally will represent something monstrous and adominable. But now it is not a matter of the ideal justification of the Law, which I shall examine in the last part of this book, devoted to the theory of juridical values; it is not a matter of the question of the estimative; it is a matter of something different; it is a matter only of explaining the historical being in force of a certain positive Law, or, what is the same, the reality of a State. Now, history offers us many examples of States which have been and which are, and which nevertheless, from the estimative point of view, we consider detestable, as something which ought not to have been. From the valuing point of view we deny validity and justification to such monstrous States; we label them pathological, abnormal, unjust; but we cannot deny their historical reality. One may recognize the reality of a certain State, and, consequently, the being in force of its juridical system; and notwithstanding consider that, because it is unjust and because it does not respond to social aspirations, we ought to procure its overthrow to establish tomorrow a more just State.

But even situated on the plane which I have just indicated, that is, on the plane of the knowledge of realities and not of critical estimation, one must also avoid the error of interpreting the phenomenon of predominant social power as a pure relation of material violence. Social power is a thing very distinct from physical force. Even when the social power appears making use of means of corporal and mechanical force, these do not constitute its root, but are mere instruments which the power manages, because it is precisely a social power, for otherwise it would not have them at its disposal. In short, social power is founded on factors of conscience. It does not consist purely in the possession of corporal vigor, of arms and of other material elements, but in the obedience of the persons who manage the arms and who accept money as a medium of payment. All social power rests, in final terms, on the recognition of it by those who submit to it. Nevertheless, it has to be noted that sometimes there occurs unfortunately the fact that the political dominator, exploiting the force which a rigid organization gives him, obtains the forced submission of a collectivity whose components are hostile to him for the most part; and it happens so because the dominator possesses the resort to discipline, the force of the inertia which is given to an organization, resources which isolated individuals lack, so that they are obliged to serve as instruments of that power, which they repudiate at the bottom of their conscience. But these cases of social power not elaborated nor supported effectively upon the authentic social reality, but obtained either by violence or by the scheme of an organization which annuls opposition — in so far as it eliminates those who foster it — carry within themselves the germ of their inevitable defeat. When there is a radical divorce between the power which triumphed by force — or which maintains itself artificially — and the authentic sentiment of the national community, then that power is condemned to wither, when it does not precipitously tumble. As José Ortega y Gasset says, "the State is, in short, the state of public opinion: a situation of equilibrium, of statics. What happens is that at times public opinion does not exist. A society divided into discrepant groups, the force of whose opinion is reciprocally annulled, does not give rise to what constitutes a mandate. And as nature abhors a vacuum, that emptiness which the absent force of public opinion leaves is filled by brute force." [75] But, normally, a mandate signifies the preponderance of an opinion; and so, of a spirit. A mandate finally is nothing but spiritual power. So, then, when we say at such a date and place such a man, such a group, commands, it is equivalent to saying that at such a date there predominates such a system of opinions (ideas, preferences, aspirations, propositions). Except in the case that, not having in a situation any opinion authentically predominant, what results is social chaos, and then the brute force of some adventurers comes to impose itself by bare violence.

Now, with reference to some realities of our time, it is desirable to make the following observation: this law which public opinion at the last imposes is always valid: but the term of its compliance may vary considerably. In all the historic past, from the most remote times until some twenty years ago, it has always been complied with and in rather short and rapid terms. Seldom, up to twenty years ago, has there been seen the phenomenon of a political mandate contrary to the predominant public opinion lasting for a long time. All tyrants, who were really and truly such, were defeated in a short period of time. Ingenuous people, who apply to past times the sight which they have at the moment in which they live, will be mistakenly judging certain past situations as "oppressions"; but as soon as they lose that ingenuousness, they take notice that those regimes, which today may be fancied to be tyrannical oppression, were in their time the authentic and normal result of preponderant public opinion. Otherwise, they would not have been able to last for long, especially if we take into account that all the material instruments of coercion at their disposal were very weak and scarce, to the point that the greater assortment of such instruments would not have been able to resist the assault of a movement of unarmed people, if such movement had represented the predominant authentic public opinion. But today, at the present time, it happens that the realization of this law of gravitation of public opinion may endure considerable delay in its fulfillment, due to a new fact that has developed in our epoch: the terrible potentiality of technical mechanics applied to arms. The destructive effects of machine guns, tanks, asphyxiating gases, etc., are of such

[75] Cf. José Ortega y Gasset, La rebelión de las masas. Also, Bertrand Russell, Power; a new social analysis (1938).

caliber that whoever today enjoys the possession of these instruments may maintain himself in power for a much longer period than would have occurred in former times, by brute force alone; even when of course at last it will have to succumb to the domination of a situation of authentic public opinion.

Now, even after the reservations which precede, there remains as the normal reality of the State the fact of the mandate of public opinion, which is what produces the unified instance of decision, upon which is based the normative order. Upon this actual base of social reality rests the normative system of the Law.

But the reality of the State as a complex of social phenomena we find not only in the founding and conditioning base of the normative system, but we find it acting dynamically in the maintenance and development of the Law in all its degrees. The real processes of the social will operate not only as cement for the fundamental norm or first constitution of a juridical system, but also influence its dynamic development. For a juridical order, rigorously conceived under the systematic form of a graduated or scaled hierarchy of norms and competences, is not, while it is in force, a fossil product, a static picture; but on the contrary it is a mechanism in movement, which is innovating and reforming some of its parts and creating new forms. All this, within a system of pure juridical logic, may be construed and explained formally by the theory of successive delegations — which, starting from the fundamental norm or original constitution, comes to rest, by means of multiple instances, with the individualized norms (judicial judgment, administrative resolution). Now, notice that this formal system of scaled delegations is not a living system, which possesses within itself the effective force of its dynamics; but rather it is put in motion thanks to the action of effective spiritual forces. These spiritual forces are those which, within the boundaries of the juridical system, determine and shape its contents. Many organs of the State — especially the legislative and also the regulatory — possess an extensive sphere of discretional faculties to dictate the norms whose establishment is conferred upon them. And so, the problem of why (within the whole possible repertory of determinations which the sphere of competence established by the order permits), the state organ chooses one of them and not another is a question which entirely escapes the pure theory of Law. This problem can be attacked only by study of the concrete social factors which condition the decision and of the political ideas which inspire it, understood not only as ideas, but as collective convictions in force. The legislator, within the margin of the discretion which the constitution confers upon him, dictates a law with one determined content and no other simply because, in the constellation of the politico-social factors, this was the view-point which triumphed. So, then, this law, which has been elaborated within constitutional limits, has its origin, as to its concrete contents, in a social process of a political character, in an intercrossing of social necessities and of aspirations. Think, for example, how within one single constitution and with strict regard for it, an advanced party can govern the same as a moderate party. What occurs with either is something which cannot be explained by the pure theory of Law; it is simply the effect of the fact that in the elections for Parliament this or that party triumphed; but this constitutes a social fact of a political character; in short, it is a fact which forms part of the reality of the State, and which is not reducible to the normal outline of the prior Law; because it signifies the determination which operates within its margin, in favor of one or another content, by virtue of something which does not depend upon the normative system. It is something which proceeds from the social-political reality. And the same may be said with respect to the determinations which other state organs make within the sphere of their competence: that among the various possible normations a Minister chooses one certain one and not the others is something which is not explained by the formal scheme of the juridical order — in which is sanctioned his discretional competence — but which is something founded on the reality of a social-political situation. It happens, then, that beneath the State in the strict sense — as a juridical order in force — there exists a social reality which originally produces it, which afterwards maintains it, which successively reëlaborates it, and which conditions it at every moment. The Law appears, consequently, as a kind of normative precipitate of that social reality. The Law is the crystallization in normative form of a series of processes of the collective life. And, on this account, we may legitimately speak of a sociological reality of the State, which is what creates, maintains, vitalizes, and develops the Law.

Now, it is to be understood that this reality of the State is not a natural reality; it is not physical, nor biological. Nor is it a substantive spirit: nor a collective soul in the manner which romantic mysticism supposes, nor an objective spirit, existing in and for itself, as the Hegelians pretend. It is simply a human reality: an aggregate of human relations, of human constellations, a series of forms of collective objectivated life and, at the same time, the series of dynamic processes in which those forms are produced and in which are formed other new ones, as history runs. And, as such human forms, it cannot be studied by means of a purely causal explanation, as the old Sociology pretended; but, on the contrary, as it is a matter of human facts with meaning, they have to be *understood* in the light of this. And the meaning of the facts which constitute the reality of the State is a political meaning.

Further it is necessary to note that if the state facts are full of signification, and only in the light of this can they be understood, nevertheless, the State does not consist only of an aggregate of significations, that is, of ideas, but it constitutes a reality, to wit, a reality composed of human lives, which behave in a determined way. On this account, the theory of the State, which is not a natural science, is also not a science of the spirit or of words, but a science of social realities in which are produced juridical normative meanings.

And, following the inspiration of Hermann Heller, it may be said that we find the State as something real, but of whose reality man forms a part. The State, the same as the other social entities, is an aggregate of forms of human life, created and realized by men. On one side, it is composed of human lives; and, on the other, the condensations of the social processes which make up the State act upon the destiny of those lives. Within this complex of social forms, vivified and renewed by the constant action of men, they are found, integrating by their conduct the reality of the State. In short the State consists of a complicated aggregate of interlaced forms of human life. The State presents itself as a condensation or accumulation of social processes, which repeat themselves in certain figures and complexes, and which are actually vivified by the men who participate in them. These accumulations constitute a kind of fabric of human forces: human energies gathered and interlaced, whose density and persistence are due to the effect of combination and organization. But it is to be understood that this reality of the State is not a substantive reality, does not constitute a *thing* which is here outside of us and independent of us. In short, the substance of this reality depends on there being men who make it effective. Without the acquiescence and collaboration of men, who live in the state forms, the reality of the State would disappear. The State is an aggregate of forms of objectivated human life; but the reality of the State does not consist only of those forms, but in the fact that such forms are actually vivified by men. And moreover it happens that men are not limited only to vivify, or better, to revivify, those forms, but also they bring innovations which result in new collective forms. And in such manner the State goes on transforming itself, and presents itself as something which develops in the historic process. So then a great part of the state forms and processes are constantly reappraised by men, whether they confine themselves to revivifying them or proceed to their renovation. The reality of the State consists then in a functional actualization.

The social processes which create, maintain, and renew the state forms are processes of integration of its members. And these processes join to form a superior unity — which crystallizes in the construction of the unity of the juridical order.

It is altogether erroneous to believe that the State is a subject which acts for itself alone, which moreover possesses an independent life and which is capable of engendering new social forms for itself and for its own account. None of this is true, but on the contrary is clearly erroneous. In reality, those who act are always men of flesh and blood. Those men, so far as they are members of the State and form part of its reality, act under the influence of the representations of the forms of collective-state behavior, and, consequently, integrating in this way the reality of the State and acting on its account and for it. But, I repeat that it is always the individual persons who act, if indeed they do it not as individual persons but as something for the State. Now, in spite of this, the imposing force which the State exercises upon men is explained (to the point that it seems that it constitutes something foreign to them, something as of an independent magnitude, against which men could do nothing or little), because in the State are condensed the forces of innumerable persons, the totality of which cannot be embraced by the consciousness and the action of one individual. And, moreover, it happens that the same individual who tries to confront the State finds himself acting — perhaps without noticing it — under the influence of the idea of the State, and, consequently, as an integrating element of the state reality.

I have pointed out that the State represents a collective unity, which crystallizes in the juridical order. Now, it is to be noted that this ordering — as in general all the actual orderings of conduct — constitutes a social unity, not only as regards *normativity,* but also as regards *normality,* that is, as to actual regularity, as it produces an organization. In this sense, the objective reality of the organized social unity is founded on a unified power; that is, the organization arises when there exists an established instance to resolve the cases not predetermined or which offer doubt and to assure that its mandates should be obeyed. The organization of that instance is what constitutes the fact of reality of the unification of the social order. This instance for decision is altogether necessary, for the juridical order, whether as normativity or as regular and actual normality, is sufficient only for the ordinary and foreseeable cases, but is not sufficient to determine what ought to be the social conduct in the unexpected event. For this, it is necessary that there should be an instance of power, as director of the social organization, to determine and impose the proper decision.

Now, how is constituted *in fact,* truly and actually, the unity of the social organization, which is embodied in the State? This question has not been answered in any way, either by the mystical thought of the monarchical theory, or by the strange essays of geopolitics, or by the grotesque racial dogmas, or by the attempt to explain it as the product of the class struggle. Considering all the processes which make up the State, and in which it is constituted as such, it might be said that the unity of the State has to be understood as a unity of actual and efficacious decision, which has succeeded in being formed in a real and concrete manner by a series of social processes. These social processes appear conditioned in part by natural factors; more decisively influenced by other collective orders; and shaped definitely and with precision by the state organs instituted by the Law. There are natural factors which in some way may exercise an influence upon the configuration of the human activities which integrate the State. And among these natural factors, there must be mentioned specially the geographic ones. The geographic elements are not always sole determinants of the social structures, but on the other hand they may constitute conditions (positive or negative) of certain sociological contexts. So, then, such geographical factors are in no way sufficient to create or to explain the actual unity of the State, since as the State is a human reality it cannot ever be considered as a phenomenon of nature; but such geographic elements may constitute conditions which exercise some influence upon human activities; such as, for example, the neighborhood of a territory which brings closer social relations, coördinates them, homogenizes them, and determines the adoption of certain models of conduct as to the exterior. Processes and situations strictly social exercise an influence of great weight in the formation of state unity; so, for example, the social entity of a nation, which constitutes a form of community, which already includes in itself a unity. But with the existence of the nation we do not yet have the State. That the State may arise there must be produced the unity of the normative order, which is obtained by the organization of the state instances, according to what is determined in the system of Law. But, in its turn, the fundamental base of the system of positive juridical organization we have seen issues from and is supported on a resultant of the social will. Notice that in no way is this predominant social will to be understood as a collective spiritual phenomenon, as a will independent of and apart from the wills of the men who compose the State. This notion would constitute a tremendous absurdity, against which I have already adduced in this book a sufficient number of reasons. It is not a matter in any way of this; it is a matter of something very different, to wit: in that among all the wills of the men who make up the State —

many times diverse and contradictory — in contrasting with each other, they combine, and from them arises a process in which is forged a real unified resultant, which is that which is effectively imposed. By means of all the processes which integrate the social reality of the State, is individualized that decisive instance, from which is derived the fundamental base of the juridical order in force and upon which it rests, the same in its continuity as in its transformations. The will of the persons who function as organs of the State has the extent and the significance of the common will, only because and so far as it may count on being provided in a regular fashion with the power of those represented, who habitually obey it.

Now, then, it is to be noted that from the sociological point of view, the fact that ordinarily the organ of the State is obeyed is due to the fact that its acts of power are valid as the resultant of the common will and are positively determined by it. And this common will appears as an actual sociological resultant, even for those individuals who find themselves in open opposition to it; because if they confine themselves to repudiating it subjectively, without doing anything else, it results that, in spite of their interior dissent, in fact by their conduct they contribute to support this state will; or if they move actively against it, then there will occur two possibilities: either they will succeed in imposing their rebellion, by which they will have produced a new common will; or they will fail, in which case the opposition will remain useless.[76]

And the same juridical order created by this unified resultant of the collective will contributes to individualize the later manifestations of it, by the organization of instances.

So, then — in disagreement with Kelsen — I emphasize that to understand the State fully, it is necessary to take account of the fact that its normative expression in the juridical order is founded initially, maintained successively, and conditioned in its developments, by a social reality, by some facts of the collective human life. These facts, as human, have a meaning, that is, a dimension of finality, vital motivations and proposed ends; and consequently in them are sheltered some intentions of value. It is true that from a strictly juridical point of view, the State expresses itself only as Law and by means of Law. But even when we isolate mentally this normative expression and in this way conceive of the State as the system of juridical order in force, it is altogether neces-

[76] Cf. HERMANN HELLER (former professor of the University of Frankfurt-am-Main, and, after expulsion by the Nazis, received at the University of Madrid), STAATSLEHRE, published after his death (1934). Cf. also RUDOLF SMEND, VERFASSUNG UND VERFASSUNGSRECHT (1928). Cf. also JOSÉ RIVERA, P. C., LA JUSTIFICACIÓN DEL ESTADO (Mexico, 1932).

sary not to divide it in a radical and final manner from the social reality which produces and maintains it, nor from its relation to the ideas of value, which give it its peculiar meaning, to wit, a political meaning.

5. Type of Relation between the Juridical Dimension of the State and Its Social Reality

In the first place, it is necessary to inquire what are the social phenomena which belong to the reality of the State. For it happens, as is well known, that the realm of social facts is very much more extensive than the state reality; that is, that there are numberless phenomena of collective life which do not belong to the State. What then are the social facts which constitute the reality of the State? Now to this question I answer that there belong to the state reality all those relations, all the situations, and all the social processes whose intentional meaning refers to juristics. Or, put in another way, there forms part of the state reality all behavior which tends to the creation of juridical norms, to their maintenance, to their modification, or to their overthrow. So, for example, we may say that a pure collective movement, of an artistic opinion or of a scientific current, is not included within the state reality; but, on the other hand, there evidently belongs to it every act which influences or tends to influence public opinion with regard to the government, with regard to the desirability or undesirability of a certain juridical institution; every act of compliance or noncompliance with the Law; every proposal to preserve or to procure the replacement of given juridical norms, etc. All these facts and numberless analogous ones have a state dimension, precisely to the degree that they point toward the juridical; because they are, in short, ingredients which influence the concrete formation of the Law, its maintenance, its development or its destruction. If one wishes, there may be given to these facts the qualification of *metajuridical;* but it is to be noticed that this qualification is far from supposing an absolute independence as toward the juridical, but on the contrary implies a reference to it. And, so, these metajuridical factors will be those elements which, not belonging strictly to the normative order of the Law, are, nevertheless, in contact with it, engendering it, supporting it, and empowering it.

Now then, to make precise the relations between the pure juridical theory of the State and the metajuridical study of it, the following must be noted: while the juridical study may make an abstraction of those real elements which have not attained a strict normative expression, and make also an abstraction of political criticism, and be elaborated in such way as a juridical doctrine, on the other hand, the philosophy of the State and also the general theory of it, which is considered in its metajuridical roots, cannot escape at any moment constant reference to the juridical order, because this constitutes the limiting circumference of its object; something which pertains to the state reality only to the degree to which it refers to the production, the conservation, the realization, and the transformation of the Law. Although the actual reality of the State embraces metajuridical elements, these enter into the ambit of the State only so far as they intentionally refer to the Law; for example, either because there are social desires which they aspire to satisfy by a juridical order, or because they are programs to elaborate a future Law, or because they are phenomena of public opinion, which support the existing Law or which rebel against it, etc.

It remains, then, clear, that although the state reality and the juridical order are not identical entities, nevertheless they are mutually implicated in an essential and necessary way. The State cannot be thought of without thinking at the same time of the Law. Nor also can one conceive of the Law without referring to the State, that is, without referring to an instance of social power, which inexorably imposes the juridical norms.

CHAPTER XII

THE JURIDICAL VALUATION

1. Statement of the Problem of the Juridical Valuation

Under the title of Juridical Valuation I am going to treat of the problem of the criteria for the judging of the norms of positive Law and for the progressive reëlaboration of it.

Practically, in the supreme organization of the social life and in the solution of the conflicts which it raises, the norm of positive Law in force constitutes an executive and unappealable decision. The solution dictated by the organs of Law in force is something definite, which is irresistibly imposed; it constitutes in the reality of social life a last word, since the Law is a norm which by its own essence is imposed inexorably, annihilating all resistance and rebellion. But this decisive and firm solution in the reality of life is not, on the other hand, a last word for thought. And, therefore, it happens that we always ask ourselves, with regard to law or judgment of the Supreme Court of Justice, if the solution contained in one or the other, with respect to the given problem of social relations, is a solution wholly good or, at least, if it is the best among those actually possible. That is, confronting the positive juridical precept we put the question as to its intrinsic justification. We need to ask ourselves if this precept is wise or if on the contrary it is defective or if it represents a blunder; in short, we may always put the question if a juridical precept is or is not intrinsically justified. Or, put in other words: the solutions which positive jurisprudence — which of course constitutes practically a last word of forcible application — offers may be submitted by thought to a criticism, in whose light we inquire as to their rights of justification. Thus, so to speak, we compare the positive Law with an ideal, philosophical instance, to examine its rights of justification. We cite the decision of positive Law, not before a tribunal of the Law, but before the forum of conscience, before the judgment of philosophical reflection; and we put the question whether this, which here and now, or there and then, is or was Law in force, does or does not present its rights of justification; and, thus, at the same time, we engage ourselves in finding out if there should be a reëlaboration of the current precepts in a sense of greater justice and of greater common benefit.

Now this examination, like every process of judgment, will have to be conducted in the light of some norms, which in this case cannot be positive norms, but will have to be ideal norms, values. And strictly the task of Juridical Valuation, as one of the parts of the philosophy of Law, does not consist in carrying into practice the concrete valuation of a certain positive Law, but in discovering what are the models according to which such work of criticism, of valuation, will be possible, and, consequently, in orientation. With this, will be submitted the base for the making of the concrete judgments of the positive Law, and, at the same time, the obtaining of those criteria which ought to inspire the development of the Law.

In short, this is the problem which has been known by the names of "natural law," "rational law," "idea of justice," "supreme end of Law," "Juridical Deontology," "juridical ideals," "ideal criticism of the Law," etc. I prefer to call it *Juridical Valuation,* because by this expression is denoted clearly the essence of the problem and it does not prejudge the solution which is to be given it. And, at the moment, before entering into the attempt at the solution which ought to be given to this theme, it is of highest interest to state the problem with full nicety. Before all, what is necessary is to attain a clear knowledge of the problem, without running into mental precipitations which imply any prejudice as to its solution. And, as I shall explain a few lines below, it is not sufficient only to put the problem, but further it will be necessary to justify it as such problem, that is, to show that it has a full meaning that we should put such question.

This theme of justice, of the Law which ought to be, of juridical values, has always and at every moment been a concern, not only to the vital conscience of individuals and to the public opinion of peoples, but also in a central manner in philosophical speculation.

If we contemplate in panoramic perspective the history of thought, we must take account that, except two or three exceptional occasions, philosophy has always turned its attention lovingly to this matter. It appeared already as a favorite theme in the works of the Pythagoreans. It is sketched vigorously in Socrates, in whose work on the foundation of morals beats a preoccupation with how the State ought to be — and, consequently, as to the ideal outline of the juridical order. And in Plato, his work of greatest extent, that in which his metaphysics culminates, is precisely that devoted to the theme of justice (to the theme of the State which *ought to be*), the dialogue of the *Politeia* (Republic). And Aristotle dedicates to this question Book V of his Nicomachean Ethics and his treatise on Politics, showing the difference between the naturally just and the civilly just. And the stoics elaborated the concept of natural law, which afterwards will be received in the thought of the Patristics. And this went on, being occupied centrally with the problem of justice and of the norms to judge and orientate the Law, to outline the concepts of the eternal law and of the natural ethical law. And this theme occupies a preferred place in all the scholastic philosophy of the Middle Ages, and still more in the Renaissance which developed in the splendid flowering of the Spanish jurists and theologians of the sixteenth and seventeenth centuries (Suarez, Victoria, Soto, Bañez, Molina, Alcazar, Vazquez de Menchaca, etc.). And the jusnaturalistic thought of Illuminism (Altusio, Grotius, Tomasio, Pufendorf, Locke, Sidney, etc.) represents not only the most vigorous common denominator of the intellectual preoccupations of the epoch, but, also, the effective protagonist of the historic situation, which is going to culminate — passing by way of the grand work of Rousseau — in the great event of the French Revolution, which indeed we may define, from this point of view, as the maximum and frantic apotheosis of the Natural Law. And this same theme goes on being refined and acquiring new perspectives in Kant. And it persists and develops with fertility in Fichte, the greatness of whose work is being realized in our days; and in Schelling. And in Hegel it acquires other perspectives, to the point that, on the one hand it disappears as a normative theme and on the other hand the philosophy of Law converts it into one of the capital points of his system. And the jusnaturalistic theme appears with new versions in the pages of Krause.

This theme was denied only at some exceptional moments of antiquity: in the thought of the sophists, centrally preoccupied with this question, but to deny every valid criterion of justification — animated by a restless nihilistic spirit — in the radical skepticism of Pyrrhus, which is pure suspension of all judgment, as well theoretical as practical, full abstention, and in the philosophy of the Middle Academy. On the other hand, there appeared some attempts at skeptical doubt in the Renaissance, with Charron and with Montaigne, who did not come to be well received in the thought of their epoch. And, finally, in the second third of the nineteenth century, on the arrival of the naturalistic currents (materialism, evolution, etc.), on the one hand, and positivism at all costs to the followers of that school, on the other, the thought became mutilated. Philosophy was denied, and there was installed what has been well called the terroristic tyranny of the laboratories, which operated in the field of juridical studies to suppress all Philosophy of Law. But none of these skeptical crises was final, or succeeded in installing itself permanently in thought. Rather, on the contrary, they all gave place to new flowerings much more vigorous and purified in general philosophy and in the theory of the juridical ideals. And so, to the skepticism of the sophists succeeded the very fruitful flowering of the great philosophic systems of antiquity: Socrates, Plato, Aristotle, stoicism, epicureanism. And so, to the attempts of desperation of Charron and of Montaigne there succeeded the great systems of the classic school of Natural Law of Grotius, Tomasio, Pufendorf, Locke, Sidney, etc. And after the positivist regimes on one side and the materialist on the other — which however contradictory between themselves, had in the juridical field analogous consequences — supervened a restoration of Philosophy in all fields, and with extraordinary vigor as to this problem of the Juridical Valuation. At about the year 1880 positivism began to enter its crisis; and at the end of the past century its decline was already giddily accented, and was completed definitely in the first years of the present century. An analogous process was noted with respect to the naturalistic currents (materialism, evolution, etc.), whose domination was ephemeral, for on reaching the present century not only were they displaced by the new philosophy, but they also fell into deep discredit within the advances of the natural sciences, which formerly had conciliated them; and especially in the sector of juridical studies. And so, the Philosophy of Law, as a theory of juridical ideals, after that positivistic and naturalistic eclipse, renewed itself with reborn and more intense vigor, in Cohen, Natorp, Stammler, Loening, Petrone, Giner, Posada, Rios, Geny, Hauriou, Bonnecase, Petrazciski, Del Vecchio, Laski, Radbruch, Muench, Kantorovicz, Roscoe Pound, etc. It happens, then, that the juridical thought rises strong after the skeptical purge which positivism signified, and not only comes out anew with greater force, but also more purified. The skeptical crises were not produced by chance nor did they fail to leave beneficial results, although of course they have since been superseded. Skeptical crises represent, when they come, the necessity that philosophy should purify itself of precipitations or exaggerations which it may have incurred.

If from the history of the doctrines we pass now to the annals of individual and social convictions, we may notice that human consciousness has always maintained a belief in some juridical ideals which serve as norm for the criticism of positive Law and for orientation to secure its betterment.

2. Justification of the Problem of the Juridical Valuation

The proof of how in the history of philosophic ideas — the same as in that of vital convictions — there persists always this thought of the juridical ideal cannot fail to be impressive. But, nevertheless, I do not wish to rest on such proof the justification of the estimative theme. Suffrage, which has a decisive value in political matters, does not constitute on the other hand any conclusive proof in the field of theoretical investigation. Scientific and philosophic truth are not founded democratically. Nor does common feeling constitute a full guarantee of truth. In our habitual daily life, and especially in dealing with others and in the practical problems of the collectivity, common sentiment, good feeling, are wont to constitute one of the most prudent and sure norms. But in pure theory we cannot deliver ourselves to it with too much confidence, since it must be recorded that the history of science and of philosophy record no few corrections in the face of common sentiment. Consequently, although the persistence of the theme as to the ideal criteria with respect to juristics impresses us greatly and predisposes us to accept the justification of this theme, nevertheless, with it we have not yet a full and sufficient proof. In the field of theory, we have to demand that each position, to be admitted, must have its rights very clear, and very much in order. And to reach a solid construction, we have to proceed in a manner which shall not allow anything else than we have shown with full and irrefutable justification. On this account, I shall have to proceed, above all, to ask with fullest rigor if the problem of seeking estimative criteria for the Law has meaning, that is, if the problem is justified as such problem — without at the moment entering into any basic aspect as to its solution. Especially also as the negation of this problem produced in the second half of the past century is relatively recent. On the other hand, it is to be noticed that apart from the skeptical crisis — today already passed — the present moments are of deep and terrible integral crisis, to wit, of profound disorientation. And in the conditions of terrible confusion which characterize the present days, the urgent and unescapable duty for the intellectual is to try to orient himself in the disorientation.

For the moment, it is a matter of nothing more than putting the question as to the theoretic correctness of this theme of juridical ideals. That is, it is a matter of asking ourselves if there is or is not meaning in our embarking on the undertaking of seeking directives for the process and for the progressive reform of the Law. I would compare the situation which I now put with that in which one finds himself if he tries to undertake a voyage to discover an unknown land. Before commencing the voyage, one should ask: but does this land whose discovery is sought exist? Of course, we do not know how it is; on this account we are planning to undertake a voyage to discover it; but first we need a minimum of certainty that we can pledge all our efforts to make this discovery, because we have made sure that what we seek exists, even though for the moment we do not know how it is. Before all, nothing more than this. One of the new ideas which perhaps I may offer in this treatment of the Juridical Valuation consists in separating with all clearness a series of questions which in prior doctrines have ordinarily been involved and even confused. And, therefore, at the moment, I put nothing more than the question of the justification of this problem as a problem; that is, we are going to inquire if it is a matter of an authentic problem or of a phantom problem. Philosophy cannot accept as good anything which has not paid satisfactorily and fully its intellectual customs dues; it cannot accept anything which has not justified itself in compliance with clear and firm reasons.

So, then, at the moment of this exposition, it is a question of investigating whether all that can be said upon the problems of the social life — which the Law pretends to solve — is exclusively contained in the historic positive norms; or if, on the contrary, it is possible to pass judgment on these problems from a point of view distinct from positive Law. Is there in the world of juridical problems anything more than the norms of positive Law? Let the reader notice that, at this instant, I do not ask whether or not there exists a supposed natural Law, nor even what may be the extent of its precepts, nor of what they consist. Now I limit myself to asking, is there any other juridical criterion above the positive norms? In case this question can be answered affirmatively, then will be the moment to put other problems, to wit, those which refer to the method of knowing these criteria, to their extent, to what are their principles, to their mode of application, etc.

What is the mental situation in which we find ourselves? As we have removed all prior judgment — that is, as we have left aside the vital and historical conviction that there are ideas of justice — we do not know if there are or are not orienting criteria for juristics, because this is precisely what we are asking. But, on the other hand, it seems indisputable that we know that in the world there is something which is called positive Law, to the study of whose essence the preceding chapters have been dedicated. Now, we start solely and exclusively from that, which we know with all certainty. And let us try to examine this which we possess firmly, in its very depths, in its very essential structure. Now, to practice this analysis with the data which we possess — positive Law — we must take into account that in it we find already the trace or mention of something which is not in positive Law, but a point of ideal reference, in short, of something which is witness to the criterion for which we are asking. Or, put in other words, the analysis of the concept of positive Law will show us that in it there is necessarily postulated an ideal of justice, independently of whether the concept embodies it or not. If we strike out the allusion to an ideal of justice, the concept of positive Law will become unrealizable. Without the intentional reference to a principle of justice there cannot exist any positive Law. I am going to show this with all clarity and proof.

Remember that positive Law is a form of objectivated human life of a normative character. Now, what does a normative form mean? Simply, it signifies that among various possibilities of conduct there are chosen some over others. And those are chosen over the rest, because they are preferred by virtue of something. And this preference is founded on a judgment of value, on a valuation. Although the norm of positive Law emanates from a mandate, from an actual power, it cannot be in any manner understood as a mere fact, but it is a human fact, and, as such, has meaning or significance. And this meaning consists basically in the reference to a value, in the pretension of a justification: this is commanded and nothing else, because those who decide believe that it is justified; they believe that this is preferable to the other, and, consequently, they choose it among all the other concrete possibilities. Or, put in another way, the normativity of positive Law would have no meaning if it did not refer to a judgment of value, which is what inspires it. Social conduct is regulated in a certain way, because it is believed that this is better than other possible regulations. Of course it may be that the positive Law fails in its intent; the panorama of history offers an abundant repertory of unjust laws and customs. But in these laws and customs lies the intent to realize a value of justice, although they did not succeed. It is a matter then of a failed intention; but, as intention, it existed essentially as a meaning of the norm. The mere notion of positive Law, although it does not contain within itself the juridical ideal, nevertheless presupposes it; that is, it postulates its existence; it intentionally refers to it, although it does not come to realize it. We cannot understand the meaning of juristics if we avoid all reference to ideals of justice. It is not that the definition of Law contains them in itself; because if this were so, it would lose its dimension of universality. But if indeed the definition of the Law does not harbor within itself the supreme juridical values, nevertheless it mentions them, intentionally refers to them. If we erase from positive Law this mention of non-positive principles, we do not remain with anything more than a chaotic conglomerate of pure incomprehensible facts. The essence of the Law is not intelligible except in the function of an intention to realize certain values. All normation supposes that there has been chosen one certain standard among others possible because it was considered better than they; now, this election entails a preference; and the preference supposes a valuation, that is, a criterion of value. Or, expressed in another way, a norm supposes that among the multiple things which might be done, there are some of them which ought to be done and others which ought to be avoided; supposes, as it were, a sifting of the repertory of possibilities, bringing out the worthy, avoiding the prohibited, and admitting the permitted. The work of sifting consists of a selection, but the selection can only be made on the condition that one considers preferable what is chosen. And every act of preference implies a valuation; we prefer something because we consider it more worthy than the other, better, more useful, more adequate, more just. By this it is demonstrated that if there did not exist something above the bare reality of the positive norms, those same positive norms could not exist, nor, finally, be understood. So, then, in the very existence of positive Law we find a sort of directing arrow which points us toward some valuing criteria; we find the testimony of a reference to ideas of value. In short, it may be affirmed categorically that there are criteria of value to orientate — and consequently to judge — positive Law, because otherwise there could not exist any reality in it. Now, as it is well known that there is positive Law in the world, hence we have to conclude necessarily that there are also valuing criteria for juristics. Thus there remains fully justified the theme of the investigation as to the transempiric norms for a judgment as to positive Law and for the orientation in the progressive reëlaboration of it.

It is possible to arrive at the same conclusion by another way. In every positive juridical norm — as in every norm of whatever class it may be — we discover a structure of finality: it proposes, by the conduct which it ordains, to realize a certain end. Now, to propose something to ourselves as an end, it is necessary that that something should appear to us as valuable from a certain point of view. With this we discover the intentional mention or reference in each juridical precept to the realization of a finality reputed valuable. If in our consciousness we strike out the estimative function, there disappears also the possibility of all appreciation of finality.

But, further, I ought to add another consideration. The concrete end which each juridical precept or each institution pursues ordinarily appears as something limited or hypothetical, that is, as something which represents in its turn a means to obtain another end; and again the same occurs with that other end; and so on, successively. Now, this process of going on inquiring the concatenation of the ends of the different positive juridical norms will necessarily bring us to a moment at which we shall have to ask ourselves the end of Law in its totality, or, what is the same thing, the ultimate or supreme end of juristics. And this is precisely the fundamental question of Juridical Valuation.

So, then, in short, if we eliminate that reference to the valuing criteria of Law, positive Law itself would appear to us as impossible; and would remain reduced to a pure phenomenon of brute force, analogous to the phenomena of nature, from which there would have evaporated completely its juridical essence, that is, what the Law has of Law.

In all that I have expounded up to now, I have limited myself to justifying the theme of juridical valuation with arguments of absolute rigor. And I have done it without complicating unnecessarily other philosophic points of view, which of course might also furnish a solid base for the Juridical Valuation. But I have wished to leave aside any reference to philosophic doctrine extrinsic to our matter, because if I had based myself on it, either I would have had to derive from it the considerations which at the same time would justify it, or I should have had to suppose as demonstrated some points with which I have not concerned myself here.

After what has been said, it remains perfectly established that the undertaking of asking ourselves for the juridical ideals is not chimerical but has meaning; and that, consequently, we may justifiably embark upon it.

3. Graded Articulation of the Themes Which Condition the Juridical Valuation

This first question as to the justification of the valuing search in juristics being settled, there have to be put in order four questions, which are the following:

First: To determine if the basic foundation of the Juridical Valuation can be empirical, or if, on the contrary, it has necessarily to be *a priori*.

Second: In case the foregoing question is resolved in favor of the aprioristic thesis, it will have to be asked if the *a priori* ideas for the valuation of the Law are mere subjective forms, psychological dispositions, or habits, or if, on the contrary, they constitute objective ideas with necessary validity.

Third: To determine the respective intervention which *a priori* ideas and *a posteriori* elements have in the elaboration of the juridical ideals; or rather, seek how to combine the juridical values with the process of history.

Fourth: In what does the idea of justice consist; and, moreover, if there are other juridical values; and, in case there are, what are these values and what relation do they have to the idea of justice.

I attribute superlative importance to articulating in a graded manner these questions, so that we should not enter upon the second without having solved the first, and so on, successively. If we examine the history of human thought with regard to these matters, we shall find that they were almost always put with precipitation and carelessly, jumping from one question to another without any order, because of not taking account of how each one conditions the following ones. Ordinarily, along the history of juridical thought, many authors have thrown themselves with good luck at first into a construction of natural Law, without having first resolved a series of previous questions. Others, on the other hand, adopted a posture of skepticism and exclaimed that there was no natural Law, that it constituted solely a phantasy, inadmissible in the field of science; but they took this position without having examined all the problems which condition a Juridical Valuation, limiting themselves to combating one certain thesis — for example, that of Natural Law in the Classic School — with which they took this problem as already solved definitely. Now, both the ones and the others did not approach the theme with the proper intellectual purity, nor did they examine seriously all the suppositions and implications which it carries with it.

Hence, I concede a decisive importance to a correct methodical articulation of all the suppositions and implications which the theme of the Juridical Valuation has. Before gaining access to the region of juridical values, it is necessary that we should solve a series of previous unknowns; since by not resolving them in due course, every effort on these themes would be weighed down by a series of deficiencies, which, finally, would condemn it to failure.

4. The Root of the Valuing Knowledge of the Law

Now is put the question of the root of the estimative knowledge with respect to juristics. That is, we ask ourselves as to what are the elements which have to serve as basic cement for every estimative judgment upon the Law. It is a matter in short of seeking to identify the ingredients which compose the judgments of value upon juristics.

In fine, this question constitutes a projection into the field of juristics of the general philosophical problem as to the origin of knowledge. And so, it happens that at this point of the Philosophy of Law, there is reflected, along its history, the secular dialogue between empiricism on one side and rationalism and apriorism on the other.

But it is to be noticed, above all, that the problem which is put here — the same as the general philosophical question as to the origin of knowledge — is not of a psychological nature, but is a theme of the theory of knowledge. It is a theme of a structural character, which consists in asking ourselves as to the composition of knowledge as a product, as to its objective laws. We are not making a psychological biography of the mental processes; we are not asking as to the vicissitudes and episodes through which this or that mind has passed to reach certain fixed truths; nor are we asking either as to the psychological laws of fact which govern the processes of knowledge. Before all, on the contrary, we take knowledge already made or constituted, to examine the ingredients of which it consists and what part corresponds to each of them in it, and from whence it has come.

This study is a consideration of knowledge already elaborated, as to its validity, as to its ingredients, and as to its object. The psychological fact of how the child discovers that his image in the mirror is only an image and not a reality is one thing and the objective law of refraction is a very different thing. The anecdote of the life of Newton, that in contemplating the fall of an apple there occurred to him the idea that led him to his theory of gravitation, has nothing to do with the physico-mathematical justification of that law. The psychological problems of origin, gestation, fabrication of knowledge, are certain ones; but the structural logical problems, that is, the gnosiological problems, are other and very different ones. We do not ask ourselves, then, for example, who has made a toy as such, but we are going to draw the insides out of the toy to see of what ingredients it consists, from whence each one comes, and what is the part which each one plays.

So, then, this problem as to the root of estimative knowledge is not psychological, but it consists in asking as to the type of mental acts in which is given me the thing of which I have an idea; or, rather, it consists in analyzing the elements of which the knowledge already made is composed and the connection which there is between them.

Along the history of general philosophy there is a controversy between empiricism and intellectualism (in its various forms: rationalism, innatism, apriorism, etc.).

In summary, it may be said that *empiricism* (represented by the Cyrenaicans, by the epicureans, by Locke, by Hume, by the positivists, etc.) maintains that the original source of all our ideas is experience. According to empiricism, consciousness would be a blank tablet on which nothing was written; so that everything which we find on it has come from experience, including the apparently most abstract ideas, which would have been formed by experience by way of repetition and generalization from those things given by it. Therefore, according to empiricism all knowledge proceeds from experience; and also all the ingredients of it would be derived from that.

Against the empirical thesis, another current philosophy, which runs along through most of two millennia, affirms that if indeed in knowledge there is a series of ingredients which comes from without, by means of sensible perception, there are others which do not proceed from experience; and that these are the most important and the decisive ones. So, for example, mathematical knowledge would not be based on experience. Rationalism understands that the decisive factor in knowledge is the intellect. If the ideal of knowledge consists in attaining universality and necessity, those dimensions can only proceed from the intellect, since sensible perception supplies us only a knowledge of the here and of the now, something fortuitous and contingent, and never with necessary principles nor with universal laws. On the other hand, there are fields of knowledge — precisely those most perfect and successful — in which experience does not play any part; for example, in mathematics. And, finally, with respect to those disciplines in which there intervene ingredients of an empirical origin, the important and decisive matter is not these data but the reëlaboration which the intellect makes of them. Now, if these rational and intellective elements do not proceed from experience, from whence are they derived? Descartes says they come from the soul itself, from the "treasury of my spirit." Leibnitz considerably refines this doctrine: he says that it is a matter of innate truths, but he warns at once that by this there ought not to be understood any knowledge formed in consciousness before those which would come in life, but simply those ideas for whose formation one counts always on the necessary forces, although in fact one does not know them at a given moment and even if they never arrive at being known. And so Leibnitz says that we also have to learn to know the innate truths and this demands of us sometimes superlative effort. So, it turns out that the innate truths are not ideas which we have preinserted or preshaped in our mind, but that our mind can arrive at them without the necessity of employing elements of experience; and so, an example of innate truth would be infinitesimal calculus, which Leibnitz discovered for the first time — almost simultaneously with Newton, though independently of him — infinitesimal calculus of which previously humanity had been completely ignorant. But, in spite of that, it was a matter of innate truth, because, when we examine it, it becomes evident that there are in it no ingredients of experience. Let it be well understood: there are no empirical elements in the theory already constituted, although mathematics in its mental process has perhaps been stimulated by experience. But, in spite of this, in such truths there are no components which proceed from experience. If we deprive geometry of its pencil and paper, probably we could not follow its meditations; and, nevertheless, the theorems which it discloses do not contain any empiric element: it makes use of the concrete triangle which it draws on paper, but the truth which it establishes does not refer to that singular triangle, but to all triangles in the absolute, to the triangle purely and simply, which is not given in experience, in short, to the universal concept of the triangle.

The transcendental Kantian apriorism maintains that knowledge is an active process, a construction which consists of two elements: one element *a priori,* that is, independent of and before experience, which is the form (pure intuitions of space and time and the categories) which constitutes a shaping and determining factor; and one element *a posteriori,* to wit, the material, or rather, the sensible data. For Kant, the world of sensation is a chaos, a thing without meaning, which only covers the figure of objects, their order, meaning, as far as the human mind organizes them by its pure intuitions of space and time and by the categories; in such manner that the being of objects consists of a determination of knowledge, that is, in the product of ordering by the categories the unformed mass of data.

All these philosophical currents have had a projection in the field of Ethics and of the Juridical Valuation. Let us fix ourselves fundamentally on the latter.

The radical empiricist tendency in the juridical field tries to reduce all knowledge of the problems of Law to an observation of the data which reach us by way of experience, and, in this case, by historical experience. In this way juridical knowledge is limited to historic Law, to what has been or is; and it ends in the basic negation of the valuing problem, as such, in a basic skepticism as to the knowledge of the values. This basic empiricism is already discarded in showing the justification of the Juridical Valuation and its possibility, better put, its necessity. But, even though false, it is, nevertheless, consistent with itself, it is faithful to its premises, since because it starts from the (erroneous) base that there is no more knowledge than that of empirical data, it is logical that it should deny the possibility of learning anything which is not given in experience.

But it happens that a series of manifestations of juridical empiricism have been produced which, in spite of wishing to limit knowledge to the sources of experience, have maintained the possibility of establishing a Valuation based on experience. Among the multiple examples which could be cited, perhaps the most representative would be that of the English philosopher Spencer and of the German jurist Adolf Merkel. Both are declared empiricists; and nevertheless they aspire to construct a Juridical Valuation based on experience. Spencer tries to establish a valuing criterion of fundamental Law for the ends of the conservation of the individual and of the species, according to the law of progressive evolution; and argues in this way: there is in the world a law of progressive evolution; all that is verified as functioning in the service of this law is worthy and ought to be; while on the contrary what is opposed to this law is unworthy. And Merkel proposes the establishment of criteria of juridical valuation taken from reality itself; and says: "In so far as we consider what is as something which has historically happened, which carries in itself the germ of what it has to become, we recognize that which ought to be. That which has to become and that which ought to be are identical concepts. Only knowledge of the tendency of evolution illustrates for us what ought to be." And as Medicine distinguishes between normal processes and pathological deviations, so also Juridical Sociology emphasizes the normal in the evolution of the collective life against that which has to be erased as diseased.

Now, these manifestations of juridical empiricism, which try to establish a Juridical Valuation based on experience run not only into an error but into an absurdity, into a position evidently incongruous. The world of pure and disengaged phenomena, without adding to it anything else which is not phenomenon, cannot ever furnish a criterion of preference or of valuation. The difference between Physiology and Pathology is not a datum of pure experience; it cannot in any way be based on a strictly natural knowledge; for from the exclusive angle of the science of nature, what we call health is as natural as what we call sickness, since both the one and the other are phenomena which have their causes. To distinguish between health and sickness, what we must do is to compare some data of experience with some ideas of value and of finality.

It results, then, that the world of pure nature, the world of phenomena as such and nothing more than such, is foreign to appraisals of value.

The world of pure experience, of facts, is blind to all valuation and does not know ranks and hierarchies. The perspective of rank and preferences does not spring from experience, but from its contrast with intuitions of value. In pure experience we meet what is as it is, and nothing more. There are no phenomena which are more phenomena than others. The world of experience is flat, without hierarchies. Experience gives us exclusively that which *is;* to wit, it gives us a series of phenomena casually produced. Among the phenomena — as phenomena — we cannot establish differences of normality and abnormality, of health and sickness, of good and bad, of justice and injustice. Phenomena, as such, all have the same consideration: all proceed from sufficient causes. The differences referred to can be discerned only in the light of an idea of finality or of value, which does not proceed from experience, but which is set up by our intellect. Experience gives us exclusively the is and never the ought to be. Although they ought to be, the ends and the values many times present themselves embodied in certain realities, we do not distinguish them nor learn them by drawing from experience, but by comparing the data in it with an *a priori* idea, that is, with an idea which does not proceed from experience. Of an empirical law of reality it is necessary to seek confirmation in experience; but the value of a conduct is not susceptible of such confirmation. Because the only thing which experience will give us, in some cases of value of utility, is the adequacy or inadequacy of a work for an end, but it will not give us the value of that end, nor the duty of proposing to ourselves its attainment.

When Spencer brought forth a critique of social and juridical reality by examining whether it agreed with the law of progressive evolution, he rested on an idea of value which does not proceed nor can proceed from experience; because we cannot draw from experience the criterion that evolution *ought* to produce in a certain way and no other. Evolution may signify a special rhythm or development of the phenomena in the real event. But when we talk of *progressive* evolution, in this concept is included a judgment of value, which cannot proceed from experience; because it is understood that a certain direction in the future of phenomena is good, is worthy, so far as it is directed toward an end which is considered valuable. Pure experience knows nothing with regard to progressive or regressive.

Juridical values are ideas which do not proceed from experience, although they may be realized in the facts which we win from experience. But that we should see a Law as just, a society as suitably organized, a political program as correct, supposes an *a priori* intuition of the values which are embodied in those realities. And, then, it is seen that the conduct in question agrees with something valuable. How could anything seem just to a man, if he did not have for himself an independent appreciation of the reality of that thing, which tells him that it has value? He loves, he wishes, he desires, he judges, he prefers, only by virtue of values primarily intuitive.

This exposition shows with all clarity how juridical empiricism is incapable of founding a valuation of the Law. Every Valuation has its root and the condition of its possibility in ideas of value, which are *a priori*, that is, which do not proceed from experience, although at times we perceive them by way of experience.

Let us notice, once more, that the question which we are examining is not a psychological problem, but the problem of the structure of knowledge. We do not discuss in this theme a history of knowledge, but a theory of it. And what has been said up to now signifies that the criteria to judge and to orientate positive Law have their basic foundation not in experience but in ideas of value.

But this does not signify that man to discover these criteria has to isolate himself from social experience, and live exclusively concentrated in his own mind to cause to arise from it such ideas of value. Surely, if he should do this, he would not be able to discover such estimative norms. The human mind closed within the vacancy of a diving bell — so to speak — would not succeed in establishing its knowledge *a priori*. Although this does not come from what is given in experience, the greater part of the time, it comes to us only on the occasion of experience. We do not draw it from it, but, thanks to its stimulus, we extract it from the sources of our own intellect. Experience, then, is not the source of *a priori* knowledge; but it usually constitutes the incitation and the inducement that our mind should discover it. Hence, the philosophy of Law, so far from isolating itself from social realities, ought to sink itself deeply in them, observing them carefully, living with them with intensity. Only in this manner, in intimate contact with historical experience, can there be formed in the mind adequate estimative judgments.

On the other hand, it is important to notice with all precision that, up to now, the only thing that I have affirmed is that the root or primary foundation of all valuation is an *a priori;* but I have not in any way affirmed that valuing judgments as to the Law do not include other ingredients of an empiric origin. But it is evident that to judge a historical Law or to elaborate a juridical idea, pure ideas of value are not sufficient, but it is necessary that they should be combined with the experience of the realities upon which they are going to be projected. Juristics — like all the functions of human life — is rooted always in a concrete circumstance of fact and is referred to certain determined men. Juristics — like all other human work — is a form of life to satisfy determined needs, which, if indeed they have a functional constancy, are concretely conditioned by the special circumstances of social reality, of time and of space; in short, conditioned by the concrete historical level of which they treat. The root of valuation is *a priori;* but the Law which we try to articulate in these valuing judgments will have to offer a concrete answer to the real and definite problems which are put in a certain collectivity, at a certain moment of its history; and, consequently, will have to contain a series of empirical elements, which only historical experience can furnish. The Law works upon empirical realities, that is, upon facts which are given in experience. Now, upon these materials which historical experience offers, the Juridical Valuation projects its judgments of value to select them, to arrange and articulate them for the service of the ends which have been recognized as valuable. And, consequently, the Juridical Valuation, which is founded on pure ideas, must nevertheless work with a series of real factors, which can be found only in experience. And such real factors are transcribed in some manner in valuing judgments and in juridical programs, because such judgments and such programs refer to concrete social realities in history.

But, moreover, it must be taken into account that the Law is an undertaking of practical realization. Therefore, it is not sufficient to know only the needs which it tries to fulfill and the valuing criterion for doing it, according to some valuable principles. There is moreover a problem of *efficacy,* that is, of knowing how to choose the adequate means of realization of the ends established as valuable. Juridical institutions raise not only a problem of just finality, but also the question of knowing how efficiently and fruitfully to realize that finality. And so it happens that, along juridical history, many of the changes which institutions have undergone do not signify a substitution of end, but a rectification of the means to attain more adequately the same end; because experience has continued to show that the means which tried to articulate them in the service of a finality are frustrated; and then there have to be sought new means, new institutional structures, to realize with greater efficacy that same finality.

For this, even when I have shown that a juridical empiricism, which pretends to limit itself for Juridical valuation to the pure data of experience and nothing more, is impossible, evidently erroneous, but nevertheless has produced some beneficial incitations, in spite of its essential error. Above all, the emphasizing of the historical conditionality of the Law has been very useful as a product of human life in various and changing circumstances; by which empiricism has called attention to the concrete reality of social life, which as such reality cannot be replaced by the constructions of the mind. And so, empiricism has done a good service in emphasizing that the problems of efficacy have to be solved by having in mind the data of experience. As well in the first as in the second of such aspects, which I have just indicated, empiricism represented a justified reaction against the rationalist school of natural Law, which pretended to determine the juridical ideal by pure proceedings of abstract and deductive reason, removed from every consideration of concrete historic reality. On the other hand, empiricism has contributed to develop a series of very interesting studies as to the biological and psychological genesis of juridical sentiments and also as to the social development of juridical ideas and of institutions. So then, empiricism, in spite of its capital and substantive error, has not gone in vain through the history of juridical ideas; on the contrary it has left some very desirable positive residue, by which the theory of Valuation has been enriched.

We may say, then, that in this theme we have mastered at the same time empiricism and pure rationalism. To master is the function of every scientific man, of every philosopher, in short, of every intellectual. To master means to rectify, to negate, but at the same time to conserve. One can master only what one digests; one masters only what in some manner he conserves, although he also rectifies it.

5. Objectivity of the "A Priori" Valuation

It has been shown that the Juridical Valuation is *a priori*, that is, that it does not proceed from experience. But now we have to ask, of what class of *a priori* are we treating? Is it a subjective *a priori* or is it an objective *a priori? Apriority* purely and simply does not signify necessarily objectivity. In saying that values are *a priori*, we say of them that they do not proceed from experience, nor are founded on it. Now, it may be a question of a subjective *a priori* or it may be an objective *a priori*. By subjective *a priori* we should understand a special configuration of the mind: a thing would be *a priori* because it would not proceed from experience but would be really in me as a sort of apparatus or psychological disposition, as an actual configuration of my spirit, which would force it to react estimatively in a determined manner; and then it would result that the judgments of value would consist of the projection of that peculiar structure of my soul and of nothing more. On the other hand, if the *a priori* is objective, then it will consist of some ideal principles which have validity in themselves, independently of the fortuitous fact whether I think of them or not, or that they are thought of correctly or incorrectly; and so, their truth, their validity, would not be founded on a psychological fact, but would be purely ideal.

It is now a matter of inquiring if the juridical values are the result of a mere psychological mechanism or if they are ideal entities with objectivity. In short, we ask if that *a priori* is subjective or objective. Is justice a pure feeling inserted in the human heart, a sort of law which we carry engraved in the depth of our consciousness, a kind of impulse of our soul? Or on the contrary is it an ideal principle, which I discover with my mind, perfectly or imperfectly?

This question has an enormous importance; for if it happens that all Juridical Valuation will represent the projection of some psychological mechanisms and nothing more, then the juridical values would not remain fundamental, but they would depend on the fact that some men felt them in one or another manner. But if, on the contrary, juridical values have an ideal entity, which does not depend on the fact of our representations, then the Juridical Valuation will have a solid base.

It happens that frequently and with predilection there has been employed to found Juridical Valuation (Natural Law) a reference to the data of spontaneous ethical consciousness. And so, they have spoken of a natural sentiment of the just, of seeds of justice rooted in the human heart, of a love for justice innate in souls. Now, while we limit ourselves to note the fact that ordinarily there exists a subjective tendency or vocation for the just, without drawing from this phenomenon consequences of a logical or metaphysical character, we proceed correctly. But the statement of this fact does not in any way constitute the solution of the problem of the Juridical Valuation; in fine, it is the door which opens the problem to us, the springboard which launches us to inquire if there are juridical values. Because if in Juridical Valuation there should be nothing more than this subjective psychological phenomenon, then we should have to conclude that there are no juridical values, but only some special psychical tendencies, which would produce in us the vain illusion of values.

This problem, which I have just put, represents the projection in juridical thought of a fundamental philosophical question which has been discussed through many centuries, and which was actualized at the end of the last century and the beginning of the present one. It is a matter of the dialogue between psychology and objectivism.

In a broad sense it may be said that psychology manifested itself very early in the history of philosophy. It was drawn with extreme radicalism and with maximum destructive extent in the affirmation of the sophist Protagoras, for whom the concrete individual consciousness of man is the measure of all things, by which he ends in an attitude of full nihilistic skepticism. But in a stricter acceptation we speak of psychology as the philosophic current which had its origin in the English philosopher of the seventeenth century, Locke, according to whom ideas are only the fruit of the deposit of sensations; and feelings and moral judgments are a mere habit of internal perceptions of pleasure or displeasure, an empirical thesis, which afterwards gave place to a development in a psychological direction. Psychology, properly, consists in wanting to reduce all disciplines of ideas or principles (Logics, Ethics, Juridical Valuation, etc.) to mere chapters of Psychology; because it considers that logical principles, ethical and juridical values, etc., are only the laws of the mechanics of our thoughts; that is, it understands that such ideas are nothing more than the expression of the real way in which our mind functions in its theoretical and practical judgments. For psychology, for example, the logical law of contradiction would be nothing more than the proof of a real phenomenon of our mind, the expression of the mechanics or of a habit of our intelligence, to gain the state of evidence; and a moral or juridical principle would be merely the expression of a real method of our consciousness to judge practical questions, either by virtue of a special predisposition or by virtue of a habit produced by the repetition of some sensory reactions of pleasure or displeasure. The pleasant feeling produced by certain situations and repeated in various cases would affect our consciousness in the direction of positive valuation of the act which produces this emotion of pleasure and of rejecting as antivaluable behaviors which give rise to an impression of ill-being or of maladaption.

The psychological tendency last mentioned, in its manifestations in the moral and juridical field, makes the goodness and the justice of the real context of the individual soul depend on its generic dimensions, common to all men. It does not ordinarily refer to the particular or individual concretions of each subject alone — as does the skeptical radical psychology of the Greek sophist, Protagoras — but it starts from the supposition that there is a psychic human structure in general. In this sense, man would be the measure of all things, not in what each man has of individuality and concreteness, but in what he has in common with the rest. And this psychology — different from that of Protagoras — seeks to found normative points of view on Morals and on Law; but it finds itself unsettled at its very root by a deficiency which condemns it to end in a skeptical position, although this was by no means the intention of its authors. But despite the purpose which animates it — which is that of founding a Valuation — if this psychology is developed with rigor, it must necessarily end in skepticism.

As manifestations of ethical and juridical psychology there may be cited: the sensory ethical school in England (Shaftesbury, Cumberland, Hutcheson, Hume, Adam Smith, Ferguson, etc.), although from another point of view there may be found in these authors a precedent (very remote and embryonic) for the phenomenological philosophy of values, so far as they emphasize the intuitive character of moral consciousness; also, the Morals of Schopenhauer, based on the feeling of compassion; some theories of the eminent jurist Jhering; and, in the more immediate epoch, the philosophers of Law, Schlossmann and Loening.

According to the English school of sensory ethics, morals and justice are grounded in a basic feeling, and cannot be explained intellectually in a rigorous manner. There is nothing which in itself has value or which is negligible; everything depends on the human organism, its feelings, or its passions. The final end of all human activity is happiness; and in the aspiration to that happiness the best way is to let ourselves be guided by nature, which has organized us wisely, for the measure of moral approbation or of reprobation is the feeling of pleasure or of sorrow which the act which is to be judged as good or as bad awakens in us. We experience this feeling of approbation when the act does not advance our own well-being and, in certain cases, even when it is opposed to it; because, besides egotistical feelings, there are those of sympathy, which make us feel, although in a tenuous manner, the grief and the joy of others, and in this guise to place ourselves, in general, in the situation of other men. Feeling alone is what determines morals, as the authors of this English school say; reason only shows us the adequate means to this end and draws from this sensory direction the congruent consequences. They explain the feeling of just and unjust in this manner: first we take account of the situation of the others, and then, thanks to sympathy, that is, to being able to feel with the others, to feel concordantly with them, we put ourselves in their situation. We consider acts which damage others to be unjust and punishable. The greater the implied injury, the greater the anger of the victim, the sympathetic indignation of the spectator, and the feeling of responsibility of the author of the deed. Therefore, we establish what is just and what is unjust. This judgment is formed very slowly and is based completely on feeling; reason intervenes only in the generalizations from this judgment. The feeling of justice emanates from the fundamental impulse of social equality and is nourished on the feeling of sympathy with the good of the next man. Also, for many others — as for example, Loening — the criterion of justice is emotional in extent: the realization of the manner of acting recognized as just fills us with satisfaction; while its nonfulfillment or its contradiction produces discomfort in us, and, in certain cases, even wrath or indignation.[77]

[77] The principal representatives of the English school of sentimental morals are Shaftesbury, Cumberland, Hutcheson, Hume, Adam Smith, etc. The principal work of Loening, here in question, is *Über Wurzel und Wesen des Rechtes* (1907).

Up to now, this short exposition of the psychological position has shown its consequences for Juridical Valuation. Against the psychological position has been maintained the doctrine which we might call objective, which has various representations in the history of Philosophy; but which outlined itself with vigor in a special manner and decisively installed itself thanks to the work of Edmund Husserl, published in 1900.[78] Objectivism affirms that the principles of logic, of morals, of justice, etc., are ideas with necessary and objective validity, independently of the psychic acts by which we make contact with them. In short, it is a matter of the fertile discovery of the ideal being, which constitutes one of the greatest conquests of contemporaneous thought, and of which I have already given an exposition in the first chapter of this book.

Now, here it is of interest to examine this theme in its applications to Juridical Valuation. The foundation of objectivism will be realized all the better in the course of a critique of psychology.

Of course I am not going to deny that in many cases — and even, it might be said, habitually — we find in human consciousness that which is called the feeling of justice, which in a concrete manner tends to indicate the correct solution for problems of social life, in a manner analogous to that which is wont to give a spontaneous moral sentiment. It is a very old observation that to have an apprehension of good and bad, of just and unjust, it is not necessary to have studied Philosophy. Kant records it at the beginning of his *Foundations of the Metaphysics of Morals,* saying that a countryman distinguishes good from bad spontaneously, and that what moral Philosophy adds is the knowledge of what are the reasons and the foundation of this judgment. Perhaps it is indeed more easy to know moral values than juridical values, because morals refers to the realm of conscience, whose elements may be more clearly embraced, while the juridical values, as they affect the objective social architecture and consequently demand the comparison of elements external to the person, may turn out more difficult of comprehension for an undisciplined mind. But, with all, it seems that the fact that in consciousness there is a spontaneous feeling of justice is habitual. It is true that the solutions offered by this feeling of justice may be divergent in different individuals and according to different historical situations; but it would be necessary to discriminate here between the influence which history and social environment have had in making concrete the feeling of justice. But, in any case, what seems a regular fact is the primary and spontaneous vocation of the human consciousness for justice, apart from the fact of whether or not this comes to be embodied correctly. Opinions,

[78] LOGISCHE UNTERSUCHUNGEN (1900).

concrete proofs, of the juridical feeling, may have, according to the case, greater or less truth; but, ordinarily, we always find the fact of a desire for justice, the fact that the consciousness tends toward an ideal of Law. But it is not this which is to be discussed here, but the knowledge whether it is possible to found Juridical Valuation on the pure bare fact of a feeling. And we have to recognize that it is not possible.

If the valuing appreciations are reduced purely and simply to psychological facts, to feelings, to likes, to instincts, to impulses, then properly we should have no values, but mere phenomena and nothing more. Now it begins to appear that, at bottom, psychology — although it does not wish to be — is skepticism. The psychologist is a skeptic without knowing it; and precisely for this reason, because he does not know it, it is more easy to demonstrate the falsity of his position. If the psychologist should take clear account of the consequences to which his attitude carries him and fully accept them with resignation, there would be no discussion, it would even have no meaning, because in the face of radical skepticism there is no possibility of controversy; for the skeptic does not answer the questions directed to him, but limits himself to shrugging his shoulders, in pure abstention from all judgment, either positive or affirmative. But, on the other hand, in the face of a relative skepticism, he may be led easily to the absurd, and, even more, it can be demonstrated that his doctrine contains a contradiction. And this is what may be done without difficulty with regard to the psychologist, as I shall show below.

In the first place, note the insufficiency of trying to found Juridical Valuation on the psychological fact of a feeling of justice. It is necessary to make clear the content of this feeling. To base, as some do, Juridical Valuation on the honorable feeling of every just man is a common subterfuge, inadmissible from every point of view, because precisely what the Philosophy of Law ought to seek is a criterion which permits us to qualify a certain meaning as just or unjust. In speaking of an emotion of justice, there are supposed to be feelings which may be qualified as just against others which are unjust. Now, what will be the criterion for this separation or sieve? Why do we feel that certain acts are just and others unjust? The feeling of justice consists of two ingredients: one of them real, to wit, its psychological mechanism; and the other its qualification of justice, which is not a fact, but is the relative quality which gives rise to this feeling when we compare it with an idea of value. What permits us to qualify a feeling as just is no real component of it, but is a valuing point of view.

It is true that the estimation of justice — and that of other juridical values — reveals a kind of sentimentally variegated intuition. But we ought to seek, beneath the fact of that feeling, the intuition of an objective ideal value. This it is which Pascal presented truly when he spoke of an "order of the heart" or of a "logic of the heart"; that is, a matter of discovering the *a priori* emotional ideal. And this it is which Max Scheler attempted:[79] the logic of the valuing appreciations.

The criticism which I have just developed is based on the supposition that in fact we want and it is possible to found a Juridical Valuation. Now, at the beginning of this chapter I completely justified the task of the Juridical Valuation, rebutting the skeptical attitudes in a decisive and final manner. And now we have just seen how it is not possible to found the Juridical Valuation on a pure psychological fact, since the feeling of justice is such, not for what it has of sentimental reality, but for what it has of coincidence with an ideal value. Whoever tries to enclose it in the mere fact of a feeling, without transcending it, is inexorably condemned to renounce entirely all possibility of a Valuation of Law; in short, he remains inevitably condemned to skepticism, as I shall show presently.

Now, the psychologists, whose doctrine is at root skepticism, engage themselves not to be skeptics and pretend to found a Juridical Valuation on some solitary psychological facts.

We are going to see, by four fundamental arguments — each one sufficient to show the error of psychology — what the absurdities are which lead to that position.[80]

First: If justice consists solely and exclusively of a feeling, of a mechanism in the soul, we should find ourselves before something incomprehensible from any point of view, to wit: that some facts, as facts, and nothing more than facts, had the pretension to regulate normatively other facts, as superior in rank to them. But natural facts, as facts, as realities and nothing more than pure realities, without reference to other ontological zones, have between themselves no other connection than that of causality: One fact is the cause of another or the effect of another. In the pure world of phenomena, without our adding to it any other extraphenomenal consideration, there are no ranks or hierarchies, there cannot be distinctions between justice and injustice, between good and bad, between suitability and unsuitability. One fact either is the cause of another, or is not; but it lacks meaning to ascribe to it, as a bare fact, the aspiration to guard other facts normatively. When I ascribe to a fact a normative dimension it means that already I do not refer to what it

[79] In his work—already classic—DER FORMALISMUS IN DER ETHIK UND DIE MATERIALE WERTETHIK (2d ed.) 59ff.

[80] Inspired by the thought of Husserl, who refers fundamentally to Logic, I have made an application of his arguments to moral and juridical Valuation.

has of fact, but that I am putting into it something which is not a fact, but which is a quality of coincidence with an ideal principle. The hierarchical ordering of the world, the distinctions between the normal and the pathological, between good and bad, between just and unjust, can be founded only on criteria of finality; and these, in turn, are always necessarily based on ideas of value. Precisely one of the dimensions of values — and always of the deeds of human life impregnated with them — is that they occur in a hierarchical series. While phenomena are or are not, on the other hand, values — worth-while things, and fundamentally the works of human life — are some of them worth more than others.

Second: If the juridical values — the same as moral values and logical principles — were solely and exclusively mechanisms of our psychological organization, we should have to explain why those ideas offer characters completely different from those which are peculiar to psychological laws. The principles of justice — the same as those of logic and ethics — present themselves to us with the pretension of absoluteness and universality, as exact and rigorous criteria; it is not a matter now of affirming that they have it, but only that they present themselves with this character. On the other hand, the psychological laws — for example, that of Fechner as to the relation between the increase of the stimulus and the intensity of the conscious result in the sensation — offer themselves only as approximate regularities, valid only within certain limits and with fluctuations. Then, when it is a matter of equalizing two things which apparently are disparate and heterogenous, it is not sufficient that this should be affirmed, because, first, it is necessary to demonstrate the homogeneity of these two things which present themselves as divergent; and, moreover, it is necessary to explain thereafter why in spite of being similar they appear to us as different. And none of this has been attained by the psychologists.

Third: Psychology destroys the whole meaning of Morals and of Law. If the juridical and moral values were solely and exclusively functions of the soul, it would follow that justice would have meaning and would be of value only for just men; but, on the other hand, it would lack meaning for those who did not have such emotions, or for those who had stifled them with contrary passions. By what right can we consider bound by juridical values those who do not have the feeling of justice?

Fourth: If the juridical values were solely and exclusively structural configurations of my psychic reality and nothing more than that, then all discussion as to the Law would lack meaning, and consequently every political controversy also would lack meaning. For if justice and the other juridical values were merely real mechanisms of the psychic, pure psychological realities, it would turn out that when men think or feel in a diverse or contrary manner with reference to a certain question, each one of them would be resting on the fact of his own subjective consciousness; and as there would not be any instance superior to that, there could not be adjudged a difference in favor of anyone, or, better put, it would have to be recognized that each one of them would be justified in his opinion. A discussion supposes a conflict or opposition between two opinions; to be able to judge if there is any truth and what it is, it is necessary to have recourse to an independent and objective criterion; and to examine whether any of the opinions in the polemic coincide with this instance. If justice is nothing more than a reality in me and only that, my opinion would correspond to the way in which I am constituted; and if another person thinks in a different manner, it will be because he possesses a psychological reality different from mine. And there will not be any meaning which he and I can discuss, as it cannot be that one taller person, as such, can discuss with another, shorter, because he is smaller; nor a blond with a brunet. Each is as he is, and there will be no meaning in trying to impose his own reality on the divergent realities of the others. But it is when we are discussing themes of justice — the same as any other axiological question — we suppose that besides the psychological facts of the opinion of each one, there is some instance or objective criterion, to judge. And each one of the opinions pretends to express what is determined in that instance; moreover to judge it is necessary to compare each one of the opinions with that instance, with that objectivity, and to see if it coincides with it, in which case it would appear as justified, and on the other hand the others as unjustified. Every discussion supposes the intention of appealing to something which is not subjective but is objective. Otherwise it lacks meaning. With respect to this, some psychologists have said that they refer to a *reasonable* mind and to a just moral consciousness; now here is something already added to psychology. For a reasonable mind cannot mean other than a mind adapted to objective truth; and by a just moral consciousness there can be understood nothing but a consciousness which reflects the objective ethical and juridical values, worthy in themselves, independently of who thinks them. But thus psychology has been abandoned indeed and one has entered into an objective position.

So, then, it remains clearly manifest that the juridical psychologist confounds justice with the fact of its knowledge and with the sentiments which accredit it. Consciousness of the principles of justice is certainly a fact, situated at the time and confined to the individual who thinks or feels. But the idea of justice — like the other juridical values — is not a fact: it constitutes an ideal essence, with objective validity, not dependent on the psychological facts in which it was conceived.

It is clear that inescapably the criterion of juridical valuation has to be revealed by means of the consciousness; but in no way is it to be confounded with the pure psychic phenomenon. Justice and the other juridical values are ideal qualities which may reside in real behaviors and in collective organizations. A consciousness, a conduct, or a social structure, are realities; but those realities, besides their real components, possess qualities of value (positive or negative). Now, those qualities of value do not consist of real ingredients of the consciousness, of the conduct, or of the society, but they are ideal dimensions which are embodied in those realities. That is, those qualities consist of the adjustment (or nonadjustment, in the negative case) of such realities with some ideas of value. The justice of a feeling, of a conduct, or of a social relation is the coincidence between those realities and an ideal principle. The valuing criterion of the Law, then, does not consist of a psychological reality, but in ideal values.

So, then, in this inquiry we find ourselves launched into a realm of ideal values, thanks to which the things which we do in our lives acquire meaning, and, among them, that which we call Law. And, in the light of this theme, there is confirmed the special meaning of our life, which I have already expounded in the first chapter of this book. Our life is fitted to and supported in an outline, in realities, between which, besides the world roundabout and my body, there are psychological mechanisms, with all of which I realize my acts. But my acts are referred intentionally to a realm of axiological ideas, that is, to some essences of value, which have no reality, but objective validity. My life is limited on one side by Psychology and through it by Biology and the world; and, on the other side, it is bounded by the values which give meaning to the structure and to the valuing function which my life is. And my life is an interlocking and intimate fusion of reality and value at the same time: the realm of functions with meaning. My life is a task, work; the urgency of living among things and with them and at the same time determining them for itself in a succession of valuations. My life is, then, the articulation of reality and value; and it is, at the same time, the profound and basic reality in which are present all the other beings (as well the real as the ideal), and I find all of them forming a part of my life and as ingredients of it. Now, therefore, I repeat here what I said in the first chapter, in considering values in general and introducing in the philosophy of Scheler and Hartmann as to them the following correction: in affirming that values are objective there ought to be indicated with this that they are not subjective, that is, that they do not constitute a projection of my soul, that their validity is independent of my knowledge and adherence; but it ought not to be understood that values are entities beyond human life, for that is the reality in which all beings occur. Consequently, the objectivity of values is intravital, in which there is no contradiction, because life is not subjectivity, but on the contrary it is the unavoidable articulation between the subject and objects, between the I and the universe, in a situation of correlative copresence.

6. Human Historicity and the Juridical Values

Putting of the question. We now ask: Does the Juridical Valuation submit to us some rigid, immovable criteria, valid for all societies in all circumstances, in all historic situations, in whatever state of culture and at whatever moment of time? Or, on the contrary, ought juridical ideals to take account and notice of the variable character of human existence, of the diversity of circumstances and situations, of the concrete necessities of each moment, in short, of the multiform and variegated variety of history? In these questions is implicit the problem of the historicity of Law, of the mutations and diversity of juridical regulations. It is not a matter now only of recording the fact that the juridical regimes are multiple and variant in history, with very diverse contents; moreover, it is a matter of asking ourselves if this variety and this historic change in the Law have a justification; and if they have it will be a matter of inquiring what this justification may be, which will oblige us then to ask the means by which juridical values can and ought to be articulated in the historic process. In short, we attend to the question of knowing if the juridical ideal can be alone a unique type of arrangement with absolute validity, universal and immutable; or if, on the contrary, it ought to be relative to the conditions of the epoch, the place, the historic development, and the concrete necessities.

This is the central theme of the Philosophy of Law throughout all its development, from the Presocratics to our days. It is the classic question par excellence; that which has always been considered in a preferential role. But, moreover, this theme covers a maximum actuality and a maximum degree of maturity in the light of the speculations of our time upon the historic dimension of humanity. And so, today, we are in condition to attend to this question of history in Law in the light of the historicity of humanity; consequently on a plane much deeper and more basic than was done for the preceding doctrines. And this is so because the philosophy of our days is characterized by having discovered the reality of human life as historic, that is, as possessing historicity as one of its essential dimensions.

The thought which developed from the Renaissance to the nineteenth century embarked on an undertaking of pure, abstract mathematical reason, which Max Scheler aptly called logomania. It saw in mathematics not only an illustrious science, with an outstanding history and mature results, but moreover it took it as an example and prototype for all scientific knowledge. And, therefore, the mathematical method was taken as an example for all the sciences, and it was sought to apply it to all the disciplines, among them to Ethics and to the Philosophy of Law, which is expressed in the title of Spinoza's work, *Etica more geometrico demonstrata*. And, in such fashion, the doctrines of natural Law flourished as purely rationalistic and educative knowledge. The undertaking failed, because the human as human escaped from the mathematical reasoning as water through a sieve.

History,[81] as well as reality, is as old as man. It is also very old as a relation of human facts. But, on the other hand, the full philosophic consciousness of history does not appear until the nineteenth century, with the exception of certain antecedents and the great anticipation of Vico. It is true that in many previous epochs we find works of meditation upon history. But it must be noted that generally in such works history was not conceived strictly as history — as diversity and as change — but rather with a rationalistic prejudice. This happened in two ways: either considering historic varieties and changes as the fruit of a degeneration of nature, which having lost its purity had abandoned goodness, justice, and truth; or interpreting history as progressive evolution toward the realization of absolute ideals of perfection, so that the nearer men came to these, the less would be the diversity and the change. History was seen either as the realm of evil or as the aggregate of forces for the conquest of some universal and permanent ideals. But it was not contemplated as the realm of various diversities and of various necessary human transformations.

Except the cited precedent of Juan Bautista Vico, we may say that it was in the nineteenth century that men took notice of the historic. And it was due in great part as well to the impulse of Romanticism as to the hegelian thinking; and, afterwards, as the flowering of positivist Sociology. But, with History, Romanticism accomplished a work which was fundamentally mystical (national soul, reverent adoration of tradition, etc.). And Hegel, instead of approaching history to discover what there

[81] This paragraph is from the Second Spanish edition of the book (Mexico, 1945). TRANSLATOR.

was in it and the secret of its effective resources, rather tried to invent it, substituting for its real authenticity a systematic construction. And afterwards, when as well the romantic as the hegelian tendency had fallen into discredit, there remained the knowledge of the historic in positivism, above all, the idea of relativity, of chance, of contingency. And then, the varied and changing spectacle of history constituted the principal source of a relativistic feeling with skeptical trimmings. Finding itself before this spectacle whose contents and perspectives were different in the various peoples, and changed and succeeded each other, knowledge felt itself weighed down and limited itself to recording the mutations only; and, in short, to establishing the regularities of coördination and of the succession of events, but renouncing all search for the content of historic reality. Thus, of the knowledge of history there came to remain in the second half of the nineteenth century nothing more than a feeling of relativity.

But at the beginning of the twentieth century[82] there commenced in Philosophy attempts to capture the essence of the historic, to discover the secret of the variety and the changes. Today we have already begun mentally to dominate this problem and to lead in a sure way to its solution, by having discovered historicity in the very essential structure of humanity.

Now, before expounding this theme to the depth which the thought of our epoch has reached, it is necessary to relate the principal vicissitudes through which it has passed in the course of the philosophy of other times. This is because the present thought, which in many of its dimensions offers horizons of basic newness, is not something which has been produced by spontaneous generation, fortuitously, but represents a stage of superseding, which could be reached because a series of thinkers retrod along the centuries the road necessary to arrive at the doctrine today attained. I will limit myself to relating the more important typical positions in the history of this theme.

This theme appears to us throughout Philosophy as a species of conflict or drama between Reason and History, as to their respective parts in the formation of juridical ideals, and so in the Valuation of the Law. At some doctrinal moments this issue was decided in favor of Reason exclusively, cutting off altogether any intervention of History (for example, in Plato, in the jusnaturalistic classical school of Illuminism, etc.). In other theories it was attempted to bar reason entirely and to concede an exclusive right to History (as occurred, for example, in romanticism and also in some manifestations of positivism). But in most

[82] This paragraph amended as in the Second Spanish edition of the book (Mexico, 1945). TRANSLATOR.

cases there was present in the philosophic consciousness the thought (conceived more or less clearly) that if indeed there were ideal criteria of justice, nevertheless, these were not sufficient for the elaboration of a concrete program of Law; that there had to be taken into account points of view relating to the special circumstances of the people, place, epoch, and historic situation. And so there can be noted, at every moment, expressions like these: the necessities of the times, the special circumstances, the urgent business of the instant, the height of the epoch, the adequacy of the means, the actual manner of being of a people, the practically feasible possibilities, etc.; expressions in which appear the idea that the Law is historically conditioned, not only as to its positive reality, but that it ought to be so also in its valuing criteria. Now, it is not sufficient to hold the conjecture that juridical ideals probably cannot be elaborated by the pure intellect, by geometrically rigorous criteria, with pretensions of universal application, but that besides it is necessary to also add historical perspectives. It is necessary to seek, with all rigor, in what way the two elements ought to be articulated, the ideas of value and the historic transmutation.

Plato. For Plato, authentic justice does not consist of the empirical orders which history records. They (like all the sensory world) do not constitute true being. This, the true being of each thing, consists of the pure idea of it. Law, in its positive version, in the historic outline of its institutions, is, like all the rest of the sensory world or of experience, something phantasmal, confused, contradictory, and miserable. The scheme of the authentically just is contained only in the pure idea of justice. And to attain a just Law it will be necessary to translate with all exactness and purity the structure of the idea of justice and to comply rigorously with its requirements. And so Plato devoted his dialogue entitled *The Republic* (*Politeia*) to the way in which the State should be organized to serve strictly the pure idea of justice, without concessions to the empirical, without compromises with experience, without admitting historic conditions. In this sense, Plato embodies an intellectual exasperation. But afterwards, in his dialogue *The Laws,* he takes account and consideration of the empiric and historical elements. In *The Laws* he tries to adjust the principles expressed in *The Republic* to the possibilities of the real circumstances of his time and of his people. But, in doing so, Plato does not adequately explain either the why of this concession to the empiric elements, or the way in which these are connected with the ideal principles. It seems as if when he tries to apply ideal principles to the concrete social reality of his time, they strike against an entity which does not let itself be modeled docilely by an idea; they collide brutally with some facts which impose limitations on the exigencies of the pure idea. But he does not explain to us why or how. Thus we find only the evidence that Plato himself had to recognize that it was not possible to elaborate a juridical program with purely ideal ingredients, but that it was necessary to rely in some measure on circumstances and on the possibilities of the social reality of the moment.

Aristotle. In Aristotle, this same theme is presented with a proposal of conciliation. The absolute and the historic, the fixed and the changeable, do not stage any quarrel, but rather they try to be harmonized. Both ingredients obtain a greater consideration. And Aristotle surmises already that the criterion of natural justice, on being applied to various circumstances, produces norms of diverse content, in spite of their being all inspired by the same idea.

St. Augustine. In the work of St. Augustine we find a profound and dramatic trace of the experience of a brute reality which is here, limiting the possibilities of pure reason. It is not so much the problem of history as the experience of what there is in man of empirical reality which appears in the Augustinian work. He examines the problem of knowing if Natural Law is one, sole, unique, absolute, and perpetual, or if, on the contrary, it tolerates concessions to circumstances and admits changes in their compass. And this question is treated in the light of a series of considerations which are in part philosophic and in part theological. If the nature of man were purely and exclusively rational, if the human reality were a full copy of rational principles and did not contain any factor which would contradict those principles, the law of conduct — and with it the Law — could be a full expression of absolute ideas. Such would be the situation of man in a state of grace, in paradise. But when human nature was corrupted by original sin, it remained weighted with factors which resist the absolute rule of the pure rational idea. And therefore, it happens that human nature, which in part is reason, is at the same time also an appetite, cupidity, egoism, ambition; in short, finds itself corrupted by sinful tendencies. Individually, the religious and moral meaning of life consists in stifling this legacy from hell, and striving for the triumph of the good. But in fact and in general it has to be recorded that man is a sinner. And on this account it is necessary, when discussing the theme of social organization, to consider human nature, such and as it is, nature corrupted by sin; and to study, on this basis, the possibilities of the idea of justice with respect to it. And so, the juridical order will take into account the real manner of being of man, with his passions, his limitations, and will try to reduce to the least bad this corrupted aspect of human nature; that is, will try to draw the best possible advantage from the true manner of being of man, seeking the greatest number of feasibilities for goodness and justice.

From this is derived the Augustinian conception of a double Natural Law: the primary and the secondary. The primary is an absolute Natural Law: that which would correspond to human nature in a state of grace. The secondary Natural Law is the only one to which the human creature can aspire after his fall, weighted with low passions. On this account, the secondary Natural Law is not a mere rational texture, but it contains empirical elements, organized rationally, in which it exists. In a perfect state of grace, empirical nature would not play any part in the determination of ideals of justice, because then human life would be something soaked in rationality, and so integrally moldable by Reason; and the adequate ordering would be that of the primary Natural Law, which regulates the community of goods, the elimination of arms, etc. But on the other basis of fact — corrupted human nature — there must be taken into account its exigencies, and we must draw from them the best possible advantage, which is what the secondary Natural Law does. So then, the real nature of men appears vis-à-vis Reason, not as an indifferent fact, but as a moment of sin, which is considered irremediable. In this aspect, it is not so much history with its diversities which opposes Reason but rather a degenerate human nature. Although there also appears in the thought of St. Augustine the idea that the variations of Law may find justification in the same eternal law, which demands that distinct circumstances be regulated suitably by norms of diverse content, yet that variety of circumstances is found foreseen *beforehand* in the eternal law; so that the eternal law, imperative in itself, adapts itself to the dynamics of life.

Scholastic philosophy. Francisco Suarez. This theme of the relations between different social circumstances and the rational principles of juristics is treated in a most thorough and profound way in scholastic Philosophy, whose most mature moment as to this doctrine we find in the work of Francisco Suarez.[83] His doctrine, with relation to prior thought, marks notable progress. It is true that we find the directives of his doctrine already in the work of St. Thomas; but Suarez carries them to full development, with formidable sharpness and with originality. Suarez considers this theme in asking if natural law is immutable or not; and even when he formulates the first thesis — that of immutability — nevertheless, in explaining and developing it he shows that in spite of the root of Natural Law being invariable, the precepts which are derived from it change according to the diversity of circumstances and in the rhythm of historic development. That is, what he does is to found a

[83] Cf. my book, La Filosofía del Derecho de Francisco Suárez, con un estudio sobre sus antecedentes en la Patristica y en la Escolástica (1927), chapter devoted to St. Augustine.

Natural Law of a perpetual and absolute root but with variable content. His work, in a certain way, was prepared by the moral casuistry of the Penitentiaries, which is supported on the supposition that in the ethical precept there ought to be found an expression of the concrete circumstances of life. And so, the Natural Law of Suarez presents itself with a sense of historic articulation.[84]

Suarez says that there are eternal rational principles, of absolute value for all conduct. But those principles have the character of general directions, which, by themselves, do not yet constitute norms directly applicable to the effective regulation of a society. For us to obtain norms conducive to the regulation of social life, it is necessary to refer those directions to the realities which we are trying to regulate; and to make with such rational criteria, combined with life, specific norms. In this way, the general principles of Natural Law shelter in their bosom the notion of the concrete real elements and produce the natural juridical norm for each situation.

According to Suarez, when the general principles are applied to the moral essence of man — which is common to all — they produce invariable norms; but when they are projected upon a variable social matter, they produce norms whose validity is conditioned on the existence of certain concrete situations; and so, with the changing of these, the norms of Natural Law change also. There is here, then, as he draws it, an attempt at a justified articulation of the ideal valuing criteria and objectives with the changes of social reality. The social material is something varied and changeable; and so it happens that, even if the first principles of Natural Law are immutable, on being applied to that social material, which is different here from there and which is transformed by the passage of time, they give rise to norms likewise different. And those norms, derived from the conjunction of principles with a certain social reality, are also norms of Natural Law, though indeed their validity is conditioned by the presence of some certain suppositions of fact, which on changing may cause the norm of Natural Law to change also.

But the doctrine of Suarez is not limited to what I have set forth, it reaches also a still much more refined analysis. He asks why and how social situations change; and he answers that the social material is diversified and transformed into several aspects, in two ways, or by two proceedings: (a) By virtue of a complex of circumstances and multiple factors, which constitute a complicated combination of causes, which do not respond to any plan which men may have traced beforehand; that is, he comes to recognize, in this, that there is a social reality with its own

[84] Cf. Luis Recaséns Siches, La Filosofía del Derecho de Francisco Suárez, con un estudio sobre sus antecedentes (1927).

laws of development, in which there does not always intervene in a decisive manner a deliberate purpose of men. (b) Thanks to a reflective and intentional action of the men who rule society; that is, there may be a modification of the social material carried out freely by man. This last puts the problem of what are the licit faculties of men as to the construction of social reality; or, stated another way, puts the question as to what men may determine freely, authorized by Natural Law, and what on the contrary may be that for which they have no power of decision, because of an absolute precept which prevents it. There are matters as to which Natural Law imposes taxatively one single solution, without permitting any option, as would be, for example, those which affect human dignity and the liberty which depends thereon. But there are, on the other hand, other matters with respect to which Natural Law adopts an attitude which we may call abstention, which consists of neither commanding nor prohibiting certain solutions, but permits a certain number of them, all equally licit in principle; and leaves to men an ample sphere of liberty to choose the solution which they deem the most useful, desirable, and opportune, in the light of the necessities and of the concrete circumstances of the social reality. Man, in compliance with the circumstances and according to this appreciation of collective utility, will decide to carry into effect one or another possibility, will articulate this or that institution and will mold it in one or another fashion. Now, from those institutions (neither prohibited nor commanded, but simply permitted) created and articulated by men, the most general principles of Natural Law, starting from the fact of the human decision (which produces a certain state of things) will then engender precepts of Natural Law congruent with the concrete structure of that social material (shaped by men), but will not demand their presence at any absolute moment. The logical formula of those precepts would be: if the circumstance is *a* (a situation created freely by men within the license which Natural Law grants them), then necessarily the precept *m* will govern. Now, there is no precept of Natural Law which imposes necessarily *a*, on the contrary desirability might advise the selection of *b* or *c* or *d*, etc.; to which there would then necessarily correspond respectively the norms, *n*, *o*, *p*, etc. The first principles of Natural Law do not vary; what happens is that these principles, on joining concrete social reality, give rise to precepts which govern only for that reality and for no other. When this state of things varies, by virtue of a free human decision (as to which its changing is permitted by Natural Law, because that does not regulate it either preceptively nor prohibitingly, but only in a permissive manner), the jusnaturalistic precepts which correspond to the new situations have a different content. Natural Law in itself does not change, because there is essentially inherent in its meaning the idea that different states of things require diverse regulations.

Suarez develops as an example of these concrete precepts of Natural Law — which start from the supposition of a certain state of things (which without offending the rational law might be otherwise) — those which refer to the right of property. Given the division of things and organized society as a basis, there is a series of precepts of Natural Law which articulate and protect property. Now, starting from a diverse state of things, for example, from that in which things were common, then the imperatives of the Natural Law would be very different ones. But Natural Law does not necessarily demand that there should be a regime of private property, nor does it impose one of community property; but in general leaves it for men to decide upon the regime most desirable and useful for their necessities, according to the concrete circumstances in which they live. It is clear that the election which men may make is not wholly indifferent to Natural Law; for they, in choosing among the repertory of possibilities, must be guided by considerations inspired by the common good, by general utility, in the light of the concrete circumstances of each situation. Now, once society has determined the regime which it deems the most desirable, from it is derived a series of concrete precepts of Natural Law; if a different regime had been chosen the precepts would be different.

Consequently, Suarez distinguishes two classes of precepts of Natural Law: (a) those whose content has a necessary character, independent of any prior human determination, which he calls "preceptive Natural Law"; and (b) those whose validity rests on a free human decision (with respect to their suppositions), a decision taken among a series of possibilities equally licit in principle, taking account of motives of suitability and opportuneness; and such precepts are called "dominative Natural Law," because they pertain to the free dominion and prudent election of men on adopting certain juridical formulas, among the several which Natural Law recognizes as admissible. This theory as to the part which human free will plays in the configuration of the juridical norms and upon the conditioning by the diverse situations of social reality, shows us one of the functions of positive Law, to wit: the single election among the possibilities admitted by Natural Law, on whose determination are bound afterwards the consequences of justice, which flow from it.

So, then, although the ideal root of Natural Law is absolute and unchangeable, on the other hand the concrete specifications of it are various and changing. Suarez condenses this into the form of an example, saying: "As medicine has some rules for the sick and others for the well, and some for the strong and others for the weak, and nevertheless the rules of Medicine do not on this account vary, but are multiplied and some serve now and others later, so Natural Law remaining the same commands one thing on a given occasion and another different on another, and this obliges now and not before or after." [85]

This same tendency of Suarez is manifested contemporaneously in the work of the neo-scholastic Georges Renard,[86] who says that Natural Law for the jurist is like the notion of beauty for the artist; the beautiful is not a recipe for making masterpieces; it is, like justice, a principle of discrimination. In nine out of ten cases Natural Law has no solution to propose; it confines itself to judging the solutions which are proposed; by which is emphasized still more the criterion of elective prudence referred to in Suarez.

The theory of Suarez constitutes one of the most interesting upon this theme. Even if we consider it as necessarily superseded — in the form which I shall explain further on — it has to be recognized that the pretensions of the two factors are not resolved either in the negation of one of them, nor in their admission reluctantly, nor in a painful compromise, but rather in a harmonious agreement. What happens is that Suarez has not developed the meaning of history; and although theoretically he gives a place to the exigencies derived from the variety of transformations, practically this doctrine has little concrete development in his work. On the other hand, it appears that, without prejudice to this theory, Suarez is dominated by the thought that the exigencies of reality do not constitute an indefinite repertory of possibilities, but that all the variety comes from a depth of common permanence.

The classic school of Natural Law. Modern man, from the Renaissance, gives a turn to the conception of the world and of life. He discovers his rational consciousness, as a regulating instance of every theory and every norm for practical conduct. To the realism of antiquity and of the Middle Ages is to succeed the regime of idealistic thought which will characterize all the Modern Age. In theoretical philosophy, man turns his back on experience — which is confused, doubtful, problematical — to found the universe on his own consciousness; for thought is the sole and indubitable reality. Similarly, in meditation upon juridical problems, he tries to elaborate a scheme of Law founded solely and exclusively on pure rational reflection, turning the back on history. The historic multiformity of positive Law is only the proof of the failures and aberrations of man. The authentic Law is Natural Law, which pure reason discovers. The history of Law can have meaning only as a progressive

[85] De Legibus, II, 14, 9.

[86] Cf. Georges Renard, Le Droit, l'Ordre, la Raison (1927) 120.

movement of approximation each time closer to the absolute norms of Natural Law, whose integral positive implantation constitutes the goal to which one ought to aspire. So, then, positive Law historically received ought to yield its place to the reign of authentic Law, which is Natural Law. To come upon Natural Law, it is necessary to find what is authentically human, in a state of pureness. It is believed that the historic process has degenerated and deformed man; and, consequently, man has to be sought in his pristine state, before history has put its sinning hands upon him, that is, he has to be sought in a *state of nature*. Whence it occurs that this rationalistic thought of the movement called Illuminism, or enlightenment, tends to confound what it projects as an ideal with a supposed prehistoric situation, in which man had not yet been deformed. The authors of the classic school of Natural Law — Grotius, Tomasio, Pufendorf, Wolff, etc. — on one side represent the rationalistic *pathos* which rejects history and wishes to substitute for it the schemes of pure reason. But, on the other side, they consider that the natural world is stuffed with rationality. And on seeking the fundamental of the juridical idea in human nature, they come to conceive it not as a normative essence but as a being, as a fact, like the fact of the *pure* human, not damaged by history.

And so they seek pure human nature, in order that without any artificial addition it may serve as a basis for Law. And for Grotius, the essential attribute of this human nature is the *apetitus societatis* (the tendency to sociability), upon which is based all Law, as rational consequences of this foundation. For Pufendorf, this essential attribute consists of the *imbecilitas* or feeling of weakness or abandonment which leads man to coördinate himself rationally with his kind. And for Tomasio, it is the anxiety of such. That is, for all three, it is a matter of a psychological fact, of a real phenomenon, which is absolutized to the point of converting it into a basis for a normative system. Here is the paradox which these three authors offer: representing a maximum intention of rationalism, they nevertheless found Natural Law on an empirical consideration. This draws with it the consequence that in Natural Law reason becomes sometimes confounded with an equivocal concept of nature. The word nature is employed confusedly, in a double and diverse sense: at the same time as what *is* and that which *ought to be*. But, after all, this jusnaturalism, although it implies a confused rationalization of real elements, represents in any case the absolute negation of power of the historical factor. Now, this antihistoricism presents still other paradoxes, and highly grave ones; having denied all significance to the historic and pretending to construct intellectually a detailed juridical system, nevertheless, many times it suffers the error of taking as a pure rational product that which at bottom is only a mere contingent historical datum. Thus, such authors absolutize as if things which are only institutions of their time were pure rational constructions.

Rousseau. Rousseau cannot be catalogued in the pure continuation of illuminist jusnaturalism; for if in many points Rousseau represents the maturing and purification of many of the themes of classic jusnaturalism, purging it of no few confusions, which had weighed it down in preceding authors, on the other hand, Rousseau brought radical novelties. And so, the juridical ideal founded on the social contract — which is not a fact, but, as Rousseau explicitly says, never existed, but is only a regulative idea of reason[87] — does not pretend indeed to constitute a rational code of full content, but an orientating directive; and, on the other hand, it is to be remembered that Rousseau directed his thought skillfully to the root of historicity as an essential dimension of man, when he qualified him as a person who, by being able to understand the other similar persons learned from them and was perpetually progressive.

Juridical Romanticism or the Historic School of Law. Already in the first third of the nineteenth century the rationalist tendencies — and with them the jusnaturalist systems — underwent a grave crisis, in the production of which multiple factors intervened. One of them is Romanticism.

Romanticism is not only an artistic matter, it also constitutes an integral conception of the world and of life. And, consequently, it is projected into all the sectors of human culture: in science and philosophy; in politics and law; in art and religion. A definition of Romanticism is very difficult, if not impossible. And this is so because of the very extent of Romanticism, which pretends essentially to be an antirationalist tendency, but does not cease to grasp the rigorous outlines of a concept. But I shall try to offer a descriptive characterization of the principal features of Romanticism.

There is in Romanticism an organic and totalitarian meaning, in which it tries to overcome and dissolve all antitheses. It seeks to include all objects in the idea of a supreme total and organic substance. Politics, religion, art, law, customs, idiom, etc., are the products of the functions

[87] On Rousseau, cf. JOAQUÍN XIRAU, ROUSSEAU Y LAS IDEAS POLÍTICAS MODERNAS (1923); G. DEL VECCHIO, LOS DERECHOS DEL HOMBRE Y EL CONTRATO SOCIAL, translation of Castaño (1914); LA FILOSOFÍA SOCIAL DE ROUSSEAU; HAYMANN, ROUSSEAU'S SOZIALPHILOSOPHIE (1898); LIEPMANN, DIE RECHTSPHILOSOPHIE DES ROUSSEAU (1898); STAMMLER, BEGRIFF UND BEDEUTUNG DER "VOLONTÉ GENERALE" BEI ROUSSEAU, in RECHTSPH. ABH. U. VORTR., t. 1, pp. 375–383; NATORP, ROUSSEAUS SOZIALPHILOSOPHIE, in ZEITSCH, F. R., PH. 12.

of this total substance; they are its emanations. It carries ready an exaltation of the irrational and of the irreducibly individual. It is the exaltation of life in its incalculable chances, in its mysterious concretions, as a spontaneous and sacred power, as a force of secret origins, which cannot be reduced to rational formulas. Hence, its historic and traditional orientation. History is the organic development of spirit, which reigns in it in an immanent and secret way. The romanticist is a follower of tradition in all lands. The traditional is always the exponent of the matured spirit in the secret bosom of time. The traditional is valuable because it is not the work of individual reason, always cold, static and limited; it is valuable because it is the exteriorization of an infinite vital force, which acts reconditely. Hence, Romanticism venerates everything which has an unconscious origin, which has its setting in basic strata of life, hidden from all rational penetration. And therefore it also has a predilection for the irreducibly individual; and it feels respect for the variegation of the world with all the complexity of its singular types. And it sees in the national community the concrete realization of an ineffable historic individuality, endowed with its own spirit. And this national spirit is conceived as an authentic psychic reality, both mysterious and secret. And it values highly all the spontaneous manifestations of the popular spirit, as an expression of its most intimate authenticity. And so, it proposes, as opposed to mathematical formulas, organic forms; to the mechanical, the living; to the rational intellect, feeling and intuition; to the concept, sensitiveness; to the ideal rationally constructed, the product of spontaneous evolution; to the rigid rule, the fluidity of the creative forces in the life process; to the abstract general, the concrete individual; to cosmopolitanism, nationalism; to centralization, the autonomy of social bodies; to revolution, continuous development according to the mysterious biology of nations; to the innovation proposed by thought, the line of the traditional.

Here it will be necessary to insist on some of the outstanding features of Romanticism which indeed do not exhaust its essence but emphasize the aspects which interest us most in the theme which I am treating.

There has to be noted, in the first place, the desire to unify all opposition, to overcome all dualism, to rest all divergencies in one supreme category: so Romanticism tries to save the dualism between God and the world. God would not be opposed to the world, but inserted in it; also between the subject and the object, which would be reciprocally blended; between matter and spirit, for the material would be also animated and every spirit would gain material expressions; between the inorganic and the organic. And, above all, it seeks to close the abysms cleft between the is and the ought, between life and culture, between history and reason. Ideals cannot be known by raising the eyes toward a region of rational abstraction, without hearing attentively and reverently the throbbings of history. The ideal is no further off than reality, but it has to be sought in the deep bosom of the historic process.

And this is connected directly, with respect to the theme which occupies me, with another of the most prominent characters of Romanticism: with its antirationalist tendency, exalting feeling and the mystic attitudes of belief — not of dogmatic belief, but the poetic or romantic. For Romanticism, it is not possible to take possession of the reality of the world, nor even to look into the norms of conduct by speculating abstractly with pure concepts of reason, but only by effusing sentimentally upon things, to penetrate into the deep intimacy of them. Reason which since Socrates has been considered as an essential principle of all things, and also as the supreme norm of work, and which in politics and juristics had just obtained its greatest apotheosis in the French Revolution, is considered by Romanticism as something mean, which is incapable of capturing the essence of the world and of life. Against reason — cold, limited, illusory, cadaverous, static — are exalted the emotional vital positions, the synthesis of supreme wisdom. This is not reducible to rational schemes, but consists of a living belief, inserted in the process of the world end of history. Value and the ideal are not found in a transcendent sphere situated above reality, but are found submerged in it, as its animating and vivifying spirit.

And so, in the third place, it must be noted that Romanticism tends to the justification of the individual, of the concrete, of every vital and historic particularity. In general terms, Philosophy, from its birth in Greece, and more accentuated still in the sixteenth, seventeenth, and eighteenth centuries, had disdained everything which could not be expressed in a general concept. For the romanticist, exactly the contrary occurs: the unique, the unrepeatable, the concrete, the singularity, is the essential inwardness of each thing, and at the same time the source of values. However antiromantic we may be today, it is necessary to recognize that romanticism puts thought in a condition to discover intimacy. The Renaissance brought the discovery of subjectivity; but it was a matter of an abstract, geometrical subjectivity — pure knowledge, after the transcendental I in Kant — but it did not attend to what the individual has of the basic individuality, of the unique, the singular, the unrepeatable. Now, the Romanticism which put its hand upon this so fertile theme — whose study contemporaneous thought has undertaken fruitfully — remained frustrated in this undertaking; because in place of embarking on the individuality of the human person, it attended to the historic individuality of national groups, that is, to the peculiar and different in each people.

Finally, we must note that Romanticism, which aspired to constitute an integral conception of the world and of life, is not Philosophy. Philosophy is also the desire for a conception of the world and of life — an autonomous and pantonomous conception — but one *intellectually justified*. On the other hand, Romanticism is founded on a mystical attitude of poetic belief, on a primary confession of the spirit. While the philosopher is guided always by the desire for noonday clarity, the romanticist, on the contrary, finds pleasure in mystery.

The romantic conception gives place in the field of juridical thought to the Historic School of Law, of whom the principal spokesman was Savigny. It is true that the historical tendency had antecedents. Leaving aside the remote ones, there should be recorded among the nearer ones Juan B. Vico,[88] Herder,[89] Burke,[90] Möser,[91] and Hugo[92] (the first initiator of the school which culminated with Savigny).

For Savigny, there was no meaning in seeking to oppose to historic Law a supposed Natural Law, constructed by abstract reason. We have to seek the unique authenticity of Law in history. And we cannot construct the juridical ideals intellectually, but we gather them from the reality of the spontaneous national consciousness. Law cannot be conceived in a cabinet of rational speculations, but is the product of the collective spirit of each people. There is no other Law than the positive; no other ideal of justice than that of the popular historic consciousness. It will be opportune to note here something which is wont to be frequently forgotten: the Historic School does not deny the possibility and even the necessity of a juridical valuation; it does not run into an absolute skepticism with respect to the valuing problem of Law, but rather it is saturated with a valuing criterion; but this criterion of judgment and of orientation has to be sought in the authenticity of the national soul, which is expressed in the historic consciousness. The Historic School contains a whole valuing Philosophy of Law; but it maintains that the valuing criteria cannot be discovered intellectually as ideas, nor constructed rationally, but discovered in the spontaneous manifestations of the popular juridical consciousness, which is one of the revelations of the national soul. And these spontaneous manifestations are found prin-

[88] VICO: PRINCIPII DI UNA NUOVA SCIENZA INTORNO ALLA COMUNE NATURE DELLE NAZIONI (1725); DE UNIVERSI IURIS UNO PRINCIPIO ET FINE UNO (1720).

[89] IDEEN ZUR PHILOSOPHIE DER GESCHUCHTE DER MENSCHEIT (1784).

[90] REFLECTIONS ON THE REVOLUTION IN FRANCE (1790).

[91] PATRIOTISCHE PHANTASIEN (1788).

[92] NATURRECHT ALS PHILOSOPHIE DES POSITIVEN RECHTES (1799).

cipally in the customary Law, which constitutes the authentic and unadulterated evidence of the popular juridical conviction. And the role of the sovereign ought to consist of making valid juridical customs, and, at most, of translating them faithfully into laws, though indeed it would not be right to extend the ambit of legislation too far, because this is something rigid which fossilizes the living rule and obstructs its development. Savigny understands, then, that there are juridical ideals, but that they are unattainable by the theoretical mind and intellectual methods, but the sole expression of them is to be obtained only in the historic national consciousness, at each moment and at each place. Consequently, there is no rational valuation of the positive Law; but there is a critical valuation in the historic sense, which judges to what point a certain order expresses with authenticity the intimate popular conviction. Consequently, that Law spontaneously expressed in juridical customs ought to be considered just; so also of laws — although less desirable — which are limited to translating with strict fidelity the data of the historic popular consciousness. Here is sacrificed, then, reason to reality, the ideal to history; but it has been done by the romanticist belief that it is in the real processes of history that reason is to be found. In short, they believe in a reason immanent in the evolutive process of history; and they condemn every attempt to try to form historic society rationally; and above all they detest every revolutionary proposal. In a certain aspect, the historic school is an effort to deny justification to the French Revolution — an expression of ideal jusnaturalism, to which it is opposed, maintaining that the Law develops by a customary process.[93]

Hegel. The thought of Hegel, which is one of the doctrines of greatest import on this theme, represents another form of historicism, not romantic but philosophic. While romanticism is emotional intoxication, Hegel represents the paroxysm of the dialectic. Although there are many differences and oppositions which occupy Hegel with regard to the romantic conception — which I shall explain further on — nevertheless there is some parallel between the two doctrines.

Natural Law prior to Hegel represented a dualistic idealism, that is, the division between a blind reality ignorant of values and a rational normativity transcendent of it. While in the theoretical Kantian philosophy there is a relation between the categories of reason and the empiric materials, so far as these are shaped by them, and their conjunction constitutes the world of objects and phenomena, this does not happen in moral and juridical philosophy but therein just the contrary happens. The moral and juridical philosophy of Kant, like that of Illuminism,

[93] This word is added from the Second Spanish edition of the book (Mexico, 1945). TRANSLATOR.

occupies itself exclusively with various abstract rational norms; and, on the other hand, disdains the true reality of moral and juridical life in its historical development, as if in it there had been nothing more than contingency, caprice, and chance. Commenting on this type of thought — especially that of Kant — Hegel says that this philosophy admitted that one ought to know nature as it is, but believed further that in nature there was inserted a rationality, which had to be investigated and understood as its immanent law; moreover, on the other hand, it believed that the ethical world consists of a rationality outside of real being, as something transcendent to it, and with normative pretensions over it; and so according to this philosophy of Kant, it happens that the world of the spirit, the ethical world, in its real and true development, is delivered to chance and arbitrariness, as abandoned by God, since its truth is not to be found in reality but outside it. Hegel opposes this dualism between the ideal norm and facts; and declares that in the world of ethical spirit, that is, in the reality of the State, there rules an objective reason and a regularity. For Hegel — the same as for Schelling — the separation between the ideal and the real represents a logical point of view already superseded. Hegel understands all things real as a spiritual process, as a system of dialectic thought which is revealed in the cosmos. And in his philosophy of Law Hegel says that it is necessary to understand and explain the State as something rational in itself; that is, he is not concerned with how the State ought to be, how it ought to be constructed, but only with knowing it as a moral universe. "What is rational is real; what is real is rational." This is the famous phrase which summarizes the panlogism of Hegel and which figures in the prologue to his *Philosophy of Law*. The rational is the idea or the spirit knowing itself; and there is nothing which is more real. And reality is always a revelation of the spirit, of the dialectic process of thought. The sole, universal, absolute reality is what Hegel calls spirit. To more clearly understand what spirit means in Hegel, perhaps it would be better to call it mind or thought. Hegel buds from the philosophic tradition of idealism, according to which there is no meaning in speaking of the reality of a thing, except so far as it is in thought. Only as thoughts are things true. Thought consists in taking account of itself. Now, it will be necessary that all else which does not appear as thought, that all the thought of, may be understood as a means which thought needs to take account of itself. And so thought develops dialectically, in a complicated process in which it goes seeking itself. Thought begins by thinking of itself as nature, as an infinite cosmic reversion. Then it perfects its idea and discovers itself as organic life, as an animal which is already a concentration in opposition to the reversion to the material. By means of the animal nature it discovers man, who is the subject who already takes account of himself. But the individual person (the subjective spirit as Hegel calls it) is not a sufficient idea of thought, because each one of us takes account of himself as to the element of natural contour and of the other men; I see myself as thought, but all the others seem to me as not being thought, with limitation and determination. While thought leaves something outside of itself, which it does not understand as part of itself, it does not have an adequate idea of spirit. The individuality of the person is an insufficient, partial idea. Spirit has to advance over it to another more complete and more adequate for its reality. Each one of us consists of himself, but our ideas, preferences, desires, norms, come to us in their greater part imposed by the social contour. But then it results that our *I* is less in us than in our people, that is, in the aggregate of norms and intellectual modalities which exercise pressure upon us. Outside of each individual there is a reality, which is not material but is spiritual, and which on the other hand is not of any individual person: it is the Objective Spirit, most fully realized in the State. Each people, each State, is an objective spirit, that is, a system of juridical, moral, artistic, etc., ideas, in which individuals live and learn; so that they are not in themselves but in the spirit of their people which surrounds them. And each great people is a new interpretation which the universal spirit is forming throughout history to come to understand itself as absolute reality. The various series of peoples along history is not a series of chance, but is a rigorous dialectic process, the sacred process of the Universal Spirit, which is diversified in those various interpretations which are given to it, to attain the full and adequate idea of itself as absolute reality. History is, then, the process of autorevelation of the spirit. Therefore, it can be seen clearly that there is no sense in seeking to oppose it to the historic as something distinct, as "ought to be"; because the spirit finds its autorevelation in history. History is the rigorous process of the stages which the spirit goes through to gain possession of itself as absolute reality.

To thoroughly understand [94] hegelian thought, it is necessary to direct the attention to the dynamic development of the spirit, that is, to the dialectic process. The dialectic is a kind of logic in movement. While traditional logic had considered concepts as static, as outlined and concluded, on the other hand Hegel shows that in every mental position, *thesis,* is contained what it is, but at the same time also the germ of its negation to which we find ourselves impelled; but at the time when we try to settle on this negation, *antithesis,* neither are we able to rest tran-

[94] This paragraph is from the Second Spanish edition of the book (Mexico, 1945). TRANSLATOR.

quilly in it, for it contains also the invitation for the negation of itself, which is in truth a certain manner of reaffirmation, *synthesis,* of the first position, only in return, that is, superseded, and so successively. For example, when we try to think of *being,* we conceive it as the strict essence of all things which are; but its content is not this nor that, it is *nothing* in concrete. I have here in thinking of being (thesis) produced the invitation to think the contrary, nothing (antithesis). But when we try to press that notion of nothing, we see that it is not an empty nothing; it is a not being this or that, but for what it may be it will have to be made concrete in a determined something; a not being, but which is going to be, or, what is the same thing, a becoming (synthesis). Or put in other words: pure being is the undetermined immediate (thesis); but so far as it is undetermined, it is nothing concrete (not being or nothing — antithesis). The transit from the undetermined being to the determined being is the becoming. In the becoming, the being and the nothing are superseded, in the double sense of the word supersede, that is, annulled and corrected. In this explanation, which I have presented only by way of the most typical and fundamental example to understand the hegelian dialectic, I have simplified, sacrificing much of the complexity and purity of the hegelian construction; but I have not been able to do it in any other way, within the limits of an incidental allusion. The reality of the world is spirit, that is, thought, idea, and finds itself dialectically constructed. That the real is rational means that everything which exists represents a stage in the dialectic evolution of thought or spirit. That the rational is real, means that every position of spirit, that every thought, has been, is, or will some day be reality. It is to be noted that dialectic development does not coincide necessarily, nor much, with chronological evolution.

It results, then, that the problem put — of the articulation of values in history — loses the character of such problem in the hegelian monism, which identifies the real with the rational and the cosmic and historic happening with the dialectic process. Rather than say that the problem is resolved in favor of one or the other of the extremes, or settled amicably by compromise, it may be said that the problem is dissolved as such problem, that is, it disappears: Reason and History are not two distinct personages which pretend to intervene in the shaping of the Law and which may fall into conflict, but they are one and the same thing. Thus indeed there is no possibility of conflict; and neither is there place to practice a work of bounding and a distribution of competencies, because Reason and History are the same; because reality and the dialectic process of thought coincide.

Comparison between the thought of the historic school and that of

Hegel. It might be said that between the romantic historicism of the historic school and the system of Hegel there are at the same time profound differences and evident parallelisms. Although the problem of the relation between Reason and History is resolved by both doctrines with some analogous consequences, we find ourselves before two diverse types of thought. So it is that Hegel and Savigny reciprocally scorn each other. Hegel considered that the adoration which Savigny professed for customary Law and his anticodifying *pathos* constituted the greatest insult which could be offered a civilized nation and the jurists. And the romanticist historians scorn the hegelian thought as frivolous philosophy. It is true that both positions are monist; that both raise the real to the category of value; that both reduce to zero the distance between history and the ideal. But for the romanticist antirationalism of the Historic School, the identification of the real fact with the juridical ideal is the fruit of a mystical belief that history (the same as nature) is saturated with something sacred. On the other hand, for Hegel, the identification of the real with the rational is expressed and tries to justify itself in the dialectic method. While in Savigny there is an antirationalistic *pathos,* on the contrary in Hegel there is offered the apotheosis of reason, of the spirit as dialectic development, constituting the absolute reality: the development of history is the rational process of the spirit unfolding itself dialectically. It is true that Hegel not only respects history, but it remains sanctified; but history is a rational texture, a system of ideas. While, on the other hand, for Savigny history is the revelation of a secret and mysterious reality, which it is not possible to capture in ideas of reason. This reality, called the national soul or popular feeling, is not the agent of rational acts but of instincts and of infallible feelings.

And nevertheless, in spite of the differences which I have just indicated, there is the impression that there is some parallelism between Hegel and Savigny. Even though Hegel cannot be called strictly romanticist, because romanticism is against reason and the exaltation of antirationalism, while on the contrary Hegel represents the maximum frenzy of reason, there is an evident romantic trace in Hegel, to wit, his frenzy, although it may be rational. Romanticism is a kind of state of intoxication or of paroxysm. Then in Hegel there is also a state of frenetic intoxication, although it may be a drunkenness of ideas. Moreover, it happens that, although by paths not only diverse but antagonistic, Savigny and Hegel travel to the same goal, to the divinification of the historic. And when we try to ask ourselves what may be the national soul of Savigny, it occurs to us that it is something like the objective spirit of Hegel which has escaped from its dialectic chains and goes wandering without finding any lodging. And, vice versa, the objective spirit of Hegel, embodied in the State, would be like the rationalization of the popular soul of Savigny. In short, although Hegel may not be a romanticist — because his philosophy is the exasperation of rational thought — he tries to do by rational methods the same as Romanticism seeks; and so he would appear to us as the culmination of the same romanticist spirit, but adding to it, so far as he expresses it in new rational formulas, those of dialectics.

Positivism and naturalism. Toward the second half of the nineteenth century, there were installed predominantly in thought the positivist attitude and the naturalist currents, which were projected also into the Philosophy of Law, as an attitude negativing Juridical Valuation.

I have already made allusion to positivism at the beginning of this chapter, on the topic of setting up the justification of the problem of Juridical Valuation. When positivism was consistent with its own premises it represented a skeptical position as to the Juridical Valuation. And when some positivists wished to found a Valuation — being unfaithful to the suppositions of positivism — they tried to do it by empirical methods — a thing which has been seen to be impossible. And in general terms, one could sum up the common denominator of positivism, with respect to Law, in the declaration that as to it there is necessary solely and exclusively consideration of its empirical manifestations, which may be studied either as juridical dogmatics — exposition of the current order — or as history of Law, or from the sociological point of view — that is, as one of the factors of the collective life, considering the laws of its formation, of its development and of its influence.

In this same epoch of the third quarter of the nineteenth century, there developed also a series of directions which in the aggregate we might include under the name of naturalism, in spite of there being multiple differences among them. I refer to materialism, to evolutionism, etc. Although these directions not only differed from but opposed radically the suppositions of positivism, they nevertheless coincided with it in many of their consequences, and especially in those which concerned juridical studies. I say that between these directions and positivism there was an opposition, for the following reason: while positivism denies the possibility of all metaphysics, on the contrary materialism carries a whole innate metaphysics, as it is that which presumes to identify the category of substance with matter. It is thought that there never could be constructed a datum of experience that all substantive being is material without this constituting a metaphysical hypothesis — a hypothesis otherwise undemonstrated and indemonstrable. But in spite of this antithesis between positivism and materialism, one coincides with the other in denying every instance of ideal valuation. With regard to the so-called programs and ideals of the juridical world, both propose exclusively the explanation of their existence, as psychological or social phenomena, that is, the causal explanation of their genesis; and in this way they lose all dimension of values and are reduced to mere natural phenomena, foreign to every critical estimation. That is, the so-called ideals are reduced to mere facts which are produced in the consciousness of peoples and in social movements, facts which they try to explain from the causative point of view. And consequently the problem with regard to the relation between Reason and History to elaborate the juridical ideal remains entirely negatived; simply because it is understood that one could not speak with scientific rigor of there being criteria of justice with ideal consistency; since what received this name would be mere phantasms and subjective illusions.

It would be an error to identify the thesis of positivism (and of naturalism) with the doctrine of the Historic School. While these currents of positivism and naturalism deny the valuing problem of Law, it is to be remembered that, on the contrary, Savigny believes in a Juridical Valuation, though it is neither rational nor ideal, but inspired by the criterion of historic authenticity (it will be exactly Law produced genuinely by the popular consciousness and will not be that which the legislator constructs abstractly or which the rationalist philosopher pictures). On the other hand, the Historical School avows an integral conception of the world and of life (the romanticist transcription of metaphysics), while positivism abstains from putting for itself any problem as to what there is beyond or below pure experience.

According to evolutionism, both the theoretical categories and the values are the product of the slow development of evolution, attained in a fashion purely natural and mechanical. The problem of how a purely natural evolutionary process can, nevertheless, produce a situation in which certain representations of cultural values dominate, obliges the greater part of evolutionist theories to admit certain directives of the evolutionary process, which seek, at any moment, systematic development and which are contradictions of the naturalist premises.[95] Remember what I said in previous pages concerning the concept of progressive evolution in Spencer: evolution from the pure point of view exclusive of nature is neither progressive nor regressive; and when we qualify it as progressive, then we are exceeding the field of pure natural science and resorting to criteria of value.

Karl Marx. The economic conception of history of Karl Marx is an

[95] Cf. José Medina Echavarría, La situación presente de la Filosofia Juridica (1935) 83.

essentially metaphysical doctrine. To take account of it, it is sufficient to recall the part which the idea of social substance plays in it, represented by economic production; and also to remember the use of the dialectic method which in no case and in no manner can be the result of experience, but an *a priori* principle of reason. Now, similar to what occurred with evolutionism, the thesis of Marx gives place, in part, to consequences negativing juridical valuation, although in another part the work of Marx encourages — and more than his work his life as a politician — a *pathos* of redemption and reform, when not of something more, to wit, revolution. But this is the contradiction unsurmounted until now — and inexorably insoluble — between a movement animated by the desire for social justice and of almost messianic characters, with a philosophic doctrine which blots out all notion of the ideal, all concept of the ought-to-be and all principle of value. The contradiction is always present and inevitable, and cannot be eliminated by mere capers of language or by brilliant metaphors, as some of its disciples attempt. In the man Marx there is an ideal impulse of social justice, a redemptionist and apostolic feeling which desires a better world. In his economic dialectic of history there is a note of cold fatalism, of harsh mechanical and naturalistic conception — ignorant of any idea of value — of Prussian hardness. And it is not said that it is ordained that man can act in history reforming its course and accelerating its processes and even directing them; for at the moment of saying this one has abandoned the economic dialectic. Accordingly, the true protagonist of history is economics. Karl Marx thinks that he has found the substance of society and the explanation of history in economics. The last and basic reality of each historic stage consists in the situation of the process of economic production. Each new form of this starts a new form of social organization, starts a proprietary social class of the instruments and others submitted to it. Ideas, morals, law, art, are no more than reactions of each social class according to its status in the common economic hierarchy. Neither ideas nor morals nor law nor art are forces of history, nor is man either, but on the contrary, those ideas and also the manner of acting of men are the result of economic reality. So then, at the moment in which one says that man by his own initiative and by his own forces can act upon the process of history, for reform or for revolution, at that moment one has abandoned the monistic thesis of pure social materialism, because then man, from a mere agent or vehicle of economic forces, changes to become an instance acting for his own account on history. But then economics is no longer the substance of society and the protagonist of history, since it has to share its action with politics, which would not be only its servant, but which might at times act upon it. In short, when one admits the collaboration of man, one has abandoned economic monism.

Marx explains that when the constellation of economic processes varies, there has to vary also necessarily the political and juridical superstructure. At times, the change occurs with a certain slowness because of the fossilized persistence of the juridical forms of the previous situation. But finally, when the degree of tension or discrepancy between the new economic situation and the old juridical form — corresponding to the past economic situation — is great enough, then the old structure breaks in pieces at the impact of the new economic reality. So it happens that upon contemporary economy — which is fully coöperative — there remains still an inadequate individualistic Law, that of the capitalist regime. And Marx announces as a provision, discovered by the laws of his economic-social dialectic, that capitalism will be ruined by itself, giving place to a new organization of production, which will *necessarily* determine the collapse of the bourgeois juridical system and the formation of a consistent, that is, socialistic, juridical system. But within the rigorous margin of the economic dialectic this is presented as an event which necessarily will occur and not as a program of justice, as an ideal, as an ought-to-be; that is, purely and simply foreseen as an event which perforce will have to happen, by virtue of the dialectic superseding of the capitalistic regime. And, therefore, it has no meaning within the pure dialectic of the economic substance, as the sole effective agency of history, to put a problem of juridical valuation, or of the valuing criterion of a certain social reality, since this is something which develops autonomically, by the very laws of its essence. In short, the only thing which can be done in the periods of transition from one economic structure in danger of dialectic supersession by another new one, is to predict that there will arise also a consistent change in juridical institutions; and when this is delayed by the inert persistence of the old juridical forms, the discordance may be emphasized and the birth of the new juridical regime, which is already carried in the womb of the new economic situation, may be assisted. But in order that this may be done, it is necessary that the gestation of the new regime should already have been accomplished in the depths of the economy, for it is not men who can create juridical systems at their free will, but these can be engendered only by the deep economic substance of history. Men at most may play the part of midwives for the birth of the new regime, engendered in the process of the economic dialectic.

Consequently, in the thought of Marx, the problem which concerns us tries to be solved by erecting history as a unique criterion, conceived as an expression of the dialectic play of economic forces. Marx presents the reverse of the hegelian system. This, by the identity which it establishes between idea and reality, is exposed to being transformed into naturalism, into realism, as soon as it accents the real element as against the ideal. The hegelian dialectic converted the logical categories into subjects of the spiritual and historic world, so that with respect to them men were reduced to mere predicters, to simple vehicles or means. The historic materialism of Marx — which could better be called historic realism — adopted the inverse position, so far as it considers that economic reality is the active substance of history and the producer (in its dialectic process) of the spiritual world and its forms; but in the thesis of Marx, man continues also dispossessed of all decisive acting capacity in history, for he is only the tool moved by economic forces.

This is in purity, in its authenticity, the thesis of the economic dialectic of Marx, such and as it appears in his theoretical work. Now, it would not perhaps be proper to forget that political *pathos* which animated Marx for the redemption of the proletariat classes, and which, in short, in spite of all his economic dialectic, constitutes a solicitude for social justice. Accordingly, one of the most outstanding socialist thinkers of our time, Hermann Heller, has thought to see in the work of Marx a new camouflaged manifestation of the belief in a natural Law, in dynamic transformation, understood as an order immanent in society, an order which would not only be a fact, but which would moreover be valued as something good and just.[96]

Stammler. When Stammler[97] undertakes the task of restoring the Philosophy of Law, which has been proscribed during the tyranny of positivism and of naturalism, he finds that before that devastating regime there were two types of doctrinal positions: on the one side, the diverse expressions of rationalism (which denied significance to history), notoriously, the Natural Law of Illuminism; and, on the other side, romantic historicism, hegelian historicism, and naturalism, which although differing among themselves coincided in rejecting as impossible, or at least as idle and useless, every ideal or rational valuation. And both types of doctrines appeared justly discredited.

The classical rationalistic jusnaturalism had demonstrated its failure because, having the pretension to elaborate a pure rational construction, it had introduced unduly into its bosom historic elements which had been absolutized as supposed *a priori* constructions, when in truth they were

[96] Hermann Heller, Politische Ideenkreise (1925).

[97] See an exposition of the system of Stammler and a bibliography in my book Direcciones contemporáneas del pensamiento jurídico (1928). See also, Roscoe Pound, Introduction to the Philosophy of Law (1922).

limited and contingent institutional outlines, that is, historic products. But, on the other hand, the Natural Law of Illuminism sought to supplant positive Law, putting itself in its place, annulling the Law historically received and replacing it by an absolute and eternal Law; now, the constructions elaborated to that end turned out weak and insufficient to accomplish it; they were much too small to serve as a juridical order applicable in practice, in which social life continued to set new unsuspected problems. And this double failure had rightly determined the discredit of rational jusnaturalism.

On the other hand, already at the end of the century, positivism had entered upon a frank decomposition, and from its own bosom proclaimed its failure. And something similar happened also with the naturalist currents (materialism, evolutionism, etc.) which had begun to crumble. Nevertheless, some doctrines — rationalism, historicism, and naturalism — had given lessons, which it was necessary not to forget. In rationalism there was emphasized a lasting truth, to wit, that a normative order is based necessarily on transempiric criteria. In historicism, as in positivism and naturalism, there was accented the consciousness that there exists a social reality, as an effective magnitude, as historical datum, which cannot be replaced by constructions of reason.

The problem, consequently, consists of investigating what it is which corresponds to reason and what it is which contends with history in the elaboration of juridical programs. And Stammler devotes himself to this problem. Law is an ordering of conduct, an ordering with special characteristics (social, autarchial, and inviolable, which it is not necessary to examine here; for I have already defined in this book the essence of juristics on a plane of superseding the theory of Stammler as to this theme of the concept). Now, when it is a matter of a work of ordering, there must be distinguished *that which* orders and the *method according to* which it is ordered; or, rather, one has to distinguish between the content which is ordered and the form of ordering it. What is ordered, the content or material, is constituted of the elements of the social life, in the reality given at a certain moment, to wit: by an aggregate of concrete men, with certain needs and desires, all of which is something which we find in historic experience. And it is a matter of ordering those materials, which are various for each place, moment and people, according to an absolutely valid criterion of ordering, that is, according to a necessary and universal criterion. Then, it results clearly, to understand this, that there is no meaning in Reason and History struggling antagonistically to eliminate each other in the elaboration of juridical ideals, since each of them plays a part perfectly determined. It is for history to furnish at each moment the contents or material, that is, the reality of the social life which is to be ordered, which cannot be invented or constructed by the mind, but which is given in a concrete and singular manner. It is for reason to furnish the form of ordering that social material. Therefore, the idea of justice is universally valid and absolute to order juridically any real situation of the collective life. Justice is a pure formal criterion, a mere ordering principle of contingent and variable (historic) materials. The form of justice, as a rational idea, is unique and invariable, *a priori;* the content of each Law is mutable and comes historically conditioned. And as juridical ideals are the product of ordering a historic social content with regard to a formal criterion of justice, hence the variety of possible *just Laws* is unlimited; and so, to each historical situation there corresponds a special juridical ideal, that is, a proper scheme of just Law: which results from ordering, according to the formal criterion of the idea of justice, the concrete reality of which it treats.

Stammler, in his investigation as to justice, asks himself for a universal necessary criterion, absolutely valid for juridical ordering. That is, a juridical criterion which is worthy for itself and in itself, unconditionally, and consequently, which may be applicable to all the situations which there have been in the world, are, or may be. If we seek something absolute, necessary, and universal — says Stammler — then it is clear that this criterion cannot contain any element which may be conditioned, contingent, particular, or concrete: it cannot shelter within itself any historical content, any reference to concrete situations, any mention of special material, any norm of particular character. In short, this criterion of justice must lack all concrete content, all special material; or, what is the same thing, it must be purely formal.

To seek to give universal and unconditioned validity to a particular modality of human life would represent a contradiction *in adjecto;* for it is clear that anything limited and concrete, anything particularly conditioned, cannot serve as a general and unconditioned criterion.

The only thing, consequently, which can constitute a universal and necessary criterion (that is, absolute) is a pure formal method of unified ordering. If, for example, it is desired to arrange papers, I shall not take as a criterion one of them, but I ought to adopt a method which will serve me to arrange any class of papers in question. In this sense, form and method mean the same.

Justice then, says Stammler, cannot consist of any concrete content, but in a form universally valid to order all the present and future contents; that is, a method which represents an absolute and unconditioned harmony of all the social materials (real or possible).

Stammler affirms that the representation of such absolute harmony is an idea, this word being understood in the Kantian sense. Stammler — following Kant — distinguishes between concept and idea. Both are pure forms; but they differ in that the concept is the unified and common determination of a series of analogous objects; while the idea, on the other hand, signifies the representation of the harmonious unity of all possible objects. The concept gives the generic notes of the objects in question: that is, the common representation of all of them; and consequently the concept is realized or fully complied with in each one of the objects which it includes. On the other hand, the idea tries to articulate, in a harmonious system, the totality of sensory experiences if they refer to nature, and the totality of desires (that is, of the ends) if they refer to the world of action; and, finally, the idea cannot be found manifest in any empirical object, in any single element, nor can we expect its realization in limited experience; since what the idea constitutes is a point of orientation, a regulating criterion, which does not turn out fully attainable, but is only a guide. Hence, says Stammler, the function of the idea has been compared metaphorically with that of the North Star, which serves to direct navigators but on which no one ever landed. So then, there is an idea of *correctness* which fulfills the function of ordering harmoniously all human desires, that is, all human ends. If this idea of correctness is applied to the intimate world of consciousness it produces the moral criterion. If we project it upon the world of social texture, it constitutes the idea of justice.

Stammler first expresses the idea of justice as the "community of free-willing men." What does this free-willing mean? By it he indicates that the juridical organization ought to be of such sort that no particular will determined by private or egotistic motives, no single desire, commands in it, but a purely rational will, free from all singleness, as a universal law. In this formula of the community of free-willing men, who desire with a free will, or, better put, freed from sensory motives, lies the resonance of the idea of the *general will* of Rousseau, which does not mean the real will of all, but the will which does not contain private motives, which is a purely rational will, that is, universal. And more nearly we perceive the recollection of the pure will of Kantian morals, that is, will purified of all sensory and appetitive determination of every private element, which obeys only a logical form of universality. In his later works, Stammler replaced this formula of the "community of free-willing men" by that of "permanent and absolute harmony" of the social ordering, with all its possibilities, present and future. All the manifestations of the life of man, as well those of his consciousness as those of social relations, may be directed or ordered in two ways: (a) starting from the person; or (b) letting one be guided by an objective criterion. In the first case, there is taken as supreme law the empirical I, the chance or contingency of the desire of each instant, with which one comes only to disordered and confused propositions. In the second case, we start with the idea of an absolute harmony between all pretensions and private desires, and, in accordance with this idea, we try to include without any contradiction all those individual empiric elements in the representation of an ideal totality, which articulates unifiedly all present and future ends. The idea of justice consists, then, of an absolute harmony, in conformity with which we order juridical material. This ordering according to the idea of an absolute harmony gives rise to the *pure community,* that is, of well-wishing men. A pure community is the coherence of the ends of the men who compose it, never taking as criterion a desire which has only subjective validity. In accordance with this idea, men will bind themselves reciprocally, each preserving at every moment the character of an autonomous end, that is, so that none may ever be taken as a mere means for another, but all preserve always their quality of moral persons.

The idea of justice, then, is a pure idea, a formal method, to order empirical social purposes, conceiving them in the totality of their possibilities according to an absolute harmony.

There is, then, one single and unique idea of justice, with an absolute and universal value, which, applied to the diverse contents of the social life of multiple peoples and historic moments, will engender different juridical ideals. Each one of those ideals, which has only a relative value — relative to the time, to the people, and the circumstances in the light of which it was elaborated — constitutes what Stammler calls *just Law.* There may be and there may be thought of, consequently, an unlimited quantity of just Laws, by virtue of the innumerable circumstances of fact to be regulated. The method of ordering is one and invariable; but as the materials to be ordered may be diverse in each people, time, and circumstance, hence it follows that there will also be diverse juridical ideals (or programs of just Law), which result as the product of the application of the invariable idea of justice in each social situation.

The superseding of formalism. To Stammler[98] we owe the conception that the juridical ideal of a concrete time and place can be formulated without there being established thereby an absolutely valid charter, that is, with necessary application to all peoples and to all epochs. That conception of Stammler has, excepting nevertheless some notorious diversities, an analogy with that of scholasticism, especially as formulated by Francisco Suarez, who offered also a harmonic articulation of the rational

[98] The first two sentences are from the Second Spanish edition of the book (Mexico, 1945). TRANSLATOR.

exigencies, universally valid, with the concrete necessities suitable for each social situation. Against the work of Stammler it has happened that — even appreciating the great dimensions of it and the merit which it deserves as the restorer of the Philosophy of Law, and even recognizing also that in it there are true *Leitmotifs* — with the passage of some years since publication, the advances of philosophic-juridical thought began to experience a kind of theoretical restlessness: the impression that in the Stammlerian system there is something which is not in order and which is insufficient for a Juridical Valuation.

First, there was directed against the Stammlerian doctrine of justice an immanent criticism. It was reproached, and with reason, for having suffered a formalistic illusion; that the results at which it arrived are not purely formal, but are founded on a material axiological idea, in an essence of value with content, to wit, in the ethical idea of the human personality as an autoend (an end in itself). And other times it also happens that in his thoughts he introduces in a surreptitious and subtle manner, as a sort of *deus ex machina,* an aggregate of ideas of value with concrete content.

On the other hand, they objected to Stammler also because he had unduly transferred to the field of moral and juridical philosophy the philosophy of the knowledge of reality, of the *Critique of Pure Reason* of Kant; and so as the latter inquired into the *a priori* forms of the knowledge of real objects, that is, of phenomena, and at the same time their contexture, analogously Stammler tried to determine the *a priori* forms of the juridical ideal, by a similar method. This is inadmissible, because the logic of the natural sciences is not transferable to the world of ethics and of history. And if indeed something of this objection would be valid against Kant, it is much more accentuated against Stammler; since in Kant the moral universe, in spite of logisticism, preserves an autonomy and moreover the primacy belongs to it, while in Stammler the specific characters of *practical reason* have disappeared.

But, even if all these objections are justified, none of them has succeeded in reaching the principal failure which burdens the Stammlerian doctrine. With the formalism of the justice of Stammler there happened something similar to what had long been occurring regarding the moral formalism of Kant. In the course of the nineteenth century there had been accentuated the conviction that in the formalistic and rigorous morals of Kant there had been something which was not according to rule. Many objections were directed against it, all of them impressive and well orientated; but none of them succeeded in discovering where the fundamental failure of the system lay.

The fundamental failure of the Kantian ethical formalism was decisively discovered by Max Scheler about the fifteenth year of our century.[99] And the criticism which Max Scheler developed against the moral formalism of Kant can, in the same way — although he did not do it — be applied to the formalism of the justice of Stammler. For Stammler — the same as for Kant — the *a priori,* that is, the absolute and necessary, has to be inevitably something generic and abstract and never anything with a concrete or individual content. And it is particularly this supposition which has broken down by virtue of the discoveries of the phenomenological philosophy of Husserl and of the theory of values of Scheler. Husserl and Scheler have shown that there are material ideas and essences, that is, full of content and that, nevertheless, they have *a priori* validity, that is, validity in and for themselves; validity which is not derived from experience, nor is founded on it, nor can be contradicted by it. Phenomenology has amplified the world of the *a priori* which the transcendental Kantian and neo-Kantian idealism had established. For it, the *a priori* era was an aggregate of some certain categories conceived as subjective functions and as empty logical forms, which made a limited and functional system. The phenomenology of Husserl has discovered the ideal being as an objectivity with validity in itself; and has shown also that the categories are ideal objects. And, moreover, it has discovered essences as ideal objects; it has discovered that phenomena, which are contingent as to their real existence in *a here* and *a now* might in their essence exist equally at another moment, find themselves in another place and have other form or content. And as this characterization of facts is not possible without appealing, as we see, to their essence, it results that every fact supposes, then, an essence; and the essences present themselves as ideal objects, because they are *a priori,* that is, necessary, independent (as to their ideal consistency) of the facts in which they are realized. They are *a priori* propositions, because in their very meaning they imply not having been derived from experience, not finding in it either their foundation or their confirmation or their refutation. It results, then, that phenomenology has considerably amplified the world of the *a priori.* And the essences are apprehensible by intellectual intuition, by intuitions in which ideal objects present themselves to us in an immediate manner.[100]

[99] Cf. Der Formalismus in der Ethik 78.

[100] I ought to mention the unpublished work of José Gaos, ¿Qué es la Fenomenología?, which is an excellent exposition of this theme. Also the book of the eminent Mexican philosopher, Dr. Antonio Caso, La filosofía de Husserl. Cf. further, Linke, Die phänomenale Sphäre und das reale Bewusstsein; Adolf Reinach, Vortrag über Phänomenologie, in Gesammelte Schriften; Metzger, La situación presente de la Fenomenología (Revista de Occidente, nos. 65 and 68); Teodoro Celms, El idealismo fenomenológico de Husserl (Madrid, 1931,

But starting from the phenomenological base, what has clearly shown where lay the capital failure of the Kantian moral formalism — and finally also the formalism of the justice of Stammler — has been the indicating of the grave error which tries to identify the *a priori* with the formal and the *a posteriori* with the material. The Kantian philosophy has equalized the contrasting pair formal – material with the contrasting pair *a priori – a posteriori.* The Kantian philosophy considered that what is absolute, necessary, evident, *a priori,* is necessarily formal; and that the material (what possesses content) is always contingent, empirical, *a posteriori.* Kant — sharpening a prejudice which was already traditional in philosophy from the epoch of Aristotle in favor of form as against matter — started, on the basis of his transcendental subjectivism, with every *a priori* principle having necessarily to be formal; and vice versa, that the contents, the material must be necessarily something contingent, *a posteriori.* And this is precisely a great error, the great error which radically vitiates the whole system; because the two pairs of opposites, *formal – material* and *a priori – a posteriori* do not coincide in any manner nor have anything to do with one another. Notice, in the first place, that the difference or contrast between the *a priori* and the *a posteriori* is absolute, basic, and inescapable, without there being possible any middle term between these two extremes. On the contrary, the contrast between the formal and the material is only a relative difference, in which there are innumerable degrees. The difference between formal and material is referred to the degree of greater or less generality respectively between two propositions; that is, that is considered as formal which is more general with respect to the other, which, in comparison with it, turns out more concrete. So, for example, the principles and laws of pure logic are formal with respect to those of mathematics, which with reference to them seem material. And, nevertheless, mathematics, the same as logic, is *a priori.* Accordingly, in the ambit of the *a priori* there is the contrast or, better put, the difference, between the formal and the material; because this difference is only a distinction as to the greater or less degree of generality. So it happens that the ethical and juridical values — and the norms on which they are founded — may have, and truly have, a material, that is, a concrete content, without thereby losing in any way their *apriority,* that is, their necessary validity. All the *a priori* is absolutely and necessarily valid; but this necessity does not have to be understood as a formal generality, but as a necessity within

REV. DE OCCIDENTE); GEORGES GURVITCH, LES TENDANCES ACTUELLES DE LA PHILOSOPHIE ALLEMANDE (1930); REYER, EINFÜHRUNG IN DIE PHÄNOMENOLOGIE.

its own sphere — in this case within the sphere determined by the very essence of value.

With the exposing of this error of the Kantian thought, moral formalism was mortally wounded, and also, consequently, the formalism of the justice of Stammler.

But joined to the rectification previously explained there is still another, which arises to clear a second confusion from the thought of the Kantian base. It is that Kantism has also identified—unduly—on one side the formal *a priori* with the *rational* and on the other side the *material* with the *sensory*. The Kantian affirmation that all will which is determined by the material, that is, by a principle full of concrete content, for this reason alone is not determined *a priori* but is necessarily determined by sensory, fortuitous, and contingent motives is untrue. We may and ought to affirm the contrary: the will may be determined by ideal emphases of value, objective, necessary, *a priori*, and, nevertheless, full of content; so, then, by material principles *a priori*, which have nothing to do with the motivations of sensibility, nor with the subjective tendencies of pleasure, nor with the mere appetites. And it is clear that if there are material (concrete) principles and determinations which have nothing to do with the world of sensibility and the appetites, but on the contrary are *a priori* and which nevertheless are not rational laws, but essences of value — apprehensible by an intellectual intuition — it evidently results that the coincidence which Kantism proclaims between the *a priori* and the rational is untrue. Far from the area of rational knowledge (by concepts, judgments, and inferences) coinciding totally with the boundaries of the *a priori*, it turns out that there is a large sector of the latter, there is a large part of the field of the *a priori* — and certainly the fundamental part — which is not determined by rational processes, but rather is apprehensible only by an intellectual intuition. And to this sector belong values in general, and finally also the ethical and juridical values, apprehensible by a singular kind of valuing intuition, which constitutes the intuition of an *a priori*, that is, of something which does not emanate from experience and is not founded in it. So, then, on the disappearance of the prejudice of believing also that everything *a priori* is rational (discursive) and that everything which is not rational has to be *a posteriori*, there is destroyed another of the points of formalism. Therefore, it has been discovered that there is a copious realm of ideal essences, rigorously *a priori*, which are not knowable rationally, but by intellectual intuition; among these figure the values full of content, with perfectly determined and concrete meanings; and it has been discovered that, consequently, the norms or the conducts oriented toward these values cannot be considered as determined by sensory factors *a posteriori,* but on the contrary they are pure elements, *a priori.* In this realm of values, there have been found those of an ethical character, in great number, for example, loyalty, purity, abnegation, etc.; and also juridical ones, with which we shall try here to establish contact.

With these antecedents explained, we can now turn with success, at the height of our time, to the problem of the relations between values and history. The story of the past doctrines which I have given prior to the systematic consideration of this problem will serve very efficiently to avoid falling into positions which have already been supplanted; and will serve also to appraise the degree of progress and even of maturity of the solution which I propose. It has been desirable to devote attention to all the antecedents which I have explained, because all those doctrines, today superseded, have left a positive residue of teachings, thanks to which it is now possible to put the question more correctly and to solve it in a certain manner.

7. New Foundation Proposed for Historicity in the Juridical Valuation.[101]

What I have explained as to values, as ideal objects with *a priori,* that is, necessary validity, perhaps has produced in the reader the impression that historicity runs a risk of being shipwrecked in this theory of value, since values constitute pure essences, foreign to time. Nevertheless, the reader will see that it is not so; he will see how without diminution of that ideal dimension of values there is a perfectly justified articulation of them in the varying process of history. And, to show it, I am going to offer, hereinafter, the résumé of my works dedicated to the solution of this theme.

Above all, it is to be noted with full clearness and rigor what the theme is which we have stated. In the investigation to found the juridical Valuation, we have found that the chief basis for developing positive institutions and for orientating the later production and the progressive reëlaboration of the Law is constituted of values, which are, *a priori,* objective ideas. We ask, then, how it may be possible to articulate the exigencies of these ideas endowed with necessary validity with the multiple, varied, and changing demands of the historic realities. The problem seems difficult to us at first sight, because it appears that it attempts to harmonize two ingredients of a different character: ideas, necessarily valid, *a priori,* and demands derived from contingent, diverse, and turncoat circumstances, in short, to harmonize reason and history.

[101] At the special request of the author, the translation of this section has been made from the ampler text of the Second Spanish edition of the book (Mexico, 1945).

But it must be noted that, strictly, it is not an attempt to harmonize ideas of value with historic facts, but is indeed something else. It is a matter, in so far as it refers to the realization of the ideal normative exigencies of pertinent values, of harmonizing their fulfillment with the concrete historico-social circumstances of each place and of each moment. That is, what has to be compared are not pure values and historic facts; but what has to be matched is the putting in practice of the exigencies of the values and the concrete characteristics of historic situations, in which these exigencies ought to be realized. Now, where are values realized? In human life; and as to what refers to juridical values, in the social organization. With respect to this theme of reason and history, it is a matter, then, of a problem of the *realization* of values. Diversity and change, that is, historicity, is not predicated of values, but of their realization in social human life. Bear in mind that the problem which I am now examining is not that of pure juridical values but that of juridical ideals; consequently, it is a problem concerning the realization of juridical values; the realization of them precisely where they have to be realized, which is in social human life. Human life is essentially historic. Human life is the conjunction of the subject with the objects which form its outline. And social human life is the texture formed by certain relations between multiple human lives in some special aspects. Then the two ingredients which form human lives — concrete subjects and circumstances — are subject to the law of diversity and to the law of change. Moreover, remember that we are constructing our life, in its reality of each moment, with the materials at our disposal, weaving it by a selection of some of the possibilities which concrete circumstance offers us. Bear in mind also that the objectivity of values is not an abstract objectivity but intravital; that is, that even though values are objective, they are given like all other objects in our life as components of it.

Consequently, what I have just shown as to the fact that it is a matter of realization, and moreover what I have just recalled as to the being, the structure, and the fact of our life, makes manifest the character and the extent of the question which we have put, which is a problem relating not to the essence of values but to the manner of complying with them or of embodying them in our existence.

The juridical values ought to be realized by men in their lives in respect to the organization of society by norms of inexorable imposition to obtain a certain, secure, pacific and just order. The basic and detailed understanding of this theme will show us five justified sources of historicity of juridical ideals; four of them derived precisely from the conditions of realization; and the fifth founded on a diversity of concrete values.

In the first place, as a source of historicity in juridical ideals or valuing programs for the Law, we find the diversity of social materials and their transformation. Juridical values ought to be realized by men in their lives. Now, remember that life is a conjunction between the I and its world. Also, as I have already explained, the world, which forms part of our life, which constitutes its outline or circumstance and at the same time one of the ingredients of which we are constructing our existence, is not the same for all; because it is correlative to our I; and above all it is not the same in all places, nor in all historical stages nor in all cultural situations. Notice that we call the world the aggregate of all those things with which I have to reckon in my life, with which I have to get along in some form, which constitute repertories of possibilities in some, of problems in others; some offer themselves to me as facilities, others interpose themselves as difficulties. Then at each historic moment and in each concrete situation there is a particular world which, in considerable part, is different from the worlds of other epochs and other conditions. Within the world or circumstance there is concrete society, the nearest and also the farthest other men. Precisely in the world, which is of capital importance, for what refers to the realization of juridical values is the concrete social reality; since the juridical values ought to be realized in a collective material with special characters, which is that constituted by the realities of the social life at each moment. Observe that this social material is different in each people, in each situation, and in each historic stage. But it is not only the social world, in the strict sense, as the texture of collective relations and forms, which comes in question for the theme of the realization of juridical values. True, that social world is the principal material for the fulfillment of such values; but it is not the only one, for it is influenced in an important measure also by the possibilities which the concrete cultural situation offers for human tasks, for example, scientific knowledge, technical means, abundancy or scarcity of economic goods, etc. It is clear that all these ingredients which constitute circumstance, the world in which one lives, come into question for juridical ideals not as directly exposed as science, as technique, etc., but in so far as they all condition the social life, influence it, and orient it, so far as they create problems in collective existence, so far as they offer facilities, or so far as they raise difficulties, so far as, in constituting the concrete outline of social activities, they determine the necessities which the men feel who make up the community and the ways which it offers them as possible in each case. So, then, the material upon which, or better in which and with which are going to be realized the exigencies of the juridical values, is different in each case; different, because of the concrete peculiarities of the existing social texture, of the number of its components, of their peculiar characteristics, and of the necessities felt; but also diverse because of all the other factors which in limiting life also condition social relations. And among these factors figure, on one side, the physical elements which distinguish life, the biological agents which intervene in it; and, on the other side, there figure also the cultural ingredients (religious, philosophic, scientific, technical, economic, etc.) which form the concrete historic constellation of each area determined at each one of its moments. And the social material, together with the sum of the factors which condition it and influence it, changes and alters with the passage of history. And it is with those diverse and changing materials in each situation that one must work to contrive juridical regulation, in accordance with the inspiration which adequate values may give. The world in which we live varies in form and content, it opens or closes to a greater or less number of concrete possibilities; consequently, the necessities of human life, the tasks which man feels an urgency to fulfill, and the possible ways for it also change.

Then, the diversity of social materials, their modification in the historic process, and the consequent changes which human life experiences, all deeply affect the problem of the realization of juridical values. When it is a matter of realizing a value, there comes into question not only the essence of that value, but also the conditions of the material, which and with which it has to comply. An example taken from the artistic field will illustrate this thought with all clarity. One given aesthetic value — including the application of it to a determined style — may be incarnated in architecture, in sculpture, in painting, in music and in poetry. Then, even though it is the same value — or the application of it in one given style — it will have a diverse figure of realization in each one of these arts. But, still more, within each one of these arts, the realization will vary according to what the materials may be and the technique of which each makes use; and so, one sculptural conception, for example, will not come to the same expression in marble, as in bronze, or in clay, or in cement; neither will it express the same result in miniature as in colossal dimensions, etc. Thus, the material conditions the realization of values; and the variety of material gives rise to a variety of works; and the change of material necessitates a change in the labor of fulfillment of values. Now it is clear, then, that in spite of values as pure ideas being something with validity *a priori,* on the other hand their realization has to be varied by virtue of the diversity of materials; and has to be changed according to the modification of these latter. Accordingly, in juristics, even treating of the same value, it will be very different to have to realize it in a society of small dimensions from realizing it in a nation of many million inhabitants; it will also be very different to have to apply it to a cultured people from applying it to a backward community; also very different to have to apply it in laborious, dynamic, active peoples, with increasing necessities and desire for progress, from applying it in indolent, quietistic, conformist, and decadent peoples; and it will be very different to apply it to a pastoral community than to an industrial society. Thus we take clear account of one of the sources of variety and of transmutation of juridical ideals.

Perhaps it may seem to someone that the considerations which I have just developed coincide with those of Stammler upon the diversity and mutability of the social material. And I will not say that there does not exist some resemblance, as also there is with the analogous reflections which St. Thomas and Francisco Suarez produced. But the thoughts which I offer, although with all modesty, undertake to constitute an addition to the above mentioned doctrines, without prejudice to recognizing whatever there appears in them of fertile suggestions. In fact, notwithstanding that he who writes these lines has learned much from Suarez and Stammler and owes them important stimuli, he offers this theme as an inquiry of the realization of values in human life. Therefore, on the one side, it is not a matter of a formal unique regulating criterion, as a method, in the manner of the idea of rectitude or justice of Stammler, but it is a matter of a series of *a priori* values, replete with content, which, in spite of their necessary ideal validity, raise in the face of each congruent concrete situation peculiar exigencies and peculiar proceedings for their realization. And this diversity of exigencies is derived precisely from the variety of materials in which there must be impressed or modeled the inspiration received from the values. But, on the other side, in the face of the doctrines of Suarez and Stammler — who made, each in his way, shrewd conjectures as to the variety and change of social material — I offer here an analysis of that material. Suarez limits himself to enumerating the variety of the social material, considered as a reality before us, without more. Stammler applies to the social the Kantian notion of matter, as an aggregate of empirical data. On the other hand, I offer here to clear up the sort of thing this material is with which one must work being inspired by the exigencies of values, an analysis of human life, relying at this point above all on the notion of the world with all the ingredients which compose it and in a special manner on its correlation with concrete human life.

In the second place, we must note another source of variety and change in the valuing juridical programs, which also is related to the problems of the realization of values. This is what is derived from the concrete necessities of each historic moment. What man does, looking toward juridical values, is to construct with a certain social material an institution, to attain the ends grounded in that idea of value. Consequently, positive Law which articulates, that is, the institutions which create, constitute a medium for the realization of the ends grounded in some values. Now, the nature of those media which create is determined not only by the nature of the value, but also by the nature of the things which are to be done and of the obstacles which have to be overcome to realize the proposed end. It happens then, that even though the end grounded in a value is one and the same, according to the circumstances, that is, according to what may be the obstacles which have to be cleared, the medium which is put into practice will necessarily have to vary. An example will illustrate this clearly. When in the eighteenth century an attempt was made to convert into present reality the juridical value liberty, there arose the problems of overcoming effectively the forces which were opposed to it, and of preventing them from conspiring for the annulment of that civil and political conquest. These forces were the Crown, the nobility, and the clergy (occupied with matters of State); and, consistently, on articulating the juridical institutions which had to protect liberty and guarantee it, there dominated the prudent preoccupation of creating inescapable barriers for those elements adverse to liberty. Today we can and ought to be inspired with the same end of liberty, founded on the value of human dignity; but we find that in the world of today liberty is in danger not only from the attacks of those traditionalist elements, but also from certain masses drunk with myths, in rebellion against culture and barbarically proud of the power of numbers, which may tend to realize their will without limitations, without stopping before the sacred boundary of the respect due to the individual person; and it especially suffers a grave threat from the action of fascist barbarism and from Nazi bestiality. And then it will follow that the institutions which we ought to articulate today as the consecration and safeguard of liberty will have to be of such sort that they constitute efficacious means to overcome this new danger. Thus it turns out exactly that the value being the same and also the end founded in it the same, nevertheless, the means must change, that is, the institutions to realize it. So, for example, we might say that the contemporaneous crisis of the State, in the form which this had in the near past, does not affect the values which inspired it — liberty, democracy, common good and social justice — but the institutions which long ago were made for the service of such values. The values go on being worthy; and where there continue to be civilized men who have not become insane, the ends which inspire those values must persist; but, on the other hand, it is possible that the structure of the institutions which are made as a means to realize those values and ends will vary, practically, in an effective manner, and in the circumstance of our time.

In the third place, we must note another source of change and of variety — in short — of historicity. This also refers, like the two preceding, to a source of variety and transmutation with regard to the putting into practice of the same juridical value. It consists of the following: in the modifications which flow from the lessons which practical experience furnishes us with respect to all human tasks and so much the more with respect to juridical ones. It happens that men, orientated by a juridical value, propose to themselves a certain end; and to attain it they conceive certain determined means, certain institutions, which they think will have to accomplish that end. But afterwards, on these being carried into practice, there arise unforeseen factors which make such institutions fail or function imperfectly. In such cases, the end has not varied; but practical experience counsels that other means be sought to realize with greater efficiency the same proposition. The history of Law offers multiple examples of this in the development of almost all juridical institutions.

And yet it must be said that most times the lesson derived from experience, although it does not go so far as to counsel a total or very great change in the means to be employed to attain the same end as was sought by the people of yesterday, always suggests at least some modifications, although they may be only of form, that is, of refinement or of better adjustment by virtue of what has been learned in practice. Man does not realize a second time the same thing in identical form in which he put it in practice the first time; simply because on coming to execute it the second time he has learned something from the original execution. An example of this, among the many which might be cited, is found in the fact of the modifications which one single political ideal suffers through the generations, for instance, through grandfather, father, and son. Let us imagine, or better let us remember, for we have experience of it, how a single political theory experiences modifications in passing through two or three generations: the grandfather as well as the father and the son are sincere and fervent democrats, but each one of them is so in a different manner. The grandfather believes in democracy not only as an exigency of justice, but moreover as a panacea for all ills and as a source productive of all classes of good. The father, who continues to be a democrat, sees in this form of regime the only one with any foundation of legitimacy, the only respectable one, although he knows nevertheless that it does not include in itself necessarily the power to resolve all social problems, and he knows also all the difficulties with which it struggles and the inconveniences which it brings; but he knows at the same time that in spite of them it constitutes the one which entails the least dangers and which guarantees, if not security with full certainty, at least some results of deliberation and equilibrium, so that even in the worst of cases it will represent the least of possible ills. The son continues being a democrat in full sincerity, but besides what he has learned from his father, he has acquired for himself the lesson that it is necessary to articulate the democratic constitutional State with the realization of other valuable exigencies; and also the lesson that for the essential nucleus of democracy to be able vigorously to persist it is desirable to limit the democratic decision to the great fundamental themes, that is, to the orientations about ends, and on the other hand to entrust to the executive power or to technical organs, according to the case, the elaboration of the means to obtain those ends upon which the democratic resolution has decided.

In the fourth place, we find also another source of historicity of juridical programs, and consequently of the concrete valuation or ideals of Law. It consists in the preference found in the ranking of urgency of the social necessities which each moment presents. It is a matter of what may be expressed by the bald assertion that "men cannot realize everything all at the same time," above all, they have to order their different tasks in preferential perspectives, according to the degree of pressure of the needs to which they correspond. This is true the same for the individual life as for the tasks referring to the collectivity. But here it is this last which it is important to emphasize. Men, as members of a collectivity, experience a pressing urgency which incites them to place in the first rank for attention and effort the task by which they can satisfy that necessity. Then the juridical ideal which is projected as most peremptory is the establishment of adequate norms to insure that that necessity should be met by them. When this urgency is resolved, the attention of people, now freed since the prior preoccupation has been remedied, is fixed on new necessities, and in this way the task of remedying them constitutes the theme of the immediate ideal or juridical program. And when it has been accomplished that by means of suitable norms and institutions these new necessities have been solved, then once more is experienced the urgency of attending to other needs, which are those which claim the principal vigilance, since the preoccupations have disappeared which formerly pressed them in the most emphatic manner. It might be expressed metaphorically, that one cannot undertake the ascent to the fifth floor until one has risen to the fourth. It is, in short, what is meant by the phrase that "each hour has its desire." And it is by reason of this desire that the juridical programs are aimed and built for the service of the ideal, in connection with the situation of the moment.

So, for example, there is a historic stage in which men, having attained knowledge of their individuality, having taken intimate possession of their own life, feeling the singular significance of their own life and the calling of special values to be realized in it, feel with the greatest urgency the need of obtaining a juridical guarantee of personal repose, that is, of liberty to be able to develop the designs of their own spirit autonomously. The perception of this necessity aroused in the Middle Ages and above all in the seventeenth and eighteenth centuries the magnificent elaboration of the juridical programs aimed at establishing the fundamental liberties of the human person. So, the jusnaturalistic conceptions of that epoch found themselves directed chiefly toward the consecration of the basic rights of liberty. In close analogy there was produced splendidly in the world of historic events a maturity of the Christian conscience which came to emphasize the values of the highest rank, which are those which are fulfilled in the individual person; and also the magnificent political movements of emancipation, inspired by the guarantee of liberty for the realization of the highest human values, the noble gestures of the English revolution, of the North American, and of the French, and as consequences in the other countries the struggle for the democratic-liberal regime. Now when the recognition has been accomplished that the greatest human value is based on individual dignity and consequently the effective guarantee has been obtained of the basic liberties which dignity requires essentially, then liberty ceases to be a problem. That is, then, it is not liberty which occupies the first rank, simply because it already has it and is assured; and on the other hand other preoccupations begin to appear: that of a greater justice in the distribution of economic goods, that of encouragement of a series of aspects of social prosperity on the part of the State. The good supremely desired above all, liberty, has ceased to constitute the primordial preoccupation, simply because it has conquered already, because already it is established as a reality; and, on the other hand, in the course of life, as new historic facts develop, we see that liberty alone does not suffice; we feel that there are other things needed; and so there arise new preoccupations which are molded into new juridical programs. It is not — as some frivolously and rudely believed — that liberty has lost the value which formerly was attributed to it; it is simply that it has ceased to preoccupy, because it constitutes an accomplished good and then there rise to the first level of care other needs. So it is that liberty has not lost importance, or can ever lose it, since it constitutes the necessary condition that the supreme human values may be realized; that, when the people of a nation who no longer think primordially of liberty because they enjoy it and all its guarantees lose it through a tragic back stroke of history, then all the other desires which were claiming their attention pass down to second place and there is born again as the first preoccupation of all that of recovering the lost individual liberty. We have a very plain and highly marked example of this in the French, Belgians, Dutch, Czechoslovaks, Norwegians, Danes, etc., who enjoyed for a long time the guarantee of the capital human liberties and found themselves dedicated to other desires; but who, on seeing themselves deprived of individual liberty by the work of Nazi bestiality — which deprived them not only of collective autonomy but of something much more important, of the possibility of a human life, reducing them to individual slavery — became preoccupied before all and above all, relegating to second and third places attention to any other task, with recovering personal freedoms and the necessary conditions for its maintenance by the destruction of the satanic monsters of the Third Reich. And not only was that preoccupation in the first place felt with the greatest pressure by the peoples of those nations who for several years were reduced to the most opprobrious servitude, but other nations which did not happen to fall victims to the Nazi savagery felt the seriousness of that great danger which imminently threatened the destruction of all human values; and so the British Commonwealth and the United States of North America laid to one side all the engagements to which they were dedicated, and directed integrally their preoccupations and their efforts to destroying the forces of Nazifascism, as an indispensable condition for the persistence and security of the fundamental human liberties. This purpose having succeeded and, consequently, the guarantees of individual liberty having been reaffirmed and reinforced, other problems occupied the first line of attention. Some of these were already in existence before the bloody drama and many other new ones will arise from the new historic conditions of post-war society; for the most part, they are combined problems of social justice and of economic organization to assure the indispensable means for a more equitable participation of all in their use and enjoyment. So then, it is seen that the problems with which men struggle along their historic development are innumerable. At each moment of their history, tasks are arranged in a special rank of preference as to the pressure to find a solution for them. This happens in all branches of human activities, and consequently also and certainly in a plain manner in the production of Law. Not all tasks are presented with immediate urgency, but many in a successive form. And on the other hand it happens that, although when many times problems are presented urgently, it is not possible to face them all at the same time and therefore it is necessary to establish a perspective of preference as to the order in which to seek a solution for them. Something happens similar to what occurs to the traveler who suddenly contemplates some peaks which he has to scale, but when he has arrived at their summit there become visible to him other peaks, which he had not seen before; and afterwards rivers which he has to ford, of which he had not had any suspicion; and so, successively, there go on being presented new and new landscapes in the course of his journey each one of which plants new problems.

The different rank of preference of each moment is determined by the influence of various factors. Sometimes, a task appears most urgent, principally because it treats of compliance with a value of a range higher than all the others whose compliance has been set in other problems. On other occasions, a task is presented as most urgent not because the value which is meant to be realized by it is of superior rank to other values whose putting into practice has also been set, but it happens that that value, even inferior to the others, claims greater urgency in its accomplishment, because it is basic with respect to those of superior hierarchy; that is, because it is not possible to accomplish the realization of the values of the higher rank if there have not been realized other values of a rank lower but whose accomplishment is a condition precedent to being able to attempt the realization of those others; for example, certain and secure order is a value less high than justice; but justice cannot be embodied in society except on the basis of a guarantee of a certain and secure order. On other occasions, the degree of preference of some tasks over others is determined by reason of a singular social structure effective in a concrete historic situation; that is, the special conditions and circumstances of the collective life at a certain moment provoke peculiar needs, which set a juridical program in which there figures in first rank those norms by whose accomplishment those results can be attained.

In short, the four sources of historicity of Juridical Valuation — such and as I have made them evident — constitute manifestations or consequences of historic reason; and in a special way the second, third, and fourth sources. For the better order of exposition I have numbered these sources of historicity of the juridical ideals; but I warn the reader that it is not a matter of four absolutely separate sources distinct among themselves, but rather of four sources of the fundamental historic structure of human life. That is, the essential historicity of man, and consequently of society, is manifest in many and various ways; and among those copious manifestations of historicity there stand out some forms or some schemes as types. These types, which come in question not only to explain the variety and the transformations of positive Law, but also to understand the justifying basis of the diversity and the changes in juridical ideals, are to my understanding those which I have just presented, or at least those are the principal ones, it being necessary to add another of which I shall speak after some considerations as to historicity.

I have explained already that the essence of the nature of man consists in the fact that man is not nature but is history; because while the other beings of the universe have their being already given or their inexorable trajectory to acquire it, on the other hand, man has to be making his own life each instant, deciding upon it; and man to decide among the various possibilities which circumstance offers him needs to form for himself an interpretation of it. Man, on advancing in knowledge, receives that interpretation, from the historic level of his epoch on that level man will bring his own work of addition or of rectification. Consequently, no man begins his human being, but he receives it initially with the configuration which past historic generations gave it; and on this base of historic reason, that is, on the accumulations of experience of other men, each one is going to add his own experience (which is what constitutes what is called vital reason).[102] Thus man has, so to speak, a double history: the alien which he carries on his back, which is what is properly called historic reason; and his own, his biography, which is what is called vital reason, as Ortega y Gasset has shrewdly indicated, and also Spranger.[103] When we speak here of experience as a combination of historic reason and vital reason, we employ this word experience not in the sense in which science and philosophy use it, not as synonymous with empirics, but in the acceptation which it has in habitual and daily language, to wit: as a vital record of successes and failures in the undertakings of our existence and as an aggregate of lessons drawn from life. Now, on discovering historic reason and vital reason, we lose the old prejudice that reason and history are unconnected and even antagonistic; for it appears that abstract reason is not the whole of reason; it appears that there is a vital and historic reason, which governs and explains the structure of human life as including the past of the others and one's own past, and developing from this level at each instant. When man finds society as prior to him and something which will survive him, he finds in it and with it an aggregate of representations accumulated in prior experiences, on which level he begins to live; and afterwards throughout our life we go on modifying this level with the wealth of our own experiences.

I would wish finally to add that the manner of effective being of man is modified in great measure along the process of history. There are many

[102] As José Ortega y Gasset has indicated.

[103] Cf. Eduard Spranger, Lebensformen (6th ed., 1927).

groups of thoughts, emotions, and tendencies which have been considered as part of human nature and consequently as invariable. But in reality it was a matter only of mental associations experienced at certain moments, under certain circumstances, which afterwards were disassociated, and other types of connections arose. Aldous Huxley (*The End and The Means,* 1937; chap. III) observed in this respect that many mental associations and action

which in their time seemed natural and inevitable have not existed in other places and at other times . . . There exist societies in which almost all the activities are associated with negative emotions, and in which what is socially well looked upon and worthy of praise is felt in a chronically distrusting, envious and malevolent manner. There are others in which it is no less legitimate to feel emotions of a positive character . . .

Each culture is full of fortuitous associations of conduct, thoughts and emotions. These associations may last for long periods, and while they last they are considered necessary, natural, correct, suitable to the nature of things. But there comes a moment at which, under the pressure of changing circumstances, those associations which have been maintained for such a long time, fall into disuse and yield their posts to others, which, in their turn, come to be considered as necessary and as good as the former. Let us look at a few examples. In the richest classes of medieval society and the first part of the Modern Age, there was a very close connection between the thoughts and customs relating to the sexes and the thoughts and customs relating to property and social position. The medieval noble married with a fief. The burgess of the first part of the Modern Age married with a dowry . . . The wife not only represented property but moreover she also was property. The fierce jealousy, which traditionally it was proper and just to feel, was due at least as much to an outrage to the feeling of property as to a sexual passion thwarted. Hurt pride and offended avarice combined with wounded love to produce that class of jealousy which could be satisfied only with the blood of the unfaithful spouse. Meanwhile, the faithful spouse was adorned and bejewelled, sometimes with true affection, but more commonly and principally to satisfy the desire for personal glorification of the husband. The spouse sumptuously clothed was a kind of walking advertisement which proclaimed the wealth and social position of her owner . . . This association . . . is still characteristic of our societies. Nevertheless in other aspects there has been realized an evident disassociation. Spouses are no longer considered private property; consequently it does not seem natural and legitimate to kill the unfaithful one. The idea of absolutely free unions, without relation to dowries or investments is frequent today even among the same rich . . .

The greater part of types of behavior observed in human associations may be disassociated and their elements might return to be associated in another way.

This contingency in the associations and disassociations in ideas and models of conduct and the formation of other new connections, shows in the first place an important aspect of the historicity of human life. It makes clear that what is strictly human in the manner of realization is not given by nature in a constant manner, but that it goes on being made by men in diverse ways and changing along the course of history. I have said in other passages of this book that probably man does always the same things, that is, realizes the same functions, but always in a different manner. The corporal mechanisms are given by nature, and psychological means are also given by nature. The strictly human functions are also constant and essential (knowledge, art, politics, etc.). But the manner in which man manages his physiological apparatus, his psychic dispositions, and the manner in which he realizes with them the functions of his life are different. In these differences and in their reasons we find the manifestation of the essential historicity of human existence.

In the fifth place, I must indicate another source of historicity of the Juridical Valuation. And this fifth source is not derived from problems of realization, nor from questions of efficacy, but it has its root in the varied multiplicity of the values themselves.

Before the philosophy of values arose, Nietsche, through the stormy and faded elements of his great work, referring to the values as something fully understood, said, among many interesting things, that the values are very many, in uncountable number, and that we are very far from knowing them all. Then, the contemporaneous philosophy of values, above all in the work of Max Scheler and in that of Nikolai Hartmann, has made it clear that the aggregate of values is most numerous and that we are not yet in the possibility of having exhausted their exploration. All values are ideal objects with validity in themselves and for themselves. That is, their validity does not depend on the liking which they produce in us, nor the desire that we devote ourselves to them; it does not depend on our subjectivity; it does not depend on experience nor on their foundation nor on their confirmation. They are ideal objective essences — it being understood, I add, as I have explained, they are objective in the immanence of our life, since all *is* in our life and not outside it. But the objectivity of the values is in no way diminished by the dimension which values have of referring in their own essential material to one given situation and not to another. That is, values, in their own essential ideal content, contain a reference to the concrete situations of life, for which they found certain norms. This carries with it that each one of the situations of our life is the supposition for the duty of realizing one certain value and no other. That is, the real presence of a certain situation in a certain person raises one particular norm, derived from the value corresponding to that situation; because in the very material of value there is a reference to the realities for which a norm is originated. And this is so, without any decrease in the objectivity of the values, nor in their validity in themselves and for themselves. For these values which are worthy in themselves and for themselves — that is, whose ideal validity does not depend on me, nor on any experience — give rise to norms which ought to be complied with, not by the generality of all persons at every moment, but perhaps only by some persons in a determined situation and not by others, nor in other circumstances.[104] Remember that I have already explained this doctrine of Scheler in treating of the theme of the human person.

There are ethical and juridical values which found norms of general character for all men and for all societies, respectively. But there are, on the other hand, other values which, having ideal validity, in themselves and for themselves, imply in their own matter or content a particular indication or destiny for one person, for one nation, or for one historic situation. And so only with respect to that person, from that collectivity or from that historic moment (which function as objects of the duties which the value founds), arises the ideal normative connection. Thus, in this sense, it is proper to say that there are moral values which constitute a good in themselves, but a good in themselves which creates a duty of realization only for certain persons and at a certain moment, and not for others or at a different time. In the same way there are social and juridical values which, being objectively such values, refer only to certain situations, and solely with respect to them create the duty of their realization. And this does not affect the dimension of ideal validity of such values, because that indication of object and of substratum in which they are to be fulfilled belongs to their own ideal-objective content.

To obtain full knowledge of the scope which this discovery of the vocational values has for the Juridical Valuation, it will be desirable that we rest our attention for a moment on the consequences which it has brought to moral philosophy. In the light of this discovery of a landscape rich in ethical values — relating to particular situations — there is made evident the penury from which the moral formalism of Kant as well as the juridical formalism of Stammler suffered. If we take the categorical imperative of Kant ("Act in such way that the maxim of your conduct may serve as a universal law for every rational being") and examine it in its consequences, in its practical application, we shall

[104] Cf. Max Scheler, Der Formalismus in der Ethik 55ff.

see that it limits itself to indicating a minimum of conduct, particularly negative: what we ought not to do, the common moral of not killing, of not lying, etc., which include all equally; but it does not offer criteria of positive orientation to give to the life of each one an affirmative mission, a content which shall signify the fulfillment of one's own ethical destiny. From this Kantian moral of the categorical imperative, a mere logical form of generalization of conduct, the various ideal repertories of positive actions, of untransferable duties of each human type, of the different vocations, have escaped; there remains outside the vocational moral, the moral of the particular situations irreducible to all generalization, the moral of the proper destiny or mission which is that which implants more dramatic and important conflicts. Today it has been discovered — or rather we should say rediscovered [105] — that morals is not only a system of prohibitions and of generic duties, the same for all individuals. It is truly this, but it is also something more: it is also an immense repertory of values, which, having validity in themselves, do not all of them refer with the pretension of fulfillment to all individuals, but in each case and for each person, some or others enter upon an actualization of the *ought-to-be*. There is of course a common, generic morals, which includes all as equal, and which constitutes the indispensable minimum for all, that without which no one can be a moral being. But with those generic values, which determine the common forms of conduct, there is no criterion of orientation as to what each one ought positively to realize in his own life. There is, then, a generic morals which is the common denominator for all; but upon it there is afterwards a series of vocational morals and of concrete and individual situations which, far from contradicting or diminishing that general one, have complemented it: the morals of the ages, of each sex, of temperaments, of vocations, of situations, etc. There is the morals of the man and that of the woman; the morals of the child, of the adult, and of the old person; there is the morals of power (which affects the governor, the industrialist, etc.), the morals of Law (which is actualized in the judge and in the citizen), the morals of love (which above all the priest expresses); there is the morals of work, the morals of modesty and of temperance; there is the active morals (of the politician, of the man of affairs) and the contemplative morals (of the intellectual); the morals of struggle (which, for example, obliges the policeman), and the morals of compassion (which the sister of charity professes); there is the morals of blind submission (proper for the soldier) and the morals of the discovery of new values (which inspires the revolutionary), etc. The

[105] Cf. JOSÉ ORTEGA Y GASSET, EL ESPECTADOR IV, 189–204 (1925); MEDITACIONES DEL QUIJOTE (1914) 24–28; NIKOLAI HARTMANN, ETHIK (1926) 33–38.

actualization of the duties of each one of these complementary morals is conditioned by the particular situations, by the character, and by the vocation of each one. And this does not imply in any way either relativity or anarchy, because each one of these complementary morals (complementary to the general human one) is not founded either on caprice or on contingencies, but is founded on values in itself; but on values in itself whose structure carries a sort of indicating arrow for the concrete situation and the object of the corresponding duties.

In the same way as there are individual vocations — which are the result of the articulation of a concrete person with a contour also concrete — there are also vocations for collectivities. To the multiplicity and diversity of historic and national types there corresponds a series of congruent juridical values, to be realized for each one of them. Each situation of a historic process represents the possibility of knowledge and the duty of realization of tasks and missions founded on single values, whose juncture is not transferable and perhaps will not be repeated. There are, then, collective and historic vocations which may be diverse with regard to the different peoples and the various epochs, just as there are individual vocations. And, as from the moral point of view we could say that each individual has the duty of being authentic, of being faithful to himself, to his vocation, to the task which destiny has presented to him, in the same manner we could say that to each historic epoch and to each people there belongs the fulfillment of particular destinies.

And in this respect we may introduce a doctrine of José Ortega y Gasset, to wit, *perspectivism,* which if indeed it was elaborated fundamentally concerning the theory of knowledge, may have important resonances for our theme. Modern thought since Descartes has emphasized the dependency which knowledge has upon the person — which is an undeniable truth — but many times it seeks to interpret this dependence as a deformation or as a creation. Ortega overcomes relativistic subjectivism — without falling into the clumsinesses of the old realism — by showing how the dependency in which things are upon the persons who contemplate them, does not signify pure anarchy or relativism. The person is not a transparent medium which reflects reality, but which imposes on it its own mode of being; but this configuration of reality on the part of the person does not imply in any manner a deformation or falsification of it. When we interpose in the current of a river a net for fishing or screening, this selects some of the elements which the current brings with it. This is the function which each man and each epoch performs with reality and with the values which surround it. Of the infinity of elements which make up reality, the person takes a certain number of them, whose form and content coincide with the mesh of his interests and preferences. Each consciousness apprehends reality from a point of view which is peculiar to it. When various men contemplate the same landscape from different points of view, it forms itself before their eyes in a different manner; but this does not mean that such different visions are false or illusory: each one of them corresponds to a perspective and is legitimate. All life is a point of view, a perspective upon the universe. The false would be that each perspective should pretend to be the only true one. Then, resting on this doctrine, it may be said that, like each individual, also each collectivity has its determined place in the historic series; and that it ought not to aspire to come out of it, because this would be equivalent to converting itself into an abstract being with integral renunciation of its existence. Each life is a point of view upon the world. In truth, whatever it sees and what it does, no other can see or do exactly the same. Each individual — person, people, epoch — is an irreplaceable organ for the conquest of truth, of the good, of justice, of beauty. And so, the values which as ideas are foreign to historic variations acquire a vital dimension, integrating it in the current of history as to the actualization of their fulfillment.[106]

Now, the proof that there are these multiple values, whose duty of fulfillment is being put into the historic series, does not contradict nor ought it to make us forget that there are general juridical values which give rise to ideal norms, which govern for all collectivities, for all moments, and for all situations. And these values must have in every case a necessary preference of prior realization over all the others. For example, the norms which are derived from the idea of human dignity: the norms of liberty of conscience, of the autonomy of the person to comply with his own moral destiny — which determine a maximum respect for the individual person — must have necessarily and inescapably a preferential realization. And there can be no single historic destiny, nor national convenience, nor concrete vocation, which can put itself before the fulfillment of those norms. This is because all particularities and all concrete missions occur in human lives, and, consequently, can have meaning and justification only on the basis of respecting what is ethically essential to man, to wit, his dignity, and the correlative norms of liberty which flow from it. With the norms founded on these supreme juridical values, no pretension based on concrete situations, no appeal to national destinies, no pretext founded on the sacrifice of today's generation to obtain a greater benefit tomorrow, can interfere disturbingly. All the concrete values, conjoined with special historic situations, are inferior in rank to the values which the ethical dignity of man founds,

[106] Cf. José Ortega y Gasset, El tema de nuestro tiempo.

and therefore inferior to the norms of individual liberty which are derived from these latter. The realization of the concrete situational values, started by the particularity of each historic time, can be legitimate only on the basis of the fundamental generic values having been previously complied with: the values which refer to all Law. It is for example altogether inadmissible that one should deny the intimate liberty and the autodetermination of the life of each one on the pretext of forming a great, powerful, and strong nation, because a nation made up of slaves or of dehumanized men is something to be despised. It is also inadmissible, for example, that one should deny the supreme juridical values to the people of today on the pretext that those born tomorrow may find a better world. Individual sacrifice, spontaneous and free, in this sense would be a matter of sublime heroism; but to attempt to impose it coercitively on a collectivity is monstrous and abominable. The life of each man is something untransferable and his own, as to which each one ought to have the same right to decide; and never, never, ought man to be taken as mere material for a future social construction, in which he is not going to participate.

Now, those juridical values which give rise to general norms of necessary ideal control in all orders — and whose realization is due in every case, and is prior to and more important than any other task — do not constitute a sufficient criterion to orient estimatively all the institutions of Law. For example, the supreme ideal norms of human dignity and of individual autodetermination are not sufficient to know how we ought to orient a sanitary legislation, or a banking regulation, or an undertaking of farm colonization, or a regulation of the University, etc., because each one of those themes raises the need of attending to concrete values and finalities — of an intellectual, technical, economic character — which come in question to orient those tasks. Nor are the general and supreme juridical values sufficient to clarify the preferential mission which a people ought to realize at a given moment, and which is derived from the special historic occasion in which it is placed.

Then, without detriment to the general juridical values — of preferential and primordial realization — the concrete situation of each people, the special conditions of its life, the exigencies of the historic moment in which it finds itself, the urgencies and opportunities of it, raise the duty of realizing some certain particular values and not others.

What has been said brings us to the necessity of emphasizing the fact that the historic collectivities are realities which have their own actual laws — sociological — which the legislator ought to take into account. The legislator ought to orient his task with regard to ideal values; but his task will have to be realized in and with certain concrete social materials, that is, in and with certain determined men, who possess special characteristics — biological, psychological, cultural characteristics — who have certain needs and certain aptitudes; who live in social groups specially constituted. All these realities constitute actual magnitudes with their own laws, which cannot be entirely amenable to the proposals of the legislator, which are not easily moldable by him. Consequently, the special context of social reality and its dynamic laws have to be taken into consideration by the legislator, and, in short, by all who pretend to formulate juridical programs. For otherwise, one would incur the imminent danger that the work of the legislator would either be reduced to a dead letter, or would produce a catastrophe on colliding with a reality which would resist it with its intimate texture. But, moreover, it must be taken into account that this concrete social reality is something alive and not an aggregate of inert materials. Therefore the legislator — and, in short, the proposer of juridical reforms — ought to proceed not in a way analogous to that in which the architect or engineer works, but in a way similar to that of the doctor or hygienist. The engineer or the architect manipulate inert materials, and with them, so long as they take into consideration their physicochemical laws, they may cut, combine, and construct at their free will. On the other hand, the doctor and the hygienist work with living bodies, which cannot be molded like clay or cut like stone at their free will, but the most that they can do is to act upon these bodies so that in biology they shall produce the reactions which they desire. The labor of the legislator — and in general that of the politician — must assimilate itself more to that of the doctor and hygienist than to that of the architect, because they also work upon something living, with the men who compose a society, which has also its own laws of dynamics; and, consequently, in place of pretending to construct a finished work with trim outlines, it has to act upon the collective reality in that form which facilitates production of the reactions which lead to the proposed results.

8. The Idea of Justice and the Juridical Valuation

It has been traditional to see in justice the principal juridical value par excellence, up to the point that, most times, the problem of the Juridical Valuation has been labeled as an investigation as to justice. And, although we are not going to rectify this presidential role which belongs to justice in the Juridical Valuation, yet we shall see how an attentive examination of it will bring us to the consideration of a series of concrete values, which are necessarily implied by the idea of justice, although they are not contained in it.

If we review the history of human thought in all its periods, with respect to the theme of justice, we shall notice a great paradox. On one side we shall take account, astonished, of the fact that this theme has preserved a basic identity through all the schools: perhaps in all the history of scientific and philosophic thought there is no other theme in which such essential unanimity has been preserved. But, on the other hand, history offers, as to the problems of the practical application of the idea of justice, the most ardent theoretical controversies and the bloodiest political strifes. This contrast, in truth confusing, makes us suspect, even for the moment, that the grave problems of Juridical Valuation are not rooted in the idea of justice — in which theme it seems that a fundamental coincidence rules — but in something which is beyond this theme, although related to it. To wit, the difficulty, as will be seen, lies not in the idea of justice, but in a series of suppositions, of references, and of implications which it sets up in us. And here is where the discrepancy and the discussion commence and develop.

From the Pythagoreans, in the stage of pre-Socratic philosophy, to our day, the idea of justice has been similarly defined. The same in a restricted sense — with especial reference to the Law — as in a broad acceptation, justice has been almost always understood as a harmony, as a proportional equality, as a harmonious means of exchange and distribution. The Pythagoreans conceived it as a correspondence or proportional equality between opposing terms, which could be expressed in square numbers. For Plato, it is the fundamental virtue from which are derived all the others; and it consists in a harmony between the constituting elements of the State, by which each one of them (the governors, the military, and the artisans) ought to do what is proper for him, dedicate himself to what corresponds to him. Aristotle understands justice, in the widest acceptation, as a proportionality of acts (in just measure between excess and defect), which is the principle of all virtue; also in a general sense, but applied to the life of the State, justice is the supreme virtue, that is, the civic virtue, the sum and compendium of the other virtues so far as they relate to the community and to the persons who compose it; and, in a strict sense, it consists in a proportionality in the distribution of honors, goods, and duties, and in an equivalence in exchange (between performance and counterperformance and between transgression and punishment). In Rome, Ulpian defines it as the attributing to each one his right, giving him what belongs to him, his value; Cicero gathers similar concepts. St. Thomas Aquinas says that "it is fit for justice to order man in his relation with others, since that implies a certain equality, as its very name shows, since it says that it adjusts things which are equal and equality is with something else": and afterwards he adds that justice turns on external actions and things, in conformity with the true special reason of the object: it consists in giving or attributing to each one what is his, according to a proportional equality; understanding by his in relation to others, all that which is subordinated or attributed to his ends. And Francisco de Vitoria, commenting on this Thomist doctrine, affirms that he calls the equal just, and so he says it is already just, it becomes just, or it is adjusted, in becoming equal. And Domingo de Soto says that justice makes an equality between him who owes and the other to whom he owes; and consists in putting a mean between things, by which there is produced equality between men. Grotius also defines it as equivalence or proportionality in exchanges and in distribution; and in an analogous manner Pufendorf explains it. And similarly Vico, who also distinguishes between commutative (*aequatrix*) and distributive (*rectrix*) justice: the former is an arithmetic equality between equal terms and the latter establishes a geometric proportion between unequal terms, for the attribution of dignities and functions. Wolf explains justice as a principle of arithmetic equality. In Kant, the idea of equality is projected upon liberty, as equality in liberty: "Liberty (independence from the imposition of another's will) so far as it can coexist with the liberty of each one, according to a general law"; equality consists, then, in not being bound by another except as to that in which one is bound reciprocally. Fichte postulates the full equality of all the members of society in the State, an equality which must be produced and maintained by it. Fries considers equality as the first principle of justice. Lasson sees the essence of justice in the form of universality and in the absence of contradictions, by means of which reason reduces to harmony and unity all differences and oppositions. For Stammler — as we have already seen — justice consists of the formal idea of an absolute harmony, according to which juridical material ought to be ordered. According to Del Vecchio, justice demands that every person be recognized by the others for what he is worth and that to each one should be attributed what belongs to him.[107]

[107] Following, I give the principal references to the citations made: ARISTOTLE, ETICA A NICOMACO, Book V; CICERO, DE OFFICIIS, L. 1, C. 5, para. 15; L. 1, C. 14, para. 42; DE INVENTIONE RETH., L. II, C. 53; ST. THOMAS, SUMMA THEOLOGICA, S. S. 57, 8; S. S. 58, arts. 2, 8, and 11; FRANCISCO DE VITORIA, DE JUSTITIA, commentary on Q. 57, art. 1; DOMINGO DE SOTO, DE IUSTITIA ET IURE, Book III, Q. 1, art. 1; Q. 2, art. 7; GROTIUS, DE IURE BELLI AC PACIS, L. I, chap. 1, paras. 3 and 8; L. II, chap. XVII, para. 2; PUFENDORF, DE IURE NATURAE, ET GENTIUM, L. VIII, chap. 3, para. 5 and chap. 7, para. 10; VICO, DE UNO UNIVERSI IURIS PRINCIPIO, paras. 40–42. Cf. DEL VECCHIO, LA JUSTICIA (Spanish translation published by Edit. Góngora, 1925; EDUARDO GARCIA MAYNEZ, EL DERECHO NATURAL EN LA ÉPOCA DE SÓCRATES (México, 1939).

The coincidence of the thought upon justice is really impressive through the twenty-five centuries of the history of Philosophy. It is clear that each one of these definitions, in spite of their basic similarity, has in each of the respective systems a special extent and peculiar consequences. But, in spite of such differences of shade, all these thoughts upon justice agree in affirming that it bears in its bosom in some way an equality, a proportionality, a harmony.

Now, if it is true, as we have seen, that there is a coincidence among almost all thinkers in the definition of justice, it is paradoxical that there should be such diverse systems of Juridical Valuation — in theory — and that history should go on presenting the most passionate and even bloody strifes upon this theme. But precisely in putting this contrast between the identity of the conceptions of justice on one side, and the varieties and antagonisms in the matter of juridical ideals, on the other, we take account of the fact that the greatest difficulty which Juridical Valuation offers is not based on what may be the idea of justice, but it has to be in some other place. All the differences in the material of Juridical Valuation, all the conflicts as to the Law which ought to be, all the political strifes, arise — in spite of their agreement on the definition of justice — because the mere idea of equality and proportionality does not submit to us any criterion of measurement, that is, it does not give us the principle by which to appraise and further this proportional or harmonious equality: it does not show us what is the point of view from which one ought to consider the equalization. And according to what may be the criteria of measurement or appraisal, so will be correspondingly the conceptions of the juridical ideal or of the program of just Law. Truly, this equality is a pure formal idea, which postulates or supposes the use of criteria of measurement, according to which the equality may be determined. It is not sufficient to say equality; one has to ask: equality in what? equality from what point of view and how? So, then, the main problem which justice sets does not consist in discovering the formal outline of its idea, but in learning the means of judgment which it supposes or implies. And these criteria of measurement, these points of view of judgment to determine proportional equality, transcend the idea of justice. And this, which is so obvious and so clear, has gone unnoticed by almost all those who philosophize upon the Law. On this account I believe that, when I now indicate the root of the problem, I offer therewith the possibility that Juridical Valuation may take an appreciable advance in the future.

To gauge better the extent of what I say, it is to be noted that the concepts "equality," "proportionality," and "harmony" are not used as an expression of something which may be, as enunciative of real relations, but as normative criteria, as a guide for a task to be done. It is a matter of furthering an equality or proportionality among men; and not among men abstractly considered, but among concrete men, inserted in the most complicated mesentery of their social relations and activities. And for these relations there come into question all the preceding diversities not only of the concrete differences between individuals, but also of the different situations in which they are found. And it is a matter, as I have said, not of enunciating a situation of equality existing in reality from any point of view, but of furthering that equality in the task of the organization of social relations, from the normative point of view of certain values. It is a matter of something which is considered as *ought to become,* of something which ought to be done. In this sense, it presents itself as a task of proportional equalization, of equalizing the terms of social relations. These terms are now unequal; and it is precisely on this account that it is demanded that they should be equalized, that in some respect they should be made equivalent, bound proportionally, harmoniously.

An example will make clear the thought which I am explaining. Let us imagine a simple relation of exchange, which was precisely what the first thinkers who reflected upon justice had in mind. The Pythagoreans, the same as Aristotle — and many others — said that justice demands that in a bilateral contract of exchange one should receive from the other as much as he delivers to him. But note that this equality between what one gives and what one receives cannot be a full identity. That is, if we take this equality as identity, it would suppose that whoever gives a pound of wheat ought to receive another pound of wheat; that whoever gives to another the service of skinning an ox should receive from him the same service. Now it is evident that such a thing has no meaning; for its lack of all motive and purpose dissolves the meaning of the relation. Consequently, it is not a matter of receiving the same, the identical, but something different, which in some way corresponds to what is delivered, which will compensate it from some point of view. That is, it is a matter of receiving not the same but something *equivalent,* something which, being different, is worth in some respect the same, precisely in the respect which ought to come into question. The better to measure the value of a thing in relation to something different, a unit of measurement is necessary, that is, there is necessary a criterion in whose light there may be homogenized the appraisal of two heterogenous things. And then, equality will consist in these two things or these two services which are exchanged embodying, in spite of their diversity, a similar magnitude of value, that is, that they should be equivalent. So, then, this analysis shows that the center of gravity of the question is removed from justice — as an idea of equality — to a problem upon the criterion of valuation. What matters is to know what ought to be the criterion for establishing the equivalence; that is, to know what measure we shall have to use to measure the equality. There will perhaps be proposed, as a solution of the example given, the measure of economic value. Let us admit provisionally this reply, although with some reservations. With some reservations, because the concept of economic value is not univocal in the science of economics: moreover, because it is not a question here of a mere economic relation, but this presents itself to us as something which ought to be submitted to a norm of juridical valuation. And so it will probably occur that — except in a physiocratic conception — the economic value will not come determined solely by the free play of mere economic factors, but also by criteria of ethical, political, etc., valuation. On the other hand, many reservations also are imposed, if we reflect that the expression "economic value," far from constituting a clear concept, enunciates a multitude of grave problems. Consequently, the science of economics has discussed as to the determining criterion of economic value: if it is objective utility, if it is simple subjective utility; if it is accumulated labor, or rather the labor which would be required to produce another equal object, etc.; if in the labor there has to be evaluated only a temporal quantity, or rather in addition, its quality.

Let us pass in review, very succinctly, some of these problems, not to resolve them here, but only that the reader may take account of the complexity of them. And it is to be noted that this complexity occurs in reference to the simplest problem which we could select; and that, consequently, such complexity would be much greater in contemplating juridical relations richer in their elements. The criterion of utility, as a supposed basis for economic value, involves multiple problems. Utility value has a double relational structure. Although the values have a validity in themselves, there are those which in their very ideal contexture possess a relational dimension. Therefore, the utility value contains a validity in itself, but instrumental, that is, *for something*. And still there is in it a second structure or rational direction: they are of value for something, but also for *some one,* that is, with reference to such or such person. We think of any useful object: in it there is the qualification of utility, because it coincides with the ideal structure of that Value; but that utility — by the same essence of value — is a utility for something; and it has value with entire independence of whether or not I feel a desire for that something — an overcoat is a useful thing, although in a warm country one does not need it. But the utility value, besides the objective relationability which consists in *serving for something*, has also a second essential relationability, to wit, with a person, with the person who has need of that something: it serves for something, but moreover, *for some one*. Now, it happens that economically a thing is worth so much the more, the more urgent or intense is the necessity. But in the field of economic valuation there arise other problems, because of new factors appearing in play; so, for example, a thing objectively useful for something and subjectively for someone will not have economic price (on the exchange) if it occurs in great abundance, as does water at the banks of a river. However, it happens that the points of view of utility with all their complications do not seem to turn out to be sufficient for the determination of the economic value; for from old times the economists noted that in the face of this criterion or in interference with it, there is an evaluation according to the volume of labor involved in the thing. But then arise the questions: from what point of view ought the volume of labor to be measured? With regard to the labor actually accumulated in the production of this article or with regard to the labor which would be necessary to reproduce it? But there are also other questions: is it necessary to attend only to the temporal quantity of the labor, or ought there also to be made differences as to the quality or rank of the labor? And, in this last case, what should be the guide to establish the diverse ranks of labor? These problems would have to be resolved by considerations founded on the philosophy of values, so far as this studies the relations of hierarchy between them and moreover their methods of being related to the persons in their real concrete situations. But moreover, still other complications arise, which have reference to other criteria. So, for example, there come into question also biological values (health) and ethical values. Easy and healthy labor will not have the same economic value — in a bilateral contract — as unhealthy labor. In that case, the measure to establish the equality which justice imposes between performance and counterperformance (wages) ought not to be the quantitative magnitude of labor (we leave aside rank in this example, referring to similar manual labors). Here it is necessary to take into account other valuing criteria: the value of human health and the ethical value of the person which is the subject of that organic vitality. Why do we take health into consideration? Because health represents a biological good in some beings which have a moral dignity. Thus, something similar may be said with respect to all the considerations which the problem of just wages raises (considering the moral personality of the workman, his material and spiritual necessities, his family duties, etc.). Notice, then, how a juridical relation of exchange, in appearance so simple and lowly, gives rise to most complicated swarms of heterogenous valuations.

There has been revealed to us how in the terms, between which one tries to establish a just equivalence, there are inserted thick and complicated bunches of valuations, each one of them founded on distinct values of unequal rank. The equality which justice demands would consist in that, the diverse valuations which affect one of the terms of the relation being calculated in due combination, there should result in the other term a like total magnitude of valuation. There would have to be developed something which metaphorically we could call an algebra of valuations, thanks to which we could obtain true criteria of measurement, to arrive at an appreciation of the sum of valuations in combination, to embody in each one of the terms of the relation. And I say the sum in combination, because it may happen that the valuation founded on a superior value may annul the consequences of other valuations based on inferior values.

It has been made manifest, then, that the important thing in Juridical Valuation does not consist of discovering that justice demands an equality or proportionality, but in finding what may be the criteria of value which ought to be taken into account to further the equivalence or harmony between the terms of a juridical relationship. In such manner, the idea of justice opens to us the door to a philosophic landscape much deeper, richer, and more complicated, to wit: the field of juridical valuation. It is not sufficient to know that the terms of a relationship ought to be equalized or harmonized; the fundamental and more important thing consists in finding the criteria of value which ought to be taken into account to establish normatively that equivalence or proportionality.

It is true that justice is also a value. But its own content consists of a formal criterion which determines what to give and what to take, to give and to receive, in juridical business, in keeping faithfully the structures of rank which there are objectively among the values which come into question for the Law. Or, put otherwise: justice demands that the realization of the social values — which may be the content of juridical norms — shall keep the harmonious proportion which the objective relations of rank require between them and the result of their interferences. A juridical relation implies a situation sharing a multitude of values, which have to do with Law; and justice demands that the juridical norm should govern this situation in such way that among the concretizations of values embodied in each one of the terms of the relation there should be that proportionality which exists objectively between those values. It is not sufficient, then, to possess knowledge of the idea of justice: it is necessary in addition, to know the values created by it in the juridical field.

Arrived at this point, the first task which offers itself for Juridical Valuation — and which will have to be done in the near future[108] — is that of determining what are the values which matter for the Law and of discarding those others which do not come into question for it. Because, as we shall see, it happens that not all values determine an *ought to be* for the Law. So, for example, the religious values, the purely and strictly moral ones, the aesthetic ones, will be irrelevant for Juridical Valuation; since in a juridical relation there ought not to be concerned nor come into question the health of a person, nor whether the debtor on paying his debt does it with purity of intention and good will — thereby complying with the duty imposed by a moral value — etc. But, on the other hand, there is a series of values of a different sort which found an ought to be for the Law, for example, the ethical dimension of personality, liberty, security, social peace, solidarity, common utility in its multiple forms (culture, economic prosperity, health, etc.). These values — and many others — constitute ideal normative points of view for the Law.

This will be seen still more clearly if one refers to an example of the relations traditionally called distributive justice. An examination of those relations will bring one to the same conclusion as did the study of the relations called commutative justice (that is, of what ought to be given in exchanges). That version of justice has been called distributive justice which is concerned with the division of functions, benefits, and public offices, and, in general, with organizing the structure of the State. As to distributive justice Aristotle says[109] that it demands that in the divisions equal persons should receive equal portions and unequal, unequal portions, according to their respective dignity and merit. Therefore, distributive justice implies at least four members in relation; and is expressed in a geometric proportion. The proportion is the equality between the ratios: $a : b = c : d$. Miguel Efesio, the commentator on Aristotle, glosses this theory with the following example: If we consider Achilles twice as meritorious as Ajax and give to the former six pieces, we ought to give three to the latter, which can be expressed in the following proportion: Achilles who is worth 8 is to Ajax who is worth 4, as 6 pieces for Achilles are to 3 pieces for Ajax. The relation between what is given to Achilles and what is given to Ajax is the same as between

[108] Up to now, I have traced the program which I understand the Theory of Juridical Valuation ought to develop, and I have indicated the directions for it. There remains to be brought to completion this theoretical undertaking, whose realization I hope may be fruitful.

[109] ETICA A NICOMACO, Book V, chap. 6.

the merits of the one and the other, to wit, double. This is very simple, perfectly comprehensible, and is beyond all discussion. But the important problem is not based here, but in knowing the point of view to appreciate the diverse merits of the persons. In short, the important thing is to know the criterion for juridical valuation. What will be the basis for measuring the value of each person, for the purpose of the distribution of advantages and public offices? In what does the rule consist for measuring what determines the difference in value between Achilles and Ajax? Is it because Achilles may be more corpulent and weighs double what Ajax weighs? It is clear that this hypothesis appears grotesque to us and we discard it; as we discard also the idea that the criteria could be physical vigor, stature, or anything else similar. Shall it be physical beauty? It seems that this supposition also is inadmissible. Let us pass to examine other points of view very distant from those which we have flatly rejected. If the mentioned criteria do not come into question, shall we have to attend to the supreme values, for example, to health? Will it be because Achilles is twice as healthy as Ajax? No: it turns out that health, a supreme value, is entirely irrelevant for the Law. Will it consist in a pure moral value, as for example purity of intention? It seems that this value does not affect the greater part of juridical relations. But, on the other hand, we cannot say that all the ethical values are irrelevant for the Law, for many of them create an ought to be for the juridical norms, such as those which found the moral dignity of man, his liberty, equality in relations, etc. For certain functions we must take into account other qualities, such as honesty, industriousness, intellectual capacity, services rendered, and perhaps include physical vigor (as for example occurs in providing candidates for policemen). Which are the criteria which may come into question and which may not? In what case shall we apply some and in what case others?

Consequently, the first theme which Juridical Valuation will have to resolve, in its future development, is that of knowing what are the values which can and ought to come into question for the juridical order, and in what case some ought to be determinative or others. It seems that there will intervene ethical values (those which found the principles of dignity, of liberty, of equality); that on some occasions there ought moreover to be taken into account also other ethical values; that on other occasions there will have to be considered the points of view founded on intellectual, technical, economic, utilitarian, aesthetic, values, when for example it is a matter of the State promoting education, health, economic prosperity, etc. But it ought to be determined from what point of view, and how and in what manner, such values could be taken as criteria inspired by the juridical norms. There will have to be determined, moreover, the laws of the hierarchy between the different kinds of values, for their combination and interference in juridical regulation: when some ought to prevail and when others, and how to articulate them among themselves.

It is, then, not a mistake to define justice as harmony; but it ought to be understood that that harmony, which is sought for juridical regulation, must be based on the objective and authentic harmony which the values which can come into question for the Law keep among themselves. It is a matter of realizing not this or that value, in an isolated manner, but in articulation with the rest, which give place to a juridical ought to be, so that in the juridical order there is reflected a silhouette analogous to the structure which the orienting values of the Law keep.

Something analogous may be said with respect to the attempts to define justice as an attribution to each one of what is his; for the only thing which this does is to leap into another problem still deeper, to wit, the question as to the criteria to determine what ought to be considered his for each one. And this fixation of the his for each one must be determined by the participation of the juridical situations in the complexes of values which have orienting dimensions for the Law.

With what has been explained, I have justified the necessity of elaborating a Juridical Valuation, inspired by the doctrine of values. Its principal tasks would be: in the first place to determine the supreme values which in every case ought to inspire the Law, the values which give rise to ideal norms of a general character, applicable to every case and situation. In the second place, to find what other values may and ought to govern the elaboration of the Law, in what cases, under what conditions, and in what relation with the first. In the third place, to inquire as to the laws of the relation, combination, and interference of the valuations which converge in each one of the types of social situations. In the fourth place, to study the laws of realization of the juridical values; and, moreover, a series of questions joined with or adjacent to those mentioned. This is the program which I outline for the future tasks of Juridical Valuation. I think that I have accomplished something with having attained a clarity of ideas upon this theme, which until now has been unknown.

One of the themes which constitute the fundamental or essential root of all juridical valuation is the value of the human person for the Law. Let us examine it.

9. The Valuation of the Human Person for the Law

It is a matter of knowing what ought to be the supreme ideal orienting principle of the Law (and, consequently, the supreme end of the

State). It is a matter, in short, of knowing whether the Law, neither more nor less than all the other tasks and things which man meets and develops in his life, has meaning and justification only in the measure in which it represents a means of complying with the values which may be realized in the individual person — which is the only genuine thing which exists. Or if, on the contrary, the Law (and the State) should be an end in itself, independently of the real individual men of flesh and blood (and each with his own and exclusive soul), who would so function singly as mere means or instruments for the realization of that transpersonal end, which would be embodied in the State. Or, put otherwise, it is a matter of knowing: whether the Law and the State are for man, or whether, on the contrary, man is for the Law and the State. It is a matter of deciding between these two antithetic and irreconcilable positions which I have just sketched, and which have been called respectively personalism and transpersonalism. And this question inserts itself in another of greater volume and extent: that of the valuation of culture and society in relation to man (it is understood, with the only man whom we know, which is the individual man). According to *personalism* (which I would prefer to call *humanism*), culture and the collectivity ought to converge upon man and take him as substratum, since only so do they have meaning and are they justified; they ought to be converted into conditions or means to elevate man in his values. According to *transpersonalism* or *totalism*, on the contrary, man would be a mere instrument to produce works of culture with an objective substratum — science, art, technique, etc. — or for the aggrandizement or power of the collectivity; man would be degraded to a pure mass of dough at the service of some supposed objective functions to be realized in power, in state glory, in the race, in culture, that is, in transpersonal magnitudes.

In fine, this is the theme upon the rank or hierarchy of values which man ought to realize in his life. One tries to ascertain what may be for human life the hierarchy between the different values, in relation to the substrata in which they are embodied. That is, one tries to know if in human life the supreme values are those which can be embodied only in the spiritual person, so that all the others are subordinate to them; or if, on the contrary, those values are superior in rank which are shaped in the objective works of human activity, so that the values which dwell only in the individual ethical person are subordinate to them, as means or instruments. If it is understood that the authentic substratum of values is man, that culture is based on him and is for him, then the values realized in the individual, as such, will be supreme; and all the other values, as to their realization, will remain at the service of the individual, because this is the seat in which can be embodied those of supreme rank. And in this way all the works of culture (Science and Art, Law and State, Fatherland and Society, Technique and Economics, etc.) will represent goods inferior in rank to those which are shaped in the individual consciousness, and will have meaning only as means or instruments put at the service of man. But if on the contrary it should be understood that the substratum of realization of the superior values is not the individual consciousness, but is an objective transpersonal work, then man would represent a mere means or instrument for producing such valuable objects (works of culture, powerful States, etc.); so that according to this transpersonal position it might be said, for example, that the Roman Coliseum is well paid for with the misery and punishments of thousands of slaves; and that the sacrifice of the soldier would be merely the price which the State pays for the benefits which he brings it.

According to *personalism* or *humanism,* the State (and consequently the Law) — the same as science, technique, art, etc. — will have meaning as a means put at the service of human personality (of the individual human personalities, which are the only authentic ones), as an instrument for the realization of its ends, as a food for the spirit of men (individuals), in order that in it they may embody the values for which they are destined. This may be expressed, paraphrasing some Biblical words relating to the Sabbath: "the State was made for the sake of man" and not vice versa. It is not that the personalist thesis denies that in culture, in the Law, and the collectivity are embodied very important values; but it maintains simply that those values which take shape in culture and the State, although of considerable elevation, are inferior to those values which are realized in the individual consciousness.

On the contrary, *transpersonalism* affirms that in man are embodied values only as he is part of the State or a vehicle for the objective products of culture; that is, that the individual man, as such, lacks any dignity of his own, and only comes in question as to value when he serves as the effective means for some transpersonal ends of the State (glory, power, conquest, etc.) or for objective works of culture. Transpersonalism may adopt two forms, according as it places on the pinnacle of the hierarchy those values which are embodied in the objective works of culture (cultural form, according to which not only the individual person but also society remain subordinated to those values); or enthrones as supreme those values which reside in the State (political transpersonalism).[110]

It will be necessary to insist still somewhat more on the characterization of each one of these two antithetic and irreconcilable positions.

[110] Cf. RADBRUCH, GRUNDZÜGE DER RECHTSPHILOSOPHIE (1914, 2d ed., 1932).

For political transpersonalism, which considers as supreme those values which are realized in the collectivity, it turns out that the individual appears as a mere ephemeral product of little or no importance. Numberless individuals come to fill the ranks of the collectivity and then disappear from it; and they are in it only as supports or agents of a supposed superior life of the "totality"; so that, from the point of view of values, the individual does not come into question, for he is considered solely as material for the superior collective formations. According to the transpersonalist theory, only the ends of the collectivity and its process would have importance; and the individual would acquire value only in the measure in which he should serve this process and the ends of the "totality." It is even said, for the transpersonal conception, that the collectivity ought to tolerate only those individuals whose conduct is adjusted totally to its ends, and ought to destroy the dissidents and the unserviceable (which for example is what the totalitarian States do — fascism, national-socialism). This inhuman conception has tried sometimes to seek support in an old metaphysical or rather mystical theory, according to which the division of humanity into individual beings would be something secondary, and individualization would represent an imperfect state, so that the superior destiny of man would consist in returning to the common substance, by his entire consecration to the totality.

Against this transpersonalist conception, suitable for primitive times — and sprouting again in the processes of disindividualization of the totalitarian States (in Italy, in Germany, etc.), there has been opposed the mature consciousness of the individual, founding it on this simple and evident consideration: how can the individual be consecrated to ends which are not his? In order that the ends of the collectivity should have legitimate meaning for the individual, it would be necessary at least that they be also at the same time his ends. Only the individual is capable of proposing ends to himself and of acting to realize them, because he alone has consciousness. The collectivity ought to respect the ends of the individual; and it ought to be formed in such a way that it would be a medium for these individual ends. The individual with his ends ought to be affirmed in the collectivity; but, on the contrary, he cannot affirm the collectivity. The collectivity exists for the reason and motive of the individuals; it cannot and ought not to be anything more than the *modus vivendi* of the individuals. The collectivity is something which indispensably needs the individual for its own life. Without a true life of the individuals, in which are embodied the ethical values of personality — which are the supreme ones — the collectivity lacks meaning and justification. The collectivity is an instrument, is an apparatus for the individual. The collectivity does not live, in the pure and authentic sense of that word; but those who live are individuals. And these need, for their own life, the collectivity, which ought to function as an instrument or apparatus destined only to facilitate individuals in the development of their individual existence and its perfecting.

To orient ourselves truly in the matter of Juridical Valuation — and consequently in political philosophy — it is necessary to obtain a clear knowledge of the fact that the primary, basic, and irreducible opposition is that which lies unbridgeably between personalism and transpersonalism. The other oppositions — for example that between individualism and socialism — are secondary and not basic. For individualism and socialism (humanist) both coincide on a personal basis, to wit: in considering that the State and the Law ought to be at the service of the values of man; and they diverge only as to the means which they consider conducive for the realization of that end.

Liberal individualism believes that the State will better serve human personality the more the volume of free activity which it concedes, limiting itself to guaranteeing meanwhile an efficient protection; and it considers that the spontaneous play of private initiative is the best source of social solidarity. Nonmaterialistic socialism, that is, as a program of justice,[111] seeks wholly the same end as the liberal school: to serve the greatest good of all individuals. But it believes that this is possible only by coming to attribute to the State full faculties, to organize in the fullest detail social coöperation and especially economics. The majority of authentic socialist programs (naturally excluding Bolshevism, which has been somewhat different) do not deify the State, do not convert it into the end of human activities, but what they pretend to do is to make men better and happier, neither more nor less than liberalism, although making use of other means; for the socialist programs believe that far from being able to succeed by the free interplay of spontaneous initiative, they can only succeed by a taxative juridical regulation of economic activities. So that, at bottom, the socialist theorists — not the materialists — are also humanists and not statists, since they desire that men should be more cultured, should eat better, and, in short, should elevate

[111] I refer to all socialism which does not take as a basic and exclusive foundation the strict economic interpretation of history; for example, the doctrines of St. Simon, Fourier, Owen, Lasalle, revisionism (Bernstein, Tugan-Baranowsky, Besteiro), the new socialism (Henri de Man, Radbruch, Heller, de los Rios, etc.) and the majority of the western socialist parties (English Laborism, German social democracy since 1919, etc.). In reality the majority of socialist parties have abandoned at depth the dogmatics of the materialistic conception of history. As to Bolshevism, it is not Marxism nor humanist socialism, but a form abounding in the most disparate and antagonistic elements.

the level of their spiritual and material life; to obtain which they understand that it is necessary to renounce a sufficiently large sector of personal liberty, yielding it to the State, in order that it may organize social living together. But in humanist socialism there is preserved respect for intimate liberties (conscience, thought) and for personal autodetermination. Also all the positions between liberal individualism and socialism are personalist or humanist, such as, for example, the many programs called interventionist. These, without aspiring in any manner to the statification of economics, maintain that the State cannot fold its hands before the consequences of inhuman exploitation and economic disorganization, to which the extremist liberalism of the Manchester school gave rise. There are, properly, programs which preserve what liberalism possesses of perpetual and supreme value, to wit: maximum respect for the individual conscience and personal autonomy; but they try at the same time to create conditions of collective liberty which may prevent anyone from taking advantage of his situation of vantage to the prejudice of the situation of disadvantage of others; and they admit that, for this defense, as well as to assure a greater common good, the State should intervene in the organization, control, and guarantee of a series of activities, which previously were matters of free individual and social initiative; but without annulling the individual spontaneity, which is always the source of all creation and progress.

Among all the doctrines referred to in the preceding paragraph there is some communication: it is possible to establish a contact between them, because in spite of their great divergencies, they have a common personalist or humanist inspiration.

But, on the other hand, any conciliation or compromise between personalism and transpersonalism is altogether impossible. The ultraconservative idealists, the romantic-traditionalists, the exalted nationalists, the militarists, the fascists, the national-socialists, etc., are all expressions of transpersonalism. In all these programs and political concretions the authentic human personality, that is, the individual, is fiercely and cruelly sacrificed to a mysticism exalting the collectivity as a supreme value, in itself and for itself, independent of the men who compose it. Transpersonalism[112] tends to represent the State as an organism whose parts lack individuality and represent only ingredients put at the service of the whole, from which they receive what meaning they possess. For transpersonalism, the individual is worth nothing as an individual,

[112] Transpersonalism has taken this idea principally from the *organic totality* of the thought of the Restoration (De Maistre, De Bonald) and from the philosophy of Schelling and of Hegel. Also sometimes it has taken as a base the biological organism.

but solely in the degree in which he is disindividualized, in which he participates in the totality. Man is degraded to pure alfalfa to feed the state monster, to mere cannon fodder. Transpersonalism considers man as the bearer of a transpersonal reason, which is embodied in the collectivity and in its historic process. This is, in fine, the idea which pervades hegelian political thought; which lies in extreme conservatism — which sees in the real and concrete existence of the State the supreme value and tends to deify it, believing that its history is governed by immanent reason. And it considers that history is perfecting itself not toward universal fraternity, but toward a differentiation all the time greater. And it seeks as a supreme end the maximum accumulation of power in the State, not only to serve the necessities of guardianship of the Law, but as an end in itself; and, finally, it looks upon war as a necessity of autoaffirmation of States. And above all it annihilates individual personality, to which it denies all dignity; and consequently all liberty; and so it proposes intently the equalization of all in a state thinking, which is violently imposed. This is seen clearly in the brutal forms which transpersonalism has adopted in the contemporaneous totalitarian States, to wit, in national-socialism, in fascism, and in their analogues — systems which insist that all follow one single line which produces an equalization or homogenization of consciences, imposed coercitively, and which, consequently, destroys human individuality.

10. Foundation of Personalism or Humanism

In putting the problem of the valuation of the human person, I have done something more than explain the antithetic doctrines, personalism (or humanism) and transpersonalism (or totalism); for I have indicated, moreover, some fundamental ideas which justify the first orientation and which show the essential error of the second. But it will be desirable to complete what has already been sketched with a rigorous founding of personalism or humanism.

Although idealism has been superseded — as I have explained in the first chapter of this book — it preserved as a firm truth that my consciousness constitutes the center, support, and proof of all the other realities. The consciousness is inescapably and necessarily the born center of the universe; since its vision or conception is articulated in a perspective which converges in a necessary manner on my mental pupil which contemplates it. The perspective created by the individuality is inescapable and necessary; it constitutes one of the components of reality. The universe is my universe; and I — and so each one — cannot refer to any but my universe. The world appears necessarily as a correlative of the I, as my world. And if I disappear, with me there disappears also the world, my world. But my world is the only world which exists for me. It will perhaps be said, ingenuously, that the world will continue for others after I have disappeared; but in this expression, which at first sight may seem acute, a great fraud is concealed; for the world which will follow is that of the others, but as I am the one who speaks, it turns out that on my disappearance there disappears the only world to which I can authentically refer. On the other hand, it is to be noted that the others for me are a part of the world, that is, of my world; and if this my world disappears, with it there go also all its ingredients, among which are the others (each one with his respective world). It will perhaps be said that I can by intellectual construction come to conclude that the world is something in itself, independently of me—at least up to a certain point; and at once I admit that this affirmation is correct; but it happens that this affirmation is a theory which I have fabricated, and, consequently, a part of my world. Or, put otherwise, the thought which I may have of an objective world independent of me, in itself is one of the ingredients of my world. And, so, when I disappear, and with me, my world, there disappears also the image which I have formed for myself of an independent world, which image was one of the ingredients of my world.

I have explained in the first chapter that life (the individual life, my life) constitutes the primary and basic reality, as co-present and inescapable correlation between the I and the world, between the subject and the objects. It is true that the metaphysical theory of life is not subjectivism nor idealism—as neither is it realism.

And it is not subjectivism or idealism, precisely because it discovers that life is the co-presence or coexistence of the I and objects. To live is to be occupied with a world in which I find myself necessarily; we meet each other, forcibly joined, in inexorable company. Therefore, my life requires these two essential ingredients; the world and I are like inseparable twins. But the objects of the world, the same as I, occur in the reality of my life, which is the indubitable reality, and which is also the reality which sustains and conditions all the other realities.

Now, if all that which is beyond me obtains expression only in my life; if all the other things depend on me—although it is also true that I depend on them; if all the other things occur solely in the reality of my life, it is evident that the primacy in a conception of the universe belongs to my life. And from this it follows necessarily that the realization of values has meaning only in my life, which is the individual life.

So-called culture—religion, philosophy, science, art, morals, law, state, economics, technique, etc.—is an aggregate of things and works which man makes in his life; and consequently they have meaning only in his life and for his life. And it has been shown already, in the first chapter, that the authentic life is the individual life.

Culture is constituted of human acts and works which aspire to realize ideas of value: it is integrated by actions and products which try to embody the truth, in the philosophic and scientific knowledge of the universe; to give sensible form to beauty, in art; to obtain the fulfillment of good in conduct, by morals; to obtain the reign of justice in society, by the Law; to utilize nature and overcome its resistances, thanks to technique; and so forth. Culture, then, as an intention of approaching the values of goodness, justice, truth, beauty, utility, power, etc., has meaning only for him who does not possess them in full measure, and who, nevertheless, feels the need of exerting himself in their conquest. Therefore, culture has no meaning for unconscious nature; nor has it either for God, who is by essence absolute Wisdom and Truth, total Good, supreme Justice, complete Beauty, infinite Power. What need has God of science if He knows everything in eternal actuality; and of morals if He is pure Good; and of art if He is perfect Beauty; and of technique if He is Omnipotent? But, on the other hand, culture seems to us filled with meaning so far as we regard it as a human function and work. Because man does not know, but needs to know; on this account science is constructed. Because man, who does not shelter within himself pure beauty, nevertheless desires to become related with it, art is created. Because man is a sinner, but it is necessary to redeem him from his meannesses, on this account we have ethics. Because society must be organized according to justice, on this account Law is elaborated. Because man is helpless, but experiences the need of using and dominating the elements which surround him, on this account technique is produced, etc. Therefore, man is necessarily the born center of culture and its point of final gravitation. And as the supreme values which can be referred to him are ethical, hence the idea of personal dignity must rule always above all his other tasks.

Miguel de Unamuno says, in true exaltation of the value of the human:[113]

> Who are you? you ask me, and with Obermann I answer: For the universe, nothing; for me, everything. — I am the center of my Universe, the center of the Universe; and in my supreme anguishes I cry with Michelet: my I, let them take away my I! Egoism, do you say? There is nothing more universal than the individual, since what it is of each it is of all; and it is of no use to

[113] Cf. Miguel de Unamuno, El sentimiento trágico de la vida en los hombres y en los pueblos (Madrid, Renacimiento) 50ff. and also 20.

sacrifice each one to all, but rather sacrifice all to each one. That which you call egoism is the principle of psychic gravity, the necessary postulate — I shall never deliver myself willingly and granting my confidence to any leader of peoples who has not learned that in leading a people he is leading men, men of flesh and blood, men who are born, suffer, and although they do not wish to die, die; men who are ends in themselves, not only means; men who have to be what they are and not otherwise — It is inhuman, for example, to sacrifice one generation of men to the generation which follows, when there is no feeling of destiny for the sacrificed.

If our life — the individual of each one — is the basic reality; if, moreover, as we have seen, values although objective occur in our life — as all the rest which there is in the Universe — and have therefore an intervital dimension; if the agent of the realization of values is man, alone capable of understanding them and devoting himself to their call, it follows that the realization of values has meaning only for man. Things in which values dwell — among them society which is a mechanism or instrument — constitute goods, only in the measure in which they represent apparatus serviceable for man; in the measure in which they are conditions for his consciousness being able to embody the supreme values, which are those destined for the individual as such.

I repeat that I do not deny that in the collectivity there may and ought to be embodied values; but those values, proper to the collectivity, are values so far as they constitute instruments or conditions for the realization of the values proper to the individual.

The great error committed by transpersonalism is the following: it does not take into account that the collectivity has no substantive reality, that it does not have a being for itself independent of the being of the individuals who compose it. On the other hand, the being of the individual consists of a being for itself, of an autonomous and independent being. On this account, the collectivity ought to respect the individual, in the mode of being peculiar to him, in the values which are destined for him, and to recognize his autonomy. The individual is not purely and simply a part of the whole. Although he may of course be necessarily a member of society, he is at the same time superior to it. He is superior to it because he is a person in the fullest and most authentic sense of the idea, which society can never be. The collectivity would lack meaning if it did not affirm itself as a medium for the individuals.

What has been said must not be misinterpreted in the sense — which would be an error — that it is denied that in the collectivity there can and ought to be embodied values; nor either in the sense — which also would be a mistake — that society is considered as something purely fortuitous. The individual is essentially social; even to the point that the isolated individual is not anything real, nor even possible, but a pure abstraction. The individual exists only in society; he lives on its historic level, supporting himself on it and making use of the goods which he finds in it. Both the anchorite and Robinson (Crusoe) carry the collectivity within themselves and live upon its level. The individual rests upon the values realized in history and transmitted to him by the collectivity; and almost everything which he does rests upon those communal goods; and, in most cases, he succeeds at last in raising himself a little above the historic level of those goods which the collectivity has transmitted to him.

But although the social is something essential to man, the goods which are realized in the collectivity are goods only of an instrumental character, they are means for the realization of the supreme values, which belong only to the individual and which can and ought to be fulfilled only by the individual. Without society there is no man; but man — here is understood the individual man, who is the only one who constitutes a basic and substantive reality — is axiologically superior to society. For society is something made by him and for him.

11. Democracy[114]

Although democracy and liberalism constitute, in the abstract, replies to two different questions, both ideas have a humanist or personalist root, which consists above all in the idea of the ethical dignity of man. And, in fact, the liberal idea and the democratic idea have presented themselves intimately combined in theories and in systems as *liberal democracy*. By itself alone, democracy presents itself as a mere form without content. The content must be obtained from another idea. If it is obtained from humanism, which is congruent with it, as it ought to be, then it will be put at the service of liberal principles. It will, moreover, have a social content, but without slighting the norms of fundamental liberty, annexed to the ethical dignity of the individual.

What is congruent, by virtue of the humanist or personalist root of the democratic idea, is that this is interlocked with the other humanist postulates, and consequently with those of liberty and also with those of social distributive justice. But it happens, even though it represents an unfaithfulness to the humanist or personalist principle, that democracy makes itself entirely independent of the adherence to the humanist meaning and rests exclusively on the mere formal principle of majority will, pretending that this is capable of legitimatizing any content it may

[114] This section is from the Second Spanish edition of the book (Mexico, 1945). Translator.

adopt. Then it turns out to be possible — even though monstrous — that a government founded on the will of the majority may be inspired with transpersonalist principles, that is, not humanist or antihumanist. It happens also that, without adopting a transpersonalist attitude, a democracy, which wishes to rely exclusively on the majority will without feeling itself committed to the realization of any contents determined by humanist principles, may eventually deny these at any moment. That is, abiding by the formal principle of democracy, without limitation from any liberal guarantees, and without necessarily giving itself a humanist content, it runs the danger that the people, intoxicated with a power which is attributed to them without limits, will permit no hindrances to their action, and may on occasions violate the conscience or the autonomy of the individuals of the minority.

Democracy, both in the theories and in the systems of the eighteenth and nineteenth centuries, united itself to the liberal idea, not in a purely accidental way but in intimate harmony, forming the liberal democratic complex. Democracy was conceived as a means put at the service of liberty, as the instrument for its realization and its guarantee. It proposed a government based on the popular will, but with guarantees for minorities, and with safeguards for the liberties of all, that is, limited by respect for the individual human person. Hence, the *declarations of rights* in them which combine the basic principles of liberty with the democratic justification of power, limiting the extent of it by the respect due to them. But it was not a matter solely of limiting the democratic power with respect to the rights of liberty. It was a question, also, of guaranteeing the effectiveness of them by instituting, in the organization of the State, structures whose functioning was to assure normally the defense of such rights; for example, by the principle of the division of powers, by parliamentary control of the finances and of the army, by the administration of justice by an independent entity. All this with respect to the ethical essence of the perennial principle of liberty. But, moreover, in the doctrines as well as in the positive institutions of a democratic-liberal character is perceived the decisive influence of some ideas in the historic form of modern liberalism; for example, parliament is not so much an institution of democratic origin as rather of liberal root. Parliament in the eighteenth century in England rather than a democratic representation sought to constitute the apparatus for free political discussion by enlightened men, responding to the belief that from the free opposition of thoughts springs light and greater probability of the rightness of decisions. On the other hand, democracy was conceived also as the most efficacious means for guaranteeing liberty: it was considered that it was difficult to preserve the effectiveness of the liberties of individuals unless they exercised some control over the government. Again, there was outlined a democratic interpretation of liberty, with hues distinct from those of the concept which pure liberalism had of it. For liberalism, the question as to liberty consists of the defense or guarantee against undue intromissions in the public power, that is, in finding in certain zones an exemption against the State. On the other hand, the democratic interpretation of liberty does not conform only to this negative aspect, but signifies, moreover, an active participation in the functions of government.

In the elaboration of the modern democratic concept — of the seventeenth and eighteenth centuries and part of the nineteenth — other ideas and factors besides the thoughts explained had influence. The theory and the construction of democratic institutions in the Modern Age were stimulated by the atomist quantitative individualism emanating from the physico-mathematical interpretation of the world: the individual constitutes the element of which the collectivity is composed. And with an attitude of rationalist spirit it is sought to construct by purely intellectual proceedings and with geometrical precision the edifice of the State. Also various historic factors contributed to forge the doctrines and modern democratic institutions: the sociological factors of the English Revolution (of a preponderantly liberal shade); the action of the middle class illustrated in France and in Great Britain; the passion which modern man feels for reason; a sentimental impulse of generosity; all the social progress which the French Revolution engendered; and the formation of national States.

The idea of equality plays a decisive part in the conception and in democratic institutions. It is not a question solely of liberal equality before the law, that is, of the principle of juridical parity of persons. It is a matter moreover of political equality which includes the suffrage, access to public jobs, taxation, performance of military service, and, in short, active participation in public affairs.

The liberal democratic State is not considered invested with a fixed mission of an absolute character, but — besides guaranteeing above all the fundamental rights of the individual — tries to serve the common good, interpreted by public opinion and according to its changing tides. That is, it aims for what public opinion considers the common good at each moment, with the limitations, nevertheless, which respect for individual rights requires.

Nothing logically prevents the old liberal democracy from being completed with greater attention and more efficient care in the fulfillment of the exigencies of social justice. Moreover, to correct the injustices which the application of the old liberalism brought with it and to be vigilant that actually there should be given an equality of opportunity, to assure the minimum of material conditions which make liberty possible and that parity before the law should be a real fact, and for the distribution of wealth to be ruled by just norms, are purposes which, far from contradicting the essence of the system which is founded on liberty and democracy, come to perfect its meaning and its humanist or personalist efficiency.

12. Planmaking and Liberty.[115] The Social Exigencies of Humanism

Notice that it is one thing to observe the injustices and disorders which the regime of capitalist society has provoked; and quite another to decide which are the best and most efficacious means to correct those iniquities and errors, that is, to decide if a socialist regime would be better, if an interventionist regime would be sufficient, or simply if the formula of neoliberalism would be enough. This is not a problem which I wish to put here, still less pretend to solve. In these short philosophical and sociological expositions upon the suppositions and the consequences of the principal political ideas, I try not to take sides, but only to present with the greatest clearness the foundations and the meanings of the different political programs. I will take a defined and definite position only in favor of humanism or personalism, but without going therein to pronounce taxatively and in detail a judgment of categorical preference for any determined one of its forms. It is clear that, whatever bond there may be between the various personalist ideas, which constitutes the purpose of successive steps in service of the efficacy of the humanist idea, there has to be noted and explained — as I have tried to do — that plan of progress. It is in this sense that I have made evident what the liberal idea has — in my opinion — of lasting essence, what it possesses of perennial validity (intimate liberties and decision as to one's own destiny) as against what constituted only a special historical manifestation, contingent and superseded, which it is necessary to overcome at any cost. Now, to decide as to which may be the means which we ought to consider the most adequate and efficient to accomplish this overcoming, is a problem which I do not attempt to resolve in this book, but which would belong to an extensive study of philosophy, of science, and of political technique, in which there would have to be taken into account the entire aggregate of multiple and very heterogenous factors which intervene in the question.

I would wish only to call attention to some sociological circumstances

[115] This section is from the Second Spanish edition of the book (Mexico, 1945). Translator.

of our epoch, concretely especially of the epoch which is going to follow the end of the Second World War. Although one might sympathize in principle in abstract fashion with the direction of neoliberalism, on condition that it could suppress the social injustices from which the humanity of our time suffers, it would have to be recognized today that this plan is absolutely inapplicable to our time. It seems that the present social situation and, moreover, that of the immediate future, will require inescapably a process of increasing planmaking, to cover an enormous series of peremptory necessities of justice and of the material life. It ought not to be forgotten that our epoch is a time of crisis, of gravest crisis, of the third of the great crises which universal history records; and that the phenomenon of the crisis presents itself with formidable volume and radical intensity. The crisis is a world in profound transformation, a bankruptcy of the fundamental convictions which ruled the life of the past and the absence of any new system of convictions yet installed really and effectively as the structure of society; wherefore there is confusion, not knowing what to rely on, a loss of security in life and of clarity and firmness as to the directives of conduct. The crisis is also an aggregate of profound lack of adjustment in all social structures, without there being observed clearly the silhouette of the new system which in the future may serve as a relatively satisfactory solution for the problems put today. In these circumstances, there is meaning and justification in asking if it would be wise to seek to apply to an exceptional period criteria and norms which perchance are only realizable in normal periods, in which there is a social structure relatively stable and coherent. Thinking of this, it occurs to one that perhaps the planmaking is coming to be an unescapable urgency in the near future, without its being opportune to predict where it may go and what structure and what system it may adopt. But in any case although we have to accept the peremptory necessity of a planmaking, we shall have to confront a problem of maximum importance, to wit, to make it compatible with basic personal liberty and with the creative founts of free initiative. Probably the gravest problem and most urgent of our time is to find the directives for a "planmaking for liberty," as Mannheim says, "to direct those spheres of social progress on which the collectivity depends to function without difficulties, but trying at the same time not to regulate those other spheres which offer more opportunities for creative individuality and spontaneous and free development"; and I shall insist with still greater emphasis upon the guarantee, from the point of view of humanism, of the fundamental liberties which are derived from ethics.

Without deciding among the various socialist programs, the different interventionist and even neoliberal forms, it is necessary, nevertheless, to recognize as a common denominator of all of them, and as completely justified, an aggregate of proofs and directives for the service of humanist and personalist orientation. There is no strictly effective liberty when one suffers under the burden of a peremptory economic necessity. Liberty requires, above all, to be given in fact, a minimum basis of material comfort. The principle of equality demands, not an equality of goods — which would be unjust for notoriously there are great inequalities of capacity, of application, and of merit — but an equality of opportunities. It has been said that the principle of parity does not require that all the runners arrive at the goal at the same time and receive the same reward, which so far from constituting equality would be something iniquitous; but it does demand that all shall leave from the same starting point and that the game shall be fair.

With respect to what has just been said, the following estimative principles have been proclaimed, or, rather, the following ideal directives for the progressive reform of the juridical order:

1. There ought to be established a right to the integral product of labor, interpreting it not in the Marxian sense, but taking into account its value and, consequently, the remunerations which belong to intellectual direction, to the labor of organization, to the risk and to the amortization of instruments, as well if these are privately as if they are collectively owned.

2. There ought to be conceded to every individual person the minimum base necessary for him to live as a human being, which implies, among other things, the exigencies of minimum salary, social assistance, due rest, possibility of education and instruction, in accord with the aptitudes of each individual and his vocation, etc.

3. It ought to be made sure that there be work for all and, so far as possible, in accordance with the capacity and aptitudes of each person; which implies institutions to foresee and to remedy suspension of work and to make channels for vocational labor.

In short, the State ought to project the exigencies of justice and of the juridical values upon economic relations.

Among all the humanist doctrines there is communication; it is possible to establish a contact between them, to pass from one to another, to elaborate multiple combined syntheses, because, in spite of their great divergencies, they have the common denominator of one same personalist orientation.

On the contrary, any conciliation or compromise between humanism (or personalism) and transpersonalism is altogether impossible, for they treat of diametrically antagonistic conceptions.

13. Italian Fascism.[116] German National-Socialism

The fascist and nazi totalitarianisms, like all other transpersonalist directives, present the following characters, but in a degree of maximum exacerbation: (1) They deny the meaning and the moral mission of the individual. They proclaim that man has no value except in the measure in which he serves the group as a pure instrument of it; and that, therefore, the individual lacks moral personality. (2) They deify the State; they elevate it to the category of God, of the only God; and they demand for it an attitude of religious veneration and of absolute submission. (3) They profess an exalted nationalism. (4) They are belligerent in the extreme, to the point of affirming that man has been born for war and that that is his supreme mission; they conceive the integrity of life in a military fashion, the collectivity in all its activities as a regiment, and the country as a permanent barracks. (5) They consider a petty leader as a supernatural being, sacred and infallible. (6) They aspire to an unlimited increase of power as the supreme end.

But besides presenting these special characteristics of transpersonalism, carrying it to a high and extreme degree, fascism and nazism have peculiarities, typical of the totalitarian system, that is, of the system which tries to absorb totally the life of men in the State, without reserve or excepted zone. The chief peculiar facts of fascist and nazi totalitarianism, besides their transpersonalist foundation, are the following: (a) a ferocious brutality, which brings to annihilation all human meaning of life and is the entire negation of all spiritual value, entailing especially a complete destruction of morals. (b) The violent imposition of an official dogma in all aspects of life or, rather, of a series of official dogmas, which embrace the totality of human behaviors, not only external, but also internal, as well intellectual as emotional. And this in a violent manner, persecuting with implacable rage not only any dissent, but including the least lukewarmness. That is, they elevate the State to the total organ of human life. Hence the name of totalitarianism. Remember the vile motto of Mussolini: "All within the State, nothing outside of the State, all for the State." (c) There is also a total absorption of society by the State, tolerating no least spontaneous collective manifestation of any sort which is not taxatively regulated by the public power. (d) They support themselves on a typical phenomenon of aggrandizement, of cultivation and exaltation of the human mass. In spite of its being against the principle of bossism, they grow from an abject multitude, soaked in a feeling of mass, of infuriated and drunken mass; drunk not exactly on

[116] This section is from the Second Spanish edition of the book (Mexico, 1945). Translator.

alcohol but on myths and the lowest frenzies. (e) An unbridled dictatorial despotism, in a degree which had no precedent in the civilization of the western countries. (f) The absence of any system of Law and the rule of a regime of arbitrariness. (g) A denial of human parity and a conception of the population of the earth divided radically and inescapably into two parts: the true group of the nation or race and the rest of the world; and, consequently, the proclaiming that they have duties only with respect to their own group and that the rest of all peoples have to be considered essentially as enemies.

14. Consequences of Personalism

Having founded rigorously and basically the personalist conception, it is desirable now that we determine the forms which it may take — which will depend on how there is understood the hierarchy in the realization of human (individual) values and the consequences to which personalism gives rise for the Law, in every case.

In the field of ethics, personalism may adopt various forms, according to what may be the moral conception which it takes as fundamental. It may start from a eudemonistic or utilitarian ethical doctrine (happiness as an end). But it may also be founded on a rigoristic ethical theory. In the first case, the eudemonistic values will be preferentially exalted, the attainment of the greatest possible quantity of benefits and pleasures for all, or for the greater number. In the second, the decisive idea will be the value which is embodied in the moral dignity of man; and the most important end of the State will consist in safeguarding this dignity (with its sequelae of liberty) and making possible the best fulfillment of the ethical ends of the individual. But this difference, which can assume great importance in a moral philosophy *sensu stricto*, has a minor scope for the Law; because the Law ought to be the condition which makes possible the fulfillment of the moral destiny, wherefore it has to guarantee the liberty of each individual; but it cannot be in any way the agent for the fulfillment of morality, which can be realized and has meaning only in the degree in which it is carried out freely by each person. And, on the other hand, it is to be noted that the benefits which the juridical order assures — in the order of satisfaction of material necessities, and also in the sphere of spiritual culture — may constitute favorable conditions for man to be able to ennoble himself by the realization of works of culture and complying better with his ethical values; in short, for cultivating his personality as a substratum of the moral and cultural values.

Among the personalist ethical conceptions there may also be established another distinction, according to what is valued in the individual person: according to whether we value his generic condition as possible substratum of the values; or whether we value the concrete realization of them in each single case. Man, whose greatness, that is, whose dignity, is based on his being the substratum and the agency for realization of the values — and among them the supreme ones, which are the moral ones — may also in fact turn out unfaithful to that destiny. What is it, then, which we are going to value in the human? The generic dimension which all men have of being able to act as agents for the realization of the values? Or is what we are going to value the individuality in which actually and truly the values have been fulfilled? There are doctrines (the rationalists and the formalists) which value the generic quality which all individuals have of being able to be the substratum for the realization of the values, that is, the common human condition. Other theories — for example that of Nietzsche — value most the individual according to the concrete realizations which he has attained; and from this thought there follows an exaltation of the outstanding individualities according to what they have of distinctiveness and peculiarity. Now, the divergence between these two indicated directions has a very great and decisive importance for morals; but, on the other hand, it is of less scope for Juridical Valuation. And it has not so much importance for juridical valuation, because the Law is not the agent for the realization of the moral values, but the condition that each individual may realize them freely on his own account. Thus, the Law is that which ought to guarantee the liberty of each individual, in order that he may be what he is, in order that each one may fulfill his own proper and untransferable destiny. The Law ought consequently to guarantee room for the solely individual, but it neither can nor ought to gather or translate in its norms the peculiarity of each individual destiny. For the Law there ought positively not to come into question the authentic and untransferable individuality of each person, but it may only take into account functional, common, schematic dimensions; and, therefore, every juridical valuation has a character of formalism, that is, of generalization. The Law, in the form of collective life, does not work with the authentic realities of men — which are the irreducible individualities — but only with some generic forms of them (citizens, functionaries, particular creditors, debtors, delinquents, etc.). But, moreover, the Law, as being a form of social life, ought to stop respectfully before each one of the individualities, without trying to invade them, without pretending to disindividualize them, without seeking to homogenize them; and finally to take from man nothing more than his typical human dimensions, and those categories also generic determinative of the social function in which they are situated; but without exceeding that external cloak of social functionality, and, consequently, leaving intact the bosom of the intimacy of each one.

So it turns out that, even though a person possesses a proper and exclusive individual being — to which is ascribed a congruent axiological signification — in the sphere of Law men ought to appear schematic, generalized, typical. And so, without prejudice to the inequality between individuals — which ought to remain intact as to the possibilities of realization in each one — it must equalize the moral dignity of persons in those spheres which are founded on values which universally affect all persons. And this is what happens — or ought to happen — in the juridical field. So, for example, this is what happens when one judges men in a formal way as juridical persons. The juridical values are not the highest in the valuing hierarchy, on the contrary they are notoriously inferior to others, as for example the moral ones; but precisely the juridical values, as inferior, are those which condition the possibility of realization of other superior human values. And it happens that men are so much the more equalized, the lower the rank of the values from whose point of view they are considered. Max Scheler[117] says metaphorically that aristocracy in heaven does not exclude democracy on earth. The satisfaction of the most peremptory urgencies — for example that of security, for which the Law fundamentally serves — is the condition for being able to accomplish tasks of higher value. Hence it is thought that men ought to be equalized as much as possible in the goods which correspond to these peremptory necessities — security, liberty, satisfaction of the most elemental material urgencies, etc. — precisely to put them in the possibility of each fulfilling his separate and single individual destiny, in which have to be embodied the values of superior rank.

It may, then, be affirmed that man as a subject of Law, that is, as a juridical person, represents participation in an inferior rank of values, in which all individuals are equalized; and, on the other hand, man in his authentic and full individuality, as participant in a realm of single and unequal values, occupies a rank superior to the State and to the Law. The State and the Law are of value so far as they serve as a conditioning means and assistance for the individuality to be able to fulfill the values superior to those which concern them.

It will be opportune now to examine succinctly the principal consequences which are derived from personalism or humanism for Juridical Valuation; consequences which we may consider as common to all the versions of personalism.

[117] Cf. MAX SCHELER, DER FORMALISMUS IN DER ETHIK 529ff.

Personalism centers the juridical order in the idea of human dignity, which brings with it as the first consequence the affirmation of individual liberty. This liberty seems intangible in what belongs to the most intimate bosom of the individual personality (conscience, thought). It manifests itself also in the decision as to its own destiny, that is, in that which is called personal autonomy.

As human dignity is taken as a generic condition, this brings the affirmation of juridical parity between all persons. And the Law alone can licitly consider those differences which rise above this basic plane of parity and which represent merits earned by the person as substratum of ethical and cultural values, or, put in other words: the human inequalities which personalism takes into account are those which suppose diverse concretizations of individual liberty, that is, various external and internal situations in which it may appear. If the juridical order takes charge of these differences, it is precisely because it wishes to treat all in equal proportion. Therefore, inspired especially by this criterion, it takes into consideration the differences which there are between diverse individuals — differences which are relevant for the Law — and those who are unequal it treats in an unequal way, by which it satisfies the exigencies of a well-understood parity.

15. Certainty and Security

In chapter six of this book I showed that the basic motivation which impelled man to establish rules of Law is the urgency to create a *certain* order (in the most important social relations) and of corresponding *security*. And I explained that, even though Law is devoted to the realization of values of a superior rank — in whose light they must be justified — nevertheless, it ought before all and primarily to create a situation of security. Security is also a value. The rank of this value of security is inferior to the rank of other juridical values — justice and the others implied in it. But the realization of this value of security is indispensably a condition which precedes the fulfillment of the values of a superior hierarchy. Or, put in other words, in order for there to be Law, it is necessary that there should be a *certain* order and an accomplished *security*. Moreover, Juridical Valuation requires that this certain and secure order should be just, favoring the common good, etc. But these superior qualities must be realized in a certain and secure order. Justice cannot govern in a society in which there is no certain and secure order. Dignity and liberty cannot reign in a society in anarchy. The common good cannot be furthered in a collectivity in which there is no certain and secure regulation. All these superior values of the Law must be fulfilled precisely in the Law. But there is no Law where there is no certain order and security. It is true that it is not sufficient to create a certain and secure order, but it must also be just. But there can be no justice when there is no security. Therefore, we could say that there may be a Law — an order of certainty and with security inexorably imposed — which might not be just. But it cannot be that in society there is justice without security. Security is then with respect to justice — and the other juridical values implied by it — an inferior value, but one whose realization conditions the possibility of fulfillment of those superior values. In short, it is a matter of the relation which exists between the realization of values connected in unequal rank: the fulfillment of the inferior value furnishes the possibility of raising upon its base the superior value. Without the realization of the inferior value, there would be no possibility of embodying the superior value.

Now, the important theme for Juridical Valuation is to determine what ought to be established as the certain and secure order. And it is clear that what primarily matters is to assure respect for the dignity of the person and its individual autonomy, in order that it may comply with its own authentic destiny. And then the security, which by itself alone is presented as a purely formal order, will gather plenty of meaning and will be filled with the highest worthy content. I need certainty and security in collective relations, to disengage my attention from a series of peremptory problems and, in this way, to devote myself to the fulfillment of my own destiny. I need to withdraw from the confusion which the perils of disorder produce and from overwhelming preoccupation with the most elemental urgencies, in order to enjoy that moment of ease in which I can attain to be the I to which I am called, to fulfill my authentic mission, humble or eminent, small or great, but my own, mine only. I need security to dispose of liberty and to dispose of what is necessary in the satisfaction of my needs, with which I am exempt from being in the perpetual situation of an alert sentinel or oppressed, and in order to develop my own individuality. Hence, security presents itself as a great good when it is put at the service of the supreme values of individuality. And hence also, on the contrary, when the Law — which is security — tries to include under its regulation the most intimate zones of my being, and to disindividualize it, reducing it to dough of a homogenized mass, it represents something abominable and monstrous. The mechanization which the Law imposes has meaning and justification when it limits itself to the purely external zones of living together and solidarity, because thanks to it man withdraws from the oppression of danger and preoccupations; and may conquer his most intimate liberty, for the fulfillment of his own and untransferable individual work. But if, on the other hand, juridical regulation pretends to regulate positively and taxatively the depths of personality, then it would realize the most degrading and devastating of tasks. Degrading because it means a process of dehumanization, of departing from the human to fall into beastliness. Devastating, because with such work it cuts off the sole *primarily* and *authentically* creative, source, which is individuality.

II

PHENOMENOLOGY OF THE DECISION

BY CARLOS COSSIO

Professor of the Philosophy of Law in the National University of La Plata, Member of the International Institute of the Philosophy of Law and of Juridical Sociology, Member of the Argentine Institute of Juridical and Social Philosophy

Being the Introduction to his book, *The Egological Theory of the Law and the Juridical Concept of Liberty*

TRANSLATED BY

Gordon Ireland, Visiting Professor of Law, Catholic University of America, School of Law

TRANSLATOR'S NOTE: None of the Author's Comments has been altered (Notes 4, 6, 7, 8, 10, 17), but the bibliographical references and quotations have been anglicized (Notes 5, 12, 16) and the case citations have been amplified and completed (Notes 11, 13, 14, 17, 18, 19, 20).

PHENOMENOLOGY OF THE DECISION

1. The Decision as the Object of this Introduction

We have to begin by making firm contact with juridical experience, although unfortunately, by reason of the limitations of the present work, not at all the points in which this contact should be made, but at the most significant of them, the judicial decision.

We need this contact with experience as a starting point, since the egological Theory is precisely in radical opposition to the traditional juridical thinking, which, like rationalism, dispenses with such contact, and with empiricism and historicity falsifies itself with various unauthentic contacts.

The egological [1] Theory considers that the Dogmatic Science of the

[1] An inquiry of Professor Cossio whether he might be willing to define further the meaning in which he uses *egological* in this work elicited a very courteous letter, with a copy of a short note by him in the *Revista de la Universidad Católica Bolivariana* (Medellín, Colombia), Nos. 40–41 (1945), of which the following is a translation.

"It is worth while to clear up the meaning of this word, used as a neologism in my work, for its use has provoked uncertainty and doubts among the serious public. What is egological? Why have I resorted to such a word? I have tried to solve two problems with it: one terminological, the other conceptual.

"The terminological problem was that it was essential that I have an adjective corresponding to the substantive 'object.' If for the egological theory the Law is conduct and the object of dogmatic knowledge is conduct in intersubjective interference; if the datum to know, as such, is the plenary man so far as he is the actuating subject—for the human person, his phenomenalized metaphysical liberty and his effective actions are inseparably one and the same thing, as is explained at length in my book—it is clear that finding myself always with the actuating subject as the object of knowledge, I would always need an adjective corresponding to the subject. Etymologically, this adjective is given by the word 'subjective.' But the development of philosophic thought has turned in such manner on the word 'subject' and, in a different sense—and with still greater vigor—upon the adjective 'subjective,' that today this adjective has multiple meanings, all of them independent of its corresponding substantive. Imagine the confusion which I should have brought upon myself in saying 'the subjective Theory of the Law.' Almost as much would have resulted if, working from the substantive 'person' I should have said 'the personalistic Theory of the Law.' Thus the need for remaining aside from all the philosophic resonances today deposited in the adjective 'subjective,' and equally the necessity of obtaining the original qualification which belonged to that word, brought me to the word 'egological,' derived from ego, I.

"Here arises the conceptual problem. Was the extension which I was going to give to the use of this technical-philosophical word correct? Did it carry with it ade-

Law is a science of reality, and insofar a science of experience; but of cultural or human experience and not of natural or causal experience. In this the egological Theory differs profoundly from the rationalism as well as from the empiricism dominant in juridical knowledge. Rationalism believes that the objects to be known by the jurist are rules and that positive Law does not represent or acquire them by the senses;

---

quately the characteristic significance of my doctrine of the Law, so as to make it an eponym?

"Egological: Husserl uses it to refer to that belonging to the I and to the knowledge of the I (egology). So he tells us of a constitutive transcendental egology in the most Kantian moments of his *Cartesian Meditations*. But with that we are always in the theoretical I or the knowing I and in their categorical plane.

"But as in all knowledge transcendental reflection puts in evidence the presence of the 'I think' (the theoretical transcendental subject), so in every action we meet an 'I act' as the practical transcendental subject. On this point, the doubt which we share with Croce and Gentile is great and lasting. (Benedetto Croce, Filosofia della Practica (Bari, 1923), p. 10, Giovanni Gentile, Los Fundamentos de la Filosofía del Derecho (Buenos Aires, 1944), Introduction and chap. 3.)

"On the other hand, the analysis of the dialectic act of comprehension with its reference to a meaning and to a substratum of meaning; and the distinction between mundane and egological objects, let us see that what characterizes the latter is not the human meaning of understand—common in essence to both—but the fact that the substratum of the meaning is a portion of Nature in the mundane objects, as it is the very conduct of man in egological objects. Thus in the egological objects we have contained the knowing I and the acting I while it is a question of the knowledge of conduct as conduct, a unique modality of the knowledge of the practical. We may, as the jurist does, who does not need to transgress to recognize a crime as a crime, place ourselves in a purely knowing position; but it is always that knowledge of the practical; and this supposes in the delinquent not an automatism, but that superposition of the acting and the knowing I's, which the jurist will measure with his knowledge, and which he will measure with a greater degree of truth as he can hold the delinquent above himself. But the conceptual reproduction, which is normative, of this situation does not at all contradict the indicated fact that the egology pertaining to the acting I is identical with the egology pertaining to the knowledge of that I. Or, to put it in the words used on page 200 of our book, in alluding briefly to this question: What in the acting subject is valid as a category (that of thought) constitutive of the object, to the jurist—knowing subject—appears as one of the essentials of the constituted object.

"Let us illustrate the point with the following example. One who commits a robbery will be able to tell us with great assurance why he committed the act; but his reply is explanatory or causal. On the other hand, if he is asked what dogmatic significance or, what is the same thing, what existential meaning his act has, it must be supposed, necessarily, that he also might be able to answer—and in fact he will answer with rough truth or flagrant error, it does not matter—why he acted knowing, in some degree, what he was doing; and this knowing what he does is the normative meaning of the act itself. At bottom, he only tries to explain the meaning of the act. But no one can fail to see that the jurist is in better condition, by his greater knowledge, to explain the not very well understood meaning of the act.

"But here are these two things which confirm the propriety of having resorted to

according to which the Dogmatic Science is a science of ideal objects, since the rules are known by thought, like the objects in Mathematics, but one does not see nor touch them. Empiricism, on the contrary, opposes this ideality in the Law and accepts its reality, so that juridical knowledge is founded on what juridical experience reveals; but empiricism does not recognize any other contact with experience except the sensory intuition which enables us to know Nature, so that juridical knowledge acquires the knowledge of its datum by its reference to another actual event; as when, for example, a law is interpreted by the

---

the adjective egological not only for the Law but also for the Science of the Law:

"(1) The jurist does not commit the robbery, notwithstanding which he explains its meaning. By this he integrates theoretically the robbery—if he is a Judge, the integration is real and effective—because he puts in it the dogmatic meaning as reality. The thought of the Judge, indeed, does not subsist in the part of spectator of the robbery from without, as a being apart, but it transfers itself to the act of the delinquent and inserts itself in it, giving it its dogmatic meaning. And this is possible only because the delinquent also is an I—an acting I—with a common base or nucleus of thought—the surrounding valuations—which the act of comprehension has to explain, be it whoever it may who realizes the comprehension. Consequently, the normative thought, which can be scientifically formulated, is going, so, to integrate the datum itself; the norm conceptualizes those valuations.

"(2) The jurist does not commit the robbery, notwithstanding which he explains its meaning. The jurist is, then, a purely knowing attitude—although of a knowledge of the practical; and, in that, of conduct as conduct.—Is it to be said, then, that if his knowledge is true it would have to be the same for the whole world, including the delinquent? Or would it be proper to speak of as many different knowledges as there are jurists who think of it, the integrating egological meaning of the delinquent act being of their creation?

"Thus can be understood the importance which the structural normativism of Hans Kelsen has for the Dogmatic as a science, for it fixes limits to the possibilities of creation of the organs; that is to say, the various jurists cannot differ among themselves beyond certain limits, without someone incurring thereby a contradiction of himself. And it is understood also that no dogmatic science can be made without taking into account the concrete valuations of jurisprudence, which are decisive facts of juridical experience; that is, giving significance to what is called jurisprudence, in the dogmatic construction, makes disappear the antithesis which the preceding questions raised.

"In some degree this has made clear the correctness of having resorted to the term egological. It suffices to think that the acting I is the plenary human person. Nor do we leave the sphere of knowledge; we treat only of the knowledge of the practical, and, in that, of conduct as conduct, which is what decides and clarifies the question.

"Egological signifies, then, at the same time, in unison, that the object of knowledge is the plenary man or acting subject and that this object, as what it is, is integrated in its meaning with knowing thought—or rather with the norm—with which it is thought of in his liberty by the knowing subject who knows it by comprehension. The norm, then, for an egological foundation, integrates the meaning of the datum to be the conceptualization of the axiological liberty of the datum itself."

true intention of those who enacted it, with regard to the mere connection in existence which there is between this fact and the law.

Unlike juridical rationalism, the egological Theory considers that the objects to be known by the jurist are not rules, but human conduct viewed from a certain particular angle. In the same manner as the objects of astronomy are the stars and not the laws of Kepler and Newton, because these are only concepts by which the stars are known, so in the Dogmatic Science the objects of knowledge of the jurist are not rules but human conduct in its intersubjective interaction, since juridical rules are only concepts by which that conduct is known as conduct. Rules are simply the concepts by which we think of that conduct. In themselves, as concepts, they are ideal objects of a logical type, like all concepts; hence the study of rules as such is the care of formal juridical Logic, of which the investigations of Kelsen, which are known as the pure Theory of the Law, contain the outlines and general fundamentals. But the Dogmatic Science, so far as it is a science of reality, contains something beyond juridical Logic, which proceeds directly and immediately from human experience, just as natural experience puts into Physics something which does not proceed from the mere logical structure of the knowledge of Nature, as the following example illustrates: With the same logical structure and without violating the formal laws of thought (which would *ipso facto* invalidate the knowledge) we may conceive that if the distance between two bodies *A* and *B* is diminished, it is because *A* has approached *B* or because *B* has approached *A*. The two possibilities appear equal in the logical laws of thought; and if the fact is that *A* has approached *B*, and not the reverse, this is something more in knowledge which is added by intuition to the logical structure as a determination which experience supplies.

Again, unlike juridical empiricism, the egological Theory considers that human conduct is an object of experience radically different from natural objects, since while they constitute an experience necessarily governed by the identity of causes with effects, human conduct constitutes an experience of liberty, in which the creation of something original appears every instant. It is for this reason that we cannot think of conduct as conduct, that is to say, conduct at liberty, as a being, as empiricism pretends, but as an existing ought-to-be. And only by holding concepts which show or represent conduct as it ought to be can we have a Dogmatic Science which shall be a science of reality, as the egological Theory maintains. Therefore the egological Theory accepts the normative Logic of the pure Theory of the Law which has shown us that rules are precisely such concepts. But it regards the special intuition of the Law, which is the intuition of liberty—and therefore an axiological intuition — as something more in knowledge which is added to the logico-juridical structure by virtue of human experience.

The purpose of this Introduction is simply to show all these things which have been asserted of the egological Theory of the Law; to show them without argument on their dominant conceptions, by their mere neutral exposition. And as such exposition tends not only to bring out the novelties with which the egological conception enriches juridical theory, but also to show its fertility for the jurist, it must be a concrete exposition: that is to say, an exposition which shall be so close to the work which engages the practical jurist (judge or lawyer) that it may aid him immediately to know better what it is that he is doing or what it is that occurs in that reality in which he takes conscious part. For this reason there has been chosen as the subject of the egological exposition the subject of the judicial decision, which is not only concrete and immediate for every man of Law, but is also the most dramatic and conclusive, whether one looks at it from the theoretical side or from the practical side.

Consequently, it could also be said that the purpose of this Introduction is to show the decision as it is a piece or fragment of juridical experience. To see it, then, from within as living; not from without, as rationalism and empiricism do in different ways. It is a matter of showing it as an act based on that which constitutes its *existence,* not on the *thought* impressed in the procedural codes where rationalism stops; since plainly a procedural code contains only thoughts concerning the decision, there being as much difference between thought about a fact and the fact itself, as Bergson suggests, as between a man who knows many things about Paris from travel books without ever having been in that city and one who knows it from having trod its streets. It tries also to describe that act in its *material essence* as a juridical fact, which does not consist in the facts of reading or hearing, thinking and writing, as empiricism tells us, because that which makes the fact of reading to be reading, of thinking to be thinking, and of writing to be writing, is a factualness totally different from that which makes the decision a fact of juridical experience, since the factualness of the decision is the same as that of the Law (factualness of conduct in its intersubjective interaction), while in the factualness of reading, thinking, and writing as such another essential is made real. And in all this, naturally, there will be left to one side the contingent contents of the Dogmatic, which have to be considered by the scientist, and only by him, in relation to a positive regimen; since the task of the philosopher ends on this plane of necessary forms and contents where the scientist takes his stand for his own task.

But to fulfill our purpose, we must first equip ourselves with certain methodical knowledge which will clear the road and provide us with a common language.

2. Objects and the Methodical Approach to Their Knowledge

In the first place, since the Law is unquestionably culture, it is desirable to distinguish well between the most general families of objects, in accordance with Husserl's idea of regional ontologies; understanding by object anything which may be the motive for an assertion after a judgment: a number, a tree, a historic personage, a mythological being, a law, are objects.

We distinguish, then, in accordance with that idea, between ideal, natural, cultural, and metaphysical objects by a triad of characteristics.

Ideal objects are unreal, that is to say, they simply are of this or that sort, consist of this or that, but do not have existence; moreover, they are not in experience, they are out of time; and finally they are neutral in value, their composition implies no axiological qualification. Among them are the objects to which Logic and Mathematics refer. For example, the object "triangle" which Geometry studies consists simply of pure space closed by three lines, but it does not exist anywhere; it is not in experience because the triangle of the geometer is none of those which may be drawn in the books and on the slates; and finally it is neutral in value because the properties of that object which can only be geometrical properties lack any quality seen as beauty, health, justice, etc.; the properties which Geometry studies, which are geometrical properties, are all the properties which the triangle has so far as it is an object.

Natural objects, studied by the various natural sciences are, for their part, real: they have existence; they are in experience; they are in time; and they are neutral in value: in themselves their being is not good or bad, just or unjust, handsome or ugly, useful or useless. If we consider a stone or a bird, we shall verify freely all these things.

Cultural objects or goods created in some manner by man motivated by preferences are, in their turn, real: they have existence, they are in experience; they are in time; but they are enriched with a positive or negative sign: just or unjust, handsome or ugly, useful or useless are properties which may qualify their being and such being has always to have at least one qualification of that class. A statute, a tool, a decision fully possess these characterizations.

Finally, metaphysical objects are real, they have existence; they are not in experience and they are appraisable. So, for example, God, who is conceived as the most real reality and the highest good, is not in experience since he cannot be seen anywhere nor can we attain to him by the operation of any of our senses.

The following table exhibits what we have just said:

REGIONAL ONTOLOGIES

Objects	Character I	Character II	Character III
Ideal	Unreal: have no existence	Are not in experience	Neutral in value
Natural	Real: have existence	Are in experience	Neutral in value
Cultural	Real: have existence	Are in experience	Valued positively or negatively
Metaphysical	Real: have existence	Are not in experience	Valued positively or negatively

We leave aside metaphysical objects, which can give us no useful assistance for the object of this dissertation. On the other hand, since it is clearly evident that an object has to be treated by a method adequate to its nature, we must elucidate the various gnosiological methods which correspond to the ideal, natural, and cultural objects, as well as make clear the act of knowledge of which these methods are composed. Both things are fundamental: the first, that is the methods, because without correlation between object and method, scientific work has no effective perspective and because the ontological differences are so immense and so marked between such objects that they have no common method. And the second, that is the act of knowledge of which the method is composed, because that act is the meaning which is translated into each method as such, so that if we do not know it we shall not know what it is we obtain by employing the method.

The truths regarding ideal objects, as Logic and Mathematics show, are obtained by a rational-deductive method. To deduce is to start with one or more general truths and to draw from them as a conclusion some particular truth. This proceeding from the general to the particular is valid rationally; it is valid because it is founded on reason as a conformity with reason; and hence the conclusion can never be contrary to the premises. Therefore when practiced on rational truths, the deductive method is wholly valid to obtain truths. There must then be taken into account the distinction of Leibnitz between rational truths and factual truths. Rational truths are apodictical; that is to say, they not only are as they are, but they could not fail to be so, it being impossible that they should be in any other manner. For example: $1 + 1 = 2$ is so, and cannot be in any other manner. On the other hand, a factual truth is declaratory; that is, it is as it is only because things happen so, but there is no contradiction in thinking that it might have been different. For example, when I affirm that metals expand when heated, I tell a truth because actually it happens in fact, but there is nothing impossible in supposing that metals should contract when heated. In factual truth experience speaks; if I do not inquire of experience, I cannot know of what the truth consists. On the other hand, in rational truth, thought speaks; to know that $1 + 1 = 2$ it is not necessary to put out two tangible balls, since it is sufficient for me to think of the matter.

We find, then, that the deductive method is a complete instrument of truth when it is practiced upon rational truths. But if deduction requires a general principle as a starting point, as we say (we deduce always of or from something), this means that the method demands, at its origin, a rational truth. In Mathematics there are the axioms, in Logic there are, among other things, the so-called supreme logical Principles, such as identity and noncontradiction. These axiomatic truths, as is well known, are indemonstrable; but they do not need demonstration, because they are directly evident.

This is the point to explain what is the act of knowing or gnosiological act which constitutes the rational-deductive method and from which it receives its meaning. This act is called *intellection* or intellectual intuition. Intuition in general is direct and immediate contact of the knower with the object known; it is a nonconceptual apprehension of the object, in a manner which happens not because it is thought of or because thought mentions it or directs itself toward the object in a merely representative manner, but which happens because the object is before us and we have it here in our presence. Intuition knows colors, for example; hence a person blind from birth cannot be made to know what blue is as such. Intuition knows things which we see or touch. In general, all the organs of our senses are sources of intuitions. But this is sensory intuition; it is to be noted that sensory intuition differs from mere sensation in that the former affirms or predicates the existence of that which provokes the sensation. We have no sensation of the existence of things; but existence, in general and without exception, recognizes sensations by sensory intuition and only by it: existence also is before us, in an immediate form; and therefore lends itself to sensory intuition.

But there is also intellectual intuition when the object of knowledge is an ideal object. Here, one sees the object not with his eyes but with his intelligence; now the object of knowledge is directly present before the intelligence. Let us consider the following example:

$$1 + 1 = 2 \qquad \begin{array}{r} 12396 \\ +\ 15983 \\ 17740 \\ \hline 46119 \end{array}$$

These two sums are equally rational truths; in such sense they are equally apodictical and both can be demonstrated as to their truth by the use of the same mathematical laws in the same manner. But it can escape no one that, besides, the first presents itself to us with an immediacy and fullness of evidence which we do not have from the second. And this is why we know the second only by thought so far as we think conceptually, while the first, moreover, we apprehend as it were seeing the very sum with our intelligence; the sum and its internalness are there before our intelligence, in full clarity and in direct and immediate form. This is the evidence possessed by the mathematical axioms, for which reason they do not need to be demonstrated. This is the meaning of the rational-deductive method which always presupposes intellection at its starting point, to give us full truths. This is the evidence possessed also by all the numerous logical principles, so that logical intellection accompanies always every kind of truth because, whatever be the act of knowledge which the mind performs, in it there is applied always, besides other things, a logical principle.

We may now define intellection as a seeing with the intelligence without doing more than seeing. And by seeing with the intelligence we now apprehend not the existence but the essence of objects; being able to have, also, a blindness of the intelligence for ideas equal to the blindness of the senses for things.

All intuition, sensory or intellectual, has alike something personal; and is therefore incommunicable and intransmissible, different from the concept or significance which may be the same for all minds. For example, the concept of a mammal or of a right angle may be the same for all of us; but the intuitive verification of what is meant by such concepts has to be seen with the eyes of each person or given effect by the intelligence of each one. Hence it is that the intuitive is not demonstrated but simply is shown. It cannot be demonstrated that this slate is black; it can only be shown that it is so. Thus it is clear that intuition in general is the instrument which permits us to describe the object we are trying to know; it being evident that the description of the object, to know to what we should attend to understand what it is, is a stage prior to any later conceptual elaboration in the scientific work, however little may this be the custom among jurists, as we shall prove later, in the description of the decision so far as it is a juridical fact, as we shall describe it in this work.

Intellection or intellectual intuition is, then, seeing with the intelligence, the ideal object or essence, without doing anything more than seeing. Common to all intuition, intellectual or sensory, is that "seeing" (in the widest sense), without doing anything more than seeing. That is, it is a question of a neutral act in which I, the knower or investigator, am a simple spectator; an act of mere apprehension in which the knowing subject takes passively what the object gives him, and, without introducing himself into the datum, taking a position or attitude toward it or creating it as an object with any reference to any position taken by him.

Let us look now at truths with reference to natural objects. As the different Natural Sciences prove, these truths are obtained by an *empiric-inductive* method. To induce is to start from facts and to obtain from them, by abstraction and generalization, a principle which is conceptual and general. This proceeding from the particular to the general and from the concrete to the conceptual, is valid in its factualness; valid because it is founded on natural experience in conformity with experience itself, which is something given and created once and forever, since all the variations and transformations which we observe in phenomena are appearances of that identity and are known as a function of it in invariable causal constancy. Here the conclusion is a declaratory, not an apodictical truth, because the starting point is facts; and already we know what characterizes factual truths. Operating from this starting point, the empiric-inductive method is a complete instrument of truth; and so we obtain the truths which we know about Nature.

Seeking now the act of knowing or gnosiological act of which the empiric-inductive method consists and from which it receives its meaning, we shall say that it is called *explanation*. To explain something is to break it up into its elements for analysis. Also it is — and this is what most interests us here — to refer something as effect to something else as cause. In both cases, says Pucciarelli with perfect conciseness, "we turn the attention beyond the object itself: toward its cause or toward its elements. To explain consists, then, in referring a fact to something outside, to something it is not, and to reconstruct it as a synthesis of factors foreign to the fact itself." [2] Explanation also is a neutral act: the knowing subject does not introduce himself into the object or take any position toward it. But in explanation the object is not described because we refer it to something which is not itself; that is, we go forward from

[2] Eugenio Pucciarelli, *La comprensión en Dilthey*, in the review HUMANIDADES (La Plata, 1938), 26, 320.

intuition of it to some other intuition, and we know it as a function of this other. To clarify this, we may consider the knowledge of what it is to give birth, so different on the part of the mother who delivers (intuition) and the doctor who helps her with his conceptual wisdom.

Let us look now at cultural objects, among which we find the Law. We say that those objects have existence, that they are in experience and that they have values. These three are evident characteristics; think, for example, of the Venus de Milo, which is in the Louvre, draped, armless, beautiful to serenity. The fact that these objects are real and in experience requires little attention from us after the foregoing explanations. We shall recall, only, that knowledge of them requires, consequently, a perceiving intuition. This has to be remembered with regard to the Law, for since Savigny the jurist knows that the sole and only Law is positive Law, which is a tangible human reality and which is human experience within arm's length of us.

But the other character, the fact that cultural objects have values, must detain us a moment. Cultural objects are not values, since these are not realities. The value resides or appears as a quality in the goods. The Venus de Milo, for example, is not beauty; it only shares this value and we say that it is beautiful, just as we do not say that it is whiteness, but only that it is white, since that is the color of its marble.

But here arises a difference from the natural world, which is neutral to values. The beauty which we assign to the Venus de Milo makes us see that this object, as a cultural object, implies the existence of a meaning which we call Beauty. All cultural objects exist so: as the existence of a meaning in some aspect. If it is a statue, it will be beautiful or ugly in greater or less degree; if it is a tool, it will be useful or useless; if it is a law, it will be just or unjust. Neutrality or indifference to these valuations does not occur; its possibility is a necessary constant. And without this axiological meaning the cultural object does not exist as such, but as Nature: apart from its meaning, the Venus de Milo is a certain number of pounds of marble which possesses in the laboratory the same properties as any other piece whatever of marble.

But a meaning only exists as living in the psychological consciousness of someone. That is to say that the existence of a meaning demands necessarily a living being. The result is surprising because it signifies that the existence of a cultural object — an evident thing, as we see — requires not only the existence of the substratum or the something in which the meaning appears, but also the existence of the living phase of the meaning, which is an existence necessarily psychological and personal. This conclusion is confirmed on seeing that every truth which declares something neutral of its object may be expressed in an independent judgment, without need of making any reference to the subject which, finally, makes the noted declaration. For example, if I say that the earth travels around the sun, this truth does not depend in any degree upon me, and to be understood it does not have to be completed with any reference to the person who utters it. On the other hand, when I say that the Venus de Milo is beautiful or that a fur overcoat is useful to protect from the cold, complete understanding of those judgments requires necessarily reference to a subject included in them: the Venus de Milo is beautiful for me or for someone else; the fur overcoat is useful to protect someone from the cold (by which is meant not only that it is efficient for that purpose, but that my utilitarian activity so understands it); but it is not useful for a stone or for a polar bear or even for a dog, although he obtains warmth from it (the meaning of the efficiency just mentioned), because the action of the dog which covers up in it does not require the utilitarian meaning to be known as such.

This shows that in the knowledge of cultural objects the knowing subject is not a spectator who merely perceives the datum, but in some form introduces himself into the datum to animate the meaning, since such animation is necessary for the existence of the meaning and since the existence of the meaning makes it a cultural object. Expressing it in another way, let us say that this gnosiological act is not an act of apprehension, but a taking of a position on the part of the knowing subject because he penetrates into the known object and sees it from within, from this or that angle, from this or that position; but always from inside; that is he sees the cultural object as well as the meaning; he sees in what the cultural object consists, since its being is to be a meaning.

This act of the consciousness or gnosiological act by which is constituted an adequate method to understand cultural objects, is called *comprehension*. Let us explain Nature, let us understand Culture, was the motto of Dilthey. We can now say that comprehension is to see a meaning in something, but saying at the same time that it is seen because a meaning is somehow alive: the knowing subject puts in the reality which he understands and the meaning does not exist except as living. It follows from this that comprehension seems somewhat like intellection: it also is a seeing with the intelligence; but it is not a seeing which implies nothing more than the seeing, for it is a seeing which sees the coming to see which refers the seeing to the I; that is, which sees what it sees as seen, just as what we love we love as beloved and what we desire we desire as desired; something which does not happen in intellection where the seen is seen as it is, but not with the quality of seen since this quality does not constitute the being of what is seen here. On the other hand, in the comprehension of what is seen it is seen with the quality of seen because this quality forms the being of what is seen: if what we love we love with the quality of beloved it is because that being beloved forms the very object loved.[3] This example is particularly illustrative, since if indeed it is true that the lover does not put in all that there is in the loved object, it is also undeniable that being loved is a quality which the lover puts in and which forms the object, since he loves it as something which is loved. We should say that not only is it loved because he loves it, but at the same time that he loves it because among other things it is loved; thus in the comprehension of the phenomenon of love cannot be seen a mere effect of associationist psychology, as if the beloved object were a cause foreign to the loving feeling which produces such sentiment as an effect in the lover, since it is clear that this sentiment qualifies the object and from it the being loved acts as loved. In the same manner, when we characterize a law as just or unjust on thinking of the conduct which it predesigns, the characterization is not an effect of the law on the knowing subject, but is the meaning of the conduct noted by the law, and as such a quality of that conduct, the more as that meaning is imparted by the awareness of the knowing subject and exists only as the awareness of some one: also here the being

[3] This passage is so fantastic, with the exaggerated use of the *figura etymologica,* that we reproduce the original text, and those who know Spanish may try their own versions. "Ella también es un ver con la inteligencia; pero no es un ver que ponga nada más que el ver, sino que es un ver que ve el viendo del ver puesto que refiere el ver al yo; es decir, que a lo que ve lo ve como visto, tal como a lo que amamos lo amamos como amado y a lo que queremos lo queremos como querido; cosa que no ocurre en la intelección donde a lo visto se lo ve como es, pero no con la calidad de visto porque esta calidad no constituye el ser de lo que aquí se ve. En cambio, en la comprensión a lo que se ve se lo ve con la calidad de visto porque esta calidad integra el ser de lo que se ve: si a lo que amamos lo amamos con la calidad de amado es porque eso de ser amado integra el propio objeto amado." P. 37. Cf. Don Quixote, pt. I, chap. I, para. 2: "La razón de la sinrazón que a mi razón se hace, de tal manera mi razón enflaquece, que con razón me quejo de la vuestra fermosura." Professor Cossio has also kindly supplied a version in German of these two sentences, by his friend, Professor O. E. Langfelder, now of Buenos Aires, as follows: "Es ist ebenfalls ein Sehen (Wahrnehmen) mit dem Verstand, aber es ist nicht ein Sehen, das nur das Sehen setzt (nichts anders als), sondern eines, das das Sehendsein des Sehens sieht (wahrnimmt), da es das Sehen auf das Ich bezieht. Das heisst also, dass es das, was es sieht, als Gesehenes sieht, ebenso wie wir das, was wir lieben, als Geliebtes lieben, und das was wir wollen möchten als Gewolltes, Gemochtes wollen möchten, ein Umstand, der bei der Einsicht (Intellektion) nicht zutrifft, die das Gesehene so sieht wie es ist, nicht hingegen mit der Qualität (Bestimmung) 'Gesehenes,' da diese nicht das Sein des diesfalls Gesehenen ausmacht. Im Verstehen hingegen sieht man das Gesehene mit der Eigenschaft (Bestimmung) des Gesehenseins, weil diese Eigenschaft (Bestimmung) das Sein dessen, was man sieht, integriert. Wir lieben das, was wir lieben, mit der Eigenschaft (Bestimmung) 'Geliebtes,' weil dieses Geliebt-zu-sein das geliebte Objekt selbst integriert." TRANSLATOR.

just or unjust forms the being of the conduct noted by the law and in it we come to value it as just, so that the valuation which the subject makes is part of what he sees in the object valued. It results, then, even on first examination, that we appreciate the Venus de Milo not only because it is beautiful, but also at the same time that it is beautiful because *in itself and so* we appreciate it. The same is true for a decision and the justice of it. But in either example we may still express ourselves better, detaching the unity from both dialectic moments; we should say, strictly, that we appreciate a decision because it is just, understanding already that it is just because in it and so we appreciate it: by which we know it as an object: wherefore we say *in it* and *so*. We know it, it is clear, with a knowledge of comprehension, which is that which corresponds to its ontological nature. Thus, to appreciate is exactly to know.

Naturally this gnosiological act of seeing in something its meaning but putting in it at the same time that it is seen, implies, in some way, removing from the meaning to get it from a certain perspective; precisely from the perspective which imposes the substratum of meaning for being in this form and not in that, for having this peculiarity and not another, etc., all of which we shall explain presently.

Again, it follows also that comprehension somewhat resembles explanation. Comprehension, in fact, also refers something to another thing which is not the same as that something. We have already seen that the cultural object demands the existence of a substratum where appears the meaning and the existence of the reality of the meaning. One thing is as real as the other, and there are no things without both realities. It does not matter that the substratum may be a fragment of the physical world as occurs in mundane objects (the canvas and the colors in the painting, the sound vibrations in music or poetry, etc.) or that the substratum may be the very acts of human conduct as occurs in egological objects. Then, in the gnosiological act of comprehension we refer one of those events to the other, whether from the materiality of the substratum we rise to its meaning, as occurs with things already created; or from the meaning we pass to the substratum, as occurs in the creative moment of the thing which is called inspiration.

But while the explanation proceeds, without retrocession, in the same direction indicated at its moment of departure (for example: from the effect to its causes and from them to their respective causes and so each time more remote; or from the whole to its elements and from them to their respective elements and so each time to something more simple), comprehension, on the other hand, returns after the first reference to its point of departure and from here again to the former reference and so successively in an indefinite circular movement which goes from the substratum to its meaning and vice versa. Knowledge by explanation is constituted and concluded with a departure at some point from the direction which the explanation takes, so that what it sums up in synthesis is always the known object and something which is not it; on the other hand, knowledge by comprehension, which is constituted and concluded also by a departure at some moment from that circular movement, sums up in synthesis the known object as a whole, but without going outside of it. In knowledge by explanation, whoever goes back in the direction taken by the knowing mind does not increase the knowledge, since what was already explained remains wholly known. On the other hand we are going to learn that each return in direction with respect to its previous stage increases knowledge by comprehension.

With all that we have been saying it has already been made clear that the adequate method to know a cultural object is an *empiric-dialectic method,* since it is this which is constituted by the gnosiological act of comprehension. Dialectic in general is the synthesis realized by the spirit by its own spontaneous activity, of a thesis and an alternative thesis[4] in the function of a mutually totalizing implication. In this way we have access to cultural objects provided we see that their comprehension circulates from the substratum to the meaning and vice versa, making one the thesis and the other the alternative thesis. Things as such are not known by induction, since nothing is generalized in their knowledge; to rest on induction, the man who has always seen ugly statues would conclude that the Venus de Milo is ugly also when he is placed before it for the first time; of which, certainly, there is no evidence or necessity; on the contrary, the experience is otherwise which we all have on discovering unexpectedly a positive value for the first time. And no more are things as such known by deduction since for them we lack the intellectual evidence which would have to serve as starting point for deductive reasoning, unless we should admit, with more conviction than that with which Plato speaks to us, a metaphysics of reminiscence, as to that seen by the soul before our birth.[5] Things as such are known in dialectic form passing from the materiality of the sub-

[4] It is not necessary that there should be an antithesis as Hegel thought. The antithesis is only one particular case of peculiar modality, of heterothesis.

[5] Plato; Meno, Dialogue, *Of Virtue,* 85 d. "And this spontaneous recovery (of knowledge) in him (boy slave of Meno) is recollection?" 85 e. "But if he did not acquire this knowledge in this life, then clearly he must have had and learned it at some other time." (Jowett's Translation.)

stratum to the reality of their spiritual meaning, and vice versa; accrediting the empirical character of the substratum as by the reality of their being.

If we observe mathematical knowledge and its process, we note that one acquires it as a *simple and closed whole,* without passing through different stages or separate parts; for example, whoever knows the rules of addition and has to add a non-intuitional sum, begins his operation and continues without transitions or interruptions to the end, where he finds all at once what he was seeking: it is of no value to add the tens and not the hundreds which are not independent of them; immediately the result is obtained there is nothing more to seek; and this knowledge does not increase if one proves it by doing the operation again; and it is as total and full for a mathematical specialist as for a young student. Again, observing natural knowledge and its process, we note that one acquires it as a *compound and open whole,* passing through separate stages or different parts; for example, when one tries to determine the forces which have caused a movement, the determination of each factor intervening as a cause or a component of the result is accomplished in a separate step from those concerning the other factors, which reveals nothing as to them and which may be pursued separately and apart whenever desired: immediately the result is obtained, that is, immediately on establishing the causes of the movement one may still ascertain the causes of the causes, and so on; and this knowledge increases in the degree in which one continues toward the open horizon.

On the other hand, if we observe cultural knowledge and its process, we note that one acquires it as a *simple, but open, whole;* without passing through separate stages or parts, but with a continuous and fluid increase of knowledge. We have already seen the simplicity of the cultural object, because the substratum and its meaning are not two alien and external things between themselves, but two things which intermingle in a single unity. Notwithstanding this, each time that cultural knowledge, in its circular movement, passes from the substratum to its meaning and then from the latter to the former, and so on, cultural knowledge increases and knows the object better and better. Think of the athlete who plays better the more he practices his sport, in which there is not a mere muscular automatism or an improvement of the organic substratum, but also a finer understanding of the meaning of the sport. Think of music which we understand better the more we hear it, or, on the contrary, after having dazzled us with its sonorousness, on hearing much we find that it was dullness or monotony without depth. Think of the nuances which we find in a great book of science or philosophy, each time that we reread it; nuances which the author put there and which were there, but which we did not appreciate in the preceding readings and which carry us further or disclose to us the error of the work, unnoticed until then. In all this we see how knowledge is increased and affirmed by comprehension each time that it returns from where it is found (in substratum or in meaning) to the other dialectic term which constitutes it, since to return is for the spirit to gain in intimacy with what it treats of. It is nothing different which occurs to the Judge when he is going to declare a decision: the Judge considers the case in all its complex of circumstances; then its juridical meaning which will appear in the decision as he outlines a rough draft of the decision; then he returns to the case to see if this corresponds in fact to its meaning; then he returns again to its formation, perhaps emphasizing some circumstance which passed unnoticed the first time; then he returns once more to the case and its circumstances, perhaps giving weight to what some lost article of the code says or perhaps only with a greater refining of the juridical meaning of the case; and so he continues in this circular movement which goes from one member to the other, his knowledge gaining in firmness and clarity, which is knowledge by comprehension, whether it confirms the juridical meaning of its first formation, or whether it has been replaced even after having been found technically founded on the laws, because of finding that, in spite of this, it is not adequate to the case for not being truly the meaning of the case. The truth is that the decision comes forth as a comprehension of the case in its ought-to-be, representing precisely that in conceptual form when the conviction of the Judge is complete; which signifies that the human conduct which constitutes the solution of the case insofar as it is a consequence imputed to its antecedents is understood in its meaning of order, of security, of power, of peace, of coöperation, of solidarity and of positive justice, all of which is what the decision describes or represents insofar as the concept of the Judge refers to such conduct as object.

Naturally this estimative meaning of the conduct described by the decision and whose existence is in the being of the Judge, is not a capricious meaning left unlimited to judicial pleasure. In no cultural knowledge is the meaning a capricious whole, since, in the dialectic process of comprehension, not only is the substratum judged from the meaning, but immediately the meaning is judged from the substratum, so that this point of view which furnishes the materiality of the substratum in both instances, respectively takes away all extravagance in the direction of the meaning and gives an objective point of support to the accommodation between both within a circumscribed frame of possibilities. Each time that the substratum is judged from the meaning, the latter is established for the knowing subject by re-creation in his life;

but each time that the meaning is judged from the substratum, there is a judgment of comparison in logical terms which raises the valuation to an objective plane; in both cases one seeks an accommodation between the substratum and its meaning. So, for example, the "Träumerei" of Schumann, with a being so simply expressed that it consists of the repetition of the same motive seven times, may be comprehended and interpreted in different manners by different performers, but only within certain limits, since not even the most famous musician could make the "Marseillaise" heard out of it. So also the Judge, as we shall see further on, has a limited fringe of possible meanings with respect to the conduct which he describes or represents conceptually in the decision.

The description of the decision so far as it is a fact of juridical experience, which we shall accomplish in this work by showing it to be a structure of the concrete validity of the Law, will show what of intellection and of comprehension there is in it. Hereby we shall not have emerged from the world of facts, like rationalism, for we shall not limit ourselves to thoughts about the decision which brings in its articles a Code of Procedure. We shall consider those facts on which juridical significations, are constituted in experience, so that neither shall we allude at all to the facts without intrinsic juricity such as reading, thinking, and writing, like empiricism, because it is clear that if some juridical signification occasionally touches these, it is in the degree in which they themselves are involved in the factitious and necessary structure which we are going to consider.

3. The Judge and the Law

Before entering upon this topic, we have still to refer to another supposition of the egological Theory. But this will take us less time than the preceding because we have to go on gradually verifying it in the course of the exposition.

The pure Theory of the Law has shown us that the juridical order constitutes a gradation of norms by which one descends by stages from the logico-juridical hypothesis or fundamental norm, through norms more or less general, to individual norms,[6] the only ones which describe

[6] Interrupting with this Note the character of this Introduction, we have to emphasize the existence of individual norms in the juridical order (for example: the decision, administrative resolutions and juridical matters), since juridical rationalism has grievously extended on this point its last line of theoretical defense, in its eagerness to identify the Law and the statute with the purpose of presenting the Judge as a mere applier of the Law.

But there is no doubt whatever that the decision is an individual norm, as Kelsen has shown, because, on being constituted with the connective ought-to-be, it has all the essence of normativity. Moreover, a contract has never been denied the character of norm in spite of being equally individual; and so it is that from ancient times it has been seen as the source of obligations.

We see now the two errors with which juridical rationalism combats individual normativity, making use of the proposition denounced above. We may use at this point the work of Sebastian Soler, *Algunas Observaciones a la doctrina de Hans Kelsen,* for in his double capacity of jurist and philosopher he makes his objections particularly lively and weighty, and because Soler heads in Argentina the most respectable resistance to rationalism.

I. The first objection of Soler will consist in saying that the decision is not a hypothetical norm, since that character is found only in general norms or statutes. With this he finds an incongruence in the doctrine of Kelsen for that author affirms the character of hypothetical judgment for the juridical norm in general.

But the word hypothetical has three meanings, of which Soler misses the third, which is precisely that which is interesting at this point, for it is the one which Kelsen uses.

(a) Hypothetical in the popular meaning signifies a probable thesis or a fact to be verified. In this sense Soler says: "What only *ought to be* will not constitute more than a hypothesis in relation to what really is." And he adds that this is not the meaning which Kelsen uses. Undoubtedly it is not, because in this meaning of the term judgment is considered for its modality and judgment will logically be problematic, not hypothetical. Kelsen has expressly put himself on guard against this misinterpretation in his monograph, *The Pure Theory of Law and Analytical Jurisprudence,* showing that the confusion between the problematic character and the hypothetical character of a judgment means that a normative proposition has been made to lose its specific character and has been diluted in a sociologism, as if the Dogmatic should make declarations of probability as to social life. But it is strange that Soler falls into this confusion (pp. 295, 297, and 311), as we shall see presently, when he says that the statute is hypothetical in this sense and the decision is not.

(b) Hypothetical in the gnosiological sense signifies solely the unconditioned presupposition or condition of the validity of juridical knowledge without which that knowledge cannot come into play. In this respect Soler says: "That all juridical reasoning should have meaning, it is necessary that there be given as an incontrovertible supposition the act of the first original legislator. That norm may be called hypothetical *because the possibility is manifest that it might be otherwise.* In fact, there coexist as many regimes as nations and even within one single nation there are many juridical regimes which have succeeded one another. *The fundamental norm, then, is not necessary in itself.*

"On this broad base are being placed new norms ever less general, until they build the figure of a true normative pyramid. Now, if we cut through this pyramid at any height to examine the structure of any norm whatever which is not the fundamental norm, we shall see that *that norm does not by itself possess a hypothetical character* but that is accorded it by the fundamental norm upon which it was placed."

We cannot say that in these passages there is a comprehension of the thought of Kelsen. It is not true that the fundamental norm is hypothetical for the manifest possibility that it might be otherwise. And it is not true that the fundamenal norm is not necessary in itself. The fundamental norm is hypothetical because it is the *a priori* gnosiological hypothesis which the jurist makes in order to be able to think as a jurist of a positive law; that is, because it is the gnosiological condition of his own thought. And it is necessary in itself insofar as it is the starting point which avoids a return to the infinite in the thought of the jurist: without it, indeed, there would be no dogmatic knowledge. Contingent alone are the concrete contents judged or thought of normatively with the fundamental norm, but not the hypothetical imputation of these contents which the jurist makes to have a positive starting point (see CARLOS COSSIO, EL CONCEPTO PURO DE REVOLUCIÓN 204–206 and 214). These contingent contents alone explain that the concrete fundamental norms of two States are diverse, but without putting in question the equal necessity of one for each of them as points of support for the dogmatic knowledge which the jurist will give us from those orders. For example, the only manner of judicializing dogmatically our battle of Caseros,* so far as it is the antecedent of our National Constitution, is *to suppose* that battle as the normative antecedent of the Constitution, in a norm which shall say: "Given the battle of Caseros, there ought to be the Constitution of 1853." Only so is the battle of Caseros the commencement of a new juridical order and not the transgression of the preceding juridical order. It is evident that juridico-dogmatic thought presents itself as a chain of norms in subordination: To the question "why a decision of our judges ought to be?" we answer because there is a statute which that decision carries out. And to the question "why ought the statute to be?" we answer because there is a constitution which that statute carries out. And if now we reach the fundamental norm asking why ought the Constitution to be, there is only one inescapable and necessary response: because the original Legislator has to be obeyed. It being evident that the Public Power which triumphed at Caseros follows the original Legislator only if to that battle is imputed, by hypothesis, the Constitution of 1853; since if such hypothetical imputation is not made, the battle of Caseros would not be the dogmatic antecedent of the Constitution.

It is clear that the battle of Caseros is contingent and that so also is the constitutional text of 1853. But the manner of thinking of these facts which the jurist employs is not contingent. Without doubt we may express historically the Constitution of 1853 by the battle of Caseros; but neither with one thing nor the other do we explain the mode or style of thinking which the jurist uses when he presents to us a positive dogmatic such as ours upon those facts. Therefore it appears that obedience to the original Legislator is not an exigency which the battle of Caseros or the National Constitution creates, but that it is a mental exigency of the jurist, absolutely inescapable, when he takes those facts as a starting point for the dogmatic truth which he is going to show us. Obedience to the original Legislator, which is the fundamental norm, is a conceptual exigency of that type of thought which we call normative or dogmatic thought; in this sense it is not in the facts nor has it their contingency, but it is in thought itself as the supposition which conditions the validity of the knowledge which the jurist gives us. Similarly, the normative exigency, in spite of its necessity, is not a positive norm but the obligatory starting point which the dogmatic jurist has and which reveals by itself the nature of the logical mechanism upon which this knowledge is sustained. Or, as we have said before, the fundamental norm is a gnosiological hypothesis.

(c) Hypothetical in the logical sense is the judgment whose enunciation depends on a condition which does not form a part of or is foreign to the enunciation itself. It is a matter, here, consequently, of two judgments, one of which is made of a thesis and the other of a condition, in such form that the thesis of the first is not valid except when it has complied with the condition to which it is subordinated. Hypothetical is, then, the form of the judgment as such because it is conditioned; that is, it is not a matter of the validity of the knowledge as in the case of the gnosiological hypothesis on which under the logical hypothesis rests the material to be known, but of the validity of the thought because the material known is conditioned by other known material and this relation is that which is thought of in the hypothetical judgment.

In this sense Kelsen says that every positive juridical norm possesses by itself a hypothetical character, reasoning in the following manner. Traditional opinion, considering that the Law was an order, understood that the State sought fulfillment of juridical duties: that one should not kill, should not rob, etc. (categorical propositions). But Kelsen notes that it cannot seek conduct of another, but only its own conduct. (It can at the most desire certain conduct of another; but neither can the State have these desires because it lacks psychological consciousness.) So that the will of the State can seek only those acts which compose its will, that is, those acts which are imputed to it as being acts of the State. According to this the State only wishes to apply the sanctions; but this wish is not unconditional: the State wishes to apply the sanctions only if there are produced certain circumstances which we call a wrong or transgression. Hence the juridical will (application of the sanction) which enunciates the norm, appears in a hypothetical judgment because it is subordinated to the fulfillment of a condition (realization of the wrong) which is expressed in the connected judgment integrating and conditioning the principal. Hence, for Kelsen, the juridical norm says simply, "Given the wrong, there ought to be the sanction"; or, as Kelsen explains, the juridical norm only expresses a conditional coactive act; if one robs, the thief ought to be imprisoned. The wrong is thus the logical condition of the sanction in which the will of the State consists and which the norm enunciates. For this reason of formal Logic and not that other gnosiological reason, is why Kelsen says that the juridical norm is a hypothetical judgment. The proof is the circumstance that Kelsen makes this affirmation upon the direct analysis of the norm, long before and in entire independence of his stating the gnosiological-juridical problem of the fundamental norm which concerns the manner of thinking by which the jurist addresses himself to positive Law to know it.

It is clear, then, that in the thought of Kelsen, the law as well as the decision turn out to be hypothetical judgments in themselves, for in both the sanction, so far as it is the will of the State, is subordinated to the logical condition of the wrong. And the wrong interpretation of the pure Theory of the Law into which Soler falls appears when he tells us that positive norms do not possess by themselves a hypothetical character, but that this is accorded them by the fundamental norm in the conception of Kelsen, because Soler does not notice the logico-formal problem propounded by Kelsen. The problem of the fundamental norm is entirely independent of this. Precisely—and Schreier is strong on this—the fundamental norm is not hypothetical in the logical sense because it enunciates simply a *duty:* that of administering the sanction as the original Legislator has provided. And it could not be so, being, as it is, a gnosiological hypothesis; that is, being the unconditional condition of juridical thought in order that the latter may have value as juridical knowledge.

From the hypothetical formulation of the juridical norm which Kelsen makes, there follows another thing which Soler also does not notice and whose difficulties we overcome in presenting the juridical norm as a disjunctive and not a hypothetical judgment. It is the following: For Kelsen, as we have said, the norm strictly by itself is the regulation of the sanction, although that is conditioned by the realization of the wrong. According to this, the juridical duty or performance which is simply the contrary of the wrong—is something which is given as a fact but which is not conceived normatively by the Law. The juridical duty is a fact foreign or strange to the juridical norm since it is not included in what the latter enunciates imperatively. While the wrong is a positive condition of the sanction, the duty appears as a negative condition of it and therefore the norm does not enunciate it. When one wishes to think normatively of the duty, he recurs to what Kelsen calls the secondary norm; and this is an intellectual artifice without proper juridical significance because it thinks in reverse what the norm thinks directly. Thus the idea of juridical duty has a very modest theoretical part and the correlative idea of juridical faculty loses all significance. Our position as to the true significance of all these things will be seen fully in the course of this book.

II. The second objection of Soler will consist in saying that the decision is not an individual norm because there are no individual norms. "There is nothing individual which may be a juridical norm in the true meaning of the word and therefore we ought to reject the doctrine of the individualized juridical norm" (p. 300).

To found this affirmation Soler thinks he is supported by Pfänder when he says that "from the moment in which a concept is referred to individual objects, it ceases to have extension. This detail alone—adds Soler—warns us of some profound transformation which the concept experiences; but with respect to the very change from the general to the individual, let us see what Logic teaches us. As to this Romero and Pucciarelli say: Extension in the logical sense leaves aside concrete individuality, consequently (citing Pfänder), to determine the extension of a concept it is doubtless necessary to consider the circle of objects which fall under it, but to *stop before arriving at the individual objects* and to remain on the lowest planes of the general objects" (p. 299).

But the fact is that none of these authors denies the existence of individual concepts. In the same passages quoted they affirm it, for in them they only say that individual concepts lack extension; which is highly astute. The existence of individual concepts (and for us the decision is an imputative individual concept) is affirmed by all logicians. No one less than Husserl says that the individual, in his logical expression, is also a species. And the great significance of Rickert is in having set the gnosiology of history on the basis of individual concepts.

It is said in Logic that a concept has extension when any inferior species falls under it; "extension is determined by the number of inferior species which fall under it" (PFÄNDER, LOGIK 179); from which it is clear that the individual concept lacks extension. Soler finds himself upset by this technicality of logical language, since the only transformation which the concept experiences by lack of extension is the qualitative difference which comes between the general and the individual. But Soler delivers to the lay reader a ratiocination which leads him to believe that for lack of extension the concept has disappeared, so that there cannot be individual concepts. Nevertheless, the only thing which disappears is generality.

Combining these two objections, which as we have seen rest on two mistakes, Soler draws the conclusion that "the decision is not a norm in itself" (p. 300), because, he says, the decision has not the same formal structure as the law. And he presents this affirmation with the following argument: "In the scheme of the pure juridical norm the first part of it functions as a hypothesis, precisely because it is constituted of a concept endowed with extension. The decision does not preserve that same formal structure, because in it the first part disentangled from coaction consists in the affirmation of a fact as given and not as merely possible" (p. 300).

If we illustrate this by an example, we shall perceive that Soler's error is complete. Let the norm be "he who kills another shall be imprisoned from 8 to 25 years," as our Penal Code says. This means, as is obvious, the following: if anyone shall kill another, the homicide ought to be shut up in prison for from 8 to 25 years. Soler believes that the first phrase of this norm ("if anyone kills another") functions as a hypothesis because this concept has extension; that is, because it is a fact merely

reality in direct and immediate form because every kind of effective reality is constituted of individual things; the universal belongs to thought, but not to existence. For example, "the" mammal does not exist, but these or those mammiferous animals; "the" marble does not exist, but these or those pieces of marble in the quarries or in objects. So the law does not exist except in individual acts (decisions, administrative resolutions, juridical business); without this realization, perforce individual, the law is a mere thought. Our Civil Code has a special rule for inheritance from a natural grandparent (Article 3582). It is not difficult to think that there might have been a special rule for inheritance from an ancestor of the tenth generation; but it is clear that such a hypothetical article would not be a living law; for that would not be strictly a law but only the thought of a law, that is a simple thought and nothing else.

---

possible. The hypothesis for him is the problematic character of the phrase, not the logical conditionality which is what restores the hypothetic to the norm. In this way Soler's argument is totally apart from the logical meaning of the word hypothetic which is the only one of interest and the only one which can decide the disputed question.

When in the individual norm the condition is affirmed—not simply enunciated—; that is, if the decision says "this man has killed another and ought to be imprisoned for 18 years," there does not disappear the hypothetical character of the second part, which continues to be conditioned by the first. And if the condition is affirmed as a given fact, it is because the norm is individual and not general as a concept, since as Romero and Pucciarelli (LOGICA 43) show, as the individual concept lacks extension, *its object is contingent,* so that it needs to be affirmed to overcome its contingency. Concepts with extension, or general ones, which describe species and genera, have no contingency to overcome because species and genera are ideal objects and, in such sense, as objects, have no logical contingency because they are outside of time: they are pure significations.

If, as Soler mistakenly believes, the problematic character of the judgment should constitute its hypothetical character, he ought to have noted that, in the individual norm, the problematic character arises again in the second part since it is only merely possible that the individualized homicide will be imprisoned (he may take flight, etc.). But all this concerns the discussion of liberty which composes the juridical norms; which has to be studied in the text.

* [General Justo José de Urquiza, Governor of Entre Rios Province, who had revolted May 1, 1851, met and defeated the forces of President (Dictator, Tyrant) Juan Manuel de Rosas, Feb. 3, 1852. Rosas resigned, fled to England, and died near Southampton Mar. 17, 1877. Caseros is a small town in Entre Rios Province, about 140 miles north of Buenos Aires, 130 miles east-northeast of Rosario, and 20 miles west of the Uruguay River. A Convention in Santa Fé adopted, May 25, 1853, a federal Constitution much like that of the United States of North America. See further, 3 LUIS V. VARELA, HISTORIA CONSTITUCIONAL DE LA REPÚBLICA ARGENTINA (La Plata, 1910) 515.

Given that the pure Theory of the Law is formal juridical Logic, the teaching of the concept of the juridical pyramid makes us see that juridical Logic is a logic of individualization. Indeed, according to that conception, the passing from one stage of norms to another lower, is done by an act of normative creation, since the application and the creation of the Law are logically relative terms in that Logic, which are co-implied in such manner that the application of a higher norm consists in the creation of a subordinate norm. Consequently, the logical meaning of juridical creation is to go toward the individual or concrete. As we have said, it is a logic of individualization; not a logic of integration, as might be that of History; nor of formalization, like that of Mathematics; nor of generalization, like that of Nature.

What we have said is important because it signifies that the Judge (to limit ourselves to the decision) is not a being strange to the Law nor is outside of the Law, looking at or knowing it from the exterior as a thing concluded and fixed and, so, taking it to apply it when the case appears, like one who impresses the seal in the wax, as follows for the Logic of being. On the contrary, if decisions compose the normative creation in which juridical order consists, it is clear that the Judge, as creator of the decision, *is within,* and not outside of, the order; and *is in* its structure as part of that structure, not as a contingent content built by it. For the first, it is understood that the Judge looks at the Law from within with the Logic of the ought-to-be; and so, not as something concluded and already made, but as something which is constantly being made in its character of living human life. For the second, it follows that he looks at it not only as something which is being made, but as something to the making of which the very Judge is contributing; that is, that, in part, the Law is the very deed of the Judge. Precisely this circumstance that the Judge is the structure of the Law and not merely something accidental built by the Law, gives its ontological meaning to the truth of reason, within the Logic of the ought-to-be, which says that the Judge ought always to decide whatever may be the obscurity or deficiency which he finds in the legal order.

This immanence of the Judge in the Law which follows from the conception of the Law as living human life maintained by the egologic Theory becomes more arduous and peremptory in rectifying the traditional vision the more it is put in connection with what we have said concerning knowledge by comprehension; since if the Judge were an extra-mural spectator, without taking the position of apprehending the object by his own knowledge, he could attain the Law only by intellection or explanatory knowledge. With a wealth of detail it must be seen, then, that the scientific knowledge which the Dogmatic Science expresses is a knowledge by comprehension.

4. Juridical Experience in General

Let us enter the subject. For it, we are not going to commence with the refutation of the dominant juridical rationalism, so far as it believes that the norms are objects which the jurist has to know. Rationalism will be implicitly refuted by all that is said, since for the egological Theory the object of juridical knowledge is human conduct considered in its intersubjective interference; and the norms are only the imputative concepts which that conduct refers to in its ought-to-be, or what is the same thing, which represent it as phenomenalized conduct or liberty. On this account the norms have to be verified by conduct if we are going to speak of the Law in a positive sense. For the egological Theory, the Dogmatic Science of the Law is a science of empirical reality, but of human experience and not of natural experience. And it is so much the more remarkable, at this opportunity, not to take notice of juridical rationalism since, from Savigny on, it is the unanimous conviction of jurists that the Dogmatic is directed toward real and existing Law, which is the positive Law and only that. Whatever may be the gnosiological errors into which the schools — among them the historicism of Savigny — have fallen in conceiving it, all agree on that realistic inspiration; so that we may go at our task taking directly the course of the original moment in which Savigny directs the attention of juridical thought to juridical experience, by the ontologization of positive Law which he brings to a head. We shall try, in consequence, to retrace the route which Savigny found and which, also lost by him, has continued lost until the present time. For us it is a question, then, of reaching juridical experience directly.

On the other hand, to understand this theme well we have to begin with a reference to natural experience, since both cases treat of experience; so that comprehension of what is different between them is transformed into an unescapable and fundamental question.

Let us consider any physical law; for example, that which tells us that metals expand with heat. It was Kant, on breaking down, by analysis, natural experience into its elements, who made us see that in a proposition like the foregoing we always find related two classes of heterogenous elements: on one side, a conceptual structure which is, by itself, intelligible or rational provided that the concepts are thought of by the intellect and share in all of which the intellect consists; and, on the other hand, an empiric content which our sensible intuition grasps.

The conceptual structure of our example would consist in the following scheme or form of thinking: *Given A, B is,*[7] and the empirical content would be in the fact that, as a real datum to put that law to the proof, I have before me a piece of iron and not of copper, I have a flame and not a live coal, etc. Referring to my concrete case I should have to say, then: Given this piece of iron and this flame which approaches it, the expansion of the iron is necessary.

Kant used a double order of characterization to signify unmistakably the differences which separate what corresponds to the structure from what corresponds to the content of natural experience, as is shown in the following table:

I. Characterization	Elements of Natural Experience	II. Characterization
Formal	Logical structure	Necessary
Material	Empiric content	Contingent

In accordance with the first characterization, the structure is formal and the content is material. The structure of experience consists in its form and nothing more; it is *the how it is* of experience; so that the structure in itself is of maximum emptiness in its unreality. On the other hand, the content of experience is the matter which it offers our knowledge: it is *the what it is* in experience; so that the content in itself is blind like an amorphous mass. Natural experience which science reveals to us in its authenticity and fullness is a synthesis of both elements in the relation of form to matter.

In accordance with the second characterization, the logical structure is necessary and universal, so that, invariable, it appears constant in Nature, whatever may be the portion of it which we take for examination. On the other hand, the content is contingent and we can consider

[7] For the purposes of this Introduction it is not necessary to distinguish in this conceptual or logical structure between what is formal Logic or mere legalistic thinking as such and what is transcendental Logic or the intelligible ingredient of knowledge in its apprehension of the object by judgment (in the example, the causal relation between the subject of the proposition and the predicate), because it is known that for Kant both Logics are products of a single activity of the knowing subject, while we are conscious of the first and not of the second. The transcendental Logic of being is reconstructed, in fact, by a gnosiological hypothesis starting from the scientific knowledge already produced and considering in it, as signs of the subject, the synthesis effected by the intellect. But this difference is irrelevant for our theme. It is more important to point out that contemporaneous Logic has well established that formal Logic also is gnosiological, since it involves always the idea of the object in general, it being erroneous to believe that it studies the laws of an empty thinking in the absolute and free from all reference to the whole object.

it effective only when sensible intuition has communicated to us its existence by present action.

This analysis of natural experience as physical science (an analysis which breaks it down into a logical structure and an empirical content) offers us the following peculiarities:

In the first place it is an exhaustive analysis. There is not, in fact, in the existing experience which we have made the object of our inquiry, anything more than that necessary form and that contingent matter. If we suppress the iron, the flame and the expansion and all that was necessary for us for the ideation of these things, there still remains to us, of the example, the logical structure as a possible object of study. But if we also suppress the logical structure, there now remains to us nothing of what the datum of experience had offered to us at the beginning in real unity.

In the second place we would say that the analysis is descriptive of the experience which we know, since it takes it intuitively as it is offered to knowledge, without referring it to other explanatory notions which are not patent in its presence. In the experience of this case we find, in fact, a formal structure and a material content; and both things will be considered because they are found in experience but only in the limits in which they occur, that is, descriptively, adjusted to the experience itself. In Kant the notion of form has a merely descriptive use; amply ratified by modern science which recurs to this word with identical purpose; and such is today its most accredited and diffused acceptation. In this Kantian and scientific meaning, purely descriptive, the notion of form is in richest use since we find it in all parts: geometric forms in bodies, forms of movement whether slow or rapid, etc. Also perception is something, Kant notes with originality, and has to have its forms (logical form in this case). Kant's interest was directed to these seeking the foundation of science, by which to distinguish certainly between forms of knowledge and forms known by knowledge; forms of knowledge turn out to be logical forms of experience in general, so far as that, being known, is thought of always in the same manner and therefore these forms are equal in all experience known as its structure *a priori;* on the other hand, geometric, kinetic, thermic, etc., forms of things, which are integral parts of the things, are forms known in the very experience of the things, and, like them, are contingent contents of experience, but they are not forms of the same experience taken as an object of reflection because here it is not possible to speak of form except as logical or conceptual form of the declaration enunciated in the knowledge. The distinction between the knowing form and the known form marks, then, in the first place, the ambit and function of Logic in the description of scientific work. The knowing forms are thought and, therefore, they are thought of; the known forms are intuitive. A different thing occurs in Aristotelian scholastic language where matter and form are notions bound to those of power and act, and that of the act bound to the notion of purpose; so that the form which things that we see have brings an inherent purpose to them, provided that it is the attainment of a certain degree of being. But it is clear that here we treat of a metaphysical interpretation of the known in experience and not of a positive description, the only point of departure for scientific knowledge.

Finally — and it is the most important for our purpose — let it be noted that the two characterizations of natural experience are superposed perfectly: the formal is necessary and the material is contingent. As the first refers to the conceptual structure, it is enunciated in truths of reason, that is, in truths which are *a priori* and independent of experience itself. On the other hand, the material or contingent is enunciated in truths of fact, which are *a posteriori* to the experience on which they are founded. It is thus that the equivalence between formal, necessary, and *a priori* is constantly used by Kant in his *Critique of Pure Reason,* in a use wholly unobjectionable provided that his investigation concerns the problems arising in Euclidean Mathematics, Newtonian physics and rational Metaphysics, it being true that the knowledge of Nature, as to form or structure of natural experience enjoys those three qualities.[8]

[8] Since Savigny this Kantian conception of Nature gravitates to the way in which the jurists wish to conceive of the Law. This gravitation is so strong that the excision of matter and form in those terms passes as evidence among the jurists, who understand that such excision is descriptive and exhaustive of juridical experience; and that form admits equality with the necessary and *a priori* to be rational, as matter admits equality with the contingent and *a posteriori* to be empirical. "Every legal relation is composed of two elements: first, a given matter, the relation itself; second, the idea of law which regulates this relation. The first may be considered as the material element of the legal relation, as a simple fact; the second as the plastic element, which ennobles the fact and imposes on it the form of the law" (1 SAVIGNY, TRAITÉ DE DROIT ROMAIN, Paris, 1840, 327). As is known, in Jhering is emphasized this dogmatic knowledge which, so far as it is dogmatic, passes over contents to bear down on forms, in conscious rationalism (1 JHERING, EL ESPÍRITU DEL DERECHO ROMANO, Madrid, n.d., sec. 3).

The following passage from Guasp regarding the conception of procedural Law gives an idea of such gravitation in the juridical disciplines. The Barcelonan professor asks: "To what matter does the activity of the Judge apply? Upon what suppositions or elements does it turn? . . . This material is integrated, in the first place, by the juridical norms; in the second place, by facts . . . The two groups of such elements which concur in every procedure *do not operate separately;* some have logically to intrude on others and this rational operation or subsumption, to employ the most accepted terminology, has been generally pictured as a syllogism

Let us compare now any datum whatever of juridical experience and proceed to characterize it in the same manner we have just done with natural experience. Let us take as an example what our Civil Code refers to when it says that at the age of 22 years one attains civil capacity without there being any formality necessary for it. Describing this datum, with intuitive confirmation, we find it composed of three classes of heterogenous elements, and not of two, as happened in natural experience.

In fact, we find there, in the first place, a logical structure. Supposing that the datum, stating it rigorously, says: "Given the fact of being 22 years old and of normal psychic functioning, there should be full civil capacity," it is evident that the logical structure consists in this scheme or form of thinking: *Given A, B ought to be.* In his investigations, Kelsen has studied the novelty and peculiarity of the words *ought to be* as a copula which founds a whole Logic of ought-to-be valid for the Law, very different from the Logic of being which is valid for the sciences which the *Critique of Pure Reason* studies.

We find also an empiric content which consists in the various dogmatic references included in the enunciation: thus: the number 22 (it might have been 21 or any other); the solar year (the time might have been determined in another way, for example by the death of the *pater familias* as happened in Rome, etc.); the normal psychic functioning clear and even (it might have been bound to conditions of sex, blood, race, etc., or to the realization of some productive economic activity, etc.); full civil capacity (it might have been a capacity with degrees as happens with the emancipated or the commercial minor, etc.). All these dogmatic contents are, indubitably, empiric and only by the conduct of the juridical reality which we are investigating can we know what and how they are.

But with these two things is still not exhausted all that we had before us with our datum. To reach majority at 22 is, in fact and in that itself, an order, a security, a power; it leads to a peace; it implies a certain cooperation and a certain solidarity; it constitutes a certain justice. In a word, it means to say that our datum is also a positive juridical valuation, so that if, by abstraction, we take away from the unity with which it presents itself to us first the logical structure and then the dogmatic contents, we have not done away with all which we had before us leaving us with nothing, but there will still remain for our reflection those estimated or valuable qualities which were integrating the datum.

If we now proceed to characterize these three integral elements of

---

whose major premise would be the juridical norm, the minor the factual elements, and the conclusion the result of such subsumption or insertion" (JAIME GUASP, JUEZ Y HECHOS EN EL PROCESO CIVIL, Barcelona, 1943, 11–12).

juridical experience, with the same characterizations which Kant used for natural experience; and if we set parallel the two results, as in the following table, to bring out their differences, the result is very surprising and much more useful still for the scientific study of the Law in a dogmatic sense:

I. Characterization	Elements of Natural Experience	II. Characterization
Formal	Logical structure	Necessary
Material	Empiric content	Contingent
	of Juridical Experience	
Formal	Logical structure	Necessary
Material	Juridical valuation	Necessary
Material	Dogmatic contents	Contingent

Considering the first characterization it is clear that the logical structure of the Law is a purely formal element: it is a form of thinking: it is the form in which juridical experience presents itself to us in scientific-dogmatic knowledge. And we know that it is in the normative form: without normative knowledge there is no dogmatic science; and this may be science only so far as it is normative knowledge, neither more nor less. On the other hand, juridical valuation and the dogmatic content which its substratum defines, are the material elements which shape and build that form: they are the things known by the jurist and represented intellectually by his juridical concepts. The dogmatic contents are the circumstances of fact taken into account by the author of the norm and which the norm assigns among themselves as antecedents and consequences in the logical web of normative representation. In such a sense the juridical valuation becomes penetrated with the dogmatic contents, as the marble of a statue is penetrated with the lines which the sculptor has given it, though the dogmatic contents bound only the outlines of human conduct; wherefore the conduct so bounded is the substratum of the juridical valuation but not the living meaning of it.

Considering the second characterization it follows that only the dogmatic content is contingent as we have already seen. The logical structure is not so, since from the form of thinking *Given A, B ought to be,* comes a series of truths of reason, *a priori* and necessary like all logical truths. And neither is juridical valuation with all its complexity contingent, as one verifies directly on remembering that the dogmatic figures not only may vary infinitely in their determinations, but even that they may not exist since each one of them has no ontological necessity for existence. For example, in our Law there might not have been mortgage or agency or injuries as there is no emphyteusis;[9] on the other hand, all Law, whatever may be its dogmatic contents, is always order or disorder, security or insecurity, power or anarchy, peace or strife, coöperation or isolation, solidarity or insolidarity, justice or injustice. One will say, perhaps, that the dogmatic contents may vary and even disappear, but that always there has to be some dogmatic content. This is true; but this empty notion of some dogmatic content in general does not afford any material knowledge to the jurist and is only a correlative of the formal juridical Logic which, like the formal Logic of being, always presupposes the empty idea of an object in general, since thought always is thought of something and never a floating thought of nothing. It is different with the consideration which juridical valuation offers us, which cannot come to be an empty reference to an indeterminate juridical value in general but is always an immediate reference to all the values previously enumerated and whose meaning is given to us fully in any datum as invariable material, whether its realization be this or that or whether the sign of its realization be negative. We always understand the meaning of juridical values fully and in their concrete significance; never as an indeterminate meaning or an absence of meaning. It is difficult, and even impossible in well credited opinions, to say in what true justice consists, but it is not difficult to characterize a situation, with truth, as just or unjust or as more or less just than another.

All this makes it evident that juridical valuation, at the same time as a material element, is a necessary element of juridical experience. As a constant content of this datum, it is the meaning of the Law because the Law is conduct; therefore it cannot disappear from the contingent mood as dogmatic figures can be made to do; it disappears with Law itself, neither before nor after; not within nor without the Law while the Law lasts. Without doubt juridical valuation, being bound to dogmatic contents as the marble to the lines of the statue, as we have explained, may vary its contents with the dogmatic variations, but in all this we do not refer to any true ideal of the Law, but to the positive valuation of it; what was positive justice in slaveholding Rome is a different thing from what positive justice is for us heirs of the French Revolution. But those two so different justices have the same meaning of giving to each person what is his, according as they existed with that meaning.

At this point the egological Theory makes it evident that juridical valuation is immanent in the Law and not something transcendental toward which the Law would tend as toward its purpose. The Law does

[9] In Spanish civil law, a long or perpetual lease of land, originally agricultural, for its cultivation or upkeep, an annual rent, and other conditions. TRANSLATOR.

not seek nor tend to realize justice because the Law itself already is positive justice; and the same is true for all the other juridical values. To say that justice is the end of the Law, to whose realization it tends, is a result of naturalistic scientificness which ingenuously believes that all the sciences of experience refer us equally to Nature, since it does not conceive any empiric knowledge except naturalistic knowledge. In this way positive Law signified a natural datum (not a human datum, since the human was already dissolved in Nature), which the jurist would have to know by a causal explanation. But thus there was cut from the Law everything which is the motive of a knowledge by comprehension; that is, the juridico-positive valuation was left outside of the task undertaken by the jurist. And with this the reference to the meaning of the Law so far as that meaning is a positive ideal integral essence of the Law, was replaced with the transcendental reference to an ideal of a true metaphysical or social type, always foreign to the objectivity of the datum. Only by putting justice in this transcendental form can it be said that the positive Law tends to it as towards its purpose. But all that we are writing lets it be very clearly seen that it does not attain the dogmatic knowledge of the Law but comprehension of the positive valuation which is immanent in it. It explains to us perfectly whence comes the juridical valuation which fixes the meaning of laws in their interpretation and by what always breaks out in decisions, sometimes in unexpected form and even ill-conceived by the practical jurist who invokes it as a superior purpose, accomplishing in such burst, a triumphant imposition of the practical life upon theories which have no place for it because they do not adequately conceive the dogmatic phenomenon, since this only has its effective reality in experience.

From the foregoing characterization of the elements which make up juridical experience, it follows that the first characterization is not superposed on the second, contrary to what happens with natural experience. In juridical experience there is not established equivalence between the formal and the necessary, nor between the material and the contingent, since juridical valuation is material and necessary. The gravest errors of Stammler and his notorious sterility for dogmatic thinking, come precisely from the fact that he carries over to the Law the critical structure of natural experience and considers that in juridical experience all that is necessary is formal and all that is material is contingent. But herein Stammler pays the price for having misinterpreted Kant by not taking as a starting point the pure intuition of the Law;[10] with that defect his

[10] Although Kant has not investigated this pure intuition necessary for his critical system, he has described it in unmistakable form in Los Principios metafísicos del Derecho (Buenos Aires, 1943) 49.

juridical concepts would have to be void concepts, as the philosopher of Königsberg noticed with so much wisdom and as every jurist proves who seeks in vain support for his scientific need in the philosophy of Stammler.

Our breaking down of juridical experience into its integral elements permits us now to draw the following conclusions, of fundamental methodic importance, which we can understand without necessity for further development.

The logical structure of juridical experience, considered abstractly and apart, is an ideal object because it is a logical object: it is a typical class of concepts which the jurist uses to describe juridical reality in scientific knowledge; or, what is the same thing, it is the form of judgment by which his intellect works in forming those concepts. To understand by intellection this datum which is the logical structure of the Law, whose essence is normativity and which, as to the imputative concept, is a norm, the attitude which the investigator needs is a necessary and fixed adequateness: that of an essentially normative analysis. On this basis, by the rational-deductive method, he will obtain as a result juridical Logic.

Juridical valuation, considered apart in its turn, carries us into the realm of cultural objects: it is the meaning of an egological object as an integral part of such object; it is the meaning of human conduct in its intersubjective interference. Here the attitude which the jurist needs to apprehend this datum by comprehension is also a necessary and fixed adequateness; it is that of an estimative aliveness. On this basis, by the empiric-dialectic method, he will obtain as a result the positive Estimation of the Law.

Finally, the dogmatic content of juridic experience, considered apart in its turn, brings us the most diverse objects, among which are those which are described by the normative imputation: brings us ideal objects when they become figures as in prescription or in hereditary legal portions or when they become logical objects like analogy; brings us natural objects as in the example of the solar year or professional infirmities; brings us cultural objects as when the norm refers to good usage or to a lessor. This lets us see that, on this point, the attitude of the jurist is a contingent and occasional adequateness according to what may be the nature of the object which the empirical datum gives him. Therefore here we have to speak of an empiric-objective method to refer to the fact that the object (ideal, natural, or cultural) dogmatically reported, is reported by and in the datum of juridical experience; and that its apprehension demands the method adequate for nature itself. For example, to know what 4/5 parts are, we have to recur to the rational-deductive method; but as to the legitimacy of children, it is necessary, besides, that that mathematical reference be given in fact in the norm which makes up the datum in experience. This lets us see that when the object imputed by the normative concept is in its turn a cultural object (for example, if the law refers to the honesty of a person or to the beauty of an avenue), in juridical knowledge there are two valuing moments: one common and unavoidable which corresponds to the juridical valuation; and the other contingent which corresponds to the knowledge by comprehension of the object imputed by the norm. By this empiric-objective method dogmatic contents are known. This, and its logical disposition, is what was attempted, from Savigny on, with the varying fortune which the rhythm of knowledge follows as the various sciences go on attaining knowledge of their objects (think, for example, of the investigations of paternity and the haematological investigations). The result has been the Dogmatic Science as it has come to us.

But precisely at this point the egological Theory interposes the decisive question to replace the problem of the Dogmatic Science on a definite and proper base. The egological Theory makes it firmly appear that the dogmatic contents are not independent references which would allude to those objects of other sciences by themselves, but which are all taken to bound or outline certain conduct; so that what is alluded to by them or referred to by means of them, is this conduct. Juridical knowledge, then, is not fulfilled with the knowledge of the dogmatic contents, as traditional Dogmatics has believed, but with the knowledge of the conduct which they bound. This is to say, then, that all these dogmatic contents have to be valued by juridic valuation because without such valuation there is no knowledge of the conduct and those contents only bound or outline that conduct. The object of dogmatic knowledge is conduct as such in its intersubjective interference. This conduct is the material of the egological substratum to be known, as is the marble in the statue; and the dogmatic contents are the forms which bound and make concrete that material, like the forms which the sculptor gives to the marble. So that the conduct and the dogmatic contents — unified or mingled in the relation of material to form — both constitute the material substratum which is known by comprehension for the juridical valuation and whose meaning exists in the aliveness of that valuation, as we have seen. This form of egological substratum which the dogmatic contents give us is not to be confused with the logical structure or form of juridical experience which we have studied further back, since now it is a question of known or constructed forms and not of forms of knowledge itself as well of the structure as of the constructed. The known forms are also the material of knowledge, since nothing exists in the concrete except with a material substance and a form of that substance; so, in a billiard ball, there is, equally, material or object of my knowledge, as well the spherical form as the marble material. On the other hand the forms of knowledge give the logical structure of experience, so that it cannot be thought of nor conceived except with that structure, whatever may be the known content in the known substances or in the forms, also known, of those substances. It is well known, for example, that space is a structure of physical reality and that we know *a priori* with apodictic force that every physical phenomenon has to present itself in this manner, since the contrary is unthinkable. On the other hand, the spherical or cubic form which this stone has is contingent, since both things are spatial constructions.

Leaving to one side, then, the logical or conceptual structure of juridical experience, which now determined in its place and function cannot confuse us, the egological Theory demands that, within that structure, we give due attention to the juridical meaning which valuation sets up and which exists in an estimative aliveness; and attend to the egological substratum of that meaning made, at the same time, the substratum, by its conduct as material substance and by the dogmatic contents as known forms of that substance. The knowledge by comprehension which Dogmatic seeks, provided that it refers to conduct as such, is, then, a function of that concrete substratum and of its juridical valuation. This makes clear, then, the necessity of valuing the dogmatic contents and the reason which the egological Theory invokes to refer all dogmatic contents to human conduct so far as they alone are the bounding or outlining of conduct. In place of this reference to conduct, the egological Theory finds traditional Dogmatics — and in no small part operating at the edge of the logical structure of juridical experience — referring the dogmatic contents to the norms so far as they are ideal possibilities substantive in themselves; or to social facts where conduct itself is materialized as one being more among those which have to be explained and not comprehended; or to historic facts, claiming as the meaning of the Law the meaning of what has been precisely for having been, without understanding that the meaning of juristics, for being the reality of a living life, is a meaning of perpetual presence: only in this do we find the Law in its reality and as a reality of ought-to-be. Those three attitudes are the faults of rationalism, of empiricism, and of historicism which the egological Theory seeks to uproot, to reformulate fundamentally the problem of Dogmatic Science.

5. The Decision as the Structure of the Concrete Validity of the Law

We may now complete our task upon the decision. To this end let us consider the case which is most typical, as being normal, that is, that of the decision which applies a law directly. Other cases, as for example that of the decision which applies directly the constitution for lack of an intermediate law, or that of the decision which applies a regulation or that of a decision founded on a norm of usage, are modalities which do not change the essence of what we are going to say. At any rate it should be taken into account that to judge or decide a case is not to decide by chance nor to decide arbitrarily, but to decide in accordance with a principle or norm regulative of the case.

As we have said, the three components of juridical experience in general have to appear in the decision, since it is a portion of that experience. So it is that we find in the decision, in the first place, a structure of it which is given before it, that is, which is *a priori* as to it. This structure, in our hypothesis, is the law, understanding by law not only the procedural laws but also the substantive laws, since the complete norm of the legal normation of our case is made up by the coördination of both things on a plane of equality. The existence of separate legislations for procedure and for substantive matter only indicates a division of legal work and a technical decentralization, but no superiority or subordination between the two legislations.

Law, understood in this manner, is, evidently, *a priori* to the decision; it is given to the Judge beforehand. The law, moreover, forecasts or predetermines to some degree what the decision will say, for it guides the judicial resolution marking out for it a closed circle of possibilities as those to which the Judge has to accommodate himself. The Law is, then, the ambit of the decision; and, in this sense, contains its whole structure. But as the law is a thought which enunciates general things for indefinite cases, it follows that the law is formal with respect to the decision which is concrete. Or put in another way: the law is not the perceptible form which the decision is going to have in the concrete, but it is the form of that juridical experience which is going to become actual in the decision and only in it. The *a priori* character of the law with respect to the decision makes us see that the Judge has to descend from the law to the decision by the deductive method, in such manner that anything of the law which appears in the decision has to have that rational conformity of the general to the particular which is common to all deduction.

In the second place we find in the decision the circumstances of the case. They are an empiric ingredient, given in fact to perceptive intuition, which places the Judge in the presence of reality and which the Judge necessarily has to consider, since, if he did not, we could not speak of the adequacy of the norm for the case. The occasional and accidental reference which some laws contain saying that the Judge has to apply them with consideration of the circumstances of the case, becomes, then, wholly superfluous and useless, since, whether the law says so or not, there is an ontological necessity that they should be considered by the Judge, since the Dogmatic is a science of reality. So, in fact and against its conceptual unity, the intellectualist theory of subsumption entertained as well by juridical rationalism as by juridical empiricism recognizes, when they affirm that the law is the major premise, the circumstances of fact are the minor premise and the decision is the conclusion of a syllogism. For between this theory of subsumption and that occasional reference to the circumstances of the case which laws sometimes carry, there is a conceptual incongruence which will aid us to see our problem, well obscured here by juridical rationalism and juridical empiricism which have not brought to the decision their methodical points of view in not having analyzed it as to the datum of juridical experience; but on the contrary have merely conceived it in that manner (as a syllogism) with a concept which in no way corresponds to reality.

In truth, if the circumstances of the case are the totality of circumstances of fact with which the case presents itself to the Judge in reality, we may divide them into three classes for our purpose:

(1) Those circumstances of fact which have been considered by the law and which are imputed by it, making up the structure of the decision; that is, the circumstances described or represented in the legal concept. For example, if the law says: "he who kills another shall be imprisoned for twenty years" or "the seller ought to deliver the thing to the buyer," there has to be in the facts to apply these norms someone who has committed homicide and someone who is a seller and nothing else. These circumstances produced in the facts are represented or described by the law as we have said; and imputed by it they form the structure of the decision, it being noted that they are general or common, that is, they are repeated from case to case. The traditional theory of the deduction alludes only to these circumstances, by which it commits a triple error: First, if it obtains from them a datum of existence, it is not to return to the norm to deduce its possible consequences in the abstract, as the traditional theory believes, but to remain in the reality of which the norm is indeed an actual conceptual representation; that is, as we shall see, to understand or value the norm itself requires that

that reality, being conduct, shall be known by comprehension. Second, because there are circumstances of fact which the case presents, which are not described in the conceptual representation of the law and which the Judge considers or always may consider, so that the basis which the decision takes from these circumstances cannot be conceived in any way as a syllogistic deduction; which also we are going to see. And third, because the phrase "circumstances of the case," occasionally brought in by the law and the authors, becomes equivocal if we do not notice that it is not going to be extended to the circumstances described and imputed by the law, in spite of their being also circumstances of the case with consequences which we shall soon verify. On that account, we exclude from that phrase, in the conventional or strict sense, the empirical circumstances described and imputed by the law, subject to express statement to the contrary when the nature of our problem falls equally upon one or the other.

(2) There are circumstances with which a case presents itself in reality, which are also general or common because they are repeated in multiple cases, but which are not described by the law which *is applied* in the case to allow or reject a claim. So, to give for the present but one example, Article 1113 of the Argentine Civil Code establishes the indirect responsibility of the employer for damages caused by those who are under his control; but in the Argentine courts, unanimously and in accordance with doctrine, this article applies only when the wrongful act is committed by the employee "in the exercise of his duties," it not being sufficient that it should be "on the occasion of them," as in France. Now, the Argentine law does not carry the concept "in the exercise of his duties" as our civilians acknowledge, it being obvious that it alludes to common and general circumstances of fact which may be repeated in innumerable cases.[11] Consequently, Article 1113 of the Argentine Civil Code does not contain a conceptual representation of our juridical experience except when it is a question of the acts of an employee done in the exercise of his duties, which is a reference to certain circumstances of the cases not described by the law but which make up the reality of the cases as they occur in experience.

(3) Finally, there are circumstances with which a case presents itself in reality, which are not described by the law but which are, nevertheless, not general or common, but are special and unique to the case which is being considered.

It is clear that these unique and special circumstances have very much

[11] Rodríguez c. Bunge y Born, S. A. (Cam. Civ. II Cap.), June 11, 1942; 27 La Ley 629, with doctrinal note by Dr. Arturo Acuña Ansorena. Action for damages for death in fight with fellow employee.

less importance for juridical theory than the common and general circumstances not described by the law to which we have before referred. Therefore we have to omit them in this dissertation, in the interest of brevity. But we have to say that both classes of circumstances, unique and special, and common and general, not included in the legal concept, constitute the circumstances of the case in the conventional and strict sense. Their common characteristic consists in the conceptual representation of both in the knowledge of the Judge which the decision will express being an *a posteriori* representation, that is a representation founded on juridical experience and given by the reality of the case, in distinction from the *a priori* representations contained in the law, which, as conceptual representations, are given to the Judge in advance. In what way the circumstances of the case in the strict sense discharge for the Judge the same part that the dogmatic contents of the law discharge for the Legislator may be gathered from what we are saying and will be seen even better further on.

In the third place, we finally find also in the decision the juridical valuation as a necessary content, in the judicial valuation which the Judge inevitably makes on estimating the totality of circumstances of the case in the broad sense. Indeed, the decision ought to be, in its intrinsic meaning, an expression of all the current juridical values, from the positive order to positive justice: the decision is, so, that order, that security, that justice, etc. As the judge is a structure of the juridical order, as we have already said in Paragraph 3, and not a datum or contingent content of it, the Law is for the Judge, in the first place and in direct form, positive order, security, power, peace, coöperation, solidarity, and justice, all of which is the necessary content of the Law. This point of view which discovers in the Judge the necessary content of juridical experience so far as it is estimative experience, is fully confirmed by a verifiable observation which comes down as stated from time immemorial and which has entered into common speech, namely: the Judge, in a lawsuit or out of it, is not the incarnation of this or that legal figure; it cannot properly be said that a Judge is the incarnation of a mortgage or of a public service concession. On the other hand, it may be said with profound truth that the Judge is the incarnation of positive order, security, justice, etc.[12]

We may now summarize, in the following provisional table, the elements constituting the decision so far as made of juridical experience, in accordance with what we have said:

[12] Aristotle, Nicomachean Ethics, V. iv. 7. "To go to a judge is to go to justice, for the ideal judge is, so to speak, justice personified." (Rackham's translation, London, 1926.)

Constituting elements of the decision	
	Legal structure: The law given *a priori*
	Contingent representations: Circumstances of the case
	Reality of the Judge: Juridical valuation

Proceeding to the functional examination of these things, it is readily to be noticed that the Judge's valuation considers, on the one hand, the circumstances of the case: it takes these or those and ranks them among themselves *a posteriori;* that is, first are the facts or circumstances and then the imputation which unites them in some bond with the ought-to-be. Thus, as the law ranks the circumstances which it describes, so also, with the same imputative bond, the Judge ranks the circumstances of the case so far as the decision is based on them; only the imputation of the law is *a priori* and that of the Judge is *a posteriori.* When we say that the judicial valuation ranks the circumstances of the case among themselves, we say that the Judge gives them juridical effects, since the judicial valuation which determines the ranking is not the merely intellectual act of a recognition of rank in favor of the ranked circumstances and against those not ranked, but it is *a choice* which confers the rank: it is a choice which the judge makes among the circumstances because he *understands* them in the juridical meaning which they have and to their meaning he gives life. Necessarily to rank these circumstances as antecedents to these others as consequence, disregarding the other circumstances, is to confer on the first a juridical value which is not assigned to those which are disregarded: in which there is a normative creation of the same type which the Legislator accomplishes in his sphere with respect to the circumstances which thereafter remain described and ranked in the law.

When the judicial imputation falls upon singular and unique circumstances, there appears for us in the decision the problem of equity, which is not the justice of the particular case, as is said, for every decision is the justice of a particular case, but which is a single act of justice. On the other hand, when the judicial imputation falls upon general and common circumstances in the broad sense, there appears in the decision the problem which underlies that peculiar phenomenon of the Law which is called jurisprudence. But, for the present, we are considering only the problem of general and common circumstances in the strict sense, which is part of it.

To put vividly the truth of all that we have just been saying, that is, that the Judge values the circumstances of the case *stricto sensu* and that on that he makes *a posteriori* a normative creation whose meaning is the current juridical values, it is sufficient to reflect how judges, commonly, give the custody of a minor whose parents have lost the *patria potestas,* to his respectable relatives although the law does not impose such obligation on them: the circumstance of being a relative is valued in positive form and to it is imputed the juridical consequence of legal custody, constituting it thus a datum of experience fully juridical. The same thing is noted when the confiscatory character of a tax on a gratuitous transfer was fixed formerly, by our courts, at 10 per cent and today at 33 per cent of the value of the real property subject to the transfer.

As we have said, we are considering, for the present, the judicial valuation which is directed to the circumstances of the case in the strict sense, without considering yet the valuation of the law; that is to say, we are considering a juridical valuation which plays freely within the region of possibilities bounded by the law, in search of a simple individualization of the juridical content of the law which perforce has to be realized in individual form. In this play upon the circumstances of the case *stricto sensu,* the juridical valuation ends in an imputative creation which judges or represents in its ought-to-be the juridical reality of the case at hand. Here then, the juridical valuation creates the imputation and is fundamental. And it is important for us to insist that the meaning of this axiological reality so created is the positive (not negative) meaning of all the current juridical values, and nothing else. In the following decision of the Supreme Court of the Province of Buenos Aires, in which is discussed the extent of *chose jugée,* the members of the court thought of the matter in irreproachable form when they said: "When having to resolve a question of chose jugée whose requisites are not specified either in substantive or in adjective laws, the judges called to decide are sovereign to appreciate the juridical situation, without adjusting it to any objective norm of the law, for in absence of any norm they are obliged to endeavor by following the principles of the legislation in force or basic norms of what may be considered just, to arrive at a decision founded on a conception of justice." [13] Or this other decision of the full Civil Chamber of the Federal Capital in which they discuss the police power of the Municipality in emphatic language filled with a certain well-known sociological notion, which does not conceal the nature of the valuation which grounds the decision: "The Deliberative Council, on exercising the authoritative power delegated to it by Congress, although it deals with acts of the police power, must adjust it to the principles of justice and public utility, because, as the Supreme Court has recognized, the people are not simple sources of revenue for governments but

[13] Catinari c. Provincia de Buenos Aires (Supreme Court), May 18, 1943; 30 La Ley 723, 1943 Jurisprudencia Argentina II. 533. Action involving question of criminal decision as res judicata in civil case.

are collective beings which develop, become moral and prosper only in the shadow of justice, under the protection of the laws and of the constitutional authorities which the people themselves have created." [14]

But moreover the juridical valuation of the Judge evaluates the statute since the valuation evaluates all the circumstances of the case and we have already seen that the dogmatic contents of the statute are also circumstances of fact given in a case. Now the juridical valuation does not create the normative imputation which unites these facts as antecedents and consequence, but it values the imputation itself given *a priori* by the law. The valuation refers, doubtless, to the circumstances described by the law so far as they represent human conduct; but it does not refer to them separately, dissecting and choosing them, but refers to them in the rigid web in which the legal norm has united them. The result of this gnosiological act of comprehension is, now, to declare that the law refers to the case or does not refer to it, restricting the effect of the precept by reference to some general circumstances not mentioned by the law.

For its frequency and importance in the constitution of juridical experience, this problem is perhaps the most difficult which the Dogmatic Science holds. For as the judicial option comes to accept or reject a legal structure the Judge, in case of rejecting it does not remain free in the vacuum, but falls upon some other legal structure, provided that the juridical order is logically finite, or as they say dogmatically, of hermetic completeness. To illustrate with an example this necessary finiteness which circumscribes the movement of the Judge, making him always fall on some legal structure when his valuation rejects a certain other structure, it will suffice to recall the case of the Singer machines,[15] very famous in the annals of Argentine courts: the Singer company delivered to seamstresses its sewing machines for monthly payments which, by the delivery contract, were to be credited to their rental; only when a certain number of installments had been paid, the contract ended,

[14] Rocca c. Municipalidad de la Capital (Cam. Civ. Cap.), Aug. 2, 1942; 31 LA LEY 345. Action over municipal charges for inspecting vacant lands.

[15] Compañia Singer v. Chacra (Cámara Comercial de Buenos Aires, Nov. 15, 1913), 32 JURISPRUDENCIA ARGENTINA 373, note. Cf. National Paper & Type Co. v. Kuperschmid (Cámara Comercial de la Capital, Dec. 4, 1929), 32 JURISPRUDENCIA ARGENTINA 364, 83 GACETA DEL FORO 298. *Savignón v. Chevalier* (Civil Court of the Capital, Oct. 4, 1940), Note by Alberto G. Spota, 74 JURISPRUDENCIA ARGENTINA 770. As to the *pactum reservati dominii* in general, see RAMÓN S. CASTILLO, CURSO DE DERECHO COMERCIAL, 4a Ed., II. 80–84 (Buenos Aires, 1939). ROBERTO N. LOBOS, VENTAS A CREDITO DE MUEBLES CON RESERVA DE PROPIEDAD, 19 LA LEY (Doctrina) 45 (Buenos Aires, 1940). RAYMUNDO L. FERNÁNDEZ, CÓDIGO DE COMERCIO COMENTADO, II. 321 (Buenos Aires, 1945). 39 SCHWEIZ. JURISTEN-ZEITUNG 192 (Zurich, 1943). TRANSLATOR.

and the machine remained the property of the seamstress. In this way, if the payments were not made in the agreed form, the Singer company recovered its machines without delay or further questions. But in a case brought to the courts by a seamstress in default on one of her last installments, the Judge rejected the structure of hiring which the contracting parties had set up as the law of their relations, and decided the case upon the structure of sales, where, without any doubt, lay the just meaning of the reality created by the parties, in spite of the contractual declaration of annulling it by the structure of hiring. The rejection of one legal structure, then, does not leave the Judge free in an empty space, without any juricity given beforehand. There are no lacunae or spaces without juricity; and each new structure brings before the Judge the same valuing problem. The Judge does not supplant the Legislator nor create justice at his will or the order which perhaps he would desire, since he operates only by choosing structures already created within a closed whole, so that he works on the complete order making alive the meaning of that order which is, in its fullness, an objective substratum. And the positive juridical values also are here always the basis of the position which the Judge takes within the order, since they are the meaning of the order itself, the more that they exist in the unescapable reality of the Judge who forms it. In this manner the phrase of Hobbes takes on unexpected significance: "For the legislator is he, not by whose authority the Lawes were first made, but by whose authority they now continue to be Lawes." [16] In this manner is made clear in its foundation the known truth that, with an unjust law, the Judge of Law fulfills his mission by choosing the least unjust of the solutions and in no other way.

We have already seen above, in connection with Article 1113 of the Argentine Civil Code, how the responsibility of the employer, for the unlawful act of his employee which the law imposes, is limited to an act done "in the exercise of his duties"; and how this notion, limiting the validity of the law, alludes to general and common circumstances of the case not specified in the law but which are not alien to it, provided they are within and not outside of those specified by the law. Now it is seen how when the Judge values the law, the legal imputation is restricted to those cases in which are present those circumstances included within the idea of "in the exercise of his duties." Or, put another way: the Judge values the legal imputation as just when those circumstances exist and unjust if it extends to cases in which those circumstances do not occur, so that the meaning of the order, security, justice, etc., of the law is defined by the valuation of all the circumstances, in such manner that the

[16] Hobbes, *Leviathan*, Part II, chap. 26, para. 5 (London, 1914).

law is order, security, justice, etc., in the first hypothesis, and disorder, insecurity, injustice, etc., in the second; for which reason the courts act on it only in the first manner and only by the first manner does it contribute to Argentine judicial experience, since this experience has a meaning — that of juridical valuation — and the meaning is given by the activity of the Judge.

The dominant rationalism has succeeded in spreading conceptually the error that there are laws which admit of but one interpretation, as if in such cases the Judge did not value the law and only knew how to deduce its consequences by mechanical application. But, even so, juridical experience witnesses daily the presence of juridical valuation as a positive foundation of the decision, with frequent judicial declarations such as the following:

> The defendant recalls in his expression of points that the laws however hard they may be ought to be applied and that it is prohibited for the judges to consider their equity, with which I am in accord. But here is no question of that but of choosing between two interpretations to which the ambiguous language of an article of the Code gives rise, as we have seen, and in that sense the judges have the right and the duty of accepting the one which agrees more with the principle of equity and which at the same time favors the progress of the country.[17]

If to this is added that all law always permits two interpretations at least — that of being applicable and that of not being applicable to the case — we see restored to juridical experience the part which juridical valuation has in it, since, however much it comes phrased in locutions as general as those of the common good, public utility, public order, progress of the country, and such, it is always a question of the bilateral values of conduct which as an active starting point, decide the application or

[17] Deferrari c. Bonorino (Cam. Civ. II Cap.), July 29, 1943; 31 La Ley 535, 1943 Jurisprudencia Argentina III 395. Action to compel neighbors to share costs of fencing rural lands. The opinion of Magistrate Dr. Perazzo Naón, with regard to art. 2742 of the Civil Code, says: "In the country, boundary fencing ought to be done by sharing costs, if the two properties are enclosed. When one of the properties is without any fence, its owner is not obliged to contribute for the dividing walls, ditches or fences." In this case the question was whether the defendant ought to contribute to the wire fencing because his parcel was fenced for three-quarters of its perimeter and whether the Rural Code, which under such circumstances imposed such an obligation, was or was not contrary to the quoted provision of the Civil Code. The court decided unanimously that the Rural Code applied and that it was not contrary to the Civil Code, since this art. 2742 only contemplated extreme cases (total enclosure and no enclosure), but not the case of partial enclosure, and moreover a rural property, partially fenced by the neighboring ones, is not in a condition to be duly exploited by its owner.

non-application of a law, whether the juridical meaning of the case is comprehended within the structure being valued, or if it is better comprehended within a neighboring structure or within the fundamental structure that all which is not prohibited is juridically permitted. In whatever manner it is always the valued meaning of the datum as to positive order, security, justice, etc., which determines the solution of the case; and knowing which legal structure succeeds in conceptualizing that meaning is what inevitably brings valuation of the law declaring it applicable before causing it to play deductively upon the case.

This situation is repeated in all the ambits of the Law. For example, Article 2588 of the Argentine Civil Code says that the owner of land, where another has planted in good faith, may take the crop for his, indemnifying the planter, who may not destroy the crop. But the courts have refused the application of this article in the case in which the planter was a tenant with an expired lease and judgment of eviction, notwithstanding that the planting had been done after the judgment but pending an appeal. The courts have said that here there is a contractual bond between the proprietor and the planter, so that this Article 2588 does not apply, because, notwithstanding the breadth of its terms, it refers only to cases in which there is no contractual relation between proprietor and planter.[18] Also here the juridical valuation of the law considers it just when there is no contractual bond and considers it unjust in the contrary case, wherefore the judges realize it only in its positive or valuable sense, undertaking to consider, to limit its meaning, the general or common circumstance of fact, that there is no contractual bond, notwithstanding that thereby they restrict the application of this norm. It is to be noted that Salvat, with a rationalistic attitude and on a basis which the law does not recognize, urges the unlimited application of that norm, without considering whether both cases have or have not the same meaning of order, of peace, of justice, etc.

Let us look at a very clear and interesting example from Administrative Law: Article 37 of Law 4349 as to civil pensions says that "He who has been dismissed from the service for poor performance of the duties of his position shall not have the right to a pension." No other legal provision clarifies or restricts this precept. The case of a public employee several times removed and reinstated, — once with seven years between the removal and his later reinstatement — being brought before the Supreme Court of the Nation, it had to be decided if the pensionable term was to be computed by adding all the periods of the different times when he occupied the place or only from the time elapsed

[18] Cimolando c. Zavaleta (Cam. Civ. I Cap.), Mar. 25, 1941; 22 LA LEY 157, 74 JURISPRUDENCIA ARGENTINA 242. Action for part of crop of corn.

since his last reinstatement. Both interpretations were possible; and it was possible also, as a third interpretation, that the cited norm was an absolute sanction in the sense that a removed employee could not be pensioned, whether with an excess of time he had committed the infraction after the necessary length of service, or whether he had completed the legal period wholly after his infraction. The two latter interpretations are strictly the more literal, however much the severity of the third tends to disregard the reform in conduct, but the first is humanely more just because a man who reaches the end of his life cannot be abandoned by demanding of him that he spend a time, which he cannot supply, in another way than he has spent it. The Supreme Court took the law in its valuable or positive sense of justice, solidarity, etc., accepting the first interpretation,[19] it being clear that the foundation of the preference was such valuation, in spite of the fact that the tribunal, dominated by rationalism, did not come to express it happily dogmatically but presented it as a deduction which is on all counts incorrect for scientific Logic. The Court, in fact, on stating it, confined itself to saying that "reinstatement supposes either that the faults imputed to the removed employee did not exist" — something which, without investigating it, even if it is a truth in fact, in good deductive logic cannot be affirmed as a truth; and the Court did not investigate it — "or that they were not of the seriousness necessary to justify removal" — a thing which the law does not indicate and which cannot be discussed before the removal produced by such cause; and here we are in the face of another truth in fact which was not investigated and which did not even fall within the dogmatic possibilities of a deduction. The truth is that by the judicial valuation by the Court, our juridical experience does not fit Article 37 of Law 4349 when there is reinstatement of the infringing employee. The lower courts have amplified still more this valuation by saying that the same criterion persists even if the reinstatement has been by another organ of the State.[20]

If we think how problems of warm discussion among the criminalists, such as the famous one of the nonresponsibility for other conduct, clear up, revealing their true meaning, on being cast into this field of juridical valuation, it will show the fecundity of the egological theory for the dogmatic knowledge of the Law. In truth, the nonresponsibility for other conduct implies the nonapplication of the penal law when, in fact, the person has found himself with the alternative of choosing conduct not

[19] Cerveceria Argentina de Quilmes c. Gobierno (Supreme Court), Dec. 4, 1925; 145 FALLOS 287, 18 JURISPRUDENCIA ARGENTINA 795. Action for return of taxes paid.

[20] Manrique c. Gobierno (Cam. Fed. Cap.), May 14, 1941; 22 LA LEY 764, 74 JURISPRUDENCIA 493. Action for pension to postoffice employee.

criminal but which is certain to bring upon him greater damage or choosing conduct which, not certainly but probably, will cause a blameworthy injury, which, by reason of that uncertain character appears as lesser damage to the actor at the moment of acting. When there is extended to wrong the idea of nonresponsibility for other conduct, then the second member of the alternative is, certainly, an unlawful act according to the legal concept taken in its full logical extent, but which preserves for the actor its character of a damage lesser than the first member of the alternative. Whatever may be the success which Dogmatics attains in securing an objective foundation of these two so different things, it is indubitable that the question rests on a valuation of the law and that as a basis for the empirical circumstance of the greater damage attached to the lawful alternative, it is desired to declare *a posteriori* that the penal law is not applicable to the second member of the alternative notwithstanding that this conduct might be subsumed in the legal statement: with it there is sought an affirmative sense of justice as the meaning of the law.

What is important to consider in this as in all cases of valuation of the law, is that the valuation of order, of security, of justice, etc., is immanent in and not transcendent to the law; that it is within and not outside of it. The dominant intellectualism understands precisely the valuation as something transcendent to the law in assigning to it a supra-legal character, whether calling it a norm of culture, or invoking it in a claimed purpose of the Law superior to the Law itself. In whatever way it is clear that thus is broken the unity or purity of the juridical method, since if the law is already Law for itself it cannot be understood how, as is claimed, that supra-legal element would have to be above the law but not above the Law. In all this there does not appear to be anything more than a play upon words to escape the qualification of metajuridical which is assigned to the supra-legal in erudite polemics; a qualification undoubtedly exact since the juridical valuation would turn out transcendent to the law, since once rationalism has affirmed that the objects of juridical knowledge are norms or laws, it is obliged to transcend towards life, in some form, from the rigid and neutral ideal world each time that it treats of life. It is true that for this rationalism it becomes a mystery that in penal Law for example, there are only two and no more supra-legal causes which correct the strict application of the law. And it is surprising that it has come to declare that these two "supra-legal" causes have opened great respective vents in legal formalism, tempering it with life,[21] as if the Law were not living human life

[21] 2 Luis Jiménez de Asúa, El Criminalista (Buenos Aires, 1942) 297.

ab initio and as if the artifice of the supra-legal causes did not denote only a vicious rationalistic comprehension of what the law is as a modality of the Law. To us it seems incontrovertible that the Law does not change its nature because it follows the technical modality of enacted law.

For the egological theory, the difficulty is resolved with great simplicity, since if the law is only a normative concept which represents certain conduct and if conduct as such is known by comprehension, it is clear that the juridical valuation is immanent in the law and always — not only occasionally — is within it integrating the conceptual knowledge which it gives. This immanence of the juridical valuation we have to look at very closely not only to avoid any mistake, but principally for the decisive importance of the matter for the dogmatic conception. The question has made itself manifest in all the examples which we have been giving, from which follows the extraordinary and incontrovertible fact that the thought of the Judge not only refers the case to the law by deductive subsumption, but also refers the law to the case by estimative dialectic: the case is submitted to the law by subsumption only after the law has been declared suitable for the case by valuation. What we said above that anything of the law which appears in the decision must have deductive form so far as the law is the structure of the decision, undergoes now a first complementation: it is thus always that the juridical valuation of the Judge has accepted the law as the structure of the case, so that the deductive part of a decision has its starting point also in juridical valuation. The importance of this affirmation is precisely that which obliges us to show that juridical valuation is within the law, immanent in it; and not outside, transcending it. Let us see how:

Considering first the substratum of the juridical object, that is the conduct of the person to whom the law is to be applied; or what is the same thing, considering the dogmatic contents which the law enunciates representing that conduct, it becomes evident that the general circumstances not enunciated by the law and which may determine that the law should not be applied to a case, are factual circumstances which are within and not outside of the circumstances, also of fact, enunciated by the law as dogmatic contents; they are not circumstances independent of those enunciated by the law; but, on the contrary, circumstances which can be considered only after those of the law have been considered. For example, in the compass of Article 1113 of the Argentine Civil Code, previously analyzed, the factual circumstances comprehended in the idea of "in the exercise of his duties," cannot be considered apart and by themselves, since then one could not know what article of the Code they would have to limit. These circumstances presuppose that there have been produced those which the cited article contemplates; that is, that it is a question of an employer and an employee and that the latter has done some illicit act. Within these facts which play as a legal class in the thought of the Judge, may be distinguished *a posteriori* two kinds, according to whether or not the illicit act was committed by the employee "in the exercise of his duties." The distinction in kind is, by logical necessity, internal to the class; and this shows beyond reply that the judicial valuation of the law, on the side which touches the substratum of the egological object, is immanent and not transcendent to the law since the factual circumstances which go to limit objectively the scope of the law are circumstances which are produced within the circumstances which the law itself mentions and imputes.

Considering now the nature of the juridical meaning of the law, the juridical valuation of the Judge also remains immanent in the law. We have already seen that a meaning exists only as a reality and that the Judge is not an external spectator of the Law, but an agent who, as the structure of it, contributes to make it.

Then if at this point of our discussion, going deeper into the table which we gave on page 384 for the constituting elements of the decision, we should ask what in turn is the law as a fact of juridical experience, in the same sense in which we have asked this question as to the decision, we should find, *mutatis mutandi,* the same formal and material, necessary and contingent, elements of juridical experience in general, in accordance now with the following table:

Constituting elements of the law	Constitutional structure: the positive constitution given *a priori*
	Contingent representation: Legislative dogmatic contents
	Juridical valuation: Activity of the Legislator

The activity of the Legislator selects and imputes the contingent circumstances of his case (the dogmatic contents are notoriously circumstances of this sort for the Legislator); but as the activity of the Legislator is extinguished as a fact once the law has been approved, it is understood without difficulty that of this total structure of the law there pass into the decision, together with the constitutional structure, only traces of the valuation of the Legislator; that is, the imputations it made as to the contingent and which, hardened into concepts, are specified in the dogmatic contents given *a priori* to the Judge as the description of a substratum of conduct. Clarifying, then, the structure of the decision with this which has come to it from the act of the law, we shall have to complete in the following manner the table of page 384 as to the constituting elements of the decision:

Law	*Decision*	*Statute*
Due conduct in accordance with the decision	Legal structure	Constitutional structure
	Circumstances of the case Juridical valuation	Dogmatic contents

But in turn, for the same motives, we should have to ask what is the positive constitution as to the fact of juridical experience. And we should find, *mutatis mutandi,* the same formal and material, necessary and contingent, elements of juridical experience in general, in accordance with the following table:

Constituting elements of the constitution	Pure normative structure: Juridical Logic given *a priori*
	Contingent representations: Constitutional dogmatic contents Juridical valuation: Activity of the Constituent Assemblyman

But as the activity of the Constituent Assembly is extinguished, in fact, once the positive constitution has been approved, it is understood also that of this total structure of the constitution there pass into the law, together with the pure logico-juridical structure, only traces of the valuation of the Constituent Assemblyman; that is, the imputations it made as to the contingent, to wit: the contents of the constitutional dogmatic given *a priori* to the Legislator as the description of a substratum of conduct.

In consequence, the complete description of the decision as to the structure of juridical experience will be finally expressed in the following table:

Law	*Decision*	*Statute*	*Constitution*
			Pure normative structure
		Constitutional structure	Constitutional dogmatic contents
Due conduct in accordance with the decision	Legal structure	Legal dogmatic contents	
	Circumstances of the case *Juridical valuation*		

Now we see our problem in its entirety. Now we are in a position to recapitulate and put in order what we have said; and also to bring to completion certain things which have been only partially completed above and which refer to the deductive foundation of what appears in the decision proceeding from the law or from the constitution.

Immediately it has to be noticed (first) that the decision, so far as it is an individual norm according to the rigorous and fruitful investigations of Kelsen, is an imputative concept which represents or describes as conduct a certain particular portion of juridical experience.

In the second place, that the meaning of all juridical experience, when it concerns those pieces which are thought of normatively with a decision, is a meaning which the Judge gives actuality and which, by such conduct, depends on the Judge for its reality in inalienable ontological form. In the decision, the valuative instant necessary to constitute juridical experience is in the Judge and not in the legal structure which is formed in another valuative instant, but which comes to the Judge only as structure.

In the third place, that the Judge values not only the circumstances of the case by creating *a posteriori* the individual imputation, but that he values also the law and the constitution which are given to him *a priori*, the juridical valuation which both different functions make being one and the same because the act of deciding is a single one. Thus, then, reality and unity of the juridical valuation.

Finally, that in decisions there are empirical truths, purely dialectic; they are those constituted *a posteriori* upon the circumstances of the case in the strictest sense. There are also deductive truths merely declaratory because they depend on the dialectical acceptance by the Judge of this or that legal or constitutional structure; they are those which are constituted empirically by the Legislator or the Constituent Assemblyman at other stages of juridical creation and which, after judicial valuation, appear included in the decision. And there are also deductive truths of an apodictic nature which figure in the decision as a valid manner of thinking, totally foreign to every juridical valuation, because they are conceptual forms of any juridical valuation; they are the truths of juridical Logic which appear in the decision as its inevitable gnosiological structure: whatever may be the valuative reality which the Judge sets up for that imputative dialectic or for that declaratory deduction, he cannot ever be excused from the intellection of normativity which his own decision requires as to the norm. In a certain sense it may be said that with all the implications which the total development of juridical Logic supposes, the fundamental norm of Kelsen appears in the decision as an individual norm.

6. Summary: Judicial Interpretation and the Reality of Contradiction

Doubtless this phenomenological analysis of the decision which we have just completed must seem of an unmitigated realism. Nothing else could be expected within the egological conception, for which the Law is living human life and the Dogmatic Science, in consequence, is a science of experience; but of human experience and not of natural experience. The decision, as has been shown, is a conceptual representation of a portion of juridical experience: it describes in the concrete a conduct in its ought-to-be. The decision, as an individual norm, is that and nothing else according to the egological theory. As a fulfillment of a task so outlined, we believe the reader will remain satisfied with the foregoing analysis.

But in another sense perhaps he does not remain satisfied and perhaps, on the contrary, he is vexed at the immense power with which the Judge is left according to the ideas which we have developed. Let us hasten to say that the egological theory does not give the Judge any new power, nor propose that there should be conferred on him any new power. The egological theory limits itself to uncovering theoretically a power which the Judge has always had, as all who know the practice of the Law are very well aware. It is true that the dominant intellectualism, in its forms of rationalism and empiricism, borne by an ideology of juridical security, has hidden the existence and the nature of that immense power which the Judge retains, by presenting magistrates as syllogistic automatons of legal precepts. But for the progress of a science, hiding, consciously or unconsciously, of the truth, is worth nothing. There has circulated in Argentine universities, for several decades, a reproachful anecdote which until now no one has contradicted, though it ought to have been nullified the same day it began to circulate. It is the case of an eminent professor of civil law in the University of Buenos Aires who, to the worst possible examination of a pupil, gave his approval, declaring that if indeed the candidate did not make a very good showing for a lawyer, made a sufficiently good showing for a Judge. We think that there is no greater crime against the juridical culture of a country than the point of view which this anecdone reflects, endorsing the judicial automatism which intellectualism theorizes. And if the egological theory reveals all the power which Judges have in their hands, perhaps it will serve to teach that the Law requires that there should go into the magistracy only those who are absorbed in the study of the Law moved by a superior calling toward the juridical values. If the Law is a human reality which the Judge shares and to whose creation the

Judge contributes with his activities, it can be understood that for the reality of that reality neither the wisdom of the Judge nor his sensitiveness to juridical valuation is immaterial. In the world of the Law, the quality of man is not foreign to the Law itself; and this is as true for the law as for the decision.

Without changing this center of gravity of juridical experience, which the egological theory locates in the Judge, we say, nevertheless, that the complete development of the theory would placate, in great measure, the uneasiness which may overtake the theorist accustomed to the intellectualist conception, in the face of the revelation of the immense power creative of reality which the Judge has in juridical experience and before the constant fact that the Dogmatic Science is a science of experience. But as we cannot now complete this development, limited as we are by the theme of this Introduction, let us be permitted to outline a summary of the matter on the following bases.

We have already seen that when the judicial valuation of the law declares that a certain law does not apply to the case submitted for decision, the Judge does not remain in a clear field, owner and master to create normative imputations, but that, on escaping the structure of the inapplicable law, he enters another legal structure also given beforehand, which in its turn again sets its valuatory problem. The Judge, then, passes always from one legal structure to another, for the reason that the juridical order is a full and hermetic whole. This necessary accommodation of the juridical valuation to one of the legal structures of the order, which is perhaps the most arduous dogmatic problem, is not arbitrary because each structure, so far as it describes a conduct, gives an objective substratum to the meaning which, integrating juridical reality, will appear in this substratum; and the correlation between the substratum and the meaning, however it may be created, is not artificial nor arbitrary, since it treats of the meaning of the substratum. As a dogmatic problem, we see easily, then, this accommodation, governed by the logical unity of the juridical order; that is, creating parcels of juridical reality without contradiction among the parts, in such form that the admission of the law in some cases and its exclusion in others harmonizes perfectly with the totality of existing juridical figures of which the entire order is composed. There is, then, at the base of the arduous dogmatic problem, the hermetic completeness of the order with the ontological axiom implied in it that everything which is not prohibited is juridically permitted.

Upon this point of incontrovertible support, which is fundamental to juridical Logic and Ontology, the scientific problem presents these two questions: is there objectivity in that judicial valuation of the law which confirms the law to that limit and not to any other? With what factual circumstances not enunciated by the law is duly conceptualized the valuation of which it is the object and which objectively limits the extent of its application? Both questions are dogmatically connected and are equally essential, since notwithstanding that the second is founded on the first, it is obvious that if the juridical theory does not succeed in dealing with the general and common circumstances which express the affirmative meaning of the judicial valuation by which the law lives in juridical experience, this latter, for lack of an empirical conception, will seem chaotic and the existing Law cannot be taught, analyzed, or discussed. It is the theory which permits such control.

But it is from the first query which one has to start if one wishes to have success with the second, since the first contains its foundation. On this point it is not sufficient, as empiricism believes, to verify simply that the facts are produced thus or so, because it is not a matter of given facts, but of created facts; or, what is the same thing, they are not neutral facts but valued facts which, as such, have to be judged to be known. Therefore no jurist can accept mere custom as a source, but only good customs.

Nor is the merely formal criterion of the noncontradictory unity of the juridical order, previously described, sufficient for the juridical theory, as rationalism believes, because formal juridical Logic — as formal Logic in general — supplies the negative criterion of juridical truth, but not its positive criterion; that is, it supplies only the normative structures which juridical thought cannot cease to hold to be juridical; but nothing more.

The positive criterion of juridical truth creates, within the normative structures, the very existence of the Law. It creates, then, the human life which it values, because valuing is how it comes to be. It creates life by adapting it to its world making it for itself or by making its world adapting it to itself. And it is exactly at this point that it illumines the problem to which we shall have briefly to address ourselves.

Human experience is a datum of reality which contains thought, since in it, conduct being as such the object of knowledge, this object is also a subject and as such has to be apprehended by conceptual representation. Hence it is that the validity of the juridical thought of the jurist is also the logical validity of the Law itself, since the same type of thought which the jurist employs in his work (normative or dogmatic thought) is met with in known conduct: who lives the Law knows what it does and this doing comes to be thought of as the norm, as the ought-to-be. But this evident immanence of thought in conduct — of which peculiar logicalness it is not for us to speak — lets it be understood that the thought expressed in a law — and the law so far as it is a norm is nothing more than imputative thought — may have been introduced in the conduct of the Judge who is going to decide. When this occurs, as in the case of enacted Law, it follows that the juridical valuation of the Judge, which is living human life, has in its interior a conceptual nucleus. But since the valuation, within it, has a concept, the activity of the Judge may come to be the nature of a contradiction if the resulting valuation does not constitute its meaning in accord with the concept, but denying thereby the reality which it creates. The nature of the contradiction is not, then, the logical contradiction between two concepts, but the contradiction between a human reality and its meaning so far as this is in part determined by the legal concept.[22] When the effectiveness of a structure is limited to certain cases, declaring that the law does not refer to the case under consideration, there is a logical contradiction between two specific concepts and therefore one remains excluded; but there may be no actuality of juridical contradiction if the law not taken into account remains as a structure of the order which conceives other segments of juridical reality, since in this way the law not considered subsists and forms part of the juridical valuation, whose unity we have already pointed out, because the law goes on being some part of the order and because the Judge, on deciding a case, always decides it with the totality of the order and not with one only of its parts, as we also have seen. On the other hand, there would be an actuality of contradiction in the juridical meaning if the excluded law should have an immediate conceptual reference to the case of the decision or if by its exclusion it should remain without any reference to the juridical experience which the order fully outlines, as if the valuation should accept it but there were no logical possibilities of applying it.

This actuality of contradiction explains the miracle of the juridical security which complies with enacted Law and which constitutes its immense advantage over customary Law. This actuality of contradiction is the power; the only power but the effective power, which the laws have over the judges because the ontological nature of the rational being which man has, leads him always to resolve contradictions by relating them to some higher noncontradictory plane. In no other manner appears always the unity of each life.

And now, with the actuality of contradiction we should have to pass from the decision as fact to the theory of the interpretation of the law. This is not our theme; it remains merely alluded to with this reference. The parallel which we drew before with the musical interpretation, where the violinist who is playing Schumann has various noncontradictory

[22] On this point, see Carlos Cossio, *La egológia en la Ciencia,* in LA TEORIA EGOLÓGICA DEL DERECHO (Buenos Aires, 1944), chap. II, d (6), p. 228.

possibilities with the opening but who, notwithstanding his skill, cannot draw from it "La Marseillaise" because then he falls into a contradiction with it, illumines sufficiently for our purpose the theme which we leave in suspense. What is important is to notice that the interpretation of the law, which is the capturing of a meaning, ends in a gnosiological act of comprehension and not in an act of any other sort. On arriving from the decision at the interpretation of the law which it brings about, we have seen the fundamental part which juridical valuation plays in the creation of experience and we understand that the positive criterion of juridical truth has to seek it in juridical valuation while the jurist has to seek it in data, as is proper inasmuch as it is a science of reality.

III

THE EIDETICS AND APORETICS OF THE LAW
PROLEGOMENA TO THE PHILOSOPHY OF LAW

BY JUAN LLAMBÍAS DE AZEVEDO

Professor of Philosophy of Law in the University of Montevideo

TRANSLATED BY
Gordon Ireland, Visiting Professor of Law, Catholic University of America, School of Law

THE EIDETICS AND APORETICS OF THE LAW

PREFACE

THIS small book which I now publish is not a system of philosophy of law, but, as the subtitle (Prolegomena to the Philosophy of Law) indicates, contains only two preliminary chapters which, with their necessary connection, constitute the indispensable points of support for the construction of a system not yet formulated and, as I believe, for the construction of any system. I do not submit a "theory" but "data" immediately verifiable and problems set by these data, with which any theory later has to concern itself. In fine, all that I have done has been to see and to hear; to see what is given intellectually, and to hear its spontaneous questioning. Then: to describe the one and to formulate the other.

Therefore, I have set myself in the "realist" point of view, which is that of natural knowledge, that is, I consider the Law on a par with any other subject — with the exception of the humanities — as transcendent, independent of knowledge. In this sense, this book is at the antipodes from gnosiological or metaphysical idealism, which is always theory, construction. Nevertheless, realism is not formulated nor defended in any part of the book: it is simply its primary supposition. Its grounding is not the task of juridical philosophy but of the theory of knowledge, for which I can do nothing better than to refer to the work of N. Hartmann, Grundzüge einer Metaphysik der Erkenntnis, the most complete and profound which I know.

The general conception of this work dates from the summer of 1938 and its ideas were developed and expounded in the autumn and winter of the same year in the Institute of Higher Studies, before a group of students whose assiduity and coöperation were the chief inducement which I had to carry through my determination.

In 1939 the Faculty authorized me to deliver an elective course upon the subject, and this repetition enabled me, in thinking it over again, to modify some parts and to adjust the whole.

Besides the methodical inspiration received from the works of E. Husserl and N. Hartmann, in particular developments I have received various suggestions from the latter, some from R. Ingarden and A.

Reinach, and above all the peculiar concept of value, outlined by the incomparable genius of Max Scheler.

The mention of these names ought not, nevertheless, to lead to any error as to the nature of this investigation: it is not a matter of a phenomenology of the law. Its object is not the ways of knowledge in which the law is given to us, but law itself. Consequently, the method employed was not that of phenomenological reflection, but that of eidetical reduction to direct positions.

I know well that my work suffers from insufficiencies, perhaps also from excesses. The introduction and the first paragraph might have been reduced to short indications or references. I gave them a certain expositional breadth, however, considering that those ideas, which constitute the methodical principles of the investigation, are little or not at all diffused in our atmosphere. Aporetics, on the other hand, is susceptible of more ample development. What I have written is only an essential minimum. But tasks other than philosophy which for a year and a half have weighed upon me absorbed nearly all my strength, and deprived me not only of time, but of that peace and that leisure of the spirit indispensable for the perfect decantation of ideas.

In spite of all I publish my work, in the conviction that it may bring light upon some points and with the hope that serious criticism may afford me the opportunity to improve it and to continue the development of the system.

Juan Llambías de Azevedo

MONTEVIDEO, April, 1940

I. INTRODUCTION

Eidetics, Aporetics, and Philosophy

Philosophy, so far as it is theoretic speculation, and like every theory, is a system of judgments which claim to be true. Its ideal is that the system should be really true and, consequently, be itself a system of truths. Indeed, this is not always within the power of the philosopher to realize, but that ideal is the ultimate purposeful reference for his efforts. His particular task consists of approximating more and more that goal.

But a theory does not arise "because." The system of judgments which form it is in itself a complex of solutions of certain mysteries or enigmas. Only so is Philosophy a need with authentic meaning. Without problems, it would not only lack justification, but it would degenerate into a capricious and empty fantasy.

There is a theory then because there are problems.

Plato saw rightly the true feeling of the philosopher in wonder and approved the ancient myth which made Iris the daughter of Thaumas, the messenger of the gods, who knows everything, daughter of wonder. The meaning of the myth is, then, that wonder is the origin of knowledge, that the problem is what engenders the solution. All Philosophy is always a response to certain problems, an effort which man makes to mitigate his wonder and to reëstablish in his mind the equilibrium which that feeling disturbed.

But wonder requires, in its turn, that something should provoke it; it is necessary that there should be something about which to wonder. This something is things in their widest acceptation: phenomena. "Men," says Aristotle, "began by marveling that things were as they were." It is necessary to seek, now, then, the meaning of problems.

Problems are questions, But they are not any kind of questions. A problem is a question which the phenomenon itself directs to us.

There are problems, then, because there are phenomena. Just as theory is aroused by a problem, so also a problem is aroused by the phenomenon. Finally, then, theory is the reply which man gives to the question of the phenomenon. The problem is the bond between them; it is the point at which the phenomenon which asks and the theory which responds meet. On the incorrectness or justice of the solution depends whether the phenomenon shall dominate man, ensnaring him in its meshes, or whether man shall free himself, subjugating the phenomenon.

To find the solution, however, man has to be guided by the phenomenon itself, for the truth is hidden in the terms of the problem. Therefore, the relation between the philosopher and the phenomenon presents itself also in inverse order: in a certain sense, it is the theoretic which asks and the object which responds. The phenomenon is like a medal on whose face is written the question and on whose reverse is written the answer. The task of the philosopher must consist, then, of turning over the medal and reading its reverse. The philosopher does not answer from his own depth; he has to read the answer in the phenomenon. "Truth is not invented, it is discovered." Only the response of the phenomenon is couched, at best, in the language of the Sibyl. Truly, every phenomenon carries written in itself its categorical answer, but man cannot always understand it totally or even with conspicuity. The judgment is not in things but in human nature corrupted by original sin. The solution is written in the depth of things: it has to be read from a distance and, still, in a foreign language. Man perceives only those signs which are cut in large characters, and with them he has to reconstruct the rest. Reading is not enough: to find the truth requires a wearisome labor of interpretation. Hence it has been said rightly that there is no royal road to Philosophy.

This situation of abandonment in which theory is found shows us that to obtain exact or at least approximate solutions there is necessary the determination of the problems, and, for the determination of the problems, there is necessary the apprehending of the phenomena. Philosophy has, then, to travel a road which consists of three successive stages: it has first to describe phenomena; it has to elaborate, second, the problems, to investigate, finally, the solutions. To have seen the necessary connection between these three steps is the merit of the contemporaneous philosopher Nikolai Hartmann.[1]

It is needful for us now to clear up all this in detail and with greater rigor.

(1) We speak of the description of phenomena; but by this we do not allude to empirical phenomena, to the individual objects which exist here and now in the real world and which we perceive by our senses, but to the esesntial traits, to the essence of phenomena. The individual and empiric is shifting and passing: it cannot be an object for Philosophy which is interested only in that which is permanent, universal, and necessary.

Such consideration of phenomena is possible because, as Husserl has

[1] In his work GRUNDZÜGE EINER METAPHYSIK DER ERKENNTNIS.

definitely shown, there exist, in truth, universalities of essence, which do not have the mere factitious consistency of spatial-temporal facts, but which possess a peculiar necessity, a necessity of essence: they are so and cannot be in any other fashion (objective *a priori*).[2]

Every contingent, every individual, object, is not only something individual, it has in itself its peculiarity constituted in such or such a way, that is, its essence, and therefore a pure *eidos*. As in "being," there have to be attributed to it certain essential predicables in order that in their turn they may attribute to it other secondary determinations. So, for example, a tree has an essence in itself and for itself, and yet above it all we find the general essence "tree."

"Essence" is, then, what is found in the very being of an individual object. But everything which belongs to the essence of an individual another individual also may have. Therefore, everything which can be put in an idea may be apprehended in its universality; the intuition of the individual may be exchanged for the intuition of the essence. What is contemplated is then the pure essence or *"eidos,"* whether of the superior category or a particularization of it.

The essence or *eidos* is a new class of object: A universal object or species, ideal, nontemporal, perfectly distinct from the individual object, which is real and exists, consequently, here and now.

The distinction between two classes of objects is guaranteed in the most absolute form by evidence. Naturally, "object" is not to be understood in the sense of "thing" nor does the "distinct" object mean an object "separate" from a being. If we understand by "object" every subject of possible true predications, everything which is recorded directly by an intentional act of knowledge, then we see with ample evidence that when we record the general essence "tree," our attention (intentional act) is directed to something distinct from that to which it is directed when we record "this tree" (this orange tree which grows in our garden), that not all the qualities which belong to the latter belong to the former; that, for example, the essences, the specified unities, the universal objects, are distinct from the facts, the individual objects, and cannot be reduced to them.

The essences are also phenomena, since they are given to knowledge with the same originality as individual objects. Just as these latter are given with an individual intuition, so the former are given directly with an essential intuition or "ideation." On the basis of an individual repre-

[2] See as to what follows: E. HUSSERL, IDEEN ZU EINER REINEN PHAENOMENOLOGIE UND PHAENOMENOLOGISCHEN PHILOSOPHIE, Sec. 2. And also: LOGISCHE UNTERSUCHUNGEN, vol. II, especially the second Investigation. In the text, only the chief thoughts are reproduced.

sentation, which truly is necessary, we can record always the species, the corresponding universal object, and this without the need of making any comparison, any intuition of equality, any induction with individual objects of the same species. But in the universal intuition, the singular objects which we perceive or imagine are simple supports for our mental intention. Thus, if indeed the intuition of the essence is kindled on the base of individual intuition and takes from it clarity and proof, it cannot be said on this account that it springs from the individual intuition. We apprehend the specific unity "tree" (in general) directly, "of itself," on the basis of the singular intuition of a tree (which may be given as well in perception as in fantasy). We look at the individual tree, but we are doing a particular act whose intuition is directed toward the "idea," toward the "universal." This peculiar knowledge which apprehends directly the specific unity on the intuitive base is abstraction in its strict sense (logical and gnosiological), ideative abstraction or simple ideation.[3]

Every concrete empirical objectivity is subordinate in its material essence to a supreme material class, to a "region" of empirical objects. So, Uruguayan positive law is subordinate to the material essence "law." To pure material essence then there corresponds a regional eidetic science. It is this science which we call simply Eidetics.[4]

Eidetics is, according to what has gone before, the science of essences; not, then, the science of an empirical phenomenon, but of a phenomenon put into an idea, of the general essential traits of the phenomenon, in the face of which the empirical phenomenon is no more than a particular case. Its object is the ideal phenomenon, the *a priori* essence.

[3] The conception which empiricism has of the abstract is completely different and erroneous.

[4] The name has been mentioned by Husserl himself, although he and some of his disciples (e.g., G. WALTHER, ZUR ONTOLOGIE DER GEMEINSCHAFT 1, 4, 5, 8) call this science "Regional Ontology." But in view of the confusion which that name may cause with the traditional Ontology which studies Being in its metaphysical consistency, or with general or formal ontology which describes the pure form of the object in general and its laws, it is preferable not to use it to designate the science of material essences. N. Hartmann calls it "Phenomenology," but that word also invites mistakes, since the eidetic science devotes itself to the description of the essence of objects, while Phenomenology, according to the mission which Husserl has assigned to it, has to return to the forms of knowledge in which essences appear. For the first, eidetic reduction or ideation suffices, but the second demands, besides, phenomenological reduction, a reflection and a suspension of judgment upon the existence of the transcendent objects whose forms of knowledge are examined. Husserl himself has repeated the desire that the word phenomenology be reserved to denote descriptions of transcendental positions, "denn ohne die Eigenheit transzendentaler Einstellung erfasst und den rein phaenomenologischen Boden sich wirklich zugeeignegt zu haben, mag man zwar das Wort Phaenomenologie gebrauchen, die Sache hat man nicht," IDEEN, p. 179.

Eidetics describes essences. It is a descriptive science; it neither theorizes nor constructs: it stands on this side of all theories and solutions. It has to rely exclusively on what is given immediately to essential intuition and to describe it. It does not have to use demonstrative arguments. But also it is on this side of the formulation of the problems themselves. It is clear that as it has a task to perform, it may be objected that it resolves problems; in fact, however, these are not problems in the sense previously determined, for all problems require a known term, and in philosophical problems the known term is the essence of the phenomenon. In short, one may speak here of pre-problems.

Even though its task is one of description alone, Eidetics has to carry it out rigorously. It has to make a rigorous description (a possible task thanks to the *apriority* of its object) because on it depends a responsibility of greater import, since the description is the initial support for problems and theories. "The phenomenon . . . has to be described in such fashion that the connection of its essential traits may be seen as a whole."[5] Therefore it is necessary to make the ideative abstraction or reduction before explained.

(2) The *eidos* of a phenomenon having been described, it will be necessary to advance to the analysis of the problems which it raises. This new step constitutes a science by itself, Aporetics. The word comes from "aporia" which in Greek means literally "lack of roads" or "without a way." Aristotle was the inventor of this science. His idea is found in his *Metaphysica,* B 1. Aporetics consists in the examination of two opposed theories and their respective reasonings, derived from a single question.

Before investigating the solutions the doubts have to be enumerated, fixed, discussed, their hidden aspects discovered, and opinions already formed upon the point compared and arguments examined. This task is inescapable to advance toward the solutions. Aristotle saw it clearly. "No one can undo a knot who does not know it absolutely, and the doubts of our thought are the knots which tie it fast and prevent it from moving onward. To investigate without studying the problems is the same as to walk without knowing whither, without direction." He saw, moreover, that not only the solutions but also the correct clarifying of the problems offers serious difficulties.

The aporetics conceived and practiced by Aristotle was continued during the Middle Ages. Abelard was then its renewer. His *Sic et Non* is a work intentionally aporetic, although restricted to theological themes. In the prologue are to be read these words: "Incipiunt sententiae collectae ab eodem, quae contrariae videntur. Pro qua contrarietate hanc

[5] N. Hartmann, *op. cit.* chap. 4.

collectionem sententiarum ipse SIC et NON appellavit."[6] Alexander de Hales and St. Thomas Aquinas practiced it indeed with consummate mastery; and in general all the scholastic tradition practiced it. But modern philosophy, following the Cartesian indication of making *tabula rasa* of alien thought and seeking an absolute beginning from which to philosophize, forgot it almost altogether.[7] In our days it has been revived and practiced successfully by N. Hartmann.

Aporetics is, then, the pure science of problems. Alongside the description of the essence of phenomena, Eidetics, Aporetics constitutes a second investigation before the strictly philosophic stage, the construction of the theory. It is precisely that which, investigating the doubts which the phenomena present, fixes the points which have to be understood in the philosophic theory. But this analysis of the problems ought to be supported on the essential description of the phenomena, as Hartmann well says. In fine, every problem has to have a known element and another unknown. The unknown is what is sought, that which the theory has to resolve; but the problem cannot arise if it does not contain in itself a known element, a datum from which to start, since that which is absolutely unknown, obscure, that of which we do not have the least information, cannot be an object of any difficulty for us, cannot present any problem to us. It lacks the necessary matter for that, and that matter is exactly the phenomenon.

But, although based on Eidetics, Aporetics is independent of it, as it is independent of the theory, for its task does not consist in treatment either of the known or of the unknown, but of the connection which exists between the two. On this account, its method is also distinct. It is not description. It has to examine, to sift the data, to compare them with analogous phenomena — and also opposite ones — to record the contradictory or that not at once explainable. Aporetics completes its task when it shows us the obstacle to the continuation of the thought, when it leads us exactly to the depth of the doubt, to that point where there is no road.

It is in this field recently studied by Aporetics that the theory can advance successfully. And it is this which constitutes the strictly philo-

[6] PETRI ABELARDI, OPERA OMNIA (in MIGNE, PATROLOGIA LATINA, vol. 178).

[7] With full knowledge Kant has indicated the necessity of an exact putting of the problems. "It is indeed a great and necessary proof of prudence and penetration to know what reasonably has to be asked. For when the question is absurd in itself and requires unnecessary answers, it has sometimes the inconvenience, aside from shaming the one who asks it, of leading him who hears it without attending well to it, to absurd answers and of giving to both the ridiculous aspect which the old saying expresses as one milks the goat and the other has the pail" (CRITIQUE OF PURE REASON, Second Part, Introduction, III).

sophic attitude: speculative construction which leads finally to the solutions. Eidetics and Aporetics are no more than preliminary tasks, but also necessary tasks. And their importance rests more than on their necessary character — this can only be appreciated when in fact one tries to theorize before fixing the doubts — on its condition as preliminary task. Because of Eidetics leading to Aporetics and because of the latter's making clear the difficulties which the essence of the described phenomena raises, it becomes evident that beyond them there is something which sustains or justifies them; incites one to follow until one meets or glimpses the other side of things, the reverse of the medal, the region of what is or is worth absolutely as absolute.

These are the two preliminary tasks which we seek to accomplish with positive law.

Our work is divided, then, naturally into two parts: (1) The Eidetics of the law, which has to describe the essential traits, the *eidos* of positive law, and (2) the Aporetics of the law, which has to analyze and fix the problems, the doubts which the essence of that phenomenon raises.

II. EIDETICS OF THE LAW

1. The Essential Questions as to Positive Law and Correction of an Ambiguity

The name "Law" is used with different meanings which are usually distinguished by more or less adequate adjectives which are added. "Objective law" may be opposed to "subjective law" (a term which leaves much to be desired), or positive law (and within this human law to divine law) to natural, rational, ideal, pure law, etc. (the final opposition being transverse to the first, which permits the combining of the terms of the two groups).

Our theme is positive Law. More exactly: objective positive Law. This is the phenomenon which can be given to all of us immediately, because we live in lasting contact with its prescriptions. It is of it of which we have to describe the essence, when we seek to know what it is.

But the question "What is it?" does not have a single signification. Ingarden[8] has shown that this interrogation may be used with various meanings, which of course must be separated carefully. A simple example taken from Mathematics will serve to establish the distinctions for us. If anyone asks with respect to the mathematical object "square," "what is it?," he may mean to indicate these interrogative contents:

(1) What is the meaning of the word "square"? He who asks has heard

[8] R. Ingarden, Essentiale Fragen, Ein Beitrag zum Wesensproblem.

the word, but he does not know what it means; he is ignorant of the object denoted. The exact response,[9] better than any verbal description, would be to put before his eyes a "square" figure and to say to him: the word "square" means this: □ The correct formulation of this question is: What does "the square" mean?

(2) With what word is designated the mathematical object which we all call "square"? He who asks has seen representations (drawings, for example) of that object, but he does not know its name, he does not know what it is called. The reply says: that is called "square" or its name is "square." The question correctly formulated is: What is the name of this: □ ?

(3) What is the nature, the strict determination of an individual example of a "square?" He who asks has seen a representation of an individual square (drawn on the slate, for example) but he does not know what its constituent nature is. He may very well know the word "square" and even its general concept but he has never connected them with the individual representation which he has before him. The reply is: this is a square. The correct formulation of the question is: What is this (indicating) □ ?

(4) To what class of objects does an individual example of the square belong? He who asks knows perfectly its individual constitutive nature, and he knows also the scheme of classes to which all objects belong, but he does not know what role the square plays in this scheme. We may formulate this question, to distinguish it from the following one, thus: What is a square? Reply: it is a mathematical (or rather ideal) object.

(5) What is the essence of the square? He who asks inquires here for an object not individual, for the species or universal object "square." Correct question: what is the square? Reply: it is a parallelogram which has equal sides and equal angles.

If we leave aside cases (1) and (2), which are questions as to the word, and reduce the other three to universal terms, we shall have the following enumeration of the related meanings of the essential questions:

(1) What is this?
(2) What is an *X*?
(3) What is the *X*?

We shall see now what are in general the characteristics of each one of these questions.

(1) The question "What is this?" called by Ingarden the question as to determination, may occur in two cases (a) when he who asks perceives an individual object until then unknown and the interrogated person

[9] The answers are indicated, because they help to clarify the difference in the questions.

"knows" what it is; (b) when, without perceiving it, he who asks has heard someone speak of it (I saw something so and so). Nevertheless, there are characteristics common to these two cases: (a) that the "this" signifies an individual object; (b) that he who asks possesses a series of things known (provided that in every question there has to be always a known element); (c) that, in spite of this, the object remains unknown for him who asks.

The elements of this question are the following:

(a) The known is an individual object apprehended by means of a subjective scheme which constitutes the correlate of the indication "this" and which does not know its nature;

(b) The unknown is the same individual object apprehended in its constitutive nature.

It is not true, as some theories maintain, that in the question "What is this?" the unknown is the name of the object. Without doubt, in formulating it, it may have been intended to ask for the name, but then the correct question is, as we have seen, "What is this called?" or "What is the name of this?" But the question "What is this?" has a significance of its own distinct from that which is attributed to it when it is mistakenly identified with the question for the name. The peremptory reason is this: that in the reply ("This is a square") the "this" implies the identity of the object-subject with the object-predicate. If the reply, then, should be the name, it would be absurd; the reply "This is an *A*" would signify "This is identical with the name *A*" ("This is a square" would signify "This is identical with the name square"). But "this" is not a name. Consequently, in the question the unknown is not a name, but the nature of the object, the τι, the individual moment constitutive of the object;

(c) The question itself consists of the identity between the known and the value sought of the unknown;

(d) But the question has a presupposition: that every individual object is constituted by an individual nature.

(2) The question "What is an *X*?" or question as to the scheme or as to the class, breaks down into the following elements:

(a) The known is a determined individual object which is apprehended by its individual constitutive nature;

(b) The unknown is the "role" or "post" of the object indicated under (a), which it has in itself, as an individual of a determined kind;

(c) The question itself consists in the appearance of the known in the "role" or "post" of the class, which constitutes the unknown;

(d) This question has various presuppositions: (1) That the subject of the question may fall and falls within a class; (2) That there is this class and that the nature of the object permits its reference to that class; (3) That the known of the problem determines the system of classes under which the object may fall; (4) That there is a "role" which is constituted by the reference between the subject of the question as an individual and as a class.

(3) The question "What is the *X*?", or question as to the essence, is distinguished from the two preceding, above all, in that the *X* is not an individual object, a specific object.

(a) The known of this question is constituted by the content of a general or particular idea, but one apprehended only by means of its immediate form (μορφή).

(b) The unknown is a special system of constants of the same contents of ideas, which is necessary and sufficient in order for there to exist identity between the known and the unknown;

(c) The question itself constitutes the existence of that identity between the known and the unknown.

In general the reply to this question, with the exception of the cases in which the *X* is a simple idea, will have the form of the judgment: *X* is a *Y* with the characteristics *a, b, c,* etc.

Finally, it is necessary to make clear that the question of the essence is logically prior to the question of the scheme. Truly, in order to know to what class an X belongs, there has to be known, first, what the *X* is.

These distinctions of the essential questions are those which we have to keep in mind with regard to positive Law when we ask what it is. We shall have, then, to distinguish:

(1) The question of the determination: "What is this?" (in which the "this" means a particular Law, the Uruguayan Law or the French Law, for example) whose unknown term is the constitutive nature of that individual "this" (which according to the case will be the Uruguayan Law or the French Law);

(2) The question of the scheme: "What is a Law?", in which the unknown consists of the post which the Law as an individual of a determined sort has in itself; and

(3) The question as to the essence: "What is the Law?", whose unknown term is constituted by the special system of constants, necessary and sufficient that there should exist the identity between it and the content of the general idea "Law."

As we know, to the first question the answer is: "This is a Law" (if truly it is). There remains for us, then, as a task the solution of the other two. But it is not immaterial whether we begin with one or the other. There is a logical order necessary in their treatment. If, as we have seen before, the question "What is an *X*" is logically subordinate to the question "What is the X," we have to know first what is the Law to be able to determine then to what class a Law belongs. The essential of the Law has to be described before determining the post of the law in a system of kinds.

With this, however, we have not avoided all the possibilities of confusion. If we observe the use which in Philosophy and in the Science of the Law is made of the term "Law," — "objective Law" — we shall find that in reality there are two significations which belong to it, and consequently two distinct objects are signified by it, in such way that, as almost never is one conscious of this duplicity of meanings, the concept of Law ends by being converted into an ambiguity, which is a factor in no few errors in the determination of its essence. In fact, "Law" often signifies the aggregate of juridical norms or rules; other times, on the other hand, it means the element of that aggregate, the juridical norm or rule. It would be superfluous to cite examples of this duplicity of meanings, which juridical literature employs currently. Doubtless in both cases what is meant is the universal: not this aggregate of norms, but the aggregate of norms in general; not this juridical norm, but the rule of law. But in the first case the concept of law alludes to a collective object, while in the second it refers to a solitary object. The distinction between the two classes of objects is well known.[10] A collective object is a whole constituted by a plurality of homogeneous objects: a flock, an army, a library. A solitary object is any object whatever of the objects which in a homogeneous plurality constitute the corresponding collective object; a bird, a soldier, a book. In general, the possibility of falling into a mistake is excluded because, as in the examples cited, distinct terms are used to name the collective and the solitary object. From the diversity of the objects follows the difference of the terms. On the other hand, if in juridical material a mistake arises or is maintained it is precisely because the same name "Law" signifies sometimes a collective object and at other times a solitary object. Now, the importance of this distinction is based on the fact that the true predicates which may correspond to the respective subjects of the judgments in both classes of objects are not the same. Not all that can be predicated with truth of the subject-collective object can be predicated with truth of the subject-solitary object, and vice versa. The judgment "This flock has a triangular form" may be true, but it does not follow from this that "Each bird in this flock has a triangular form" must be a true judgment. And the same may be said of the Law so far as it contains those two meanings which we have disclosed before. So it is that Kelsen, for example, an author trained in

[10] See PFÄNDER, LOGIK.

the rigor and the precision of his concepts, although perfectly conscious of the distinction, does not notice, nevertheless, that predicates which are true of the Law as a collective object cannot be transferred without modification to the Law as a solitary object. From him come these thoughts: "The juridical order is a system of norms of Law . . . the nature of all ought to be investigated, as it is reflected in each one of its parts: for each juridical norm, to be such, has to reflect the nature of Law considered in its totality. If the Law is a coactive order, each juridical norm will have to regulate and prescribe the practice of coaction." [11] Kelsen, then, distinguishes between the Law as a system of norms and each norm of the system, but he pretends to attribute to it the same determinations for the whole and for the part. We have shown, nevertheless, that nothing guarantees *a priori* that it is so. Therefore, to describe exactly the essence of the Law, we have to distinguish carefully Law in its significance as a collective object and in its significance as a solitary object. Each of them is a distinct object; each of them has to have, therefore, its own essence. If to a certain point there is a coincidence between the two it is a thing which legitimately can be proved only at the end.

2. The Essence of Positive Law

A. The Law as Collective Object

If on the basis of the representation of any particular Law we make the ideative abstraction and apprehend intuitively the universal essence "positive Law" we shall discover in it the following moments:[12]

(1) The Law refers to human conduct.

Further on I will make clear of what this reference consists; but it is at once evident that human conduct is the object or material of Law. Conduct, however, is not something separated from man, although it may have effects upon other objects which outlast it in duration and consequently are separable from it. Conduct, in itself, is something *in* the man: it is always his conduct. The reference to conduct is, then, simultaneously a reference to man.

(2) The conduct of man permits a fundamental division, according to whether or not it supposes for its realization the existence of another man. To eat, to plant a tree, to discover and formulate a mathematical

[11] Teoria General del Estado, Sec. 10 A, pp. 61–62 of the Spanish edition. Cf. Hauptprobleme, p. 238, note.

[12] It is not a matter here of a demonstration of the essence, which, as Aristotle saw, is impossible. Proof of the truth of the description of the essence must consist in finding if it is truly identical with intuitive essence.

theorem are tasks which one man may execute though he be alone in the world. The aggregate of such actions we call individual conduct. Better: "asocial conduct."

On the other hand, to buy or to assassinate, to promise or to injure, to abandon a child or to teach a science require necessarily the existence of another; they are actions directed toward another. Their aggregate we call "social conduct."

The material of Law is not any conduct whatever, but is only social conduct. The Law refers necessarily to a plurality of subjects.

The determination of "social" in conduct embraces also the sphere of thought (in the full meaning, cogitations). The opposition "action-thought" does not coincide with the opposition "social-individual"; rather it is transverse of it. There are social purposes, desires, thoughts, as there are social actions. There are individual, asocial actions as there are asocial, individual thoughts, desires, and purposes. And law may refer, and in fact does refer, to purposes, desires, and thoughts, in spite of their originally internal character, with regard to how they are oriented toward another. The penal concepts of fault, blame, extra and super intention are divers forms of purpose and desire; the rules of the civil Law as to the interpretation of laws (Articles 16 to 20 of the Uruguayan Civil Code) and those of procedural law as to the formation of the demand, answer, pleadings, judgment, etc. (Uruguayan Code of Civil Procedure, Articles 284, 297, 325, 462, 466, etc.), refer to thoughts.[13]

The plurality of men may be more or less extensive, may have this or that constitution (community, society, etc.), but it has to form a circle in which each one is in relation to the other and to which the Law must be referred.

The circle of men and their social conduct is an indispensable supposition of the Law. All Law necessarily makes reference to them. But the reciprocal is not true. The circle itself and its social conduct are independent of the Law. Then neither in the essence of man, nor in that of the circle, nor in that of social conduct does there enter at all the determination of the juridical. The life of the circle is the primary thing and the Law is something which adverts to that life.

(3) Looked at from another angle, the Law is an object made by man. Man is not only the material of the law. He is also its creator. Just

[13] The paradoxical destiny of procedural Law consists in its regulating acts which are found at the opposite poles of human conduct: on the one side, attachment, delivery of a thing, deprivation of liberty to go and come (imprisonment), etc.; and on the other, complaint, defense, judgment, interpretation, etc.; actions there, thoughts here.

as he makes instruments and houses, squares and sciences, morals and religions, so he also makes Law. In this is rooted its "positive" character. For this we call it positive law. To its essence there belongs the being something put in, something dictated by man. By this we do not allude in any respect to the State. Law may be dictated in any circle of men; in the church, in the association, in the family, in the international community. The State is only one of the objects which dictate Law; unless it is understood: State, a subject which dictates Law. Then, of course, all law would be of a state, but it would have to be added that the church, the association, the family, etc., are States.

The essential thing is that positive Law supposes on one side a circle of men to whose social conduct it refers, and on the other a man or group of men who make it. At what point this group coincides or not with that circle is for the moment absolutely indifferent and does not alter in any way the essentiality of that "face to face" of both terms, as in knowledge is not altered the necessary correlation of subject and object, by the circumstance that the object may be at the same time the subject itself.

But originally positive Law needs to distinguish between the man who dictates it and the man whose social conduct is the material of Law.

(4) And nevertheless the Law itself is nothing (not even a part) either of him who makes it nor of those whose conduct is its material.

Social conduct is not the material of the Law, in the way that wood is the material of the tree, but in the same way that wood is the material of the science which studies trees, of Botany.

And in the same way, law is not made by man, as he makes some action, or an automobile, but analogously to the way he makes Chemistry or a novel.

Law is an aggregate of thoughts.

To say, then, that social conduct is the material of the Law signifies that that conduct is the necessary objective correlate of the thoughts which constitute the Law. And to affirm that the Law is an aggregate of thoughts is as much as to say that it is composed of significations — concepts — connected by a bond, significations whose objective correlate has to be social conduct.

(5) But science also is a tissue of thoughts, and the Law is not a science. No doubt there is a science of Law; but in no way should it be confounded with Law itself. The latter is the object of the former; consequently, it is a necessary supposition. Science describes or explains its objects. To a certain point it may be said that its thoughts have a reproductive character, they are thoughts of adaptation, which have to turn into logical form the ontological connections which they have be-

fore them. The Law, however, is not a description nor an explanation of conduct. There are sciences which do that: Sociography and Sociology. On the other hand, the Law does not have for object conduct as it is; it does not say to us what actions are nor how they happen, but how they ought to be. It is not a phenomenon of adaptation, but adapting: it is conduct which has to adapt itself to the law, and not the Law to conduct. The thoughts of science are judgments; the thoughts of the Law are dispositions. The Law is an aggregate of dispositions.

But the adapting character of the Law does not signify any compulsion. The Law does not force man to move in its channel. It is not, like the ontological categories, an internal principle of being, which leads it irresistibly over steel rails. Conduct does not let itself be dominated so by the Law; it may submit to its dispositions, but it also may rebel against them or ignore them. In itself conduct is independent in the face of law. But law is also independent in the face of conduct. Its essence remains intact before all transgression of its dispositions: for these are not principles "in" but "upon" conduct. An ontological law would cease to be such if it could be transgressed, but a Law violated goes on being Law. It is more: the Law has to take account of this hiatus between conduct and its dispositions for it has no meaning to say what the action ought to be, if already by itself the action is what it ought to be. Violability then belongs to the essence of law.

(6) It is not sufficient to consider the Law as an aggregate of dispositions upon social conduct. The dispositions of the Law have a heterogenous structure which binds the conduct of the members of the circle in a peculiar way. It is not a matter here of a mere reciprocity. Reciprocity is an equal conduct of all for all, and for it dispositions of homogeneous structure are sufficient.

The Law prevents on one side the realization of certain conduct and on the other side makes possible the execution of other actions. To some it indicates what is not prevented; to others it indicates that they ought not to prevent what is not prevented. To one it opens a free sphere of action, another it restricts, exactly in the same measure in which it has opened up to the first. On one side the obligation arises, the juridical duty, on the other side, the loosening, the juridical faculty (the so-called "subjective law"). It does not regulate, then, a uniform reciprocal conduct, but a complementary conduct.

The structure of the law is analogous to that of a sphere with its concave and convex faces. This essential trait is bilateralness.

Hence it results that the relation of the subjects which the Law presupposes is more complex than that of mere placing face to face—man so far as he makes law and man so far as his conduct is regulated by the

Law. In the juridical circle of those regulated there is also a facing of two irreducibly distinct positions: that of the empowered and that of the compelled. And the fact that the same man may be the carrier at the same time of duties and of rights does not modify the opposition, since the two situations of the compelled and the empowered are always essentially opposed.

The Law is, then, a relation with a triple aspect; in it man is supposed in three essentially necessary and essentially distinct situations: as a subject who makes the law (Subject D),[14] as a subject with faculties or active subject (Subject A), and as a subject with obligations or passive subject (Subject P).

(7) The law not only regulates social conduct but it also offers the motives for determining the effective adaptation of it to its dispositions and contains a consideration of their respective deviation and the fixing of its consequences.

These motives and consequences are also the content of its dispositions and consist of a new social conduct of certain men whose effects have to fall upon those who have adjusted themselves to or have deviated from its dictates. By this we have named retributions or sanctions, which are called penalties or punishments when they consist of ills, and premiums or rewards when they consist of goods. Therefore the ancients said: "Two divine lights govern all things, reward and punishment."

It would be a deplorable mutilation to present Law as implying exclusively the method of damaging retribution, the penalty. The essence of the Law implies retribution, but this may be not only by punishment but also by reward. And the history of positive law shows us actual examples of retributions which are premiums: the laurel branch (Greece) and the elogy and the prize (Medieval Spain), promotion and increase of salary, decoration, grace pensions, economic rewards, and exemptions. If they pass unnoticed by us it is because they have not been unified in a Code as have penalties.

On this account there has been urged with reason the creation of a reward Law, as opposed or complementary to the penal Law.[15]

Certainly penalties are found in juridical reality with much greater frequency than rewards, and this has its basis — which it is not possible to clarify now, because it requires elements not yet known. But in the essence of juristics is implied the constant of retribution in gen-

[14] An exact name would be "jurislator," but the word is exotic. If we call him "legislator" it has to be remembered that thereby we do not refer to any state category.

[15] See L. Jimenez de Asúa, La recompensa como prevención general. El Derecho premial.

eral, not a special manner of it. On this account we say that law is the retributor.

(8) The qualities of bilateralness and of retribution reveal that the law has necessarily a systematic structure. The heterogeneity of its dispositions and, consequently, its complementary nature, united to the essential necessity of the law to be a relation with a triple face, make it evident that the Law is not a mere aggregate of dispositions all cut after the same model, but a union of members which exercise distinct functions within the whole and which complete each other reciprocally.

The Law is always a system: a bilateral system, and retributor of dispositions.

(9) We know that the Law is an object made by man. It would be an exaggeration to affirm that every human activity is determined by ends. There is a sector of it which is produced unconsciously, and that, without doubt, is not determined by ends set by man. But all conscious activity is oriented toward ends. In this sphere man realizes a finalistic activity: toward an ax to cut down trees, toward science to dominate natural phenomena. As an active and conscious being, man is a teleological entity.

The end is the form of a pro-position, of a putting before the progress toward realization: the position of the end is a putting above and beyond what is.

The subject alone by himself can propose his end. Only he is capable of a tendency, for which the position of the end has meaning. The position is reflexive: it is the position of the subject for the subject.

But the subject also may propose ends for another subject, with the purpose that he in his turn should propose ends reflexively. The position of the ends is here double and reflexive in the two subjects.

If the law is a product of the conscious activity of man, it has also to serve certain ends. The law may be cleared up somewhat here under a new light, so far as it is a means for the service of ends. For only knowledge of the end permits perfect comprehension of the means. It does not avail to argue that the end is external to the object and consequently is independent of it. Perhaps this may be justified with respect to the objects of nature. But in objects made by man, the reference to the end — or at least the indication of the type of end — is inescapable to comprehend their essence and to distinguish them from other human products.

(10) The ends which man proposes to himself are multiple and of distinct extent, but it is clear that they have to have a valuable content. And not only can what is not judged as valuable not be sought or proposed as an end, but it cannot either be recognized as a mandate or exigency. The end of all action and aspiration, of the norms themselves,

has its basis in a form of special kind and manner of its own being: value.[16]

It is impossible to propose an end without considering the value of that end. Man may make an end only of that which he feels as valuable. Without doubt he may err in his feeling of value: then the end proposed does not correspond to a true value. Also, he may for his end depart from the highest values and direct himself toward lower ones. But he cannot pursue as an end what in general he does not feel as worthy.

The end is the position of the value for the subject.

This signifies that the Law is, in last analysis, a means at the service of values, and given that its object is human conduct, Law appears now as a phenomenon of mediation between values and conduct.

(11) The sphere of value contains a plurality of forms of different quality and kind. Values are, for example, justice, prudence, beauty, holiness, tragedy, love, loyalty, etc. There are values of goods, ethical, aesthetic, religious, but the law is not a medium which proposes all values as ends. Its possibilities are limited at two extremes: one is a peculiarity of values, the other, the structure of law itself.

Not every value can be the content of an end, because not every value is a final point of an ought to be which presents to man its exigency of realization. Ends may be only those values whose realization may be possible for the subject, that is, those which can be founded on an "ought to be."

Moreover, it is clear that there can be ends for the Law only those values whose duty to be can be imposed from without. There are values which, presenting themselves as ought to be's, require, nevertheless, a spontaneous realization. So, love. These cannot be ends of Law.

Means, then, are not immaterial as to the ends. They are determined by them. To an end not any means whatsoever can be joined. And distinct series of means alone are adequate to harmonizing ends.

This same point may be considered from the point of view of the

[16] The determination of the essence of values in general falls outside of our purpose. See as to this the grand discoveries of M. Scheler in "Der Formalismus in der Ethik und die materiale Wertethik," and its later systematization and elaboration in N. HARTMANN, ETHIK. Let us record here his fundamental determinations:

Values are *a priori* material essence.

Values are absolute.

Values have an ideal not real being in themselves.

Values are principles and appear to man as an ought to be.

Values are irrational essences, not wholly reducible to concepts, and are apprehended emotionally.

There are positive values and negative ones, or not-values.

Values form a peculiar sphere in which each one has distinct quality, complexity, force, and depth. This is the hierarchical order of values.

means. The end is realized from an adequate causation, and cannot be realized except by competent means. No means can arrive at accomplishing ends which do not follow from the very nature of the means being employed. A category of means cannot evolve with respect to an end greater than the power which rises from its own structure.

The Law, then, can be put as a means at the service of only those ends which are compatible with its structure.

If we call ethical values all those whose material is human conduct, it is evident that not all of them can be ends for the Law. Law has to serve those whose material refers to the plurality of men as such. So individual values are excluded. But also so are social values. These are values of the individual which require for their completion the presence of a plurality. They are values which one individual has to realize in the presence of another. Individual and social values are ends of morals. But as the Law is a system of complementary dispositions which imply a relation with a triple front, it can only be at the service of values which can be realized in a plurality itself as such. Such are justice, order, soldarity, peace, security. We call them values of the common good or values of the community. (The term "community" has to be understood in a broad sense, without any regard to its internal constitution, and also as not opposed to "society.") The social values are values of the individual of a community, the values of a community are values of a community of individuals. It is true that this is not a definition of the group: it is only the minimum which has to be taken for them in any more positive determination. But it is sufficient to provide the criterion for a distinction between Law and morals. The Law is directed toward the values of the community.

If now we wish to sum up the result of our inquiry in a single formula, we may define positive law — as a collective object — as a bilateral and retributive system of dispositions proposed by man to regulate the social conduct of a circle of men and as a means of realizing the values of the community.

B. The Law as Single Object

Having described the whole, we have now to direct ourselves to the part and to describe also the essence of the juridical disposition, understood in the sense of the third of the essential questions, that is, as to what is or aspires to be an adequate reply to the question, "What is the juridical disposition?"

If we attend to the objective complex in which the disposition appears and examine its elements we shall have to distinguish:

(1) A subject who makes the disposition. He is the origin of its

positiveness. It is possible that it is formed by one or by various individuals — this is for the moment immaterial — ; but without it there is no positive disposition. He is the disposing subject.

(2) The act of the subject in which he makes the disposition. It is a matter of a particular psychic act, distinct in its essence from every other act of the subject, from desiring, from feeling, from judging, etc. It is the act of disposing.

(3) The disposition itself, which constitutes the content of the act of disposing, but which is distinct from that act; which is evidenced in the fact that various subjects may make the same disposition: then the disposing content is the same in all, it is only one, so far as the act of disposing is distinct in each subject; there are as many acts as there are subjects.

(4) The expression of the disposition, which also it is necessary not to confound with its content: one same disposition may be expressed in various idioms, or in the same idiom in different words, that is, one disposing content may be manifested in signs completely different among themselves. The expression of the disposition is, then, something entirely distinct from the disposition expressed. The signs in which a disposition is expressed constitute the disposing proposition.

(5) The objective correlate of the disposition. We know that the disposition is a thought, and a thought consists of significations. In the significations something is recorded: it is the thing signified, the objective correlate of all thought. In the disposition, this objective correlate is a determined human conduct, recorded in the specific form of the disposition.

Our interest has to be directed toward an examination of the disposition itself, that is, to the element which in the enumeration above appears under subd. (3).

If on the basis of the representation of any individual juridical disposition we perform ideation and apprehend intuitively the universal essence "juridical disposition" we shall discover in it three constant elements: the concept of a subject or person to whom it is directed, the concept of a bond, and the concept of a duty or exigency. This lends to the disposition a physiognomy similar to that of a judgment, which as is well known also consists of three elements: a concept-subject, a concept-bond, and a concept-predicate. But there is no more than a likeness. A disposition is not a judgment. What radically distinguishes one from the other is the bond. In the disposition the bond not only is different from the bond of the judgment, but it determines as well certain peculiarities and limitations in the other two elements.

In the disposition the bond is the "ought to be"; in the judgment it is the copula "is." The ought to be is an indefinable. It is a matter of a final element which, like being, it is not possible to reduce to other concepts without falling into tautology, or without employing notions which, far from explaining it, only explain it on the basis of its own concept. The use of concepts is here only an auxiliary means of letting us approach from different quarters an object which can be fully comprehended in its fullness only by intuition. The ought to be records something which is not, and which nevertheless is not a pure is-not. It signifies the necessity that something should be, but not with causal necessity. Thus, although it may never be, it does not lose its validity as an ought to be. And even when it comes to be neither does it disappear as an ought to be: it is also as well an ought to be: so it ought to be.

But the "being" which here is opposed to the "ought to be" is not the being of ontology, the being in its concept of existence. This is the error of idealism applied to norms, inevitable in it, by reason of the fact that for it the categories of thought are constitutive of the objects. But the realist conception is free from that. The authentic opposition is merely logical. It is the opposition of two different bonds between the elements of a thought. From the ontological point of view, the ought to be (as bond) is, as the being (as bond) also is. (Without this last it would be a tautology.) The logical sphere has also its own existence, if indeed a peculiar one, and of all its elements there can, consequently, be predicated being.

In the judgment the bond unites the concept-predicate with the concept-subject as actually belonging to it: it enunciates the predicate of the subject. In the disposition, the bond does not unite the exigency to the subject as belonging to it in fact, it is not an enunciation. It indicates that the subject has to conform to what is demanded. I would say that in the judgment it is the subject which draws toward itself the predicate; in the disposition it is the demanded which draws toward itself the subject. But in the last analysis it can only be understood intuitively that the judgment expresses its content as being, and that the disposition expresses its content as ought to become.

Hence the different relation in which the judgment and the disposition stand with regard to their corresponding objective correlates. The judgment has to coördinate itself to its respective correlate. If the judgment "this sheet is white" is true, it is because the object "sheet" belongs actually to the determination "white." The primary thing here is the objective situation: the judgment has to conform to it. Every judgment is reproductive,[17] it is a thought of adaptation. It is guided by the object, it has the pretension of being true, and in fact it is true or false.

[17] Although the expression is not strictly exact, since it is known that judgments are neither reproductions nor copies, I use it here to indicate its opposition to disposition.

On the other hand, the disposition has nothing to do with coördinating itself to its objective correlate, above all, it is the coördinating element. If I say "every debtor ought to perform his obligation on the date and at the place indicated in the contract," I do not mean, nor pretend to mean, that in fact the debtor acts in this way, but that he has to coördinate his conduct to the content of the disposition. The disposition is not reproductive, but efficacious. It is not a thought of adaptation, but an adapting. It is not true or false, but in force or not in force, just or unjust. The judgment goes after its objective situation; the objective situation goes after its disposition.

According to this, Kelsen[18] and Duguit[19] commit an error in maintaining that the norm of law is a judgment, an error more surprising in the former, who maintains that the norm falls in the category of ought to be. Kelsen understands that the proposition "you ought" (*du sollst*) is a judgment in that of the subject "you" is enunciated a predicate "ought" (*sollen*), which excludes his being able to consider it imperative. But it is evident that that proposition of ought to be is copula and not predicate. For if it were predicate what would be the copula? The juridical disposition would be a juxtaposition of subject and predicate without a bond. And that is not a judgment.

In the propositions with ought to be there is strictly no predicate. The third element — which corresponds to the predicate of the judgment — is the concept of a conduct determined by the bond.

The origin of this confusion between the disposition and the judgment lies — to my way of thinking — in the circumstance that dispositions are expressed in propositions, like judgments. Assimilate then what is expressed to the expression and say that dispositions are judgments because they are expressed in propositions. Meanwhile, the truth is that if indeed every judgment is expressed in a proposition, not every proposition expresses a judgment. Our previous analysis has shown us the radical difference there is between the disposition and the judgment, which is evidenced further by the fact that propositions express at least two classes of thoughts: enunciative ones (judgments) and disposing ones (dispositions). But there are moreover two other classes of contents which are expressed in propositions and which are not judgments: they are interrogative and optative thoughts.[20] When I think "What is paper?" I do not make a judgment, for in that there has to be a predicate, while in that thought one notes the absence of any predicate. In the same way when I think "Oh that tomorrow would be a pleasant

[18] HAUPTPROBLEME DER STAATSRECHTSLEHRE 211.

[19] I TRAITÉ DE DROIT CONSTITUTIONEL (3d ed.) 82.

[20] See PFÄNDER, LOGIK.

day" I do not make a judgment, I do not enunciate a predicate of a subject, I express a desire, which is a different thought from a judgment, although it also has the form of a proposition.

Propositions may express, then: (1) Enunciative thoughts; (2) Interrogative thoughts; (3) Optative thoughts; (4) Disposing thoughts.

Judgments are enunciative thoughts only, that is, the only one of the four classes of thoughts which are expressed in propositions. The same language offers different grammatical forms which accommodate themselves to the different classes of thoughts: the indicative, the subjunctive, and the imperative are the proper moods to be employed respectively for enunciative, optative, and disposing thoughts. In fact, however, this correspondence does not always occur. Sometimes laws are expressed in the indicative mood, proper for judgments.[21] It is a matter of a defective form of expression, strictly speaking, since the meaning of every law is to be a disposing and not an enunciative thought. Therefore one has to distinguish always the disposing content from its verbal expression.

Nor should the disposition be identified with any article of a law. An article may contain several dispositions,[22] and inversely, it may not contain one complete disposition[23] which has to be integrated then with particulars from other articles.

If the disposition is not a judgment, it is clear that neither is it a hypothetical judgment as Kelsen believes.[24] And if we try to rectify the first error and maintain that the disposition, as disposition, only occurs in the hypothetical form of a relation, that is, the content of its exigency is necessarily subordinated to the fulfillment of a condition — analogously to the hypothetical judgment — nothing will have been gained. Like the judgment, the disposition does not necessarily have to be hypothetical: its essence permits perfectly the three forms of relation.[25] And in positive law we frequently find dispositions which are not submitted to any hypothesis, which are, consequently, categorical.[26] And also there are disjunctive dispositions, that is, those in which there are two or more exigencies, reciprocally exclusive, so that the realization of one of them invalidates the other.[27]

[21] Examples abound. At random I cite Arts. 703, 704, 708 of the Civil Code. There are Codes which use systematically the indicative mood, such as the Code of Obligations and the Civil Code of Switzerland.

[22] For example, the Civil Code, Art. 602.

[23] For example, the Civil Code, Art. 608.

[24] KELSEN, *op. cit.*, pp. vii, 207, 228.

[25] As to this, see my study, "Sobre la distinción entre las normas de los usos sociales y el derecho."

[26] See Constitution, Arts. 8, 9, 72, 73, Civil Code, Arts. 1, 7, 127, 128.

[27] E.g., Code of Commerce, Art. 287, Civil Code, Arts. 1431, 394.

It is clear that there are also hypothetical dispositions. What is not true is that the juridical disposition is essentially hypothetical.

For every disposition there is essential a concept-subject. But the kind of subject is here limited by a peculiarity of the bond: the very ought to be of the disposition implies that only man can be its subject. For the meaning of the dispositive ought to be consists in a determined objective correlate (subject) being adapted to the content of its exigency by virtue of the knowledge of that content itself put as an ought to become. And to adapt itself to what is disposed by virtue of knowledge of its content only a conscious and at the same time free being is capable, to wit, a man. This shows us a new difference from a judgment: that may have as subject any kind of objects, but a disposition, only man.

This has been sometimes denied. A. Reinach,[28] for example, maintains that the disposition has nothing to do necessarily with the conduct of men. Such would be the case with a disposition which establishes: "majority is attained at 21 years." But this is not a complete disposition, but a formula or a fragment of a disposition which must be coördinated with all the dispositions which turn upon the conduct of subjects differentiated into "adults" and "minors." It is a matter then of a technical proceeding of abbreviation by which are determined the two concepts of subjects to which are referred all the dispositions of that law or of a certain sector of it. Formulas of this sort abound in all positive law:[29] all must be understood in the sense just indicated.

In the same way if an article establishes: "dogs unattended may not roam in cities and towns," this thought does not constitute a disposition which turns upon animals and their conduct, but it is a manner of expressing a disposition which fully developed would say: "It is prohibited for the inhabitants of cities and towns to let their dogs roam at large," in which it appears evident what is the subject of the disposition and what conduct is demanded of it.

Let us consider now the extent of the disposition.

Sometimes it has been maintained that to the juridical disposition there belongs essentially the note of universality.

This thesis is equivocal in its vagueness. To understand it correctly and judge it there must be distinguished in it, at least the following meanings:

(1) The subject of the juridical disposition is universal.

Universal subject may mean:

(a) The concept of man in all its generic extent. Explicitly or implicitly the subject of every disposition would be: "All men . . ."

It is not necessary to waste much argument to reach the conviction

[28] Fundamentos apriorísticos del Derecho Civil, Sec. 8.

[29] See Civil Code, Arts. 1 (subd. 1), 2, 3, 5, 6, 7, etc.

that in this meaning the thesis is false. The disposition cannot refer to more subjects than those which belong to a determined juridical circle, that is, to the point to which the effect of the disposition reaches, which is limited by territory, time, and other circumstances. Only the dispositions of desired and nonexistent universal law could attain that extension; but, even so, as we shall see, the essential character of universality would not be demonstrated.

(b) With the limitation explained under (a): the concept of man belonging to a determined juridical circle.

But neither is it true that the necessary subject of the disposition should be all men of the community in which the disposition has its effect.

The subject of judicial sentences and of many administrative acts (designation of an official, concession of a patent of invention) is an individual concept.

To sustain the thesis, in the face of these phenomena which contradict it, there would have to be excluded from the concept of juridical disposition the sentence and the decree, limiting it to the law. But such an exclusion would be arbitrary, for the simple difference of quantity in the thoughts may serve to found species or subgenera within the genus, but not to create a new genus. If we do not consider the organ which dictates them — a contingent and variable moment — the only difference between the sentence and the law — considered in their intrinsic elements — would be the quantity of the subject concept, for both fall under the category of the ought to be which refers to the values of the community. If the sentence is not a juridical disposition, what is it then? If it is admitted that the sentence is a juridical phenomenon and that law consists of dispositions, it is not possible to maintain without contradiction that the sentence is not a juridical disposition. To exclude the sentence and the decree from the concept of disposition because their subject is individual would be equivalent in the field of logic to maintaining that only those enunciative thoughts whose subjects are universal are judgments but not those whose subject is individual or particular.

And, nevertheless, even reduced to the concept of law, the thesis of the universality of the disposition would not come out better off. There are also laws whose concept-subject is individual, like that which grants a pension to *A* or which authorizes the Head of the State to absent himself temporarily from the country; or whose concept-subject is particular — as one which requires a conduct only of some of the individuals comprised in the concept-subject, like the prescription in the 3rd subdivision of Article 112 of the Code of the Organization of the Courts.[30]

[30] Art. 112, subd. 3, Código de Organización de los Tribunales Civiles y de Hacienda. (Draft presented, Feb. 23, 1915; approved, Feb. 15/19, 1933, Law No.

(c) It is clear that in the majority of laws the concept-subject is universal, but this does not imply in any way that the objective correlate of that universal concept-subject should be that indicated under (b).

The concept-subject is universal when it extends to all the individuals who compose that concept: every owner, every buyer, every minor, every citizen — and it is clear then that none of these concepts has cause to coincide with that of "every man belonging to this juridical circle." That would depend on what the positive law should establish as to who might be owner, citizen, etc. And the exclusion of certain men from one of these concepts, as in the Roman law with its distinction between citizens and strangers, or in the (recent) German law which distinguishes between Aryans and Hebrews, shows that simultaneously the subject of one disposition may be universal in the meaning under (c) and will not be so in the meaning under (b).

Of course, if we understand by law only the dispositions whose subject is universal in the meaning under (b), it will have to be admitted that universality is an essential note of the disposition. That would not be anything more than the expression of a tautology: "universal dispositions are universal." And no one can prevent that event. Only a person who should so understand universality, to be consistent with his own thesis, would have to come to the conclusion that Roman law is not law.

(d) From all these senses in which may be interpreted the thesis that the subject of a disposition is universal, there must be distinguished carefully the question of whether the Law ought to recognize and to establish equality among all subjects, which would entail the consequence that certain dispositions ought to be universal in the meaning under (b). Then it would be a matter of a deontological exigency for the Law — admitted in the majority of modern legislations, but not an essential note of the disposition.

Conclusion: the thesis that the subject of the disposition is universal has been shown inadmissible: there are, it may be, in this sense — the same as in judgments — individual dispositions, both particular and universal. These are differences in the quantity of the subject which do not affect — nor above all presuppose — the essence of the disposition.

(2) The validity of the juridical disposition is universal.

In this sense universality signifies that the disposition is valid for every subject.

9164, in effect Jan. 1, 1934. Registro Nacional, 1933, p. 1053.) Art. 112. (1) The presence of all the (three) members of the (Appellate) Tribunal and unanimity of votes is necessary for the dictation of final judgments. (2) To dictate interlocutory judgments (etc.) . . . (3) Decrees of substantiation may be dictated by one alone of the members of the (Appellate) Tribunal. [TRANSLATOR.]

It is not the subject who has to realize the conduct which is universal here, but the validity of the disposition so far as it is a content with a meaning which aspires to be fulfilled. It is the respect due to the disposition from every subject, not only from the subject of the disposition.

The disposition which establishes that in bilateral contracts one of the parties may ask rescission if the other has not complied with his obligation, is not of value only for him or them who find themselves in that situation, but for all other subjects the meaning of that disposition is valuable and has to be respected by all.

Universal is a predicate not of the subject but of the bond of the disposition. In this sense, the thesis is true.

But, so understood, it is evident that the dispositions whose concept-subject is individual or particular are universal as well as those in which it is universal.

The only sense, then, in which it may be said with truth that the juridical disposition is universal is: every juridical disposition possesses universal validity.

The third element of the disposition is also limited as to its kind by the bond. The dispositive ought to be which has as concept-subject man can only have as third element the conduct of that subject. "Conduct" is the concept sufficiently ample to include in itself acts and omissions, individually considered or in series, internal or external.

We have said that conduct presents itself to the subject as an exigency. This term is, nevertheless, defective, for it signifies only one of the two forms in which the dispositive ought to be may manifest itself: duty.

Ought to be (in German, *sollen*) and ought or obligation (*Pflicht*) are distinct concepts. Ought to be is the supreme category opposed to the category of being. The ought (obligation) is the concept opposed to the permitted (lawful, power).

The ought to be determines the difference between the disposition and the judgment and other classes of thoughts. The ought, on the other hand, is a concept and a difference within the category of the ought to be. Then, the connection between the subject and the conduct may be manifested in two forms: determining an obligation or a power.

In this the only point which needs clarification is that in fact the permitted (*the "Dürfen"*) also falls within the category of the ought to be.

Article 510 of the Civil Code establishes that "The usufructuary may enjoy the increase which alluvion brings to the thing enjoyed . . ." There is created in him a power and not an obligation, a right and not a duty.

But the disposition does not signify that in fact usufructuaries do enjoy the increase brought by alluvion. In fact, they may see themselves prevented from that enjoyment by the acts of third persons. And nevertheless, even so, juridically the usufructuary has this power. This signifies that we are not in the presence of a judgment which binds the predicate to the object as actually belonging to it. The meaning of the disposition is that the usufructuary ought to be able to enjoy the increase by alluvion, although in fact he does not enjoy it. It does not signify a possibility of being, but a possibility of ought to be.

There is then a permitting ought to be, as there is a compelling ought to be. The power and the obligation both fall, then, within the category of ought to be, but one cannot be reduced to the other. A mandate and a prohibition may be reciprocally reduced, because both are different forms of expressing the obligation. But the permissive disposition contains an ought to be distinct from that of the obligation. The efforts made by Kelsen and Duguit to reduce subjective right to objective have demonstrated precisely that the permissive disposition falls under the concept of ought to be, but in no way under that of ought.

The double form of ought to be does not signify, however, that the juridical disposition should be bilateral, rather it demonstrates that it is not. A bilateral disposition would be one which should be at the same time an obliging ought to be and a permitting ought to be, which we have just seen is impossible.

But in the Law, power and obligation are reciprocally implied; for if there is anyone who is compelled to a certain conduct, there must also be another who can demand it.

The system then is bilateral, the law is a collective object, because in it are found two classes of dispositions. It is a system of complementary dispositions, in which the bilateralness arises from the joining of duties and powers (rights).

Hence then comes the following classification:

(1) Dispositions of obligation, which found a duty to be obliged;

(2) Dispositions of power, which found a duty to be permitted.

In the quality of bilateralness are hidden the following axioms as to dispositions implied by others:

(1) Every disposition of power implies a disposition of obligation for all other subjects, to respect the exercise of this power;

(2) Every disposition of obligation implies for the same subject the disposition of power to realize the act (if I have the duty, I have to have the right);

(3) Every disposition of obligation implies for all other subjects a disposition of obligation not to prevent the fulfillment of the obligation of the first;

(4) Every disposition of obligation implies for any subject a disposition of power to demand the fulfillment of the obligation of the first.

In consequence, there are no acts indifferent to the law.

The foregoing analysis, nevertheless, is not sufficient to distinguish the juridical disposition from other classes of disposition.

These three elements are common to every disposition, but not every disposition is a juridical disposition. It may be distinguished from the others by its content so far as it regulates the material of the values of the community. In the isolated disposition this content may not appear patent, because, as it is only an element of the system, it is directed toward the values of the common good only as a member of the whole.

Its specific quality can be appreciated only in connection with other dispositions, and, in any case, with the entire system.

Digression upon Compulsion

The eidetic description of the Law does not for a moment attribute to it the quality of compulsion.

Nevertheless, in the course of the history of juridical Philosophy are to be found various attempts to consider compulsion as belonging to the essence of the Law. It is true that it is a doctrine which has appeared only since the eighteenth century: it has scarcely two hundred years of existence. The first who makes mention of this element is Tomasio[31] and then Kant. For until then that thesis had not occurred to anyone. But in the nineteenth century many philosophers and theorists of the Law maintained that compulsion is an essential element in the juridical phenomenon and indicated it as a criterion of distinction from the moral norms.

There does not exist, nevertheless, a unified doctrine upon the question. Compulsion has been conceived in different manners and connected to different qualities of the Law, so that a correct clarification of the point can have success only if it take account of all the views.

(1) "The Law is the objective *ethos,* the exterior form of life. According to that, its outstanding feature is constant realization, that is, the inevitable fulfillment in the individual of the determination imposed by all. The Law is not a mere norm, but truly an ordering, that is, precisely,

[31] TOMASIO: "Jus dividitur in perfectum, quod Grotio facultas dicitur et imperfectum, seu aptitudinem secundum eundem. Illud est, cuius vi alterum, qui obligatione suae non vult satisfacere, cogere possum ad implendum debitum. Hoc contra se habet et illuis qui obligationem huic juri respondentem possidit, pudori ac conscientiae saltem relinquitur eius adimpletio." INSTITUTIONES JURISPRUDENTIAE DIVINAE. "Obligatio juris correspondens semper externa est metuens coactionam aliorum hominum." (FUNDAMENTA JURIS NATURAE ET GENTIUM, bk. I, chap. V, sec. XXI.)

a realized norm, constantly followed. That necessity of inevitable fulfillment is externalized in the face of resistance by the individual as physical compulsion. Compulsion appeared therein always as the principal and most easily understood difference between the law and morals." [32] In these thoughts of Stahl, the physical compulsion is that which appears not only as an essential element but also as constituting the very substance of the Law.

Then the law is converted into a physical phenomenon, that is, exactly, into the contrary of what the preceding analyses have shown us that it is. The Law is composed of dispositions and dispositions are thoughts. The thesis thus appears in all its falsity. To maintain that physical compulsion is the essence of the Law would be the same as to affirm that gravity is the essence of numbers.

When the Law is identified with physical compulsion, it would appear like the cause of an effect — conduct — like a phenomenon of nature. But the Law is not the cause of anything, precisely because it is not a physical object, a spatial-temporal being. It may, indeed, be the real motive for the completion of an action, but the motive is indeed a psychic and not a physical phenomenon, and in any case carries the possibility of being followed or not.

On the other hand, in affirming that the Law is a realized norm, constantly followed, Stahl disregards the fundamental distinction between the existence and the realization of the Law. We know that it does not cease to be law from the circumstance that individuals do not follow it. The characteristic of every ought to be, including a normative ought to be, is that its content ought to be, even if in fact it is not. According to the thesis of Stahl, one would have to admit that a law which is not constantly followed is not law, since that it should be followed belongs to its essence. And hence this other consequence: that the juridical sanctions lack all meaning, since they suppose basically the violation of the Law.

(2) A different form of the theory of compulsion is expounded in the work of Jhering *The End in Law.* Compulsion is "the realization of an end by means of subjection to an external will." He explains that there are two classes of compulsion: the physical and the psychical. The first is material pressure in that the act is executed by him who exerts the compulsion. On the other hand, in psychic compulsion the act is done by the one compelled.

Jhering explains the genesis of the State and of the Law by means of compulsion. The Law springs from force; his definition is famous: "The Law is the policy of force." Without force the Law does not arise

[32] 2 STAHL, RECHTS- UND STAATSLEHRE 196ff.

nor is realized. The Law would be "the aggregate of norms by virtue of which compulsion is practiced in a State." So that there would have to be distinguished in it two elements: the norm and the realization of it by compulsion. And compulsion, says Jhering, is the only thing which distinguishes the Law from morals and from custom. It is true that Jhering admits that the sovereign or title holder of the public Power does not have anyone who compels him, and, nevertheless, he maintains that the norms to which he refers are also juridical norms, (1) because they are a feeble part within an aggregate which is juridical, (2) because according to the intention of the legislator they claim the same submission without reserve as the other norms.[33]

It is not very difficult to observe that the doctrine of Jhering fails at its base, since he himself recognizes that there is a point in Law where compulsion is impossible: the very power which exercises the compulsion. This has been constantly pointed out by the adversaries of the *Zwangstheorie.* "The State has not only the right but the duty to punish, and nevertheless this duty is uncoercible" (Binding). And the arguments of Jhering to save the difficulty are of evident insufficiency.

The methodical position of Jhering is also erroneous, because instead of examining what it is that is absolutely and unfailingly united in the essence of the Law, he takes the point of view of its genesis, that is, he investigates how the Law originated. The essence of an object and its origin are distinct questions. Even admitting that the law springs from force, this does not signify that the law has force as an essential element. But even from his point of view the thesis of Jhering is not true: the law cannot spring from force, because a physical phenomenon cannot produce a series of thoughts.

On the other hand, he affirms that force is the basis of the realization of the Law. But then we are confronted with another problem: it is now not a matter of the essence of the law, but of the manner of applying it. Then, as Jhering himself says, the compulsion has to come from back of the disposition for the case in which the latter is violated. Consequently, compulsion supposes the existence of the juridical disposition and, if it comes from back of it, it will never be an essential element of it, but something which associates itself with it from without and comes to its support. Compulsion shows itself so in its true essence, not as a constitutive element, but as a phenomenon of accompaniment of the juridical disposition.

Of course the name of law might be used to designate the permanent connection of disposition and compulsion. But apart from the fact that

[33] R. IHERING, DER ZWECK IM RECHT, I, Nos. 113, 118, 145, 147.

one would designate with the same name an amalgam of objects of distinct essence, it would be necessary to know if that phenomenon of accompaniment is constant and effective, with respect to every juridical disposition.

Physical compulsion fails in entire circles of juridical dispositions. All international law, many constitutional provisions, natural obligations, are examples of it. To be consistent he would have to deny juridical character to those dispositions.

But with it little is gained, because there where compulsion is foreseen and exercised it is not effective to prevent transgressions. Compulsion always arrives too late to cause the substantial obligation to be fulfilled. What compulsion can force the artist to execute a portrait which he has promised and refuses to make; the witness who keeps silent or lies, to tell the truth; the apostate from his faith to become a convinced believer? What compulsion can avoid the commission of a crime? Nothing can prevent a man's preferring to be a martyr, a delinquent, or a recalcitrant to a submissive complier with the Law. This shows that every action is no more than the external manifestation of a spiritual attitude, by incompellable essence.

The conclusion shows then the opposite: the law is never complied with by physical compulsion.

It is true that the debtor who does not pay may be compelled to liquidate his goods — if he has any — and to meet his debt, and the homicide may be caught, jailed, and shut up in a prison. In all these cases — foreseen by the law — the physical compulsion shows its effectiveness. But what is it which is fulfilled compulsively in them? In the case of the delinquent who is led to prison against his will, it is not the juridical disposition which imposes respect for the life of another which is fulfilled by the compulsion. Plainly the penalty supposes that the juridical duty has been violated. The distributive sanction is coercive. Compulsion then is the means of making truly effective not the principal juridical disposition but the penalty provided for its transgression.

In the case of the debtor obliged to pay against his will, the compulsion is exercised in the sale of his goods and the delivery of the proceeds to the creditor: it is the execution. It seems that here the juridical disposition which obliges the debtor to pay his debt is fulfilled coercively. But it is not so. In this the subject who has to fulfill the obligation is the debtor, in the execution it is an official; the obligation has its time and place for performance, the execution is realized at another day and in another place.

Consequently, in the Law only those dispositions are coercive whose content is the sanction or forced execution.

Jhering invokes also psychic coercion. But whoever seeks to defend the theory of coercion in this form already confesses his failure. For psychic coercion is not coercion. It differs from it as much as the representation of a prison differs from a real prison. The so-called psychic coercion is the motive created by the representation of a sanction so far as it determines an action. Truly, such a motive may occur in the fulfillment of the Law. But not always. Like every motivation, its determining efficiency is not irresistible. It is always possible that the subject should decide in another direction for other motives which weigh more and so persuade him to run the risk of the sanction. On the other hand, this coercion is not exclusive with the Law. The fulfillment of moral rules or of customs may also be motivated by the representation of sanctions which do not have to be juridical sanctions. Punishments and other worldly rewards, the verdicts of public opinion, the exclusion from certain circles, may not only constitute a psychic coercion but not rarely are stronger than the representation of juridical sanctions and may induce the subject to violate the Law to comply with other orders more powerful for him. There are produced then those strife-torn situations of which History is full.

(3) If, as a result of the preceding analysis, only those dispositions are coercive whose content is the sanction or forced execution, it is explainable how one should fall into the temptation to invert the limitation and to conceive of Law as constituted only of that class of dispositions. Kelsen has succumbed to this temptation,[34] for he, recognizing the errors of the *Zwang* theorists previously explained, nevertheless propitiates this new form. The Law is a coercive order, composed of coercive norms. But for Kelsen this does not signify "dispositions whose violation is guaranteed by coercion," but precisely and exclusively "norms regulative of coercion." The coercion is not a phenomenon of accompaniment of certain juridical dispositions, but the proper and exclusive content of the norms of the Law. Every juridical proposition consists of a condition and of a consequence, so that, in case of fulfillment of the first, the second has also to be complied with, and "the consequence connected with the juridical precept on a given condition is the state coercive act, that is, the penalty and the civil or administrative forced execution."[35] In his *Hauptprobleme* Kelsen has not been so radical. The norm regulative of coercion was only that which obliged the subjects, excluding the State; the juridical proposition in the strict sense. But the law knows also "the juridical proposition in the fullest sense": every proposition which enacts a will of the State as to its own conduct. Coercion is only one form of the

[34] KELSEN, HAUPTPROBLEME 212ff.; Prologue, p. xi.

[35] KELSEN, REINE RECHTSLEHRE.

conduct of the State. It may do other things besides coerce: construct railroads, aid the sick and the aged, etc. So then the juridical proposition in the strict sense is only one case within the juridical proposition in the fullest sense: the former is contained in the latter. The essential in a juridical norm is that it should enact a duty of the State, and in this consists the juridical proposition in its widest sense. The juridical proposition in the strict sense also enacts a duty of the State (the coercion) and moreover — as a consequence of this — a duty of the subjects.[36] Although this doctrine starts from two false premises, (1) that the juridical proposition is an expression of the will of the State and (2) that the State cannot will more than its own actions,[37] still it does not present coercion as an essential content of the Law.

But later Kelsen abandoned the doctrine of the juridical proposition in the fullest sense[38] and preserved as essential to every juridical norm the characters of the juridical proposition in the strict sense.[39] According to this theory the juridical proposition does not have the form "*A* ought to do *Y*," nor does this proposition found a juridical duty. For it to do so, it is necessary that there should be another proposition which should have the form "If *A* does not do *Y*, the State will do *Z*, in which *Z* is a coercive proceeding against *A*. That is the juridical proposition which creates the juridical duty of the subjects. The juridical duty is no more than the contradiction of the condition of the juridical proposition. "As the content of a juridical duty there can be recognized only the action or omission of a man when the conduct contradictorily opposed is threatened with a juridical consequence, when in some part of the legislation there is imposed on that conduct a penalty or execution." [40] So then, the proposition "*A* ought to do *Y*" is a mere auxiliary proceeding, to express the contradiction of the condition. It is a "secondary norm." The primary norm is that which binds the coercive sanction with the condition, that is, the norm regulative of the coercion.

If one has understood the theory, immediately he notices that it is a "construction" — useful perhaps for certain ends of dogmatic juristics, but which does not agree with the natural intuition of the juridical phenomenon. It is at the same time a mutilation and an inversion of the object "Law" as it presents itself immediately to consciousness. Mutilation, because it suppresses the axiological and teleological consideration of the Law. But we have already seen that value and end are qualities

[36] Kelsen, Hauptprobleme 251ff.
[37] Kelsen, Hauptrobleme 189.
[38] Kelsen, Hauptprobleme (2d ed.), Prologue, pp. xi and xii.
[39] Kelsen, Reine Rechtslehre.
[40] Kelsen, Hauptprobleme 242.

which are essentially connected with it. Inversion, because eidetically that which Kelsen calls secondary is the primary juridical disposition and vice versa. These two defects go together and the second is the result of the first. The essential in the Law cannot be the juridical "consequence," the sanction, precisely because it is a consequence. The central essential has to be the eidetic precedent of the consequence, that is, the juridical condition. The sanction, since it is a consequence, is dependent on the condition. The condition exactly because of being such is independent of the consequence. But the condition — to the contrary of what Kelsen thinks — is no more than the contradictory opposite of a disposition in the form of *A* ought to do *Y*." Only so the condition shows its independence. Put in another way: in the meaning of every sanction — as a proceeding dangerous for a subject — is the presumption of the nonfulfillment of a duty, and consequently the disposition which constitutes that duty. Otherwise the sanction is dissolved as such — it lacks justification — and is converted into a pure deed of him who executes the action which constitutes it. It is clear that the disposition "*A* ought to do *Y*" so far as put by man can also not have its justification in itself. That will have to be sought in its end, which in its turn can rest only on an ideal ought to be, according to which in some way *Y* ought to be. In the sphere of dispositions, then, "*A* ought to do *Y*" is the primary proposition and not the secondary as Kelsen wishes. The secondary is necessarily that which enacts the sanction. The sanction is the last link of a complex whose members in the order of eidetic succession are the following: (1) *Y* ought to be; (2) *Y* is proposed as an end; (3) *A* ought to do *Y*; (4) If *A* does not do *Y*, *E* ought to do *Z*. This is a whole in that any of the propositions becomes inexplicable if those in order before it are suppressed, but not if any later ones are suppressed. But it was inexplicable that Kelsen — after having abolished the axiological and teleological qualities — should wish to begin on the opposite side. But it is clear that the proposition under (3) by itself cannot be sustained.

On the other hand, and considered by itself, the theory leads to the absurd. This was shown in conclusive form by the Russian (Polish) philosopher Petrazycki in his *Allgemeine Rechts und Staatstheorie,* published some years before Kelsen constructed his system. It is an analysis which for its precision and clarity deserves to be known.

According to the theory of coercion as an essential note of the Law, the rule of Law (X) is no more than a rule of a particular kind which, not being complied with spontaneously, supposes the existence of another rule (X^1) which determines the coercitive means to take, for example, it orders such or such a person (policeman, bailiff, etc.) to take such a measure of coercion. But this rule (X^1) in its turn cannot, according to this theory, be considered as a rule of Law, unless there exists a third rule (X^2) which, in case rule X^1 should not be complied with, determines the coercive means to take (for example, in case the agents charged with executing an act of coercion refuse, it imposes on other agents to intervene to sanction that dereliction). The rule X^2 ought in its turn to be sanctioned by a rule X^3 and the rule X^3 ought to be supported by the rule X^4 and so successively to infinity. The theory of coercion as a necessary note of the Law leads to a superposition to infinity of rules which institute the coercion. Hence would follow the following conclusions, whose absurdity is evident: supposing that in any social medium whatsoever there exist certain rules of Law it has to be affirmed that they exist in infinite number. To prove that a rule has truly the juridical character becomes absolutely impossible, for this would require a verification to infinity; every pause caused by the absence of a superior rule which would regulate once more the coercion, must be regarded as a demonstration that none of the preceding rules is a rule of Law (if, for example, one arrives as a consequence of this verification at rule X^{20} and does not find any rule X^{21}, which in case of infraction of rule X^{20} determines the means of coercion to take, rule X^{20} for lack of sanction would be no longer a rule of Law; but for that reason also rule X^{19} which is supported by rule X^{20} will have lost its juridical character, etc.). In other terms, if coercion is an indispensable note of the Law, it is easy, proceeding by way of verification, to be persuaded with respect to every rule without exception that it is not a juridical rule, etc. But also without such verification it is evident that there does not exist nor can there exist any rule which should conform to the exigencies of the theory of coercion consistent with itself.[41]

(4) Kant [42] maintains that "the Law implies the power of coercing him who attacks it." This power to coerce is just because "resistance opposed to an obstacle to an effect serves to aid and agrees with that effect." The effect would be Law, the obstacle, the contrary attitude of an individual, and the resistance opposed to the obstacle, the coercion. As according to Kant the Law is liberty, the coercion which the Law implies is resistance to an obstacle to liberty and is consequently just.

Further on Kant maintains that strict law, that is, stripped of every ethical element, is no more than this faculty of coercing, so far as it can coexist according to universal laws along with the liberty of each one. As the Law has for object only "what there may be external in actions," strict law does not demand any other principles of determination than external principles, because only then is it pure and unmixed with ethics.

This doctrine of Kant is not altogether consistent, for it is not the same to say that Law implies the power of coercing as to say that the law

[41] Cited by GURVITCH, L'IDÉE DU DROIT SOCIAL 109ff.

[42] KANT, METAPHYSISCHE ANFANGSGRÜNDE DER RECHTSLEHRE, Sec. D.

is no more than that same power. The two thoughts are exclusive. In the first, coercion is conceived as an element which accompanies the Law; in the second, as a constituent of the very essence of the Law.

The first thesis in reality is indicating that the law is not coercion, that it is independent of it, because the power of coercion supposes an attack on the Law and consequently the Law itself. On the other hand, the reasoning of Kant is not directed to showing coercion as an integral part of the Law, but to demonstrating that that coercion is just, that is, that its use is not contrary to the principle of the Law. In this Kant is right, but then he demonstrates not that coercion is a constant of the Law but that it is a just means for its application.

And the second thesis, although literally it identifies the Law with coercion, does not mean that it is (or belongs to) the essence of the Law, in the meaning which "essence" has for us. For the thing, now, is seen by Kant not in itself but from its action. The Law appears here — in opposition to morals — as that determining motive of action which is not moved by its ethical content but by the coercion which accompanies it, which Kant considers — separating it from that content — as constituting exclusively the Law. This only signifies considering the Law as psychic coercion, a doctrine which we have already analyzed critically.

The doctrine of Kant has been revised and finally purified by Del Vecchio.[43] Del Vecchio maintains that "the possibility of compelling the observance of the Law is an integral and characteristic element of the Law itself." This is his thesis whose foundation is also similar to that of Kant. One observes in it the same vice which we indicated in that one. The possibility of compelling the observance of the Law supposes precisely Law already: one cannot cause the observance of an object which does not yet exist. Coercion consequently already presupposes the Law, that is, it is not an essential note of it. It would be as if we should say that to the essence of truth belongs the possibility that men should believe in it. This would evidently be a false proposition, because the possibility that men should believe in the truth already supposes its essence.

Del Vecchio emphasizes that what belongs to the essence of the Law is not the coercion but the coercibility, that is, the possibility of a coercive action to force respect for a law. But to replace the concept of coercion with that of coercibility is precisely to pronounce against the thesis; for the juridical disposition is then not a coercive disposition.

What is the possibility of coercion? The reply of Del Vecchio is equivocal, for once he defines it as the power to constrain, the lawfulness

[43] Del Vecchio, El concepto del Derecho, chap. V.

of coercion, and again as coercion not in act but in power. The two determinations are not identical. In the first is affirmed the justice of coercion. Possibility equals lawfulness. Then it is the thesis of Kant and the same observations are applicable to it. In the second "possibility" is taken as the category opposed to "reality." In a certain sense, all the essential notes and the essence itself of an object are no more than mere possibilities with respect to the existence of that object. Then the essence of an object does not necessarily signify its existence *hic et nunc*. But that such is not the sense in which Del Vecchio applies the concept of possibility to coercion is evident from the fact that he employs it only for this note and not for the others. Now considered not as to existence but as parts of the very essence, the notes are not possibilities: they have to occur as constants which actually integrate the essence. In this sense they are real. If then coercion only as a possibility composes the Law this is to say that it does not belong to its essence. On the contrary, it could also be said that the possibility of regulating sale, property, etc., belongs to the essence of the law. And the essence of the Law would be composed of an infinite series of possible contents.

If now we cast a retrospective glance over the aggregate of our investigations, we shall have to verify the lack of total coincidence between the essential constants of the juridical disposition and those of the system of dispositions which constitute the Law: the qualities of bilateralness and of the sanction and the direct reference to the values of the community have been recognized as essential elements of the system, but not as integral parts of each one of its members considered separately. The result then not only has confirmed the usefulness of the distinction between the collective object and the single one, but it has revealed moreover that the juridical collective is a whole and not a mere sum of dispositions, that is, a unity in which the parts only acquire their full meaning as integral parts of that whole. The Law as a collective object is the primary thing, and therefore ought to be the point of support for Aporetics.

Finally, I call attention to the fact that what we have said in this paragraph of the Law is not "theory." It is a matter solely of a conceptual description — prior to any theory — of necessities of essence, indissolubly enclosed in an object intuitively knowable directly by consciousness.

3. The Validity of the Law

The foregoing description of the essence of positive Law does not offer any basis for inferring that a Law so exists in any part of the world. The essence of an object is a mere possibility in the face of existence. Nothing can exist which does not have an essence, but the essence is determinable without relation to its existence. Therefore, even after determining it totally, the essence is not sufficient to prove its existence.

Positive Law has an essence — that which we described in the preceding paragraphs — but it is not only an essence.

It exists and may exist in the real world, which is more ample than the physical world, which is within it. There exists a Uruguayan law and another German one. More than two thousand years ago there existed the Roman Law of the XII Tables. The Law has, then, its existence.

But the existence of the Law is of a peculiar sort. It is called validity. Validity is the manner in which Law exists.

Valid Law is not synonymous with positive Law. Validity is something more than positiveness. This indicates an essential note of the Law: that of being put in effect, dictated. But the fact that someone has dictated Law does not suffice to consider it existing in a circle of men. Roman Law is a positive Law, but not a valid Law. It was valid in the time of Labeo and in that of Justinian. But not now nor here. A law recently promulgated is positive law, but if it is yet valid law is a question which will have to be examined.

Nor should validity be confused with the fulfillment or application of the Law. The subject complies with the Law if he adjusts his conduct to the juridical precepts. The judge applies the Law when he orders the sanction of the forced execution against him who has not complied with it. Truly, no law can be considered valid, if it is not complied with or applied at least in part. But the fulfillment and the application are not constitutive of the validity. If this should consist of those qualities, never could a Law be spoken of as valid because no Law is complied with or applied in its totality by all. We know moreover that every ought to be, according to its essence, may be violated. To demand then that a law to be such should have to be always complied with, means to deny its belonging to the category of ought to be.

Furthermore, the fulfillment and the application of a law suppose already that that law is valid. He who commits a crime does not comply with the Law; but, truly, it can be affirmed that the reason he does not comply with it is because that Law exists, is valid.

The validity of the Law is, then, something more than its positiveness, but something less than its fulfillment and application. Better put: the fulfillment and the application are nothing "in" the Law, but the relation of adaptation between conduct and the juridical system.

This shows us that validity is a peculiar manner of existence, different from that of physical or psychic objects. A table or a recollection do not have validity. They exist or do not, simply or totally. But a juridical disposition to exist has to possess something more than the mere essence, without, nevertheless, its full realization being necessary. Only that which pertains to the category of the ought to be exists as valid: morals, law, the rules of social usages.

Validity is the special manner of existence of a system of ought to be which contains the possibility of adapting the conduct of men to its dispositions. Valid Law has to imply, then, the possibility of adapting the conduct of certain men to its contents. And that possibility consists in a determined circle of men agreeing on the same juridical contents as constituting their Law, that is, that those contents shall be the criteria for consideration of their conduct whether to adjust it or to judge it, and including evasion of them. Not only he who complies with the Law lives it and makes it valid. Also he who violates it has to take it into consideration and coöperates in this way in its validity. The delinquent who prepares his alibi and takes precautions not to leave traces of his acts, the debtor who thinks up ways to hide his property and keep it from the reach of his creditors, have to be guided in their purpose by certain juridical contents — exactly because they wish to realize the opposing contents — and, in truth, by the same contents which others are going to take into consideration to judge their conduct and eventually to apply sanctions to them.

Observation shows us that over every group of men in which reciprocal action exists a Law grows up. It is the valid Law of that community.

So far as it is valid a Law presents these principal characteristics:

(1) It is a superindividual formation. The individual does not create it; he always encounters in his turn an existing Law, which he receives and adopts in dealing with the other members of the group. Man is not born with any juridical idea. He brings into the world only the capacity to comprehend and adapt the Law for himself.

There is a penetration of this into the individual. So far as man begins to act for himself in his life of relation, he receives the Law in a more or less slow process of learning. In it he assimilates a spiritual good, a legacy of the strictly human sphere;

(2) It is not inherited by the blood, but it is adopted in a progressive experience. Only that can be received, adopted, learned, which can be transmitted. Consequently the Law is not inherited but is only transmitted: it extends by transmission to adoption across the generations. Valid Law does not know any other way of propagating itself. Fixing it by writing is no more than a method of making more available the transmission. The penetration, then, is here a learning and a conquering.

In organic life there is inheritance; in conscious life transmission. He who inherits does not have to do anything to inherit. Transmission requires an activity in him who is to appropriate the thing to himself;

(3) The contents of valid Law not only refer to the common life of the circle, but they are in intimate connection with other contents whose bearer is also that circle; with morals and usages, with the common beliefs, judgments, and feelings of the members of the same group;

(4) It is a living formation, which as such has a process. Valid Law is not quiet, it changes slowly. But its life is not a second life apart from or above that of man. It consists in living always anew the juridical tendencies of the individuals. Only that life is not exhausted in one individual. For its process occurs in units of time greater than those of the human life. But its support is not a collective consciousness, a superindividual subject, but the individuals. And the individual is not only its bearer but also the creative and moving impulse of its change; as legislator, contractor, or judge. It is clear only in small part. For the individual alone can move and create the Law so far as he moves within a preëxisting mass of juridical dispositions. What he creates is always a small part compared with what he adopts or receives.

4. Positive Law in the General System of Objects

The determination of the genus of positive Law supposes — as we have already made clear — the knowledge of the essence of the Law, on the one hand, and, on the other, that of a system of genera under which law may fall. Now we know the first; it is necessary for us to determine the second.

The determination of a system of genera falls within the most ample task of the classification of objects. The totality of thinkable objects may be classified in infinite ways, according to the *principium divisionis* adopted. But the *principia divisionis* themselves may be differentiated into two groups: (1) those which do not refer to the constitutive nature of the objects to be classified but which are constituted by any exterior quality chosen arbitrarily by the one who is classifying. I can classify all objects under the principle of what is and what is not my property. Then there would belong to this latter class the sun, the moon, God, the spirits, the field of my neighbor, the money of my lender, logical principles, etc.; to the former, my clothes, my books, my savings, etc. These are the principles of all arbitrary classifications or simply classifications. These may be complete so long as they take as principle a contradictory opposition — as in the example given — but they do not tell us anything about the essence of the thing classified; (2) those which refer to the constitutive nature of the objects or to a quality of it. From them arise the generic classifications, or those by genera.

These are the ones which interest us. The question "What is a Law?"

alludes to the role which this thing occupies in a total classification of objects according to their chief genera.

If in accordance with the terminology already established[44] we call being or object[45] in general every subject of possible true predications, the most general exclusion which can be made of it offers us the quality of temporalness. There is a temporal being, that of the beings which begin and end which have a process, a future, whose existence is spent in an irreversible direction, within whose limits the "before" and the "after" are not interchangeable without more. They pass, they are in time. Temporalness founds the genera of real objects. To it belong the planets, the trees, the representations, the thoughts. And there is an untemporal being, that of the immutable beings, which have neither beginning nor end, which are those which they are and as they are perennially. Time does not enter into them as a constitutive quality. Extratemporality founds the genera of ideal objects. It is the realm of the essences and the values, of numbers, of relations and of geometrical figures.

Every object[46] is real or ideal, then necessarily it is temporal or untemporal. Ideality and reality are the two most extensive genera of being.

A law is a real object. Temporality is a constitutive element of it, for we have seen that it has a life, that it is made and unmade, that is, it becomes. The Law has its place within the genera of the real.

The sphere of the real being is divided also into two halves — truly of a distinct radius — with regard to the quality of having space. For there is a spatial temporal being and an unspatial temporal being.

The first is the being of extensive, material, and organic objects, which consist of juxtaposed or interlaced parts in the function of a whole, but which however it may be have three dimensions, possess a constitution primarily spatial, susceptible, in principle always of being measured. A stone and a horse, a star and a protozoa, have, in spite of their enormous differences, this common note. Spatiality founds the genera of corporeal objects. It is the sphere of things and of organisms, of matter and of life, of the physical and the biological.

The second is the being of inextensive objects which do not permit being reduced or compared with any spatial measure. Nor can there be found in them any formation of parts or of members. Hence they are also far from the ambit of all laws which are founded on a spatial con-

[44] See the Introduction.

[45] Present ontology distinguishes between "being" and "object" and rightly. See N. HARTMANN, ZUR GRUNDLEGUNG DER ONTOLOGIE. But for our purposes the distinction is immaterial.

[46] Metaphysical objects have been expressly excluded from the classification.

stitution. The perception of a mountain is no more nor less great than that of an ant. The predicates of extension do not have meaning for it. And what is true of perceptions is true also of thoughts, of recollections, of fantasies, of opinions and feelings, of judgments and prejudices, of knowledges and valuations. All these formations are spaceless. Unspatiality founds the genera of incorporeal objects.

A law is an incorporeal object. No doubt it is linked to space, for it is necessarily borne by a circle of men who, as bodies, are extensive. But in itself it is non-spatial, since it consists of thoughts. The world is not increased or diminished in size when a law is promulgated or repealed.

The term "incorporeal" is purely negative. In fact the only real incorporeal beings which we know are those which, like sensations, representations, or thoughts, rest solely on the base of animal life, and more especially on human life. Man and the animal are their only carriers. Positively they could be designated as cogitations, provided there is conceded to this term a very ample meaning which permits it to embrace this whole sphere.

And here again we encounter two genera: that of animate objects and that of spiritual objects, the sphere of the soul and of the spirit.[47] To desire and to perceive, to represent, to value, and to think, in general all acts and processes, all which come under the categories of subjectivity and of knowledge are animate objects.[48] Representations and thoughts, the ends of the will, beliefs, valuations, and judgments, and in general all that which like the contents of art, of science, of the *ethos* and of the social community is submitted to laws irreducible to those which rule the life of the consciousness, are spiritual objects.

The animated being is always an esoteric being of the individual, intimate and untransmittable. When I think a thought, my act of thinking is mine alone, no one else can possess it; another subject can, it is true, think that thought in an equal act, but that act of thinking is not my own. On the other hand, the thought which I have thought another individual may think, if he has apprehended it. And it is the same thought and not another equal one. The spiritual being is, then, expansive, objective, transmissible. Spiritual objects constitute a common sphere as against individuals. Hence Hartmann says that spirit binds and consciousness isolates.

What characterizes spirit is that it goes beyond the person, constituting

[47] We refer to objects which are given to us, of which we have some sort of experience. Metaphysical objects which are designated by the same words "soul" and "spirit" are excluded from this classification.

[48] In this and in what follows, I am guided by the exposition of N. Hartmann in his book Das Problem des geistigen Seins.

an interpersonal sphere, which is not the work of an individual, but which is already found by him.

It is a sphere of community, which is above individuals, which binds them and sustains them and is the land of their growth and differentiation. Spiritual objects are above all superpersonal.

Doubtless there is also a personal spirit. But in it there are already traces which lead to the objective spirit. The spiritual "contents" — in contrast to the "acts" in which they occur — the propositions, opinions, representations, judgments, prejudices, concepts, and intuitions, have a tendency to constitute themselves in forms objectively drawn, and come to possess in the spirit a certain objective consistency. Those contents are separable not only from acts, but also from the first subject which has borne them. They may be transferred from person to person and come to be a common possession of many. Where this is perceived with greater clarity is in concepts and judgments, which are the most fixed mintings among spiritual contents and possess great objectivity. But also the nonlogical manifestations of the representation — even though less objective — have a certain separability and communicability: observations, experiences, and doings of other persons which have been communicated and of which one can form an image. And the same may be affirmed of the ends, desires, and tastes: we can understand them and make them ours, independently of their objective value.

On this transfer of spiritual contents from person to person is founded "tradition," one of the central phenomena of the objective spirit. But besides this transmissibility, spiritual contents possess an intersubjectivity, a quality which does not coincide with the former, and which is even more deep. Intersubjective is not what passes from person to person, but what beforehand is common to all, as a structure and legality of the spirit which binds all. It is this: what I know of certain events others also know, what I know of facts and phenomena others also know. From one single experience I and others independently deduce the same conclusions. Even the image of the world — as an internal spiritual form — in its fundamental traits is also the same in all individuals. Only by this can we understand about things. The intersubjectivity rests on the identity of the laws of thought, above all of ratiocinations. We may form, *a piacere,* concepts and judgments but not ratiocinations. These are bound by a law which dominates private thinking. There is then not an individual reason but a community of *logos* and of categories. And all this occurs independently of communication and transferability. These are just the things which rest on the identity of reason and of the categorical forms.

But these superindividual traits of the personal spirit are not the most characteristic of the spirit. This is above all objective spirit. Its own territory forms customs, language, knowledge, morals, political life, religious beliefs, art, all those objects which the "sciences of the spirit" study, like philology and historiography, the sciences of literature and of politics. Here is where we find the common living spirit, in rise and fall across the times. It is not a matter of a mysterious entity, but of apprehensible phenomena. We speak of the spirit of Hellenism, of the spirit of the Middle Ages, of the spirit of the Renaissance; in general of the "spirit of the time" and by this we allude to the system of ideas, ends, tendencies, and convictions of an epoch. Also we speak of the "spirit of a people" as of a national peculiarity as compared with other peoples. This is a concrete, apprehensible phenomenon. Doubtless it is difficult to perceive the spirit of the people in which one lives, but this is precisely because we are absorbed in it. When we go to a foreign land, we experience the spirit of that people and at the same time there is illuminated also that of our own. At once we see that the system of ideas, convictions, and habits which we have does not serve to move us in this new country. Now we have to live in a new spirit, we have to comprehend it and to learn to manage ourselves within it if we wish to live in that land. It is a power which reaches us, surrounds us, and presents exigencies to us; and with other powers we have to agree with it. We perceive then that it is a unitary something, which is in everything and binds the most heterogenous things, from courtesy to political passion. And as a people has a common spirit so also has a city, a town, a ward, a battalion, a class. But the common spirit is not the community. This is an aggregate of individuals, that an aggregate of forms and of spiritual contents: intuitions, convictions, valuations. It is true that the objective spirit necessarily requires a collectivity as support. But that is not the collective. It is not the sum nor the whole of the individuals. Common is exactly what each individual can possess in total, without division. On the other hand, the individuals do not precede the common spirit. In every collectivity, the individual depends on a language, on certain customs, which he has not invented, but which, on the contrary, he receives and has to adopt. The individual meets a common spirit and it grows within him. This does not increase with the increase of persons. They may change but this is maintained. Its change is distinct from the fluctuation of the generations.

A law is a spiritual object. It is objective spirit.

It does not have the intimate being of subjectivity which animate objects possess. It does not isolate, it binds. It is a common reality created as such by a circle of individuals. It is transmissible, supraindividual. The characteristics which we have heretofore met in the current Law show that it is so.

III. APORETICS OF THE LAW

5. Elaboration and Fixing of the Philosophical Problems Raised by Positive Law

I. The Law is a system of dispositions for the service of the values of the community. Between Law and values there exists a relation of means and end (Sec. 2, Nos. 10 and 11). But with this we have not said what relation there has to be between the content of the mean and the content of the end. The problem commences here, then, with the nature of that relation. Is it a matter of a reproduction, of a perfect coincidence between the exigencies of the values and the dispositions of the Law? The question presents itself as to all the values of the community, but it attains special relief with respect to justice, which seems to be the central value of this group. If the problem is answered affirmatively, a system of dispositions which did not reproduce those values would not be Law. So thought the representatives of the classic Scholastic school, of natural law, of the social contract. However many differences there may be between the conceptions of justice of a St. Thomas Aquinas, of a Grotius, and of a Rousseau, they are in one thing in agreement: the law which is not just is not law. In fact, here the juridical system is identified with justice, and the Law loses all unitist autonomy. Hence may be derived two consequences radically opposed to the historical existence of positive Law, according to the plane on which the values are placed. If justice is an ideal being constituted alongside the data of the real world, then many ordinances of social life cannot pretend to a juridical character. Further: strictly, no real order would be Law. One would have to wait for a total change in the very constitution of the groups. Such is the opinion of Plato, of Rousseau, etc. If, on the contrary, the real world is already grasped in the exigencies of the ideal, so that the Laws of the one are the laws of the other, as Hegel and the historical school see, then all positive Law is just, all real ordering of the groups is Law. Sociologism and juridical positivism come to the same result. For them there not only does not exist the tension between the real and the ideal but one of the terms has disappeared entirely. It is seen here that behind all these theories what is in play is nothing less than the radical disparity of two opposed conceptions of the universe: monism and dualism.

If the problem is resolved negatively, that is, if the relation between

Law and values of the community is not a relation of reproduction, this means that the content of the Law is or may be distinct from the content of the values. The means has only to realize the end by reproducing it. Then the autonomy of the Law remains intact. The difference of content may be merely quantitative, and this in such way that the favorable balance may be as well on the side of the values as on the side of the Law: it may realize the end in reproducing only part of the content of the values, or in reproducing all and adding something more, or combining these two possibilities.

But the difference may also be qualitative, and then there will be set up an opposition between the exigencies of the values and the content of the Law. In other words: there may be nonvaluable Law, unjust Law (Stammler).

But the foregoing formulation contains an equivocation. The relation of the contents may be determined from two points of view: as a real relation and as an exacted relation, as a relation in fact and as a deontological relation. Therefore to formulate the problem strictly there must be separated the two questions:

(1) How is the content of the Law in relation to the content of the values?

(2) How ought the content of the Law to be in relation to the content of the values?

II. Positive Law constitutes a mediation between the values of the community and human conduct (Sec. 2, A. 10). This means that the exigencies of the values are in some way realized in the juridical forms and so imposed on man for their fulfillment. But that mediation is also human work (Sec. 2, A. 3) and man in making it has to be guided precisely by those same values. The Law presents itself thus with two faces: as to man it is a system of exigencies which have to be realized in human conduct: as to the values it has to be the same realization in the spiritual world of the exigencies of the values. This implies that man before making law has already learned the values. Then there is offered to meditation the thought whether the Law will not be something superfluous, something which lacks all justification. What is here in play is not the justification of one determined content of the Law in opposition to another, but the justification of the very phenomenon itself of the Law whatever may be its content. The problem, then, reads: Is it justifiable, is it "legitimate" that man should make the Law? or How is it possible to justify the dispositions of positive Law if man already learns the values directly?

The question may present itself also in the form of an antimony:

Thesis: the Law is justified because values of the community exist.

Antithesis: the Law is not justified because values of the community exist.

In the face of the enormous mass of theories which disregard the problem or declare themselves for its justification, anarchy arises, or better that form of anarchy which, without denying the existence of ethical principles, visits upon the Law the strongest condemnation. Proudhon recognized justice as the supreme law of the community, but in the name of that same justice he rejected all the laws of the State. "What can be the laws for him who thinks for himself and is responsible for himself, that he should be free and feel himself worthy of it? I defend myself against every precept which imposes on me a superiority which pretends to be necessary." "How can one get along with few laws? How can it be avoided that even the best of them should immediately become abominable?" (*Idée Générale de la révolution.*) Consequently: "Every one who puts his hands on me is a usurper and a tyrant: I declare him my enemy." (*Confessions.*) In a similar way Bakunin: The State "even when it commands the good, takes away its value by the very command of it . . . from the moment that the good is commanded by imposition it is changed into evil for true morals." (*God and the State.*) These anarchists do not reject all Law (they admit free contracts) but only the Law of the State. But this is, truly, that which has acquired the greatest volume and importance in the present collectivities. And they roundly condemn it in the name of the values as an enemy which prevents the direct and free apprehension of their exigencies and a responsibility which alone can be reclaimed by that ideal realm.

Whatever may be the judgment which this doctrine merits as to its intrinsic justice, its methodic value cannot be disregarded for the Philosophy of the Law. For its own negation sets this problem with full sharpness, as a problem of justification.

The doubt of justification does not coincide with the question: "Why does man make Law?" The ready proof is that even if the solution of the first should be negative, the second would remain open. If the recognition of the Law as an evil did not annihilate it *ipso jure,* man would continue to make Law, and before his position one could always ask: Why does man make this evil thing? This is a psychological problem, sociological and even of metaphysical anthropology, if it is set in the last instance. Methodically it is identical with these: Why does man sin, make poems, construct habitations? The doubt of the justification is, on the other hand, of an axiological character. To justify means to recognize an object as axiologically positive.

The problem is not set in the same way for all the manifestations of the objective spirit. What makes it burning for the Law and gives it a peculiar physiognomy is not only the character of dispositive ought to be, but above all the quality of retribution, especially of damaging retribution, which the positive law possesses. The philosophic consideration cannot rest so long as it takes no account of this.

III. The Law is an object among the objects whose totality constitutes the universe: it is here, joined to the stars and the protozoa, beside numbers, feelings, morals, religion. Truly it has its defined place in the system of supreme genera in which that totality is gathered: it is a spiritual object, objective spirit (Sec. 4). But this is an eidetic discrimination. And the world is not only an unfolding of beings grouped in genera. Those beings are worth some of them more than others, that is: the world has an axiotic hierarchical order, it is a hierarchy of goods (or evils). Then arises the problem of what is the axiological grade which the Law occupies in the general system of objects. This system is neutral in the face of the doubt: it only submits its material. Now it is a matter of an axiological system, not a generic one.

The problem is not the same as that of the justification. This is a problem of a sign: positive or negative. What now occupies us is a problem of grade, of altitude. Let the first be resolved in one way or the other, there can always then be asked, in what grade of good or of evil is the Law.

The determination of that grade does not have the same importance in the face of all objects. To know if the Law is a good superior or inferior to that of the stars is a question which may leave us cold. But if we compare it with morals, with the rules of social usages, with life or liberty, then the problem becomes urgent. Morals and usages are systems like the law, which present to us exigencies with no less pressure than it, whose content, nevertheless, may be in opposition to that of the juridical system. Life and liberty are constitutive of our very being and the Law may also (in fact) demand their sacrifice. Theoretically this means that the Law may enter into conflict directly or indirectly with certain values. Practically the question which is set is whether or not its dictates merit unconditional respect, or, as the scholastics say, if they oblige our "conscience." And the practical decision is, of course, subordinated to the theoretical solution. The question was set with all clarity in *Crito*. Socrates and his disciple there discuss whether disobedience to the laws is legitimate. And if Socrates defends the thesis of absolute obedience, it is precisely because he believes that the laws are the expression of justice and that in the world there is nothing superior to that. If this affirmation be recognized as erroneous, it is clear that the practical solution would have to be otherwise. All the questions, then, relative to resistance to the Law whether passive or active (the so-called right of revolution), depend on the grade of Law in the system of goods, especially in the system of objects of culture, or, as sometimes this doubt has been called, of the meaning of law for human life.

IV. The place of Law in the general system of objects is also one of the points of departure for a new doubt. That system is neutral not only in the face of the axiological problem, but also before the ontological one. By ourselves we cannot determine when objects exist, much less upon what bases their existence rests, the connection between the existence of some of them and that of others. For among the possible worlds there is one really existing with its ontic structure, in which the objects which form it are not simply some at the side of others, but they are in multiple connections, and above all in connections of existential dependence. The existence of some is conditioned on the existence of others.

This occurs also with the Law. There is a current Law and a Law not current — which never existed, which does not exist yet or which does not exist now. And if indeed we know in what currency consists (as also noncurrency) — that is, in the common being of certain juridical contents in a circle of men, — this tells us nothing as to the existential bases of it (Sec. 3). It is true that the very determination of currency informs us that the Law requires to exist the presence of a circle of men. This is an ontological base necessary for the Law. But it is not sufficient. The problem remains in the search for the conditions which are required in order that this circle of men may have the common life of a juridical system: on what bases does the currency of the Law depend. It is one thing to know what a current Law is and another, when and how it is current. The first is a datum for the second, which is the true problem. This is perceived more clearly if one recalls that there is a birth, a flourishing, and a death of the Law within the same community, and that the individual has the initiative in its creation without his sufficing to make it current (Sec. 3).

Is the currency founded on the fact that the process of juridical creation is developed in conformity with the already current rules which regulate that creation? In the power of those who dictate the Law? In the recognition of those regulated? In the confidence that those who impose it have also to submit to it?

V. The Law is an object made by man (Sec. 2, A. 3). He is not only regulated by the Law, he is also the regulator. But the Law is a mediation between values and conduct, and the dispositive essence (of ought to be) of that mediation supposes that man does not realize those values spontaneously, that he does not respond docilely to their call (Sec.

2, A. 5). In fact man deviates his conduct from the directives of value. But this is true not only for the regulated one; the same deviation may affect the regulator (Sec. 2, A. 10). He who makes the Law may also be deaf to that call, for, after all and finally, to make law is also a mode of conduct. What should we have gained then by the mediation? Here is where the new problem opens. There is no doubt that the confrontation of the regulator and the regulated one is inexorable, for it constitutes the very essence of the positiveness of the law. But it is possible to choose the regulator. ("To choose" not in the juridical sense of designating by the votes of such and such persons, but in the sense of ontic possibility of various solutions.) Positive Law demands necessarily the essence, that there should be someone who dictates it, but not who has to dictate it. The problem then is: who ought to be those who dictate the Law in order that the Law dictated should be adequate for the values of the community? In what conditions must they be placed, what qualities must they have to prevent deviation from their true end, in order that the law may not cease to be just?

What is sought then is the political equivalent of the values of the community, especially the political equivalent of justice. The question of the ideal State, of the best form of government, is grasped here. Only this formulation of the problem is too narrow, because the State is not the only community in which Law is dictated. The problem is set for every circle of men in which Law arises. To the point where it is soluble, it is a thing which exceeds the ambit of Aporetics, but this has not only determined the exact terms of the problem and its extent but it has shown also that positive Law is its point of departure. The problem, then, cannot be treated as belonging to a political science independent of the philosophy of law. By its origin and by its ends its place is within that.

VI. The foregoing doubts refer to positive Law. But, as a result of their very setting, the solution of the greater part of them supposes an estimative consideration. Behind them there opens a world of principles, of values; and only by looking from this point does the juridical phenomenon acquire full meaning in its totality (Sec. 2, A. 10 and 11).

If the Law is a means at the service of certain values, the inquiring glance has to be directed also to that axiotic sphere and to consider it in itself. The doubts of the Law conduce, then, to the pure axiological doubt. Here is the ultimate instance of the philosophic interrogation of the Law. But the task becomes more complex at this height because it treats not of one but of various doubts, though indeed closely connected among themselves.

It will have to be faced above all, with each one of the values of the community, to examine and to describe them to the point where one reaches the power of intuition. The question does not consist of demonstrating the existence of the values. This seems to me a false problem. Without doubt, they have sometimes been radically denied. The extreme representative of this position was Stirner. His anarchism — different from that of Proudhon and the Russians — is no more than the logical consequence of his robust nihilism in the face of every value. "Men are not 'called' to anything, nor do they have any 'mission' to fulfill, any 'destiny,' as likewise the plant and the animal are not 'called' to anything." Man alone has forces which are externalized, which cannot remain inactive. There is no duty, no truth, no right, no liberty, no humanity. "I do not have in my heart anything more than I myself." And "my things are not either the divine or the human; they are not the true, the good, the right, liberty, etc., but exclusively mine and not general things, but they are unique, the same as I also am unique. Nothing is above me." (The unique and his property.) But this "nothing is above me" means "I am above all" and with this I already recognize a value. And against this "nothing is above me" the fact of the judgments of value which man gives upon conduct gives testimony. If man judges actions just or unjust, prudent or imprudent, etc., this means that there is a criterion of the just and the prudent. Distinct from this evidence of its existence is the inquiry as to the nature of those criteria. But this is a matter of general Axiology.

The fact, then, that some deny values does not prove anything against them. It only confirms the opinion that there is an intellectual blindness for the axiological region, as there is a blindness for certain colors. Perhaps Stirner suffered from it.

The authentic problem consists in determining what are the values of the community, in describing the material and the valorative quality proper to each one, to explain their exigencies, to indicate the possible conflicts between the ought to be of one and of another, and in clarifying the hierarchical order between them. Can there be deduced in this sphere material, universal, and immutable principles, as the millenary doctrine of natural law affirms? Or is there here only a purely formal principle from which may be inferred diverse and even opposed norms (a "natural Law of variable content"), but not concrete exigencies of absolute validity? And even there will have to be examined a third possibility: whether the juridical formations have — independently of what positive law says about it — a certain material *a priori* structure, necessities of the essence inherent in their very concepts (A. Reinach and W. Schapp).

There has to be investigated then the general characteristic common to the whole group of values of the community, and consequently their difference from the other values, especially the moral ones.

Is it a matter in reality of an autonomous sphere, independent of the other values, or is there in them an essential reference or dependence in the face of the values of the individual, so that these are the ones which in final analysis decide as to the content of the former?

The indispensable complement of this has to be the determination of the essence of the community and its problematic autonomy as against the individual. The antithesis of the theory between the community as sum and the community as all has to meet its adequate solution here. But even when the solution shall recognize the autonomy of the community as against the individual, this does not yet import any judgment as to the grade of good which there is in one or the other. This only an ultimate investigation can decide: the determination of the place of values of the community in the general hierarchical order of the ethical values, and in all the dimensions which that order possesses; that is, the differences of height, strength, complexity, which exist between the values of the person and those of the community.

However distinct may be the direction of the pure axiological doubts and that of the doubts of the Law, it is easy to observe their indissoluble connection and that the latter cannot be resolved if the former have not been. Not only the problem of the relation, but also that of the justification, that of the grade, and that of the political equivalent contain a reference to value.

The pure axiological doubt is, then, the last which is set, but it is the first which has to be resolved. In its solution is the foundation of the solution of the rest. The medullar problem of the Law is axiological.

6. The Mission of the Philosophy of Law

If there has been perceived the internal bond which exists between Aporetics and Eidetics, set forth in the preceding paragraph, if it has been understood that the doubts of the Law are not arbitrary questions, but real problems peremptorily set by the juridical phenomenon itself, it will have to be agreed that the very material upon which the Philosophy of Law has to work is that offered by Aporetics. Its theme consists of the treatment and the solution of the doubts which positive Law presents. Its mission, then, is not only traced beforehand, but it is also demanded as an *ex officio* duty of the philosopher. Since these problems exist, one has to meet them and try to resolve them. Before them one cannot close his eyes, as does positivism, or be silent, like the Viennese school.

There is no doubt that this mission does not imply the forced attainment of solutions. These may be, in some cases, inaccessible. Perhaps some doubts are antinomian; perhaps some principles are irrational. But even then the Philosophy of Law has to test them, because it has to prove the authenticity of the antinomies and of the irrationality and to say why they are not soluble.

That the result of its recommendations should crystallize into an original system is a secondary question. The immanent end of the philosophic undertaking is not novelty, but the truth. "Seek above all the kingdom of God and the rest shall be given you in addition." For the philosopher the kingdom of God is primarily the truth. If then that principle is valid also for him, its meaning must be "Seek above all the realm of truth, that originality shall be given you in addition." Originality cannot be "proposed" as an end beforehand. He who seeks it so will never encounter it. Only he who pursues the truth, for the truth itself, without being concerned if it is old or new, is in grace for the arrival of originality. Unless he contents himself with mere originality, which is, surely, the originality of error.

The final result of our investigations is that the center of gravity of the Philosophy of Law is not in the delimitation of the concept of positive Law, as positivism thinks. Positive Law is not the problem, but the phenomenon which sets problems. If indeed in a very broad sense that determination belongs as an introductory theme to the Philosophy of Law, its medullar theme is not that, but the principles or fundamentals of positive law.

Therefore on closing these preliminaries we cannot say "here ends" but "here begins the Philosophy of Law."

IV

THE PHILOSOPHICAL-JURIDICAL PROBLEM OF THE VALIDITY OF LAW

BY EDUARDO GARCÍA MÁYNEZ

Professor of Philosophy of Law, National University of Mexico

TRANSLATED BY

Miguel A. de Capriles, Professor of Law, New York University School of Law

and

Milton R. Konvitz, Associate Professor of Industrial and Labor Relations, Cornell University

CHAPTER I

THE JURIDICAL PROBLEM OF THE VALIDITY OF LAW

THE phrase validity of law may be taken in two principal ways; namely, in its technical juridical sense, or in its meta-juridical or philosophical sense. The object of this chapter is to define the phrase in its technical juridical sense.

Validity in the formal juridical sense. Ordinarily a statute is said to be valid when it has been duly promulgated, and its validity continues as long as there is no supervening act of derogation.

The constitutions of the various states generally contain a set of rules relating to the mode of statutory enactment. The process of lawmaking consists of the acts performed by proper governmental organs in their exercise of the legislative function.

Validity, in the formal juridical sense, when applied to any precept,[1] means that the precept exists. A bill adopted by the legislative organs and approved by the executive becomes a mandate immediately upon enactment, or upon the date stated in the act. At that moment, the precept acquires juridical life. This means that the norm enters into the total juridical order, and will thereafter play the role of a concrete formulation of the will of the state.[2] The new norm may be attributed to the state itself, and the conduct prescribed by the norm becomes obligatory.

It does not matter that the law in question is not known to all persons to whom it relates; and its imperative quality is not impaired by the fact that persons subject to it consider the law an arbitrary fiat. From the formal juridical viewpoint, knowledge or ignorance of the norm does not affect its validity. Its validity is not rooted in its observance; its validity is to be found in the fundamental law, namely, the Constitution.

Absolute validity is inherent in the precepts of law; hence the legislator is not concerned with the question whether those to whom the law

[1] The author uses the words "precept," "norm," "law," and occasionally "rule" as interchangeable terms. (TRANSLATORS' NOTE.)

[2] We understand the expression "will of the State" in the same sense as Hans Kelsen. See ALLGEMEINE STAATSLEHRE 52.

is applicable recognize as just and legitimate the conduct the law requires of them. Not only juridical norms but also the conventional, religious, and aesthetic norms aspire to command unconditional observance and present themselves as imposing inescapable duties. Thus it is wrong to say that the norms of fashion and etiquette, and the social conventions generally, are mere invitations, the observance or violation of which is left to the judgment of the individual. The claim of absolute validity is an essential attribute of every heteronomous norm.

Validity and effectiveness. Is it correct to attribute the quality of validity to laws which have been promulgated in accordance with the procedures and requisites prescribed by the fundamental norm or constitution? Doubtless it would be more appropriate to say only that such laws exist, or that they are in force. These two statements have the same meaning. To say that a duly enacted law is valid is, from the formal juridical viewpoint, a pleonasm. For what is meant is that the precept is a part of the juridical order and constitutes a concrete formulation of the will of the state. Each proposition which states "Such a law was duly enacted," and "Such a law exists," indicates that the law in question is obligatory, since the imperative quality is inevitably united to the existence of the rule.

The lapse of time between the moment of enactment and that of derogation is known as the period of effectiveness. It may be said, therefore, that a law is effective or "in force" as long as the conduct it prescribes constitutes a juridical obligation.

Positive or factual quality of law. Some authors, when they say that a norm is positive, mean that it forms part of positive law. Positive law usually means the aggregate of juridical norms which effectively govern the life of a people at a given moment in history (G. del Vecchio). This definition contains a new element, which is not found in the concept of validity. The positive quality is not ascribed to every juridical system, but only to the aggregate of norms which govern, in an effective manner, the life of a community at a given period of its history. In the concept we are now examining, a new note is implicit; the factual quality of law.

In order that a system of law may be called positive, it is not enough that its norms be juridically valid, i.e., that they be adopted in accordance with the provisions of the supreme norm; it is, in addition, required that such norms evoke conduct in consonance with the "ought to be" formulated by the norms.

Innumerable treatise writers, who fail to consider these distinctions in meaning, use the terms "positive" and "in force" as if they were synonymous, and thereby often cause lamentable confusion. Most frequently the formal juridical attribute of validity is confused with the fact of observance. There is a widespread view that a norm of positive law, to merit such designation, must in fact be observed by those to whom it applies. Thus the validity of law (which is a postulate of juridical science) is made to depend upon an external phenomenon; namely, the fact of compliance. Kelsen has energetically protested against such confusion in terminology.

The validity of the laws — without which it would be impossible to attribute the positive quality to any juridical order — does not consist in universal or inevitable observance; for a system of law which would be always obeyed, without any exception whatever, would lose its essential character. Norms, of whatever kind, prescribe a course of conduct which in all cases "ought to be," but in fact sometimes may not be, observed. Juridical precepts would lack meaning if, in relation to them, there were no possibility of violation. Inviolable are the laws of nature, not legal norms.

The positive quality (we prefer the term "factual quality") implies only observance more or less general, but never total. It represents an intermediate zone of enforcement, which never reaches the maximum limit of universal observance, nor descends to the minimum limit of complete failure of observance (Kelsen).

A precept never followed by individuals, nor ever enforced by the authorities, would lose its normative character. Sometimes, the written law is derogated by custom (that is, it falls into disuse, or the practice is contrary to the law). Such a phenomenon is very similar to that which George Jellinek called the normative force of facts (*die normative Kraft des Faktischen*). The results of both processes — the law falling into disuse and the practice which is contrary to the law — are different,[3] but the causes are identical. In the one case, the constant repetition of a certain practice gives birth to an "ought to be," to a norm; in the other, the complete failure to observe a precept turns it into a mere theoretical statement, devoid of any normative significance.

The mere failure of compliance, on the part of those under obligation, does not, however, destroy the formal juridical validity of a norm. To destroy it, it is necessary, in addition, that the authorities should fail to enforce the norm. Experience offers many examples of laws which were always violated, but which were always actively and constantly enforced. And that is because the imperatives in the law are not exclusively addressed to private persons, but also to the organs of the state who must enforce them. As long as a norm is enforced, its normative char-

[3] The original reads "opposite." (TRANSLATORS' NOTE.)

acter subsists, even though individuals may always violate it. The violation does not destroy its formal juridical validity. It is clear that the violated law may be unjust and that, if it be considered from a viewpoint other than the formal juridical, it may appear as an indefensible mandate. But this is a different problem, and we shall examine it at length in later chapters of this essay.

Validity of juridical acts. The term "validity" is applied not only to norms of a general character but also to specific juridical acts. In the latter sense, it may be said, e.g., that a certain testament is valid, or that a certain contract is invalid. By these expressions, one means that the act was done in accordance, or not in accordance, with the norms of law then in force. Upon this conformance or nonconformance depend the validity, the consequences, and in certain cases the absolute or relative nullity of the act.

In the absence of certain essential legal requisites, which are essential to the creation of the desired juridical form sought, it is said that the act is nonexistent. The word "act" in this connection is used in its popular significance, and the adjective "nonexistent" means that the act in question does not exist in law and is, therefore, devoid of any legal effect.

The distinction between relative and absolute nullity is based upon the gravity of the causes of invalidity and upon the possibility or impossibility of correcting the defects from which the act suffers (e.g., vitiation of consent, lack of capacity, illegality of the object of the contract, etc.). In all these cases, the criterion relating to nullifiability, validity, or nonexistence must be found in the law. We are dealing, therefore, with a purely formal criterion — the same criterion which permits us to say that a statute is valid if it has been promulgated in accordance with the provisions of the supreme norm or the constitution.

Normative imputation. The relation existing between juridical acts and their consequences is always determined by a norm which connects the consequences with the juridical act. Such a connection is called normative imputation (Kelsen). Normative imputation is a logical process which consists in connecting a fact with a rule, or specific consequences with a juridical act. Legal facts (*Tatbestände*) are either human actions or natural phenomena (*Ereignisse*). Consequences, however, may consist of only human actions, since it would be senseless to impose norms upon nature.

The expression "legal consequences" is preferable to the term "effects." Effect is the result of cause; it is a link in a causal chain. Legal consequences, on the other hand, can be imputed to an action only by a logical process; they are not a necessary effect from an anterior phenomenon (cause), but rather the enunciation of an "ought," the existence of which is dependent upon a given legal fact.[4]

A norm provides, e.g., that "legally made contracts must be precisely fulfilled." The fulfillment of a contract, or better, the duty to fulfill it, is one of its consequences. If I have received money as a loan, I am obligated to return it on the date of maturity. The juridical duty of return (a consequence) is imputed to the contractual act, because a given precept so provides. That I return the money loaned to me is not a natural and necessary effect of the contract, but conduct pursuant to a legal duty. The best demonstration that there is no relation of necessity between the legal act and its consequences may be found in the fact that the consequences do not always follow. In every case I am obligated to fulfill my juridical duties; but in fact I may fail to comply. To this new situation (the failure to comply) the law attaches new consequences: if the creditor has recourse to his right of action against the debtor, the courts must receive the complaint, summon the parties, hear the controversy, and render a decision. The judgment pronounced in the suit will in turn produce further consequences, the last of which, in the absence of voluntary compliance with the judgment, will be execution.

Delegation. Just as there is a connection between legal acts and consequences, so there is a relation among the various norms which constitute the juridical order. The bond existing among these norms is achieved through delegation. The constitution of a state provides, e.g., that certain matters shall be governed by a statute. In this case, the fundamental norm or constitution delegates to a statute the power to regulate given situations. In other instances, the delegation is by a statute to a regulation.

There is delegation from one norm to another, and from one authority to another; but these delegations are legitimate only if they are sustained by the precepts of the law in force; whence it follows that every delegation rests in the last instance upon the provisions of the supreme norm or constitution.

Frequently a precept refers to another of an inferior rank, which determines the conduct to be followed in certain circumstances by those whom it affects. The superior norm provides sometimes for a pure or broad delegation; in other instances it sets the limits within which the delegated norm must operate, and fixes the criteria which must be used by the legislator. Those in the first group, that is, those which make a broad delegation, are styled by the German theorists "blanket rules" (*Blankettrechtssätze*).

[4] Kelsen, Allgemeine Staatslehre 47.

Delegation is effective between precepts of different categories. The delegated norm is subordinate to the delegating norm; the latter is superior in rank to the former. Juridical norms may also be of the same rank; these are said to be coördinate. Constitutional laws, for example, are coördinate as between themselves, since they have identical rank.

The relation of superior and subordinate rank permits the establishment of a hierarchy of norms. This hierarchy constitutes the juridical order, i.e., the total aggregate of the precepts belonging to positive law.

The hierarchical order of norms. The problem of the hierarchical order of norms was first posed in the Middle Ages, but soon thereafter was relegated to oblivion. In modern times Bierling revived the old question. This jurist analyzes the possibility of establishing a hierarchy of the precepts of law, and considers, as integral parts of the juridical order, not only the totality of norms in force, but also the concretization and individualization of these norms in acts such as testaments, administrative decisions, and judicial judgments.

The development of Bierling's ideas, and the creation of a theory of a hierarchy of norms, are to the credit of Professor Adolf Merkl of Vienna. Hans Kelsen has incorporated the theory of Merkl into his system and Professor Verdross, another famous representative of the same school, has produced interesting works on the same theme.[5]

The discussion that follows is an exposition of the ideas of Merkl. The *Stufentheorie* [hierarchy theory] is of interest to our study, since, as we shall see later, it shows the manner in which the problems relating to the juridical validity of acts and norms must be solved.

Theory of the hierarchy of norms. The widespread belief among scholars and laymen, says Merkl, that the juridical order is exhausted by or consists of a more or less large aggregate of precepts of general observance is an error. For beside the laws, or rather subordinate to and conditioned by them, are the juridical acts in their infinite variety and multiplicity. Such acts, as Bierling says, are nothing more than the individualization or concretization of general precepts. Merkl gives to the said acts the name of special or individualized norms, in order to distinguish them from laws, which he calls general or abstract norms. Both these types of norm constitute the total juridical order.

The precept which prescribes that, e.g., in certain circumstances the lessee of a city house is obligated to make certain repairs or in the alternative to indemnify the lessor for damage done to the estate, is a general norm. It is also an abstract principle, which may be applied to

[5] Merkl, Die Lehre von der Rechtskraft; Kelsen, *op. cit.;* Verdross, Die Einheit des rechtlichen Weltbildes (1923), and Gesellschaft und Recht (Studies in the pure theory of law, a work dedicated to Kelsen), 1931.

an unlimited number of concrete situations. On the other hand, the judgment which declares that John Doe, tenant, shall make, within a period of one month, certain repairs to a certain house, or else pay to Richard Roe, owner, a stated sum as damages, is an individualized and concretized norm. In joining both adjectives — "individualized" and "concretized" — in one phrase, we are not guilty of a pleonasm or useless repetition. It is correct to speak of concretizing a general norm in a special act because the abstract (or ideal) juridical situation foreseen by the norm is then converted into a concrete (or real) juridical situation. The judgment in our example no longer refers to a lease in the abstract, but to a concrete juridical transaction, from which certain consequences follow. It is also correct to speak of individualizing a general norm, since the norm refers to an abstract juridical person (owner, tenant, co-tenant, etc.), whereas juridical acts create legal relations between real, existing persons (*X* company, buyer *Y*, secured creditor *Z*, etc.).

The process whereby an abstract juridical situation is transformed into a concrete one, and a general rule is individualized, is denominated application of the law. If we examine the law in the light of its application, we shall discover, according to Merkl, the criterion which permits us to see a hierarchic order among the various norms of law and between the norms and specific juridical acts.

The conception of law as a mere aggregate of general precepts is a static conception; that which regards it as a continuous process of creation and application is of a dynamic character. Only the latter is capable of offering us a faithful image of the life of the law, and it is the only one which explains how the abstract rules formulated by the codes pass into practice, and make possible the actualization of law. (Employing Aristotelian expressions, one might say that every abstract provision of law potentially contains an infinite series of concrete norms, and that every juridical act is an actualization of a general precept.)

The process of application is a long series of legal situations, tending toward an increase in the degree of concretization. Every concrete juridical situation is conditioned by an abstract norm. Norms of general observance, which in relation to juridical acts are conditioning, are in their turn conditioned by higher precepts. A norm conditions another when the existence of the latter depends upon the former. Juridical acts are conditioned by the norms of law, since their formation as well as their validity and consequences are derived from those norms, and are based upon them. The existence of a contract, for example, is conditioned by certain provisions of a general character, which establish the forms of contract, the rules of capacity, the requisites of validity, and the legal consequences of various transactions. A concrete juridical transaction, which in relation to such norms lies in a subordinate position, constitutes, nevertheless, in relation to the parties, and in reference to the consequences of the action, a determining norm or aggregate of norms. In this sense it is said that a contract constitutes the law between the parties (*lex inter partes*). The contract (an individualized norm, according to the terminology of the Viennese jurists) determines the consequences of the transaction, and the consequences are conditioned by the contract.

Every conditioned norm constitutes, relative to the conditioning norm from which it derives, an act of application. The juridical order is a long hierarchy of precepts, each of which performs a dual role: In relation to those of a lower order, it has a normative character; in relation to those of a higher order, it is an act of application. Any norm,[6] whether general or individualized, abstract or concrete, has, like the head of Janus, two faces: if examined from above, it appears as an act of application; if from below, as a norm.

The juridical order, however, is not an endless succession of controlling precepts and controlled acts; it is not a chain of an infinite number of links, for it has an upper and a lower limit. One limit is the fundamental norm or the constitution; the other is the final act of execution, which does not provoke further consequences. It follows, therefore, that not all norms, or juridical acts, present a dual aspect.

The fundamental norm is itself not an act of application for, as its name indicates, it is a limiting principle; that is, a norm above which there is no precept of higher category. On the other hand, the last act of application has no normative significance, since it represents a definitive realization of a juridical duty — consequently, a fact.

Application may be achieved voluntarily or by compulsion. Voluntary individualization, carried out by a private person, is called compliance; compulsion, accomplished by the organs of power, is termed execution or punishment, according to the case. Execution and punishment are the two principal forms of sanction.

When the "ought" enunciated by a precept is actualized, the precept loses, in relation to the act, its character as a norm.

Normative application constitutes a bridge between two worlds: The ideal of the "ought to be" and the world of reality. Every "ought to be," when complied with, penetrates into the sphere of fact. In the act of application, the transition is achieved.

Let us clarify the foregoing propositions by an example: The precept whereby one who has received a loan is under a duty to return it on

[6] Exceptions are considered in the following paragraph. (TRANSLATORS' NOTE.)

maturity represents, in relation to the other party, an "ought" of juridical nature. If I have received a loan of twenty pesos, I am obligated to return it. The duty established by the rule is valid for all possible cases, and its validity is not impaired if I do not fulfill my contract. But, if I do fulfill it, the norm loses, in relation to my conduct, all its normative force, since there would be no sense in asserting that I must do what I have already done, or that I am obligated to return a sum which I have already returned. Norms are valid as to future cases, not as to those already completed.

A norm may, of course, serve as a criterion to judge the legitimacy or illegitimacy of a past action; very frequently it is said, for example, that a certain action was illegal, or that a certain procedure was unjust. On these occasions, the precept is used simply as a rule of evaluation or judgment of conduct. If the conduct is in accord with the norm, it is said to be legitimate; if contrary thereto, it is illicit or illegitimate. But this is not the form of application which we have previously discussed. In our view, a norm is applicable to a concrete case only so long as the norm retains its normative quality. Since this normative quality disappears automatically when there is compliance with the "ought" formulated by the precept, it follows that the precept is no longer valid with respect to the concrete case, even though it is used as a measure of value with respect to the same case. We must be careful to make a distinction, therefore, between the normative quality of a precept and its use as a criterion of legality.

Rules on validity. Let us now see whether the *Stufentheorie* of Merkl and Kelsen furnishes a solution to the problems arising in relation to the formal validity of acts and norms.

We have said that the precepts of law are inter-connected in a hierarchical order, and that the existence of each precept is conditioned by a superior one. It is these conditional or determining relations that make possible the construction of a hierarchy. From these relations we derive as well the criterion of validity.

An act of execution is juridically valid only when it is based on a valid norm (the writ or mandate of execution). This mandate is revealed as a juridical consequence, in a suit at law, when there is a failure of voluntary compliance, and is conditioned by the respective judgment. The judgment rests upon a series of general norms, and the validity of these is derived from the fundamental norm. It follows that every act of application seeks support, directly or indirectly, in the constitution. The constitutional laws represent, so to speak, the foundations upon which is built the edifice of the juridical order.

From the foregoing exposition it is possible to deduce the following principles, which are valid in any case:

1. A juridical act is valid if it represents the application of a valid norm.

2. An individualized norm is valid if it is an application of a valid general norm.

3. A general norm is valid if it constitutes an application of the fundamental norm.

4. The validity of the fundamental norm does not depend upon any superior juridical norm.

Naive and critical positivism. But, it may be asked: "What is the foundation of the limiting norm? From what principle is derived the validity of the total juridical order?"

The foregoing questions have been answered in very different ways. We shall first analyze the solution of the jurist Bergbohm.[7]

Bergbohm attempts to solve the question by reference to the positive quality of law. A system of law is valid, he says, if it is effectively in force. Here we see the briefest résumé of the thesis which Verdross calls naive positivism, as distinguished from the critical positivism of Kelsen. According to Bergbohm, law is a historical phenomenon, a real happening. An event is converted into a juridical phenomenon when it appears under the form of law. There is a formal criterion for distinguishing historical or positive law from ideal or desired law. This criterion is supplied by the concept of competence. Every norm enacted by a competent power is a juridical norm; every system of law established by a legitimate power constitutes positive law.

In making these assertions, Bergbohm is guilty of a contradiction which automatically destroys his original thesis; for if law is valid only when imposed by a legally competent authority it follows that its validity does not rest upon the material fact of power, nor upon the effective enforcibility of the juridical order, but rather on the norm or aggregate of norms determining the legal competence of the ruler. Hence it is not the positive quality of law, but rather the principle which constitutes the rules a legitimate authority, that legitimizes his commands.

Now then, every judgment upon competence or incompetence presupposes the existence of a norm. Competence is not a natural fact but a normative creation. In the sphere of nature there are no competent or incompetent authorities; hence the statement of Spinoza that "In the state of nature, the right of each is coextensive with his might," is paradoxical.

[7] Jurisprudenz und Rechtsphilosophie.

To justify the existence of any system of law, it is not enough to say that it is effective; it must be proved legitimate. But to speak of legitimacy is equivalent to assuming, as stated above, the preëxistence of a normative order. And if such order exists, it is necessary to discover the foundations of its validity. In other words: We must find the principle which permits us to consider as valid the fundamental norm.

The hypothetical fundamental norm in Kelsen's theory. Sometimes it is possible to refer a constitution which is in force to one or more earlier constitutions, and to find in the latter the foundations of the former. Positive law establishes the rules of its own creation; and these do not refer exclusively to the enactment of statutes but also to the establishment of constitutional norms. If we imagine a series of successive constitutions, each of which was established in accordance with the precepts of an antecedent one, we may go back to the original constitution, upon which all subsequent constitutions have been based. Kelsen calls this first constitution the hypothetical fundamental norm.

Experience teaches us, however, that in the history of states there is no uniform juridical order, no regular succession of constitutions. As a general rule, the political history of every state shows numerous revolutions, many of which caused a violent rupture of the juridical order. Nevertheless the unity of the state may be sustained, despite the changes of government produced by revolutionary movements, if one admits the existence of a juridical order superior to the state.

If one accepts the premise of the international juridical order, the principle of the integrity of the state is preserved. In accordance with a tacit rule of public international law, a victorious revolution is considered as an extraordinary procedure for reform of the existing order. When a revolution triumphs, and a juridical order is replaced by a different one, the other states usually declare whether or not they will recognize the new government. Such recognition constitutes, in the ultimate instance, an application of the tacit norm mentioned by the head of the Viennese School. This norm furnishes a juridical explanation for revolutionary movements and, at the same time, justifies them legally.

But Kelsen's ingenious doctrine simply shifts the problem of validity of law. Whether one affirms the supremacy of the international order, or accepts the premise of national juridical order, the old difficulty continues, for each hypothesis deals with limiting norms which cannot be justified in juridical terms. There is no way out but to assume the validity of the limiting norms, as Kelsen does. But this simply renounces a solution of the problem.

Kelsen tells us that the fundamental norm is a hypothesis. Let us examine up to what point this terminology may be correct. Procedure by hypothesis performs a most important role in the physical and mathematical sciences. From the scientific viewpoint, hypothesis may be defined as an anticipation of natural law. In order to explain the phenomena of nature, the investigator imagines a hypothetical relation, that is, he assumes that the phenomena in question are related in a given manner. This ideal relationship acquires the character of a scientific principle when experience shows that the real relationships of the physical world conform to it. It follows, therefore, that every hypothesis, to be valid, must be confirmed by reality.

Kelsen's phrase "hypothetical fundamental norm" cannot be understood in this sense. Such a norm is, by definition, a command or an imperative. But an imperative cannot be proved or destroyed by experience, as Kant has demonstrated. The juridical hypothesis of Kelsen is not, therefore, a scientific hypothesis. He uses the term in its popular meaning as an assumption, or, better, as a postulate of his normative structure.

A theory of positive law may start with an admission of this hypothetical fundamental norm; but a philosophy of law must go even further, and discover what is the meta-juridical norm or principle on which the validity of the laws is based or supported.

Kelsen establishes with transparent clarity the distinction between validity and factual quality of law, and demonstrates the impossibility of basing the former upon the latter. At the foundation of Kelsen's doctrine lies the anxiety of justifying positive law as positive law; that is, independently of every value judgment concerning the content of its norms. We believe, however, that the structure of that illustrious jurist is not wholly exempt from value considerations. Behind the theoretical hypothetical assertion of the supreme norm there stands an evaluating will, to wit, the desire to assert the imperativeness of a positive order. Kelsen departs from the factual quality of law and affirms without reservation the obligatory character of law. To suppress the most transcendental problem of juridical philosophy, that of validity, or to claim to solve it by the assumption of a hypothetical norm, means in the final analysis an apotheosis of the law in force, and the placing of a halo over the head of the legislator.

CHAPTER II

VALIDITY OF LAW IN THE PHILOSOPHICAL SENSE

The formal juridical problem of the validity of law is relatively simple. It deals with a merely technical question the solution of which is contained in the fundamental norm. It is, so to speak, an immanent problem of positive law. To solve it, it is unnecessary to go beyond the limits of the legislation in force. The supreme law points out in every case the criteria according to which must be decided the validity or nullity of the acts and laws thereto subordinated.

The philosophical question is of a very different nature, and its solution is less easy. The norms in force in a country, at a given moment, are not always recognized as intrinsically just principles of action. As a general rule they are debated, and are usually subjected to more or less severe criticism. Without reservation we may accept their legal existence, their formal juridical validity, but we may not blindly admit their intrinsic or philosophical validity. Such a law exists, it is said, but it ought not to exist, because it is unjust. Such value judgments are possible only when, besides the formal juridical criterion previously studied, we make use of a new, non-juridical criterion. This is generally a substantial axiological criterion, as distinguished from the former, which is purely legal. Thus arises the parallelism between legality and morality which often turns into sharp opposition.

This opposition is a typical instance of incompatibility between norms belonging to different systems. When the commands included in two different systems are mutually exclusive, it is impossible to decide which should be obeyed and which disregarded, unless reference is made to a principle of evaluation foreign to the rival systems and superior to them. In other words: the criterion of preference must in such cases transcend the systems in conflict. The foregoing may readily be understood if it is remembered that one of the essential attributes of any norm of action is its claim of absolute validity. Every normative order purports to be valid unconditionally and aspires to complete observance. It denies, furthermore, the validity of systems opposed to it; the latter are for it nonexistent.[8]

Every norm is in reality a dogma. Dogmas are the principles of religion, and the canons of the church, the imperatives of morals, the conventions of society, and the legislation of the various states.

Social life is a stage on wheels, wherein a thousand contradictory im-

[8] On this point, see FELIX SOMLÓ, JURISTISCHE GRUNDLEHRE.

peratives fight one another; and, in the perennial battle of dogma, the most reckless claims and the most absurd prejudices, parading under the shining and deceptive shield of the "ought to be," usually fight for preeminence against the supreme principles of morals, religion, or law.

The arduous task of the philosopher consists precisely in unmasking prejudice and dissipating error, in order to establish with incontestable clarity which norms of conduct have absolute and universal validity and which have only derivative validity.

The hierarchical scale exists not only within the limits of an isolated system but as well among the various normative systems which compose the realm of duty. Even though it may be argued that law and morals constitute groups of mutually independent norms, we must perforce recognize the need for a superior criterion, a new pattern, a supreme principle, the function of which shall be to resolve the incompatibilities that so often arise between juridical rules and the imperatives of ethics.

Crime committed for the sake of conscience is nearly always the result of conflict between the dictates of moral conscience and the mandates of positive law. In order to remain faithful to his principles, the person may be unfaithful to the laws of the State. Coming to the crossroads, where one way leads to punishment and internal peace, the other to compliance with juridical law and remorse, he elects the first, and with resignation awaits the consequences which will ensue from his disobedience of the law.

Occasionally, the conflict between legality and morality is extremely difficult to resolve. The two contending mandates appear to merit, for reasons of equal weight, the most meticulous and respectful obedience. When contradictory interests are equally high and noble, the situation takes on an intensely tragic character, and throws the individual into a painful perplexity. Hence the writers, and particularly the dramatists, of all time have seen in the discordance between law and conscience a literary motif of extraordinary richness and deep philosophical sense.

The two most beautiful classical works which make use of this conflict as the crisis of their drama are the *Antigone* of Sophocles and the Platonic dialogue in which Crito suggests that Socrates flee from jail and leave the city. There is nothing strange in the fact that these two superior works, whose artistic merit and moral fullness are equally admirable, should have opposite solutions. In the first instance, the internal voice pronounces the decisive word, and external law is rejected; in the second, the collective interest represented by the law is placed ahead of the moral interest of the individual. In Sophocles' tragedy, the victory is won by feeling — the spontaneous impulse of a woman's heart, compassionate and loving; in the Platonic dialogue the victory is won by the cold reason of the philosopher, who affirms the superiority of general juridical value over private interest, and considers it a lesser evil to suffer a wrong than to commit one.

The opposition between the legal "ought" and the moral "ought" has been placed in relief in numerous philosophical-juridical writings. In Hellenic philosophy we find interesting considerations of this ancient problem. Unfortunately the solutions suggested are not always satisfactory. The defects from which they suffer are derived, in general, from an error in posing the problem.

In philosophical (as in mathematical) problems, correct statement of the problem is as important as the true solution. The only difference is that, while mathematical problems are nearly always possible of solution, philosophical problems rarely are. The philosopher must be content with approximate solutions, the value of which is more or less debatable. The path which leads to truth is not only rough and winding; it may be said that it is endless as well. Human strength is hardly sufficient to traverse it; the obstacles and difficulties become ever greater; the goal appears every day more distant. The charm of philosophizing dwells precisely in such difficulties. Far from sapping the energies of the thinker, they stimulate, just as the hazards and dangers of an unexplored road act as a spur to the hiker.

The alleged right of the strongest. The philosophical-juridical thesis of the Greek sophists may serve as an example of an erroneous statement of the problem we are examining. Callicles develops his doctrine around the concepts of natural law and written law. The latter is the work of man and, as such, is contingent and mutable; the former is the child of nature, and therefore superior to any convention. A different concept of justice applies to each of these types of law. In the legal order, the just is a result of the judgment of the legislators: it is a matter of convention imposed by the weak as a means of defense against the strong. Written law is artificial law; its supreme postulate is to assert a fictitious equality. In the natural order there is no equality, and justice demands that the strong shall have supremacy. If the inferiors unite, they do not thereby destroy or dim the dignity of the elect; the will of a host of slaves is incapable of denting the strength of the superman. Law is founded on power; force is the highest reason, the decisive argument. It is just that the large fish shall eat the small, and it is just that the lion shall devour the lamb. It is just, likewise, that the handsome and strong Hercules shall seize the oxen of Gerion. Because it is natural, inequality is good. Democracy, stepdaughter of fear, is a despicable lie. Only the spontaneous is true; only the acts of the powerful are just.

Now, undoubtedly, between positive law and moral law there is sometimes the conflict to which Callicles seems to refer. The error, however, lies in the dogmatic assertion that written law is always artificial and that justice rests upon force. Power is a fact, and a norm cannot be based on fact. What is and what ought to be are two entirely different worlds, two diverse sectors of existence.

But the chief mistake of Thrasymachus and Callicles lies in taking as known what is sought to be known, that is, in the present instance, the essence of justice. The point of departure of these thinkers is in reality the following: We already know what is just. But here is the grave error. The problem of the validity of law must be stated in another form. It is a question of finding the justification of positive law and not of establishing generalizations, more or less awkward, based upon observation of certain natural phenomena. Experience tells us that there is a positive law, and that this law may usually be compared with a given criterion of justice. When an individual finds that legislation is in harmony with this meta-juridical criterion of what is just, he asserts the validity of that law; and, if not, he denies it.

Callicles in fact proceeds in a similar manner. Upon discovering that written law does not accord with his idea of justice, he declares that the former is artificial and unjust. His assertions would be irrefutable if they rested on a foundation of certainty. That is, the denial of the validity of positive law would represent the solution of the problem, if power were the essence of natural law. That the foundation of law must not be sought in force was demonstrated by Socrates, a contemporary of the Sophists. In the Platonic dialogue *Gorgias* and the first book of *The Republic,* we find the definitive refutation of all the arguments which may possibly be advanced in favor of the doctrine that power is the essence of natural law.

Statement of the problem. The philosophical problem of the validity of law must be examined from two points of view: in relation to the total juridical order, and in relation to concrete juridical norms.

It is possible, therefore, to set down the following premise: Any norm whatever is valid, and therefore justified, if the conduct it prescribes constitutes an "ought to be." [9]

We are not dealing with an "ought" in the juridical sense, but an

[9] On the philosophic concept of the "ought to be," see KITZ, SEIN UND SOLLEN (1869), p. 74; SIMMEL, EINLEITUNG IN DIE MORALWISSENSCHAFT. Says Simmel: "The 'being' as well as the 'ought to be' are primary categories; and just as 'to be' or 'to think' cannot be described, neither is there a definition of the 'ought to be' . . . The 'ought to be' is, like the future or preterit, the subjunctive or the conditional, a form of thought."

"ought" in the philosophical sense. In other words: a precept prescribing that which "ought to be" unconditionally is a precept with objective validity.

The fact of the nonobservance of a norm does not destroy its intrinsic validity: the possibility that the normative precept may be violated is an essential condition of its existence. It would be senseless to assert an "ought to be" in relation to anything which could not be otherwise than it is. The concepts of physical necessity and moral duty are mutually exclusive.

These observations are valid for any moral norm. Let us now investigate whether such principles are applicable to juridical laws.

Autonomous norms and heteronomous norms. Since Kant, two types of fundamental norms are usually distinguished: the autonomous or absolute and the heteronomous. Those of the first kind are the ones which the subject gives to himself. Those of the second kind are formulated by a will outside of the subject under obligation.[10]

Autonomous norms seem to the individual as self-evident; the heteronomous, on the other hand, appear as the exigencies of an external power, that is, as claims which need justification.

We have already said that every norm possesses an absolute claim to validity. A precept which aspires to compliance only in certain instances, and whose enforcement depends upon the judgment of certain men, is not a true norm, but simply an invitation or advice. Juridical laws, as well as religious and moral precepts, claim to be unconditionally valid. It is not true, as Rudolf Stammler believes, that social conventions are mere invitations, the acceptance of which depends on individual caprice. Society wants to have its norms obeyed in all cases, and in every case the state aspires to attain unconditional observance of its commands.[11]

A careful distinction must be drawn between objective validity and alleged validity. Between the two there is a relation similar to that which obtains between the concepts of price and value in economic theory. Price, as the expression of a thing's exchange value, is usually higher than the thing's use-value. But the relation between value and price is not always the same; as a general rule price is superior; occasionally it is inferior, and sometimes equivalent. Something similar happens with respect to the expressions "objective validity" and "alleged validity." The claim

[10] "The autonomy of the will is the constitution of the will whereby it is for itself a law, independently of how the objects of desire may be constituted." KANT, FUNDAMENTACIÓN DE LA METAFÍSICA DE LAS COSTUMBRES (FUNDAMENTALS OF THE METAPHYSICS OF MORALS, Calpe, Madrid, 1921) 97.

[11] STAMMLER, WIRTSCHAFT UND RECHT (1906) 2 AUFL. 121. Against the quoted thesis of Stammler, see KELSEN, HAUPTPROBLEME DER STAATSRECHTLEHRE 37.

to validity may or may not correspond to an objectively valid norm. If it corresponds, the norm is justified; if not, it lacks value and justification.

Validity and efficiency of the juridical order. When can it be said that a juridical precept is valid?

Certain authors erroneously believe that every effective juridical order is valid. But the validity of a norm or of a normative system cannot be based upon the phenomenon of compliance. In the first chapter of this essay we said that a precept is in force and has the positive quality when the conduct it prescribes is observed generally and constantly. This does not mean that observance of law does not tolerate exceptions. Juridical norms, as we have seen, claim to be valid in every case; but this claim is not always realized absolutely. It is most unlikely that any law of man has ever achieved universal obedience among those to whom it applied. If the norms of morals or law were invulnerable they would cease to be authentic norms and would acquire the necessary character of physical law and mathematical formulae.

The factual quality of law is not absolute: it consists simply of the more or less general and durable observance of the conduct prescribed by the laws.

The effectiveness of a precept does not, however, suffice to support its validity. The orders of a despot are frequently obeyed, if not from conviction, at least from fear. Such orders, nevertheless, are usually arbitrary: they have a factual quality, but they are not justified in that, far from expressing an "ought to be," they unjustly demand certain conduct.

The preceding considerations compel us to reject any theory such as that of Thrasymachus and Callicles which attempts to base the validity of law on the might of the governors. The well-known saying of Lasalle that, "If the first time I have the power to do something, the second time I also have the right to do it," is paradoxical and false. From a fact it is impossible to derive the validity of a norm. It is not lawful to base a right to domination on the fact of domination. A precept is not valid in itself; it may be justified only if it is based upon another precept, which in turn must have objective validity.

It may be objected that the observance of juridical imperatives is generally the result of conviction and only exceptionally the product of force. In the heart of this statement there is a profound truth. Most men comply with the law spontaneously. This indicates only that the validity of the law is commonly recognized by those who are subject to its power: but this does not solve the problem. The reference to observance by conviction of the legislator's precepts is to a given fact or psychological phenomenon, which explains why juridical norms are usually obeyed. This explanation clarifies the factual quality of juridical norms but does not demonstrate their validity.

Objective validity and subjective belief in the validity of a precept. Nor should the validity of a norm be confused with the belief in its validity. The validity of a normative precept does not depend upon human judgment. The intrinsic validity of an imperative may be recognized or denied; but neither the recognition nor the ignorance or negation thereof can influence in the least the existence and dignity of the norm.

According to W. Windelband norms which enunciate an absolute duty appear to the conscience of the obligated subject as self-evident, and they arouse in him the conviction that they must be complied with.[12] That a normative precept presents itself with the character of self-evidence does not mean, however, that the intrinsic validity of the imperative in question is derived from its self-evident aspects. The norm is not valid because it is self-evident; on the contrary, it appears self-evident because it is valid.

Commands emanating from a will outside the obligated subject are recognized by him only when they agree with the demands of his conscience. This is the case of juridical norms. But on such occasions what is self-evident is not the external juridical law, but the internal voice which orders us to respect such a law and obey it.

Nevertheless nothing prevents the admission that a juridical norm which we accept may sometimes lack objective validity. Belief in the justice of a precept may be absolutely false: it may be a moral optical illusion. And the aspect of self-evidence may also be misleading.

The foregoing considerations demonstrate the urgent necessity of distinguishing most carefully between what is just *per se* (objective value) and what is just for me (subjective appreciation). The note of self-evidence is solely an external sign, the subjective echo which certain values produce upon the mind. But the validity of a norm does not necessarily follow from the existence of this self-evidence.

From the foregoing it follows that juridical laws, as heteronomous precepts, have need of justification. One must investigate whether they have objective validity, or what is the same thing: to make clear whether they are the expression of an authentic "ought to be."

Some authors see in every juridical norm a moral imperative politically sanctioned; others, like Duguit, distinguish between juridical norms having moral content and purely technical norms. Duguit calls the first

[12] Windelband, *Normen und Naturgesetze,* in PRÄLUDIEN (1884) 211.

normative rules, and the second constructive rules.[13] In Kant's terminology the former may be said to be categorical imperatives and the latter hypothetical imperatives.[14] The juridical categorical imperatives constitute the ethical minimum of George Jellinek; the juridical hypothetical imperatives represent the technique of the jurist.

If the question be thus stated in Kantian terms, it would be easy to resolve the debated problem of the validity of law in accord with the viewpoint of the German philosopher. The Kantian solution would run as follows: The normative juridical rules (categorical imperatives) are objectively valid, and consequently justified, because they represent the practical necessity of an act good in itself, e.g., give to each what belongs to him, fulfill promises, etc.; the constructive juridical rules (hypothetical imperatives) are valid because they represent the practical necessity of a possible act as a means of obtaining a desired end, or an end which possibly may be desired, e.g., the achievement of a contract, for which the law prescribes stated requirements.

But Kant states differently the problem which concerns us. In his eyes, law is absolutely independent of morals, and, according to him, lacks ethical content.

Moral law always prescribes internal conduct; juridical legislation demands only external concordance of an act with the law. The legislator does not take into account the secret springs of action.

The concordance of an act with a norm—when the motive of such act is the idea of a duty—Kant calls morality; the purely external concordance of act and law, legality.[15]

In this way the philosopher contrasts the externality of law and the internality of morals:

> An action is just if, in accord with its maxim, the liberty of each may coexist with the liberty of all. But it does not follow that this principle of all maxims is at the same time my maxim. I cannot be required to make this principle the maxim of my action, for each one may be free (although I may

[13] In the Napoleonic Code there are, according to Duguit, only three normative rules, if family law is omitted: liberty of contract, respect for property, and reparation for injury based on fault. 1 DROIT CONSTITUTIONNEL 7.

[14] "The representation of an objective principle in so far as it is restrictive upon a will is called a command (of reason) and the formula of the command is termed an imperative . . . All imperatives command, either hypothetically or categorically. The former represent the practical necessity of a possible action, as a means of obtaining something else which is desired (or which it is possible may be desired). The categorical imperative would be one which represented an action *per se,* without reference to any other end, as objectively necessary." KANT, *op. cit.,* pp. 54ff.

[15] METAPHYSISCHE ANFANGSGRÜNDE DES RECHTSLEHRE (1893), p. 13.

be wholly indifferent to his liberty or I may wholeheartedly desire to attack it) if in fact I do not attack it by my external conduct. That I convert observance of the law into the maxim of my acts is a requirement of ethics.[16]

Juridical duties are therefore indirect ethical obligations (*indirekt-ethische Pflichten*); moral duties are direct ethical obligations (*direkt-ethische Pflichten*). It follows that compliance with a juridical norm has moral significance only in the cases where the motive of the action is the idea of duty.

This doctrine, however, does not resolve the problem of the validity of law. The morality described by Kant simply reveals the purity of a motive, but does not demonstrate the validity of a norm which has been complied with "out of respect for the law." The law which I respect and obey, even against my personal interests, may be bad or unjust. Autonomous legislation would be objectively valid only on the hypothesis that the legislator is infallible. But the auto-legislator described by the author of the *Metaphysics of Morals* is not the real man but an abstract entity gifted with divine omnisapience.

A law is not just because it has been complied with in obedience to a law which the subject has imposed upon himself; neither is it just by reason of the fact that it accords with a universal maxim. The categorical imperative is a psychological fiction, as has been demonstrated with abundant reasons by Beneke, Brentano, and Scheler.[17]

[16] Die Metaphysik der Sitten, p. 32.

[17] "In the *Fundamentals of the Metaphysics of Morals,* Kant presents to us the categorical imperative in the following formulae: 'act only pursuant to such a maxim as you would at the same time posit as a universal law,' and 'act as if the maxim of your action were to be converted into a universal law of nature.' In the *Critique of Practical Reason,* he says: 'act in such a manner that the maxim of your conduct may always be valid at the same time as a principle of universal legislation,' that is, as Kant himself explains, that the maxim raised to universal law does not lead to contradictions and does not end by nullifying itself. The consciousness of this universal law would be, for Kant, a fact (*factum*) of pure reason, which in this fashion would show itself to be legislative (*sic volo, sic jubeo*). But Beneke, in his *Grundlinien der Sittenlehre,* has already observed that it is but a psychological fiction, and today no judicious person doubts it. It is quite characteristic that even philosophers, like Mansel, who feel the greatest veneration for Kant, confess that the categorical imperative is an absolutely untenable fiction. The categorical imperative has in addition another and no lesser defect. The deductions attempted by Kant fail him, as Mill says, 'in a manner which is almost grotesque.' His favorite example of deduction is the following: 'May one, he asks, keep a thing which has been received for deposit without having given a receipt or any other evidence of deposit?' And he answers: 'No, for if the contrary maxim were to be law, no one would trust another in such circumstances. The law would then remain without possibility of application; that is, unrealizable and nullified by itself.' It is easy to

On the other hand it is also false that juridical legislation lacks moral content, that it is simply form without substance, or form capable of enclosing any content whatever (as Kelsen holds). Neither the subjectivism or formalism of Kant, nor the pure theory of Kelsen offers a firm criterion for clarifying the questions which we have been studying. An action is justified if it is good in itself, that is, if it is valid *per se*, and a norm is valid only in case it constitutes an expression of an ought-to-be. In this way we again set down the principles we had provisionally enunciated at the beginning of this chapter, and we find ourselves suddenly confronted with a new and difficult problem: In which cases can it be asserted that a norm is the expression of an "ought to be"?

The problem of duty has been resolved by modern philosophy in terms of the concept of value. Every "ought" refers directly or indirectly, mediately or immediately, tacitly or expressly, to a value to be realized by the subject. Norms express precisely the moral necessity that the subject addressed realize a value or series of values, the realization of which depends upon the judgment and capacity of the subject obligated.

Every "ought to be" is related to a value to be realized; consequently, we must analyze the relations between the two concepts to which we have referred. But inasmuch as the analysis of the relations existing between two concepts presupposes knowledge of the concepts to be related, we are constrained to study in another chapter the modern theory of values, the doctrine which in the end will permit us to solve the difficulties which have appeared in the course of our work.

The problem of the validity of the total juridical order. Earlier we stated that the problem dealt with in this essay may be stated in two different forms: in relation to an isolated juridical precept, and in relation to the total juridical order.

The Greek philosophers generally stated the problem of the validity of law in the latter form. Socrates and his disciple, Plato, always saw in the laws the essence of the Hellenic *polis,* and in the legal order a homogeneous aggregate of duties to be zealously fulfilled by the individual, even at the cost of his private moral interest. When the normative conflict appears, and ethical value clashes with general juridical

---

ascertain that Kant's argument is false and even absurd. If, in consequence of the law, certain actions are omitted, then the law produces an effect, and therefore it is real and is in no way nullified. Notice how ridiculous it would be if the following question were asked: 'Should I listen to one who attempts to bribe me?'; and the same kind of answer were given: 'Yes; because if you thought of the opposite maxim raised to a universal law of nature, no one would attempt to bribe anyone, and consequently the law would be without application, and therefore would be nullified by itself.' " BRENTANO, EL ORÍGEN DEL CONOCIMIENTO MORAL. (Translation by Manuel G. Morente, in REVISTA DE OCCIDENTE, Madrid, pp. 83 and 84.)

value, Socrates does not hesitate to sacrifice ethical value. The belief in the superiority of juridical value over the moral interest of the subject prevented him from heeding the pleas of his friend Crito, and impelled Socrates to accept with resignation the consequences of a sentence which, though morally unjust, adhered strictly to the precepts of Athenian law.

The formidable Socratic argument, reproduced by Plato in the Crito dialogue, is the best which has been formulated up to the present in support of the Greek thesis whereby, what is now called the value of security or order, must be given precedence, in case of conflict, over the moral interest of the citizen.

Since this whole argument rests upon value judgments, and refers to values considered to be objective, we again find ourselves compelled to interrupt the thread of our reasoning in order to make an exposition in the following chapter of the theory of value. In this way we shall clarify many important concepts and shall be able later to pick up the thread of the argument and resolve satisfactorily the problems which concern us. Subsequent developments will demonstrate that the problem both of the validity of the isolated juridical precept and of the validity of the total juridical order may be solved only in terms of a theory of values.

CHAPTER III

THE PHILOSOPHY OF VALUES

The modern theory of values may be considered the richest and most interesting chapter of contemporary philosophy. It was born in Germany, and in Germanic lands has achieved its most seasoned fruits. The first serious studies of the value problem appeared a few years prior to the great war.[18] Whoever is familiar with the admirable work of Oscar Kraus, *Die Grundlagen der Wertheorie,* will appreciate the notable development attained by research on this theme twenty years ago.[19]

The theory of values courageously entered the lists of philosophical

[18] World War I. (TRANSLATORS' NOTE.)

[19] The literature on this subject is already quite voluminous. Among works of a historical character, the following merit special attention: August Messer's small book *Deutsche Wertphilosophie der Gegenwart,* worthy of recommendation for the clarity of its exposition and the beauty of its style; the work of Kraus cited above; Wiederhold's study, *Wertbegriff und Wertphilosophie* (Ergänzungsheft der Kant-studien, 1920, 52), and Ortega y Gasset's elegant essay, "¿Qué son los valores?" in *Revista de Occidente.* Sources: 1 RICKERT, SYSTEM DER PHILOSOPHIE; MÜNSTERBERG, PHILOSOPHIE DER WERTE (1908); STERN, WERTPHILOSOPHIE (1924).

contention, to confront subjectivism and, in general, all the currents of relativism so much in vogue in the later decades of the past century (historicism, nominalism, sociological relativism, etc.).

The fundamental work on values appeared in 1913, the year before the European war. I refer to Max Scheler's famous book, *Der Formalismus in der Ethik und die Materiale Wertethik*. This work signalized the beginning of a new epoch in the history of moral philosophy, and marked a radical change in the orientation, method, and tendencies of this discipline. It may be asserted, without fear of exaggeration, that from thence on moral philosophy is no longer *formalistic* but has become substantial. Scheler in the above-mentioned work gathers, reinforces with new reasons, and explains with inimitable clarity, the arguments with which, many years before, Brentano had fenced against Kantian ethics. Scheler's work consists of two parts: a critical part (against Kant) and a constructive part (the fundamentals of the theory of values). In the latter we find an interesting application of the phenomenological method, which the author considers the most adequate for the treatment of moral questions.

Scheler never regarded his book as a definitive work. The study we have referred to was conceived as a preparatory essay for a later work on ethical values.

This undertaking, which Scheler never completed, has been carried out in masterly fashion by Nicolai Hartmann, one of the most illustrious thinkers of our time. His *Ethik* (1926) is one of the three best fruits of contemporary philosophy, alongside Scheler's *Der Formalismus in der Ethik* and Husserl's *Logische Untersuchengen*. Hartmann's treatise represents the most successful application of the method of the great logician to the study of morals, and constitutes at the same time a synthesis of the central ideas of Scheler and Husserl.

In the present chapter we shall sketch in broad strokes the theory of values, in order to achieve, in the last part of our study, the application of this theory to the philosophical problem of the validity of law.

The theory of values is far from being a rounded philosophy, a complex of ideas definitively articulated. In reality there is not only one doctrine concerning these questions; the doctrines are numerous, and they differ from one another in detail and shadings of greater or lesser degree. The only point where authors meet is that respecting objectivity; but the opinions separate and clash as soon as there is an attempt to set up a hierarchy of values, or to determine how a value judgment may be made.

In the following lines we shall briefly and as faithfully as possible describe the ideas of Hartmann. His doctrine is one of the most complete, and it possesses, among other merits, the very great quality of clarity. Philosophy's mission, according to Hartmann, is to answer satisfactorily the following three questions: What can we know? What ought we to do? What may we justly expect?

Of these three, the second constitutes the central problem of ethics. Its object does not consist in studying existence, but in discovering the meaning of existence. This moral discipline occupies the middle ground between the hard realities of life and the distant ideals of spiritual contemplation; and although it does not immediately refer to what is real, it is nevertheless closer to experience than any abstraction or any hope. Its roots dig into the deepest ground, yet never does it lose sight of the ideal realm of absolute values which, in imposing and sublime majesty, rises above it as do the heavens over the confines of the world.

The problem of duty arises in almost every moment of life, in the most insignificant as well as the gravest; in every new situation, existence poses before us the eternal problem, and demands the taking of a position. The traveler on life's way, arriving at the crossroads, cannot remain indifferent; he must choose one of the paths opening before him; each appears to beckon to him; each has its own appeal, its own perspective, and its special attractions; but the decision is left exclusively to the traveler. If his choice is unwise, if he depart from the straight path, he must bear the evil consequences of his error. This is the price of the autonomy of the will.

Every new action is a new answer that we give to life. Once consummated, our acts enter the sphere of the irrevocable. What once achieves reality, what once appropriates an instant in the cosmic process, can never be annihilated; it becomes eternal. What happens once never again will be the same; yet no supernatural or human power is strong enough to banish it from history. Every event has its place in the process of existence, and this place belongs to it exclusively and will be its own until the end of time.

Ethics does not indicate what we should do in every concrete situation; it only shows in a general way how we may discover what our duty is. It offers simply a general citerion; it is a high vantage point from which we may get a bird's-eye objective view of things in the aggregate. It does not proffer a new norm for every special situation and every new conflict; nor does it show the way in which we must decide; it points out only the criteria which should guide us in making a decision. It does not enunciate definitive judgments, but it teaches us how to judge. Therefore, it is not a collection of barren norms nor, like the law, a code of prohibitions and commands. It is addressed to the most sublime, creative element in man. Ethics is not casuistic; nor should it be, for, if it were, it would kill all moral spontaneity.

"In the human heart," Hartmann says, "there is an intricate mixture of the chaotic and demiurgic; in the chaotic lie its possibilities, but its dangers as well; in the demiurgic is its vocation. To realize its vocation is to be a man."

The question concerning duty poses only the first part of the ethical problem. The other is less apparent; though it does not as readily come into view, it is more universal and no less important. Faced with the question of duty, man is compelled to take a position. It is not a matter of facing a theoretical question, but an unavoidable vital problem. Whoever has no ear to listen to an imperative, and no eye to contemplate what is valuable, lives this life in vain. What is deeply significant does not move him; what is sublime does not elevate him; he is incapable of discovering the hidden meaning of vital relations, the inexhaustible wealth of situations, and the value of actions and men.

Besides the demand that he take a position, man is faced with another challenge: that of taking part in the fullness of existence, and with love opening his senses to all that has significance and value. Traditional ethics did not take this into account. Imperativist morals also commits this traditional fault and likewise places itself on the periphery of life's fullness and richness. Moral dazzle and obfuscation, deplorable blindness to the valuable: this is the ethics of duty. It is not strange that pessimism steps upon its heels. It is difficult to bear life in a world devoid of values, in a world where the good and the holy have been degraded to the category of a barren formula.

The problem of values is as important as the one of duty; its metaphysical significance is, however, deeper and its content richer and broader. The problem of values bears in its womb the problem of duty. I cannot know what my conduct ought to be if I know not what is valuable and what lacks value. The solution given to the problem of duty, therefore, depends on the solution of the problem of values.

The metaphysical transcendence of the problem of values is beyond measure. Human action would lack meaning if it exhausted itself in work. And if what is created by mortals had no significance whatever, the creative act would be inexplicable and superfluous. His cosmic smallness, his transitoriness and impotence do not divest the human being of his metaphysical greatness, nor do they destroy his undeniable superiority over the other forms of existence. He is a subject among objects, actor and spectator, cosmic mirror, creature and demiurge. *Homo sapiens,* to whom God gave no wings, has learned nevertheless how to soar into azure heights; he plows over the depths of the sea, and in his impetuous daring attempts the most portentous feats. He thus asserts his power over the forces of nature, which in his hands are transformed into the docile instrument for the realization of his desires.

The participation of the human being in the coming and going of events is not indifferent: in that participation there is interest, there is sympathy, there is an apprehension of the valuable. We must reckon as by-products the impartial sobriety of thought and the cold neutrality of philosophical reflection.

The apprehension of the valuable is generally very narrow. For the majority of mortals the limits of their most urgent interests, and of their most immediate vital relations, are also the limits of their moral existence. Their life is a limited, dwarfed life; a caricature of humanity.

When the poet shows us a situation, we discover without effort its entire moral fullness; we observe instantly its value-meaning, even though very often we may not be clearly conscious of its special and complex value structure.

But real life differs from the dramatic art: the former lacks the wise hand of the master, the guiding hand which imperceptibly puts in the foreground everything that is important, that is significant, so that it becomes visible even to the most naive eye. The insignificant, the banal, and the superfluous are, on the other hand, relegated by the artist to the background; they make up, as it were, the gray backdrop of existence, against which stand out in clear colors the beauty of situations, the interest of conflicts, and the significance of positions taken. Despite this difference between life and art, life is always and everywhere an intense drama. If we would but contemplate the situation in which we find ourselves, in a manner as plastic as the poet's, it would appear to us as rich and colorful as the creations of art.

With great frequency, in casting a retrospective glance over our existence, our attention is held by certain concrete situations which at another time seemed insignificant; and with a surprise that is not free from melancholy we discover in these situations a hidden and deep meaning, an unsuspected richness. And we then experience a profound and secret sorrow, in thinking of what has irrevocably gone by, which was ours and yet never belonged to us. This *indifferent passing-by* of the valuable is a curious chapter in the history of men. If we cast to one side everything which we passed by without noticing — without a glance of sympathy, without the slightest feeling, — we could consider as spiritually ours only a minute portion of the totality of life.[20]

[20] HARTMANN, ETHIK.

The problem of duty and the problem of values are the fundamental themes of ethics. It does not deal with two independent problems. Between them there is the most intimate and closest relation. Rather than of two independent problems, we should speak of the two central aspects of one major problem — the two faces of the same coin. The problem of duty can be resolved only in the light of the theory of values. Every "ought," every norm, is founded upon the existence of a value and postulates the obligation to realize it.

What are values? For many centuries it has been admitted that, in addition to the world of matter, there is a world of immaterial entities, a realm of the ideal. Plato termed it the realm of Ideas; Aristotle, that of form (εἶδος), and the Scholastics, that of the essences (*essentia*). After being denied by the subjectivism triumphant in recent times, the existence of this ideal world is almost unanimously recognized and affirmed by contemporary thinkers.

The immaterial entities which compose the ideal world are the *essences* of phenomenology. The German word *Wesenheit* is a faithful translation of the term *essentia* used by the Scholastics. Both concepts, the ancient and the modern, coincide in fundamentals.

The mode of being of Platonic Ideas is that of a 'οντωςόν, that is, the mode of being whereby whatever shares in them is as it is. The archetypes of Plato comprehend the principles of ethics and the values studied by morals. In so far as their mode of being is concerned, values are Platonic Ideas. They belong to that ideal world discovered by Plato, to that supersensory sphere which may be known intuitively or regarded intellectually, but which cannot be seen with the eyes nor touched by the hands.

We may say of values what is affirmed of archetypes: they are that whereby whatever shares in them is as it is. Or, expressed in modern language, *values are essences.* This proposition synthesizes the results achieved in the field of ethics by the Kantian critique. Values do not depend either on the subject or external things; neither realism nor subjectivism explains their mode of being But they are not forms without content; rather substance and structure which determine a specific quality in the objects, persons, and relations wherein they are found.

The apprehension of the valuable. Values are accessible only through an intellectual glance or intuition. The Platonic motive of the *glance,* which the philosopher uses as a *Leitmotiv* in his beautiful *Allegory of the Cave,* is at bottom equivalent to what contemporary ethics terms the sense or apprehension of the valuable (*das Wertfühlen*).

The apprehension of the valuable [writes Hartmann], is the annunciation of the existence of values to the person; the annunciation of the ideal being which is characteristic of values. The *a priori* character of the knowledge in question is not reflective or intellectual, but emotional and intuitive.

The goods. Things in which a value is inherent are called goods. Speaking in Kantian terms, we might say that values, in so far as they relate to things, are *conditions of the possibility of goods.* The values of things (*Dingwerte*) may be known only intuitively in valuable things (*Wertdinge*); but the knowledge of the valuable qualities is not based on our experience with the goods. Experience leads us to consider certain objects as useful and agreeable; others as disagreeable and useless. This commerce of experience simply indicates that certain things are adequate or inadequate means to something whose value was known beforehand. *A priori* knowledge of the valuable is precisely what permits us to call certain things *goods,* and others *ills.* It would be impossible to recognize given objects as good unless there were some judgment possible independent of such objects. The faculty of judgment in the human being divides things into the good and the bad; but the reality of the latter and the former are identical. If man is able to distinguish and contrast the good and the bad, it is only because he has an apprehension of the valuable. This original sense which exists in us is what makes possible the selection and classification of objects which appear within the ambit of our life.

Relations between the a priori and the absolute character of values. A careful distinction must be drawn between the thesis affirming the *a priori* character of values and that which sustains their absolute character. Their absolute character refers to their mode of being or their essence; their *a priori* character is related to the knowledge of value. The doctrine which states that such knowledge of value is independent of experience would not be destroyed, even were every judgment shown to be subjective or arbitrary. In the latter hypothesis, values "would become *prejudices* or, better stated, *predispositions* of the subject; but would still lack an empirical basis and experimental correlation." Realities as such do not contain any measure of value; they are simply that which can be measured and evaluated, that which is measured and judged.

The values of action. Human acts do not relate solely to goods. The highest ethical phenomena consist of acts of another kind, and relate to values of a different sort; namely, the values of action, or moral values.

What is valid in relation to certain necessities must be valid in relation to higher aspirations, which have no relation to goods. The object of desire has, to the volitional conscience, the form of an end or purpose. It is in the nature of the end that its content have, or at least appear to have, value. It is impossible to set any goal whatever without recognizing some merit in it. Whenever a selection of means is made, with a view to accomplishing an end, it is because of a belief that some value has been discovered in that end. The prior judgment of valuation is an essential condition of the teleological act. It is an *a priori* condition, for the end as such is not, and cannot be, proved by experiment. The end is something unreal, something not realized; for at the stage of realization, it is no longer an end.

The deeper one digs into the problem of ethical phenomena, the more evident the essential character of values becomes, and the clearer their *a priori* nature. The determination of will; the projection or statement of ends; moral approval or disapproval, do not as yet constitute the most profound part of the problem. Conscience does not limit itself to considering and testing acts and intentions; it also imputes to persons qualities and defects, virtues and vices. And just as the tree is judged by its fruits, so the actor is judged by his conduct, and the maintainer of a purpose by the intention embodied in the purpose. The tribunal of conscience not only judges; it also condemns. It imputes to the actor responsibility and guilt; and these imputations are not directed exclusively to others, but also to oneself. "Conscience shows itself uncompromising with self, it forces self-denial in the painful feelings of guilt, self-devouring repentance and desperation; or else it leads to moral regeneration, transformation and renovation of oneself."

The relation existing between value and reality is clearly revealed in this phenomenon. The experience of value "accredits its autonomy within the subject," as a power to which natural and rebellious impulses must submit. The real person in this way feels himself placed before an Idea of a person, capable of judgment; and the synthetic self is torn into an empirical self and a moral self. The empirical self respectfully bows to the moral self, acknowledging the latter's superior rights, and bearing the guilt pronounced by the judge.

What we vulgarly call the *voice of conscience* is nothing other than the primary experience of values. That certain things are considered good or bad; that the impulse aspires toward them or away from them; that there are ends of desire, which are the determinants of our conduct; and that this experience raises its insinuating voice in the depths of our spirit — are phenomena which can be understood only if one admits that values are a power which influences the life of men. The doctrines of classical ethics, referring to goods and to virtue, are implicitly based on this thought; but their authors never had a clear idea of these facts; they lacked a concept of value.

The determination derived from values is far from being an absolute determination like that from natural law. Values do not *necessarily* determine human conduct; man may or may not realize the valuable. The moral determination produced by values is essentially different from the determination existing in the physical world. A natural law allowing of exceptions would not be an authentic law. The exceptions, far from proving the principle, would demonstrate its falsity. Moral imperatives, on the other hand, express something that "ought to be" in every case, but which in fact very often is not. The factual quality of ethical norms tolerates exceptions, as previously stated; yet their validity suffers no diminution, even though no reality may correspond to the ideal they postulate.

Values do not directly determine human conduct. The requirements and duties that flow from them can penetrate into the sphere of reality only if a real power makes them effective.

The meeting point between the realm of value and the world of matter can exist only in a being which has these three attributes: first, he must be a real entity, found amidst the flow of life, and subject to the determination of nature; second, he must be able to experience the valuable and consequently to listen to the voice of an imperative; and, finally, he must be capable of realizing the values he experiences intuitively, thus obeying the mandates of his conscience.

Realization of values appears under the category of finality. Finality is precisely the capacity to set a goal which is still unreal, and the ability to select the means adequate to achieve the objective.

Of all living beings only man embodies the above three attributes. The human being thus constitutes a bridge between the realm of value and the world of reality. Those attributes make him a moral entity and assure his privileged cosmic position.

Human power is revealed in all its transparency in the teleological act. Finality means, in a certain sense, predestination and providence, since every realization of an end lies in the future. "The past remains static and cannot be modified; the present is already made. Only the future is yet to be made; only the hereafter remains open to the voluntary activity of men." [21]

In this capacity of setting goals and selecting means lies the undeniable superiority of the human species. Finalistic activity permits *homo sapiens* to become the lord of the universe and to guide the course of events.

[21] HARTMANN, SYSTEMATISCHE SELBTSDARSTELLUNG (1933) 327.

The flow of things does not obey any finality; it is a flow indifferent and blind, a flow without goal. If it were a finalistic process, there would remain to us no radius of action; what is would be directed toward a point foreordained by divinity, and man could not set his own finalities nor find means of realizing them.

In a world teleologically ordered, there never could be a free being. This is not true in a world causally ordered. In the sphere of causality nothing is predetermined; nothing is foreknown; each new determinant may change the direction of the process.[22]

Relativity of values. Values are exposed to the suspicion of subjectivism. Goods have value only for a subject, and the moral qualities of intentions and acts exist solely in relation to persons.

But the relativity of goods to subjects is not the result of individual valuation. That an object be for me a good or an ill is something entirely independent of my will and my power. In the power of men there is simply the possibility of aspiring toward the good and the faculty of rejecting what is bad.

The relativity of goods to the subject does not imply a relativism of values. Man cannot vary the goodness of an object. If he is unaware of it, or ignores it, the value of the object is neither altered nor diminished. The nature of things (their being good or bad) is not relative to persons as subjects who value and judge, but relative to persons as such. It is not the individual who determines the value of things; the subject is simply one of the points of reference of a relation founded in the substance of a value. The thing has value for the person, even though he may not know it; or, knowing it, may fail to appreciate it. In this case, we are dealing with the same "for" which is implied in so many categorial structures. As Hartmann says:

> That geometric truths have value only for the spatial, mechanical laws for real bodies, and the physiological for organisms, does not imply relativism in the categorial content of those laws. This is not a question of laws created by the objects or by men, but of laws to which the subject *for whom* they have value must submit unconditionally.

[22] "In such a world, man can direct what without him would pass by blindly, he can impress into his service the forces of nature, and he can make them work toward the achievement of his ends. Man is the administrator of values and of the 'ought to be' in the world. If it were not thus, if values could by themselves determine what is in existence, man would find himself also determined by them and would have no freedom to pronounce himself for or against them. On that supposition, he would not be a superiorly organized natural being, nor would he occupy a position of privilege in the world. If values were not impotent before reality, men would be impotent before values. Consequently men would be slaves, irresponsible, and would find themselves, like animals, subject eternally to the laws of their species." SELBSTDARSTELLUNG, p. 328.

Relativity of moral values. The highest values are not those of things, but those of persons and their actions. They reside not in objects and relations but in human conduct, will, intentions, and acts.

The fact that the moral values of a person or of an attitude may be valid only in relation to a subject does not, however, show that these values are subjective. Their validity is not derived from the estimation by an individual, but is independent of it and subsists even in case the person is unaware of the existence of the valuable qualities.

The relativity of ethical values is manifested in three principal directions:

(a) In the first place, every moral value is mediately a good, and as such is relative to a subject, and exists for other persons. Charity, for example, is a good for the recipient; fidelity is a good for the person who has reposed his trust in us; and love is a good for the loved one. But in this *being good for someone* does not lie the ethical value of one who shows love, charity, or trust. The moral value of actions rests on itself; it exists for itself or in itself. And this is true even on the hypothesis that the individual for whom such value constitutes a good does not recognize it.

(b) Every moral value is value of conduct, and all conduct is relative to someone. Conduct has a real object, and this object is either a person or a community of persons. This relativity to an object (the person toward whom conduct is directed) lies in the structure of the content of the value itself. My friendship is a value to my friend, but this value is not created by the person whom it favors.

(c) The third and most important form of relativity is that which exists between the value and its bearer or support. Certain values are always referred to a special bearer; for example, "thing values" to valuable things, "life values" to living beings, and "moral values" to persons.

Only a being capable of desire, an entity susceptible of setting finalities for itself and selecting means of realization, can be the subject of conduct. Moral values do not simply attach themselves to acts; they reside in the actors. Frequently it is said that a procedure was magnanimous and noble; in that case the valuation of the attitude necessarily transcends the individual; the latter is also, by virtue of his acts, magnanimous and noble. And this is because every moral imputation in the last analysis rests upon a subject; the judgments of approval or censure refer to him, and he is in every case the one entitled to reward or punishment.

But this does not imply any relativism of values. It does not mean, for example, that the value of common sense depends upon the existence of certain men who act sensibly. On the contrary, certain acts are sensible because the value of common sense exists. The relativity to the person, as the bearer or support of some valuable quality, lies exclusively in the substance of value itself. In the substance of the value of *courtesy* there is implicit a reference to a person.[23]

Relations between value and the "ought to be," according to Brentano and Scheler. In the sphere of the "ought to be" we must distinguish the *ideal "ought"* from an "ought" which formulates a command and directs a will (*normative "ought"*). This latter category of "ought" depends upon the former, since every obligation is always the ideal "ought to be" of an act of will. "When the content of an ideal 'ought' is placed in relation to a want, a demand follows from the former addressed to that want. But the demand in question is not the ideal 'ought' but only one of its consequences." [24]

Every demand is founded *immediately* upon an ideal "ought," and *mediately* upon a value. It may appear either under the form of an internal command (consciousness of the obligation), or under the form of an external command.

The expression: "You shall behave in this or that way" has several meanings. In certain circumstances, it contains only the simple statement that the speaker desires that we do one thing or another. The appropriate form to phrase such a desire would be this: "I tell you that I want you to do such a thing." This formula bears a double meaning: first, the affirmation that the act of the other corresponds to an ideal "ought to be"; and, second, the announcement of the will of the speaker, in the sense that the other, obeying that demand, will act in a given

[23] "The thesis according to which values are essences has gained clarity in two of its aspects. First, values are a *prius* determining all moral phenomena (in relation to which the *a priori* character of the value conscience is only a partial phenomenon). In the second place, values have, as to the subject, an absolute character. We have demonstrated that every 'relativity as to the subject' rests simply upon the structure of the substance of value. But the value of the substance, and its structure, are different things. The moral value of trust, to pose an instance, is not trust itself. This is only a specific relation between two persons, a relation which can be perfectly characterized in a general way.

"Values exist in themselves and by themselves. This thesis is the formulation of the results which we have previously obtained in our critique of Kantian subjectivism. Values exist independently of consciousness. The preceding assertion does not refer to the substance of values. The subject may undoubtedly, within certain limits, create the substance of a value (for example, he may establish a relation of trust with another person); but he can neither make that substance have or lack value, nor prevent it from having or lacking value. Value is what it is, independently of the will of the subject, and even despite any contrary estimation of the latter." HARTMANN, ETHIK, chap. V.

[24] SCHELER, DER FORMALISMUS IN DER ETHIK 210.

way. This is the interpretation to be placed upon the commands of an authority.

The relation existing between value concepts and the "ought to be" is governed by two axioms: (a) every positive value ought to be; (b) every negative value ought not to be. The foregoing relation is not reciprocal but unilateral. As Scheler says: "Every 'ought' is fused into a value, but values are not fused into an ideal 'ought.' "

The values which are found in relation to a normative "ought" are those which consist in the being or not being of something valuable. This statement, according to Brentano, follows from two axioms: (a) the being of a positive value is a positive value; (b) the being of a negative value is a negative value.

In principle, values are indifferent to existence or nonexistence. Every "ought to be," on the other hand, refers to the existence or nonexistence of some value. The "ought to be" is not, like values, indifferent to the being or non-being of its content.

Every "ought to be" is an ought-to-be-something. That is why whenever we say that something ought to be, we consider that this something is nonexistent, something that should be realized. And inversely: when we state that something ought not to be we consider it as existing.

Concept of obligation. Every obligation is based upon a command. It makes no sense to speak of an obligation which does not exist in relation to anyone, or which does not derive from some authority. Likewise it makes no sense to speak of *auto-obligation,* as Kant does. There are obligations *toward oneself,* but there are no *auto-obligations,* that is, obligations in which the commander and the obligated are the same person.

For this reason, imperativist ethics, which sees in the concept of obligation the original ethical phenomenon, and attempts to derive from it the ideas of the good and the bad, of virtue and vice, has only a negative, repressive, and critical character.

We have briefly explained, in the preceding lines, the theory of values, and we are now in a position to go back over the ground covered in order to apply this theory to the problem of the validity of law.

We are not unaware that the philosophy of values is exposed to much criticism, nor have we forgotten that it is impossible to demonstrate absolutely several of its capital affirmations.

Theoretical reason is incapable of proving, in an entirely satisfactory manner, the existence of objective values. The thesis of objectivity is a metaphysical thesis, which is the same as saying that the problem it refers to has an irreducible nonrational bottom.

It is often said that the philosophy of value, far from constituting an authentic scientific position, is simply an act of faith. The objection lacks force, for all philosophical doctrines repose, in the last instance, upon some belief, and as a general rule reflect a given temperament. The Platonic doctrine of the archetypes, for example, is derived from a mystic attitude. And in the pages of *Fundamentals of the Metaphysics of Morals* it is easy to discover under the dry reasoning of the austere Kant the religious fervor of the pious man and the idealism of the believer. The famous categorical imperative of the thinker of Koenigsberg is the Kantian expression of the precept of the Gospel: "Do not unto others what thou dost not want for thyself."

With justice it is said that every philosophy is the intellectualization of a temperament. The deceitful mask of the most arid of rationalisms unavoidably hides behind itself a will or a purpose. What we call a metaphysical system is but the conceptual crystallization of a human soul. Behind the writer is the man with his virtues and his vices, his disillusions and his hopes, his triumphs and his defeats. The ideas of the writer are a shadow or a reflection of the hopes and aspirations of the man. The best men were always the most profound philosophers. Tell me what you think, and I shall tell you who you are!

The objectivity of values is theoretically undemonstrable, yet it imposes itself upon the conscience with the compelling clarity of the self-evident. The recognition of that objectivity, and the admission of the *a priori* character of value knowledge, are not simple affirmations, ephemeral and gratuitous, of a few contemporary thinkers. The conviction that there are values independent of any subjective consideration, capricious and mutable, is implicit in the metaphysics of all religions, and is the essence of the most sublime creations of art. The so-called modern philosophy of values is really very ancient, as ancient as the *Allegory of the Cave*. And the conviction of the objectivity of values, which more than a belief is a metaphysical necessity of the human spirit, has never been strange to artistic creation. Faith in the invulnerability of the ideal, and its location in a world beyond matter, in the world of becoming, and in the world beyond death, shines like an inextinguishable flame in the most beautiful work in Castilian literature. The noble Don Quixote is the victim of the cruelest contretemps, but adversity never abates his strong spirit. And if his lance bursts into a thousand fragments in its clash with the blades of the windmill, or if the tired limbs of the knight errant are beaten by the blows of the vulgar rabble, the value of the ideals which move him issues intact from all the struggles and all the adventures, and the beauty of those ideals reaches its maximum splendor in contrast with the meaner realities.

CHAPTER IV

THE PROBLEM OF THE VALIDITY OF LAW EXAMINED IN THE LIGHT OF THE PHILOSOPHY OF VALUES

In the second chapter of this essay we had stated provisionally the following principle: *Every norm which expresses an "ought to be" is a valid norm.* And in the third chapter, in studying the relations between the concepts of value and the ought-to-be, we reached the following conclusions:

(a) Every norm or *normative "ought"* is based upon an *ideal "ought."*

(b) Every ideal "ought" is related to an *objective value.*

We said also that a *normative "ought"* refers to the existence or nonexistence of something valuable, and that, when it is stated that something "ought to be," this something is considered to be nonexistent, that is, something which has not been realized. It follows from all that has been said that *norms, to be valid, must postulate the realization of objective values.*

If it is admitted, for example, that justice is a value, it is necessary to accept the validity of the following principle: Give unto each what belongs to him. The norm just stated is valid because it demands the realization of the value referred to.

We are not unaware that the verb *to realize* is far from being wholly adequate for the idea to be expressed, nor do we ignore the possibility that the phrase may easily lead us into error. The reader should remember the exposition in the preceding chapter concerning the mode of being or essence of values. When we say that a given procedure *realizes* the value of justice, we do not mean that the subject of that action creates that value. The subject may simply create the substance of such procedure (in this case, give to each what is his own); but he cannot prevent the substance so established from *supporting* a valuable quality. If I give to a person what is due him in justice, my action is valid and justifiable, and its validity subsists even though I am mistaken in evaluating my conduct.

The same results we have reached in relation to isolated norms may be applied to any normative system, and consequently also to law. *Every juridical order which realizes objective values must be considered as a valid order.*

The principles we have now established raise at once a series of problems: What are the values which law must realize? Are there special juridical values, or may law realize any value? If law can realize only certain values, what are they, and how can they be distinguished from the others?

The preceding questions have been answered very differently.[25] We shall limit ourselves to an exposition of the principal solutions which have been advanced in relation to the problems posed. Such solutions may be stated thus:

I. Law must realize moral values.

II. Law has as its end the realization of justice.

III. The supreme finality of law is the establishment of peace and order (juridical security).

IV. Law's desideratum is the realization of the common good.

Doctrine that the finality of law is the realization of moral values. The first of the enumerated theses presents a few variants. Some writers assert that law must realize only certain moral values (the moral values of a social nature); others deem the finality of the juridical order to be the realization of an ethical minimum, that is, the aggregate of principles strictly indispensable to the conservation and development of a community at a given moment of history.[26]

Against these doctrines numerous objections have been correctly stated. In relation to the first variant it has been said, for example, that it is incorrect to limit the end of law to the regulation of ethical values of a social nature, and that individual ethical duties are not, and never have been, wholly foreign to juridical regulation. And against the second it is objected that the equiposition of law and morals, in so far as content is concerned, is an unjustifiable equiposition, since juridical principles and ethical rules, far from coinciding in every case, are very often in conflict, which gives rise to greater or lesser incompatibilities. The existence of crimes committed for the sake of conscience demon-

[25] As yet, essays in the application of the doctrine of values to the philosophy of law are rather scarce. Among the best known is the one made by Gustav Radbruch in his books, *Einführung in die Rechtswissenschaft* and *Rechtsphilosophie*. The application is interesting, particularly where it touches on the problem of validity, but Radbruch does not explain in those works the fundamental principles of the theory of values, nor does he clearly define his concept of the valuable which therein appears vacillating and changes frequently, like the face of Proteus.

The reader should consult the interesting book by Juan José Bremer, *Teoría Crítica, Teoría Axiologica, y Teoría Integral del Derecho*, a work which discusses several of Radbruch's principal theories. (This was published by the National University of Mexico, in 1933.)

[26] TRENDELENBURG, NATURRECHT AUF DEM GRUNDE DER ETHIK; JELLINEK, DIE SOZIALETHISCHE BEDEUTUNG VON RECHT, UNRECHT UND STRAFE (1878).

strates eloquently, according to Radbruch, the falsity of Jellinek's theory. The tragic clashes sometimes presented between moral and juridical demands clearly indicate the essential difference in content between the two norms.

These arguments are derived from the study of the relations between morals and law. Law and morals are regulations of human conduct; but while the latter refers essentially to the intimate life of the individual, the former refers to his external conduct. This distinction is usually expressed by the following formula: *Externality of law, internality of morals* (*Äusserlichkeit der Rechts, Innerlichkeit der Sittlichkeit*). However, the distinction is not absolute, inasmuch as morals is not limited exclusively to a definition of the duties of man toward himself; nor is law wholly indifferent to the internal life of the subject.

When the legislator takes into account purposes and intentions, he does so with a view to a social end; never for reasons of an ethical nature. The interests of morals and law follow different paths, as Radbruch has well stated. The former is interested in the internal life of a person, and in his external acts only in so far as they reveal the goodness or badness of his intention; the latter is essentially interested in external acts, and incidentally in those of an intimate nature, but only in so far as they are important to the community. The jurist is above all concerned with the objective aspect of conduct; the moralist is primarily interested in its subjective aspect. The former takes into account the social significance of the subject's actions; the latter examines the purity of purpose and the righteousness of will. Or, stated in other terms: law refers to the realization of social values, whereas morals pursues the realization of individual values. Modern philosophy calls the latter *values of personality* (*Persönlichkeitswerte*), and the former *transpersonal values.* Radbruch divides the transpersonal into work values (*Werkwerte*) and community values (*Gemeinschaftswerte*).

The distinction between values of personality and transpersonal values is not absolute, however, since every individual value is indirectly a *good* for the group, and every social value a *good* for the individual. But, whereas law's desideratum is the realization of transpersonal values, the supreme finality of morals is the perfecting of individuals, that is, the realization of the values of the person, considered as an ideal ethical entity. When the state establishes universities and other centers of education and culture, it undoubtedly promotes the vocations and aptitudes of the citizens, and indirectly contributes to the realization of the values of personality; but the fundamental objective which is in prospect in such cases is the common good, the general interest. Every human action has its motives and consequences, which may bear upon either the actor or other persons. The jurist is fundamentally interested in the consequences of conduct and, more specially, in its social consequences; the moralist is above all concerned with motives.[27]

From the foregoing considerations it follows that the thesis that the end of law is the realization of moral values (or of certain moral values) is false, because, first, the imperatives of morals and law may be mutually exclusive, and second, the values to be realized by law are not those of personality but those which are transpersonal.

Doctrine whereby the desideratum of the law is the realization of justice. Generally it is asserted that the supreme end of law is the realization of justice. According to this conception, the intrinsic validity of a juridical law depends upon its concordance with the demands of absolute justice. Every norm, which postulates the realization of the value of the just, will consequently be valid; and the same criterion must be employed in deciding upon the validity of positive law.

The thesis thus stated rests upon the following principles:

I. Justice is an absolute value, and is independent of individual valuation.

II. The written law is the work of man; consequently it never corresponds in a wholly satisfactory manner to the demands of justice.

III. The incompatibilities between *what is just per se* and *what is legally just* result from the narrowness or limitation of the value-conscience of the authors of the law.

[27] "Reviewing whatever has been written in the modern age on that question (that values are called upon to realize law and the state), we can discuss two chief trends under which it is possible to classify, in broad terms, the several doctrines. Either the starting point is the belief that the supreme values are values belonging to the individual, and that all others are nothing more than means toward the realization of ethical personality, or it is admitted that besides the values belonging to the individual there is an independent value, typically a social value, the realization of which is achieved by means of the juridical order. In the first instance, law is conceived as an external regulation of human conduct, the end of which is to make possible the realization of ethical values appertaining to personality. In the second type of doctrine, the common life is deemed to possess a special dignity of its own, of an independent character which finds no *raison d'être* in a derivative process starting from individual ethical values; it is admitted that in the sphere of absolute values there is one which is autonomous and independent, which constitutes the polar star of social reality, and the latter is conceived as an entity independent of the individuals. The first of these conceptions, which may be called personalistic, has achieved its most acute expression in Kantian philosophy and the schools which have sprung from it. The most radical form of the second has been stated by Hegelianism." RECASÉNS SICHES, LA FILOSOFÍA DEL DERECHO DE FRANCISCO SUÁREZ (1927), pp. 60 and 61.

Let us examine these three principles in order:

I. Justice is an objective value because it exists in itself and by itself, independently of the subjective considerations of men. Men may establish among themselves relations which may be just or unjust; but their justice or injustice does not depend upon human valuation. Individuals create simply the substance which supports value, not the valuable quality.

The just is an absolute value, because it is identical with itself everywhere and at all times. Experience, in revealing to us the great diversity of juridical conceptions among different peoples at different times, seems to contradict this. What according to one system is just and good is elsewhere an iniquity; and the dominating concept of justice in one period of history appears later to be modified or destroyed by a different concept. But these various conceptions of the just, which follow and fight one another through the years and in different places, are not justice but the contingent appreciations of it by individuals and peoples. Doctrines and opinions change in aspect, like the mythological figure of Proteus; but the value of justice remains immutable, because it is independent of those doctrines and of any valuation. And, precisely as the infinite series of human errors does not destroy the existence and dignity of truth, so the aberrations of legislators and judges are not valid as testimony against the existence of the just.

Justice is always the same, even though the factual conditions in which this value may be realized are different. This is possible because the just is a relation, and like all relations may be identical with itself even though its terms may vary to infinity. Two equal objects may be three times larger than other objects, but the latter, though three times smaller than the former, may still be equal among themselves. The terms of the two relations are different, but the relation of equality does not change. What is asserted of equality must also be asserted of justice. This is a special form of relation, and this relation is always the same, even though its terms may change.

Several philosophers have tried to express by means of formulae the essence of the just. The most famous definitions and formulae are those of Aristotle, who distinguishes three classes of justice: legal justice (or justice in the broad sense), and its two special forms, the distributive and the commutative.[28]

Distributive justice of honors and fortune is subjected to the following principle: Give unto each what his merit deserves. It follows hence

[28] " 'The just' therefore means that which is lawful and that which is equal or fair, and 'the unjust' means that which is illegal and that which is unequal or unfair." Nicomachean Ethics, Book V. i. 8 (Loeb translation).

that equals must be treated equally, and unequals in an unequal manner, in proportion to their inequality. He who is worth more should receive more than the one who is worth less, and *vice versa*.[29]

Commutative justice, which regulates private relations (and repressive justice, which serves the legislator as a norm for the establishment of penalties corresponding to crimes), is subject to another principle. This is the principle of *equality of treatment* even in cases where the persons are different.[30]

Justice may be considered in its subjective aspect (as virtue) and in its objective aspect (as a social value). The former is always, as Aristotle said, "relative to a third person." More than a good for the one who practices it, it is a good for others, because it is practiced in relation to them.

The foregoing formulae do not exhaust the essence of the just. They are simple formulae, abstract principles to which reality never absolutely corresponds. Each case is different, and the two most similar cases imaginable differ between themselves as the two most alike leaves of the same tree. Written laws are also abstractions, general statements incapable of foreseeing every situation which might arise in practice. The norm and life do not always coincide, and what is legally just sometimes varies from what is absolutely just. A new case does not fit squarely into

[29] (1) "Now since an unjust man is one who is unfair, and the unjust is the unequal, it is clear that corresponding to the unequal there is a mean, namely that which is equal; for every action admitting of more and less admits of the equal also. If then the unjust is the unequal, the just is the equal—a view that commends itself to all without proof; and since the equal is a mean, the just will be a sort of mean too. Again, equality involves two terms at least. It accordingly follows not only (a) that the just is a mean and equal [and relative to something and just for certain persons], but also (b) that, as a mean, it implies certain extremes between which it lies, namely the more and the less; (c) that, as equal, it implies two shares that are equal; and (d) that, as just, it implies certain persons for whom it is just. It follows therefore that justice involves at least four terms, namely, two persons for whom it is just and two shares which are just. And there will be the same equality between the shares as between the persons, since the ratio between the shares will be equal to the ratio between the persons; for if the persons are not equal, they will not have equal shares; . . ." NICOMACHEAN ETHICS, V. iii. 1–6.

(2) "All are agreed that justice in distributions must be based on desert of some sort, although they do not all mean the same sort of desert; democrats make the criterion free birth; those of oligarchical sympathies wealth, or in other cases birth; upholders of aristocracy make it virtue." NICOMACHEAN ETHICS, V. iii. 7.

(3) "Justice is therefore a sort of proportion; for proportion is not a property of numerical quantity only, but of quantity in general, proportion being equality of ratios, and involving four terms at least." NICOMACHEAN ETHICS, V. iii. 8.

[30] "But the just in private transactions, although it is the equal in a sense (and the unjust the unequal), is not the equal according to geometrical but according to arithmetical proportion." NICOMACHEAN ETHICS, V. iv. 3.

the old mold, and if the judge does not want to be unjust in applying the law strictly, he must resort to equity and seek in its principles an adequate corrective.[31]

II. All positive law represents an attempt, happy or unhappy, to realize justice. The goal of the legislator consists in the establishment of a just juridical order, and as a general rule this ideal really determines the behavior of those who are called to exercise the legislative function. But since legislators are not and never have been infallible, laws sometimes lack intrinsic validity and occasionally turn out to be bad or unjust. Thus is born the conflict between the legally just and the absolute just, a conflict which we mentioned in the second chapter of this work.

III. The discrepancy between ideal law and legislation is explained in most cases in terms of the narrowness or limitation of the value-conscience of the legislators. The general thesis of the limitation of the apprehension of the valuable, maintained by Hartmann, must be applied to knowledge of juridical values. Besides this general limitation, Hartmann speaks of the *"narrowness of the sense of justice."* This phenomenon explains the multiple judgments, many of them contradictory, which are usually made about the essence of the just. And that limitation gives origin, as we have said before, to the incompatibilities and discrepancies which so frequently arise between the demands of legality and the dictates of justice.

[31] "Justice and equity are therefore the same thing, and both are good, though equity is better.

"The source of the difficulty is that equity, though just, is not legal justice, but a rectification of legal justice. The reason for this is that law is always a general statement, yet there are cases which it is not possible to cover in a general statement. In matters therefore where, while it is necessary to speak in general terms, it is not possible to do so correctly, the law takes into consideration the majority of cases, although it is not unaware of the error this involves. And this does not make it a wrong law; for the error is not in the law nor in the lawgiver, but in the nature of the case: the material of conduct is essentially irregular. When therefore the law lays down a general rule, and thereafter a case arises which is an exception to the rule, it is then right, where the lawgiver's pronouncement because of its absoluteness is defective and erroneous, to rectify the defect by deciding as the lawgiver would himself decide if he were present on the occasion, and would have enacted if he had been cognizant of the case in question. Hence, while the equitable is just, and is superior to one sort of justice, it is not superior to absolute justice, but only to the error due to its absolute statement. This is the essential nature of the equitable: it is a rectification of law where law is defective because of its generality. In fact this is the reason why things are not all determined by law: it is because there are some cases for which it is impossible to lay down a law, so that a special ordinance becomes necessary. For what is itself indefinite can only be measured by an indefinite standard, like the leaden rule used by Lesbian builders; just as that rule is not rigid but can be bent to the shape of the stone, so a special ordinance is made to fit the circumstances of the case." NICOMACHEAN ETHICS, V. x. 2–7.

These discrepancies result from other causes, such as, for example, the generality of norms, which makes impossible a perfect adaptation to all cases and a provision for all situations; or the evil nature of certain legislators, who legislate to their own advantage or in favor of the few, in grave prejudice to the interests of the majority.

Doctrine that the supreme finality of law is the realization of the juridical value of security and order. In studying, in the first chapter of this essay, the formal-juridical problem of the validity of law, we arrived at the conclusion that a law is valid when it has been promulgated in accordance with the applicable provisions of the supreme norm. But upon analysis of the philosophical problem we were able to perceive that norms which are *formally* valid are sometimes unjust and therefore lack intrinsic value. Thus was defined the conflict between legality and absolute justice, to which we have so often made reference in the course of this work.

The possibility of this conflict authorizes the investigator to distinguish, in every juridical norm and in any system of law, two different values: a *value of form* and a *value of substance.* Both may coincide in a law, but it is also possible that there is no valuable content in the legal form, or that such form may contain an unjust substance.

The fault or lack of intrinsic value in a precept, and the immorality of its content, usually provoke serious conflicts. Such conflicts arise at the moment of application or on the occasion of compliance. The judge, required to apply a law which he considers unjust, is at once faced with the following dilemma: either the fulfillment of his professional duty and the causing of injustice; or the observance of a moral duty and the consequent violation of the law. Which position must be taken in the face of this clash of duties? The defenders of the theory of juridical security do not vacillate in holding that, in such a case, the good judge must shut his ears to the demands of conscience and apply the positive law even though it may be reprehensible and bad.[32] Furthermore, say the partisans of that doctrine, the judges have undertaken, under oath or affirmation, to exercise their mission and to decide controversies in accordance with the precepts of the prevailing law. The juridical duty of applying a given norm is thus reinforced by a moral duty derived from the oath of office.

[32] "It is precisely with respect to this right, unpleasant because of its perniciousness or inhumanity, that the highest virtue of the jurist is demonstrated; the capacity of abstracting his reason from every influence, even that of the deepest personal convictions and most fervent desires of the heart, expecting the satisfaction of the same only through the transformation of law." BERGBOHM, JURISPRUDENZ UND RECHTSPHILOSOPHIE 407.

The same incompatibility of duties arises with private persons when the time comes to comply with a provision which is contrary to ethical demands. On the hypothesis of juridical security, the individual must obey the commandments of the state, even at the cost of his most profound and deeply rooted convictions.

The judge as well as the lawyer, or the simple addressee of a legal precept, has capacity to estimate critically its intrinsic goodness; and in his position as a free being has the power to comply with it, or to violate it if it is opposed to his personal convictions or private interests. In relation to this conflict between [legal] imperatives and [moral] principles, the defenders of the thesis of juridical security categorically affirm the necessity of sacrificing private moral interest at the altar of the collective interest represented by legislation. The foundations of this assertion cannot be other than the profound conviction that the *juridical order is valid per se, as order, independently of the goodness or badness of its content.* And not only is it valid but, in case of conflict, it must be given precedence over any demand of the individual conscience.

The thesis above sketched was brilliantly defended by Plato, and at present has very numerous and illustrious partisans.[33]

One of the modern jurists, who with the greatest ardor and enthusiasm has upheld the superiority of formal value over value of substance, is Bergbohm, who, in his book *Jurisprudenz und Rechtsphilosophie,* poses the following problem: Which law must the judge apply, and what must be his position in cases where the law contradicts his personal convictions? The first part of the question he resolves by saying that the applicable law is the one which exists in reality, that is, which effectively regulates the life of the community. And as to the second part of the inquiry, he holds that the judge is obliged to obey unconditionally the provisions of positive law. If it should be admitted that anyone may reject the precepts of this law which he considers unjust — argues Bergbohm — the juridical order would lose all its force, because then everybody would believe himself authorized to modify or correct it; which in the end would produce complete anarchy.

The ideas of Bergbohm rest upon a value judgment, namely, the con-

[33] In one of his most beautiful dialogues, Plato depicts Socrates, the beloved master, as he awaits in prison the hour of his death. A rich and generous friend arrives at the jail, and announces that the jailer will be bribed, and that the prison must be abandoned that very night. "What would we do, Crito," argues Socrates, "if at the moment of flight, the laws of Athens, like outraged queens, should appear before us and say: 'Socrates, what are you doing? The act you are about to commit, does it not tend to disturb us and the entire state, in so far as it depends upon you? For, what state can subsist if the judgments rendered have no force and are evaded by private persons?' "

viction that *order is the fundamental juridical value.* According to this conception, social order requires that positive law be fully complied with; and the judge who is charged with its enforcement has no reason to examine the intrinsic value of each isolated precept.

Those called to judge must take this position, because the intrinsic justice of the laws does not constitute the essential and particular value of law. Law is valid *per se,* in so far as it is effective; it produces order and engenders security in social relations.

The problem we have posed, which Bergbohm resolves in the manner indicated, has no meaning, according to Kelsen, as a juridical question. The inquiry, why must a precept of law be complied with and enforced, does not state a juridical problem, but an ethical one. The foundation of the validity of the laws is the supreme norm; and the latter is not derived from any superior juridical precept. Hence the question formulated above may be answered only in terms of a meta-juridical principle, and therefore belongs to morals. The moralist may inquire whether or not a law is intrinsically just, but the law-man should not pose that problem to himself. He must always start from an indisputable assumption, from a dogmatic truth: the normative character of the juridical precept. The jurist may consider that a law does not coincide with the requirements of his morals, and nevertheless judge that the law must be followed and enforced; any other attitude on his part "would be the same as cutting off the limb on which he is perched."[34] The appeal to a superior moral order would mean renouncing an independent juridical order and denying an autonomous juridical science.

Another defender of the doctrine of juridical security is Radbruch, according to whom law has a proximate and a remote end. The latter is the realization of the value of justice; the former is the securing of peace and order. Both values, security and justice, are often mutually exclusive, which gives rise to the difficult problem of preference. In case of a conflict, which of the two values should be preferred?

Radbruch concludes that juridical security should have precedence over justice. The arguments which lead him to this result, and which have great weight and merit attentive consideration, are as follows: If men could know without doubt the essence of the just, any law which embodied an injustice could be regarded as a simple theoretical state-

[34] "The jurist must not question the material foundation of the validity of the juridical order; his inquiry may have only a *formal* character; he must not investigate the foundation, *why?*, but only *how?*. 'What principles,' he asks, 'shall be applied as juridical principles by the organs of the state and obeyed as such by the subjects? How may those principles be recognized? What is their logical form?' " HAUPTPROBLEME DER STAATSLEHRE (1911) 353.

ment devoid of any obligatory character. But experience shows that human beings, far from knowing intuitively, with the desired clarity, what the essence of justice is, hold multiple and quite contradictory opinions about it. Science does not tell us which are the values that law is called upon to realize; will and power must, therefore, pronounce the decisive word, in order to prevent anarchy. Practical reason indicates that peace must reign in society, that order must exist within it. But this could never be achieved if individuals would recognize no norm of action but their own personal opinions. It is indispensable that an authority prescribe what is law, since individuals and science are incapable of settling absolutely what is just and what is unjust. If we systematize individual subjective valuations in order to rise to an objective point of view we shall find that there are two dominating positions: personalism and transpersonalism. According to the first conception, the individual is the supreme value, and law must be limited to protecting the integral development of personal values. For transpersonalism, on the other hand, the community is the highest value. Law should not be simply the limitation of the liberty of each in order to achieve the liberty of all (as Kant would have it); its role must be positive: to promote the perfecting of collective life and to favor the realization of cultural values.

Radbruch believes that the two positions are theoretically undemonstrable, and that it is permissible, therefore, to postulate either of them. The important thing is that the one as well as the other recognizes the necessity for the existence of law. For each position, law is a means; and, as a means to valuable ends, it is also valid and is preferable in every case to anarchy. Radbruch starts from relativist premises but reaches an absolute conclusion: Law is valuable, independently of its content, by the sole fact of existence.

A corollary of this doctrine is the denial of the *right to resist* arbitrary laws, and the degradation of the citizen to the category of an unconditional subject, who is denied the right to criticize and the power to learn intuitively the essence of the just. The thesis of Radbruch, which interpreted in moderation appears very exact, may lead to dangerous extremes if carried to its ultimate conclusion. In effect, dictatorship and despotism may find in it their absolute justification. The grave error of Radbruch consists in forgetting that the first requisite for the establishment, and particularly for the consolidation, of any order is precisely its justice. We cannot pretend to place in issue the fact that in certain cases the requirements of juridical security are opposed to those of ideal law; such a phenomenon is undeniable. But it is also beyond doubt that the opposition is relative, and that it may be granted only in isolated cases; never in the majority of situations. An order is more nearly perfect the more just it is. Without justice there is no order, and the principal cause of every disorder is precisely injustice. The most important revolutions recorded by history had as their principal motive the hope of substituting, for a reprehensible regime, a better one. It may be objected that in many cases the process is blind, and that individuals and peoples are the victims of their own illusions and hopes; that they revel in conquering ghosts, and that they consider as indisputable values their subjective appreciations and their personal interests. This is the eternal objection of relativism, which modern philosophy has combated with so much energy and so brilliant a chain of argument. Science is perhaps incapable of proving conclusively the existence of those values; but value-conscience, despite its limitations, tells us that they exist; and instead of submerging us into the sorrowful skepticism of those spirits who expect everything from reason, it fills us with hope and enthusiasm; and in discovering the immovable ideal, it defines for us the sense of life and points out the lighthouse which should guide our steps in the world.

Radbruch's entire argument is based on the study of the phenomenon which we have called, paraphrasing Hartmann's expression, "the narrowness of the sense of justice." Radbruch's error consists in denying to this sense of the just the power of conveniently perceiving by intuition the value under consideration. Limitation of the apprehension of the valuable does not mean value blindness. Without any doubt, there are many men who completely lack such apprehension, and are in consequence blind to values. But this is not the rule; it is an exception.

It is possible that order may reign in an unjustly organized society; power may perhaps impose it momentarily; but the apparent peace, founded on fear, and order imposed by force, will have a very brief life. The conflict between justice and juridical security is granted always within certain limits, each very close to the other. When an arbitrary power attempts to cross them, and to create a state of security on the foundations of a wholly unjust system of law, security disappears, the bad law is violated, resistance is organized, culminating, in extreme cases, in revolution and the consequent violent rupture of an untenable situation. What is affirmed with respect to every juridical system may be asserted in relation to any isolated norm. Authority is capable of actively enforcing an unjust law; but if the injustice of the precept goes beyond certain limits, its addressees resist compliance with it, and violate it systematically.

The right of a people to revolution and the subject's power to resist arbitrary laws cannot be recognized by juridical science; but they are justified in certain cases as requirements of ethics.

The rights of resistance and revolution have been categorically asserted by numerous writers, and on certain occasions have obtained a kind of consecration in the very sanctuary of positive law, as if they were authentic rights. The *Declaration des Droits de l'homme et du citoyen* of the French Constitution of 1783 contains, for example, an article on the individual's right of resistance, and another on the people's right in insurrection.[35]

Another example is offered by the English Magna Carta of 1215, in Article 61. This provision instituted a Committee of Resistance, composed of twenty-five barons, who had the right to intervene against the monarch in case of a juridical violation, but always protecting his person and family.[36]

In the thought of the Church fathers, and in scholastic philosophy, we

[35] Art. 11: "Every action taken against a man except in the cases and with the formalities determined by the law is arbitrary and tyrannical; he against whom it might be attempted with violence has the right to repel it by force." Art. 35: "When the government violates the right of the people, insurrection is, for each of its parts and for the people as a whole, the most sacred of rights and the most indispensable of duties."

The works most worthy of recommendation, with respect to the doctrine of the right of resistance, are: WOLZENDORFF, STAATSRECHT UND NATURRECHT IN DER LEHRE VOM WIDERSTANDRECHT DES VOLKES GEGEN RECHTSWIDRIGE AUSÜBUNG DER STAATSGEWALT (1916); MURHARD, UEBER WIDERSTAND, EMPÖRUNG UND ZWANGSÜBUNG DER STAATSBÜRGER GEGEN DIE BESTEHENDE STAATSGEWALT IN SITTLICHER UND RECHTLICHER BEZIEHUNG; HERRFAHRDT, REVOLUCIÓN Y CIENCIA DEL DERECHO (Spanish translation by Antonio Polo, Madrid, 1932).

[36] 61. "And whereas, for the honour of God and the amendment of our kingdom, and for the better quieting the discord that has arisen between us and our barons, we have granted all these things aforesaid: willing to render them firm and lasting, we do give and grant our subjects the underwritten security, namely, that the barons may choose five-and-twenty barons of the kingdom, whom they think worthy; who shall take care, with all their might, to hold and observe, and cause to be observed, the peace and liberties we have granted them, and by this our present charter confirmed; so that if we, our justiciar, our bailiffs, or any of our officers, shall in any circumstance fail in the performance of them, towards any person, or shall break through any of these articles of peace and security, and the offence be notified to four barons chosen out of the five-and-twenty before mentioned, the said four barons shall repair to us, or our justiciar, if we are out of the realm, and, laying open the grievance, shall petition to have it redressed without delay: and if it be not redressed by us, or if we should chance to be out of the realm, if it should not be redressed by our justiciar, within forty days, reckoning from the time it has been notified to us, or to our justiciar (if we should be out of the realm), the four barons aforesaid shall lay the cause before the rest of the five-and-twenty barons; and the said five-and-twenty barons, together with the community of the whole kingdom, shall distrain and distress us in all possible ways, by seizing our castles, lands, possessions, and in any other manner they can, till the grievance is redressed according to their pleasure; saving harmless our own person, and the persons of our queen and children; and when it is redressed, they shall obey us as before." (Magna Carta.)

find many doctrines concerning the right of resistance. The same may be said of Spanish juridical philosophy.[37] The right of revolution appears to be explicitly embodied in the writings of Origen. He strongly asserts the legitimacy of resistance to an unjust precept and the propriety of overthrowing a tyrant. Other authors have gone even further, and some, like St. Thomas, declared justifiable the assassination of a despot. "Whoever kills the tyrant in order to liberate the fatherland is praised and rewarded."

In modern times also, the people's right of revolution has been upheld. Emge speaks of the *ethical right of revolution*,[38] and Sauer, in his *Grundlagen der Gesellschaft*, holds that in certain cases the violent upsetting of an unjust and decrepit regime cannot even be considered a violation of law, since "the old law is no longer law."

Resistance to unjust laws and revolutionary movements should never be recognized as legal powers, for it would be senseless, speaking juridically, to assert an alleged *right to violate the law.* Juridical philosophy, on the other hand, can and should recognize resistance and revolution, not as powers granted by the legislator, but as prerogatives founded upon the demands of justice.

In reality, it is impossible to decide, by means of simple formulae, in which cases it is proper to exercise the right of resistance and in which cases a revolution may be justified. Each situation is unique, and the sole criterion offered by value philosophy is the very vague one stated elsewhere in this work: When two values are mutually exclusive, the higher one must be preferred. Selection implies a judgment of preference, and this is possible and valid when the hierarchy of conflicting values is known.

We have already expounded the opinion of certain authors that the formal value of law should be given precedence over its value of substance, but the considerations outlined later showed us the falsity of the doctrine. This doctrine is valid only in cases where the breach between legal form and the requirements of the just is not very deep, but it lacks force otherwise. The supreme finality of the legislator must be the realization of justice; if he achieves it, however imperfectly, he will have accomplished also the consolidation of order and the cementing of peace,

[37] The reader should consult the famous work of Father Juan de Mariana, *Del Rey y de la Institución Real* (1598, translated from the Latin by Barriobero); and the study of Treumann on the king-makers, *Die Monarchomachen* (1903).

[38] ARCHIV FÜR RECHTS UND WIRTSCHAFTPHILOSOPHIE, XIV, 159. To the same effect, 1 JHERING: DER ZWECK IM RECHT (Law as a Means to an End) (2d ed. 1884) 251ff.

since order and peace are but the crowning glory of justice and its best fruits.

Positivity should not be considered an absolute value, nor an end in itself. Positive law is only a means, and consequently may be justified only if it serves valuable ends.

Doctrine that the end of the law is the realization of the common good. Here we are dealing with a doctrine, numerous forms of which ascribe to the law, as its highest finality, the achievement of social welfare—the only point on which they agree; otherwise they present multiple divergences and infinite shadings.

The doctrine whereby law must set for itself the realization of the common good is broader and less precise than the doctrines previously examined and, in a certain sense, embraces them. This fact is readily explainable, inasmuch as justice as well as order are indispensable elements in collective welfare. Thus, for example, St. Thomas considers the common good as a finality to the realization of which peace and justice are means; and in this way he writes a prelude, as Professor Recaséns correctly states, to the modern distinction between the value of justice and the value of security, or between the intrinsic value and the formal value of law.[39]

Very interesting is the thesis of Aquinas; however, we cannot pause to examine it in detail; first, for lack of space, and second, because our study is not historical but systematic. Briefly, St. Thomas distinguishes between the *formal cause* and the *final cause* of the state; the former consists in authority, the latter in the common good. The achievement of the common good must be the desideratum of every member of the community and particularly the objective of those who govern. The common and the individual interests sometimes are opposed; but in case of conflict the general good must have precedence over the private good. This preference does not mean, however, the annihilation of the individual before the public authority. Private persons have certain rights which authority may not attack or destroy. In every case, the state must respect the moral dignity of the individual, and must never look upon him simply as a means.

The common good does not represent a simple sum of all private interests; neither does it consist in the greatest good of the greatest number, but it possesses, in the Thomistic philosophy, a special dignity, and a character in some way independent. The common good is a specific

[39] Recaséns Siches: La Filosofía del Derecho de Francisco Suárez, con un estudio previo sobre sus antecedentes en la patrística y en la escolástica, chap. VII, pp. 54ff.

good of the state, not of the sum of individuals. But the interests of individuals and those of the state are not mutually exclusive; private persons find in the assurance of welfare by means of peace and justice the best guarantee of their own happiness.

As to the modern doctrines concerning this point, we have already said that they may be classified in two large groups, one of personalist theories, the other of transpersonalist theories; that the former see in the individual the supreme value, and in law a simple means for his protection and the guarantee of his liberty; and that the latter consider cultural values as the highest, and set for the law a much broader function, not simply negative or of limitation, but a positive function, the realization of values.

We have said also that the distinction between values of personality and values of the community is not between opposites, since the values of personality represent indirectly a good for the group and the values of the community a good for the individual.

Law should be oriented principally toward the achievement of cultural values, while morals is concerned with the individual's perfection. In this way, morals and law fulfill their destiny, realizing, at the same time, in different directions, a common task.

The interests of the community coincide, in the final analysis, with those of the individual. If often they seem to be opposed, and even mutually exclusive, such opposition is apparent only, or is derived from a false appreciation of the values in conflict: we speak of incompatibilities existing between the general interest and private interest, and we do not stop to consider the true nature of the clashing interests; we employ those formulae antithetically, and try to hide behind them the mean interests of individuals or of classes. Proceeding in this fashion we forget that *individual* and *society* are but abstractions; that individuals can exist only in the community, and that the community without them would be nothing.

Once more, the thesis of the limitation of valuc-conscience finds in this fact its palpable demonstration; and, in making us meditate upon the true causes of the quarrels and dissensions of men, strengthens again our faith in the existence of absolute values, at the same time pointing out to us that the source of all relativism is within us, and not in values.

V

LIBERTY AS RIGHT AND AS POWER

BY EDUARDO GARCÍA MÁYNEZ

Professor of Philosophy of Law, National University of Mexico

TRANSLATED BY

Jorge Roberto Hayzus, Advocate, University of Buenos Aires; Bachelor of Laws, Yale University

FOREWORD

Invited by the Executive Committee of the Faculty of the National School of Jurisprudence, at the *Universidad Nacional Autónoma de México,* I delivered in the Pallares Auditorium of that school, on October 4th, 11th, 18th, and 25th, and on November 1st, 1939, several lectures on the subject of "Liberty, as right and as power. A positive definition and an essay on the philosophical justification of the right of liberty."

As the title indicates, these lectures were aimed at showing — as against the thesis of the Italian proceduralist, Ugo Rocco — that a positive definition of the right of liberty is not only possible, but necessary. I attempted to survey, besides, the problem of justifying philosophically the existence of juridical liberty, and reached the conclusion that it can only be solved in the light of the theory of values.

If every juridical authority is a function of each individual's duties, and liberty is a subjective right, it is impossible to separate it from the obligations of the individual. For that reason, the contradictory notion of natural freedom — which so many thinkers have sought to oppose to the concept of juridical liberty — is inadmissible. Liberty, as power, is merely an attribute of man's will, not a subjective right. To expect the validity of the legal order to stand upon discretional human will completely denies the essence of law. A system of rules cannot support itself on the acceptance of those to whom it is addressed, because the duties it imposes have meaning only if they exist independently of their recognition.

The breadth and importance of the subjects connected with the main theme of these lectures compelled me, of course, to set down without prior criticism or demonstration a series of assumptions, which I have partly examined in other writings, and which I also hope to develop later on. Especially where the problem of the philosophical justification of the right of liberty is concerned, I want to point out that when I refer to a theory of values, I have in mind only the doctrines of Max Scheler and Nikolai Hartmann, as expounded in their respective works: *Formalism in Ethics and the Material Ethics of Values* (1913) and *Ethics* (1925). My monograph *El problema de la validez del Derecho* endeavors to show how these theories can be applied to the main issues of legal philosophy.

LIBERTY AS RIGHT AND AS POWER

CHAPTER I

POSITIVE AND NEGATIVE DEFINITIONS OF THE RIGHT OF LIBERTY

PRINCIPAL MEANINGS OF THE WORD "LIBERTY"

THERE are probably few words in the vocabulary of science, philosophy, and even the everyday language as equivocal as the term *liberty*. It could be compared to those instruments devised by man for a special purpose which are then used, with more or less success, to reach other ends. A letter opener, for instance, could be used as a weapon; a lectern, as a trestle. Similarly, expressions which at first had a clearly defined meaning, in time acquire different ones, until a day comes when the original sense is no longer known. With them, says Jellinek, it happens as with certain old coins: they go through so many hands that they wear off and in the end it is difficult to tell whether they are still legal tender.

The concept we referred to is so flexible, has so many shadings, that it has been applied not only to the human being and its conduct but also to animals and inanimate objects, sometimes in a physical sense, at other times to express moral or juridical ideas.

In everyday conversation, liberty is understood as the absence of restraints upon the possible motions of a person, an animal, or an object. We say of the prisoner locked in his cell that he is not free, and in the same way we state that the gas emanating from a test tube in the course of a chemical reaction, or a bird escaping from its cage, becomes free.

Here the connotation is purely mechanical. It refers to a simple possibility of motion, before which there are no obstacles capable of destroying or limiting it. For this reason, the English writer Hobbes says that the man who is prevented from moving (a paralytic, for instance) or the stone that lies on the road, could not be properly thought of as deprived of liberty.[1]

The term is also used to indicate a lack of occupation, or the extinction of a pain, as when we speak of the free existence of the vagabond, or we say that someone has been liberated of a great pain.

[1] THOMAS HOBBES, LEVIATHAN (Everyman's Library, 1937) 110.

In the everyday language the term has also a moral connotation, and in that sense it applies to persons who follow a scandalous conduct or lead a life at odds with the exigencies of decorum. The word is then synonymous with license or indecence.

The meanings of this protean expression are no less numerous in legal and philosophic terminology. A distinction is of course advisable between liberty as an *attribute of man's will,* and liberty as *right.* The former is generally conceived as a *power* or natural faculty of self-determination. It could be defined as the ability to act on one's own volition, without submitting to any force or determining motive. It is, as Kant would say, a causativeness whose first moment is itself cause, and not the effect of another cause.

We cannot enter here into a discussion of the difficult problem of free will, nor even mention the many ways in which it has been approached through the ages. We merely wish to distinguish freedom of the will, as a fact, from juridical liberty, which is the faculty derived from a norm. We realize that the term "faculty" itself is ambiguous; it is generally employed to designate various aptitudes and natural predispositions, that have nothing to do with the right of liberty. We praise, for instance, the extraordinary faculties of a virtuoso of the violin, and in an even broader sense we speak of the faculties of the soul. In those contexts, the term means the same as aptitude or attribute.

Juridical liberty is not *power,* nor a *capability* drawn from nature, but *right.* We could say, quite justly, *authorization.* To be authorized means to have the right of doing or omitting certain acts. The Germans express this idea with the verb *dürfen,* which has no equivalent in Spanish.

It is often stated that, from a juridical point of view, one is free to do or not to do what is not forbidden. As we shall attempt to show later, this is not correct. There are many actions not barred by the law which nevertheless do not belong to the realm of liberty. We are referring to the acts prescribed by law, those which come under a juridical duty. Where they are concerned, there is no such liberty. Anyone who is obliged to follow a predetermined course of conduct is not able (normatively speaking) to depart from it, even when, in fact, he fails in his duty. Violation of the norm is then a manifestation of free will, but does not amount to the exercise of juridical liberty.

At various times many authors have presumed to counter juridical liberty with a certain natural freedom, untouched by any regulation, whose limits would extend as far as the power of each individual. Using the term in this sense, Spinoza says that in the state of nature the right of everyone reaches as far as his power remains effective. This concept has played an important part in the history of legal philosophic doctrines, and especially in the evolution of political theory. In opposition to a normatively limited juridical liberty, it postulates the ***absolute freedom of nature***. In this manner, the former is made to appear as a distortion of true liberty; law becomes a shackle and the state an evil. It is not strange, therefore, that the anarchists should be the most energetic defenders of that so-called absolute freedom.

This notion has also been put to use by the supporters of the social compact doctrine, who, under color of explaining the origin of the political community, attempt to refer the validity of a juridical order to the individual will. They see in the law the outcome of a pact to which each one agrees in the exercise of his self-determination. From this it follows that the contractualist doctrine and the ***theory of recognition*** appear on the same level and pursue identical ends.

Traditional Definition of Juridical Liberty

Liberty is usually defined in legal theory as the authority to do or omit that which is not commanded or forbidden.

Prescribed acts (1)

(3) Permissible acts

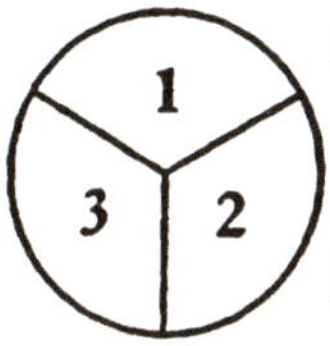

Forbidden acts. (2)

This definition stems from a classification of the possible behavior of a given subject, in relation to the rules of law ("objective law"). Such behavior necessarily falls into one of these three categories: prescribed, forbidden, permitted. (See illustration.) The first sector covers the positive duties of a person (obligations which consist in doing or giving); the second, its negative duties (obligation to abstain or not do); the third, its privileges. According to the traditional theory, juridical liberty manifests itself in the performance or withholding of those acts which are neither prescribed nor prohibited.

The aphorism "What is not forbidden is permitted," points out instead that it is lawful to perform the actions included in sectors "1" and "3." For there is not only the normative possibility of doing what objective law neither commands nor forbids, but also that of effecting what it ordains. Between the acts within these two sectors there exists, however, a difference. To fulfill a duty is just as lawful as to perform an act not commanded or prohibited; but while the right to satisfy an obligation merely authorizes the obligee to do what is required of him, those acts figuratively presented in the third sector may not only be performed, but also omitted. To make that clear, there should be drawn a distinction between the broad and strict senses of the term "permissible." In the first sense, it is permissible (a) to perform obligatory acts; (b) to abstain from prohibited conduct; (c) to carry out or omit that behavior which does not belong to any of the preceding groups. The concept here merges with that of lawfulness. In a strict sense, that which is permissible covers the performance or nonperformance of any acts which objective law neither prohibits nor requires. We may therefore speak of the *lawful-compulsory* (privilege of doing one's own duty), and the *lawful-optional* (right of following or departing from all behavior not included in sectors "1" and "2"). That right is juridical freedom.

Positive Definition of the Right of Freedom

In his book *L'Autorità della cosa giudicata e I suoi limiti soggetivi*, Ugo Rocco states that liberty can only be defined negatively.[2] This position is incorrect. The right of liberty can and must be defined in a positive way, for otherwise, though its limits be indicated, its essence is not. That the authors who have approached the subject should have determined the area of freedom by exclusion, results from the erroneous belief that the said right is one among several on the same level, within the general classification of subjective rights.[3] For instance, Georg Jellinek, referring to the status of persons, says that it comprises three types of legal faculties: (a) rights of liberty; (b) rights which confer the ability to claim State intervention in favor of individual interests; (c) political rights.[4]

What proves that juridical liberty does not stand for an independent group of privileges — within the range of subjective rights — is the fact that it manifests itself in the exercise of all other rights, whichever they may be. He who has a right of judicial action, or a creditorial right, is also authorized to exercise or not to exercise it. No one can legally demand (or prevent) that he exercise it. He is free in regard to the operation thereof. And this liberty is not to be confused with his rights as a plaintiff or a creditor, even though it manifest itself in the exercise or nonexercise of the same. The analysis of this simple example reveals

[2] Ugo Rocco, L'Autorità della cosa giudicata e i suoi limiti soggetivi 346n.

[3] An amplification of the author's views on the general classification of subjective rights may be found in 1 García Máynez, Introducción al Estudio del Derecho (Mexico, 1940) 247.

[4] 2 Jellinek, L'Etat Moderne et son Droit (Paris, 1913) 51.

the possibility of defining in a positive manner the right under consideration: juridical liberty is the authority which every subject has of exercising or not exercising (at his discretion) his subjective rights.

The foregoing definition is a positive one, and does not contain any reference to the breakdown of human actions into those ordained, forbidden, and permitted. It holds, further, that liberty does not concern itself directly with the rights of an individual, but with their use or nonuse. Because of this, we cannot consider liberty as one among several species of rights, or as a group of normative possibilities within a common gender. It is a categorial form of manifestation of any subjective right, be it absolute or relative, private or public.

CHAPTER II

LIBERTY AND SUBJECTIVE RIGHTS

Rights and Their Exercise

At this point [5] we may ask, what difference is there between a right and the exercise of the same? The elucidation of this question requires a small digression.

As regards their logical structure, the rules of law are hypothetical. This means that every juridical precept states one or several assumptions, and if any of them is effectively realized, diverse normative consequences follow. These in turn, may signify the creation, transmission, change or extinction of duties and rights. We may state, therefore, that legal duty and subjective right are the two logical categories within which juridical consequences are framed.

If we examine a given rule of law, in its structural as well as its operative aspects, we shall discover the following relations:

Between the hypothesis stated by the rule and the actual occurrence of the event it postulates, there is a contingent relation, because the event may or may not become a reality. But when the hypothetical fact does occur, the consequences provided for by the rule arise as of course. We can therefore say that between the happening of the assumption and the rise of the legal consequences there is a logically necessary

[5] Having been originally presented in the course of a lecture series, this material originally contained introductory remarks which served as a recapitulation of the main points made at the previous meeting. Wherever this occurred in the printed text of the lectures, the pertinent paragraphs have been omitted by the Editors, to avoid the repetitive effect of their content.

connection. (Juridical causativeness, in Fritz Schreier's terminology.) [6]

The rise of normative consequences does not compel their actual realization. It may happen, in effect, that the duties established by the rule are disregarded, or that the rights it confers remain unused. For this reason, the relation between the legal consequences and the realization of the same is contingent.

For example: Section 877 of the Civil Code for the Federal District and Territories of Mexico provides, in these or similar words, that he who discovers a treasure in the land of another, is entitled to one half, and must deliver the rest to the owner of the estate. The hypothesis contemplated by this provision, is that of a treasure being found by a person other than the owner of the land. That is a mere supposition, a contingency that may or may not occur. But let us imagine that an individual, "*X*," digs up on "*Z*'s" land a chest full of gold coins. This fact, the finding of the treasure, produces *ipso facto* various normative consequences. *X* has a right to half the treasure, and *Z* may claim from him the other half. By the same token, the discoverer is obliged to deliver one half of his find to the landowner, and the latter falls under a duty to recognize the former's right to the balance. But the actuality of those consequences, does not signify — unavoidably — the exercise of the proper subjective rights nor a submission to the correlative obligations. For that reason we said earlier that between the "rise" and the "effective realization" of legal consequences there is a contingent relation. For instance, the owner of the land where someone else has found a treasure, feeling liberally inclined to give up the share he is entitled to, may say to the finder, "Take it all, I give you my part, man lives not by bread alone." Or, on the contrary, the finder, without waiting for such selfless generosity, may prefer to conceal his good fortune.

This simple example illustrates most clearly the difference between a right and the exercise of a right. A right is simply a normative possibility, an authority to proceed in this or that direction; the exercise of a right is a factual occurrence, the coming into existence of what the norm allows. The right of liberty is founded upon some other right, and consists in the faculty of choosing between exercise or nonexercise of the latter.

Having thus outlined the concept of "exercise," we may now return to the question we formulated before, and ask ourselves whether the positive definition of the right of liberty really applies to all subjective rights. In the elucidation of this point, we shall refer to the several kinds

[6] FRITZ SCHREIER, GRUNDBEGRIFFE UND GRUNDFORMEN DES RECHTS. ENTWURF EINER PHÄNOMENOLOGISCH BEGRÜNDETEN FORMALEN RECHTS- UND STAATSLEHRE (Wien, 1924) 93.

of juridical powers, within the general classification commonly accepted by legal doctrine.

Liberty and the First-Degree Rights

Civil-law writers usually divide *private* subjective rights into two categories, real and personal, the latter also being called creditorial rights.

The right *in personam* confers upon one individual, called the creditor, the authority to exact from another, called the debtor, an act of behavior, a forbearance, or the delivery of a thing. Of this type, for instance, is the right of the buyer to have the goods turned over to himself, once he and the seller have agreed upon the object and the price therefor. The right *in personam* is a limited authority (paucital right), since it exists not as against all persons but only against the debtor, an individually determined person. The creditorial right, furthermore, is the basis of another juridical power which consists in choosing between the exercise or quiescence of the former right. If I have bought a hat I have the right to claim it from the seller, but at the same time I have legally the option of doing or not doing so. And this second right, founded upon the creditorial one, is no longer relatively limited, but is instead absolute in scope, because it exists as against everyone, and is the correlative of a universal negative obligation.

The definition we have put forward applies equally well to rights *in rem*. These are generally thought of as an authority to obtain from a thing (*res*) all or some of the advantages it is able to afford. Real rights are multital, since the juridical faculties of the title holder correspond to a duty of respect, imposed by law upon everybody else. Now, upon that right there is always grounded another right, equally broad, which expresses itself in the exercise or nonexercise of the first. If I am the owner of a tennis table, I am as such entitled to use it (*jus utendi*); but I also have the choice of playing or not playing upon it. In other words, no one can legally prevent me from enjoying it, if I want to do so, nor compel me, in the opposite case, to use it.

Another example: if I am the owner of a plot of land in favor of which there exists a right of way, I am entitled to travel the road that leads to the public highway, but at the same time I am authorized to choose between using or not using the road.

Let us now apply our definition to *public* subjective rights. We shall deal first with the right of judicial action. It may be conceived of as the privilege of seeking from State organs invested with jurisdictional functions the application of the rules of law to concrete cases, either to ascertain juridical situations that are doubtful, or to obtain the compulsory fulfillment of an obligation. The right of action is a limited right, since it exists not *erga omnes* but as against the juristic person of the state, represented by its jurisdictional organs. Founded upon this limited right and concerning its exercise, we find a multital right of liberty. Any being endowed with juridical personality may be invested with rights of action, and may in consequence choose between their use or non-use. "As the correlative of a universal obligation," says Ugo Rocco, "this faculty presents the absolute (multital) side of all, including relative (limited), rights." Herein, the mistake of the Italian proceduralist lies in considering a limited right as capable of having an absolute aspect. What really happens is that the right of action serves as the basis for a different right, that of juridical liberty.

What we have asserted in regard to the right of action may also be said of the right of petition. Every citizen has that right, and may further elect freely between its exercise or nonexercise.

We must inquire, finally into whether our proposed definition of liberty is applicable to political rights. These are characterized by Jellinek as the citizen's authority to participate, as an individual organ, in the life of the State. The archetype of rights of this kind is the right of suffrage. Whoever has that right enjoys the legal possibility of exercising it; but may we say further that he also is qualified to choose between effective exercise and abstention therefrom? Undoubtedly not. Why? Because voting is not only a right but also a duty; in other words, it is a political right directly founded upon a duty. We must admit, therefore, that a surprise was in store for us where political rights are concerned. Our definition does not suit them. It must either be amended or else declared invalid. We shall choose the first course. The amendment in any case is a simple matter. To carry it through it will suffice to determine precisely the meaning of the expression "subjective right" within our formula, since those words may be used in a broad and in a restricted sense.

The Right of the Obligee and the Right of the Claimant

In its broad connotation, "subjective right" applies to the fulfillment of one's own duty as well as to the privileges correlated with someone else's obligation; in a strict sense, the term is reserved for the latter. The distinction will be made clearer by a couple of examples.

The tenant, obliged to pay the rent for the house he lives in, has, besides, the right of paying it, because an imperative which both ordains and forbids the same conduct would be logically inconceivable. The right of the landlord, instead, is not referred to any duty of his, but to the tenant's obligation. Now, juridical liberty only exists in connection with those subjective rights which do not exhaust their content in the fulfillment of the person's own obligation. Were we to draw up a new terminology we should perhaps oppose the *right of the obligee* to the *right of the claimant.* The first covers the privileges of the passive subject of a legal relation, in regard to the accomplishment of his duty. The right of the claimant, on the other hand, goes beyond the mere fulfilling of an obligation.

The right of the obligee is absolute in scope, since it exists *vis à vis* the whole world. This privilege is logically founded upon a legal duty. Resorting to the vocabulary so often used by the jurists of the phenomenological school, particularly Gerhart Husserl and Fritz Schreier, we could say that the right of the obligee is the *supported privilege,* while the duty of the same person is the *supporting obligation.* But since the said privilege amounts merely to the normative possibility of submitting to one's own duty, excluding the right of not doing so, it is unquestionable that liberty cannot be thought of in relation to the right of performing the obligations to which one is subject. In the case of the claimant's right, the contrary is true. When the content of a subjective right is not reduced to the fulfillment of a duty, its holder enjoys the possibility of exercising or not exercising it. Thus, the right of liberty appears superimposed on another right, which we call "supporting privilege" and consider a subjective right in the first degree. The "supported authority" is a subjective right in the second degree. Juridical liberty must therefore be placed at this level, since it is founded upon a first-degree subjective right. The supporting privilege may be, as we have seen, a limited or a multital right. In the latter case we find two multital rights, the first of which serves as a basis for the second; in the former, the multital right (juridical liberty) is founded upon a limited right, public or private in nature.

If we bring these ideas to bear upon the special case of political rights, we may see that, in our legal system at least, these fall within the category of rights of the obligee. In other words, the political right is coextensive with the privilege of fulfilling one's political duty. As a citizen, I have the right to vote, but not the right of not doing so. It would be otherwise if the right in question were founded upon another right, instead of an obligation. We may well imagine a legal system within which the political rights of citizens are not at the same time duties. In such a situation, those rights, being in the first degree, could serve as a basis for the right of liberty. Or, what amounts to the same thing, the titular holder of the rights would be privileged to choose between the exercise or nonexercise of the same.

The foregoing development allows us to draw our definition more tightly: we understand juridical liberty to mean the authorization extended to every person to exercise or not to exercise his subjective rights, when the content of the latter is not limited to the fulfillment of a duty. From this it may be inferred that liberty, as a second-degree right, is always founded upon a right in the first degree, and never upon a duty to which the holder is subject. Expressing the same in another way, we might say that the right of liberty has as its scope the area of the *lawful-optional* and not of the *lawful-compulsory* (fulfillment of one's own duty).

CHAPTER III

THEORIES OF ROCCO AND KELSEN ON JURIDICAL LIBERTY

Positivistic and "Natural Law" Interpretations of the Right of Liberty

Before developing the views of Ugo Rocco and Hans Kelsen on juridical freedom, we should point out, in order to avoid misunderstandings, that our definition is valid within both the positivistic conception of law and the doctrines of natural law. Such adaptability is readily explained by the fact that the concept we have propounded rests upon a purely logical analysis of the existing relationship between the ideas of legal duty and subjective right.

From a positivistic point of view, it can be said that juridical liberty is the authority conferred upon every person by the rules of law, to exercise or abstain from exercising the subjective rights it enjoys under positive law, whenever those rights amount to more than the fulfillment of a duty. It is of course clear that the term "positive law" covers not only the sum total of legislative precepts which effectively regulate the life of a community at a given moment in its history, but also the customary rules created by the community itself.

In the perspective of natural law, our definition would appear in the following terms: juridical liberty is the authority granted by the rules of a just or objectively valid system of law, to every person for the exercise or nonexercise of its first-degree subjective rights. Within this position we must consequently admit the possibility of conflicts between the positive legal order and natural law. Thus, instead of granting recognition to the right of liberty, positive law may conceivably restrict it beyond reason, and even annul it completely. The sphere of legal faculties conferred upon the individual by each system of positive law never coincides entirely with that of the rights which — in justice —

it ought to recognize. Speaking metaphorically, we might say that there are two eccentric circles, of different size, whose overlapping areas increase or decrease in the course of time. The natural-law ideal would be the total coincidence of both circles, or, what amounts to the same, the elimination of their disparities of center and radius, while the supporters of the positivistic attitude begin by denying such duality, and do not accept the existence of any subjective rights other than those established by law or recognized by state-sanctioned custom.

The discrepancies between the ideals of justice and the precepts of positive law result in the fights — often bloody — which the conquest of liberty brings about. Every time men or nations succeed in obtaining recognition of a new right, their freedom correspondingly expands; whenever their legal faculties are restricted, their freedom is reduced. To borrow the style of mathematics, we could say that liberty is, in every case, a function of subjective right. If the number of such rights changes, the volume of liberty necessarily varies. And this is because to be free means nothing other than having rights concerning the conduct of others, and consequently, being in a position to choose between exercising or not exercising them. Closing this digression, we may now proceed to state and discuss the thesis of Ugo Rocco in regard to the right of liberty.

Theory of Ugo Rocco

This famous Italian proceduralist says that when individual freedom is protected by objective law, it turns from "liberty in fact" into "juridical liberty." The latter confers upon the person a privilege of "acting within the limits of that which the rules of law neither command nor forbid, and preventing others from hindering the development of that activity, or interfering with it . . . Every act not opposed to a prohibition, and every abstention not contrary to a juridical directive belong to the area of juridically free behavior." [7]

Rocco's starting point, as the foregoing sentences indicate, is the distinction between freedom, in the current or physical sense, as opposed to juridical liberty. The freedom-in-fact to which the Italian jurist refers is not freedom in a normative sense, but only the actual possibility of deploying one's activities according to and in the measure of one's own power. From this it follows that juridical liberty must appear as a restraint upon freedom-in-fact. If the latter is limited by the rules of law, such limitation answers to the need of providing a juridical safeguard for the liberties of all. For that reason, limitation and protection acquire the same operative meaning.

[7] Rocco, L'Autorità della cosa giudicata e i suoi limiti soggetivi, p. 299.

The right of liberty, in Rocco's opinion, is an aggregate of *facultates agendi,* because every person is authorized to do what is not forbidden and to omit what is not required. This authorization is linked to the claim which the holder of the right can enforce as against the passive subjects of the legal relationship, so that no one may hinder his activity or disturb his inactivity. The right of liberty exists *erga omnes,* and consequently its correlative is a universal negative obligation. In its multiple forms, it represents a capacity of action which in turn reflects itself in everyone else's duty to respect its exercise. The procedural right of action, instead, covers a group of *facultates exigendi* which correspond to the special obligations cast by law upon the state organs entrusted with jurisdictional functions. We can see that the defendant's duty to respect the plaintiff's right of action is not a special duty imposed upon him alone, but a general obligation which he shares with every other member of the community. This suggests that besides his right of action the plaintiff has another right (liberty), before which all other persons (including the defendant) must bow, refraining from any interference with the exercise of the first right. The privilege which has as its correlative a universal duty, says Rocco, "is the absolute side of every right, even the relative right." [8]

We think the Italian master is mistaken when he states that juridical liberty comprises a number of *facultates agendi,* while the right of action amounts to a series of *facultates exigendi.* All multital rights really present two aspects, one consisting of various authorized courses of behavior, and the other implying certain exigencies or claims. To urge that liberty is only an assemblage of *facultates agendi* is just as serious an error as to say that property is simply the relationship of a person and a thing, without taking into account the legal ties between the owner and all the other persons whose duty it is to respect the privileges granted by the rules of law to the owner of the thing.

The right of ownership covers a great number of *facultates agendi* because the title holder is legally authorized to obtain from the thing all the advantages it is capable of providing; but that shows only the *internal side,* so to speak, of the owner's right. There is also an *external side,* where we may notice the title holder's claim to everybody else's respect for the exercise of his ownership. And in its external aspect the right of ownership is unquestionably a sum-total of *facultates exigendi,*

[8] It is unquestionable that the right of action must not be confused with the right of liberty, which manifests itself in the exercise or nonexercise of the former; for that very reason, it would be contradictory to maintain that liberty is the multital aspect of a limited (paucital) right. Limited rights can have no such aspects, although they do serve as basis for a distinct multital right.

or *claims*. The owner would lack the right of using, enjoying, and disposing of his property if others were not juridically obliged not to prevent it. This essential aspect of the multital right is often forgotten, perhaps because its correlative is purely a negative universal duty, and no occasion arises to enforce it as long as the duty is observed. There can be no claim founded upon a negative obligation while the latter is properly fulfilled by abstention. To become an actual legal exigency, the duty of respect must be breached by some of the obligees, by their standing in the way of the *facultates agendi,* or doing something that they are obligated not to do under the law.

With juridical liberty the same thing happens. In its internal aspect it is a bundle of *facultates agendi* (for instance, to have a drink or to go to the opera); in its external aspect it consists of a series of *facultates exigendi.* I have, for example, the right to read a book; but I may also choose between doing and not doing so. While I remain seated on a park bench and read a novel unmolested, the duty which corresponds to the right I am exercising is not the basis of a legal claim, precisely because the strollers in the park, by leaving me alone, are fulfilling their obligation. But if any of them should presume to interfere with my reading, I could *ipso facto* demand from him that he refrain from doing so; my claim would be founded upon my right of liberty.

Denial of the Right of Liberty
Hans Kelsen's Doctrine

We shall now refer to a famous theory, according to which liberty is not a genuine right, but simply an unnecessary duplication of the concept of juridical duty. It has been developed by the Viennese jurist Hans Kelsen in several of his works; we shall begin by taking the statement of his views from his *General Theory of the State.*

In the "will" theory,[9] there is noticeable the trend that carries the concept of subjective right to its own destruction. When this doctrine states that subjective right is a juridically protected power of willing, it has in view several things which differ sharply among themselves. The will, under legal safeguards, recognized as "subjective right," addresses itself either to the subject's own conduct, or to the conduct of someone else. What is made effective, therefore, as subjective right is a "legal authorization" or a "juridical power." I have the "right" of freely disposing of my property; I have the "right" to do everything that is not legally forbidden. But I have also the "right" of demanding performances from my debtor, or of excluding third parties from interference with the things of which I have free disposition. I "can," ("I am

[9] Referring to Bernard Windscheid's theory of subjective rights, as developed in his *Pandektenrecht.*

authorized," therefore, to) "will" to do or omit this or that, or "will" that others do it or cease from doing it. Under the notion of subjective right, however, the "will" theory also includes the fact that I may express a determination which is linked by law to the effect I am seeking to bring about through the expression of my will. Therefore, what is here called a "subjective right" is not "being legally authorized" but having "juridical power." The legal order confers upon the individual the power of attaining the purposes in which his interest lies, by means of juridical dealings with others; it enables him to impose his own will in order to obtain economic advantages. Through the exercise of my will — at least by means of the expression of my will in legal bargaining — I oblige another to perform a certain obligation; in similar fashion, by exercising my right of action I compel the state authorities to issue execution against a defaulting debtor.

The diversity of the elements included within the notion of subjective right deprives it in the end of all its usefulness. The "right" of doing as one wishes with one's own property, the same as the "right" to do what is not prohibited, is nothing but the subordinate reflection of the rules that establish juridical duties. The juridically relevant content of any affirmative expression of such "subjective rights" disappears as soon as we postulate the existence of someone else's duty to abstain from any interference in "my" things (which become "mine" precisely because of that duty). In this way there may appear a legal right upon inanimate things, a right to use, enjoy and dispose of them. But when we say: I have a right to breathe, to work, to relax, to love, etc., it means nothing more than the non-existence of any legal rule which compels me to the contrary. Any attentive consideration of "power" (in the sense of "being authorized") will disclose in both the cases stated that it is simply a "shall be" expressed by a legal rule: subjective right is objective law and only in that capacity does it enjoy any juridical recognition. My right in regard to someone else's conduct, consisting merely in that I can demand — therefore, "will" — the act of the other person or the omission of his interferences in my range of competence, is the objective norm when seen through my own eyes, as the rule happens to favor me by requiring from the other that conduct which I "want" from him. It matters little, however, that I want it; all relevancy is upon the fact that the obligee must do something because the law, objective law, commands it, even though it may be true that the reason for the existence of the rule is the thought that I (as the party whose interests are sought to be protected) do want or presumably may want what the rule provides for.[10]

The foregoing paragraphs reveal that Kelsen's criticism aims not only at the utter negation of juridical liberty but also denies any need for the concept of "right in rem," and especially for the notion of ownership. The point of departure for Kelsen's argument is the distinction — open to argument, to say the least — between rights to one's own con-

[10] KELSEN, TEORÍA GENERAL DEL ESTADO (Ed. Labor, 1934) 73.

duct and rights upon the conduct of others. According to the traditional view, the rights to one's own conduct resolve themselves into a group of operative capacities (*facultates agendi,* in Rocco's terminology), while the others always mean a "juridical power," or *facultas exigendi.* As an example of the first group of rights, we may mention the rights of property and liberty; as instances of the second, the right of action and creditorial rights. The Austrian jurist, it is plain, denies that the former are genuine rights. He says they are simply "the reflection" of a universal duty of respect imposed upon everyone by objective law. As the owner of a house, I have the right to live in it, but this privilege is just the complement, the rear view, of the legal obligation under which all other people find themselves in regard to allowing me an undisturbed use of what belongs to me. Similarly, the privileges I possess in connection with going to the movies or reading a book are not in themselves subjective rights, but the consequence of everyone else's obligation not to prevent my doing so.

What value should we give to this thesis?

It must be recognized from the outset that the complementary or reflected nature of the capacities mentioned above is uncontrovertible. Liberty and property, for instance, are the correlative of a negative universal obligation. But this does not prove that they are not rights. If they were not, how could they be correlated with the obligations of others? Besides, it is not true that such rights as these amount only to *facultates agendi.* We have already seen that they also serve as the basis for a series of claims that may be addressed to other persons. That this aspect of multital rights should often be forgotten is a consequence of the negative nature of their corresponding duties. For a claim founded upon a negative obligation arises only when the latter has been breached. As long as it is respected, there is no sense in requiring performance from the obligee. It would be, however, a serious mistake to think that multital rights are born when the correlative obligation ceases to be fulfilled. For the existence of a multital right is one thing, and the enforceability of the correlative duty is another. There are legal duties that can be immediately claimed and others where the claim is deferred in point of time,[11] so that the creditor may not demand satisfaction until the debt matures. But in that case, regardless of the delay, his right exists from the instant the contract is perfected. Similarly, from the moment he acquires title to it, the owner of a thing enjoys as against all other persons, the right of using it, selling it, etc., in correlation with the obligation of the latter to respect that right; but performance of

[11] See Invrea, Parte Generale del Diritto (Padova, 1936) 166.

such obligation could not be judicially exacted except in the case where the obligees failed to observe their duty.

The breakdown of subjective rights as between those pertaining to one's own conduct and those upon the behavior of others, is entirely artificial, because, as we have shown, in every legal power there is an "inside" referring to the activity of the person so empowered, and an "outside" that is seen in relation to the conduct of third parties, from whom may be claimed, depending upon the case, a positive act, a forbearance, or the delivery of something.

But the fundamental mistake of Kelsen's theory consists in his assumed identity between the notions of objective law and subjective right. To say that a subjective right is simply the rule of objective law connected to a juridical subject [12] is to confuse a norm with the authority it confers. Just because every right arises from a norm, it does not follow that norm and authority are one and the same. Subjective right is a possibility of action conforming to a rule, or, in other terms, a legal authorization afforded to a person. The rule, instead, is the foundation of the operative capacity. Kelsen's sophism compares with the one which would say that, since there exists a necessary relation between the ideas of father and son, they are identical.

It should be pointed out, finally, that with his criticism of the distinction between rights to one's own conduct and upon someone else's, the leader of the Austrian school proves a point quite different from that which he had in mind. We agree with the famous jurist in that liberty and property are correlative to a duty imposed on everyone; but we do not believe that they amount to an unnecessary duplication of the concept of duty, and less still that they are not genuine rights. The conclusion to which the Kelsenian argument logically leads is that those privileges, as any other subjective right, are correlatives of certain duties, or, in Kelsen's own words, "reflections" of the same. Even allowing the use of this term, the thesis should be rejected, because a right can never be the copy, image, or reproduction of an obligation. Besides, we fail to see why Kelsen does not apply to creditorial rights, for instance, the objection he flourishes in his denial of liberty and property as rights. For creditorial rights are the correlative of obligations, even though the latter be particular instead of general. The theory we have discussed should apply, in strict logic, to personal rights. They too are "reflections" of certain obligations. But this does not mean that as rights

[12] Kelsen defines subjective rights in these terms: ". . . the same rule of law, referred to the person upon whose statement of decision the application of coercive State action is made to depend." See HAUPTPROBLEME DER STAATSRECHTSLEHRE (Tübingen, 1911) 618.

they do not exist, nor that they are the useless duplicate of the corresponding duty. My right to demand delivery of what I have bought is correlative to the seller's duty to perform, and yet we cannot say that such a claim merely restates the obligation of the seller. All we can say, in the case of creditorial rights, as all others, is that the subjective right is a correlative of a duty — general or special — imposed upon one, several, or all persons.

CHAPTER IV

PHILOSOPHICAL VIEW OF THE RIGHT OF LIBERTY

Philosophical Justification of the Right of Liberty

Prior analysis of our subject led us to state that juridical freedom confers the authority of exercising or not exercising one's own subjective rights, when the content of the same amounts to more than the fulfillment of a duty. But we do not yet know how this faculty can justify itself under the fundamental criticism of philosophy. The Law may recognize liberty, and — within certain limits — protect it, but that does not answer the question one way or the other. What we ask now is not whether such a right exists, but whether it ought to exist or not. The difficulties of this inquiry might prove merely superficial if one thought of the right of liberty as not being original, but derivative. It could be said then, that liberty is not one species of subjective right, among others within the same family; it is the categorial area where every right appears. As an authority, it does not exist of itself; it rests upon another right which serves as its precondition. To justify the first it should suffice, therefore, to establish the philosophical foundation of the second, for once the supporting right is duly justified, there can be no doubt about the philosophical acceptance of the supported authority.

The investigation should begin, then, on the question of whether subjective rights, regardless of type, represent arbitrary claims, or whether they are capable of justification. In the case of the right of the obligee the answer is easy. He who is under obligation to do something is, logically enough, authorized to do it. This statement impresses itself upon our minds with the overwhelming persuasion of self-evidence. For otherwise, how could we be subject to any duty, if we were forbidden to submit to it? What duty commands, cannot be forbidden in the name of duty without giving to the same imperative rule, two contradictory contents. The right of the obligee is a *conditio sine qua non* of the rule's effectiveness. The person who is disabled from fulfilling the obligation imposed by the norm, could not be under the duty of doing so. For example, the rule that calls upon the father to provide sustenance for his child implicitly gives him the right of doing what this norm requires.

To justify the right of the obligee is simple. Can the same be said of the faculties of the claimant? In a brilliant doctoral thesis, José M. de Semprún y Gurrea[13] has urged the point that every right must be understood as the function of a juridical duty. This seems to be entirely correct. We believe, with the distinguished Spanish jurist, that any right can be referred back to an obligation of the same person, and that, consequently, the justification of the former must be sought within the latter.

Fulfillment of a legal precept indicates that he to whom the rule is addressed has made of its observance an end of his own conduct. Between the exigency of the rule and actual behavior (conforming or deviational) there is a contingent relationship. This is so on account of the free determination of the person's will. As a free entity, he is able to do or to leave undone what is prescribed. In one case, the objective of his conduct is obedience, in the other it is departure from the rule. This teleological element, it has been aptly said,[14] is the categorial form of duty whenever it is fulfilled. And also, we might add, whenever it is breached.

Before the legal rule is submitted to, this submission must be postulated as an end. But the attainment of an end presupposes the use of certain means. It must be admitted, therefore, that the *right to fulfill a duty justifies the right of using the means conducive thereto*. How would it be possible from a normative point of view to require the end without authorizing the actions which lead to it? In so far as I am under a duty to preserve my own life, I have the right of turning that obligation into an end of my conduct, and no one can deny me the use of the necessary means.

In this manner, the right to realize a prescribed end serves as basis and justification for the right of employing the means that bring about that result. Generally, legal rules prescribe certain acts or omissions, without indicating any of the permissible directions in which one may go to fulfill the command or submit to the prohibition. But such silence does not implicitly deny the authorization to proceed in search of an objective, when finding it is compulsory.

The relationships which we have been tracing so far have a purely

[13] SEMPRÚN Y GURREA, SENTIDO FUNCIONAL DEL DERECHO DE PROPIEDAD (Ed. Revista de Derecho Privado, Madrid, 1933).

[14] N. HARTMANN, ETHIK (2 AUFLAGE) 181.

logical basis, and stand independently of their recognition or nonrecognition by positive law. There may be, for instance, no express provision authorizing the seller to deliver the goods sold, but that right exists, as a necessary derivation of the duty to deliver. Neither are there laws that regulate in all detail the methods by which the seller may fulfill his obligation, and yet there is no reason to deny him the right of following that which he thinks best among the lawful ones, since such a privilege is also the logical consequence of the duties imposed on him by his contract. In the same way, even though the Civil Code does not say that the buyer is legally authorized to pay the contract price, that right exists, indissolubly linked to the duty of making payment. What we have stated in regard to the faculties of the buyer (as an obligee) we can also say of his other rights, when they manifest themselves in a claim. In the absence of specific provisions on the medium of payment, for instance, he may choose between different types of money or coin, providing they are legal tender.

The right to fulfill a duty serves, then, as the point of departure for the practical use of the means which lead to the legally required end. We have in mind *lawful* means, because the faculty of choice does not extend to those forbidden by law. This limitation is not hard to understand, if it is considered that the legal order does not aim at the conduct of an isolated individual, but instead covers the reciprocal relations of a plurality of subjects. The legal order does not take human beings in the fullness of their reality, but only in certain aspects of their conduct, the rest remaining beyond its scope. In other words, it does not refer to *man,* but to the *person.* Now, recognition of the forms of human activity in which juristic personality manifests itself implies the existence of equal rights in regard to fulfillment of duties and the use of means conducive thereto. The person is legally capable of being under obligation, and cannot, therefore, fail to be recognized as the holder of rights. Such rights are referred to its obligations as well as to the use of those means which permit their fulfillment. But since there exists only a more or less limited range of means, in regard to duties of equal rank, the right of resorting to those means cannot be allowed exclusively to one or several subjects. It must inure to the benefit of all, in proportion to their obligations. The problem of justice amounts to an investigation of the criteria according to which duties are to be imposed, and the use of means is to be authorized. The abstract formulas of justice, presented in the past, are nothing but an attempt to solve that problem: to determine the obligations of each, and provide the limits and manner in which they shall be fulfilled (or, to the same effect, the forms and limitations of the rights granted to each person as against other persons).

With the foregoing in mind, we may now return to our original question and ask ourselves how the right of liberty can be justified.

If it be allowed that the right of reaching a legally compulsory end is the foundation of the right to put into operation the means conducive to that purpose, then it follows that, among the several appropriate means, the obligee is entitled to choose. Let us suppose that a person has within his reach five different methods equally suited to attaining an end prescribed by law. The legal precept commands submission to a certain duty, but does not indicate through what means. This omission, of course, would not excuse a lack of performance. Neither does the existence of alternative choices release the person from its obligation. He can choose; not only *can* he, but he *must*, and consequently he has the right of resorting to any one particular means. It may be well to point out that this right cannot be confused with the faculty of employing the means conducive to a certain purpose, nor with that of complying with the command of the norm. Having the right of traveling a road is not the same as being authorized to choose among several roads in order to get to a certain place. This faculty of choice is precisely what we understand as juridical liberty. Returning now to our example, we may say that, as long as the means are lawful, the person has a right to resort to numbers one, or two, or three, it being assumed that the legal rule does not prescribe the use of one to the exclusion of the others; but, furthermore, the person also has the *right of choosing* the means he thinks best. Liberty then appears as the right of selecting the means upon which the fulfillment of a duty depends, either directly or remotely. On the other hand, the right to put such means into operation is termed a "claim," or subjective right in the first degree.

The ideas we have presented so far may be condensed in this manner:

(a) The right of placing the fulfillment of a duty as an end of one's own conduct is the privilege we have previously referred to as the right of the obligee.

(b) The capacity of putting into operation the means that lead to fulfillment of a duty constitutes the *right of the claimant.*

(c) Finally, the right of selecting lawful means which are appropriate for the achievement of a legally required purpose, is called juridical liberty.

This concept is not to be taken only with reference to the means directly conducive to the observance of a rule, but applies also to indirect means. The same can be said of subjective rights that extend to claims against other subjects: they are not always concerned with direct means. The relation between juridical claim and supporting duty is sometimes quite remote. The means which a claim refers to and the end required by law may be separated by a number of links, each of which is both means and end within the chain, until the ultimate end: the performance of a duty is finally reached. Now, if the fulfillment of the duty is a final end, the means subordinate to it are simply the steps that lead to it, in effect relative ends. As to compliance with the command, they will be means, but with respect to the means that precede and precondition them, they will be ends. This circumstance is precisely what complicates the task of determining the necessary relationship which exists between every right and the duties of its holder. The gap from the means to the ultimate purpose it subserves is on occasion so broad that the right exercised in the use of such means appears to be independent of any duty. But such independence cannot be admitted without depriving subjective rights of their only justification, which would leave them as purely arbitrary claims. The only thing that supports a claim as genuine right is its connection, immediate or remote, with the duty that serves as its basis. Were a legal capacity to be divested of its content of means directed toward the observance of a normative precept, it would be impossible to furnish it any logical justification.

Perhaps a simple example may show that this theory, despite its seemingly artificial outlines, is easy to understand. Let us suppose that I must take a streetcar in order to go from my home to my place of business. If anyone attempted to prevent me from boarding the streetcar, I would object, on the basis of my right of liberty. No legal rule compels me not to use that means of transportation, therefore, I have the right of using it. But, upon what basis am I so authorized? What connection is there between that privilege and my juridical duties? The answer is almost obvious: I have the right to ride a streetcar to my office because I must go to work. Now, since I am faced with the necessity of using certain means in pursuance of that end, it follows that I have the possibility of choosing the means I like best. My option extends to the automobile, the bus, or any other lawful system of transportation. Someone may say that I am not really obliged to get to my office. I would deny it, because I must work at that particular place. The next question would then be why am I under such a duty. The answer: I must work because I am under a duty to support myself, and this because I must preserve my own existence. The first of the faculties mentioned above, that of choosing the means of transporting myself from home to office, is immediately founded upon my duty to reach the latter point; more remotely, it is founded upon all my other duties: work, eat, subsist.

Does this mean that the juridical duties of a person form an endless series? If each obligation is explained by another, and every right is founded upon a duty, how can we grasp the ultimate duty, the one on which all others rest? Going back to our illustration, we might ask: What is the foundation of my right of self-preservation? The answer would have to go beyond the duty of conserving one's own life, into the area of values, the value here being life itself. The philosophy of values teaches that the notion of duty is not, as Kant believed, irreducible to any other term, but is instead a concept that can be explained in relation to the idea of value. The ultimate justification of our duties must therefore be sought in certain objective values (values which exist independently of their recognition or appreciation by any individual, and possess — in Nikolai Hartmann's words — a *being in itself*). The thesis that subjective rights are a function of duty, advanced by Semprún y Gurrea, must therefore be complemented by the statement that duty, in turn, is a function of value. And since values are of different sorts, we may add that the attribution of duties under the rules of law ultimately represent the concrete embodiment of a system of values.

The relationship between compulsory ends and the means (direct or indirect) which lead to them has nothing to do with the recognition or nonrecognition thereof by the holders of the respective rights. In general, the titular holder of a legal claim is not conscious of whatever relation exists between the object of his rights and the fulfillment of his duties. Of course, such ignorance or unawareness does not affect the relationship in question. Besides, it is not too difficult to discover in any case.

The Abuse of Right

Against the theory that we have so far developed, an objection may be raised on the ground that the exercise of a subjective right can be aimed, not at the fulfillment, but at the breach of a duty. And so, for instance, an individual has the right of buying a dagger for himself the eventual use of which, in his own designs, may be murder.

The objection is ineffective, because the right to acquire a weapon only justifies itself in so far as it tends to secure (mediately or immediately) a legally compulsory end. In connection with the duty to preserve one's life, it may be necessary to put into operation certain means, which include instruments of self-defense.

It should be borne in mind that our earlier analyses have a purely normative value, and do not take into account the practical consequences which may follow the use of whatever object one happens to own; we merely seek to justify certain types of juridical powers. The one who buys a dagger may be capable of employing it as the means to commit a murder, but in such a case our judgment of his right of ownership is certainly independent of his eventual behavior. Aside from its circumstantial subservience to an unlawful purpose, this right stands as an authority which leads, directly or indirectly, to the fulfillment of prescribed ends. To deny all justification to the right of property, because of the results which its unlawful use might bring about, is to confuse the juridical issue with a completely separate question of fact.

Returning to the case of the dagger, we can say there is a right to buy one, but not to employ it in a prohibited manner. That a murderer may happen to use a weapon of his in order to kill his victim does not prove anything against the right of ownership. As a juridical power, property justifies itself only when it applies to objects used in the fulfillment of duties. For that reason, the owner is not authorized to put his property to any use he wishes, but only to use it in a manner not inconsistent with his duties. In other words: *the illegal use of an object can never be considered as the exercise of a right.* Stabbing somebody with one's own dagger is not the proper exercise of a right of ownership.

The foregoing thoughts point out the impropriety of speaking, as some authors do, of the *abuse,* or the *abusive exercise of a right.* No one can abuse his legal faculties, because they exclude by definition any unlawful use. The facts upon which this assumed abuse of right is made to rest have nothing to do with it; they are the negation of all right. There is consequently no abuse of right, but only violation of a duty, which is quite another matter.

CHAPTER V

LIBERTY AS RIGHT AND AS POWER. THE IDEA OF NATURAL FREEDOM

Liberty as Right and as Power

As "right," liberty is a purely normative concept; as "power" it is an attribute of the will. The time has come to examine the relations between both aspects of the term. These relations appear only in the exercise of juridical freedom, since prior to that moment it does not acquire the reality of fact.

The exercise of liberty assumes, logically speaking, a specific determination of free will, either in the direction of performance or of omission of the authorized act. In order to enjoy his right of liberty, the individual must choose between the exercise or nonexercise of the underlying authority he possesses. Such a choice reveals, in its volitional nature, the existence of freedom as power. The scope of this freedom, however, is much broader than that of freedom as right. Juridical liberty appears in connection with the use or nonuse of first-degree subjective rights; freedom-as-power can apply instead to the fulfillment or denial of duties as well as to pursuing or abstaining from a legally authorized course of action (rights of first and second degree, or in sole degree).

Returning to the threefold classification of human acts: prescribed, forbidden, and permitted, we submit therefore that the right of liberty only exists in regard to the last, while freedom as power exists in regard to all three.

The expression of free will, in its relevant legal aspects, can take three forms: (a) exercise or nonexercise of a subjective right; (b) commission or omission of forbidden acts; (c) obedience or disobedience of a precept.

The boundary of freedom-as-right runs together with that of the lawfully optional, while freedom of will can go beyond the lawful-compulsory and enter the domains of prohibitory rules.

Furthermore, two different moments of human conduct show the operation of free will: in the first, certain ends are postulated, in the second, proper means are chosen. The objectives of our activity are theoretically infinite in number; man cannot fulfill them all, so he must necessarily choose the most valuable ones and disregard the rest, even at a sacrifice. This selection, in each case, depends upon the value that may be recognized in various ends. Among all possible ones, the law prescribes some, excludes others by prohibition, and allows the remainder, either by expression or implication. The right of liberty, as we have seen, is germane only to attaining or ignoring the permissible ends. We have said, also, that free will operates not only where a statement of ends is concerned, but also in the selection of means. The possibility of choice exists here as long as the individual has within his reach several processes conducive to the ends in view. If several roads are open, he may pick whichever he prefers. In a juridical sense, the normative scope of choice is limited. For even though *in fact* a person may be in a position to resort to means of any sort, juridically it only has the right of employing *lawful* means. This restriction exists for the same reason that determines the classification of ends, as prescribed, permitted, and forbidden.

The Concept of Natural Freedom

The history of political thought presents, since the distant days of the Greek sophists, as a recurring *leitmotiv,* the old theme of the struggle between juridical liberty and natural freedom. This conflict finds its most striking and dramatic expression in Callicles' discourse upon the right of the strongest, in Plato's *Gorgias*.[15]

Juridical liberty, in the view of some philosophers, appears as a limitation or compression of natural freedom. The latter, they conceive, is an absolute freedom, escaping all regulation and coextensive with the power of each individual. This attitude would seem to reveal a desire to turn the freedom of the will into the source of a new right, of a power of decision which is a rule unto itself, untrammeled by any restriction. From this point of view, perfect liberty would be a right to do, in every case, what one wills, purely and simply because one wills it. The natural-freedom thesis attempts to resolve, by suppression, all conflicts between the aims of decision and the imperatives of duty. Losing therefore its original content, the idea of what is compulsory becomes identical with an unregulated development of self-determination. The view we have been stating appears most drastically put forth in the anarchist principle: There is no obligation other than to do what one wishes.

With such a starting point, the conclusion must then be reached that juridical liberty, hemmed in by rules of conduct, narrows down the scope of natural freedom. But since an unqualified postulation of the latter would be incompatible with the existence of any legal order, the supporters of that doctrine have endeavored to state a formula which might overcome the antithesis of absolute freedom and liberty under law. In Kelsen's words,

the idea of liberty is in the background of all speculation about society, notwithstanding that it is in the nature of society to unify and inter-relate, which amounts to a negation of freedom. Nature rebels against society, against the constraint inherent to all social order, against the outside pressure of imperative rules, and cries out for freedom. The burden of alien wills, cast upon man by the social order, becomes unbearable in so far as he experiences more directly the primary feeling of his own value, as the subject manifests most impulsively against the ruler his reaction: If he is a man like myself, I am his equal; whence his right to command me? In this manner, the negative idea of equality comes to the support of the similarly negative concept of freedom.

Now, if liberty is the outcome of society (including the State) although denied by it, the reason must be found in a change of meaning; negating no longer that which is social (and particularly, of the State), liberty becomes the conceptual framework within which, together with its dialectical antithesis, are represented all the possible forms of State and Society, democracy and autocracy.

[15] See García Máynez, El Derecho Natural en la época de Sócrates (Mexico, 1939).

The existence of Society and State requires that order be imposed upon the reciprocal conduct of men; this implies a dominant and effective *imperium*. But if we must be dominated, we want to do it ourselves. From natural freedom, social or political liberty derives. He is politically free who, being subject, obeys no other will but his own.[16]

Self-Rule and Democracy

The concept of autonomy[17] furnishes one of the answers to the problem under consideration. The aim of its proponents would be to establish a juridical order within which, although subject to a complex of rules, the individual follows only his own determinations. How is this possible? It is possible — the answer goes — if the precepts embodied in the legal order originate in the decisions of the same individual who is meant to observe them, and not in someone else's. The subject and the lawmaker must therefore be one person.

These views lead straight to a political doctrine of the democratic type. Democracy is a political formula which attempts to conciliate the external imperativeness of a normative structure with the ideal of absolute freedom. But the antithesis does not seem to be overcome in this manner, not even where all citizens participate in the discussions and vote in legislative bodies. By saying that the support of every rule must be found in the free choice of those subject to it, the theoreticians of popular government are bound to follow with a recognition of equal value in each and all individual wills. Were they to do otherwise, they would acknowledge as a possibility the imposition of one will upon another, thereby falling again into the tangle of imperativeness. Therefore, they necessarily combine the idea of absolute freedom with that of absolute equality. The product of this combination is the majority principle, according to which, in the event of disagreement among free and equal wills, the decision belongs to the greater number. Truly enough, the views of the minority are not any less valuable, but since the decision of the whole cannot be self-contradictory, the principle of majority rule is resorted to in order to secure the freedom of a greater number of citizens.

> The majority principle [says Kelsen] should be derived from the idea of freedom, and not, as sometimes happens, from the idea of equality. The majority principle assumes, of course, that the opinions of various individuals are all of equal value. But such equality is purely figurative, since it cannot

[16] Kelsen, *op. cit. supra* n. 10, at p. 530.

[17] The terms "autonomía" and "heteronomía" provide, in the original, the necessary contrast between conduct that is self-determining and conduct that must take into account the impositions—from without—of a normative order.

signify the effective measurability of human persons and their wills, nor the possibility of adding these up. It would be no justification of the majority principle to say that more votes are worthier than less votes. From the purely negative proposition that one is not worth more than another, it cannot be positively inferred that the majority view must prevail. If the majority principle were to be deduced from the sole notion of equality, it would acquire the mechanical and non-spiritual taints which the supporters of autocracy claim to find in it; it would merely remain as a poor statement of the fact that the many are superior to the few, and with this the aphorism "Might before Right" would be superseded only to receive legal recognition. It is the idea that, if not all, then the greater number of men should be free, in other words, that the fewest possible should be opposed to the general will established by the social order, that leads logically to the majority principle. This is a fundamental concept of democracy, as evidenced by the fact that liberty is not given to this or that person because it is worth more than the next, but that instead the greatest possible number of men is sought to be made free.[18]

In its application, the majority principle admits, however, of its own insufficiency to resolve systematically the antithesis of personal freedom and legal rule to which we have been referring. The will of the majority governs as a general will, but it is not everyone's will. The minority remains nevertheless subject to whatever decisions are validly made. As far as the minority group is concerned, such decisions amount to coercive legislation. This objection has been met with the somewhat fictitious assumption that all citizens agree beforehand to submit themselves to the prevailing view; on this basis, it is argued, what the assembly resolves embodies the will of all its members. Such an interpretation would lead to this strange conclusion: *democracy is a system within which every individual agrees to follow the majority view, regardless of how different it may be from his own.*

The antithesis in question cannot even be overcome in regard to the voters who agree with the majority, for once their decision acquires the dignity of an obligatory rule, it rises above the will of its creators and stands before them as an inescapable imperative. The difficulty we are pointing out is greater still where parliamentary democracies are concerned, since the acts of a legislature, as private citizens see them, are always stamped with the seal of compulsory observance. And this last problem cannot be solved either, by saying that an agent's decision takes the place of the principal's will, because voters are bound by such decisions even when in conflict with their own views.

"The English people think that they are free, but they deceive themselves, because they only are so when they elect their representatives; once these are

[18] Kelsen, Vom Wesen und Wert der Demokratie (2n ed. 1929) 22.

chosen, they fall back into serfdom and political void." Rousseau deduces this well-known statement from the indirect processes of English democracy. Although the will of the political organs of the State has been shaped by direct popular decision, the individual has been free during only one moment: the election of his representatives, and even that assumes he has voted with the majority and not with the defeated minority. It would seem therefore that the democratic principle of freedom calls for a reduction to the minimum of those instances where the wishes of the minority are overpowered, and to that effect, such safeguards of individual liberty as qualified majorities and, if possible, complete unanimity, are considered appropriate. This, however, is so difficult in the face of the diversity of interests present in political practice, that an apostle of freedom such as Rousseau only required unanimity for the social compact through which a State was constituted.[19]

It should be observed, however, that the French writer did not take the social compact to be a historical fact, but considered it instead as the hypothesis which provides a philosophical basis for the external validity of the legal order, as opposed to the subjective will of individuals; the argument does not lend, in consequence, any support to the conciliation of natural freedom and the idea of normatively conditioned liberty.[20] The opposition between *citoyen* and *sujet* clearly indicates this failure. In his capacity as a citizen, sharing in the creation of the common will, every individual is free; but as he enjoys his liberty in this manner, he actually forges his own chains, since in regard to the juridical order he helps create, he is simply a subject. In other words: *what is self-rule for the citizen becomes, for the subject, binding legislation.*

Criticism of the Natural-Freedom Theory

The problems we have thus far examined cease being such when the issues are properly framed and the contradictory notion of natural freedom is eliminated. If this freedom consists of the *power of doing as one wishes,* there is no valid reason for considering it a *right* at the same time. And if it is not a right, but sheer power, the restrictions placed upon it in the name of duty could never appear unwarranted, nor constitute an infringement of the immunities due to the dignity of the human being. Juridical liberty cannot be absolute or arbitrary, precisely because it is a right, that is, a legal authority indissolubly linked (even when indirectly so) to the duties of each person.

The supporters of the natural-freedom theory err in allowing normative significance to an external manifestation of man's will, disconnecting

[19] Kelsen, *op. cit. supra.*

[20] Rousseau, Discours sur l'origine et les fondements de l'inégalité parmi les hommes.

it entirely from the idea of duty and confusing the power which carries into execution the designs of free will with a legal authority to choose between the exercise or nonexercise of those rights whose content is not limited to performance of a duty.

If the false notion of natural freedom is discarded, the concept of external imperativeness loses its oppressive meaning and gains a new relevance, which — far from antagonizing human dignity — becomes one of its most helpful conditions. For the true imperativeness of law lies not in the fact that one person may command another, but in the subordination of will power to a group of rules which carry the intrinsic justification of their own validity. For this reason, the limitations imposed by objective law upon the scope of self-determining power do not negate the worth of the individual, but rather amount to a recognition of his juridical essence, as the subject of rights and duties.

Conclusions

Turning a retrospective glance upon the road we have traveled we can summarize the development of our journey as follows:

We recognized at the outset that the traditional view of the right of liberty is clearly defective, for it outlines the scope of the concept without indicating its essence. To state that liberty is an authority to perform or omit what is neither prescribed nor forbidden tells us nothing about the content of the same.

A positive definition was therefore the object of our next efforts. Analyzing the relations between rights, on the one hand, and their exercise, on the other, we found that juridical liberty is not a self-sustaining possibility of action, but a second-degree right, which consists of the normative range of choice between the exercise or nonexercise of primary authorizations.

This is no doubt our most important finding. Beyond demonstrating that a positive definition of juridical liberty can be attained, it also reveals that this is not one among several species in a general classification of subjective rights, but a separate category within which all rights manifest themselves. As we observed thereafter, our proposed definition applies to multital as well as paucital rights (both public and private).

In the analysis of one specific situation, that of political rights in the context of Mexican law, we had occasion to settle the scope and direction of our definition. When it speaks of an authority to choose between the exercise or nonexercise of subjective rights, the expression "subjective right" is used in a narrow sense. This is because there are two kinds of legal authorizations: those which refer to the fulfillment of one's own duty, and those which relate to someone else's duty. We distinguish between them through the terms *right of the obligee* and *right of the claimant*. The right of the obligee, which amounts to the possibility afforded him by law, to abide by his duties, cannot provide a basis for a right of liberty. It is not therefore a right of first or second degree, but a right in sole degree. On the other hand, those rights which go beyond the person's fulfillment of its duty always serve as the foundation for a second-degree right, namely, the choice between using or not the underlying authority.

Since the positive definition of the right of liberty derives — through a purely logical process — from the concept of subjective right and its relations with the fact of its exercise, we were able to support the possibility of applying our thesis in the area of a positivistic conception of law as well as in the area of natural-law theory. We discussed at that time the doctrines of Ugo Rocco and Hans Kelsen. Comparing our positive definition of juridical liberty with Rocco's views on the right of action, we stated that the latter, as an authority limited in object and primary in degree, can have no absolute aspect or facets, although it does serve as the basis of a different right (liberty) paired with a universal duty of noninterference. Against Kelsen's thesis we argued that with the reasons brought forth by the leader of the Viennese School to show that liberty and property are not genuine rights, one can only prove the conceptual correlation of legal duty and subjective right. Saying that freedom is merely the reflex-image of a universal duty of respect, is simply giving a new name to multital rights.

A philosophical justification of the right of liberty, within the framework of the theory of values, was our next objective. We outlined the categorial form with reference to which the violation or observance of duty takes place, namely, the teleological connection between behavior and its ends, and thus were able to establish the relations which link the subjective rights and the obligations of every person. We saw that juridical authorizations of every type are in final analysis a function of the duties to which the individual may be subject. Between a right and the duty or duties that provide its basis and justify its existence, there may be a direct relation, as in the case of the obligee's privileges, or an indirect one, as in that of the right of liberty. For liberty appears — from the legal-philosophical point of view — as the authority to choose among the lawful means which lead, directly or circuitously, to the observance of the legal precepts by which everyone is bound.

We finally examined the contradictory notion of natural freedom, and pointed out the impossibility of bringing it into harmony with the concept of juridical liberty. Freedom, in a physical sense, cannot, as we noted, have any normative significance. It is not right, but power. It is therefore improper to rest the validity of the legal order upon individual free will, and to consider objective law as a limitation or deviation of true liberty. As the function of duty, right can never support itself on the self-determination of men. Duty, and the legal order that prescribes it, draw their validity from an objective structure of values.

INDEX

INDEX

Bei Fragen zur Produktsicherheit wenden Sie sich bitte an:
If you have any questions regarding product safety,
please contact:

Walter de Gruyter GmbH
Genthiner Straße 13
10785 Berlin
productsafety@degruyterbrill.com